THE LAW OF NATIONS

NATURAL LAW AND
ENLIGHTENMENT CLASSICS

Knud Haakonssen
General Editor

Emer de Vattel

NATURAL LAW AND
ENLIGHTENMENT CLASSICS

The Law of Nations,
Or, Principles of the Law of Nature,
Applied to the Conduct and Affairs
of Nations and Sovereigns, with Three
Early Essays on the Origin and Nature
of Natural Law and on Luxury

Emer de Vattel

Edited and with an Introduction
by Béla Kapossy and Richard Whatmore

LIBERTY FUND

Introduction, annotations, translations, bibliographies, index © 2008 by Liberty Fund, Inc.

21 22 23 24 25 C 8 7 6 5 4
23 24 25 26 27 P 10 9 8 7 6

Frontispiece courtesy of the Bibliothèque publique et universitaire, Neuchâtel, Switzerland.

Library of Congress Cataloging-in-Publication Data
Vattel, Emer de, 1714–1767. [Droit des gens. English]
The law of nations, or, Principles of the law of nature, applied to the conduct and affairs of nations and sovereigns, with three early essays on the origin and nature of natural law and on luxury/Emer de Vattel; edited and with an introduction by Béla Kapossy and Richard Whatmore; translated by Thomas Nugent.
p. cm.—(Natural law and enlightenment classics)
Includes bibliographical references and index.
ISBN 978-0-86597-450-0 (hc: alk. paper)   ISBN 978-0-86597-451-7 (pbk.: alk. paper)
1. International law.   2. War (International law)   3. Natural law.
I. Kapossy, Béla, 1965–   II. Whatmore, Richard.   III. Title.   IV. Title: Law of nations.
V. Title: Principles of the law of nature, applied to the conduct and affairs of nations and sovereigns, with three early essays on the origin and nature of natural law and on luxury.
KZ2414.A3D7613   2008
341—dc22   2007048362

LIBERTY FUND, INC.
11301 North Meridian Street
Carmel, Indiana 46032
libertyfund.org

CONTENTS

Introduction   ix

A Note on the Texts   xxi

Acknowledgments   xxv

THE LAW OF NATIONS, OR, PRINCIPLES OF THE
LAW OF NATURE, APPLIED TO THE CONDUCT
AND AFFAIRS OF NATIONS AND SOVEREIGNS   I

Additional Essays

Essay on the Foundation of Natural Law and on the
First Principle of the Obligation Men Find Themselves
Under to Observe Laws. *Translated by T. J. Hochstrasser*   747

Dissertation on This Question: Can Natural Law Bring
Society to Perfection Without the Assistance of Political
Laws? *Translated by T. J. Hochstrasser*   773

Dialogue Between the Prince of **** and His Confidant,
on Certain Essential Elements of Public Administration.
Translated by Kenneth Goodwin   783

Biographical Sketches of Authors Referred to by Vattel   797

Bibliography
    Works Referred to by Vattel   813
    Writings on Vattel   827

Index   831

INTRODUCTION

Life of Vattel

Emer[1] de Vattel's *Le droit des gens. Ou Principes de la loi naturelle, appliqués à la conduite & aux affaires des nations & des souverains* (*The Law of Nations, or Principles of the Law of Nature, Applied to the Conduct and Affairs of Nations and Sovereigns*) (1758) was the most important book on the law of nations in the eighteenth century. It was in great measure thanks to this work that the practical and theoretical influence of natural jurisprudence was extended down through the Revolutionary and Napoleonic eras. Indeed, it was Vattel who was cited as a major source of contemporary wisdom on questions of international law in the American Revolution and even by opponents of revolution, such as Cardinal Consalvi, at the Congress of Vienna.

Emer de Vattel was born at Couvet, in Neuchâtel, a principality ruled by the kings of Prussia, on April 25, 1714, as the youngest son of David Vattel and Marie de Montmollin.[2] His father, ennobled in 1727 by the king of Prussia, Friedrich Wilhelm I, was a Protestant clergyman and head of the local congregation of ministers; his mother was the daughter

---

1. Vattel was christened "Emer." Modern authors have mistakenly given him a German name, "Emerich."

2. The most authoritative biography of Vattel is still E. Béguelin, "En souvenir de Vattel," in *Recueil de travaux offert par la Faculté de Droit de l'Université de Neuchâtel à la Société Suisse des Juristes à l'occasion de sa réunion à Neuchâtel, 15–17 septembre 1929,* 35–176; in English, the most informative account is A. de Lapradelle's introduction to the Carnegie edition of *The Law of Nations or the Principles of Natural Law,* iii–lix. For a concise summary, see also S. Beaulac, "Emer de Vattel and the Externalization of Sovereignty," *Journal of the History of International Law* 5 (2003): 237–92; especially pp. 242–47.

of the principality's ambassador to the Prussian court. From 1728 to 1730 Vattel was enrolled as a student of the humanities at the University of Basel, where he seems to have attended courses on Samuel Pufendorf given by the Huguenot minister Pierre Roques. In 1733 he went to Geneva to pursue theological and metaphysical studies; one of his teachers was Jean-Jacques Burlamaqui, and it was under Burlamaqui's tutelage that Vattel first studied in detail the principles of natural law and the law of nations. Little is known of the following years, but in 1740 and 1741 Vattel wrote a series of essays, several of which appeared in Switzerland's leading literary journal, the Neuchâtel-based *Journal Helvétique*.[3] The same year also saw his lengthy defense of the philosophy of Leibniz against the accusation of atheism made by the Lausanne professor of philosophy and mathematics Jean-Pierre de Crousaz.[4] Vattel's *Défense,* which he dedicated to Friedrich II ("the Great"), earned him an invitation from the French ambassador in Berlin to come to the court of the prince whose subject he was by birth. However, he failed to obtain a diplomatic position and, pressed by financial difficulties, in 1743 he moved to Dresden, where he was promised employment by Count Brühl, first minister of Elector Friedrich August II of Saxony (who as August III was also the elective king of Poland). Vattel spent the next three years in Neuchâtel, writing essays and studying the works of the

3. Vattel, "Apologie de la médisance"; "Essai sur l'utilité du jeu"; and "Relation d'un jugement rendu sur le Mont Olympe" appeared in the October and December 1740 issues of the *Journal Helvétique.* In 1741 Vattel wrote a number of essays explaining the relation between self-love and friendship, in which he put forward some of the arguments later developed in his discussion of the foundation of obligation: "Lettre à Mademoiselle de M . . . sur les sentimens délicats, généreux et désintéressés"; "Lettre sur la nature de l'amour"; and "Sur la différence de l'amour et de l'amitié." They were included in the *Pièces diverses* (see note 5) and *Le loisir philosophique* (see note 6).

4. Vattel, *Défense du système leibnitzien contre les objections et imputations de Mr de Crousaz, contenues dans l'Examen de l'Essai sur l'homme de Mr Pope. Ou l'on a joint la Réponse aux objections de Mr Roques, contenues dans le* Journal Helvétique, *par Mr Emer de Vattel* (Leyde: Jean Luzac, 1741). See S. Zurbuchen, "Die schweizerische Debatte über die Leibniz-Wolffsche Philosophie und ihre Bedeutung für Emer von Vattels philosophischen Werdegang," in *Reconceptualizing Science, Nature, and Aesthetics,* ed. P. Coleman, A. Hofmann, and S. Zurbuchen, 91–113.

German philosopher Christian Wolff, while waiting for orders from Dresden. These essays, which included his *Dissertation sur cette question: Si la loi naturelle peut porter la société à sa perfection, sans le secours des loix politiques* (*Dissertation on This Question: Can Natural Law Bring Society to Perfection Without the Assistance of Political Laws?*) as well as the *Essai sur le fondement du droit naturel, et sur le premier principe de l'obligation où se trouvent tous les hommes, d'en observer les loix* (*Essay on the Foundation of Natural Law and on the First Principle of the Obligation Men Find Themselves Under to Observe Laws*), were published in 1746.[5] In 1747, finally, after dedicating the second edition of the *Pièces diverses* to Brühl,[6] he was granted a modest annual pension of 500 *écus* and sent as a permanent minister to Berne. The purpose of his mission remains unclear; some of his compatriots speculated that it was to negotiate the acquisition of Neuchâtel by the elector of Saxony,[7] but it is more likely that he was to facilitate renegotiation of a loan of 700,000 Reichsthaler that Saxony had received from the city the year before. In fact, Vattel's stay in Berne lasted no longer than a few weeks.

For much of the next ten years Vattel remained in Neuchâtel. From here he sent a stream of letters to Brühl complaining of his ill health and dire financial circumstances. Nevertheless, this turned out to be the most productive period of his life. In 1757 he published a further collection of essays that included dialogues between Diogenes and Marcus Aurelius and between Henry IV of France and his adviser Sully.[8] Also during this period he wrote his masterpiece, *Droit des gens,* which appeared in Neuchâtel at the end of 1757, though the title page says London 1758.[9] The work quickly established Vattel as a major authority on nat-

5. Vattel, *Pièces diverses, avec quelques lettres de morale et d'amusemens* (Paris: Briasson, 1746).

6. Vattel, *Le loisir philosophique ou Pièces diverses de philosophie, de morale, et d'amusement* (Genève [in fact, Dresden]: Walther, 1747); see Béguelin, "En souvenir de Vattel," 106n112.

7. Béguelin, "En souvenir de Vattel," 47.

8. Vattel, *Poliergie ou mélange de littérature et de poësie* (Amsterdam: Arkstée et Merkus, 1757).

9. Vattel first mentions the work in a letter to Brühl from March 1758; see Béguelin, "En souvenir de Vattel," 131.

ural jurisprudence.[10] It also changed his personal situation. In 1759 the elector of Saxony finally recalled Vattel to Dresden, appointed him to the Privy Council, and made him chief adviser to the government of Saxony on foreign affairs. During his stay at Dresden, Vattel published two further works, *Mélanges de littérature, de morale, et de politique* (1760, reprinted in 1765 as *Amusemens de littérature, de morale, et de politique*) and *Questions de droit naturel et observations sur le traité du droit de nature par le Baron de Wolf* (1764), a detailed critique of Wolff's *Ius gentium methodo scientifica pertractatum* that Vattel had completed already in 1753. In 1764 he married Marie de Chêne, the daughter of a Huguenot noble family, with whom he had a son. Due to ill health, Vattel was unable to cope with his office and retired to his native Neuchâtel, where he died in December 1767 at the age of fifty-three.

Influence of Swiss Heritage

Although a subject of the king of Prussia by birth, and a servant of the elector of Saxony by profession, Vattel was first and foremost Swiss. However, that description was more complicated in the eighteenth century than it is today. What foreign observers often referred to as the Swiss republic was in fact a loose federation of independent and highly diverse entities, some aristocratic, some democratic, some monarchical, all of them small, some no bigger than a town. The federation was held together by fear of foreign aggression, a complex web of treaties, jointly ruled territories, and military and trade agreements to contain conflict between individual cantons. Although Swiss thinkers frequently invoked a universal society of nations, they remained highly suspicious of projects for perpetual peace in Europe, whether a benevolent hegemony or a European federation. Instead, they saw their best chances of survival in the more fragile order provided by a balance of power between large commercial nations constantly in need of Swiss mercenaries for their

---

10. The numerous editions of *The Law of Nations* in French, English, German, Spanish, and Italian are listed in Lapradelle, introduction, lvi–lix. To these should be added Greek, Russian, Polish, Chinese, and Japanese.

armies and Swiss investments for their public coffers. Swiss attachment to state autonomy was so great that, during the 1750s and 1760s, a small but highly vocal minority flirted with Rousseau's ideas of strict isolationism as the only way to defend Swiss liberty from the aggressiveness of modern commercial politics. Like Vattel, the majority of eighteenth-century Swiss thinkers, however, saw clear military and cultural benefits in commercial progress and ridiculed Rousseau and his followers' infatuation with the alleged virtuousness of ancient Sparta.[11] They hoped to adapt the humanist heritage of Swiss politics to the realities of a modern economy by showing how new forms of Christian patriotism, assisted by wide-reaching legislative reforms, were able to arrest and dissolve the dangerously "unsocial" tendency of commercial states.[12]

Vattel's Theory of Natural Law as Applied to the Law of Nations

Against the background of this Swiss debate, we can understand not only Vattel's vision of a workable European order but also the importance he attributed to political economy for establishing and maintaining a regime of international justice. In a famous passage, Vattel claimed that commerce had transformed Europe from a "confused heap of detached

11. See especially Vattel's "Réflexions sur le Discours de M. Rousseau touchant l'origine de l'inégalité parmi les hommes" (*Amusemens de littérature, de morale, et de politique,* 79–89), where he attacked Rousseau's elaborate critique of the idea of sociability. Although Vattel, in *The Law of Nations,* does not mention Rousseau by name, he repeatedly rejected arguments that contemporaries immediately associated with the latter. See, for example, Preliminaries §10, where Vattel argued against the Rousseauvian image of solitary natural man: "Each individual, moreover, is intimately conscious that he can neither live happily nor improve his nature without the intercourse and assistance of others." See also bk. I, §113, where he defended the arts and the sciences: "Let the friends of barbarism declaim against the sciences and polite arts; let us, without deigning to answer their vain reasonings, content ourselves with appealing to experience."

12. For a discussion of mid-eighteenth-century Swiss reform discourse, see B. Kapossy, *Iselin contra Rousseau: Sociable Patriotism and the History of Mankind.* For the wider European context of Vattel's theory, see F. Stephen Ruddy, *International Law in the Enlightenment: The Background of Emmerich de Vattel's "Le Droit des Gens."*

pieces" into a kind of large republic, where all members were united "for the maintenance of order and liberty" (bk. III, §47). An "eternal and immutable law of nature" obliged a state not only to respect and to treat other states as equals but also to provide mutual aid "so far as that other stands in real need of its assistance, and the former can grant it without neglecting the duties it owes to itself" (bk. II, §3). Here Vattel claimed to be following Christian Wolff who, in his *Ius gentium methodo scientifica pertractatum,* derived the duty to mutual aid from analogy between the state of nature and the realm of international relations: the law of nations was simply the law of nature of individuals in the state of nature applied to states (Prelim. §3–9). The primary duties of states were, first, to preserve and perfect themselves, and, second, to assist each other in fulfilling those duties each state owed to itself. States should "cultivate human society," primarily through trade, as long as the development of commerce did not conflict with their primary duties to themselves. Vattel argued that states that acted upon the principles of natural law alone would ultimately come to form a universal republic: "A real friendship will be seen to reign among them; and this happy state consists in a mutual affection" (bk. II, §12).

Although Vattel claimed that this "delightful dream" was derived directly from human nature, in *The Law of Nations* he acknowledged that "most nations aim only to strengthen and enrich themselves at the expense of others" (bk. II, §16). Accordingly, prudence prevented existing states from making mutual aid the guiding principle of foreign politics. Instead, states ought to content themselves with a morally less appealing, but nevertheless workable, order based on the balance of power. Vattel explained this acknowledgment of the realities of modern European politics on two grounds. The first was the theoretical incoherence of previous natural law theories with regard to the duties of perfectly independent states. Here he turned against Wolff's idea of a *civitas maxima,* as we will see.[13] Vattel claimed that Wolff had rightly distinguished between two forms of the law of nations: first, an immutable or *necessary*

13. N. Greenwood Onuf, "Civitas Maxima: Wolff, Vattel, and the Fate of Republicanism," *American Journal of International Law* 88 (1994): 280–303.

law of nations, signifying the law of nature applied to individual states; second, a *voluntary* law of nations, which defined the necessary limitations of natural law within the realm of international relations and which, he argued, had to be tolerated in order to avoid greater harm.[14] Although states, like individuals, were bound to assist others, this duty was limited by the perfect right of a state to self-preservation. The implication this had for trade was clear enough: while a state was obliged to trade with all other states and sell its products at a "fair price," considerations of self-preservation allowed it to limit its trade, establish trading companies, or even refuse commerce with another state altogether. Wolff had also rightly recognized that since the law of nations applied to all states in the same way, those states affected by trade sanctions could merely point out breaches of the *necessary* law of nations. Refusal to trade, however, did not provide any legal ground for the commencement of military hostilities. The situation was different when a state was not just incapable of self-preservation but lacked any resources to exchange for vital goods. Here, the perfect right of preservation of a potential donor nation was bound to clash with the equally perfect right of preservation of a state on the brink of starvation. It is in this context that one needs to read Vattel's often-cited justification of the appropriation of uncultivated land by European settlers in America.[15]

Given the increasingly economic dimension of European politics, there was a constant danger that peaceful trade would be subjected to the logic of warfare. Vattel's main task in *The Law of Nations* was to define as clearly as possible the limits individual states were allowed to impose on freedom of trade. Wolff hoped to derive such understanding from the image of a *civitas maxima,* a universal republic instituted by nature, whose civil law was the expression of the right reason of civilized nations. In the preface, Vattel rejected Wolff's *civitas maxima* as fictitious and incompatible with the idea of state sovereignty (preface, 14). While civil society could be said to be natural in that it originated in

---

14. For a detailed treatment of Vattel's theory of international law, see Emmanuelle Jouannet, *Emer de Vattel et l'émergence doctrinale du droit international classique.*

15. Vattel, *Law of Nations,* I §81; II §86–87, 97; *Questions,* 71–72.

human need, no such thing could be said of the relation between sovereign states: "I acknowledge no other natural society between nations than that which nature has established between mankind in general" (ibid.). In contrast to individuals, nations enjoyed greater autonomy and because of this had no pressing reason to subject themselves to a higher authority. Furthermore, their absolute liberty was necessary "properly to discharge the duties [the state] owes to herself and to her citizens" (preface, 15).

Vattel's defense of a natural law of nations together with his insistence on state sovereignty earned him a reputation for incoherence, the view of Kant, or, as many international law theorists writing after the First World War maintained, for being an unconditional supporter of reason of state who "disguised his evil intentions through words of sublime charity."[16] Although in *The Law of Nations* Vattel dealt with this issue only in passing, he discussed it at length in several of his other writings, notably his *Essay on the Foundation of Natural Law and on the First Principle of the Obligation Men Find Themselves Under to Observe Laws.* Here he sought to explain how humans could be under an obligation to natural law even in the absence of a punitive superior. Vattel's main move, primarily aimed at Jean Barbeyrac, was to derive obligation not from any external source, but from what he claimed was man's most basic motive, namely self-love and a desire for the happiness of a perfect soul.[17] Ultimately it was from man's obligation to himself to attain the highest degree of happiness, which in turn required commerce with other rational beings, that the duty of mutual aid and friendship could be derived.[18] This also applied to the obedience citizens owed to the state:

16. C. Van Vollenhoven, *Du droit de paix. De iure pacis,* 99. See Emmanuelle Jouannet, "La critique de la pensée classique durant l'entre-deux guerres: Vattel et Van Vollenhoven," in *Miskolc Journal of International Law* 1 (2004): 45–63. Kant, in his "Perpetual Peace: A Philosophical Sketch," had famously labeled Vattel, together with Grotius and Pufendorf, as "sorry comforters," in *Political Writings,* 103. See also R. Tuck, *The Rights of War and Peace: Political Thought and the International Order from Grotius to Kant,* 191–96; and T. J. Hochstrasser, *Natural Law Theories in the Early Enlightenment,* 177–83.

17. Vattel, *Essay on the Foundation,* 752.

18. See also Vattel's essays on friendship from 1741 (see note 3, below).

"The love and affection a man feels for the state of which he is a member, is a necessary consequence of the wise and rational love he owes to himself, since his own happiness is connected with that of his country" (bk. I, §120). In *The Law of Nations* Vattel used the same argument with regard to states. As in the case of individuals, a nation's duty of self-preservation and of self-perfection could be derived only from its basic self-interest and its desire to attain the highest level of national happiness. Moreover, like individuals, nations could attain national happiness only by developing more enlightened forms of self-interest, forms that took into account the well-being of other nations.[19] Vattel claimed that the highest degree of national happiness consisted in "true glory" (bk. I, §§186–88). It was acquired through the positive reputation a state enjoyed among well-intentioned nations, and through the respect it received from those seeking to violate the laws of nations. A truly glorious nation, Vattel hoped, would set an example others would wish to emulate. In so doing, it would gradually shift the pathological rivalry between states in the direction of a system based on virtuous competition.[20]

As a further measure for reducing the tensions between self-preservation and mutual aid, Vattel called upon European rulers and their ministers to implement a wide range of legislative reforms that would allow modern nations to break out of the vicious cycle of public borrowing and taxation and to create a healthier balance between income and expenditure (bk. I, §183). Instead of relying on the distributive effect of luxury and conspicuous consumption, rulers should initiate a new culture of virtuous moderation and encourage agriculture so as to procure "abundance in every thing" (bk. I, §73).[21] Although he accepted

19. Note the revealing subtitle added to the pirated edition (Leyden, 1758), which suggested that Vattel's treatise should be read as "a work tending to display the true interest of powers." This additional subtitle seems to have been included only in the German edition of 1760, the first English translation of 1759, and the second American edition of 1805.

20. Vattel dealt with the distinction between true and false glory at length in his "Dialogue entre Pierre le Grand & Charles XII sur la gloire des conquérans," published in the *Amusemens de littérature* (La Haye: Pierre Gosse, 1765), 1–19.

21. See Vattel's essay *Dialogue entre le prince de **** & son confident, sur quelques parties essentielles de l'administration publique,* reproduced in this edition, p. 783.

certain protectionist measures with regard to foreign trade, Vattel insisted that states should intervene as little as possible in the domestic economy and grant individual citizens the maximum amount of natural liberty: "Liberty is the soul of abilities and industry" (bk. I, §74). He also expressly recommended the role of learned societies for the dissemination of technological know-how (bk. I, §76). Vattel believed that of all modern nations Britain had come closest to implementing a system worthy of emulation, and in *The Law of Nations* he repeatedly singled it out as an example for the rest of Europe, not only with regard to its economy but also with respect to its "admirable constitution." In contrast with the constitutions of patrimonial states, Britain allowed its citizens to recognize themselves as part of both the nation and the universal society of men (bk. I, §24).[22]

Contemporaries would have recognized Vattel's stance on perhaps the central issue of European politics at the time: whether Britain or France would prove the stronger in the international rivalry for supremacy. In supporting Britain's advocacy of an ongoing European balance of power, rather than French hegemony on mainland Europe that was associated with the peace projects of the Abbé de Saint-Pierre and Victor Riqueti de Mirabeau, Vattel was taking a stand on the domestic stability of mixed government as much as he was on the consequences of such a polity for international affairs. In advocating mixed government in commercial monarchies he was going against the grain of the majority of writers, such as Montesquieu and Rousseau, for whom Britain's mixed government, with its parties, corruption, and factions, represented an institutionalization of civil war domestically that would have dire consequences if transposed into the dominant form of state internationally. Praise of Britain also allowed Vattel to emphasize the greater modernity of Protestant states by contrast with the backwardness of the religious, moral, and economic practices that he associated with Catholicism. In an openly polemical fashion, Vattel often linked such backwardness with reason of state, or amoral policy, in the international

---

22. On Vattel's critique of the patrimonial state, see Frederick G. Whelan, "Vattel's Doctrine of the State," *History of Political Thought,* 9 (1988): 59–90.

sphere and was always ready to provide examples of the violation of natural law from the history of the papacy. Catholic writers were, however, willing to use Vattel for his broader arguments about the independence of small states. One key example is Cardinal Consalvi at the Congress of Vienna, who employed Vattel's arguments to justify the sovereignty of the Vatican over the papal states.

Vattel was convinced that if Britain played a more active role in the relations between European states, French aspirations to universal monarchy would be countered. This was expected in turn to safeguard the sovereignty of the smaller states, and especially the Swiss republics, the legitimacy of whose existence was increasingly questioned as public credit allowed the larger monarchies to employ mercenary armies too strong for the old republics, however great their republican valor and virtue. Vattel's case for the survival of small states in the modern world is one of his main themes, especially in *The Law of Nations.* Vattel's association of the law of nations with the defense of small states against more powerful neighbors was illustrated in February 1758, after the Prussian army had destroyed castles belonging to the duke of Saxony. Vattel announced to Brühl that his recently published work proved the legitimacy of Saxony's complaints and also showed that "all powers are obliged to unite and punish the one who wishes to introduce such wicked customs."[23] Prussia should be held accountable, he explained in a letter addressed to the avoyer[24] and Small Council of Berne, for violating the established rules of war that permitted armed conflict only as a last resort after all diplomatic options had been exhausted. Given that Saxony had not only disarmed but even granted passage to Prussian troops, Friedrich's systematic plundering of Saxony's riches and forced enlistment of the "entire flower of youth"—a practice that Vattel described as being without precedent among Christian princes—threatened the very possibility of peaceful coexistence among European nations.[25]

23. Béguelin, "En souvenir de Vattel," 131; see *Law of Nations,* III §168.
24. Berne's chief magistrate.
25. Béguelin, "En souvenir de Vattel," 172.

Conclusion

Vattel's ideas of modern patriotism and encouragement of the economy are not among the most original in *The Law of Nations.* Nevertheless, they are important because they show the weakness of any attempt to capture Vattel's position within the analytical framework of retrospective histories of international law or international relations.[26] Besides clarifying more thoroughly than previous thinkers the proper relationship between the natural law of individuals and of states, Vattel used his unusually broad intellectual interests to comment on the cultural, political, and economic conditions required for a viable system of international justice. Vattel saw his magnum opus as a contribution to a great European debate on the science of legislation, a debate that analyzed the possibilities available to modern nations to secure liberty and cultural advancement against constant interruption by war. The importance of *The Law of Nations* therefore resides both in its systematic derivation of international law from natural law and in its compelling synthesis of the modern discourse of natural jurisprudence with the even newer language of political economy. These features help to explain the continuing appeal of this text well into the nineteenth century among politicians, international lawyers, and political theorists of every complexion.[27]

26. For two opposite interpretations, see A. Nussbaum, *A Concise History of the Law of Nations,* 152, and Q. Wright, *A Study of War,* 336–37.

27. For the reception of Vattel, see C. G. Fenwick, "The Authority of Vattel," *American Political Science Review* 7 (1913): 395–410; F. S. Ruddy, "The Acceptance of Vattel," *Grotian Society Papers* (1972): 177–96; and H. Thévenaz, "Vattel ou la destinée d'un livre," *Schweizerisches Jahrbuch für Internationales Recht,* 14 (1957): 9–16.

A NOTE ON THE TEXTS

English Editions of *The Law of Nations*

Vattel's *Law of Nations* was translated anonymously into English several times in the eighteenth century. The first edition of 1760 was based on the French original *Droit des gens* of 1758. A Dublin translation of 1787 is remarkably fluent and elegant, but it does not include the substantive notes of the original nor, more importantly, the notes added to the posthumous French edition of 1773 and intended by Vattel for a second edition he did not live to complete. Several English editions, including the 1916 Classics of International Law edition, are similarly flawed and based on the edition of 1760. However, two English editions from the end of the eighteenth century include Vattel's later thoughts. One, from 1793, contains a pagination error. This has been corrected in the revised version, London 1797, and the latter forms the basis for the present edition. The 1797 edition has the benefit of a detailed table of contents and margin titles for subsections.

There is no modern edition of *The Law of Nations*, but facsimiles of the popular nineteenth-century editions by the London barrister Joseph Chitty have appeared in recent times. These annotated editions (first in 1834) and their reissue with further notes by Edward Ingraham (first in 1852) were based on the 1797 London edition. Chitty helpfully identified the notes that distinguished the 1797 edition from the earlier English translation. He sought, however, to add much more to the text, as he explained in a preface written in Chancery Lane in November 1833:

> Many years have elapsed since the original work was published, long before the invaluable decisions of Sir William Scott, Sir C. Robinson, and Sir John Nichol, and other eminent Judges in the Courts of Ad-

miralty, and Prize and other Courts; and the last edition upon which any care was bestowed, was published in A.D. 1797; since which time, and especially during the last general war, many most important rules respecting the Law of Nations were established. The object of the present Editor has, therefore, been to collect and condense, *in numerous notes,* the *modern rules and decisions,* and to fortify the positions in the text by references to other authors of eminence, and by which he hopes that this edition will be found of more practical utility, without interfering with the text, or materially increasing its size.

In consequence, Chitty's text is overloaded with legal citations based on the case law of the sea that emerged in the Napoleonic era. Vattel's work had become a textbook for law students in both Britain and North America.

Some of Chitty's notes remain useful and have on occasion been incorporated into the editorial apparatus for this edition. The present edition includes new footnotes, elucidating dates, events, works, and persons referred to by Vattel. Posthumous additions to the French edition of 1773, which were then translated in the edition of 1797, are identified as such in the new notes. Translations of Vattel's Latin citations have come from the best modern editions, particularly from the Loeb Classical Library. For each translation, reference to the edition used can be found in the bibliography of authors cited. In cases where no translation could be found, or where the context of Vattel's work required an amended translation, the editors undertook the translation, and this is signaled in the text by "trans. Eds." All of the preceding new material has been added to the 1797 text as numbered notes or as double squarebracketed inserts within Vattel's original notes.

Chitty lamented in 1833 that "he proposed to form an Index, so as to render the work more readily accessible; but, in that desire, he has been overruled by the publishers." The present edition adds bibliographical and biographical details of authors cited in the text, following up Vattel's own sometimes obscure references. The bibliography of authors cited includes and explains the short titles employed by Vattel in his footnotes.

Page breaks in the 1797 edition have been indicated in the body of the text by the use of angle brackets. For example, page 112 begins after <112>.

Three Essays by Vattel

The first two essays included here, *Essay on the Foundation of Natural Law*[1] and *Can Natural Law Bring Society to Perfection Without the Assistance of Political Laws?*[2] date from the early and formative phase of Vattel's career and anticipate many of the themes of *The Law of Nations*. Both essays were originally published in the collection *Le loisir philosophique ou pièces diverses de philosophie, de morale et d'amusement* (Geneva, 1747). The second dissertation was a response to the Academy of Dijon's prize competition of 1742.

The two translations, both for the first time in English, are based on the texts as appended to a nineteenth-century edition of the *Le droit des gens: Nouvelle édition, précédé d'un essai et d'une dissertation (de l'auteur), accompagnée des notes de Pinheiro-Ferreira et du Baron de Chambrier d'Oleires, augmente du discours sur l'étude du droit de la nature et des gens par Sir J. Mackintosh (traduction nouvelle), complèté par l'exposition des doctrines des publicistes contemporains mise au courant des progrès du droit public moderne et suivie d'une table analytique des matières, par M. P. Pradier-Fodéré* (3 vols.; Paris: Saint-Denis, 1863).

The third essay, *Dialogue Between the Prince of **** and His Confidant*,[3] was first published in *Amusemens de littérature, de morale, et de politique par M. de Vattel* (The Hague: Pierre Gosse Junior & Daniel Pinet libraires de S.A.S, 1765, 21–48). It is translated here in English for the first time.

The text of this essay is important because it shows Vattel to have

---

1. Emer de Vattel, *Essay on the Foundation of Natural Law and on the First Principle of the Obligation Men Find Themselves Under to Observe Laws* (*Essai sur le fondement du droit naturel, et sur le premier principe de l'obligation où se trouvent tous les hommes, d'en observer les lois*), translated by T. J. Hochstrasser.

2. *Dissertation on This Question: "Can Natural Law Bring Society to Perfection Without the Assistance of Political Laws?"* (*Dissertation sur cette question: "Si la loi naturelle peut porter la société à sa perfection, sans le secours des loix politiques?"*), translated by T. J. Hochstrasser.

3. Emer de Vattel, *Dialogue Between the Prince of **** & his Confidant, on certain Essential Elements of Public Administration* (*Dialogue entre le prince de **** & son confident, sur quelques parties essentielles de l'administration publique*), translated by K. Goodwin.

been participating fully in the debates about economic and administrative reform that took place all over Europe at the time. The *Dialogue* also shows that Vattel's theory of international law (and especially his assessment of Europe's chances of having a workable system of international justice) can be fully understood only when seen in the light of his ideas about domestic reform.

In all three essays the original notes have been preserved as numbered notes. New material added by the volume editors is enclosed in double square brackets.

ACKNOWLEDGMENTS

The editors would like to thank Nikolas Funke, Ken Goodwin, Tim Hochstrasser, Amanda McKeever, Norman Vance, and Stefania Tutino for extensive scholarly labors which have immeasurably improved this edition. Ian Gazeley, Julian Hoppit, Istvan Hont, Michael Sonenscher, Gabriella Silvestrini, and Brian Young deserve thanks for help on specific points of fact. Thanks are also due to Laura Goetz, Diana Francoeur, and the editorial team at Liberty Fund, who saw the manuscript through press with outstanding professionalism. Support for the research underpinning this edition was provided by the School of Humanities Research Fund at the University of Sussex, the British Academy, the Arts and Humanities Research Council, the Leverhulme Trust, and the History Department of the University of Lausanne. As is always the case, a debt of gratitude is owed to our wives and families, and also to our colleagues in intellectual history at Sussex, Fribourg, and Lausanne. Our greatest debt, however, is to Knud Haakonssen who, master editor that he is, guided us with patience and good humor through the minefield of modern editorial practice.

Béla Kapossy
Richard Whatmore

THE LAW OF NATIONS

THE
LAW OF NATIONS,
OR,
PRINCIPLES
OF THE
LAW OF NATURE,

Applied to the Conduct and Affairs

OF NATIONS AND SOVEREIGNS.

FROM THE FRENCH OF MONSIEUR DE VATTEL.

Nihil est enim illi principi Deo qui omnem hunc mundum regit, quod quidem in terris fiat, acceptius, quam concilia coetusque hominum jure sociati, quae civitates, appellantur.[1]   CICERO, Som. Scip.[2]

A NEW EDITION,

Revised, corrected, and enriched with many valuable Notes never before translated into English.

LONDON:

PRINTED FOR G. G. AND J. ROBINSON, PATERNOSTER-ROW.

1797.

---

1. "For to the Supreme God who governs this whole universe nothing is more pleasing than those companies and unions of men that are called cities."
2. Somnium Scipionis (Scipio's Dream) in Cicero, *De republica.*

ADVERTISEMENT

In undertaking this new edition of Monsieur De Vattel's treatise, it was not my intention to give what might strictly be called a new translation. To add the author's valuable notes from the posthumous edition printed at Neuchatel in 1773,—to correct some errors I had observed in the former version,—and occasionally to amend the language where doubtful or obscure,—were the utmost limits of my original plan. As I proceeded, however, my alterations became more numerous: but whether they will be acknowledged as amendments, it must rest with the reader to determine. Even if his decision should be more favourable than I have any reason to expect, I lay no claim to praise for my humble efforts, but shall esteem myself very fortunate if I escape the severity of censure for presenting the work to the public in a state still so far short of perfection. Conscious of its defects, I declare with great sincerity—

> . . . . Veniam pro laude peto,—laudatus abunde,
> Non fastiditus si tibi, lector, ero.[3]

LONDON,   THE EDITOR
May 1, 1797.

---

3. "I ask forgiveness not praise,—I will be praised in full, if you don't despise me, reader" (Ovid, *Tristia* I, VII).

PREFACE

The Law of Nations, though so noble and important a subject, has not hitherto been treated of with all the care it deserves. The greater part of mankind have therefore only a vague, a very incomplete, and often even a false notion of it. The generality of writers, and even celebrated authors, almost exclusively confine the name of the Law of Nations to certain maxims and customs which have been adopted by different nations, and which the mutual consent of the parties has alone rendered obligatory on them. This is confining within very narrow bounds a law so extensive in its own nature, and in which the whole human race are so intimately concerned; it is at the same time a degradation of that law, in consequence of a misconception of its real origin.

There certainly exists a natural law of nations, since the obligations of the law of nature are no less binding on states, on men united in political society, than on individuals. But, to acquire an exact knowledge of that law, it is not sufficient to know what the law of nature prescribes to the individuals of the human race. The application of a rule to various subjects can no otherwise be made than in a manner agreeable to the nature of each subject. Hence it follows that the natural law of nations is a particular science, consisting in a just and rational application of the law of nature to the affairs and conduct of nations or sovereigns. All those treatises, therefore, in which the law of nations is blended and confounded with the ordinary law of nature, are incapable of conveying a distinct idea or a substantial knowledge of the sacred law of nations.

The Romans often confounded the law of nations with the law of nature, giving the name of "the law of nations" (*Jus Gentium*) to the law of nature, as <iv> being generally acknowledged and adopted by all civilised nations.* The definitions given by the emperor Justinian, of the law of nature, the law of nations, and the civil law, are well known. "The law of nature" says he, "is that which nature teaches to all animals":† thus he defines the natural law in its most extensive sense, not that natural law which is peculiar to man, and which is derived as well from his rational as from his animal nature. "The civil law," that emperor adds, "is that which each nation has established for herself, and which peculiarly belongs to each state or civil society. And that law, which natural reason has established among all mankind, and which is equally observed by all people, is called the law of nations, as being a law which all nations follow."‡ In the succeeding paragraph the emperor seems to approach nearer to the sense we at present give to that term. "The law of nations," says he, "is common to the whole human race. The exigencies and necessities of mankind have induced all nations to lay down and adopt certain rules of right. For wars have arisen, and produced captivity and servitude, which are contrary to the law of nature; since, by the law of nature, all men were originally born free."§ But, from what he adds— that almost all kinds of contracts, those of buying and selling, of hire, partnership, trust, and an infinite number of <v> others, owe their origin to that law of nations,—it plainly appears to have been Justinian's idea, that, according to the situations and circumstances in which men were placed, right reason has dictated to them certain maxims of equity, so founded on the nature of things, that they have been universally acknowledged and adopted. Still this is nothing more than the law of nature which is equally applicable to all mankind.

---

* Neque vero hoc solum natura, id est, jure gentium, &c. Cicero de Offic. lib. iii. c. 5.

† Jus naturale est, quod natura omnia animalia docuit. Instit. lib. i. tit. 2.

‡ Quod quisque populus ipse sibi jus constituit, id ipsius proprium civitatis est, vocaturque jus civile, quasi jus proprium ipsius civitatis: quod vero naturalis ratio inter omnes homines constituit, id apud omnes peraeque custoditur, vocaturque jus gentium, quasi quo jure omnes gentes utantur. Ibid. §1.

§ Jus autem gentium omni humano generi commune est: nam usu exigente et humanis necessitatibus, gentes humanae jura quaedam sibi constituerunt. Bella etenim orta sunt, et captivitates secutae et servitutes, quae sunt naturali juri contrariae. Jure enim naturali omnes homines ab initio liberi nascebantur. Ibid. §2.

The Romans, however, acknowledged a law whose obligations are reciprocally binding on nations: and to that law they referred the right of embassies. They had also their *fecial* law, which was nothing more than the law of nations in its particular relation to public treaties, and especially to war. The *feciales* were the interpreters, the guardians, and, in a manner, the priests of the public faith.*

The moderns are generally agreed in restricting the appellation of "the law of nations" to that system of right and justice which ought to prevail between nations or sovereign states. They differ only in the ideas they entertain of the origin whence that system arose, and of the foundations upon which it rests. The celebrated Grotius understands it to be a system established by the common consent of nations; and he thus distinguishes it from the law of nature: "When several persons, at different times and in various places, maintain the same thing as certain, such coincidence of sentiment must be attributed to some general cause. Now, in the questions before us, that cause must necessarily be one or the other of these two—either a just consequence drawn from natural principles, or a universal consent. <vi> The former discovers to us the law of nature, and the latter, the law of nations."†

That great man, as appears from many passages in his excellent work, had a glimpse of the truth: but as he had the task of extracting from the rude ore, as it were, and reducing into regular shape and form, a new and important subject which had been much neglected before his time, it is not surprising, that,—having his mind burthened with an immense variety of objects, and with a numberless train of quotations which

---

* *Feciales,* quod fidei publicae inter populos praeerant: nam per hos fiebat ut justum conciperetur bellum (et inde desitum), et ut foedere fides pacis constitueretur. Ex his mittebant, antequam conciperetur, qui res repeterent: et per hos etiam nunc fit foedus. Varro de Ling. Lat. lib. iv. [["The *Fetiales* [herald-priests] because they were in charge of the state's word of honor in matters between peoples; for by them it was brought about that a war that was declared should be a just war, and by them the war was stopped, that by a *foedus* [treaty], the *fides* [honesty] of the peace might be established. Some of them were sent before war should be declared, to demand restitution of the stolen property, and by them even now is made the *foedus.*" *De lingua Latina* V.XV]]

† *De Jure Belli & Pacis,* translated by Barbeyrac: Preliminary Discourse, §41.

formed a part of his plan,—he could not always acquire those distinct ideas so necessary in the sciences. Persuaded that nations or sovereign powers are subject to the authority of the law of nature, the observance of which he so frequently recommends to them,—that learned man, in fact, acknowledged a natural law of nations, which he somewhere calls the *internal* law of nations: and perhaps it will appear that the only difference between him and us lies in the terms. But we have already observed, that, in order to form this natural law of nations, it is not sufficient simply to apply to nations what the law of nature decides with respect to individuals. And besides, Grotius, by his very distinction, and by exclusively appropriating the name of "the law of nations" to those maxims which have been established by the common consent of mankind, seems to intimate, that sovereigns, in their transactions with each other, cannot insist on the observance of any but those last-mentioned maxims,—reserving the *internal* law for the direction of their own consciences. If—setting out with the idea that political societies or nations live, with respect to each other, in a reciprocal independence, in the state of nature, and that, as political bodies, they are subject to the natural law—Grotius had moreover considered that the law must <vii> be applied to these new subjects in a manner suitable to their nature,—that judicious author would easily have discovered that the natural law of nations is a particular science; that it produces between nations even an *external* obligation wholly independent of their will; and that the common consent of mankind is only the foundation and source of a particular kind of law called the *Arbitrary Law of Nations.*

Hobbes, in whose work we discover the hand of a master, notwithstanding his paradoxes and detestable maxims,—Hobbes was, I believe, the first who gave a distinct though imperfect idea of the law of nations. He divides the *law of nature* into that of *man,* and that of *states:* and the latter is, according to him, what we usually call the law of nations. "The maxims," he adds, "of each of these laws are precisely the same: but as states once established assume personal properties, that which is termed the natural law when we speak of the duties of individuals, is called the law of nations when applied to whole nations or states."* This

---

* Rursus (*lex*) *naturalis* dividi potest in naturalem hominum, quae sola obtinuit

author has well observed, that the law of nations is the law of nature applied to states or nations. But we shall see in the course of this work, that he was mistaken in the idea that the law of nature does not suffer any necessary change in that application,—an idea from which he concluded that the maxims of the law of nature and those of the law of nations are precisely the same.

Puffendorf declares that he unreservedly subscribes to this opinion espoused by Hobbes.* He has not therefore separately treated of the law of nations, <viii> but has every-where blended it with the law of nature properly so called.

Barbeyrac, who performed the office of translator and commentator to Grotius and Puffendorf, has approached much nearer to the true idea of the law of nations. Though the work is in every body's hands, I shall here, for the reader's convenience, transcribe one of that learned translator's notes on Grotius's Law of War and Peace.† "I acknowledge," says he, "that there are laws common to all nations,—things which all nations ought to practise towards each other: and if people choose to call these the law of nations, they may do so with great propriety. But setting aside the consideration that the consent of mankind is not the basis of the obligation by which we are bound to observe those laws, and that it cannot even possibly take place in this instance,—the principles and the rules of such a law are in fact the same as those of the law of nature,

---

dici *Lex Naturae,* et naturalem *civitatum,* quae dici potest *Lex Gentium,* vulgo autem *Jus Gentium* appellatur. Praecepta utriusque eadem sunt: sed quia civitates semel institutae induunt proprietates hominum personales, lex quam, loquentes de hominum singulorum officio, *naturalem* dicimus, applicata totis civitatibus, nationibus, sive gentibus, vocatur *Jus Gentium.* De Cive, c. xiv. §4. [["Again, the Natural Law may be divided into that of men, which alone hath obtained the title of the Law of Nature, and that of cities, which may be called Law of Nations, but vulgarly it is termed the Right of Nations. (The precepts of both are alike, but because cities once instituted do put on the personal proprieties of men, that law, which speaking of the duty of single men, we call natural, being applied to whole cities, and nations, is called the Right of Nations. And the same Elements of natural law, and right, which have hitherto been spoken of, being transferred to whole cities and nations, may be taken for the Elements of the laws, and Right of Nations." Hobbes, *De Cive,* ed. Warrender, 28.]]

* Puffendorf's Law of Nature and Nations, book ii. chap. iii. §23.

† Book i. chap. 1, §14, note 3.

properly so called; the only difference consisting in the mode of their application, which may be somewhat varied, on account of the difference that sometimes happens in the manner in which nations settle their affairs with each other."

It did not escape the notice of the author we have just quoted, that the rules and decisions of the law of nature cannot be purely and simply applied to sovereign states, and that they must necessarily undergo some modifications in order to accommodate them to the nature of the new subjects to which they are applied. But it does not appear that he discovered the full extent of this idea, since he seems not to approve of the mode of treating the law of nations separately from the law of nature as relating to individuals. He only commends Budaeus's method, saying, "it was right in that author to point out,* after each article of the law of nature, the application which may be <ix> made of it to nations in their mutual relations to each other,—so far at least as his plan permitted or required that he should do this."† Here Barbeyrac made one step at least in the right track: but it required more profound reflection and more extensive views in order to conceive the idea of a system of natural law of nations, which should claim the obedience of states and sovereigns,— to perceive the utility of such a work, and especially to be the first to execute it.

This glory was reserved for the baron de Wolf. That great philosopher saw that the law of nature could not, with such modifications as the nature of the subjects required, and with sufficient precision, clearness, and solidity, be applied to incorporated nations or states, without the assistance of those general principles and leading ideas by which the application is to be directed;—that it is by those principles alone we are enabled evidently to demonstrate that the decisions of the law of nature respecting individuals must, pursuant to the intentions of that very law, be changed and modified in their application to states and political so-

* In his Elementa Philos. Pract.

† Note 2 on Puffendorf's Law of Nature and Nations, book ii. chap. 3, §23. I have not been able to procure Budaeus's work, from which I suspect that Barbeyrac derived this idea of the Law of Nations.

cieties,—and thus to form a natural and necessary law of nations:* whence he concluded, that it was proper to form a distinct system of the law of nations,—a task which he has happily executed. But <x> it is just that we should hear what Wolf himself says in his Preface.[1]

"Nations,"† says he, "do not, in their mutual relations to each other, acknowledge any other law than that which nature herself has established. Perhaps, therefore, it may appear superfluous to give a treatise on the law of nations, as distinct from the law of nature. But those who entertain this idea have not sufficiently studied the subject. Nations, it is true, can only be considered as so many individual persons living together in the state of nature; and, for that reason, we must apply to them all the duties and rights which nature prescribes and attributes to men in general, as being naturally born free, and bound to each other by no ties but those of nature alone. The law which arises from this application, and the obligations resulting from it, proceed from that immutable law founded on the nature of man; and thus the law of nations certainly belongs to the law of nature: it is therefore, on account of its origin, called the *natural,* and, by reason of its obligatory force, the *necessary* law of nations. That law is common to all nations; and if any one of them does not respect it in her actions, she violates the common rights of all the others.

"But nations or sovereign states being moral persons, and the subjects

---

* If it were not more advisable, for the sake of brevity, of avoiding repetitions, and taking advantage of the ideas already formed and established in the minds of men,—if, for all these reasons, it were not more convenient to presuppose in this instance a knowledge of the ordinary law of nature, and on that ground to undertake the task of applying it to sovereign states,—it would, instead of speaking of such application, be more accurate to say, that, as the law of nature, properly so called, is the natural law of individuals and founded on the nature of man, so the natural law of nations is the natural law of political societies, and founded on the nature of those societies. But as the result of either mode is ultimately the same, I have in preference adopted the more compendious one. As the law of nature has already been treated of in an ample and satisfactory manner, the shortest way is simply to make a rational application of it to nations.

† A nation here means a sovereign state, an independent political society.

1. Christian Wolff, *Ius naturae et ius gentium* (Halle, 1740–46).

of the obligations and rights resulting, in virtue of the law of nature, from the act of association which has formed the political body,—the nature and essence of these moral persons necessarily differ, in many respects, from the nature and essence of the physical individuals, or men, of whom they are composed. When, therefore, we would apply to nations the duties which the law of nature prescribes to individual man, and the rights it confers on him in order to enable him <xi> to fulfil his duties,—since those rights and those duties can be no other than what are consistent with the nature of their subjects, they must, in their application, necessarily undergo a change suitable to the new subjects to which they are applied. Thus we see that the law of nations does not in every particular remain the same as the law of nature, regulating the actions of individuals. Why may it not therefore be separately treated of, as a law peculiar to nations?"

Being myself convinced of the utility of such a work, I impatiently waited for Monsieur Wolf's production, and, as soon as it appeared, formed the design of facilitating, for the advantage of a greater number of readers, the knowledge of the luminous ideas which it contains. The treatise of the philosopher of Hall[[e]] on the law of nations is dependent on all those of the same author on philosophy and the law of nature. In order to read and understand it, it is necessary to have previously studied sixteen or seventeen quarto volumes which precede it. Besides, it is written in the manner and even in the formal method of geometrical works. These circumstances present obstacles which render it nearly useless to those very persons in whom the knowledge and taste of the true principles of the law of nations are most important and most desirable. At first I thought that I should have had nothing farther to do, than to detach this treatise from the entire system by rendering it independent of every thing Monsieur Wolf had said before, and to give it a new form, more agreeable, and better calculated to ensure it a reception in the polite world. With that view, I made some attempts; but I soon found, that if I indulged the expectation of procuring readers among that class of persons for whom I intended to write, and of rendering my efforts beneficial to man-kind, it was necessary that I should form a very different work from that which lay before me, and undertake to furnish an original production. The method <xii> followed by Monsieur Wolf has had the effect of rendering his work dry, and in many respects incomplete. The different subjects are scattered through it in a manner that is extremely fatiguing to the attention: and as the author had, in his "Law of Nature," treated of universal public law, he frequently contents himself with a bare reference to his former production, when, in handling the law of nations, he speaks of the duties of a nation towards herself.

From Monsieur Wolf's treatise, therefore, I have only borrowed whatever appeared most worthy of attention, especially the definitions and general principles; but I have been careful in selecting what I drew from that source, and have accommodated to my own plan the materials with which he furnished me. Those who have read Monsieur Wolf's treatises on the law of nature and the law of nations, will see what advantage I have made of them. Had I every-where pointed out what I have borrowed, my pages would be crowded with quotations equally useless and disagreeable to the reader. It is better to acknowledge here, once for all, the obligations I am under to that great master. Although my work be very different from his (as will appear to those who are willing to take the trouble of making the comparison), I confess that I should never have had the courage to launch into so extensive a field, if the celebrated philosopher of Hall[[e]] had not preceded my steps, and held forth a torch to guide me on my way.

Sometimes, however, I have ventured to deviate from the path which he had pointed out, and have adopted sentiments opposite to his. I will here quote a few instances. Monsieur Wolf, influenced perhaps by the example of numerous other writers, has devoted several sections* to the express purpose of treating of the nature of *patrimonial* kingdoms, without rejecting or rectifying that idea so degrading to human kind. I do not even admit of such a denomination, which I <xiii> think equally shocking, improper, and dangerous, both in its effects, and in the impressions it may give to sovereigns: and in this, I flatter myself I shall obtain the suffrage of every man who possesses the smallest spark of reason and sentiment,—in short, of every true citizen.

---

* In the VIIIth Part of his Law of Nature, and in his Law of Nations.

Monsieur Wolf determines (Jus Gent. §878) that it is naturally lawful to make use of poisoned weapons in war. I am shocked at such a decision, and sorry to find it in the work of so great a man. Happily for the human race, it is not difficult to prove the contrary, even from Monsieur Wolf's own principles. What I have said on this subject may be seen in Book III. §156.

In the very outset of my work, it will be found that I differ entirely from Monsieur Wolf in the manner of establishing the foundations of that species of law of nations which we call *voluntary*. Monsieur Wolf deduces it from the idea of a great republic (*civitatis maximae*) instituted by nature herself, and of which all the nations of the world are members. According to him, the *voluntary* law of nations is, as it were, the civil law of that great republic. This idea does not satisfy me; nor do I think the fiction of such a republic either admissible in itself, or capable of affording sufficiently solid grounds on which to build the rules of the universal law of nations which shall necessarily claim the obedient acquiescence of sovereign states. I acknowledge no other natural society between nations than that which nature has established between mankind in general. It is essential to every civil society (*civitati*) that each member have resigned a part of his right to the body of the society, and that there exist in it an authority capable of commanding all the members, of giving them laws, and of compelling those who should refuse to obey. Nothing of this kind can be conceived or supposed to subsist between nations. Each sovereign state claims and actually possesses an absolute independence on <xiv> all the others. They are all, according to Monsieur Wolf himself, to be considered as so many individuals who live together in the state of nature, and who acknowledge no other laws but those of nature, or of her Great Author. Now, although nature has indeed established a general society between mankind, by creating them subject to such wants as render the assistance of their fellow-creatures indispensably necessary to enable them to live in a manner suitable to men,—yet she has not imposed on them any particular obligation to unite in civil society, properly so called: and if they all obeyed the injunctions of that good parent, their subjection to the restraints of civil society would be unnecessary. It is true, that, as there does not exist in mankind a disposition voluntarily to observe towards each other the rules of the law of nature, they have had recourse to a political association, as the only adequate remedy against the depravity of the majority,—the only means of securing the condition of the good, and repressing the wicked: and the law of nature itself approves of this establishment. But it is easy to perceive that the civic association is very far from being equally necessary between nations, as it was between individuals. We cannot therefore say that nature equally recommends it, much less that she has prescribed it. Individuals are so constituted, and are capable of doing so little by themselves, that they can scarcely subsist without the aid and the laws of civil society. But as soon as a considerable number of them have united under the same government, they become able to supply most of their wants; and the assistance of other political societies is not so necessary to them as that of individuals is to an individual. These societies have still, it is true, powerful motives for carrying on a communication and commerce with each other; and it is even their duty to do it; since no man can, without good reasons, refuse assistance to another man. But the law of nature may suffice to regulate this commerce, and this <xv> correspondence. States conduct themselves in a different manner from individuals. It is not usually the caprice or blind impetuosity of a single person that forms the resolutions and determines the measures of the public: they are carried on with more deliberation and circumspection: and, on difficult or important occasions, arrangements are made and regulations established by means of treaties. To this we may add, that independence is even necessary to each state, in order to enable her properly to discharge the duties she owes to herself and to her citizens, and to govern herself in the manner best suited to her circumstances. It is therefore sufficient (as I have already said) that nations should conform to what is required of them by the natural and general society established between all mankind.

But, says Monsieur Wolf, a rigid adherence to the law of nature cannot always prevail in that commerce and society of nations; it must undergo various modifications, which can only be deduced from this idea of a kind of great republic of nations, whose laws, dictated by sound reason and founded on necessity, shall regulate the alterations to be made

in the natural and necessary law of nations, as the civil laws of a particular state determine what modifications shall take place in the natural
law of individuals. I do not perceive the necessity of this consequence;
and I flatter myself that I shall, in the course of this work, be able to
prove, that all the modifications, all the restrictions,—in a word, all the
alterations which the rigour of the natural law must be made to undergo
in the affairs of nations, and from which the voluntary law of nations
is formed,—to prove, I say, that all these alterations are deducible from
the natural liberty of nations, from the attention due to their common
safety, from the nature of their mutual correspondence, their reciprocal
duties, and the distinctions of their various rights, internal and external,
perfect and imperfect,—by a mode of reasoning nearly similar to that
which Mon-<xvi>sieur Wolf has pursued, with respect to individuals,
in his treatise on the law of nature.

In that treatise it is made to appear that the rules, which, in consequence of the natural liberty of mankind, must be admitted in questions
of external right do not cancel the obligation which the internal right
imposes on the conscience of each individual. It is easy to apply this
doctrine to nations, and—by carefully drawing the line of distinction
between the internal and the external right—between the necessary and
the voluntary law of nations—to teach them not to indulge themselves
in the commission of every act which they may do with impunity, unless
it be approved by the immutable laws of justice, and the voice of
conscience.

Since nations, in their transactions with each other, are equally bound
to admit those exceptions to, and those modifications of, the rigour of
the necessary law, whether they be deduced from the idea of a great
republic of which all nations are supposed to be the members, or derived
from the sources whence I propose to draw them,—there can be no reason why the system which thence results, should not be called the *Voluntary Law* of nations, in contradistinction to the *necessary*, internal,
and consciential law. Names are of very little consequence: but it is of
considerable importance carefully to distinguish these two kinds of law,
in order that we may never confound what is just and good in itself, with
what is only tolerated through necessity.

The necessary and the voluntary law of nations are therefore both established by nature, but each in a different manner; the former as a sacred law which nations and sovereigns are bound to respect and follow in all their actions; the latter, as a rule which the general welfare and safety oblige them to admit in their transactions with each other. The necessary law immediately proceeds from nature; and that common mother of mankind recommends the obser-<xvii>vance of the voluntary law of nations, in consideration of the state in which nations stand with respect to each other, and for the advantage of their affairs. This double law, founded on certain and invariable principles, is susceptible of demonstration, and will constitute the principal subject of this work.

There is another kind of law of nations, which authors call *arbitrary,* because it proceeds from the will or consent of nations. States, as well as individuals, may acquire rights and contract obligations, by express engagements, by compacts and treaties: hence results a conventional law of nations, peculiar to the contracting powers. Nations may also bind themselves by their tacit consent: upon this ground rest all those regulations which custom has introduced between different states, and which constitute the *usage* of nations, or the law of nations founded on custom. It is evident that this law cannot impose any obligation except on those particular nations who have, by long use, given their sanction to its maxims: it is a peculiar law, and limited in its operation, as the conventional law: both the one and the other derive all their obligatory force from that maxim of the natural law which makes it the duty of nations to fulfil their engagements, whether express or tacit. The same maxim ought to regulate the conduct of states with regard to the treaties they conclude, and the customs they adopt. I must content myself with simply laying down the general rules and principles which the law of nature furnishes for the direction of sovereigns in this respect. A particular detail of the various treaties and customs of different states belongs to history, and not to a systematic treatise on the law of nations.

Such a treatise ought, as we have already observed, principally to consist in a judicious and rational application of the principles of the law of nature to the affairs and conduct of nations and sovereigns. The study of the law of nations supposes therefore a pre-<xviii>vious knowledge of the ordinary law of nature: and in fact I proceed on the supposition that my readers are already, to a certain degree at least, possessed of that knowledge. Nevertheless, as it is not agreeable to readers in general to be obliged to recur to other authorities for proofs of what an author advances, I have taken care to establish, in a few words, the most important of those principles of the law of nature which I intended to apply to nations. But I have not always thought it necessary to trace them to their primary foundations for the purpose of demonstration, but have sometimes contented myself with supporting them by common truths which are acknowledged by every candid reader, without carrying the analysis any farther. It is sufficient for me to persuade, and for this purpose to advance nothing as a principle, that will not readily be admitted by every sensible man.

The law of nations is the law of sovereigns. It is principally for them and for their ministers that it ought to be written. All mankind are indeed interested in it; and, in a free country, the study of its maxims is a proper employment for every citizen: but it would be of little consequence to impart the knowledge of it only to private individuals, who are not called to the councils of nations, and who have no influence in directing the public measures. If the conductors of states, if all those who are employed in public affairs, condescended to apply seriously to the study of a science which ought to be their law, and, as it were, the compass by which to steer their course, what happy effects might we not expect from a good treatise on the law of nations! We every day feel the advantages of a good body of laws in civil society:—the law of nations is, in point of importance, as much superior to the civil law, as the proceedings of nations and sovereigns are more momentous in their consequences than those of private persons.

But fatal experience too plainly proves, how little regard those who are at the head of affairs pay to the <xix> dictates of justice, in conjunctures where they hope to find their advantage. Satisfied with bestowing their attention on a system of politics which is often false since often unjust, the generality of them think they have done enough when they have thoroughly studied that. Nevertheless we may truly apply to states a maxim which has long been acknowledged as true with respect to individuals,—that the best and safest policy is that which is founded on virtue. Cicero, as great a master in the art of government as in eloquence and philosophy, does not content himself with rejecting the vulgar maxim, that "a state cannot be happily governed without committing injustice"; he even proceeds so far as to lay down the very reverse of the proposition as an invariable truth, and maintains, that, "without a strict attention to the most rigid justice, public affairs cannot be advantageously administered."*

Providence occasionally bestows on the world kings and ministers whose minds are impressed with this great truth. Let us not renounce the pleasing hope that the number of those wise conductors of nations will one day be multiplied; and in the interim let us, each in his own sphere, exert our best efforts to accelerate the happy period.

It is principally with a view of rendering my work palatable to those by whom it is of the most importance that it should be read and relished, that I have sometimes joined examples to the maxims I advance: and in that idea I have been confirmed by the approbation of one of those ministers who are the enlightened friends of the human race, and who alone ought to be admitted into the councils of kings.[2] But I have been sparing in the use of such embellishments. Without ever aiming at a vain parade of erudition, I only sought to afford an occasional relaxation to the reader's mind, <xx> or to render the doctrine more impressive by an example, and sometimes to shew that the practice of nations is conformable to the principles laid down: and whenever I found a convenient opportunity, I have, above all things, endeavoured to inspire a love of virtue, by shewing, from some striking passage of history, how amiable it is, how worthy of our homage in some truly great men, and even productive of solid advantage. I have quoted the chief part of my ex-

---

* Nihil est quod adhuc de republicâ putem dictum, et quo possim longius progredi, nisi sit confirmatum, non modo falsum esse istud, sine injuriâ non posse, sed hoc verissimum, sine summâ justitiâ rempublicant regi non posse. Cicero, Fragment. ex lib. de Republica.

2. Vattel is probably referring to his so-called protector Count Brühl. As Vattel considered Brühl to be the very opposite of his idea of a good minister, the remark is one of pure flattery.

amples from modern history, as well because these are more interesting, as to avoid a repetition of those which have been already accumulated by Grotius, Puffendorf, and their commentators.

As to the rest, I have, both in these examples and in my reasonings, studiously endeavoured to avoid giving offence; it being my intention religiously to observe the respect due to nations and sovereign powers: but I have made it a still more sacred rule to respect the truth, and the interests of the human race. If, among the base flatterers of despotic power, my principles meet with opponents, I shall have on my side the virtuous man, the friend of the laws, the man of probity, and the true citizen.

I should prefer the alternative of total silence, were I not at liberty in my writings to obey the dictates of my conscience. But my pen lies under no restraint, and I am incapable of prostituting it to flattery. I was born in a country of which liberty is the soul, the treasure, and the fundamental law; and my birth qualifies me to be the friend of all nations. These favourable circumstances have encouraged me in the attempt to render myself useful to mankind by this work. I felt conscious of my deficiency in knowledge and abilities: I saw that I was undertaking an arduous task: but I shall rest satisfied if that class of readers whose opinions are entitled to respect, discover in my labours the traces of the honest man and the good citizen. <xxi>

CONTENTS[1]

PRELIMINARIES
Idea and general Principles of the Law of Nations.

Sect. 1. What is meant by a nation or state,   page lv

2. It is a moral person,   lv
3. Definition of the law of nations,   lv
4. In what light nations or states are to be considered,   lvi
5. To what laws nations are subject,   lvi
6. In what the law of nations originally consists,   lvi
7. Definition of the necessary law of nations,   lviii
8. It is immutable,   lviii
9. Nations can make no change in it, nor dispense with the obligations arising from it,   lviii
10. Society established by nature between all mankind,   lix
11. and between all nations,   lx
12. The object of this society of nations,   lxi
13. General obligation imposed by it,   lxi
14. Explanation of this observation,   lxi
15. The second general law is the liberty and independence of nations,   lxii
16. Effect of that liberty,   lxii
17. Distinctions between internal and external, perfect and imperfect obligations and rights,   lxii
18. Equality of nations,   lxiii
19. Effect of that equality,   lxiii
20. Each nation is mistress of her own actions, when they do not affect the perfect rights of others,   lxiii
21. Foundation of the voluntary law of nations,   lxiii
22. Right of nations against the infractors of the law of nations,   lxiv

1. The page numbers in the Contents are those of the 1797 edition.

Sect. 23. Measure of that right,   page lxiv

24. Conventional law of nations, or law of treaties,   lxv

25. Customary law of nations,   lxv

26. General rule respecting that law,   lxv

27. Positive law of nations,   lxvi

28. General maxim respecting the use of the necessary
and the voluntary law, <xxii>   lxvi

BOOK I

Of Nations considered in themselves.

CHAPTER I
Of Nations or Sovereign States.

1. Of the state, and of sovereignty,   1

2. Authority of the body politic over the members,   1

3. Of the several kinds of government,   2

4. What are sovereign states,   2

5. States bound by unequal alliance,   2

6. or by treaties of protection,   2

7. Tributary states,   3

8. Feudatory states,   3

9. Two states subject to the same prince,   3

10. States forming a federal republic,   3

11. A state that has passed under the dominion
of another,   3

12. Objects of this treatise,   4

CHAPTER II
General Principles of the Duties of
a Nation towards herself.

13. A nation ought to act agreeably to her nature,   4

14. Preservation and perfection of a nation,   4

15. End of civil society,   5

16. A nation is under an obligation to preserve herself,   5

17. and to preserve her members,   5

18. A nation has a right to every thing necessary for her
preservation,   6

19. She ought to avoid every thing that might occasion
her destruction,   6

Sect. 20. Her right to every thing that may promote
    this end,   page 6
21. A nation ought to perfect herself and her condition,   6
22. and to avoid every thing contrary to her perfection,   7
23. The rights she derives from these obligations,   7
24. Examples,   7
25. A nation ought to know herself,   8

CHAPTER III
Of the Constitution of a State, and the Duties and Rights of a Nation in that respect.

26. Of the public authority,   8
27. What is the constitution of a state, <xxiii>   8
28. The nation ought to choose the best constitution,   9
29. Political, fundamental, and civil laws,   9
30. Support of the constitution, and obedience to
    the laws,   9
31. Rights of a nation with respect to her constitution
    and government,   10
32. She may reform the government,   10
33. and may alter the constitution,   10
34. Of the legislative power, and whether it can alter
    the constitution,   11
35. The nation ought not to attempt it without
    great caution,   12
36. She is the judge of all disputes relative to
    the government,   12
37. No foreign power has a right to interfere,   12

CHAPTER IV
Of the Sovereign, his Obligations, and his Rights.

38. Of the sovereign,   12
39. He is solely established for the safety and advantage
    of society,   13
40. His representative character,   14
41. He is intrusted with the obligations of the nation,
    and invested with her rights,   14
42. His duty with respect to the preservation and
    perfection of the nation,   14
43. His rights in that respect,   14

Sect. 44. He ought to know the nation,   page 15
    45. Extent of his power:—prerogatives of majesty,   15
    46. The prince is bound to respect and support the
         fundamental laws,   15
    47. He may change the laws not fundamental,   16
    48. He is bound to maintain and observe the
         existing laws,   16
    49. In what sense he is subject to the laws,   16
    50. His person is sacred and inviolable,   17
    51. But the nation may repress a tyrant, and renounce
         her allegiance to him,   17
    52. Arbitration between the king and his subjects,   20
    53. Obedience which subjects owe to a sovereign,   21
    54. In what cases they may resist him,   21
    55. Ministers,   23

CHAPTER V

Of States Elective, Successive or Hereditary,
and of those called Patrimonial.

56. Elective states,   23
57. Whether elective kings be real sovereigns,   24
58. Successive and hereditary states:—origin of the
     right of succession,   24
59. Other origin of that right, <xxiv>   24
60. Other sources, which still amount to the
     same thing,   24
61. A nation may change the order of the succession,   24
62. Renunciations,   25
63. The order of succession ought commonly to
     be observed,   26
64. Regents,   27
65. Indivisibility of sovereignties,   27
66. Who are to decide disputes respecting the
     succession to a sovereignty,   27
67. The right of succession not to depend on the
     judgment of a foreign power,   29
68. States called patrimonial,   30
69. Every true sovereignty is unalienable,   31
70. Duty of a prince who is empowered to nominate
     his successor,   32
71. His nomination must be sanctioned by at least the
     tacit ratification of the people,   32

CHAPTER VI
*Principal Objects of a good Government; and first,
to provide for the Necessities of the Nation.*

Sect. 72. The object of society points out the duties
of the sovereign:—he is bound to procure
plenty, page 33
73. to take care that there be a sufficient number
of workmen, 33
74. to prevent the emigration of those that are useful, 33
75. Emissaries who entice them away, 34
76. Labour and industry must be encouraged, 34

CHAPTER VII
Of the Cultivation of the Soil.

77. Utility of Agriculture, 34
78. Regulations necessary in that respect:—for the
distribution of land, 34
79. for the protection of husbandmen, 35
80. Husbandry ought to be placed in an
honourable light, 35
81. Cultivation of the soil a natural obligation, 35
82. Public granaries, 36

CHAPTER VIII
Of Commerce.

83. Domestic and foreign trade, 37
84. Utility of domestic trade, 37
85. Utility of foreign trade, 37
86. Obligation to cultivate domestic trade, <xxv> 37
87. Obligation to carry on foreign trade, 38
88. Foundation of the laws of commerce:—right
of purchasing, 38
89. Right of selling, 38
90. Prohibition of foreign merchandises, 39
91. Nature of the right of purchasing, 39
92. Each nation to determine for herself how she will
carry on commerce, 39
93. How a nation acquires a perfect right to a
foreign trade, 40
94. Simple permission to carry on trade, 40

Sect. 95. Whether commercial rights be subject
       to prescription,   page 40
    96. Imprescriptibility of rights founded on treaty,   41
    97. Monopolies, and trading companies with
        exclusive privileges,   42
    98. Balance of trade, and attention of government in
        that respect,   43
    99. Import duties,   43

CHAPTER IX
Of the Care of the public Ways; and of Tolls.

100. Utility of highways, canals, &c.   43
101. Duty of government in that respect,   43
102. Its rights in that respect,   44
103. Foundation of the right to demand toll,   44
104. Abuse of that right,   44

CHAPTER X
Of Money and Exchange.

105. Establishment of money,   45
106. Duty of the nation or prince with respect to
      the coin,   45
107. Their rights in that respect,   46
108. How one nation may injure another in the article
      of coin,   47
109. Exchange, and commercial laws,   47

CHAPTER XI
Second Object of a good Government,—to procure the true Happiness of a Nation.

110. A nation is bound to labour after her
      own happiness,   47
111. Instruction,   47
112. Education of youth,   48
113. Arts and sciences,   48
114. Freedom of philosophical discussion,   49
115. Love of virtue, and abhorrence of vice, to
      be excited,   51

Sect. 116. The nation may hence discover the intention
of her rulers, page 51
117. The nation, or public person, bound to perfect her
understanding and will, <xxvi> 52
118. and to direct the knowledge and virtues of the
citizens to the welfare of the society, 52
119. Love for their country, 53
120. in individuals, 53
121. in the nation or state itself, and in the sovereign, 53
122. Definition of the term, "country," 53
123. How shameful and criminal to injure our country, 54
124. The glory of good citizens.—Examples, 54

CHAPTER XII

Of Piety and Religion.

125. Piety, 55
126. It ought to be attended with knowledge, 55
127. Religion, internal and external, 56
128. Rights of individuals:—liberty of conscience, 56
129. Public establishment of religion:—rights and
duties of the nation, 56
130. when there is as yet no established religion, 57
131. when there is an established religion, 57
132. Duties and rights of the sovereign with respect
to religion, 58
133. where there is an established religion, 59
134. Objects of his care, and the means he ought
to employ, 60
135. Toleration, 60
136. How the prince is to act when the nation is
resolved to change her religion, 60
137. Difference of religion does not deprive a prince of
his crown, 61
138. Duties and rights of the sovereign reconciled with
those of the subjects, 61
139. The sovereign ought to have the inspection of the
affairs of religion, and authority over those who
teach it, 62
140. He is bound to prevent the abuse of the
established religion, 63
141. His authority over the ministers of religion, 63

Sect. 142. Nature of that authority,   page 64

143. Rule to be observed with respect to ecclesiastics,   64

144. Recapitulation of the reasons which establish the
     sovereign's rights in matters of religion, 64—
     Authorities and examples,   65

145. Pernicious consequences of the contrary opinion,   65

146. Abuses particularised.—1. The power of the popes,   66

147. 2. Important employments conferred by a
     foreign power,   68

148. 3. Powerful subjects dependent on a foreign court,   68

149. 4. Celibacy of the priests:—Convents,   69

150. 5. Enormous pretensions of the clergy:—
     Pre-eminence,   70

151. 6. Independence, immunities,   71

152. 7. Immunity of church possessions,   72

153. 8. Excommunication of men in office,   73

154. 9. and of sovereigns themselves,   74

155. 10. The clergy drawing every thing to themselves,
     and interrupting the course of justice, <xxvii>   75

156. 11. Money drawn to Rome,   76

157. 12. Laws and customs inimical to the welfare
     of states,   76

CHAPTER XIII
Of Justice and Polity.

158. A nation is bound to make justice flourish,   77

159. to establish good laws,   77

160. to enforce them,   78

161. Functions and duties of the prince in that respect,   78

162. How he is to dispense justice,   78

163. His duty to appoint upright and enlightened
     judges,   78

164. The ordinary courts should determine causes
     relating to the revenue,   79

165. Necessary to establish supreme courts, from whose
     sentence there shall be no appeal,   79

166. The prince bound to observe the forms of justice,   80

167. to support the authority of the judges, and enforce
     their decrees,   80

168. Distributive justice:—distribution of
     employments and rewards,   80

Sect. 169. Punishment of transgressors:—foundation of the
    right of punishing,   page 81
    170. Criminal laws,   81
    171. Degree of punishment,   82
    172. Execution of the laws,   82
    173. Right of pardoning,   83
    174. Internal police,   83
    175. Duel or single combat,   84
    176. Means of putting a stop to that disorder,   84

CHAPTER XIV
Third Object of a good Government,—
to fortify itself against external Attacks.

177. A nation ought to fortify herself against external
    attacks,   87
178. National strength,   87
179. Increase of population,   87
180. Valour,   88
181. Other military virtues,   89
182. Riches,   89
183. Public revenues and taxes,   90
184. The nation ought not to increase her power by
    unlawful means,   90
185. Power is but relative, <xxviii>   90

CHAPTER XV
Of the Glory of a Nation.

186. Advantages of glory,   91
187. Duty of the nation.—How true glory is acquired,   91
188. Duty of the prince,   91
189. Duty of the citizens,   92
190. Example of the Swiss,   92
191. Attacking the glory of a nation is doing her an
    injury,   93

CHAPTER XVI
Protection sought by a Nation, and her voluntary
Submission to a Foreign Power.

192. Protection,   93
193. Voluntary submission of one nation to another,   94

Sect. 194. Several kinds of submission, page 94
195. Right of the citizens when the nation submits
to a foreign power, 94
196. These compacts annulled by the failure
of protection, 95
197. or by the infidelity of the party protected, 95
198. and by the encroachments of the protector, 95
199. How the right of the nation protected is lost by
her silence, 96

CHAPTER XVII

How a Nation may separate herself from the State of which she is a Member, and renounce her Allegiance to her Sovereign when she is not protected.

200. Difference between the present case and those in
the preceding chapter, 96
201. Duty of the members of a state, or subjects of a
prince, who are in danger, 97
202. Their right when they are abandoned, 97

CHAPTER XVIII

Establishment of a Nation in a Country.

203. Possession of a country by a nation, 98
204. Her right over the part in her possession, 98
205. Acquisition of the sovereignty in a vacant country, 99
206. Another manner of acquiring the empire in a
free country, 99
207. How a nation acquires the property of a
desert country, 99
208. A question on this subject, 99
209. Whether it be lawful to take possession of
part of a country inhabited only by a few
wandering tribes, 100
210. Colonies, <xxix> 101

CHAPTER XIX

Of our Native Country, and various Matters relating to it.

211. What is our country, 101
212. Citizens and natives, 101

Sect. 213. Inhabitants, page 102

214. Naturalisation, 102

215. Citizens' children born in a foreign country, 102

216. Children born at sea, 102

217. Children born in the armies of the state, or in the
house of its minister at a foreign court, 103

218. Settlement, 103

219. Vagrants, 103

220. Whether a person may quit his country, 103

221. How a person may absent himself for a time, 105

222. Variation of the political laws in that respect:—
they must be obeyed, 105

223. Cases in which a citizen has a right to quit
his country, 105

224. Emigrants, 106

225. Sources of their right, 106

226. If the sovereign infringes their right, he
injures them, 107

227. Supplicants, 107

228. Exile and banishment, 107

229. The exile and the banished man have a right to
live somewhere, 108

230. Nature of that right, 108

231. Duty of nations towards them, 108

232. A nation cannot punish them for faults committed
out of her territories, 109

233. except such as affect the common safety
of mankind, 109

CHAPTER XX

Public, Common, and Private Property.

234. What the Romans called *res communes*, 109

235. Aggregate wealth of a nation, and its divisions, 109

236. Two modes of acquiring public property, 110

237. The income of the public property is naturally at
the sovereign's disposal, 110

238. The nation may grant him the use and property of
her common possessions, 110

239. or allow him the domain, and reserve to herself
the use of them, 110

240. Taxes, 111

Sect. 241. The nation may reserve to herself the right
       of imposing them,   page III
   242. Sovereign possessing that power,   III
   243. Duties of the prince with respect to taxes,   II2
   244. Eminent domain annexed to the sovereignty,
       <xxx>   II2
   245. Dominion over public property,   II3
   246. The sovereign may make laws respecting the use of
       things possessed in common,   II3
   247. Alienation of the property of a corporation,   II3
   248. Use of common property,   II4
   249. How each member is to enjoy it,   II4
   250. Right of anticipation in the use of it,   II4
   251. The same right in another case,   II4
   252. Preservation and repairs of common possessions,   II5
   253. Duty and right of the sovereign in that respect,   II5
   254. Private property,   II5
   255. The sovereign may subject it to regulations
       of police,   II5
   256. Inheritances,   II6

CHAPTER XXI

Of the Alienation of the public Property, or the Domain, and that of a Part of the State.

   257. The nation may alienate her public property,   II6
   258. Duties of the nation in that respect,   II6
   259. Duties of the prince,   II7
   260. He cannot alienate the public property,   II7
   261. The nation may give him a right to do it,   II7
   262. Rules on that subject with respect to treaties
       between nation and nation,   II7
   263. Alienation of a part of the state,   II8
   264. Rights of the dismembered party,   II8
   265. Whether the prince has power to dismember
       the state,   II9

CHAPTER XXII

Of Rivers, Streams, and Lakes.

   266. A river that separates two territories,   I20
   267. Bed of a river which is dried up or takes
       another course,   I2I

Sect. 268. Right of alluvion,   page 121
269. Whether alluvion produces any change in the right
  to river,   121
270. Consequence of a river changing its bed,   122
271. Works tending to turn the current,   122
272. or generally prejudicial to the rights of others,   122
273. Rules relative to interfering rights,   122
274. Lakes,   123
275. Increase of a lake,   123
276. Land formed on the banks of a lake,   125
277. Bed of a lake dried up,   125
278. Jurisdiction over lakes and rivers,   125

CHAPTER XXIII
Of the Sea.

279. The sea, and its use, <xxxi>   125
280. Whether the sea can be possessed, and its
  dominion appropriated,   125
281. Nobody has a right to appropriate to himself the
  use of the open sea,   125
282. A nation attempting to exclude another, does her
  an injury,   126
283. She even does an injury to all nations,   126
284. She may acquire an exclusive right by treaties,   126
285. but not by prescription and long use,   127
286. unless by virtue of a tacit agreement,   127
287. The sea near the coasts may become property,   127
288. Another reason for appropriating the sea bordering
  on the coasts,   128
289. How far that possession may extend,   128
290. Shores and ports,   129
291. Bays and straits,   129
292. Straits in particular,   130
293. Right to wrecks,   130
294. A sea inclosed within the territories of a nation,   130
295. The parts of the sea possessed by a sovereign are
  within his jurisdiction,   131

BOOK II

Of a Nation considered in her
Relation to other States.

CHAPTER I
Of the common Duties of a Nation towards other States, or the Offices of Humanity between Nations.

Sect. 1. Foundation of the common and mutual
duties of nations, page 133

2. Offices of humanity, and their foundation, 134

3. General principle of all the mutual duties
of nations, 135

4. Duties of a nation for the preservation of others, 135

5. She is bound to assist a nation afflicted with famine
or any other calamity, 136

6. She is bound to contribute to the perfection of
other states, 136

7. but not by force, 137

8. The right to require the offices of humanity, 138

9. The right of judging whether they are to
be granted, 138

10. A nation is not to compel another to perform those
offices of which the refusal is no wrong, 138

11. Mutual love of nations, 138

12. Each nation is bound to cultivate the friendship
of others, 138

13. to perfect herself with a view to the advantage of
others, and to set them good examples, 139

14. to take care of their glory, 139

15. Difference of religion ought not to preclude the
offices of humanity, 139

16. Rule and measure of the offices of humanity,
<xxxii> 140

17. Particular limitation with respect to the prince, 141

18. No nation ought to injure others, 141

19. Offences, 142

20. Bad custom of the ancients, 143

CHAPTER II
Of the mutual Commerce between Nations.

Sect. 21. General obligation of nations to carry on
    mutual commerce,   page 143
22. They are bound to favour trade,   144
23. Freedom of trade,   144
24. Right of trading, belonging to nations,   144
25. Each nation is sole judge of the propriety of
    commerce on her own part,   144
26. Necessity of commercial treaties,   145
27. General rule concerning those treaties,   145
28. Duty of nations in making such treaties,   145
29. Perpetual or temporary treaties, or treaties revocable
    at pleasure,   145
30. Nothing contrary to the tenor of a treaty can be
    granted to a third party,   146
31. How far lawful to give up by treaty the liberty of
    trading with other nations,   146
32. A nation may restrict her commerce in favour of
    another nation,   146
33. A nation may appropriate to herself a particular
    branch of trade,   147
34. Consuls,   147

CHAPTER III
Of the Dignity and Equality of Nations,—
of Titles,—and other Marks of Honour.

35. Dignity of nations or sovereign states,   149
36. Their equality,   149
37. Precedency,   149
38. The form of government is foreign to this question,   150
39. A state ought to retain her rank, notwithstanding
    any changes in the form of her government,   150
40. Treaties and established customs are to be observed
    in this respect,   150
41. Name and honours given by the nation to
    her conductor,   151
42. Whether a sovereign may assume what title and
    honours he pleases,   152
43. Right of other nations in that respect,   152

Sect. 44. Their duty,   page 152

45. How titles and honours may be secured,   153

46. We must conform to general custom, <xxxiii>   153

47. Mutual respect due by sovereigns to each other,   153

48. How a sovereign ought to maintain his dignity,   154

CHAPTER IV
Of the Right to Security, and the Effects of the Sovereignty and Independence of Nations.

49. Right to security,   154

50. It produces the right of resistance,   154

51. and that of obtaining reparation,   155

52. and the right of punishing,   155

53. Right of all nations against a mischievous people,   155

54. No nation has a right to interfere in the government
of another state,   155

55. One sovereign cannot make himself judge of the
conduct of another,   155

56. How far lawful to interfere in a quarrel between a
sovereign and his subjects,   156

57. Right of opposing the interference of foreign
powers in the affairs of government,   157

58. The same right with respect to religion,   157

59. No nation can be constrained in religious concerns,   158

60. Offices of humanity in these matters:—
missionaries,   158

61. Circumspection to be used,   159

62. What a sovereign may do in favour of those who
profess his religion in another state,   159

CHAPTER V
Of the Observance of Justice between Nations.

63. Necessity of the observance of justice in
human society,   160

64. Obligation of all nations to cultivate and
observe justice,   160

65. Right of refusing to submit to injustice,   160

66. This right is a perfect one,   161

67. It produces—the right of self-defence,   161

68. the right of doing ourselves justice,   161

Sect. 69. The right of punishing injustice,   page 161
70. Right of all nations against one that openly
    despises justice,   161

CHAPTER VI

*Of the Concern a Nation may have in
the Actions of her Citizens.*

71. The sovereign is bound to avenge the wrongs of the
    state, and to protect the citizens,   161
72. He must not suffer his subjects to offend other
    nations or their citizens,   162
73. The acts of individuals not imputable to the nation,
    <xxxiv>   162
74. unless she approve or ratify them,   162
75. Conduct to be pursued by the offended party,   162
76. Duty of the aggressor's sovereign,   163
77. If he refuses justice, he becomes a party in the fault
    and offence,   163
78. Another case in which the nation is guilty of the
    crimes of the citizens,   164

CHAPTER VII

Effects of the Domain, between Nations.

79. General effects of the domain,   164
80. What is comprehended in the domain of a nation,   165
81. The property of the citizens is the national property
    with respect to foreign states,   165
82. A consequence of that principle,   165
83. Connection of the domain of the nation with the
    sovereignty,   165
84. Jurisdiction,   166
85. Effects of the jurisdiction in foreign countries,   166
86. Desert and uncultivated places,   167
87. Duty of the nation in that respect,   168
88. Right of possessing things that have no owner,   168
89. Rights granted to another nation,   168
90. Not allowable to expel a nation from the country
    she inhabits,   168
91. nor to extend by violence the bounds of empire,   169

Sect. 92. The limits of territories ought to be
      carefully ascertained,   page 169
    93. Violation of territory,   169
    94. Prohibition to enter the territory,   170
    95. A country possessed by several nations at the
      same time,   170
    96. A country possessed by a private person,   170
    97. Independent families in a country,   170
    98. Possession of certain places only, or of certain
      rights, in a vacant country,   171

CHAPTER VIII
Rules respecting Foreigners.

    99. General idea of the conduct a state ought to
      observe towards foreigners,   171
    100. Entering the territory,   172
    101. Foreigners are subject to the laws,   172
    102. and punishable according to the laws,   172
    103. Who is the judge of their disputes,   173
    104. Protection due to foreigners,   173
    105. Their duties,   173
    106. To what burthens they are subject,   174
    107. Foreigners continue members of their own nation, 174
    108. The state has no right over the person of a
      foreigner, <xxxv>   174
    109. nor over his property,   174
    110. Who are the heirs of a foreigner,   175
    111. Will of a foreigner,   175
    112. Escheatage,   176
    113. The right of *traite foraine*,   177
    114. Immovable property possessed by an alien,   177
    115. Marriages of aliens,   177

CHAPTER IX
Of the Rights retained by all Nations after the Introduction of Domain and Property.

    116. What are the rights of which men cannot
      be deprived,   178
    117. Right still remaining from the primitive state
      of communion,   178

Sect. 118. Right retained by each nation over the
property of others, page 178
119. Right of necessity, 178
120. Right of procuring provisions by force, 179
121. Right of making use of things belonging
to others, 179
122. Right of carrying off women, 179
123. Right of passage, 180
124. and of procuring necessaries, 180
125. Right of dwelling in a foreign country, 180
126. Things, of which the use is inexhaustible, 181
127. Right of innocent use, 181
128. Nature of that right in general, 182
129. and in cases not doubtful, 182
130. Exercise of that right between nations, 182

CHAPTER X

How a Nation is to use her Right of Domain, in order to discharge her Duties towards other Nations, with respect to the Innocent Use of Things.

131. General duty of the proprietor, 183
132. Innocent passage, 183
133. Securities may be required, 184
134. Passage of merchandise, 184
135. Residence in the country, 184
136. How we are to act towards foreigners who desire a
perpetual residence, 185
137. Right accruing from a general permission, 185
138. A right granted as a favour, 186
139. The nation ought to be courteous, 186

CHAPTER XI

Of Usucaption and Prescription between Nations.

140. Definition of usucaption and prescription, 187
141. Usucaption and prescription derived from the law
of nature, <xxxvi> 187
142. What foundation is required for ordinary
prescription, 189
143. Immemorial prescription, 189

Sect. 144. Claimant alleging reasons for his silence,   page 190
    145. Proprietor sufficiently shewing that he
         does not mean to abandon his right,   190
    146. Prescription founded on the actions of
         the proprietor,   190
    147. Usucaption and prescription take place
         between nations,   190
    148. More difficult, between nations, to found them on
         a presumptive desertion,   190
    149. Other principles that enforce prescription,   191
    150. Effects of the voluntary law of nations on
         this subject,   191
    151. Law of treaties, or custom, in this matter,   192

CHAPTER XII

Of Treaties of Alliance, and other public Treaties.

    152. Nature of treaties,   192
    153. Compacts, agreements, or conventions,   192
    154. By whom treaties are made,   192
    155. Whether a state under protection may
         make treaties,   193
    156. Treaties concluded by proxies or plenipotentiaries,   193
    157. Validity of treaties,   194
    158. Injury does not render them void,   194
    159. Duty of nations in that respect,   194
    160. Nullity of treaties which are pernicious to
         the state,   194
    161. Nullity of treaties made for an unjust or
         dishonest purpose,   195
    162. Whether an alliance may be contracted with those
         who do not profess the true religion,   195
    163. Obligation to observe treaties,   195
    164. The violation of a treaty is an act of injustice,   196
    165. Treaties cannot be made, contrary to those
         already existing,   196
    166. How treaties may be concluded with several
         nations with the same view,   197
    167. The more ancient ally entitled to a preference,   197
    168. We owe no assistance in an unjust war,   197
    169. General division of treaties:—those that relate to
         things already due by the law of nature,   197

Sect. 170. Collision of those treaties with the duties
we owe to ourselves, page 198
171. Treaties in which we barely promise to do
no injury, 198
172. Treaties concerning things that are not naturally
due:—equal treaties, 198
173. Obligation to preserve equality in treaties, 199
174. Difference between equal treaties and
equal alliances, 200
175. Unequal treaties, and unequal alliances, 200
176. An alliance with diminution of sovereignty may
annul preceding treaties, 202
177. We ought, as much as possible, to avoid making
unequal alliances, <xxxvii> 203
178. Mutual duties of nations with respect to
unequal alliances, 203
179. in alliances where the inequality is on the side of
the more powerful party, 203
180. How inequality of treaties and alliances may be
conformable to the law of nature, 204
181. Inequality imposed by way of punishment, 205
182. Other kinds, of which we have spoken
elsewhere, 205
183. Personal and real treaties, 205
184. Naming the contracting parties in the treaty does
not render it personal, 205
185. An alliance made by a republic is real, 205
186. Treaties concluded by kings or other monarchs, 206
187. Perpetual treaties, and those for a certain time, 206
188. Treaties made for the king and his successors, 206
189. Treaties made for the good of the kingdom, 206
190. How presumption ought to be founded in
doubtful cases, 207
191. The obligations and rights resulting from a real
treaty pass to the successors, 208
192. Treaties accomplished once for all, and perfected, 208
193. Treaties already accomplished on the one part, 209
194. The personal alliance expires if one of the parties
ceases to reign, 211
195. Treaties in their own nature personal, 211
196. Alliance concluded for the defence of the king and
royal family, 211

Sect. 197. Obligation of a real alliance, when the
 allied king is deposed,   page 212

CHAPTER XIII

Of the Dissolution and Renewal of Treaties.

198. Expiration of alliances made for a limited time, 213
199. Renewal of treaties, 213
200. How a treaty is dissolved, when violated by
 one of the contracting parties, 214
201. The violation of one treaty does not
 cancel another, 214
202. The violation of one article in a treaty may cancel
 the whole, 215
203. The treaty is void by the destruction of one of the
 contracting powers, 216
204. Alliances of a state that has afterwards put herself
 under the protection of another, 216
205. Treaties dissolved by mutual consent, 217

CHAPTER XIV

*Of other public Conventions,—of those that are
made by Subordinate Powers,—particularly
of the Agreement called in Latin* Sponsio,—
*and of Conventions between the Sovereign
and Private Persons.*

206. Conventions made by sovereigns, <xxxviii> 218
207. Those made by subordinate powers, 218
208. Treaties concluded by a public person,
 without orders from the sovereign, or without
 sufficient powers, 219
209. The agreement called *sponsio*, 219
210. The state is not bound by such an agreement, 220
211. To what the promiser is bound when it
 is disavowed, 220
212. To what the sovereign is bound, 223
213. Private contracts of the sovereign, 226
214. Contracts made by him with private persons,
 in the name of the state, 226
215. They are binding on the nation, and on
 his successors, 227

Sect. 216. Debts of the sovereign and the state,   page 227
217. Donations of the sovereign,   228

CHAPTER XV

Of the Faith of Treaties.

218. What is sacred among nations,   229
219. Treaties sacred between nations,   229
220. The faith of treaties is sacred,   229
221. He who violates his treaties, violates the law
of nations,   229
222. Right of nations against him who disregards the
faith of treaties,   230
223. The law of nations violated by the popes,   230
224. This abuse authorised by princes,   231
225. Use of an oath in treaties.—It does not constitute
the obligation,   232
226. It does not change the nature of obligations,   232
227. It gives no pre-eminence to one treaty
above another,   232
228. It cannot give force to a treaty that is invalid,   233
229. Asseverations,   233
230. The faith of treaties does not depend on the
difference of religion,   233
231. Precaution to be taken in wording treaties,   233
232. Subterfuges in treaties,   234
233. An evidently false interpretation inconsistent
with the faith of treaties,   234
234. Faith tacitly pledged,   234

CHAPTER XVI

Of Securities given for the Observance of Treaties.

235. Guaranty,   235
236. It gives the guarantee no right to interfere unasked
in the execution of a treaty,   236
237. Nature of the obligation it imposes,   236
238. The guaranty cannot impair the rights of a
third party,   236
239. Duration of the guaranty,   237
240. Treaties with surety,   237
241. Pawns, securities, and mortgages,   237

Sect. 242. A nation's right over what she holds as a
            pledge, <xxxix>   page 237
     243. How she is obliged to restore it,   238
     244. How she may appropriate it to herself,   238
     245. Hostages,   238
     246. What right we have over hostages,   239
     247. Their liberty alone is pledged,   239
     248. When they are to be sent back,   239
     249. Whether they may be detained on any
            other account,   239
     250. They may be detained for their own actions,   240
     251. Of the support of hostages,   240
     252. A subject cannot refuse to be a hostage,   241
     253. Rank of the hostages,   241
     254. They ought not to make their escape,   241
     255. Whether a hostage who dies is to be replaced,   242
     256. Substitute for a hostage,   242
     257. Hostage succeeding to the crown,   242
     258. The liability of the hostage ends with the treaty,   242
     259. The violation of the treaty is an injury done to
            the hostages,   242
     260. The fate of the hostage when he who has given
            him fails in his engagements,   243
     261. Right founded on custom,   243

CHAPTER XVII
Of the Interpretation of Treaties.

     262. Necessity of establishing rules of interpretation,   244
     263. First general maxim—it is not allowable to
            interpret what has no need of interpretation,   244
     264. Second general maxim—if he who could and
            ought to have explained himself, has not done it, it
            is to his own detriment,   245
     265. Third general maxim—neither of the contracting
            parties has a right to interpret the treaty according
            to his own fancy,   245
     266. Fourth general maxim—what is sufficiently
            declared, is to be taken for true,   245
     267. We ought to attend rather to the words of
            the person promising, than to those of the
            party stipulating,   245

Sect. 268. Fifth general maxim—the interpretation
  ought to be made according to certain rules, page 246
269. The faith of treaties imposes an obligation to
  follow those rules, 247
270. General rule of interpretation, 247
271. The terms are to be explained conformably to
  common usage, 248
272. Interpretation of ancient treaties, 248
273. Quibbles on words, 249
274. A rule on that subject, 249
275. Mental reservations, 249
276. Interpretation of technical terms, 249
277. Terms whose signification admits of degrees, 250
278. Figurative expressions, <xl> 250
279. Equivocal expressions, 250
280. The rule for these two cases, 251
281. Not necessary to give a term the same sense
  every-where in the same deed, 252
282. We ought to reject every interpretation which leads
  to an absurdity, 252
283. or which renders the act null and void of effect, 253
284. Obscure expressions interpreted by others more
  clear in the same author, 254
285. Interpretation founded on the connection of
  the discourse, 254
286. Interpretation drawn from the connection and
  relation of the things themselves, 255
287. Interpretation founded on the reason of
  the deed, 256
288. Where many reasons have concurred to
  determine the will, 256
289. What constitutes a sufficient reason for an act
  of the will, 257
290. Extensive interpretation founded on the reason
  of the act, 257
291. Frauds tending to elude laws or promises, 258
292. Restrictive interpretation, 259
293. Its use, in order to avoid falling into absurdities,
  or into what is unlawful, 259
294. or what is too severe and burthensome, 260
295. How it ought to restrict the signification agreeably
  to the subject, 260

Sect. 296. How a change happening in the state of
things may form an exception, page 260
297. Interpretation of a deed in unforeseen cases, 262
298. Reasons arising from the possibility and not the
existence of a thing, 262
299. Expressions susceptible of an extensive and a
limited sense, 263
300. Things favourable, and things odious, 263
301. What tends to the common advantage, and to
equality, is favourable: the contrary is odious, 264
302. What is useful to human society, is favourable: the
contrary is odious, 265
303. Whatever contains a penalty, is odious, 265
304. Whatever renders a deed void, is odious, 265
305. Whatever tends to change the present state of
things, is odious: the contrary is favourable, 265
306. Things of a mixed nature, 266
307. Interpretation of favourable things, 266
308. Interpretation of odious things, 267
309. Examples, 268
310. How we ought to interpret deeds of pure liberality, 270
311. Collision of laws or treaties, 271
312. First rule in cases of collision, 271
313. Second rule, 271
314. Third rule, 271
315. Fourth rule, 272
316. Fifth rule, 272
317. Sixth rule, 273
318. Seventh rule, 273
319. Eighth rule, <xli> 274
320. Ninth rule, 274
321. Tenth rule, 274
322. General remark on the manner of observing all the
preceding rules, 274

CHAPTER XVIII
*Of the Mode of terminating Disputes
between Nations.*

323. General direction on this subject, 274
324. Every nation is bound to give satisfaction
respecting the just complaints of another, 275

Sect. 325. How nations may abandon their rights and
    just complaints,   page 275
   326. Means suggested by the law of nature, for
    terminating their disputes:—amicable
    accommodation,   276
   327. Compromise,   276
   328. Mediation,   276
   329. Arbitration,   277
   330. Conferences and congresses,   278
   331. Distinction to be made between evident and
    doubtful cases,   278
   332. Essential rights, and those of less importance,   279
   333. How we acquire a right of recurring to force in a
    doubtful case,   280
   334. and even without attempting other measures,   280
   335. Voluntary law of nations on that subject,   280
   336. Equitable conditions to be offered,   281
   337. Possessor's right in doubtful cases,   282
   338. How reparation of an injury is to be sought,   282
   339. Retaliation,   282
   340. Various modes of punishing, without having
    recourse to arms,   283
   341. Retortion,   283
   342. Reprisals,   283
   343. What is required to render them lawful,   284
   344. Upon what effects reprisals are made,   284
   345. The state is bound to compensate those who suffer
    by reprisals,   285
   346. The sovereign alone can order reprisals,   285
   347. Reprisals against a nation for actions of her
    subjects, and in favour of the injured subjects,   285
   348. but not in favour of foreigners,   285
   349. Those who have given cause for reprisals are
    bound to indemnify those who suffer by them,   286
   350. What may be deemed a refusal to do justice,   287
   351. Subjects arrested by way of reprisals,   287
   352. Our right against those who oppose reprisals,   288
   353. Just reprisals do not afford a just cause for war,   288
   354. How we ought to confine ourselves to reprisals, or
    at length proceed to hostilities, <xlii>   288

BOOK III
Of War.

CHAPTER I
Of War,—its different Kinds,—and the
Right of making War.

Sect. 1. Definition of war.   page 291
   2. Public war,   291
   3. Right of making war,   291
   4. It belongs only to the sovereign power,   292
   5. Defensive and offensive war,   293

CHAPTER II
Of the Instruments of war,—the raising of Troops,
&c.—their Commanders, or the Subordinate
Powers in War.

   6. Instruments of war,   293
   7. Right of levying troops,   294
   8. Obligation of the citizens or subjects,   294
   9. Enlisting or raising of troops,   294
  10. Whether there be any exemptions from
       carrying arms,   294
  11. Soldiers' pay and quarters,   296
  12. Hospitals for invalids,   296
  13. Mercenary soldiers,   297
  14. Rule to be observed in their enlistment,   298
  15. Enlisting in foreign countries,   298
  16. Obligation of soldiers,   299
  17. Military laws,   299
  18. Military discipline,   299
  19. Subordinate powers in war,   299
  20. How their promises bind the sovereign,   300
  21. In what cases their promises bind only themselves,   300
  22. Their assumption of an authority which they do
       not possess,   300
  23. How they bind their inferiors,   301

CHAPTER III
Of the just Causes of War.

Sect. 24. War never to be undertaken without very
cogent reasons, page 301
25. Justificatory reasons, and motives for making war, 301
26. What is in general a just cause of war, 302
27. What war is unjust, 302
28. The object of war, 302
29. Both justificatory reasons and proper motives
requisite in undertaking a war, 303
30. Proper motives—vicious motives, <xliii> 303
31. War undertaken upon just grounds, but from
vicious motives, 303
32. Pretexts, 304
33. War undertaken merely for advantage, 304
34. Nations who make war without reason or
apparent motives, 305
35. How defensive war is just or unjust, 305
36. How it may become just against an offensive war
which was originally just, 305
37. How an offensive war is just in an evident cause, 305
38. in a doubtful cause, 306
39. War cannot be just on both sides, 306
40. Sometimes reputed lawful, 306
41. War undertaken to punish a nation, 307
42. Whether the aggrandisement of a neighbouring
power can authorise a war against him, 307
43. Alone, and of itself, it cannot give a right to
attack him, 308
44. How the appearances of danger give that right, 309
45. Another case more evident, 310
46. Other allowable means of defence against a
formidable power, 311
47. Political equilibrium, 311
48. Ways of maintaining it, 312
49. How he that destroys the equilibrium, may be
restrained, or even weakened, 312
50. Behaviour allowable towards a neighbour preparing
for war, 313

CHAPTER IV
Of the Declaration of War,—and of War in due Form.

Sect. 51. Declaration of war:—necessity thereof,   page 315
52. What it is to contain,   315
53. It is simple or conditional,   316
54. The right to make war ceases on the offer of equitable conditions,   316
55. Formalities of a declaration of war,   316
56. Other reasons for the necessity of its publication,   316
57. Defensive war requires no declaration,   317
58. When it may be omitted in an offensive war,   317
59. It is not to be omitted by way of retaliation,   317
60. Time of the declaration,   317
61. Duty of the inhabitants on a foreign army's entering a country before a declaration of war,   317
62. Commencement of hostilities,   318
63. Conduct to be observed towards the enemy's subjects who are in the country at the time of the declaration of war,   318
64. Publication of the war, and manifestoes,   318
65. Decorum and moderation to be observed in the manifestoes,   319
66. What is a lawful war in due form,   319
67. It is to be distinguished from informal and unlawful war,   320
68. Grounds of this distinction, <xliv>   320

CHAPTER V
Of the Enemy, and of Things belonging to the Enemy.

69. Who is an enemy,   321
70. All the subjects of the two states at war are enemies,   321
71. and continue to be enemies in all places,   321
72. Whether women and children are to be accounted enemies,   321
73. Things belonging to the enemy,   322
74. continue such every-where,   322
75. Neutral things found with an enemy,   322

Sect. 76. Lands possessed by foreigners in an
          enemy's country,   page 322
      77. Things due to the enemy by a third party,   322

CHAPTER VI

Of the Enemy's Allies,—of warlike Associations,—
of Auxiliaries and Subsidies.

 78. Treaties relative to war,   323
 79. Defensive and offensive alliances,   323
 80. Difference between warlike alliances and
     defensive treaties,   324
 81. Auxiliary troops,   324
 82. Subsidies,   324
 83. When a nation is authorised to assist another,   324
 84. and to make alliances for war,   324
 85. Alliances made with a nation actually engaged
     in war,   325
 86. Tacit clause in every warlike alliance,   325
 87. To refuse succours for an unjust war, is no breach
     of alliance,   326
 88. What the *casus foederis* is,   326
 89. It never takes place in an unjust war,   326
 90. How it exists in a defensive war,   326
 91. and in a treaty of a guaranty,   326
 92. The succour is not due under an inability to
     furnish it, or when the public safety would
     be exposed,   326
 93. Other cases:—two of the parties in an alliance
     coming to a rupture,   327
 94. Refusal of the succours due in virtue of
     an alliance,   327
 95. The enemy's associates,   328
 96. Those who make a common cause with the enemy
     are his associates,   328
 97. and those who assist him, without being obliged to
     it by treaties,   328
 98. or who are in an offensive alliance with him,   329
 99. How a defensive alliance associates with
     the enemy,   329
100. Another case,   329

Sect. 101. In what case it does not produce the same
effect, <xlv>   page 330
102. Whether it be necessary to declare war against the
enemy's associates,   331

CHAPTER VII

*Of Neutrality,—and the Passage of Troops through
a Neutral Country.*

103. Neutral nations,   332
104. Conduct to be pursued by a neutral nation,   332
105. An ally may furnish the succour due from him,
and remain neuter,   333
106. Right of remaining neuter,   333
107. Treaties of neutrality,   333
108. Additional reason for making those treaties,   334
109. Foundation of the rules of neutrality,   334
110. How levies may be allowed, money lent, and every
kind of things sold, without a breach of neutrality, 334
111. Trade of neutral nations with those which are
at war,   335
112. Contraband goods,   336
113. Whether such goods may be confiscated,   337
114. Searching neutral ships,   339
115. Enemy's property on board a neutral ship,   339
116. Neutral property on board an enemy's ship,   339
117. Trade with a besieged town,   339
118. Impartial offices of neutrals,   340
119. Passage of troops through a neutral country,   340
120. Passage to be asked,   340
121. It may be refused for good reasons,   341
122. In what case it may be forced,   341
123. The fear of danger authorises a refusal,   342
124. or a demand of every reasonable security,   342
125. Whether always necessary to give every kind of
security required,   342
126. Equality to be observed towards both parties, as to
the passage,   343
127. No complaint lies against a neutral state for
granting a passage,   343
128. That state may refuse it from fear of the
resentment of the opposite party,   343

Sect. 129. and lest her country should become the
    theatre of war,   page 343
130. What is included in the grant of passage,   344
131. Safety of the passage,   344
132. No hostility to be committed in a neutral country,   344
133. Neutral country not to afford a retreat to troops,
    that they may again attack their enemies,   345
134. Conduct to be pursued by troops passing through
    a neutral country,   345
135. A passage may be refused for a war evidently
    unjust, <xlvi>   345

CHAPTER VIII

Of the Rights of Nations in War,—and first, of what we have a Right to do, and what we are allowed to do, to the Enemy's Person in a just War.

136. General principle of the rights against an enemy in
    a just war,   346
137. Difference between what we have a right to do,
    and what is barely allowed to be done with
    impunity between enemies,   346
138. The right to weaken an enemy by every
    justifiable method,   347
139. The right over the enemy's person,   347
140. Limits of that right:—an enemy not to be killed
    after ceasing to resist;   347
141. A particular case, in which quarter may be refused,   348
142. Reprisals,   348
143. Whether a governor of a town can be punished
    with death for an obstinate defence,   349
144. Fugitives and deserters,   351
145. Women, children, the aged, and sick,   351
146. Clergy, men of letters, &c.   352
147. Peasants, and, in general, all who do not
    carry arms,   352
148. The right of making prisoners of war,   353
149. A prisoner of war not to be put to death,   354
150. How prisoners of war are to be treated,   354
151. Whether prisoners, who cannot be kept or fed,
    may be put to death,   355
152. Whether prisoners of war may be made slaves,   356

Sect. 153. Exchange and ransom of prisoners,   page 357

154. The state is bound to procure their release,   357

155. Whether an enemy may lawfully be assassinated
or poisoned,   358

156. Whether poisoned weapons may be used in war,   361

157. Whether springs may be poisoned,   361

158. Disposition to be entertained towards an enemy,   362

159. Tenderness for the person of a king who is in arms
against us,   363

CHAPTER IX

Of the Right of War, with respect to Things belonging to the Enemy.

160. Principles of the right over things belonging to
the enemy,   364

161. The right of seizing them,   364

162. What is taken from the enemy by way of penalty,   364

163. What is with-held from him, in order to oblige
him to give just satisfaction,   365

164. Booty, <xlvii>   365

165. Contributions,   366

166. Waste and destruction,   366

167. Ravaging and burning,   367

168. What things are to be spared,   368

169. Bombarding towns,   368

170. Demolition of fortresses,   369

171. Safeguards,   369

172. General rule of moderation, respecting the evil
which may be done to an enemy,   369

173. Rule of the voluntary law of nations on the
same subject,   369

CHAPTER X

Of Faith between Enemies,—of Stratagems, Artifices in War, Spies, and some other Practices.

174. Faith to be sacred between enemies,   371

175. What treaties are to be observed between enemies,   372

176. On what occasions they may be broken,   372

177. Lies,   372

178. Stratagems and artifices in war,   373

Sect. 179. Spies,   page 375
    180. Clandestine seduction of the enemy's people,   376
    181. Whether the offers of a traitor may be accepted,   377
    182. Deceitful intelligence,   377

CHAPTER XI

Of the Sovereign who wages an unjust War.

183. An unjust war gives no right whatever,   378
184. Great guilt of the sovereign who undertakes it,   378
185. His obligations,   379
186. Difficulty of repairing the injury he has done,   379
187. Whether the nation and the military are bound to
    any thing,   380

CHAPTER XII

*Of the Voluntary Law of Nations, as it regards the
Effects of Regular Warfare, independently of the
Justice of the Cause.*

188. Nations not rigidly to enforce the law of nature
    against each other,   381
189. Why they are bound to admit the voluntary law
    of nations,   381
190. Regular war, as to its effects, is to be accounted
    just on both sides,   382
191. Whatever is permitted to one party, is so to
    the other,   382
192. The voluntary law gives no more than impunity to
    him who wages an unjust war, <xlviii>   383

CHAPTER XIII

*Of Acquisitions by War, and particularly
of Conquests.*

193. War a mode of acquisition,   384
194. Measure of the right it gives,   384
195. Rules of the voluntary law of nations,   385
196. Acquisition of movable property,   385
197. Acquisition of immovables,—or conquest,   386
198. How to transfer them validly,   387

Sect. 199. Conditions on which a conquered town
    is acquired,   page 387
200. Lands of private persons,   388
201. Conquest of the whole state,   388
202. To whom the conquest belongs,   391
203. Whether we are to set at liberty a people whom the
    enemy had unjustly conquered,   391

CHAPTER XIV

Of the Right of Postliminium.

204. Definition of the right of postliminium,   392
205. Foundation of that right,   392
206. How it takes effect,   393
207. Whether it takes effect among the allies,   393
208. Of no validity in neutral nations,   393
209. What things are recoverable by that right,   394
210. Of those who cannot return by the right
    of postliminium,   394
211. They enjoy that right when retaken,   394
212. Whether that right extends to their property
    alienated by the enemy,   395
213. Whether a nation that has been entirely subdued
    can enjoy the right of postliminium,   396
214. Right of postliminium for what is restored at
    the peace,   397
215. and for things ceded to the enemy,   397
216. The right of postliminium does not exist after
    a peace,   397
217. Why always in force for prisoners,   397
218. They are free even by escaping into a
    neutral country,   397
219. How the rights and obligations of
    prisoners subsist,   398
220. Testament of a prisoner of war,   398
221. Marriage,   398
222. Regulations established by treaty or custom,
    respecting postliminium,   398

CHAPTER XV
Of the Right of private Persons in War.

Sect. 223. Subjects cannot commit hostilities without
the sovereign's order, page 399
224. That order may be general or particular, 399
225. Source of the necessity of such an order, 399
226. Why the law of nations should have adopted this
rule, <xlix> 399
227. Precise meaning of the order, 400
228. What may be undertaken by private persons,
presuming on the sovereign's will, 400
229. Privateers, 400
230. Volunteers, 401
231. What soldiers and subalterns may do, 401
232. Whether the state is bound to indemnify the
subjects for damages sustained in war, 402

CHAPTER XVI
*Of various Conventions made during the
Course of the War.*

233. Truce and suspension of arms, 404
234. does not terminate the war, 404
235. A truce is either partial or general, 404
236. General truce for many years, 404
237. By whom those agreements may be concluded, 405
238. The sovereign's faith engaged in them, 406
239. When the truce begins to be obligatory, 406
240. Publication of the truce, 406
241. Subjects contravening the truce, 406
242. Violation of the truce, 407
243. Stipulation of a penalty against the infractor, 407
244. Time of the truce, 407
245. Effects of a truce:—what is allowed, or not,
during its continuance.—First rule—Each party
may do at home what they have a right to do in
time of peace, 408
246. Second rule—Not to take advantage of the truce
in doing what hostilities would have prevented, 409
247. for instance, continuing the works of a siege, or
repairing breaches, 409

Sect. 248. or introducing succours, page 409

249. Distinction of a particular case, 410

250. Retreat of an army during a suspension
of hostilities, 410

251. Third rule—Nothing to be attempted in contested
places, but every thing to be left as it was, 411

252. Places quitted or neglected by the enemy, 411

253. Subjects inclined to revolt against their prince not
to be received during the truce, 411

254. much less to be solicited to treason, 411

255. Persons or effects of enemies not to be seized
during the truce, 411

256. Right of postliminium during the truce, 411

257. Intercourse allowed during a truce, 411

258. Persons detained by unsurmountable obstacles
after the expiration of the truce, 412

259. Particular conditions added to truces, 412

260. At the expiration of the truce, the war
recommences without any new declaration, 412

261. Capitulations; and by whom they may be
concluded, <1> 412

262. Clauses contained in them, 413

263. Observance of capitulations, and its utility, 414

264. Promises made to the enemy by individuals, 414

CHAPTER XVII

*Of Safe-conducts and Passports,—with Questions on
the Ransom of Prisoners of War.*

265. Nature of safe-conducts and passports, 416

266. From what authority they emanate, 416

267. Not transferable from one person to another, 416

268. Extent of the promised security, 416

269. How to judge of the right derived from a
safe-conduct, 417

270. Whether it includes baggage and domestics, 417

271. Safe-conduct granted to the father does not
include his family, 417

272. Safe-conduct given in general to any one and
his retinue, 417

273. Term of the safe-conduct, 418

274. A person unavoidably detained beyond the term, 418

Sect. 275. The safe-conduct does not expire at the
death of him who gave it, page 418
276. How it may be revoked, 418
277. Safe-conduct, with the clause, "for such time as
we shall "think fit," 418
278. Conventions relating to the ransom of prisoners, 419
279. The right of demanding a ransom may
be transferred, 419
280. What may annul the convention made for the rate
of the ransom, 419
281. A prisoner dying before payment of ransom, 419
282. Prisoner released on condition of procuring the
release of another, 420
283. Prisoner retaken before he has paid his
former ransom, 420
284. Prisoner rescued before he has received his liberty, 420
285. Whether the things which a prisoner has found
means to conceal, belong to him, 421
286. Hostage given for the release of a prisoner, 421

CHAPTER XVIII
Of Civil War.

287. Foundation of the sovereign's rights against
the rebels, 421
288. Who are rebels, 422
289. Popular commotion, insurrection, sedition, 422
290. How the sovereign is to suppress them, 422
291. He is bound to perform the promises he has made
to the rebels, 423
292. Civil war, 424
293. A civil war produces two independent parties, 425
294. They are to observe the common laws of war, 425
295. The effects of civil war distinguished according
to cases, 426
296. Conduct to be pursued by foreign nations, <li> 427

BOOK IV

Of the Restoration of Peace;
and of Embassies.

CHAPTER I
Of Peace, and the Obligation to cultivate it.

Sect. 1. What peace is,   page 429
   2. Obligation of cultivating it,   430
   3. The sovereign's obligation in that respect,   430
   4. Extent of that duty,   430
   5. Disturbers of the public peace,   431
   6. How far war may be continued,   431
   7. Peace the end of war,   432
   8. General effects of peace,   432

CHAPTER II
Treaties of Peace.

   9. Definition of a treaty of peace,   432
  10. By whom it may be concluded,   432
  11. Alienations made by a treaty of peace,   433
  12. How the sovereign may, in a treaty, dispose of what
     concerns individuals,   435
  13. Whether a king who is a prisoner of war, can
     make a peace,   435
  14. Whether peace can be made with a usurper,   436
  15. Allies included in the treaty of peace,   436
  16. Associates to treat, each for himself,   437
  17. Mediation,   437
  18. On what footing peace may be concluded,   437
  19. General effect of the treaty of peace,   438
  20. Amnesty,   439
  21. Things not mentioned in the treaty,   439
  22. Things not included in the compromise or amnesty,   439
  23. Former treaties, mentioned or confirmed in the
     new, are a part of it,   440

CHAPTER III
Of the Execution of the Treaty of Peace.

Sect. 24. When the obligation of the
treaty commences, page 440
25. Publication of the peace, 440
26. Time of the execution, 441
27. A lawful excuse to be admitted, 441
28. The promise is void when the party to whom it was
made has himself hindered the performance of it, 441
29. Cessation of contributions, 442
30. Products of the thing restored or ceded, 442
31. In what condition things are to be restored, \<lii\> 442
32. The interpretation of a treaty of peace is to be
against the superior party, 443
33. Names of ceded countries, 443
34. Restoration not to be understood of those who have
voluntarily given themselves up, 444

CHAPTER IV
*Of the Observance and Breach of the
Treaty of Peace.*

35. The treaty of peace binds the nation and successors, 444
36. It is to be faithfully observed, 444
37. The plea of fear or force does not dispense with the
observance, 445
38. How many ways a treaty of peace may be broken, 446
39. by a conduct contrary to the nature of every treaty
of peace, 446
40. To take up arms for a fresh cause is no breach of the
treaty of peace, 446
41. A subsequent alliance with an enemy is likewise no
breach of the treaty, 447
42. Why a distinction is to be made between a new war
and a breach of the treaty, 447
43. Justifiable self-defence is no breach of the treaty, 448
44. Causes of rupture on account of allies, 449
45. The treaty is broken by what is contrary to its
particular nature, 449
46. by the violation of any article, 449

Sect. 47. The violation of a single article breaks the
          whole treaty,   page 449
      48. Whether a distinction may here be made
          between the more and the less important articles,   450
      49. Penalty annexed to the violation of an article,   450
      50. Studied delays,   450
      51. Unsurmountable impediments,   450
      52. Infractions of the treaty of peace by the subjects, 451
      53. or by allies,   451
      54. Right of the offended party against him who has
          violated the treaty,   452

CHAPTER V
*Of the Right of Embassy, or the Right of sending
and receiving public Ministers.*

      55. It is necessary that nations be enabled to treat and
          communicate together,   452
      56. They do that by the agency of public ministers,   453
      57. Every sovereign state has a right to send and receive
          public ministers,   453
      58. An unequal alliance, or a treaty of protection, does
          not take away that right,   453
      59. Right of the princes and states of the empire in
          that respect,   453
      60. Cities that have the right of banner,   454
      61. Ministers of viceroys, <liii>   455
      62. Ministers of the nation or of the regents during
          an interregnum,   455
      63. Sovereign molesting another in the exercise of the
          right of embassy,   455
      64. What is allowable in that respect in time of war,   455
      65. The minister of a friendly power is to be received, 456
      66. Resident ministers,   456
      67. Admission of an enemy's ministers,   457
      68. Whether ministers may be received from or sent to
          a usurper,   457

CHAPTER VI
*Of the several Orders of public Ministers,—of
the Representative Character,—and of the Honours
due to Ministers.*

Sect. 69. Origin of the several orders of public
    ministers, page 459
70. Representative character, 459
71. Embassadors, 459
72. Envoys, 460
73. Residents, 460
74. Ministers, 460
75. Consuls, agents, deputies, commissioners, &c. 461
76. Credentials, 461
77. Instructions, 461
78. Right of sending embassadors, 461
79. Honours due to embassadors, 462

CHAPTER VII
*Of the Rights, Privileges, and Immunities of
Embassadors, and other public Ministers.*

80. Respect due to public ministers, 464
81. Their persons sacred and inviolable, 464
82. Particular protection due to them, 465
83. When it commences, 466
84. What is due to them in the countries through
    which they pass, 466
85. Embassadors going to an enemy's country, 467
86. Embassies between enemies, 467
87. Heralds, trumpeters, and drummers, 468
88. Ministers, trumpeters, &c. to be respected even in
    a civil war, 468
89. Sometimes they may be refused admittance, 469
90. Every thing which has the appearance of insult to
    them, must be avoided, 469
91. By and to whom they may be sent, 470
92. Independence of foreign ministers, 470
93. How the foreign minister is to behave, 472
94. How he may be punished for ordinary
    transgressions, 475
95. for faults committed against the prince, 475

Sect. 96. Right of ordering away an embassador who
is guilty, or justly suspected, <liv> page 475

97. Right of repressing him by force, if he behaves
as an enemy, 476

98. Embassador forming dangerous plots
and conspiracies, 476

99. What may be done to him according to the
exigency of the case, 478

100. Embassador attempting against the sovereign's life, 479

101. Two remarkable instances respecting the
immunities of public ministers, 480

102. Whether reprisals may be made on an embassador, 481

103. Agreement of nations concerning the privileges
of embassadors, 482

104. Free exercise of religion, 483

105. Whether an embassador be exempted from
all imposts, 484

106. Obligation founded on use and custom, 485

107. A minister whose character is not public, 485

108. A sovereign in a foreign country, 486

109. Deputies to the states, 487

CHAPTER VIII
Of the Judge of Embassadors in Civil Cases.

110. The embassador is exempt from the civil
jurisdiction of the country where he resides, 488

111. How he may voluntarily subject himself to it, 489

112. A minister who is a subject of the state where he
is employed, 490

113. Immunity of the minister extends to his property, 491

114. The exemption cannot extend to effects belonging
to any trade the minister may carry on, 492

115. nor to immovable property which he possesses in
the country, 493

116. How justice may be obtained against an
embassador, 493

CHAPTER IX
Of the Embassador's House and Domestics.

117. The embassador's house, 494

118. Right of asylum, 495

Sect. 119. Exemption of an embassador's carriages, page 496
120. of his retinue, 497
121. of his wife and family, 497
122. of the secretary of the embassy, 497
123. of the embassador's couriers and dispatches, 498
124. The embassador's authority over his retinue, 498
125. When the rights of an embassador expire, 500
126. Cases when new credentials are necessary, 500
127. Conclusion, <lv> 500

THE
LAW
OF
NATIONS

꩜ PRELIMINARIES ꩜

Idea and general Principles of the Law of Nations.

Nations or states are bodies politic, societies of men united together for the purpose of promoting their mutual safety and advantage by the joint efforts of their combined strength.

§1. What is meant by a nation or state.

Such a society has her affairs and her interests; she deliberates and takes resolutions in common; thus becoming a moral person, who possesses an understanding and a will peculiar to herself, and is susceptible of obligations and rights.

§2. It is a moral person.

To establish on a solid foundation the obligations and rights of nations, is the design of this work. The *law of nations* is *the science which teaches the rights subsisting between nations or states, and the obligations correspondent to those rights.*

§3. Definition of the law of nations.

In this treatise it will appear, in what manner states, as such, ought to regulate all their actions. We shall examine the obligations of a people, as well towards themselves as towards other nations; and by that means we shall discover the rights which result from those obligations. For, the right being nothing more than the power of doing what is morally possible, that is to say, what is proper and consistent with duty,—it is evident that right is derived from duty, or passive obligation,—the obligation we lie under to act in such or such manner. It is therefore <lvi> necessary that a nation should acquire a knowledge of the obligations incumbent on her, in order that she may not only avoid all violation of her duty, but also be able distinctly to ascertain her rights, or what she may lawfully require from other nations.

§4. In what light nations or states are to be considered.

Nations being composed of men naturally free and independent, and who, before the establishment of civil societies, lived together in the state of nature,—nations or sovereign states are to be considered as so many free persons living together in the state of nature.

It is a settled point with writers on the natural law, that all men inherit from nature a perfect liberty and independence, of which they cannot be deprived without their own consent. In a state, the individual citizens do not enjoy them fully and absolutely, because they have made a partial surrender of them to the sovereign. But the body of the nation, the state, remains absolutely free and independent with respect to all other men, all other nations, as long as it has not voluntarily submitted to them.

§5. To what laws nations are subject.

As men are subject to the laws of nature,—and as their union in civil society cannot have exempted them from the obligation to observe those laws, since by that union they do not cease to be men,—the entire nation, whose common will is but the result of the united wills of the citizens, remains subject to the laws of nature, and is bound to respect them in all her proceedings. And since right arises from obligation, as we have just observed (§3), the nation possesses also the same rights which nature has conferred upon men in order to enable them to perform their duties.

§6. In what the law of nations originally consists.

We must therefore apply to nations the rules of the law of nature, in order to discover what their obligations are, and what their rights: consequently the *law of nations* is originally no other than the *law of nature applied* to nations. But as the application of a rule cannot be just and reasonable unless it be made in a manner suitable to the subject, we are not to imagine that the law of nations is precisely and in every case the same as the law of nature, with the difference only of the subjects to which it is applied, so as to allow of our substituting nations for individuals. A state or civil society is a subject very different from an individual of the human race: from which circumstance, pursuant to the law of nature itself, there result, in many cases, very different obligations and rights; <lvii> since the same general rule, applied to two subjects, cannot produce exactly the same decisions, when the subjects are different; and a particular rule which is perfectly just with respect to one subject, is not applicable to another subject of a quite different nature. There are many cases, therefore, in which the law of nature does not decide between state and state in the same manner as it would between man and man. We must therefore know how to accommodate the application of it to different subjects; and it is the art of thus applying it with a precision founded on right reason, that renders the law of nations a distinct science.* <lviii>

* The study of this science presupposes an acquaintance with the ordinary law of nature, of which human individuals are the objects. Nevertheless, for the sake of those who have not systematically studied that law, it will not be amiss to give in this place a general idea of it. The natural law is the *science of the laws of nature,* of those laws which nature imposes on mankind, or to which they are subject by the very circumstance of their being men; a science, whose first principle is this axiom of incontestable truth—"The great end of every being endowed with intellect and sentiment, is happiness." It is by the desire alone of that happiness that we can bind a creature possessed of the faculty of thought, and form the ties of that obligation which shall make him submit to any rule. Now, by studying the nature of things, and that of man in particular, we may thence deduce the rules which man must follow in order to attain his great end,—to obtain the most perfect happiness of which he is susceptible. We call those rules the natural laws, or the laws of nature. They are certain, they are sacred, and obligatory on every man possessed of reason, independently of every other consideration than that of his nature, and even though we should suppose him totally ignorant of the existence of a God. But the sublime consideration of an eternal, necessary, infinite Being, the author of the universe, adds the most lively energy to the law of nature, and carries it to the highest degree of perfection. That necessary Being necessarily unites in himself all perfection: he is therefore superlatively good, and displays his goodness by forming creatures susceptible of happiness. It is then his wish that his creatures should be as happy as is consistent with their nature: consequently it is his will that they should, in their whole conduct, follow the rules which that same nature lays down for them, as the most certain road to happiness. Thus the will of the creator perfectly coincides with the simple indications of nature: and those two sources producing the same law, unite in forming the same obligation. The whole reverts to the first great end of man, which is happiness. It was to conduct him to that great end that the laws of nature were

§7. Definition of the necessary law of nations.   We call that the *necessary law of nations* which consists in the application of the law of nature to nations. It is *necessary*, because nations are absolutely bound to observe it. This law contains the precepts prescribed by the law of nature to states, on whom that law is not less obligatory than on individuals, since states are composed of men, their resolutions are taken by men, and the law of nature is binding on all men, under whatever relation they act. This is the law which Grotius, and those who follow him, call the *internal law of nations,* on account of its being obligatory on nations in point of conscience. Several writers term it the *natural law of nations.*

§8. It is immutable.   Since therefore the necessary law of nations consists in the application of the law of nature to states,—which law is immutable, as being founded on the nature of things, and particularly on the nature of man,—it follows, that the necessary law of nations is immutable.

§9. Nations can make no change in it, nor dispense with the obligations arising from it.   Whence, as this law is immutable, and the obligations that arise from it necessary and indispensable, nations can neither make any changes in it by their conventions, dispense with it in their own conduct, nor reciprocally release each other from the observance of it.

This is the principle by which we may distinguish lawful conventions or treaties from those that are not lawful, and innocent and rational customs from those that are unjust or censurable.

---

ordained: it is from the desire of happiness that his obligation to observe those laws arises. There is, therefore, no man,—whatever may be his ideas respecting the origin of the universe,—even if he had the misfortune to be an atheist,—who is not bound to obey the laws of nature. They are necessary to the general happiness of mankind; and whoever should reject them, whoever should openly despise them, would by such conduct alone declare himself an enemy to the human race, and deserve to be treated as such. Now, one of the first truths which the study of man reveals to us, and which is a necessary consequence of his nature, is, that, in a state of lonely separation from the rest of his species, he cannot attain his great end—happiness: and the reason is, that he was intended to live in society with his fellow-creatures. Nature herself, therefore, has established that society, whose great end is the common advantage of all its members: and the means of attaining that end constitute the rules that each individual is bound to observe in his whole conduct. Such are the natural laws of human society. Having thus given a general idea of them, which is sufficient for any intelligent reader, and is developed at large in several valuable works, let us return to the particular object of this treatise. [[Note added in 1773/1797 editions.]]

There are things, just in themselves, and allowed by the necessary law of nations, on which states may mutually agree with each other, and which they may consecrate and enforce by their manners and customs. There are <lix> others, of an indifferent nature, respecting which, it rests at the option of nations to make in their treaties whatever agreements they please, or to introduce whatever custom or practice they think proper. But every treaty, every custom, which contravenes the injunctions or prohibitions of the necessary law of nations, is unlawful. It will appear, however, in the sequel, that it is only by the internal law, by the law of conscience, such conventions or treaties are always condemned as unlawful,—and that, for reasons which shall be given in their proper place, they are nevertheless often valid by the external law. Nations being free and independent,—though the conduct of one of them be illegal and condemnable by the laws of conscience, the others are bound to acquiesce in it, when it does not infringe upon their perfect rights. The liberty of that nation would not remain entire, if the others were to arrogate to themselves the right of inspecting and regulating her actions;—an assumption on their part, that would be contrary to the law of nature, which declares every nation free and independent of all the others.

Man is so formed by nature, that he cannot supply all his own wants, but necessarily stands in need of the intercourse and assistance of his fellow-creatures, whether for his immediate preservation, or for the sake of perfecting his nature, and enjoying such a life as is suitable to a rational being. This is sufficiently proved by experience. We have instances of persons, who, having grown up to manhood among the bears of the forest, enjoyed not the use of speech or of reason, but were, like the brute beasts, possessed only of sensitive faculties. We see moreover that nature has refused to bestow on men the same strength and natural weapons of defence with which she has furnished other animals,—having, in lieu of those advantages, endowed mankind with the faculties of speech and reason, or at least a capability of acquiring them by an intercourse with their fellow-creatures. Speech enables them to communicate with each other, to give each other mutual assistance, to perfect their reason and knowledge; and having thus become intelligent, they find a thou-

§10. Society established by nature between all mankind;

sand methods of preserving themselves, and supplying their wants. Each individual, moreover, is intimately conscious that he can neither live happily nor improve his nature without the intercourse and assistance of others. Since, therefore, na-<lx>ture has thus formed mankind, it is a convincing proof of her intention that they should communicate with and mutually aid and assist each other.

Hence is deduced the establishment of natural society among men. The general law of that society is, that each individual should do for the others every thing which their necessities require, and which he can perform without neglecting the duty that he owes to himself: a law which all men must observe in order to live in a manner consonant to their nature, and conformable to the views of their common creator,—a law which our own safety, our happiness, our dearest interests, ought to render sacred to every one of us. Such is the general obligation that binds us to the observance of our duties: let us fulfil them with care, if we would wisely endeavour to promote our own advantage.

It is easy to conceive what exalted felicity the world would enjoy, were all men willing to observe the rule that we have just laid down. On the contrary, if each man wholly and immediately directs all his thoughts to his own interest, if he does nothing for the sake of other men, the whole human race together will be immersed in the deepest wretchedness. Let us therefore endeavour to promote the general happiness of mankind: all mankind, in return, will endeavour to promote ours; and thus we shall establish our felicity on the most solid foundations.

§11. and between nations. The universal society of the human race being an institution of nature herself, that is to say, a necessary consequence of the nature of man,— all men, in whatever stations they are placed, are bound to cultivate it, and to discharge its duties. They cannot liberate themselves from the obligation by any convention, by any private association. When, therefore, they unite in civil society for the purpose of forming a separate state or nation, they may indeed enter into particular engagements towards those with whom they associate themselves; but they remain still bound to the performance of their duties towards the rest of mankind. All the difference consists in this, that, having agreed to act in common, and having resigned their rights and submitted their will to the body of the society, in every thing that concerns their common welfare,—it thenceforward belongs to that body, that state, and its rulers, to fulfil the duties of humanity <lxi> towards strangers, in every thing that no longer depends on the liberty of individuals; and it is the state more particularly that is to perform those duties towards other states. We have already seen (§5) that men united in society remain subject to the obligations imposed upon them by human nature. That society, considered as a moral person, since possessed of an understanding, volition, and strength peculiar to itself, is therefore obliged to live on the same terms with other societies or states, as individual man was obliged, before those establishments, to live with other men, that is to say, according to the laws of the natural society established among the human race, with the difference only of such exceptions as may arise from the different nature of the subjects.

Since the object of the natural society established between all mankind is that they should lend each other mutual assistance in order to attain perfection themselves and to render their condition as perfect as possible,—and since nations, considered as so many free persons living together in a state of nature, are bound to cultivate human society with each other,—the object of the great society established by nature between all nations is also the interchange of mutual assistance for their own improvement and that of their condition.

§12. The object of this society of nations.

The first general law that we discover in the very object of the society of nations, is that each individual nation is bound to contribute every thing in her power to the happiness and perfection of all the others.*

§13. General obligation imposed by it.

But the duties that we owe to ourselves being unquestionably paramount to those we owe to others,—a nation owes herself in the first instance, and in preference to all other nations, to do every thing she can to promote her own happiness and perfection. (I say every thing she *can,* not only in a *physical* but in a *moral* sense,—that is, every thing that she

§14. Explanation of this observation.

---

* Xenophon points out the true reason of this first of all duties, and establishes its necessity, in the following words. "If we see a man who is uniformly eager to pursue his own private advantage, without regard to the rules of honour or the duties of friendship, why should we in any emergency think of sparing him?" [[Note added in 1773/1797 editions.]]

can do lawfully, and consistently with justice and honour.) When therefore she cannot contribute to the welfare of another nation without doing an es-<lxii>sential injury to herself, her obligation ceases on that particular occasion, and she is considered as lying under disability to perform the office in question.

§15. The second general law is the liberty and independence of nations.

Nations being free and independent of each other, in the same manner as men are naturally free and independent, the second general law of their society is, that each nation should be left in the peaceable enjoyment of that liberty which she inherits from nature. The natural society of nations cannot subsist, unless the natural rights of each be duly respected. No nation is willing to renounce her liberty: she will rather break off all commerce with those states that should attempt to infringe upon it.

§16. Effect of that liberty.

As a consequence of that liberty and independence, it exclusively belongs to each nation to form her own judgment of what her conscience prescribes to her,—of what she can or cannot do,—of what it is proper or improper for her to do: and of course it rests solely with her to examine and determine whether she can perform any office for another nation without neglecting the duty which she owes to herself. In all cases, therefore, in which a nation has the right of judging what her duty requires, no other nation can compel her to act in such or such particular manner: for any attempt at such compulsion would be an infringement on the liberty of nations. We have no right to use constraint against a free person except in those cases where such person is bound to perform some particular thing for us, and for some particular reason which does not depend on his judgment,—in those cases, in short, where we have a perfect right against him.

§17. Distinctions between internal and external, perfect and imperfect obligations and rights.

In order perfectly to understand this, it is necessary to observe, that the obligation, and the right which corresponds to or is derived from it, are distinguished into *external* and *internal*. The obligation is *internal,* as it binds the conscience, and is deduced from the rules of our duty: it is *external,* as it is considered relatively to other men, and produces some right between them. The internal obligation is always the same in its nature, though it varies in degree: but the external obligation is divided into *perfect* and *imperfect;* and the right that results from it is also *perfect* or *imperfect*. The *perfect right* is that which is accompanied by the right of compelling those who refuse to fulfil the correspondent obligation; the *imperfect* right is unaccompanied by that right of compulsion. The <lxiii> *perfect obligation* is that which gives to the opposite party the right of compulsion; the *imperfect* gives him only a right to ask.

It is now easy to conceive why the right is always imperfect, when the correspondent obligation depends on the judgment of the party in whose breast it exists: for if, in such a case, we had a right to compel him, he would no longer enjoy the freedom of determination respecting the conduct he is to pursue in order to obey the dictates of his own conscience. Our obligation is always imperfect with respect to other people, while we possess the liberty of judging how we are to act: and we retain that liberty on all occasions where we ought to be free.

Since men are naturally equal, and a perfect equality prevails in their rights and obligations, as equally proceeding from nature,—nations composed of men, and considered as so many free persons living together in the state of nature, are naturally equal, and inherit from nature the same obligations and rights. Power or weakness does not in this respect produce any difference. A dwarf is as much a man as a giant; a small republic is no less a sovereign state than the most powerful kingdom.

§18. Equality of nations.

By a necessary consequence of that equality, whatever is lawful for one nation, is equally lawful for any other; and whatever is unjustifiable in the one, is equally so in the other.

§19. Effect of that equality.

A nation then is mistress of her own actions so long as they do not affect the proper and perfect rights of any other nation,—so long as she is only *internally* bound, and does not lie under any *external* and *perfect* obligation. If she makes an ill use of her liberty, she is guilty of a breach of duty; but other nations are bound to acquiesce in her conduct, since they have no right to dictate to her.

§20. Each nation is mistress of her own actions when they do not affect the perfect rights of others.

Since nations are free, independent, and equal,—and since each possesses the right of judging, according to the dictates of her conscience, what conduct she is to pursue in order to fulfil her duties,—the effect of the whole is, to produce, at least externally and in the eyes of mankind, a perfect equality of rights between nations, in the administration

§21. Foundation of the voluntary law of nations.

of their affairs and the pursuit of their pretensions, without regard to the intrinsic justice of their conduct, of which others have no right to form a definitive judgment; so that whatever may be done by any one nation, may be <lxiv> done by any other; and they ought, in human society, to be considered as possessing equal rights.

Each nation in fact maintains that she has justice on her side in every dispute that happens to arise: and it does not belong to either of the parties interested, or to other nations, to pronounce a judgment on the contested question. The party who is in the wrong is guilty of a crime against her own conscience: but as there exists a possibility that she may perhaps have justice on her side, we cannot accuse her of violating the laws of society.

It is therefore necessary, on many occasions, that nations should suffer certain things to be done, though in their own nature unjust and condemnable; because they cannot oppose them by open force, without violating the liberty of some particular state, and destroying the foundations of their natural society. And since they are bound to cultivate that society, it is of course presumed that all nations have consented to the principle we have just established. The rules that are deduced from it, constitute what Monsieur Wolf calls "the voluntary law of nations"; and there is no reason why we should not use the same term, although we thought it necessary to deviate from that great man in our manner of establishing the foundation of that law.

§22. Right of nations against the infractors of the law of nations. The laws of natural society are of such importance to the safety of all states, that, if the custom once prevailed of trampling them under foot, no nation could flatter herself with the hope of preserving her national existence, and enjoying domestic tranquillity, however attentive to pursue every measure dictated by the most consummate prudence, justice, and moderation.* Now all men and all states have a perfect right to those things that are necessary for their preservation, since that right

---

* Etenim si haec perturbare omnia et permiscere volumus, totam vitam periculosam, insidiosam, infestamque reddemus. Cicero in Verr. ii. 15. [["The fact is that if we are prepared to reduce all these principles to chaos and confusion, we shall fill life with danger and resentment and hostility at every turn." *In Verrem.*]]

corresponds to an indispensable obligation. All nations have therefore a right to resort to forcible means for the purpose of repressing any one particular nation who openly violates the laws of the society which nature has established between them, or who directly attacks the welfare and safety of that society.

But care must be taken not to extend that right to the <lxv> prejudice of the liberty of nations. They are all free and independent, but bound to observe the laws of that society which nature has established between them; and so far bound, that, when any one of them violates those laws, the others have a right to repress her. The conduct of each nation, therefore, is no farther subject to the controul of the others, than as the interests of natural society are concerned. The general and common right of nations over the conduct of any sovereign state is only commensurate to the object of that society which exists between them.

§23. Measure of that right.

The several engagements into which nations may enter, produce a new kind of law of nations, called *conventional,* or *of treaties.* As it is evident that a treaty binds none but the contracting parties, the conventional law of nations is not a universal but a particular law. All that can be done on this subject in a treatise on the law of nations, is to lay down those general rules which nations are bound to observe with respect to their treaties. A minute detail of the various agreements made between particular nations, and of the rights and obligations thence resulting, is matter of fact, and belongs to the province of history.

§24. Conventional law of nations, or law of treaties.

Certain maxims and customs consecrated by long use, and observed by nations in their mutual intercourse with each other as a kind of law, form the *customary law of nations,* or the *custom of nations.* This law is founded on a tacit consent, or, if you please, on a tacit convention of the nations that observe it towards each other. Whence it appears that it is not obligatory except on those nations who have adopted it, and that it is not universal, any more than the *conventional law.* The same remark, therefore, is equally applicable to this *customary law,* viz. that a minute detail of its particulars does not belong to a systematic treatise on the law of nations, but that we must content ourselves with giving a general theory of it,—that is to say, the rules which are to be observed in it, as well with a view to its effects, as to its substance: and, with respect

§25. Customary law of nations.

to the latter, those rules will serve to distinguish lawful and innocent customs from those that are unjust and unlawful.

§26. General rule respecting that law.
When a custom or usage is generally established, either between all the civilised nations in the world, or only between those of a certain continent, as of Europe, for example, or between those who have a more frequent intercourse with each other,—if that custom is in its own nature in-<lxvi>different, and much more, if it be useful and reasonable, it becomes obligatory on all the nations in question, who are considered as having given their consent to it, and are bound to observe it towards each other, as long as they have not expressly declared their resolution of not observing it in future. But if that custom contains any thing unjust or unlawful, it is not obligatory: on the contrary, every nation is bound to relinquish it, since nothing can oblige or authorise her to violate the law of nature.

§27. Positive law of nations.
These three kinds of law of nations, the *voluntary,* the *conventional,* and the *customary,* together constitute the *positive law of nations.* For they all proceed from the will of nations,—the *voluntary* from their presumed consent, the *conventional* from an express consent, and the *customary* from tacit consent: and as there can be no other mode of deducing any law from the will of nations, there are only these three kinds of *positive law of nations.*

We shall be careful to distinguish them from the *natural* or *necessary* law of nations, without, however, treating of them separately. But after having, under each individual head of our subject, established what the necessary law prescribes, we shall immediately add how and why the decisions of that law must be modified by the voluntary law; or (which amounts to the same thing in other terms) we shall explain how, in consequence of the liberty of nations, and pursuant to the rules of their natural society, the *external* law, which they are to observe towards each other, differs in certain instances from the maxims of the *internal law,* which nevertheless remain always obligatory in point of conscience. As to the rights introduced by treaties or by custom, there is no room to apprehend that any one will confound them with the natural law of nations. They form that species of law of nations which authors have distinguished by the name of *arbitrary.*

To furnish the reader beforehand with a general direction respecting the distinction between the *necessary* and the *voluntary* law, let us here observe, that, as the *necessary* law is always obligatory on the conscience, a nation ought never to lose sight of it in deliberating on the line of conduct she is to pursue in order to fulfil her duty: but when there is question of examining what she may demand of other states, she must consult the *voluntary* law, whose maxims are devoted to the safety and advantage of the universal society of mankind. <1>

§28. General maxim respecting the use of the necessary and the voluntary law.

THE
LAW
OF
NATIONS

ɷɷ BOOK I ɷɷ

Of Nations considered in themselves

CHAPTER I

Of Nations or Sovereign States.

A nation or a state is, as has been said at the beginning of this work, a body politic, or a society of men united together for the purpose of promoting their mutual safety and advantage by their combined strength.

§1. Of the state, and of sovereignty.

From the very design that induces a number of men to form a society which has its common interests, and which is to act in concert, it is necessary that there should be established a public authority, to order and direct what is to be done by each in relation to the end of the association. This political authority is the sovereignty; and he or they who are invested with it are the sovereign.

It is evident, that, by the very act of the civil or political association, each citizen subjects himself to the authority of the entire body, in every thing that relates to the common welfare. The authority of all over each member, therefore, essentially belongs to the body politic, or state; but

§2. The authority of the body politic over the members.

81

the exercise of that authority may be placed in different hands, according as the society may have ordained. <2>

§3. Of the several kinds of government.

If the body of the nation keeps in its own hands the empire or the right to command, it is a popular government, a *democracy;* if it entrusts it to a certain number of citizens, to a senate, it establishes an *aristocratic* republic; finally, if it confides the government to a single person, the state becomes a *monarchy.*

These three kinds of government may be variously combined and modified. We shall not here enter into the particulars; this subject belonging to the *public universal law:** for the object of the present work,

---

* Nor shall we examine which of those different kinds of government is the best. It will be sufficient to say in general, that the monarchical form appears preferable to every other, provided the power of the sovereign be limited, and not absolute—qui [*principatus*] tum demum regius est, si intra modestiae et mediocritatis fines se contineat, excessu potestatis, quam imprudentes in dies augere satagunt, minuitur, penitusque corrumpitur. Nos stulti, majoris, potentiae specie decepti, dilabimur in contrarium, non satis considerantes eam demum tutam esse potentiam quae viribus modum imponit. [["This [sovereignty] is indeed kingly, if it confines itself within the bounds of modesty and moderation, with a withdrawal from power. The imprudent daily concern themselves to extend such power, but it is diminished and inwardly corrupted. We fools, taken in by the appearance of superior power, lurch to the opposite conclusion, not sufficiently considering that in the end that power is secure which imposes due measure on its energies" (trans. Eds.). The source is unidentified, but the last sentence quotes Valerius Maximus, *Factorum et dictorum memorabilium libri novem,* exemplum externum 8, the story of Theopompus.]] The maxim has both truth and wisdom on its side. The author here quotes the saying of Theopompus, king of Sparta [[720–675 B.C.]], who returning to his house amidst the acclamations of the people after the establishment of the Ephori,—"You will leave to your children (said his wife) an authority diminished through your fault." "True (replied the king): I shall leave them a smaller portion of it; but it will rest upon a firmer basis." [[Five Ephors were elected annually to "uphold" the rule of the kings, but instead they became a constraint on the power of the two Spartan kings; hence the comment by Theopompus's wife.]] The Lacedaemonians, during a certain period, had two chiefs to whom they very improperly gave the title of kings. They were magistrates who possessed a very limited power, and whom it was not unusual to cite before the tribunal of justice,—to arrest,—to condemn to death.—Sweden acts with less impropriety in continuing to bestow on her chief the title of king, although she has circumscribed his power within very narrow bounds. He shares not his authority with a colleague,—he is hereditary,—and the state has, from time immemorial, borne the title of a kingdom. [[Note added in 1773/1797 editions.]]

it is sufficient to establish the general principles necessary for the decision of those disputes that may arise between nations.

Every nation that governs itself, under what form soever, without dependence on any foreign power, is a *sovereign state.* Its rights are naturally the same as those of any other state. Such are the moral persons who live together in a natural society, subject to the law of nations. To give a nation a right to make an immediate figure in this grand society, it is sufficient that it be really sovereign and independent, that is, that it govern itself by its own authority and laws. §4. What are sovereign states.

We ought therefore to account as sovereign states those which have united themselves to another more powerful, by an *unequal alliance,* in which, as Aristotle says, to the more powerful is given more honour, and to the weaker, more assistance.[3] §5. Of states bound by unequal alliance.

The conditions of those unequal alliances may be infinitely varied. But whatever they are, provided the inferior ally reserve to itself the sovereignty, or the right of governing its own body, it ought to be considered as an independent state, that keeps up an intercourse with others under the authority of the law of nations.

Consequently a weak state, which, in order to provide for its safety, places itself under the protection of a more powerful one, and engages, in return, to perform several offices equivalent to that protection, without however divesting itself of the right of <3> government and sovereignty,—that state, I say, does not, on this account, cease to rank among the sovereigns who acknowledge no other law than that of nations. §6. Or by treaties of protection.

There occurs no greater difficulty with respect to *tributary* states; for though the payment of tribute to a foreign power does in some degree diminish the dignity of those states, from its being a confession of their weakness,—yet it suffers their sovereignty to subsist entire. The custom of paying tribute was formerly very common,—the weaker by that means purchasing of their more powerful neighbour an exemption from oppression, or at that price securing his protection, without ceasing to be sovereigns. §7. Of tributary states.

3. This is Vattel's sole reference to Aristotle.

§8. Of feuda-
tory states.   The Germanic nations introduced another custom,—that of requiring homage from a state either vanquished, or too weak to make resistance. Sometimes even, a prince has given sovereignties in fee, and sovereigns have voluntarily rendered themselves feudatories to others.

When the homage leaves independency and sovereign authority in
the administration of the state, and only means certain duties to the lord
of the fee, or even a mere honorary acknowledgment, it does not prevent
the state or the feudatory prince being strictly sovereign. The king of
Naples pays homage for his kingdom to the pope, and is nevertheless
reckoned among the principal sovereigns of Europe.

§9. Of two
states subject
to the same
prince.   Two sovereign states may also be subject to the same prince, without
any dependence on each other, and each may retain all its rights as a free
and sovereign state. The king of Prussia is sovereign prince of Neufchatel in Switzerland, without that principality being in any manner
united to his other dominions; so that the people of Neufchatel, in virtue
of their franchises, may serve a foreign power at war with the king of
Prussia, provided that the war be not on account of that principality.[4]

§10. Of states
forming a
federal
republic.   Finally, several sovereign and independent states may unite themselves together by a perpetual confederacy, without ceasing to be, each
individually, a perfect state. They will together constitute a federal republic: their joint deliberations will not impair the sovereignty of each
member, though they may, in certain respects, put some restraint on the
exercise of it, in virtue of voluntary engagements. A person does not
cease to be free and independent, when he is obliged to fulfil engagements which he has voluntarily contracted.

Such were formerly the cities of Greece; such are at present[5] the Seven
United Provinces of the Netherlands, and such the members of the Helvetic body.

4. Although there is no known case of mercenaries from Neuchâtel fighting
against Prussian forces, Vattel would have had in mind the battle of Novara (1500),
when Swiss troops employed by both France and the Italian states clashed. The event
acquired iconic status in Swiss historiography, and its ramifications were extensively
discussed by historians such as Wattenwyl.

5. 1758.

But a people that has passed under the dominion of another is no longer a state, and can no longer avail itself directly of the law of nations. Such were the nations and kingdoms which the Romans rendered subject to their empire; the generality even of those whom they honoured with the name of friends and allies no longer formed real states. Within themselves, they were go-<4>verned by their own laws and magistrates; but without, they were in every thing obliged to follow the orders of Rome; they dared not of themselves either to make war or contract alliances; and could not treat with nations. §11. Of a state that has passed under the dominion of another.

The law of nations is the law of sovereigns: free and independent states are moral persons, whose rights and obligations we are to establish in this treatise. §12. The objects of this treatise.

CHAPTER II

General Principles of the Duties of a Nation towards itself.

If the rights of a nation spring from its obligations, it is principally from those that relate to itself. It will further appear that its duties towards others depend very much on its duties towards itself, as the former are to be regulated and measured by the latter. As we are then to treat of the obligations and rights of nations,—an attention to order requires that we should begin by establishing what each nation owes to itself. §13. A nation ought to act agreeably to its nature.

The general and fundamental rule of our duties towards ourselves is, that every moral being ought to live in a manner conformable to his nature, *naturae convenienter vivere.* A nation is a being determined by its essential attributes, that has its own nature, and can act in conformity to it. There are then actions of a nation as such, wherein it is concerned in its national character, and which are either suitable or opposite to what constitutes it a nation; so that it is not a matter of indifference whether it performs some of those actions, and omits others. In this respect, the Law of Nature prescribes it certain duties. We shall see, in this first book, what conduct a nation ought to observe, in order that it may not be wanting to itself. But we shall first sketch out a general idea of this subject.

§14. Of the preservation and perfection of a nation.

He who no longer exists can have no duties to perform: and a moral being is charged with obligations to himself, only with a view to his perfection and happiness: for *to preserve and to perfect his own nature,* is the sum of all his duties to himself.

The *preservation* of a nation consists in the duration of the political association by which it is formed. If a period is put to this association, the nation or state no longer subsists, though the individuals that composed it, still exist.

The *perfection* of a nation is found in what renders it capable of obtaining the end of civil society; and a nation is in a perfect state, when nothing necessary is wanting to arrive at that end. We know that the perfection of a thing consists, generally, in the perfect agreement of all its constituent parts to tend to the same end. A nation being a multitude of men united together in civil society,—if in that multitude all conspire to attain the end proposed in forming a civil society, the nation is perfect; and it is more or less so, according as it approaches more or less <5> to that perfect agreement. In the same manner its external state will be more or less perfect, according as it concurs with the interior perfection of the nation.

§15. What is the end of civil society.

The *end* or *object* of civil society is to procure for the citizens whatever they stand in need of, for the necessities, the conveniences, the accommodation of life, and, in general, whatever constitutes happiness,—with the peaceful possession of property, a method of obtaining justice with security, and, finally a mutual defence against all external violence.

It is now easy to form a just idea of the perfection of a state or nation:—every thing in it must conspire to promote the ends we have pointed out.

§16. A nation is under an obligation to preserve itself.

In the act of association, by virtue of which a multitude of men form together a state or nation, each individual has entered into engagements with all, to promote the general welfare; and all have entered into engagements with each individual, to facilitate for him the means of supplying his necessities, and to protect and defend him. It is manifest that these reciprocal engagements can no otherwise be fulfilled than by maintaining the political association. The entire nation is then obliged to maintain that association; and as their preservation depends on its continuance, it thence follows that every nation is obliged to perform the duty of self-preservation.

This obligation, so natural to each individual of God's creation, is not derived to nations immediately from nature, but from the agreement by which civil society is formed: it is therefore not absolute, but conditional,—that is to say, it supposes a human act, to wit, the social compact. And as compacts may be dissolved by common consent of the parties,—if the individuals that compose a nation should unanimously agree to break the link that binds them, it would be lawful for them to do so, and thus to destroy the state or nation; but they would doubtless incur a degree of guilt, if they took this step without just and weighty reasons; for civil societies are approved by the Law of Nature, which recommends them to mankind, as the true means of supplying all their wants, and of effectually advancing towards their own perfection. Moreover civil society is so useful, nay so necessary to all citizens, that it may well be considered as morally impossible for them to consent unanimously to break it without necessity. But what citizens may or ought to do,—what the majority of them may resolve in certain cases of necessity, or of pressing exigency,—are questions that will be treated of elsewhere: they cannot be solidly determined without some principles which we have not yet established. For the present, it is sufficient to have proved, that, in general, as long as the political society subsists, the whole nation is obliged to endeavour to maintain it.

If a nation is obliged to preserve itself, it is no less obliged carefully to preserve all its members. The nation owes this to itself, since the loss even of one of its members weakens it, and <6> is injurious to its preservation. It owes this also to the members in particular, in consequence of the very act of association; for those who compose a nation are united for their defence and common advantage; and none can justly be deprived of this union, and of the advantages he expects to derive from it, while he on his side fulfils the conditions. §17. And to preserve its members.

The body of a nation cannot then abandon a province, a town, or even a single individual who is a part of it, unless compelled to it by necessity, or indispensably obliged to it by the strongest reasons founded on the public safety.

§18. A nation has a right to every thing necessary for its preservation.

Since then a nation is obliged to preserve itself, it has a right to every thing necessary for its preservation. For the Law of Nature gives us a right to every thing, without which we cannot fulfil our obligation; otherwise it would oblige us to do impossibilities, or rather would contradict itself in prescribing us a duty, and at the same time debarring us of the only means of fulfilling it. It will doubtless be here understood, that those means ought not to be unjust in themselves, or such as are absolutely forbidden by the Law of Nature. As it is impossible that it should ever permit the use of such means,—if on a particular occasion no other present themselves for fulfilling a general obligation, the obligation must, in that particular instance, be looked on as impossible, and consequently void.

§19. It ought to avoid every thing that might occasion its destruction.

By an evident consequence from what has been said, a nation ought carefully to avoid, as much as possible, whatever might cause its destruction, or that of the state, which is the same thing.

§20. Of its right to every thing that may promote this end.

A nation or state has a right to every thing that can help to ward off imminent danger, and keep at a distance whatever is capable of causing its ruin; and that from the very same reasons that establish its right to the things necessary to its preservation.

§21. A nation ought to perfect itself and the state.

The second general duty of a nation towards itself is to labour at its own perfection and that of its state. It is this double perfection that renders a nation capable of attaining the end of civil society: it would be absurd to unite in society, and yet not endeavour to promote the end of that union.

Here the entire body of a nation, and each individual citizen, are bound by a double obligation, the one immediately proceeding from nature, and the other resulting from their reciprocal engagements. Nature lays an obligation upon each man to labour after his own perfection; and in so doing, he labours after that of civil society, which could not fail to be very flourishing, were it composed of none but good citizens. But the individual finding in a well regulated society the most powerful succours to enable him to fulfil the task which Nature imposes upon him in relation to himself, for becoming better, and consequently more happy,—he is doubtless obliged to contribute all in his power to render that society more perfect.

All the citizens who form a political society, reciprocally en-<7>gage to advance the common welfare, and as far as possible to promote the advantage of each member. Since then the perfection of the society is what enables it to secure equally the happiness of the body and that of the members, the grand object of the engagements and duties of a citizen is to aim at this perfection. This is more particularly the duty of the body collective in all their common deliberations, and in every thing they do as a body.

A nation therefore ought to prevent, and carefully to avoid, whatever may hinder its perfection and that of the state, or retard the progress either of the one or the other.

§22. And to avoid every thing contrary to its perfection.

We may then conclude, as we have done above in regard to the preservation of a state (§18), that a nation has a right to every thing without which it cannot attain the perfection of the members and of the state, or prevent and repel whatever is contrary to this double perfection.

§23. The rights it derives from these obligations.

On this subject, the English furnish us an example highly worthy of attention. That illustrious nation distinguishes itself in a glorious manner by its application to every thing that can render the state more flourishing. An admirable constitution there places every citizen in a situation that enables him to contribute to this great end, and every-where diffuses that spirit of genuine patriotism which zealously exerts itself for the public welfare. We there see private citizens form considerable enterprises, in order to promote the glory and welfare of the nation. And while a bad prince would find his hands tied up, a wise and moderate king finds the most powerful aids to give success to his glorious designs. The nobles and the representatives of the people form a link of confidence between the monarch and the nation, and, concurring with him in every thing that tends to promote the public welfare, partly ease him of the burden of government, give stability to his power, and procure him an obedience the more perfect, as it is voluntary. Every good citizen sees that the strength of the state is really the advantage of all, and not that of a single

§24. Examples.

person.[6] Happy constitution! which they did not suddenly obtain: it has cost rivers of blood; but they have not purchased it too dear. May luxury, that pest so fatal to the manly and patriotic virtues, that minister of corruption so dangerous to liberty, never overthrow a monument that does so much honour to human nature—a monument capable of teaching kings how glorious it is to rule over a free people![7]

There is another nation illustrious by its bravery and its victories.[8] Its numerous and valiant nobility, its extensive and fertile dominions, might render it respectable throughout all Europe, and in a short time it might be in a most flourishing situation. But its constitution opposes this; and such is its attachment to that constitution, that there is no room to expect a proper remedy will ever be applied. In vain might a magnanimous king, raised by his virtues above the pursuits of ambition and injustice, form the most salutary designs for promoting the happiness of <8> his people;—in vain might those designs be approved by the more sensible part, by the majority of the nation;—a single deputy, obstinate or corrupted by a foreign power, might put a stop to all, and disconcert the wisest and most necessary measures. From an excessive jealousy of its liberty, that nation has taken such precautions as must necessarily place it out of the power of the king to make any attempts on the liberties of the public. But is it not evident that those precautions exceed the end proposed,—that they tie the hands of the most just and wise prince, and deprive him of the means of securing the public freedom against the enterprises of foreign powers, and of rendering the nation rich and happy? Is it not evident that the nation has deprived itself of the power of acting, and

6. In his editions from 1834 Joseph Chitty here noted: "This is indeed a flattering compliment from Vattel, a foreigner: but certainly it is just: for although, as a commercial nation, it might be supposed that each individual principally labours for his own individual gain; yet when we refer to the spirited employment of capital: building national bridges, canals, rail-roads, &c not yielding even 2 per cent, it must be admitted that great public spirit for national good very generally prevails."

7. Vattel is here positioning himself in the debate about the relative merits of Britain and of France, and the vexed question of Britain's likely prospects for survival as a mixed state.

8. Vattel is discussing France.

that its councils are exposed to the caprice or treachery of a single member?

We shall conclude this chapter, with observing, that a nation ought to know itself. Without this knowledge, it cannot make any successful endeavours after its own perfection. It ought to have a just idea of its state, to enable it to take the most proper measures; it ought to know the progress it has already made, and what further advances it has still to make,—what advantages it possesses, and what defects it labours under, in order to preserve the former, and correct the latter. Without this knowledge, a nation will act at random, and often take the most improper measures. It will think it acts with great wisdom in imitating the conduct of nations that are reputed wise and skilful,—not perceiving that such or such regulation, such or such practice, though salutary to one state, is often pernicious to another. Every thing ought to be conducted according to its nature. Nations cannot be well governed without such regulations as are suitable to their respective characters; and in order to this, their characters ought to be known.

§25. A nation ought to know itself.

CHAPTER III

Of the Constitution of a State, and the Duties and Rights of the Nation in this respect.

We were unable to avoid, in the first chapter, anticipating something of the subject of this.

We have seen already that every political society must necessarily establish a public authority, to regulate their common affairs,—to prescribe to each individual the conduct he ought to observe with a view to the public welfare,—and to possess the means of procuring obedience. This authority essentially belongs to the body of the society; but it may be exercised in a variety of ways; and every society has a right to choose that mode which suits it best.

§26. Of public authority.

The fundamental regulation that determines the manner in which the public authority is to be executed, is what forms the <9> *constitution of the state.* In this is seen the form in which the nation acts in quality of

§27. What is the constitution of a state.

a body-politic,—how and by whom the people are to be governed,—
and what are the rights and duties of the governors. This constitution
is in fact nothing more than the establishment of the order in which a
nation proposes to labour in common for obtaining those advantages
with a view to which the political society was established.

§28. The
nation ought
to chuse
the best
constitution.

The perfection of a state, and its aptitude to attain the ends of society,
must then depend on its constitution: consequently the most important
concern of a nation that forms a political society, and its first and most
essential duty towards itself, is to chuse the best constitution possible,
and that most suitable to its circumstances. When it makes this choice,
it lays the foundation of its own preservation, safety, perfection, and
happiness:—it cannot take too much care in placing these on a solid
basis.

§29. Of
political,
fundamental,
and civil laws.

The laws are regulations established by public authority, to be observed in society. All these ought to relate to the welfare of the state and
of the citizens. The laws made directly with a view to the public welfare
are *political laws;* and in this class, those that concern the body itself and
the being of the society, the form of government, the manner in which
the public authority is to be exerted,—those, in a word, which together
form the constitution of the state, are the *fundamental laws.*

The *civil laws* are those that regulate the rights and conduct of the
citizens among themselves.

Every nation that would not be wanting to itself, ought to apply its
utmost care in establishing these laws, and principally its fundamental
laws,—in establishing them, I say, with wisdom, in a manner suitable to
the genius of the people, and to all the circumstances in which they may
be placed: they ought to determine them and make them known with
plainness and precision, to the end that they may possess stability, that
they may not be eluded, and, that they may create, if possible, no *dis-
sension*—that, on the one hand, he or they to whom the exercise of the
sovereign power is committed, and the citizens, on the other, may
equally know their duty, and their rights. It is not here necessary to consider in detail, what that constitution and those laws ought to be:—this
discussion belongs to public law and politics. Besides, the laws and constitutions of different states must necessarily vary according to the dis-

position of the people, and other circumstances. In the Law of Nations we must adhere to generals. We here consider the duty of a nation towards itself, principally to determine the conduct that it ought to observe in that great society which nature has established among all nations. These duties give it rights, that serve as a rule to establish what it may require from other nations, and reciprocally what others may require from it.

The constitution and laws of a state are the basis of the public tranquillity, the firmest support of political authority, and a security for the liberty of the citizens. But this constitution is a vain <10> phantom, and the best laws are useless, if they be not religiously observed: the nation ought then to watch very attentively, in order to render them equally respected by those who govern, and by the people destined to obey. To attack the constitution of the state, and to violate its laws, is a capital crime against society; and if those guilty of it are invested with authority, they add to this crime a perfidious abuse of the power with which they are intrusted. The nation ought constantly to repress them with its utmost vigour and vigilance, as the importance of the case requires. It is very uncommon to see the laws and constitution of a state openly and boldly opposed: it is against silent and gradual attacks that a nation ought to be particularly on its guard. Sudden revolutions strike the imaginations of men: they are detailed in history; their secret springs are developed. But we overlook the changes that insensibly happen by a long train of steps that are but slightly marked. It would be rendering nations an important service, to shew from history, how many states have thus entirely changed their nature, and lost their original constitution. This would awaken the attention of man-kind:—impressed thenceforward with this excellent maxim (no less essential in politics than in morals), *principiis obsta,*[9]—they would no longer shut their eyes against innovations, which, though inconsiderable in themselves, may serve as steps to mount to higher and more pernicious enterprises.

§30. Of the support of the constitution and obedience to the laws.

9. "Resist the first advances."

§31. The
rights of a
nation with
respect to
its consti-
tution and
government.

The consequences of a good or bad constitution being of such importance, and the nation being strictly obliged to procure, as far as possible, the best and most convenient one, it has a right to every thing
necessary to enable it to fulfil this obligation (§18). It is then manifest
that a nation has an indisputable right to form, maintain, and perfect
its constitution,—to regulate at pleasure every thing relating to the government,—and that no person can have a just right to hinder it. Government is established only for the sake of the nation, with a view to its
safety and happiness.

§32. It may
reform the
government.

If any nation is dissatisfied with the public administration, it may
apply the necessary remedies, and reform the government. But observe
that I say "the nation"; for I am very far from meaning to authorise a
few malcontents or incendiaries to give disturbance to their governors
by exciting murmurs and seditions. None but the body of a nation have
a right to check those at the helm when they abuse their power. When
the nation is silent and obeys, the people are considered as approving
the conduct of their superiors, or at least finding it supportable; and it
is not the business of a small number of citizens to put the state in danger, under the pretence of reforming it.

§33. And may
change the
constitution.

In virtue of the same principles, it is certain that if the nation is uneasy
under its constitution, it has a right to change it.

There can be no difficulty in the case, if the whole nation be unanimously inclined to make this change. But it is asked, what is to be done
if the people are divided? In the ordinary manage-<11>ment of the state,
the opinion of the majority must pass without dispute for that of the
whole nation; otherwise it would be almost impossible for the society
ever to take any resolution. It appears then by parity of reasoning, that
a nation may change the constitution of the state by a majority of votes;
and whenever there is nothing in this change that can be considered as
contrary to the act of civil association, or to the intention of those united
under it, the whole are bound to conform to the resolution of the majority. But if the question be, to quit a form of government, to which
alone it appeared that the people were willing to submit on their entering
into the bonds of society,—if the greater part of a free people, after the
example of the Jews in the time of Samuel, are weary of liberty, and

resolved to submit to the authority of a monarch,—those citizens who are more jealous of that privilege, so invaluable to those who have tasted it,—though obliged to suffer the majority to do as they please,—are under no obligation at all to submit to the new government: they may quit a society which seems to have dissolved itself in order to unite again under another form: they have a right to retire elsewhere, to sell their lands, and take with them all their effects.

Here again a very important question presents itself. It essentially belongs to the society to make laws both in relation to the manner in which it desires to be governed, and to the conduct of the citizens:—this is called the *legislative power*. The nation may intrust the exercise of it to the prince, or to an assembly; or to that assembly and the prince jointly; who have then a right to make new laws and to repeal old ones. It is asked whether their power extends to the fundamental laws,—whether they may change the constitution of the state? The principles we have laid down lead us to decide with certainty, that the authority of these legislators does not extend so far, and that they ought to consider the fundamental laws as sacred, if the nation has not, in very express terms, given them power to change them. For the constitution of the state ought to possess stability: and since that was first established by the nation, which afterwards intrusted certain persons with the legislative power, the fundamental laws are excepted from their commission. It is visible that the society only intended to make provision for having the state constantly furnished with laws suited to particular conjunctures, and, for that purpose, gave the legislature the power of abrogating the ancient civil and political laws that were not fundamental, and of making new ones: but nothing leads us to think that it meant to submit the constitution itself to their will. In short, it is from the constitution that those legislators derive their power: how then can they change it, without destroying the foundation of their own authority? By the fundamental laws of England, the two houses of parliament, in concert with the king, exercise the legislative power: but if the two houses should resolve to suppress themselves, and to invest the king with full and absolute authority, certainly the nation would <12> not suffer it. And who would dare to assert that they would not have a right to oppose it? But if the

§34. Of the legislative power, and whether it can change the constitution.

parliament entered into a debate on making so considerable a change, and the whole nation was voluntarily silent upon it, this would be considered as an approbation of the act of its representatives.

§35. The nation ought not to attempt it without great caution.

But in treating here of the change of the constitution, we treat only of the right: the question of expediency belongs to politics. We shall therefore only observe in general, that, great changes in a state being delicate and dangerous operations, and frequent changes being in their own nature prejudicial, a people ought to be very circumspect in this point, and never be inclined to make innovations without the most pressing reasons, or an absolute necessity. The fickleness of the Athenians was ever inimical to the happiness of the republic, and at length proved fatal to that liberty of which they were so jealous, without knowing how to enjoy it.

§36. It is the judge of all disputes relating to the government.

We may conclude from what has been said (§31), that if any disputes arise in a state respecting the fundamental laws, the public administration, or the rights of the different powers of which it is composed, it belongs to the nation alone to judge and determine them conformably to its political constitution.

§37. No foreign power has a right to interfere.

In short, all these affairs being solely a national concern, no foreign power has a right to interfere in them, nor ought to intermeddle with them otherwise than by its good offices, unless requested to do it, or induced by particular reasons. If any intrude into the domestic concerns of another nation, and attempt to put a constraint on its deliberations, they do it an injury.

CHAPTER IV

Of the Sovereign, his Obligations, and his Rights.

§38. Of the sovereign.

The reader cannot expect to find here a long deduction of the rights of sovereignty, and the functions of a prince. These are to be found in treatises on the public law. In this chapter we only propose to shew, in consequence of the grand principles of the law of nations, what a sovereign is, and to give a general idea of his obligations and his rights.

We have said that the *sovereignty* is that public authority which commands in civil society, and orders and directs what each citizen is to perform, to obtain the end of its institution. This authority originally and essentially belonged to the body of the society, to which each member submitted, and ceded his natural right of conducting himself in every thing as he pleased according to the dictates of his own understanding, and of doing himself justice. But the body of the society does not always retain in its own hands this sovereign authority: it frequently intrusts it to a senate, or to a single person. That senate, or that person, is then the sovereign. <13>

It is evident that men form a political society, and submit to laws, solely for their own advantage and safety. The sovereign authority is then established only for the common good of all the citizens; and it would be absurd to think that it could change its nature on passing into the hands of a senate or a monarch. Flattery therefore cannot, without rendering itself equally ridiculous and odious, deny that the sovereign is only established for the safety and advantage of society.

§39. It is solely established for the safety and advantage of society.

A good prince, a wise conductor of society, ought to have his mind impressed with this great truth, that the sovereign power is solely intrusted to him for the safety of the state, and the happiness of all the people,—that he is not permitted to consider himself as the principal object in the administration of affairs, to seek his own satisfaction, or his private advantage,—but that he ought to direct all his views, all his steps, to the greatest advantage of the state and people who have submitted to him.* What a noble sight it is to see a king of England ren-

---

* The last words of Louis VI. [[Louis the Fat, r. 1108–37]] to his son Louis VII. [[Louis VII, the Younger, r. 1137–80]] were—"Remember, my son, that royalty is but a public employment of which you must render a rigorous account to him who is the sole disposer of crowns and sceptres." Abbé Velly's Hist. of France, Vol. III. p. 65.

Timur-Bec declared (as he often before had done on similar occasions) that "a single hour's attention devoted by a prince to the care of his state, is of more use and consequence than all the homage and prayers he could offer up to God during his whole life." [[Timur-Bec, or Tamurlane, ca. 1336–1405, Mongol warlord; as conqueror of much of central Asia, he founded the Timurid dynasty.]] The same sentiment is found in the Koran. Hist. of Timur-Bec, Book II. ch. xli. [[Sharaf ad-Din 'Ali Yazdi,

dering his parliament an account of his principal operations,—assuring that body, the representatives of the nation, that he has no other end in view than the glory of the state, and the happiness of his people,—and affectionately thanking all who concur with him in such salutary views! Certainly a monarch who makes use of this language, and by his conduct proves the sincerity of his professions, is, in the opinion of the wise, the only great man. But in most kingdoms, a criminal flattery has long since caused these maxims to be forgotten. A crowd of servile courtiers easily persuade a proud monarch that the nation was made for him, and not he for the nation. He soon considers the kingdom as a patrimony that is his own property, and his people as a herd of cattle from which he is to derive his wealth, and which he may dispose of to answer his own views, and gratify his passions. Hence those fatal wars undertaken by ambition, restlessness, hatred and pride;—hence those oppressive taxes, whose produce is dissipated by ruinous luxury, or squandered upon mistresses and favourites;—hence, in fine, are important posts given by favour, while public merit is neglected, and every thing that does not immediately interest the prince, is abandoned to ministers and subalterns. Who can, in this unhappy government, discover an authority established for the public welfare?—A great prince will be on his guard even against his virtues. Let us not say, with some writers, that private virtues are not the virtues of kings,—a maxim of superficial politicians, or <14> of those who are very inaccurate in their expressions. Goodness, friendship, gratitude, are still virtues on the throne; and would to God they were always to be found there! but a wise king does not yield an undiscerning obedience to their impulse. He cherishes them, he cultivates them in his private life: but in state-affairs he listens only to justice and sound policy. And why? because he knows that the government was intrusted to him only for the happiness of society, and that therefore he ought not to consult his own pleasure in the use he makes of his power. He tempers his goodness with wisdom. He gives to friendship his domestic and private favours; he distributes posts and employments according to

---

History of Timur-Bec, translated into French by de la Croix. Note added in 1773/1797 editions.]]

merit,—public rewards to services done to the state. In a word, he uses the public power only with a view to the public welfare. All this is comprehended in that fine saying of Lewis XII.[10] "A king of France does not revenge the injuries of a duke of Orleans."

A political society is a moral person (prelim. §2) inasmuch as it has an understanding and a will of which it makes use for the conduct of its affairs, and is capable of obligations and rights. When therefore a people confer the sovereignty on any one person, they invest him with their understanding and will, and make over to him their obligations and rights, so far as relates to the administration of the state, and to the exercise of the public authority. The sovereign, or conductor of the state, thus becoming the depositary of the obligations and rights relative to government, in him is found the moral person, who, without absolutely ceasing to exist in the nation, acts thenceforwards only in him and by him. Such is the origin of the representative character attributed to the sovereign. He represents the nation in all the affairs in which he may happen to be engaged as a sovereign. It does not debase the dignity of the greatest monarch to attribute to him this representative character; on the contrary, nothing sheds a greater lustre on it, since the monarch thus unites in his own person all the majesty that belongs to the entire body of the nation.

§40. Of his representative character.

The sovereign, thus clothed with the public authority, with every thing that constitutes the moral personality of the nation, of course becomes bound by the obligations of that nation, and invested with its rights.

§41. He is intrusted with the obligations of the nation, and invested with its rights.

All that has been said in chap. II. of the general duties of a nation towards itself, particularly regards the sovereign. He is the depositary of the empire, and of the power of commanding whatever conduces to the public welfare; he ought, therefore, as a tender and wise father, and as a faithful administrator, to watch for the nation, and take care to preserve it, and render it more perfect,—to better its state, and to secure it, as far as possible, against every thing that threatens its safety or its happiness.

§42. His duty with respect to the preservation and perfection of the nation.

10. Louis XII, called "Father of the People," r. 1498–1515.

§43. His rights
in this respect.

Hence all the rights which a nation derives from its obligation to preserve and perfect itself, and to improve its state, (see §§18, <15> 20, and
23, of this book)—all these rights, I say, reside in the sovereign, who is
therefore indifferently called the conductor of the society, superior,
prince, &c.

§44. He ought
to know the
nation.

We have observed above, that every nation ought to know itself. This
obligation devolves on the sovereign, since it is he who is to watch over
the preservation and perfection of the nation. The duty which the law
of nature here imposes on the conductors of nations is of extreme importance, and of considerable extent. They ought exactly to know the
whole country subject to their authority,—its qualities, defects, advantages, and situation with regard to the neighbouring states; and they
ought to acquire a perfect knowledge of the manners and general inclinations of their people, their virtues, vices, talents, &c. All these
branches of knowledge are necessary to enable them to govern properly.

§45. The
extent of
his power.

Prerogatives
of majesty.

The prince derives his authority from the nation; he possesses just so
much of it as they have thought proper to intrust him with.* If the
nation has plainly and simply invested him with the sovereignty without
limitation or division, he is supposed to be invested with all the prerogatives, without which the sovereign command or authority could not be
exerted in the manner most conducive to the public welfare. These are
called *regal prerogatives,* or *the prerogatives of majesty.*

---

* Neque enim se princeps reipublicae et singulorum dominum arbitrabitur,
quamvis assentatoribus id in aurem insusurrantibus, sed rectorem mercede a civibus
designata, quam augere, nisi ipsis volentibus, nefas existimabit. Ibid. c. v. [["For the
prince will not consider himself lord of the state and of individuals, however much
yes-men might whisper in his ear, but rather a governor with remuneration assigned
by the citizens which he will think it unlawful to increase except by their wish" (trans.
Eds.). The source is not identified.]]—From this principle it follows that the nation
is superior to the sovereign. Quod caput est, sit principi persuasum, totius reipublicae
majorem quam ipsius unius auctoritatem esse: neque pessimis hominibus credat di-
versum affirmantibus gratificandi studio; quae magna pernicies est. Ibid. [["The chief
point is, let the prince be persuaded that the authority of the entire state is greater
than that of one person in himself, and let him not believe the opposite when the
worst of men affirm it out of a desire to curry favor, which is a great evil" (trans.
Eds.). The source is not identified. Note added in 1773/1797 editions.]]

But when the sovereign power is limited and regulated by the fundamental laws of the state, those laws shew the prince the extent and bounds of his power, and the manner in which he is to exert it. The prince is therefore strictly obliged not only to respect, but also to support them. The constitution and the fundamental laws are the plan on which the nation has resolved to labour for the attainment of happiness: the execution is intrusted to the prince. Let him religiously follow this plan,—let him consider the fundamental laws as inviolable and sacred rules,—and remember that the moment he deviates from them, his commands become unjust, and are but a criminal abuse of the power with which he is intrusted. He is, by virtue of that power, the guardian and defender of the laws:—and while it is his duty to restrain each daring violator of them, ought he himself to trample them under foot?* <16>

§46. The prince ought to respect and support the fundamental laws.

If the prince be invested with the legislative power, he may, according to his wisdom, and when the public advantage requires it, abolish those laws that are not fundamental, and make new ones. See what we have said on this subject in the preceding chapter, §34.

§47. He may change the laws not fundamental.

But while these laws exist, the sovereign ought religiously to maintain and observe them. They are the foundation of the public tranquillity, and the firmest support of the sovereign authority. Every thing is uncertain, violent, and subject to revolutions, in those unhappy states where arbitrary power has placed her throne. It is therefore the true in-

§48. He ought to maintain and observe the existing laws.

* In some countries, formal precautions are taken against the abuse of power.— "Reflecting, among other things (says Grotius), that princes are often found to make no scruple of violating their promises under the stale pretext of the public good, the people of Brabant, in order to obviate that inconvenience, established the custom of never admitting their prince to the possession of the government without having previously made with him a covenant, that, whenever he may happen to violate the laws of the country, they shall be absolved from the oath of obedience they had sworn to him, until ample reparation be made for the outrages committed. The truth of this is confirmed by the example of past generations, who formerly made effectual use of arms and decrees to reduce within proper bounds such of their sovereigns as had transgressed the line of duty, whether through their own licentiousness or the artifices of their flatterers. Thus it happened to John the Second: nor would they consent to make peace with him or his successors, until those princes had entered into a solemn engagement to secure the citizens in the enjoyment of their privileges." Annals of the Netherlands, book ii. [[Note added in 1773/1797 editions.]]

terest of the prince, as well as his duty, to maintain and respect the laws. He ought to submit to them himself. We find this truth established in a piece published by order of Lewis XIV.[11] one of the most absolute princes that ever reigned in Europe. "Let it not be said that the sovereign is not subject to the laws of his state, since the contrary proposition is one of the truths of the law of nations, which flattery has sometimes attacked, and which good princes have always defended, as a tutelar divinity of their states."*

§49. In what sense he is subject to the laws.
But it is necessary to explain this submission of the prince to the laws. First he ought, as we have just seen, to follow their regulations in all the acts of his administration. In the second place, he is himself subject, in his private affairs, to all the laws that relate to property. I say, "in his private affairs"; for when he acts as a sovereign prince, and in the name of the state, he is subject only to the fundamental laws, and the law of nations. In the third place, the prince is subject to certain regulations of general polity, considered by the state as inviolable, unless he be excepted in express terms by the law, or tacitly by a necessary consequence of his dignity. I here speak of the laws that relate to the situation of individuals, and particularly of those that regulate the validity of marriages. These laws are established to ascertain the state of families: now the royal family is that of all others the most important to be certainly known. But, fourthly, we shall observe in general, with respect to this question, that, if the prince is invested with a full, absolute, and unlimited sovereignty, he is above the laws, which derive from him all their force; and he may dispense with his own observance of them, whenever natural justice and equity will permit him. <17> Fifthly, as to the laws relative to morals and good order, the prince ought doubtless to respect them, and to support them by his example. But, sixthly, he is certainly above all civil penal laws. The majesty of a sovereign will not admit of his being punished like a private person; and his functions are too exalted to allow of his

---

* [[Antoine Bilaine,]] A treatise on the right of the queen to several states of the Spanish monarchy, 1667, in 12mo, part II. p. 191.
11. Louis XIV of France, "the Sun King," r. 1643–1715.

being molested under pretence of a fault that does not directly concern the government of the state.

It is not sufficient that the prince be above the penal laws: even the interest of nations requires that we should go something farther. The sovereign is the soul of the society; if he be not held in veneration by the people, and in perfect security, the public peace, and the happiness and safety of the state, are in continual danger. The safety of the nation then necessarily requires that the person of the prince be sacred and inviolable. The Roman people bestowed this privilege on their tribunes, in order that they might meet with no obstruction in defending them, and that no apprehension might disturb them in the discharge of their office. The cares, the employments of a sovereign, are of much greater importance than those of the tribunes were, and not less dangerous, if he be not provided with a powerful defence. It is impossible even for the most just and wise monarch, not to make mal-contents; and ought the state to continue exposed to the danger of losing so valuable a prince by the hand of an assassin? The monstrous and absurd doctrine, that a private person is permitted to kill a bad prince, deprived the French, in the beginning of the last century, of a hero who was truly the father of his people.* Whatever a prince may be, it is an enormous crime against a nation to deprive them of a sovereign whom they think proper to obey.†

§50. His person is sacred and inviolable.

---

* Since the above was written, France has witnessed a renewal of those horrors. She sighs at the idea of having given birth to a monster capable of violating the majesty of kings in the person of a prince, whom the qualities of his heart entitle to the love of his subjects and the veneration of foreigners. [*The author alludes to the attempt made by Damien to assassinate Louis XV.*]

† In Mariana's work above quoted [[*De rege et regis institutione*]], I find (chap. vii. towards the end) a remarkable instance of the errors into which we are apt to be led by a subtle sophistry destitute of sound principles.—That author allows us to poison a tyrant, and even a public enemy, provided it be done without obliging him, either by force or through mistake or ignorance, to concur in the act that causes his own death,—which would be the case, for instance, in presenting him a poisoned draught. For (says he), in thus leading him to an act of suicide, although committed through ignorance, we make him violate the natural law which forbids each individual to take away his own life; and the crime of him who thus unknowingly poisons himself redounds on the real author,—the person who administered the poison.—Ne cogatur

§51. But the
nation may
curb a tyrant,
and withdraw
itself from his
obedience.

But this high attribute of sovereignty is no reason why the nation should not curb an insupportable tyrant, pronounce sentence on him (still respecting in his person the majesty of his rank), and withdraw itself from his obedience. To this indisputable right a <18> powerful republic owes its birth. The tyranny exercised by Philip II. in the Netherlands excited those provinces to rise: seven of them, closely confederated, bravely maintained their liberties, under the conduct of the heroes of the house of Orange; and Spain, after several vain and ruinous efforts, acknowledged them sovereign and independent states. If the authority of the prince is limited and regulated by the fundamental laws, the prince, on exceeding the bounds prescribed him, commands without any right, and even without a just title: the nation is not obliged to obey him, but may resist his unjust attempts. As soon as a prince attacks the constitution of the state, he breaks the contract which bound the people to him: the people become free by the act of the sovereign, and can no longer view him but as an usurper who would load them with oppression. This truth is acknowledged by every sensible writer, whose pen is not enslaved by fear, or sold for hire. But some celebrated authors maintain, that if the prince is invested with the supreme command in a full and absolute manner, nobody has a right to resist him, much less to curb him, and that nought remains for the nation but to suffer and obey with patience. This is founded upon the supposition that such a sovereign is not accountable to any person for the manner in which he governs, and that if the nation might controul his actions and resist him, where it thinks them unjust, his authority would no longer be absolute; which would be contrary to this hypothesis. They say that an absolute sovereign completely possesses all the political authority of the society, which no-

---

tantum sciens aut imprudens sibi conscire mortem; quod esse nefas judicamus, veneno in potu aut cibo, quod hauriat qui perimendus est, aut simili alia retemperato. [["Let him not be forced knowingly or imprudently to be complicit in his own death; we judge it to be unlawful that he who must perish should swallow poison in food or drink or mixed with some other substance" (trans. Eds.).]] A fine reason, truly! Was Mariana disposed to insult the understandings of his readers, or only desirous of throwing a slight varnish over the detestable doctrine contained in that chapter? [[Note added in 1773/1797 editions.]]

body can oppose,—that, if he abuses it, he does ill indeed, and wounds his conscience,—but that his commands are not the less obligatory, as being founded on a lawful right to command,— that the nation, by giving him absolute authority, has reserved no share of it to itself, and has submitted to his discretion, &c. We might be content with answering, that in this light there is not any sovereign who is completely and fully absolute. But in order to remove all these vain subtleties, let us remember the essential end of civil society. Is it not to labour in concert for the common happiness of all? Was it not with this view that every citizen divested himself of his rights, and resigned his liberty? Could the society make such use of its authority, as irrevocably to surrender itself and all its members to the discretion of a cruel tyrant? No, certainly, since it would no longer possess any right itself, if it were disposed to oppress a part of the citizens. When therefore it confers the supreme and absolute government, without an express reserve, it is necessarily with the tacit reserve that the sovereign shall use it for the safety of the people, and not for their ruin. If he becomes the scourge of the state, he degrades himself; he is no better than a public enemy, against whom the nation may and ought to defend itself; and if he has carried his tyranny to the utmost height, why should even the life of so cruel and perfidious an enemy be spared? Who shall presume to blame the conduct of the Roman senate, that declared Nero an enemy to his country? <19>

But it is of the utmost importance to observe, that this judgment can only be passed by the nation, or by a body which represents it, and that the nation itself can not make any attempt on the person of the sovereign, except in cases of extreme necessity, and when the prince, by violating the laws, and threatening the safety of his people, puts himself in a state of war against them. It is the person of the sovereign, not that of an unnatural tyrant and a public enemy, that the interest of the nation declares sacred and inviolable. We seldom see such monsters as Nero. In the more common cases, when a prince violates the fundamental laws,— when he attacks the liberties and privileges of his subjects,—or (if he be absolute) when his government, without being carried to extreme violence, manifestly tends to the ruin of the nation,—it may resist him, pass sentence on him, and withdraw from his obedience: but though this may be done, still his person should be spared, and that for the welfare of the state.* It is above <20> a century since the English took up arms

* Dissimulandum censeo quatenus salus publica patiatur, privatimque corruptis moribus princeps contingat: alioquin si rempublicam in periculum vocat, si patriae religionis contemptor existit, neque medicinam ullam recipit, abdicandum judico, alium substituendum; quod in Hispania non semel fuisse factum scimus: quasi fera irritata, omnium telis peti debet, cum, humanitate abdicata, tyrannum induit. Sic Petro rege ob immanitatem dejecto publice, Henricus ejus frater, quamvis ex impari matre, regnum obtinuit. Sic Henrico hujus abnepote ob ignaviam pravosque mores abdicato procerum suffragiis, primum Alfonsus ejus frater, recte an secus non disputo, sed tamen in tenera aetate rex est proclamatus: deinde defuncto Alfonso, Elisabetha ejus soror, Henrico invito, rerum summam ad se traxit, regio tantum nomine abstinens dum ille vixit. [["My assessment is that there must be secrecy about the extent of what public safety can tolerate, and the extent to which the prince can be privately involved with corrupted morals; otherwise if he brings the state into danger, if he stands forth as one who despises the religion of his country, and accepts no remedy, then I judge he must abdicate and another take his place. We know this has happened more than once in Spain when, as a provoked wild animal needs to be pursued by the weapons of all, human decency has been in abeyance and she has taken on a tyrant. Thus, when Peter was king, when the people were laid low on account of his excesses, his brother Henry, although from a different mother, obtained the kingdom. Thus when by the votes of the nobles Henry had been deposed by his grandson on account of his sloth and vicious morals, in the first instance his brother Alfonsus was proclaimed king, I will not argue whether rightly or wrongly but at any rate at a tender age. Then on the death of Alfonsus his sister Elisabeth assumed control of affairs despite Henry's unwillingness and was queen in all but name as long as he lived" (trans. Eds.).]] Mariana, de Rege et Regis Institut. Lib. I. c. iii.

To this authority furnished by Spain, join that of Scotland, proved by the letter of the barons to the pope, dated April 6, 1320 [[the Declaration of Arbroath, or formal confirmation of Scotland's independence]], requesting him to prevail on the king of England to desist from his enterprises against Scotland. After having spoken of the evils they had suffered from him, they add—A quibus malis innumeris, ipso juvante qui post vulnera medetur et sanat, liberati sumus per serenissimum principem regem et dominum nostrum, dominum Robertum, qui pro populo et haereditate suis de manibus inimicorum liberandis, quasi alter Maccabaeus aut Josue, labores et taedia, inedias et pericula, laeto sustinuit animo. Quem etiam divina dispositio, et (juxta leges et consuetudines nostras, quas usque ad mortem sustinere volumus) juris successio, et debitus nostrorum consensus et assensus nostrum fecerunt principem atque regem: cui, tanquam illi per quem salus in populo facta est, pro nostra libertate tuenda, tam jure quam meritis tenemur, et volumus in omnibus adhaerere. Quem, si ab inceptis desistet, regi Anglorum aut Anglis nos aut regnum nostrum volens subjicere, tanquam inimicum nostrum et sui nostrique juris subversorem, statim expellere nitemur, et alium regem nostrum, qui ad defensionem nostram sufficiet, fa-

against their king, and obliged him to descend from the throne. A set of able enterprising men, spurred on by ambition, took advantage of the terrible ferment, caused by fanaticism and party spirit; and Great Britain suffered her sovereign to die unworthily on a scaffold. The nation coming to itself discovered its former blindness. If, to this day, it still annually makes a solemn atonement, it is not only, from the opinion

---

ciemus: quia, quamdiu centum viri remanserint, nunquam Anglorum dominio aliquatenus volumus subjugari. Non enim propter gloriam, divitias, aut honores pugnamus, sed propter libertatem solummodo, quam nemo bonus nisi simul cum vita amittit. [["But from these countless evils we have been set free, by the help of Him Who though He afflicts yet heals and restores, by our most tireless Prince, King and Lord, the Lord Robert. He, that his people and his heritage might be delivered out of the hands of our enemies, met toil and fatigue, hunger and peril, like another Maccabaeus or Joshua, and bore them cheerfully. Him, too, divine providence, his right of succession according to our laws and customs which we shall maintain to the death, and the due consent and assent of us all have made our prince and king. To him, as to the man by whom salvation has been wrought unto our people, we are bound both by law and by his merits that our freedom may be still maintained, and by him, come what may, we mean to stand. Yet if he should give up what he has begun, and agree to make us or our kingdom subject to the king of England or the English, we should exert ourselves at once to drive him out as our enemy and a subverter of his own rights and ours, and make some other man who was well able to defend us our king; for, as long as but a hundred of us remain alive, never will we on any conditions be brought under English rule. It is in truth not for glory, nor riches, nor honours that we are fighting, but for freedom—for that alone, which no honest man gives up but with life itself." (Scottish nobles to Pope John XXII.)]]

"In the year 1581 (says Grotius, Ann. book III.) the confederated provinces of the Netherlands,—after having for nine years continued to wage war against Philip the Second [[king of Spain, r. 1556–98]] without ceasing to acknowledge him as their sovereign,—at length solemnly deprived him of the authority he had possessed over their country, because he had violated their laws and privileges." The author afterwards observes that "France, Spain herself, England, Sweden, Denmark, furnish instances of kings deposed by their people, so that there are at present few sovereigns in Europe whose right to the crown rests on any other foundation than the right which the people possess of divesting their sovereign of his power when he makes an ill use of it." Pursuant to this idea, the United Provinces, in their justificatory letters on that subject, addressed to the princes of the Empire and the king of Denmark,—after having enumerated the oppressive acts of the king of Spain,—added—"Then, by a mode which has been often enough adopted even by those nations that now live under kingly government, we wrested the sovereignty from him whose actions were all contrary to the duty of a prince." Ibid. [[Note added in 1773/1797 editions.]]

that the unfortunate Charles I. did not deserve so cruel a fate, but, doubt-less, from a conviction that the very safety of the state requires the person of the sovereign to be held sacred and inviolable, and that the whole nation ought to render this maxim venerable, by paying respect to it when the care of its own preservation will permit.

One word more on the distinction that is endeavoured to be made here in favour of an absolute sovereign. Whoever has well weighed the force of the indisputable principles we have established, will be con-vinced, that, when it is necessary to resist a prince who has become a tyrant, the *right* of the people is still the same, whether that prince was made absolute by the laws, or was not; because that right is derived from what is the object of all political society,—the safety of the nation, which is the supreme law.* But if the distinction of which we are treating, is of no moment with respect to the right, it can be of none in practice, with respect to expediency. As it is very difficult to oppose an absolute prince, and it cannot be done without raising great disturbances in the state, and the most violent and dangerous commotions, it ought to be attempted only in cases of extremity, when the public misery is raised to such a height, that the people may say with Tacitus, *miseram pacem vel bello bene mutari,* [12]—that it is better to expose themselves to a civil

---

* Populi patroni non pauciora neque minora praesidia habent. Certe a republica unde ortum habet regia postestas, rebus exigentibus, regens in jus vocari potest, et, si sanitatem respuat, principatu spoliari; neque ita in principem jura potestatis transtulit, ut non sibi majorem reservârit potestatem. Ibid. cap. VI. [["The defenders of the people have means of defense which are not scantier or smaller. Certainly when circumstances demand it the ruler can be brought before the law by the state from which royal power has its origin, and if he refuses to see sense he can be stripped of his power; and no power has legally transferred to the prince, so he does not reserve power to himself." *Annales et historiae de rebus Belgicis,* lib. III (trans. Eds.).]]

Est tamen salutaris cogitatio, ut sit principibus persuasum, si rempublicam op-presserint, si vitiis et foeditate intolerandi erunt, ea se conditione vivere, ut non jure tantum, sed cum laude et gloria, perimi possint. Ibid. [["It is however a salutary con-sideration, that princes should be persuaded, if they oppress the state, if through vice and foulness they are unendurable, that they live under this condition that their re-moval can be not just legal but praiseworthy and glorious" (trans. Eds.). Note added in 1773/1797 editions.]]

12. "Even war is a good exchange for a miserable peace." Tacitus, *Annales,* III.47.

war, than to endure them. But if the prince's authority be limited,—if it in some respects depends on a senate or a parliament that represents the nation,—there are means of resisting and curbing him, without exposing the state to violent shocks. When mild and innocent remedies can be applied to the evil, there can be no reason for waiting until it becomes extreme.

But however limited a prince's authority may be, he is commonly very jealous of it; it seldom happens that he patiently suffers resistance, and peaceably submits to the judgment of his people. Can he want support, while he is the distributer of <21> favours? We see too many base and ambitious souls, for whom the state of a rich and decorated slave has more charms than that of a modest and virtuous citizen. It is therefore always difficult for a nation to resist a prince and pronounce sentence on his conduct, without exposing the state to dangerous troubles, and to shocks capable of overturning it. This has sometimes occasioned a compromise between the prince and the subjects, to submit to the decision of a friendly power all the disputes that might arise between them. Thus the kings of Denmark, by solemn treaties, formerly referred to those of Sweden the differences that might arise between them and their senate: and this the kings of Sweden have also done with regard to those of Denmark. The princes and states of West Friesland, and the burgesses of Embden, have in the same manner constituted the republic of the United Provinces the judge of their differences. The princes and the city of Neufchatel established, in 1406, the canton of Berne perpetual judge and arbitrator of their disputes. Thus also, according to the spirit of the Helvetic confederacy, the entire body takes cognisance of the disturbances that arise in any of the confederated states, though each of them is truly sovereign and independent.

§52. Arbitration between the king and his subjects.

As soon as a nation acknowledges a prince for its lawful sovereign, all the citizens owe him a faithful obedience. He can neither govern the state, nor perform what the nation expects from him, if he be not punctually obeyed. Subjects then have no right, in doubtful cases, to examine the wisdom or justice of their sovereign's commands; this examination belongs to the prince: his subjects ought to suppose (if there be a possibility of supposing it) that all his orders are just and salutary: he alone is accountable for the evil that may result from them.

§53. The obedience which subjects owe to a sovereign.

§54. In what
cases they may
resist him.

Nevertheless this ought not to be entirely a blind obedience. No engagement can oblige or even authorise a man to violate the law of nature. All authors who have any regard to conscience or decency, agree that no one ought to obey such commands as are evidently contrary to that sacred law. Those governors of places who bravely refused to execute the barbarous orders of Charles IX.[13] on the memorable day of St. Bartholomew,[14] have been universally praised; and the court did not dare to punish them, at least openly. "Sire," said the brave Orte, governor of Bayonne, in his letter, "I have communicated your majesty's command to your faithful inhabitants and warriors in the garrison: and I have found there only good citizens and brave soldiers; but not a single executioner: wherefore both they and I most humbly entreat your majesty to be pleased to employ our hands and our lives in things that are possible, however hazardous they may be; and we will exert ourselves to the last drop of our blood in the execution of them."* <22> The count de Tende, Charny, and others, replied to those who brought them the orders of the court, "that they had too great a respect for the king, to believe that such barbarous orders came from him."

It is more difficult to determine in what cases a subject may not only refuse to obey, but even resist a sovereign, and oppose his violence by force. When a sovereign does injury to any one, he acts without any real authority; but we ought not thence to conclude hastily that the subject may resist him. The nature of sovereignty, and the welfare of the state, will not permit citizens to oppose a prince whenever his commands appear to them unjust or prejudicial. This would be falling back into the state of nature, and rendering government impossible. A subject ought patiently to suffer from the prince, doubtful wrongs, and wrongs that are supportable,—the former, because whoever has submitted to the decision of a judge, is no longer capable of deciding his own pretensions; and as to those that are supportable, they ought to be sacrificed to the

* Mezeray's Hist. of France, vol. II. p. 1107.
13. Charles IX, king of France, r. 1560–74.
14. August 24, 1572, when approximately three thousand Protestants were murdered at Paris.

peace and safety of the state, on account of the great advantages obtained by living in society. It is presumed, as matter of course, that every citizen has tacitly engaged to observe this moderation; because, without it, society could not exist. But when the injuries are manifest and atrocious,—when a prince, without any apparent reason, attempts to deprive us of life, or of those things, the loss of which would render life irksome,—who can dispute our right to resist him? Self-preservation is not only a natural right, but an obligation imposed by nature, and no man can entirely and absolutely renounce it. And though he might give it up, can he be considered as having done it by his political engagements, since he entered into society only to establish his own safety upon a more solid basis? The welfare of society does not require such a sacrifice; and, as Barbeyrac well observes in his notes on Grotius, "If the public interest requires, that those who obey should suffer some inconvenience, it is no less for the public interest that those who command, should be afraid of driving their patience to the utmost extremity."* The prince who violates all laws,—who no longer observes any measures,—and who would in his transports of fury take away the life of an innocent person,—divests himself of his character, and is no longer to be considered in any other light than that of an unjust and outrageous enemy, against whom his people are allowed to defend themselves. The person of the sovereign is sacred and inviolable: but he who, after having lost all the sentiments of a sovereign, divests himself even of the appearances and exterior conduct of a monarch, degrades himself: he no longer retains the sacred character of a sovereign, and cannot retain the prerogatives attached to that exalted rank. However, if this prince is not a monster,—if he is furious only against us in particular, and <23> from the effects of a sudden transport or a violent passion, and is supportable to the rest of the nation,—the respect we ought to pay to the tranquillity of the state is such, and the respect due to sovereign majesty so powerful, that we are strictly obliged to seek every other means of preservation, rather than to put his person in danger. Every one knows the example set by David: he fled,—he kept himself concealed, to secure himself from Saul's fury,—

* De Jure Belli & Pacis, Lib. 1. cap. iv. §11. not. 2.

and more than once spared the life of his persecutor.[15] When the reason of Charles VI.[16] of France was suddenly disordered by a fatal accident, he in his fury killed several of those who surrounded him: none of them thought of securing his own life at the expense of that of the king; they only endeavoured to disarm and secure him. They did their duty like men of honour and faithful subjects, in exposing their lives, to save that of this unfortunate monarch: such a sacrifice is due to the state and to sovereign majesty: furious from the derangement of his faculties, Charles was not guilty; he might recover his health, and again become a good king.

§55. Of ministers.   What has been said is sufficient for the intention of this work: the reader may see these questions treated more at large in many books that are well known. We shall conclude this subject with an important observation. A sovereign is undoubtedly allowed to employ ministers to ease him in the painful offices of government; but he ought never to surrender his authority to them. When a nation chuses a conductor, it is not with a view that he should deliver up his charge into other hands. Ministers ought only to be instruments in the hands of the prince; he ought constantly to direct them, and continually endeavour to know whether they act according to his intentions. If the imbecillity of age, or any infirmity, render him incapable of governing, a regent ought to be nominated, according to the laws of the state: but when once the sovereign is capable of holding the reins, let him insist on being served, but never suffer himself to be superseded. The last kings of France of the first race surrendered the government and authority to the mayors of the palace: thus becoming mere phantoms, they justly lost the title and honours of a dignity of which they had abandoned the functions. The nation has every thing to gain in crowning an all-powerful minister; for he will improve that soil as his own inheritance, which he plundered whilst he only reaped precarious advantages from it.

15. I Samuel 19–20.
16. Charles VI, "the Well-Beloved," r. 1380–1422.

CHAPTER V

Of States Elective, Successive or Hereditary, and of those called Patrimonial.

We have seen in the preceding chapter, that it originally belongs to a nation to confer the supreme authority, and to chuse the person by whom it is to be governed. If it confers the sovereignty on him for his own person only, reserving to itself <24> the right of chusing a successor after the sovereign's death, the state is *elective.* As soon as the prince is elected according to the laws, he enters into the possession of all the prerogatives which those laws annex to his dignity.

§56. Of elective states.

It has been debated, whether elective kings and princes are real sovereigns. But he who lays any stress on this circumstance must have only a very confused idea of sovereignty. The manner in which a prince obtains his dignity has nothing to do with determining its nature. We must consider, first, whether the nation itself forms an independent society (see chap. I.), and secondly, what is the extent of the power it has intrusted to the prince. Whenever the chief of an independent state really represents his nation, he ought to be considered as a true sovereign (§40), even though his authority should be limited in several respects.

§57. Whether elective kings are real sovereigns.

When a nation would avoid the troubles which seldom fail to accompany the election of a sovereign, it makes its choice for a long succession of years, by establishing the *right of succession,* or by rendering the crown hereditary in a family, according to the order and rules that appear most agreeable to that nation. The name of an *Hereditary State* or *Kingdom* is given to that where the successor is appointed by the same law that regulates the successions of individuals. The *Successive Kingdom* is that where a person succeeds according to a particular fundamental law of the state. Thus the lineal succession, and of males alone, is established in France.

§58. Of successive and hereditary states.

The origin of the right of succession.

The right of succession is not always the primitive establishment of a nation; it may have been introduced by the concession of another sovereign, and even by usurpation. But when it is supported by long pos-

§59. Other origins of this right.

session, the people are considered as consenting to it; and this tacit consent renders it lawful, though the source be vicious. It rests then on the foundation we have already pointed out,—a foundation that alone is lawful and incapable of being shaken, and to which we must ever revert.

§60. Other sources which still amount to the same thing.

The same right, according to Grotius and the generality of writers, may be derived from other sources, as conquest, or the right of a proprietor, who, being master of a country, should invite inhabitants to settle there, and give them lands, on condition of their acknowledging him and his heirs for their sovereigns. But as it is absurd to suppose that a society of men can place themselves in subjection otherwise than with a view to their own safety and welfare, and still more that they can bind their posterity on any other footing, it ultimately amounts to the same thing; and it must still be said that the succession is established by the express will or the tacit consent of the nation, for the welfare and safety of the state.

§61. A nation may change the order of the succession.

It thus remains an undeniable truth, that in all cases the succession is established or received only with a view to the public welfare and the general safety. If it happened then that the order established in this respect became destructive to the state, the nation would certainly have a right to change it by a new law. <25> *Salus populi suprema lex,*—the safety of the people is the supreme law; and this law is agreeable to the strictest justice,—the people having united in society only with a view to their safety and greater advantage.*

This pretended proprietory right attributed to princes is a chimera produced by an abuse which its supporters would fain make of the laws respecting private inheritances. The state neither is nor can be a patrimony, since the end of patrimony is the advantage of the possessor,

---

* Nimirum, quod publicae salutis causa et communi consensu statutum est, eadem multitudinis voluntate, rebus exigentibus, immutari quid obstat? [["To be sure, when circumstances demand it, what stands in the way of changing that which has been established for the sake of public safety and by common consent when this too is the will of the multitude?" (trans. Eds.)]] MARIANA, ibid. [[*De rege*]] c. iv. [[Note added in 1773/1797 editions.]]

whereas the prince is established only for the advantage of the state.*
The consequence is evident: if the nation plainly perceives that the heir
of her prince would be a pernicious sovereign, she has a right to exclude
him.

The authors whom we oppose, grant this right to a despotic prince,
while they refuse it to nations. This is because they consider such a prince
as a real proprietor of the empire, and will not acknowledge that the care
of their own safety, and the right to govern themselves, still essentially
belong to the society, although they have intrusted them, even without
any express reserve, to a monarch and his heirs. In their opinion, the
kingdom is the inheritance of the prince, in the same manner as his field
and his flocks,—a maxim injurious to human nature, and which they
would not have dared to advance in an enlightened age, if it had not the
support of an authority which too often proves stronger than reason and
justice.

A nation may, for the same reason, oblige one branch who removes
to another country, to renounce all claim to the crown, as a daughter
who marries a foreign prince. These renunciations, required or approved
by the state, are perfectly valid, since they are equivalent to a law that

§62. Of
renunciations.

---

* When Philip II. resigned the Netherlands to his daughter Isabella Clara Eugenia,
it was said (according to the testimony of Grotius) that it was setting a dangerous
precedent, for a prince to treat free citizens as his property, and barter them away like
domestic slaves;—that, among barbarians indeed, the extraordinary practice sometimes obtained, of transferring governments by will or donation, because those people
were incapable of discerning the difference between a prince and a master;—but that
those whom superior knowledge enabled to distinguish between what is lawful and
what is not, could plainly perceive that the administration of a state is the property of
the people (thence usually denominated *res-publica*);—and that as, in every period
of the world, there have been nations who governed themselves by popular assemblies
or by a senate, there have been others who intrusted the general management of their
concerns to princes. For it is not to be imagined (it was added) that legitimate sovereignties have originated from any other source than the consent of the people, who
gave themselves all up to a single person, or (for the sake of avoiding the tumults and
discord of elections) to a whole family: and those to whom they thus committed
themselves, were induced by the prospect of honourable pre-eminence alone to accept a dignity by which they were bound to promote the general welfare of their
fellow citizens in preference to their own private advantage. GROTIUS. Hist. of the
Disturbances in the Netherlands. Book II. [[Note added in 1773/1797 editions.]]

such persons and their posterity should be excluded from the throne. Thus the laws of England have for ever rejected every Roman Catholic. "Thus a law of Russia, made at the beginning of the reign of Elizabeth, most <26> wisely excludes from the possession of the crown every heir possessed of another monarchy; and thus the law of Portugal disqualifies every foreigner who lays claim to the crown by right of blood."*

Some celebrated authors, in other respects very learned and judicious, have then deviated from the true principles in treating of renunciations. They have largely expatiated on the rights of children born or to be born, of the transmission of those rights, &c. But they ought to have considered the succession, less as a property of the reigning family, than as a law of the state. From this clear and incontestable principle we easily deduce the whole doctrine of renunciations. Those required or approved by the state are valid and sacred: they are fundamental laws:—those not authorised by the state can only be obligatory on the prince who made them. They cannot injure his posterity; and he himself may recede from them in case the state stands in need of him and gives him an invitation: for he owes his services to a people who had committed their safety to his care. For the same reason, the prince cannot lawfully resign at an unseasonable juncture, to the detriment of the state, and abandon in imminent danger a nation that had put itself under his care.†

§63. The order of succession ought commonly to be kept.   In ordinary cases, when the state may follow the established rule without being exposed to very great and manifest danger, it is certain that every descendent ought to succeed when the order of succession calls him to the throne, however great may appear his incapacity to rule by himself. This is a consequence of the spirit of the law that established the succession: for the people had recourse to it, only to prevent the troubles which would otherwise be almost inevitable at every change. Now little advances would have been made towards obtaining this end, if, at the death of a prince, the people were allowed to examine the capacity of his heir, before they acknowledged him for their sovereign.

* Spirit of Laws, Book XXVI. chap. XXIII. where may be seen very good political reasons for these regulations.
† See further on.

"What a door would this open for usurpers or malcontents!—It was to avoid these inconveniences that the order of succession was established; and nothing more wise could have been done; since by this means no more is required than his being the king's son, and his being actually alive,—which can admit of no dispute: but on the other hand there is no rule fixed to judge of the capacity or incapacity to reign."* Though the succession was not established for the particular advantage of the sovereign and his family, but for that of the state, the heir apparent has nevertheless a right, to which justice requires that regard should be paid. His right is subordinate to that of the nation, and to the safety of the state; but it ought to take place when the public welfare does not oppose it. <27>

These reasons have the greater weight, since the law or the state may remedy the incapacity of the prince by nominating a regent, as is practised in cases of minority. This regent is, during the whole time of his administration, invested with the royal authority; but he exercises it in the king's name.

§64. Of regents.

The principles we have just established respecting the successive or hereditary right, manifestly shew that a prince has no right to divide his state among his children. Every sovereignty, properly so called, is, in its own nature, one, and indivisible, since those who have united in society cannot be separated in spite of themselves. Those partitions, so contrary to the nature of sovereignty and the preservation of states, have been much in use: but an end has been put to them, wherever the people, and princes themselves, have had a clear view of their greatest interest, and the foundation of their safety.

§65. Indivisibility of sovereignties.

But when a prince has united several different nations under his authority, his empire is then properly an assemblage of several societies subject to the same head; and there exists no natural objection to his dividing them among his children: he may distribute them, if there be neither law nor compact to the contrary, and if each of those nations consents to receive the sovereign he appoints for it. For this reason France

* Memorial in behalf of Madame de Longueville, concerning the principality of Neufchatel, in 1672.

was divisible under the two first races.* But being entirely consolidated under the third, it has since been considered as a single kingdom,—it has become indivisible,—and a fundamental law has declared it so. That law, wisely providing for the preservation and splendour of the kingdom, irrevocably unites to the crown all the acquisitions of its kings.

§66. Who are to decide disputes respecting the succession to a sovereignty. The same principles will also furnish us with the solution of a celebrated question. When the right of succession becomes uncertain in a successive or hereditary state, and two or three competitors lay claim to the crown,—it is asked, Who shall be the judge of their pretensions? Some learned men, resting on the opinion that sovereigns are subject to no other judge but God, have maintained that the competitors for the crown, while their right remains uncertain, ought either to come to an amicable compromise,—enter into articles among themselves,—chuse arbitrators,—have recourse even to the drawing of lots,—or, finally, determine the dispute by arms; and that the subjects cannot in any manner decide the question. One might be astonished that celebrated authors should have maintained such a doctrine. But since, even in speculative philosophy, there is nothing so absurd as not to have been advanced by one or other of the philosophers,† what can be expected from the human mind, when seduced by interest or fear? What! in a question that concerns <28> none so much as the nation,—that relates to a power established only with a view to the happiness of the people,—in a quarrel that is to decide for ever their dearest interests, and their very safety,— are they to stand by as unconcerned spectators? Are they to allow strangers, or the blind decision of arms, to appoint them a master, as a flock of sheep are to wait till it be determined whether they are to be delivered up to the butcher, or restored to the care of their shepherd?

But, say they, the nation has divested itself of all jurisdiction, by giving itself up to a sovereign; it has submitted to the reigning family; it

---

* But it is to be observed that those partitions were not made without the approbation and consent of the respective states.

† Nescio quomodo nihil tam absurde dici potest, quod non dicatur ab aliquo philosophorum. [["I do not know why, but nothing can be said which is so absurd, that it is not said by one or other of the philosophers."]] Cicero, de Divinat. Lib. II [[119]].

has given to those who are descended from that family a right which nobody can take from them; it has established them its superiors, and can no longer judge them. Very well! But does it not belong to that same nation to acknowledge the person to whom its duty binds it, and prevent its being delivered up to another? And since it has established the law of succession, who is more capable or has a better right to identify the individual whom the fundamental law had in view, and has pointed out as the successor? We may affirm, then, without hesitation, that the decision of this grand controversy belongs to the nation, and to the nation alone. Even if the competitors have agreed among themselves, or have chosen arbitrators, the nation is not obliged to submit to their regulations, unless it has consented to the transaction or compromise,—princes not acknowledged, and whose right is uncertain, not being in any manner able to dispose of its obedience. The nation acknowledges no superior judge in an affair that relates to its most sacred duties, and most precious rights.

Grotius and Puffendorff differ in reality but little from our opinion; but would not have the decision of the people or state called a juridical sentence (*judicium jurisdictionis*). Well! be it so: we shall not dispute about words. However, there is something more in the case than a mere examination of the competitors' rights, in order to submit to him who has the best. All the disputes that arise in society are to be judged and decided by the public authority. As soon as the right of succession is found uncertain, the sovereign authority returns for a time to the body of the state, which is to exercise it, either by itself, or by its representatives, till the true sovereign be known. "The contest on this right suspending the functions in the person of the sovereign, the authority naturally returns to the subjects, not for them to retain it, but to prove on which of the competitors it lawfully devolves, and then to commit it to his hands. It would not be difficult to support, by an infinite number of examples, a truth so evident by the light of reason: it is sufficient to remember that the states of France, after the death of Charles the Fair,[17] terminated the famous dispute between Philip de Valois and the king of

17. Charles IV, king of France, r. 1322–28.

England (Edward III.),[18] and that <29> those states, though subject to him in whose favour they granted the decision, were nevertheless the judges of the dispute."*

Guicciardini, book XII.[19] also shews that it was the states of Arragon that decided the succession to that kingdom, in favour of Ferdinand,[20] grandfather of Ferdinand[21] the husband of Isabella queen of Castile,[22] in preference to the other relations of Martin king of Arragon,[23] who asserted that the kingdom belonged to them.†

In the kingdom of Jerusalem also, it was the states that decided the disputes of those who made pretensions to it; as is proved by several examples in the foreign political history.‡

The states of the principality of Neufchatel have often, in the form of a juridical sentence, pronounced on the succession to the sovereignty. In the year 1707, they decided between a great number of competitors, and their decision in favour of the king of Prussia was acknowledged by all Europe in the treaty of Utrecht.

§67. That the right to the succession ought not to depend on the judgment of a foreign power. The better to secure the succession in a certain and invariable order, it is at present an established rule in all Christian states (Portugal excepted) that no descendent of the sovereign can succeed to the crown, unless he be the issue of a marriage that is conformable to the laws of the country. As the nation has established the succession, to the nation

---

* Answer in behalf of Madame de Longueville, to a Memorial in behalf of Madame de Nemours.

† Ibid.

‡ See the same memorial, which quotes P. Labbe's Royal Abridgement, page 501, &c.

18. The dispute was over who would succeed to the throne after Charles IV died without a male heir.

19. Francesco Guicciardini, *The History of Italy, from the Year 1490, to 1532 . . . In Twenty Books. Translated into English by the Chevalier Austin Parke Goddard* (London, 1753–56), bk. 12, vol. 6, 395.

20. Ferdinand I, king of Aragon and Sicily, r. 1412–16.

21. Ferdinand II, king of Aragon, r. 1476–1516; king of Sicily, r. 1468–1516; king of Naples, r. 1504–16; and king of Castile and León (as Ferdinand V), r. 1474–1504.

22. Isabella, queen of Castile, r. 1474–1504.

23. Martin I, king of Aragon, r. 1396–1410; king of Sicily as Martin II, r. 1409–10; uncle of Ferdinand I.

alone belongs the power of acknowledging those who are capable of succeeding; and consequently, on its judgment and laws alone must depend the validity of the marriage of its sovereigns, and the legitimacy of their birth.

If education had not the power of familiarising the human mind to the greatest absurdities, is there any man of sense who would not be struck with astonishment to see so many nations suffer the legitimacy and right of their princes to depend on a foreign power? The court of Rome has invented an infinite number of obstructions and cases of invalidity in marriages, and at the same time arrogates to itself the right of judging of their validity, and of removing the obstructions; so that a prince of its communion cannot in certain cases be so much his own master, as to contract a marriage necessary to the safety of the state. Jane, the only daughter of Henry IV. king of Castile,[24] found this true by cruel experience. Some rebels published abroad that she owed her birth to Bertrand de la Cueva, the king's favourite; and notwithstanding the declarations and last will of that prince, who explicitly and invariably acknowledged Jane for his daughter, and nominated her his heiress, they called to the crown Isabella, Henry's sister, and wife to Ferdinand heir of Arragon. The grandees of Jane's party had provided her a <30> powerful resource, by negotiating a marriage between her and Alphonsus king of Portugal:[25] but as that prince was Jane's uncle, it was necessary to obtain a dispensation from the pope; and Pius II.[26] who was in the interest of Ferdinand and Isabella, refused to grant the dispensation, though such alliances were then very common. These difficulties cooled the ardour of the Portuguese monarch, and abated the zeal of the faithful Castilians. Every thing succeeded with Isabella, and the unfortunate Jane took the veil, in order to secure, by this heroic sacrifice, the peace of Castile.*

24. Henry IV, king of Castile, r. 1454–74.
25. Alphonso V, r. 1438–81.
26. Pius II, r. 1458–64.
* I take this historical passage from M. Du Port de Tertre's Conspiracies. To him I refer; for I have not the original historians by me. However, I do not enter into the question relating to the birth of Jane: this would here be of no use. The princess had

If the prince proceeds and marries notwithstanding the pope's refusal, he exposes his dominions to the most fatal troubles. What would have become of England, if the reformation had not been happily established, when the pope presumed to declare Queen Elizabeth illegitimate, and incapable of wearing the crown?

A great emperor, Lewis of Bavaria,[27] boldly asserted the rights of his crown in this respect. In the diplomatic code of the law of nations by Leibnitz, we find* two acts, in which that prince condemns, as an invasion of the imperial authority, the doctrine that attributes to any other power but his own, the right of granting dispensations, and of judging of the validity of marriages, in the places under his jurisdiction: but he was neither well supported in his life-time, nor imitated by his successors.

---

not been declared a bastard according to the laws; the king acknowledged her for his daughter; and besides, whether she was or was not legitimate, the inconveniences resulting from the pope's refusal still remained the same with respect to her and the king of Portugal. [[Note added in 1773/1797 editions.]]

* P. 154 Forma divortii matrimonialis inter Johannem filium regis Bohemiae & Margaretham ducissam Karinthiae. This divorce is given by the emperor on account of the impotency of the husband, per auctoritatem, says he, nobis rite debitam & concessam. [["A form of matrimonial divorce between John, son of the king of Bohemia, and Margaret, Duchess of Karinthia." ". . . by authority . . . duly owed and granted to us" (trans. Eds.).]]

P. 156. Forma dispensationis super affinitate consanguinitatis inter Ludovicum marchionem Brandenburg & Margaretham ducissam Karinthiae, nec non legitimatio liberorum procreandorum, factae per dom. Ludovic. IV. Rom. imper. [["A form of dispensation in respect of affinity of blood between Ludwig, Marquis of Brandenburg, and Margaret, Duchess of Karinthia, together with a legitimation of any children to be begotten, made by the authority of Ludwig IV, Emperor of the Romans."]]

It is only human law, says the emperor, that hinders these marriages intra gradus affinitatis sanguinis, praesertim intra fratres & sorores. De cujus legis praeceptis dispensare solummodo pertinet ad auctoritatem imperatoris seu principis Romanorum. [["within the degrees of affinity of blood, especially between brothers and sisters. Dispensing of the requirements of this law is a matter for the authority of the emperor or prince of the Romans" (trans. Eds.).]] He then opposes and condemns the opinion of those who dare to say that these dispensations depend on ecclesiastics. Both this act and the former are dated in the year 1341. [[Note added in 1773/1797 editions.]]

27. Louis of Bavaria, Holy Roman Emperor, r. 1328–47.

Finally, there are states whose sovereign may chuse his successor, and even transfer the crown to another during his life: these are commonly called *patrimonial* kingdoms or states: but let us reject so unjust and so improper an epithet, which can only serve to inspire some sovereigns with ideas very opposite to those they ought to entertain. We have shewn (§61) that a state cannot be a patrimony. But it may happen that a nation, either through unbounded confidence in its prince, or for some other reason, has intrusted him with the care of appointing his successor, and even consented to receive, if he thinks proper, another sovereign from his hands. Thus we see that Peter I.[28] em-<31>peror of Russia, nominated his wife[29] to succeed him, though he had children.

But when a prince chuses his successor, or when he cedes the crown to another,—properly speaking, he only nominates, by virtue of the power with which he is, either expressly or by tacit consent, intrusted— he only nominates, I say, the person who is to govern the state after him. This neither is nor can be an alienation, properly so called. Every true sovereignty is, in its own nature, unalienable. We shall be easily convinced of this, if we pay attention to the origin and end of political society, and of the supreme authority. A nation becomes incorporated into a society, to labour for the common welfare as it shall think proper, and to live according to its own laws. With this view it establishes a public authority. If it intrusts that authority to a prince, even with the power of transferring it to other hands, this can never take place without the express and unanimous consent of the citizens, with the right of really alienating or subjecting the state to another body politic: for the individuals who have formed this society, entered into it in order to live in an independent state, and not under a foreign yoke. Let not any other source of this right be alleged in objection to our argument, as conquest, for instance; for we have already shewn (§60) that these different sources ultimately revert to the true principles on which all just governments are founded. While the victor does not treat his conquest according to those principles, the state of war still in some measure subsists: but the mo-

§68. Of states called patrimonial.

§69. Every true sovereignty is unalienable.

28. Peter I, r. 1682–1725.
29. Marta Skavronskaya, Catherine I, 1684–1727.

ment he places it in a civil state, his rights are proportioned by the principles of that state.

I know that many authors, and particularly Grotius,* give long enumerations of the alienations of sovereignties. But the examples often prove only the abuse of power, not the right. And besides, the people consented to the alienation, either willingly or by force. What could the inhabitants of Pergamus, Bithynia, and Cyrene do, when their kings gave them, by their last wills, to the Roman people? Nothing remained for them, but to submit with a good grace to so powerful a legatee. To furnish an example capable of serving as an authority, they should have produced an instance of a people resisting a similar bequest of their sovereign, and whose resistance had been generally condemned as unjust and rebellious. Had Peter I. who nominated his wife to succeed him, attempted to subject his empire to the grand signor, or to some other neighbouring power, can we imagine that the Russians would have suffered it, or that their resistance would have passed for a revolt? We do not find in Europe any great state that is reputed alienable. If some petty principalities have been considered as such, it is because they were not true sovereignties. They were fiefs of the em-<32>pire, enjoying a greater or lesser degree of liberty: their masters made a traffic of the rights they possessed over those territories: but they could not withdraw them from a dependence on the empire.

Let us conclude then, that, as the nation alone has a right to subject itself to a foreign power, the right of really alienating the state can never belong to the sovereign, unless it be expressly given him by the entire body of the people.† Neither are we to presume that he possesses a right

---

* De Jure Belli & Pacis, Lib. I. Cap. III. §12.

† The pope [[Innocent III, r. 1198–1216]] opposing the attempt made upon England by Louis the son of Philip Augustus [[Louis VIII, r. 1223–26]], and alleging, as his pretext, that John [[John, king of England, r. 1199–1216]] had rendered himself a vassal of the holy see, received for answer, among other arguments, "that a sovereign had no right to dispose of his states without the consent of his barons, who were bound to defend them." On which occasion the French nobles unanimously exclaimed that they would, to their last breath, maintain this truth—"that no prince can, of his own private will, give away his kingdom, or render it tributary, and thus

to nominate his successor or surrender the sceptre to other hands,—a right which must be founded on an express consent, on a law of the state, or on long custom, justified by the tacit consent of the people.

If the power of nominating his successor is intrusted to the sovereign, he ought to have no other view in his choice, but the advantage and safety of the state. He himself was established only for this end (§39); the liberty of transferring his power to another could then be granted to him only with the same view. It would be absurd to consider it as a prerogative useful to the prince, and which he may turn to his own private advantage. Peter the Great proposed only the welfare of the empire when he left the crown to his wife. He knew that heroine to be the most capable person to follow his views, and perfect the great things he had begun, and therefore preferred her to his son, who was still too young. If we often found on the throne such elevated minds as Peter's, a nation could not adopt a wiser plan in order to ensure to itself a good government, than to intrust the prince, by a fundamental law, with the power of appointing his successor. This would be a much more certain method than the order of birth. The Roman emperors who had no male children appointed a successor by adoption. To this custom Rome was indebted for a series of sovereigns unequalled in history,—Nerva, Trajan, Adrian, Antoninus, Marcus Aurelius,—what princes! Does the right of birth often place such on the throne?

§70. Duty of a prince who is empowered to nominate his successor.

We may go still farther, and boldly assert, that, as the safety of the whole nation is deeply interested in so important a transaction, the consent and ratification of the people or state is necessary to give it full and entire effect,—at least their tacit consent and ratification. If an emperor of Russia thought proper to nominate for his successor a person notoriously unworthy of the crown, it is not at all probable that vast empire would blindly submit to so pernicious an appointment. And who shall presume <33> to blame a nation for refusing to run headlong to ruin out of respect to the last orders of its prince? As soon as the people submit to the sovereign appointed to rule over them, they tacitly ratify the choice

§71. He must have at least a tacit ratification.

---

enslave the nobility." Velly's Hist. of France, Vol. III. p. 491. [[Note added in 1773/ 1797 editions.]]

made by the last prince; and the new monarch enters into all the rights of his predecessor.

CHAPTER VI

Principal Objects of a good Government; and first to provide for the Necessities of the Nation.

§72. The object of society points out the duties of the sovereign.

After these observations on the constitution of the state, let us now proceed to the principal objects of a good government. We have seen above (§§41 and 42) that the prince, on his being invested with the sovereign authority, is charged with the duties of the nation in relation to government. In treating of the principal objects of a wise administration, we at once shew the duties of a nation towards itself, and those of the sovereign towards his people.

A wise conductor of the state will find in the objects of civil society the general rule and indication of his duties. The society is established with the view of procuring, to those who are its members, the necessaries, conveniences, and even pleasures of life, and, in general, every thing necessary to their happiness,—of enabling each individual peaceably to enjoy his own property, and to obtain justice with safety and certainty,—and, finally, of defending themselves in a body against all

He ought to procure plenty.

external violence (§15). The nation, or its conductor, should first apply to the business of providing for all the wants of the people, and producing a happy plenty of all the necessaries of life, with its conveniences, and innocent and laudable enjoyments. As an easy life without luxury contributes to the happiness of men, it likewise enables them to labour with greater safety and success after their own perfection, which is their grand and principal duty, and one of the ends they ought to have in view when they unite in society.

§73. To take care that there be a sufficient number of workmen.

To succeed in procuring this abundance of every thing, it is necessary to take care that there be a sufficient number of able workmen in every useful or necessary profession. An attentive application on the part of government, wise regulations, and assistance properly granted, will produce this effect, without using constraint, which is always fatal to industry.

Those workmen that are useful ought to be retained in the state; to succeed in retaining them, the public authority has certainly a right to use constraint, if necessary. Every citizen owes his personal services to his country; and a mechanic, in particular, who has been reared, educated, and instructed in its bosom, cannot lawfully leave it, and carry to a foreign land that industry which he acquired at home, unless his country has no occasion for him, or he cannot there obtain the just fruit of his <34> labour and abilities. Employment must then be procured for him; and if, while able to obtain a decent livelihood in his own country, he would without reason abandon it, the state has a right to detain him. But a very moderate use ought to be made of this right, and only in important or necessary cases. Liberty is the soul of abilities and industry: frequently a mechanic or an artist, after having long travelled abroad, is attracted home to his native soil by a natural affection, and returns more expert and better qualified to render his country useful services. If certain extraordinary cases be excepted, it is best in this affair to practise the mild methods of protection, encouragement, &c. and to leave the rest to that natural love felt by all men for the places of their birth.

§74. To prevent the emigration of those that are useful.

As to those emissaries who come into a country to entice away useful subjects, the sovereign has a right to punish them severely, and has just cause of complaint against the power by whom they are employed.

§75. Emissaries who entice them away.

In another place, we shall treat more particularly of the general question, whether a citizen be permitted to quit the society of which he is a member. The particular reasons concerning useful workmen are sufficient here.

The state ought to encourage labour, to animate industry, to excite abilities, to propose honours, rewards, privileges, and so to order matters that every one may live by his industry. In this particular, England deserves to be held up as an example. The parliament incessantly attends to these important affairs, in which neither care nor expense is spared. And do we not even see a society of excellent citizens formed with this view, and devoting considerable sums to this use? Premiums are also distributed in Ireland to the mechanics who most distinguish

§76. Labour and industry must be encouraged.

themselves in their profession. Can such a state fail of being powerful and happy?

CHAPTER VII

Of the Cultivation of the Soil.

§77. The utility of tillage.

Of all the arts, tillage, or agriculture, is doubtless the most useful and necessary, as being the source whence the nation derives its subsistence. The cultivation of the soil causes it to produce an infinite increase; it forms the surest resource, and the most solid fund of riches and commerce, for a nation that enjoys a happy climate.

§78. Regulations necessary in this respect—

This object then deserves the utmost attention of the government. The sovereign ought to neglect no means of rendering the land under his jurisdiction as well cultivated as possible. He ought not to allow either communities or private persons to acquire large tracts of land, and leave

For the distribution of land.

them uncultivated. Those rights of *common,* which deprive the proprietor of the free liberty of <35> disposing of his land,—which will not allow him to inclose and cultivate it in the most advantageous manner,— those rights, I say, are inimical to the welfare of the state, and ought to be suppressed, or reduced to just bounds. Notwithstanding the introduction of private property among the citizens, the nation has still a right to take the most effectual measures to cause the aggregate soil of the country to produce the greatest and most advantageous revenue possible.

§79. For the protection of husbandmen.

The government ought carefully to avoid every thing capable of discouraging the husbandman, or of diverting him from the labours of agriculture. Those taxes,—those excessive and ill-proportioned impositions, the burthen of which falls almost entirely on the cultivators,— and the oppressions they suffer from the officers who levy them,— deprive the unhappy peasant of the means of cultivating the earth, and depopulate the country. Spain is the most fertile and the worst cultivated country in Europe. The church there possesses too much land; and the contractors for the royal magazines, being authorised to purchase at a low price all the corn they find in the possession of a peasant, above what is necessary for the subsistence of himself and his family, so greatly discourage the husbandman, that he sows no more corn than is barely necessary for the support of his own household. Hence the frequent scarcity in a country capable of feeding its neighbours.

Another abuse injurious to agriculture is the contempt cast upon the husbandman. The tradesmen in cities,—even the most servile mechanics,—the idle citizens,—consider him that cultivates the earth with a disdainful eye: they humble and discourage him: they dare to despise a profession that feeds the human race,—the natural employment of man. A little insignificant haberdasher, a tailor, places far beneath him the beloved employment of the first consuls and dictators of Rome! China has wisely prevented this abuse: agriculture is there held in honour; and to preserve this happy mode of thinking, the emperor himself, followed by his whole court, annually, on a solemn day, sets his hand to the plough, and sows a small piece of land. Hence China is the best cultivated country in the world: it feeds an immense multitude of inhabitants who at first sight appear to the traveller too numerous for the space they occupy.

§80. Husbandry ought to be placed in an honourable light.

The cultivation of the soil deserves the attention of the government, not only on account of the invaluable advantages that flow from it, but from its being an obligation imposed by nature on mankind. The whole earth is destined to feed its inhabitants; but this it would be incapable of doing, if it were uncultivated. Every nation is then obliged by the law of nature to cultivate the land that has fallen to its share; and it has no right to enlarge its boundaries, or have recourse to the assistance of other nations, but in proportion as the land in its possession is incapable of furnishing it with necessaries. Those nations (such as the ancient Germans, and some modern Tartars), who <36> inhabit fertile countries, but disdain to cultivate their lands, and chuse rather to live by plunder, are wanting to themselves, are injurious to all their neighbours, and deserve to be extirpated as savage and pernicious beasts. There are others, who, to avoid labour, chuse to live only by hunting, and their flocks. This might, doubtless, be allowed in the first ages of the world, when the earth, without cultivation, produced more than was sufficient to feed its small number of inhabitants. But at present, when the human race

§81. The cultivation of the soil, a natural obligation.

is so greatly multiplied, it could not subsist if all nations were disposed to live in that manner. Those who still pursue this idle mode of life, usurp more extensive territories than, with a reasonable share of labour, they would have occasion for, and have therefore no reason to complain, if other nations, more industrious, and too closely confined, come to take possession of a part of those lands. Thus, though the conquest of the civilised empires of Peru and Mexico was a notorious usurpation, the establishment of many colonies on the continent of North America might, on their confining themselves within just bounds, be extremely lawful. The people of those extensive tracts rather ranged through than inhabited them.

§82. Of public granaries.

The establishment of public granaries is an excellent regulation for preventing scarcity. But great care should be taken to prevent their being managed with a mercantile spirit, and with views of profit. This would be establishing a monopoly, which would not be the less unlawful, for its being carried on by the magistrate. These granaries should be filled in times of the greatest plenty, and take off the corn that would lie on the husbandman's hands, or be carried in too great quantities to foreign countries: they should be opened when corn is dear, and keep it at a reasonable price. If in a time of plenty they prevent that necessary commodity from easily falling to a very low price, this inconvenience is more than compensated by the relief they afford in times of dearth: or rather, it is no inconvenience at all: for, when corn is sold extremely cheap, the manufacturer, in order to obtain a preference, is tempted to undersell his neighbours, by offering his goods at a price which he is afterwards obliged to raise (and this produces great disorders in commerce, by putting it out of its course); or he accustoms himself to an easy life, which he cannot support in harder times. It would be of advantage to manufactures and to commerce to have the subsistence of workmen regularly kept at a moderate and nearly equal price. In short, public granaries keep in the state quantities of corn that would be sent abroad at too cheap a rate, and must be purchased again, and brought back at a very great expense after a bad harvest; which is a real loss to the nation. These establishments, however, do not hinder the corn trade. If the country, one year with another, produces more than is sufficient for the support of her inhabitants, the superfluity will still be sent abroad; but it will be sent at a higher and fairer price. <37>

CHAPTER VIII

Of Commerce.

It is commerce that enables individuals and whole nations to procure those commodities which they stand in need of, but cannot find at home. Commerce is divided into home and foreign trade. The former is that carried on in the state between the several inhabitants; the latter is carried on with foreign nations.

§83. Of home and foreign trade.

The home trade of a nation is of great use; it furnishes all the citizens with the means of procuring whatever they want, as either necessary, useful, or agreeable: it causes a circulation of money, excites industry, animates labour, and, by affording subsistence to a great number of people, contributes to increase the population and power of the state.

§84. Utility of the home trade.

The same reasons shew the use of foreign trade, which is moreover attended with these two advantages:—1. By trading with foreigners, a nation procures such things as neither nature nor art can furnish in the country it occupies. And secondly, if its foreign trade be properly directed, it increases the riches of the nation, and may become the source of wealth and plenty. Of this the example of the Carthaginians among the ancients, and that of the English and Dutch among the moderns, afford remarkable proofs. Carthage, by her riches, counter-balanced the fortune, courage, and greatness of Rome. Holland has amassed immense sums in her marshes; a company of her merchants possesses whole kingdoms in the East, and the governor of Batavia exercises command over the monarchs of India. To what a degree of power and glory is England arrived! Formerly her warlike princes and inhabitants made glorious conquests which they afterwards lost by those reverses of fortune so frequent in war: at present, it is chiefly commerce that places in her hand the balance of Europe.

§85. Utility of foreign trade.

§86. Obligation to cultivate the home trade.

Nations are obliged to cultivate the home trade,—first, because it is clearly demonstrated from the law of nature, that mankind ought mutually to assist each other, and, as far as in their power, contribute to the perfection and happiness of their fellow-creatures: whence arises, after the introduction of private property, the obligation to resign to others, at a fair price, those things which they have occasion for, and which we do not destine for our own use. Secondly, society being established with the view that each may procure whatever things are necessary to his own perfection and happiness,—and a home trade being the means of obtaining them,—the obligations to carry on and improve this trade are derived from the very compact on which the society was formed. Finally, being advantageous to <38> the nation, it is a duty the people owe to themselves, to make this commerce flourish.

§87. Obligation to carry on foreign trade.

For the same reason, drawn from the welfare of the state, and also to procure for the citizens every thing they want, a nation is obliged to promote and carry on a foreign trade. Of all the modern states, England is most distinguished in this respect. The parliament have their eyes constantly fixed on this important object; they effectually protect the navigation of the merchants, and, by considerable bounties, favour the exportation of superfluous commodities and merchandises. In a very sensible production,* may be seen the valuable advantages that kingdom has derived from such judicious regulations.

§88. Foundation of the laws of commerce.

Let us now see what are the laws of nature and the rights of nations in respect to the commerce they carry on with each other. Men are obliged mutually to assist each other as much as possible, and to contribute to the perfection and happiness of their fellow-creatures (Prelim. §10); whence it follows, as we have said above (§86), that, after the introduction of private property, it became a duty to sell to each other at a fair price what the possessor himself has no occasion for, and what is necessary to others; because, since that introduction of private property, no one can by any other means procure the dif-

* [[Louis-Joseph Plumard de Danguel,]] Remarks on the Advantages and Disadvantages of France and Great Britain with respect to Commerce.

ferent things that may be necessary or useful to him, and calculated to
render life pleasant and agreeable. Now, since right springs from obligation (Prelim. §3), the obligation which we have just established gives
every man the right of procuring the things he wants, by purchasing
them at a reasonable price from those who have themselves no occasion
for them.

We have also seen (Prelim. §5) that men could not free themselves
from the authority of the laws of nature by uniting in civil society, and
that the whole nation remains equally subject to those laws in its national
capacity; so that the natural and necessary law of nations is no other
than the law of nature properly applied to nations or sovereign states
(Prelim. §6): from all which it follows, that a nation has a right to procure, at an equitable price, whatever articles it wants, by purchasing
them of other nations who have no occasion for them. This is the foundation of the right of commerce between different nations, and, in particular, of the right of buying.

We cannot apply the same reasoning to the right of selling such things
as we want to part with. Every man and every nation being perfectly at
liberty to buy a thing that is to be sold, or not to buy it, and to buy it
of one rather than of another,—the law of nature gives to no person
whatsoever any kind of right to sell what belongs to him to another who
does not wish to buy it; neither has any nation the right of selling her
commodities or merchandise to a people who are unwilling to have
them. <39>

Every state has consequently a right to prohibit the entrance of foreign merchandises; and the nations that are affected by such prohibition
have no right to complain of it, as if they had been refused an office of
humanity. Their complaints would be ridiculous, since their only
ground of complaint would be, that a profit is refused to them by that
nation, who does not chuse they should make it at her expense. It is,
however, true, that if a nation was very certain that the prohibition of
her merchandises was not founded on any reason drawn from the welfare
of the state that prohibited them, she would have cause to consider this
conduct as a mark of ill-will shewn in this instance, and to complain of

Right of buying.

§89. Right of selling.

*§90. Prohibi-
tion of foreign
merchandises.*

it on that footing. But it would be very difficult for the excluded nation to judge with certainty that the state had no solid or apparent reason for making such a prohibition.

§91. Nature of the right of buying.

By the manner in which we have shewn a nation's right to buy of another what it wants, it is easy to see that this right is not one of those called *perfect,* and that are accompanied with a right to use constraint. Let us now distinctly explain the nature of a right which may give room for disputes of a very serious nature. You have a right to buy of others such things as you want, and of which they themselves have no need; you make application to me: I am not obliged to sell them to you, if I myself have any occasion for them. In virtue of the natural liberty which belongs to all men, it is I who am to judge whether I have occasion for them myself, or can conveniently sell them to you; and you have no right to determine whether I judge well or ill, because you have no authority over me. If I, improperly, and without any good reason, refuse to sell you at a fair price what you want, I offend against my duty: you may complain of this; but you must submit to it; and you cannot attempt to force me, without violating my natural right, and doing me an injury. The right of buying the things we want is then only an imperfect right, like that of a poor man to receive alms of the rich man; if the latter refuses to bestow it, the poor man may justly complain; but he has no right to take it by force.

If it be asked, what a nation has a right to do in case of extreme necessity,—this question will be answered in its proper place in the following book, Chap. IX.

§92. Every nation is to chuse how far it will engage in commerce.

Since then a nation cannot have a natural right to sell her merchandises to another that is unwilling to purchase them,—since she has only an imperfect right to buy what she wants of others,—since it belongs only to these last to judge whether it be proper for them to sell or not—and, finally, since commerce consists in mutually buying and selling all sorts of commodities,—it is evident that it depends on the will of any nation to carry on commerce with another, or to let it alone. If she be willing to allow this to one, it depends on the nation to permit it under such conditions as she shall think proper. For in permitting another nation to trade with her, she grants that other a <40> right; and every one is at liberty to affix what conditions he pleases to a right which he grants of his own accord.

Men and sovereign states may, by their promises, enter into a perfect obligation with respect to each other, in things where nature has imposed only an imperfect obligation. A nation, not having naturally a perfect right to carry on a commerce with another, may procure it by an agreement or treaty. This right is then acquired only by treaties, and relates to that branch of the law of nations termed *conventional* (Prelim. §24). The treaty that gives the right of commerce, is the measure and rule of that right. §93. How a nation acquires a perfect right to a foreign trade.

A simple permission to carry on commerce with a nation gives no perfect right to that commerce. For if I merely and simply permit you to do any thing, I do not give you any right to do it afterwards in spite of me:—you may make use of my condescension as long as it lasts; but nothing prevents me from changing my will. As then every nation has a right to chuse whether she will or will not trade with another, and on what conditions she is willing to do it (§92),—if one nation has for a time permitted another to come and trade in the country, she is at liberty, whenever she thinks proper, to prohibit that commerce,—to restrain it,—to subject it to certain regulations; and the people who before carried it on cannot complain of injustice. §94. Of the simple permission of commerce.

Let us only observe, that nations, as well as individuals, are obliged to trade together for the common benefit of the human race, because mankind stand in need of each other's assistance (Prelim. §§10, 11, and Book I. §88): still however, each nation remains at liberty to consider, in particular cases, whether it be convenient for her to encourage, or permit commerce; and as our duty to ourselves is paramount to our duty to others,—if one nation finds herself in such circumstances, that she thinks foreign commerce dangerous to the state, she may renounce and prohibit it. This the Chinese have done for a long time together. But, again, it is only for very serious and important reasons that her duty to herself should dictate such a reserve; otherwise, she could not refuse to comply with the general duties of humanity.

§95. Whether
the laws
relating to
commerce are
subject to
prescription.

We have seen what are the rights that nations derive from nature with regard to commerce, and how they may acquire others by treaties:—let us now examine whether they can found any on long custom. To determine this question in a solid manner, it is necessary first to observe, that there are rights which consist in a simple *power:* they are called in Latin, *jura merae facultatis,* rights of mere ability. They are such in their own nature, that he who possesses them may use them or not, as he thinks proper,—being absolutely free from all restraint in this respect; so that the actions that relate to the exercise of these rights, are acts of mere free will, that may be done or not done according to pleasure. It is manifest that rights of this kind cannot be lost by prescription on account of their not <41> being used, since prescription is only founded on consent legitimately presumed; and that, if I possess a right which is of such a nature that I may or may not use it as I think proper, without any person having a right to prescribe to me on the subject, it cannot be presumed, from my having long forborne to use it, that I therefore intend to abandon it. This right is then imprescriptible, unless I have been forbidden or hindered from making use of it, and have obeyed with sufficient marks of consent. Let us suppose, for instance, that I am entirely at liberty to grind my corn at any mill I please, and that during a very considerable time, a century if you please, I have made use of the same mill:—as I have done in this respect what I thought proper, it is not to be presumed, from this long-continued use of the same mill, that I meant to deprive myself of the right of grinding at any other; and consequently, my right cannot be lost by prescription. But now suppose, that, on my resolving to make use of another mill, the owner of the former opposes it, and announces to me a prohibition;—if I obey his prohibition without necessity, and without opposition, though I have it in my power to defend myself, and know my right, this right is lost, because my conduct affords grounds for a legitimate presumption that I chose to abandon it.—Let us apply these principles.—Since it depends on the will of each nation to carry on commerce with another, or not to carry it on, and to regulate the manner in which it chuses to carry it on (§92), the right of commerce is evidently a right of mere ability (*jus merae facultatis*), a simple power,—and consequently is imprescriptible.

Thus, although two nations have traded together, without interruption, during a century, this long usage does not give any right to either of them; nor is the one obliged on this account to suffer the other to come and sell its merchandises, or to buy others:—they both preserve the double right of prohibiting the entrance of foreign merchandise, and of selling their own wherever people are willing to buy them. Although the English have from time immemorial been accustomed to get wine from Portugal, they are not on that account obliged to continue the trade, and have not lost the liberty of purchasing their wines elsewhere. Although they have, in the same manner, been long accustomed to sell their cloth in that kingdom, they have, nevertheless, a right to transfer that trade to any other country: and the Portuguese, on their part, are not obliged by this long custom, either to sell their wines to the English, or to purchase their cloths. If a nation desires any right of commerce which shall no longer depend on the will of another, she must acquire it by treaty.[30]

What has been just said may be applied to the rights of commerce acquired by treaties. If a nation has by this method procured the liberty of selling certain merchandises to another, she does not lose her right, though a great number of years are suffered to elapse without its being used; because this right is a <42> simple power, *jus merae facultatis,* which she is at liberty to use or not, whenever she pleases.

§96. Imprescriptibility of rights founded on treaty.

Certain circumstances, however, may render a different decision necessary, because they imply a change in the nature of the right in question. For instance, if it appears evident, that the nation granting this right granted it only with the view of procuring a species of merchandise of which she stands in need,—and if the nation which obtained the right of selling, neglects to furnish those merchandises, and another offers to bring them regularly, on condition of having an exclusive privilege,—it

30. Joseph Chitty noted, "This perpetual obligation to purchase Port wines from Portugal in exchange for British wool cloths was established by the celebrated treaty of Methuen, A.D. 1703 (so called because concluded by Sir P. Methuen) with Portugal. A treaty which has been censured by some as evidently advantageous to Portugal and disadvantageous to Great Britain." Chitty cited Adam Smith, Dean Tucker, and his own *Commercial Law* in support.

appears certain that the privilege may be granted to the latter. Thus the nation that had the right of selling, would lose it, because she had not fulfilled the tacit condition.

§97. Of monopolies, and trading companies, with exclusive privileges.

Commerce is a common benefit to a nation; and all her members have an equal right to it. Monopoly therefore, in general, is contrary to the rights of the citizens. However, this rule has its exceptions, suggested even by the interest of the nation; and a wise government may, in certain cases, justly establish monopolies. There are commercial enterprises that cannot be carried on without an energy that requires considerable funds, which surpass the ability of individuals. There are others that would soon become ruinous, were they not conducted with great prudence, with one regular spirit, and according to well-supported maxims and rules. These branches of trade cannot be indiscriminately carried on by individuals: companies are therefore formed, under the authority of government; and these companies cannot subsist without an exclusive privilege. It is therefore advantageous to the nation to grant them: hence have arisen, in different countries, those powerful companies that carry on commerce with the East. When the subjects of the United Provinces established themselves in the Indies on the ruin of their enemies the Portuguese, individual merchants would not have dared to think of such an arduous enterprise; and the state itself, wholly taken up with the defence of its liberty against the Spaniards, had not the means of attempting it.

It is also certain beyond all doubt, that, whenever any individual offers, on condition of obtaining an exclusive privilege, to establish a particular branch of commerce or manufacture which the nation has not the means of carrying on, the sovereign may grant him such privilege.

But whenever any branch of commerce may be left open to the whole nation, without producing any inconvenience or being less advantageous to the state, a restriction of that commerce to a few privileged individuals is a violation of the rights of all the other citizens. And even when such a commerce requires considerable expenses to maintain forts, men of war, &c. this being a national affair, the state may defray those expenses, and, as an encouragement to industry, leave the profits of the trade to the merchants. This is sometimes done in England. <43>

The conductor of a nation ought to take particular care to encourage the commerce that is advantageous to his people, and to suppress or lay restraints upon that which is to their disadvantage. Gold and silver having become the common standard of the value of all the articles of commerce, the trade that brings into the state a greater quantity of these metals than it carries out, is an advantageous trade; and, on the contrary, that is a ruinous one, which causes more gold and silver to be sent abroad, than it brings home. This is what is called the balance of trade. The ability of those who have the direction of it, consists in making that balance turn in favour of the nation.

§98. Balance of trade, and attention of government in this respect.

Of all the measures that a wise government may take with this view, we shall only touch here on import duties. When the conductors of a state, without absolutely forcing trade, are nevertheless desirous of diverting it into other channels, they lay such duties on the merchandises they would discourage, as will prevent their consumption. Thus French wines are charged with very high duties in England, while the duties on those of Portugal are very moderate,—because England sells few of her productions to France, while she sells large quantities to Portugal. There is nothing in this conduct that is not very wise and extremely just; and France has no reason to complain of it,—every nation having an undoubted right to make what conditions she thinks proper, with respect to receiving foreign merchandises, and being even at liberty to refuse taking them at all.

§99. Import duties.

CHAPTER IX

Of the Care of the Public Ways of Communication, and the Right of Toll.

The utility of high-ways, bridges, canals, and, in a word, of all safe and commodious ways of communication, cannot be doubted. They facilitate the trade between one place and another, and render the conveyance of merchandise less expensive, as well as more certain and easy. The merchants are enabled to sell at a better price, and to obtain the preference;

§100. Utility of high-ways, canals, &c.

an attraction is held out to foreigners, whose merchandises are carried through the country, and diffuse wealth in all the places through which they pass. France and Holland feel the happy consequences of this from daily experience.

§101. Duty of government in this respect. One of the principal things that ought to employ the attention of the government with respect to the welfare of the public in general, and of trade in particular, must then relate to the high-ways, canals, &c. in which nothing ought to be neglected to render them safe and commodious. France is one of those states where this duty to the public is discharged with the greatest attention and magnificence. Numerous patroles every <44> where watch over the safety of travellers: magnificent roads, bridges, and canals, facilitate the communication between one province and another:—Lewis XIV. joined the two seas by a work worthy of the Romans.

§102. Its rights in this respect. The whole nation ought, doubtless, to contribute to such useful undertakings. When therefore the laying out and repairing of high-ways, bridges, and canals, would be too great a burthen on the ordinary revenues of the state, the government may oblige the people to labour at them, or to contribute to the expense. The peasants, in some of the provinces of France, have been heard to murmur at the labours imposed upon them for the construction of roads: but experience had no sooner made them sensible of their true interest, than they blessed the authors of the undertaking.

§103. Foundation of the right of toll. The construction and preservation of all these works being attended with great expense, the nation may very justly oblige all those to contribute to them, who receive advantage from their use: this is the legitimate origin of the right of toll. It is just, that a traveller, and especially a merchant, who receives advantage from a bridge, a canal, or a road, in his own passage, and in the more commodious conveyance of his merchandise, should help to defray the expense of these useful establishments, by a moderate contribution: and if the state thinks proper to exempt the citizens from paying it, she is under no obligation to gratify strangers in this particular.

§104. Abuse of this right. But a law so just in its origin frequently degenerates into great abuses. There are countries where no care is taken of the high-ways, and where nevertheless considerable tolls are exacted. A lord of a manor, who happens to possess a stripe of land terminating on a river, there establishes a toll, though he is not at a farthing's expense in keeping up the navigation of the river, and rendering it convenient. This is a manifest extortion, and an infringment of the natural rights of mankind. For the division of lands, and their becoming private property, could never deprive any man of the right of passage, when not the least injury is done to the person through whose territory he passes. Every man inherits this right from nature, and cannot justly be forced to purchase it.

But the *arbitrary* or *customary* law of nations at present tolerates this abuse, while it is not carried to such an excess as to destroy commerce. People do not, however, submit without difficulty, except in the case of those tolls which are established by ancient usage: and the imposition of new ones is often a source of disputes. The Swiss formerly made war on the dukes of Milan, on account of some oppressions of this nature. This right of tolls is also further abused, when the passenger is obliged to contribute too much, and what bears no proportion to the expense of preserving these public passages.

At present, to avoid all difficulty and oppression, nations settle these points by treaties. <45>

CHAPTER X

Of Money and Exchange.

In the first ages after the introduction of private property, people exchanged their superfluous commodities and effects for those they wanted. Afterwards gold and silver became the common standard of the value of all things: and to prevent the people from being cheated, the mode was introduced of stamping pieces of gold and silver in the name of the state, with the figure of the prince, or some other impression, as the seal and pledge of their value. This institution is of great use and infinite convenience: it is easy to see how much it facilitates commerce.—Nations or sovereigns cannot therefore bestow too much attention on an affair of such importance.

§105. Establishment of money.

§106. Duty of the nation or prince with respect to the coin.

The impression on the coin becoming the seal of its standard and weight, a moment's reflection will convince us that the coinage of money ought not to be left indiscriminately free to every individual: for by that means, frauds would become too common;—the coin would soon lose the public confidence; and this would destroy a most useful institution. Hence money is coined by the authority and in the name of the state or prince, who are its surety: they ought therefore to have a quantity of it coined sufficient to answer the necessities of the country, and to take care that it be good, that is to say, that its intrinsic value bear a just proportion to its extrinsic or numerary value.

It is true, that, in a pressing necessity, the state would have a right to order the citizens to receive the coin at a price superior to its real value: but as foreigners will not receive it at that price, the nation gains nothing by this proceeding: it is only a temporary palliative for the evil, without effecting a radical cure. This excess of value, added in an arbitrary manner to the coin, is a real debt which the sovereign contracts with individuals: and in strict justice, this crisis of affairs being over, that money ought to be called in at the expense of the state, and paid for in other specie, according to the natural standard; otherwise this kind of burthen, laid on in the hour of necessity, would fall solely on those who received this arbitrary money in payment: which would be unjust. Besides, experience has shewn that such a resource is destructive to trade, by destroying the confidence both of foreigners and citizens,—raising in proportion the price of every thing,—and inducing every one to lock up or send abroad the good old specie; whereby a temporary stop is put to the circulation of money. So that it is the duty of every nation and of every sovereign to abstain, as much as possible, from so dangerous an experiment, and rather to have recourse <46> to extraordinary taxes and contributions to support the pressing exigencies of the state.*

---

* In Boizard's Treatise on Coin, we find the following observations. "It is worthy of remark, that, when our kings debased the coin, they kept the circumstance a secret from the people:—witness the ordinance of Philip de Valois in 1350, by which he ordered Tournois *Doubles* to be coined 2*d.* 5⅓ *gr.* fine, which was in fact a debasement of the coin. In that ordinance, addressing the officers of the mint, he says, 'Upon the oath by which you are bound to the king, keep this affair as secret as you

Since the state is surety for the goodness of the money and its cur- §107. Their
rency, the public authority alone has the right of coining it. Those who rights in this
respect.
counterfeit it, violate the rights of the sovereign, whether they make it
of the same standard and value or not. These are called false-coiners, and
their crime is justly considered as one of the most heinous nature. For
if they coin base money, they rob both the public and the prince; and
if they coin good, they usurp the prerogative of the sovereign. They will
never be inclined to coin good money, unless there be a profit on the
coinage: and in this case they rob the state of a profit which exclusively
belongs to it. In both cases, they do an injury to the sovereign; for the
public faith being surety for the money, the sovereign alone has a right

---

possibly can, that neither the bankers nor others may by your means acquire any
knowledge of it: for if through you it comes to be known, you shall be punished for
the offence in such manner as shall serve as an example to others.'"—The same author
quotes other similar ordinances of the same king, and one issued by the Dauphin
who governed the kingdom as regent during the captivity of king John, dated June
27, 1360, by virtue of which, the mint-masters directing the officers engaged in the
coinage to coin white *Deniers* 1*d.* 12 *gr.* fine, at the same time expressly command
them to keep this order secret, and, "if any persons should make inquiry respecting
their standard, to maintain that they were 2*d.* fine." Chap. xxix.

The kings [of France] had recourse to this strange expedient in cases of urgent
necessity: but they saw its injustice.—The same author, speaking of the debasement
of coin, or the various modes of reducing its intrinsic value, says—"Those expedients
are but rarely resorted to, because they give occasion to the exportation or melting
down of the good specie, and to the introduction and circulation of foreign coin,—
raise the price of every thing,—impoverish individuals, diminish the revenue, which
is paid in specie of inferior value,—and sometimes put a total stop to commerce. This
truth has been so well understood in all ages, that those princes, who had recourse to
one or other of these modes of debasing the coin in difficult times, ceased to practise
it the moment the necessity ceased to exist." We have, on this subject, an ordinance
of Philip the Fair, issued in May, 1295, which announces, that, "The king having
reduced the coin both in fineness and weight, and expecting to be obliged to make
a further reduction in order to retrieve his affairs,—but knowing himself to be, in
conscience, responsible for the injury caused to the state by such reduction,—pledges
himself to the people of his kingdom, by solemn charter, that, as soon as his affairs
are retrieved, he will restore the coin to its proper standard and value, at his own
private cost and expense, and will himself bear all the loss and waste. And, in addition
to this engagement, Dame Joan, queen of France and Navarre [[r. 1285–1305]],
pledges her revenues and dower for the same purpose." [[Note added in 1773/1797
editions.]]

to have it coined. For this reason the right of coining is placed among the *prerogatives of majesty,* and Bodinus relates,* that Sigismund Augustus, king of Poland,[31] having granted this privilege to the duke of Prussia, in the year 1543, the states of the country passed a decree in which it was asserted that the king could not grant that privilege, it being inseparable from the crown. The same author observes, <47> that, although many lords and bishops of France had formerly the privilege of coining money, it was still considered as coined by the king's authority: and the kings of France at last withdrew all those privileges, on account of their being often abused.

§108. How one nation may injure another in the article of coin.

From the principles just laid down, it is easy to conclude, that if one nation counterfeits the money of another, or if she allows and protects false-coiners who presume to do it, she does that nation an injury. But commonly criminals of this class find no protection any-where,—all princes being equally interested in exterminating them.

§109. Of exchange, and the laws of commerce.

There is another custom more modern, and of no less use to commerce than the establishment of coin,—namely *exchange,* or the traffic of bankers, by means of which a merchant remits immense sums from one end of the world to the other, at a very trifling expense, and, if he pleases, without risk. For the same reason that sovereigns are obliged to protect commerce, they are obliged to support this custom, by good laws, in which every merchant, whether citizen or foreigner, may find security. In general, it is equally the interest and the duty of every nation to have wise and equitable commercial laws established in the country.

---

* In his [[Bodin's]] Republic, Book I. Chap. X.
31. Sigismund Augustus, r. 1548–72.

CHAPTER XI

*Second Object of a good Government,—to procure
the true Happiness of the Nation.*

Let us continue to lay open the principal objects of a good government. §110. A nation
What we have said in the five preceding chapters relates to the care of ought to labour
providing for the necessities of the people, and procuring plenty in the happiness.
state: this is a point of necessity; but it is not sufficient for the happiness
of a nation. Experience shews that a people may be unhappy in the midst
of all earthly enjoyments, and in the possession of the greatest riches.
Whatever may enable mankind to enjoy a true and solid felicity, is a
second object that deserves the most serious attention of the government. Happiness is the point where centre all those duties which individuals and nations owe to themselves; and this is the great end of the
law of nature. The desire of happiness is the powerful spring that puts
man in motion: felicity is the end they all have in view, and it ought to
be the grand object of the public will (Prelim. §5). It is then the duty of
those who form this public will, or of those who represent it—the rulers
of the nation—to labour for the happiness of the people, to watch continually over it, and to promote it to the utmost of their power.

To succeed in this, it is necessary to instruct the people to seek felicity §111.
where it is to be found,—that is, in their own perfection,—and to teach Instruction.
them the means of obtaining it. The <48> sovereign cannot then take
too much pains in instructing and enlightening his people, and in forming them to useful knowledge and wise discipline. Let us leave a hatred
of the sciences to the despotic tyrants of the east: they are afraid of having their people instructed, because they chuse to rule over slaves. But
though they are obeyed with the most abject submission, they frequently
experience the effects of disobedience and revolt. A just and wise prince
feels no apprehensions from the light of knowledge: he knows that it is
ever advantageous to a good government. If men of learning know that
liberty is the natural inheritance of mankind, on the other hand they
are more fully sensible than their neighbours, how necessary it is, for

their own advantage, that this liberty should be subject to a lawful authority:—incapable of being slaves, they are faithful subjects.

§112. Education of youth. The first impressions made on the mind are of the utmost importance for the remainder of life. In the tender years of infancy and youth, the human mind and heart easily receive the seeds of good or evil. Hence the education of youth is one of the most important affairs that deserve the attention of the government. It ought not to be entirely left to fathers. The most certain way of forming good citizens is to found good establishments for public education, to provide them with able masters,—direct them with prudence,—and pursue such mild and suitable measures, that the citizens will not neglect to take advantage of them. How admirable was the education of the Romans, in the flourishing ages of their republic, and how admirably was it calculated to form great men! The young men put themselves under the patronage of some illustrious person; they frequented his house, accompanied him wherever he went, and equally improved by his instructions and example: their very sports and amusements were exercises proper to form soldiers. The same practice prevailed at Sparta; and this was one of the wisest institutions of the incomparable Lycurgus. That legislator and philosopher entered into the most minute details respecting the education of youth,* being persuaded that on that depended the prosperity and glory of his republic.

§113. Arts and sciences. Who can doubt that the sovereign,—the whole nation,—ought to encourage the arts and sciences? To say nothing of the many useful inventions that strike the eye of every beholder,—literature and the polite arts enlighten the mind, and soften the manners: and if study does not always inspire the love of virtue, it is because it sometimes, and even too often, unhappily meets with an incorrigibly vicious heart. The nation and its conductors ought then to protect men of learning and great artists, and to call forth talents by honours and rewards. Let the friends of barbarism declaim against the sciences and polite arts;—let us, without deigning to answer their <49> vain reasonings, content ourselves with appealing to experience. Let us compare England, France, Holland, and

---

* See Xenophon, *Lacedaemon. Respublica.*

several towns of Switzerland and Germany, to the many regions that lie buried in ignorance, and see where we can find the greater number of honest men and good citizens. It would be a gross error to oppose against us the example of Sparta, and that of ancient Rome. They, it is true, neglected curious speculations, and those branches of knowledge and art that were purely subservient to pleasure and amusement: but the solid and practical sciences,—morality, jurisprudence, politics, and war, were cultivated by them, especially by the Romans, with a degree of attention superior to what we bestow on them.

In the present age, the utility of literature and the polite arts is pretty generally acknowledged, as is likewise the necessity of encouraging them. The immortal Peter I. thought that without their assistance he could not entirely civilise Russia, and render it flourishing. In England, learning and abilities lead to honour and riches. Newton was honoured, protected, and rewarded while living, and after his death his tomb was placed among those of kings. France also, in this respect, deserves particular praise: to the munificence of her kings she is indebted for several establishments that are no less useful than glorious. The Royal Academy of Sciences diffuses on every side the light of knowledge, and the desire of instruction. Louis XV. furnished the means of sending to search, under the equator and the polar circle, for the proof of an important truth; and we at present *know* what was before only *believed* on the strength of Newton's calculations. Happy will that kingdom be, if the too general taste of the age does not make the people neglect solid knowledge, to give themselves up to that which is merely amusing, and if those who fear the light do not succeed in extinguishing the blaze of science!

I speak of the freedom of philosophical discussion, which is the soul of the republic of letters. What can genius produce when trammelled by fear? Can the greatest man that ever lived contribute much towards enlightening the minds of his fellow-citizens, if he finds himself constantly exposed to the cavils of captious and ignorant bigots,—if he is obliged to be continually on his guard, to avoid being accused by innuendo-mongers of indirectly attacking the received opinions? I know that liberty has its proper bounds,—that a wise government ought to have an eye to the press, and not to allow the publication of scandalous

§114. Freedom of philosophical discussion.

productions, which attack morality, government, or the established religion. But yet great care should be taken not to extinguish a light that
may afford the state the most valuable advantages. Few men know how
to keep a just medium; and the office of literary censor ought to be intrusted to none but those who are at once both prudent and enlightened.
Why should they search in a book for what the author does not appear
to have intended to put into it? and when a writer's thoughts and <50>
discourses are wholly employed on philosophy, ought a malicious adversary to be listened to, who would set him at variance with religion?
So far from disturbing a philosopher on account of his opinions, the
magistrate ought to chastise those who publicly charge him with impiety,
when in his writings he shews respect to the religion of the state. The
Romans seem to have been formed to give examples to the universe: that
wise people carefully supported the worship and religious ceremonies
established by law, and left the field open to the speculations of philosophers. Cicero—a senator, a consul, an augur—ridicules superstition,
attacks it, and demolishes it in his philosophical writings; and, in so doing, he thought he was only promoting his own happiness and that of
his fellow-citizens: but he observes that "to destroy superstition is not
destroying religion; for (says he) it becomes a wise man to respect the
institutions and religious ceremonies of his ancestors: and it is sufficient
to contemplate the beauty of the world, and the admirable order of the
celestial bodies, in order to be convinced of the existence of an eternal
and all-perfect being, who is entitled to the veneration of the human
race."* And in his Dialogues on the Nature of the Gods, he introduces

* Nam, ut vere loquamur, superstitio fusa per gentes oppressit omnium fere an-
imos, atque omnium imbecillitatem occupavit. . . . multum enim & nobismet ipsis
& nostris profuturi videbamur, si eam funditus sustulissemus. Nec vero (id enim
diligenter intelligi volo) superstitione tollendâ religio tollitur. Nam & majorum in-
stituta tueri, sacris caeremoniisque retinendis, sapientis est: & esse praestantem ali-
quam aeternamque naturam, & eam suspiciendam, admirandamque hominum generi, pulchritdo mundi, ordoque coelestium cogit confiteri. [["For, to speak truly,
that superstition has extended itself through all nations, and has oppressed the intellectual energies of almost all men, and has betrayed into endless imbecilities. . . .
For I thought that I should be doing an immense benefit both to myself and to my
countrymen if I could entirely eradicate all those superstitious errors. Nor is there

Cotta the academic, who was high-priest, attacking with great freedom the opinions of the stoics, and declaring that he should always be ready to defend the established religion from which he saw the republic had derived great advantages; that neither the learned nor the ignorant should make him abandon it: he then says to his adversary, "These are my thoughts, both as pontiff and as Cotta. But do you, as a philosopher, bring me over to your opinion by the strength of your arguments: for a philosopher ought to prove to me the truth of the religion he would have me embrace, whereas I ought in this respect to believe our forefathers, even without proof."*

Let us add experience to these examples and authorities. Never did a philosopher occasion disturbances in the state, or in religion, by his opinions: they would make no noise among the people, nor ever offend the weak, if malice or intemperate zeal did not take pains to discover a pretended venom lurking in them. It is by him who endeavours to place the opinions of a great man in opposition to the doctrines and worship established <51> by law, that the state is disturbed, and religion brought into danger.

---

any fear that true religion can be endangered by the demolition of superstition; for it is a part of a wise man to uphold the religious institutions of our ancestors by the maintenance of their rites and ceremonies. And the beauty of the world and the order of all celestial things compel us to confess that there is an excellent and eternal Nature which deserves to be worshipped and admired by all mankind."]] *De Divinatione, Lib.* II.

* Harum ego religionem nullam unquam contemnendam putavi: mihique ita persuasi, Romulum auspiciis, Numam sacris constitutis, fundamenta jecisse nostrae civitatis, quae nunquam profecto sine summa placatione Deorum immortalium tanta esse potuisset. Habes, Balbe, quid Cotta, quid pontifex sentiat. Fac nunc ego intelligam, quid tu sentias: a te enim philosopho rationem accipere debeo religionis; majoribus autem nostris, etiam nulla ratione reddita, credere. [["I have always thought that none of these departments of religion was to be despised, and I have held the conviction that Romulus by his auspices and Numa by his establishment of our ritual laid the foundations of our state, which assuredly could never have been as great as it is had not the fullest measure of divine favour been obtained for it. There, Balbus, is the opinion of a Cotta and a pontiff; now oblige me by letting me know yours. You are a philosopher, and I ought to receive from you a proof of your religion, whereas I must believe the word of our ancestors even without proof."]] *De Natura Deorum, Lib.* III.

§115. Love of virtue, and abhorrence of vice to be excited.

To instruct the nation, is not sufficient:—in order to conduct it to happiness, it is still more necessary to inspire the people with the love of virtue, and the abhorrence of vice. Those who are deeply versed in the study of morality are convinced that virtue is the true and only path that leads to happiness; so that its maxims are but the art of living happily; and he must be very ignorant of politics, who does not perceive how much more capable a virtuous nation will be, than any other, of forming a state that shall be at once happy, tranquil, flourishing, solid, respected by its neighbours, and formidable to its enemies. The interest of the prince must then concur with his duty and the dictates of his conscience, in engaging him to watch attentively over an affair of such importance. Let him employ all his authority in order to encourage virtue, and suppress vice: let the public establishments be all directed to this end: let his own conduct, his example, and the distribution of favours, posts, and dignities, all have the same tendency. Let him extend his attention even to the private life of the citizens, and banish from the state whatever is only calculated to corrupt the manners of the people. It belongs to politics to teach him in detail the different means of attaining this desirable end,—to shew him those he should prefer, and those he ought to avoid, on account of the dangers that might attend the execution, and the abuses that might be made of them. We shall here only observe, in general, that vice may be suppressed by chastisements, but that mild and gentle methods alone can elevate men to the dignity of virtue: it may be inspired, but it cannot be commanded.

§116. The nation may hence discover the intention of its rulers.

It is an incontestable truth, that the virtues of the citizens constitute the most happy dispositions that can be desired by a just and wise government. Here then is an infallible criterion, by which the nation may judge of the intentions of those who govern it. If they endeavour to render the great and the common people virtuous, their views are pure and upright; and you may rest assured that they solely aim at the great end of government, the happiness and glory of the nation. But if they corrupt the morals of the people, spread a taste for luxury, effeminacy, a rage for licentious pleasures,—if they stimulate the higher orders to a ruinous pomp and extravagance,—beware, citizens! beware of those corruptors! they only aim at purchasing slaves in order to exercise over them an arbitrary sway.

If a prince has the smallest share of moderation, he will never have recourse to these odious methods. Satisfied with his superior station and the power given him by the laws, he proposes to reign with glory and safety; he loves his people, and desires to render them happy. But his ministers are in general impatient of resistance, and cannot brook the slightest oppo-<52>sition:—if he surrenders to them his authority, they are more haughty and intractable than their master: they feel not for his people the same love that he feels: "let the nation be corrupted (say they) provided it do but obey." They dread the courage and firmness inspired by virtue, and know that the distributor of favours rules as he pleases over men whose hearts are accessible to avarice. Thus a wretch who exercises the most infamous of all professions, perverts the inclinations of a young victim of her odious traffic; she prompts her to luxury and epicurism, she inspires her with voluptuousness and vanity, in order the more certainly to betray her to a rich seducer. This base and unworthy creature is sometimes chastised by the magistrate; but the minister, who is infinitely more guilty, wallows in wealth, and is invested with honour and authority. Posterity, however, will do him justice, and detest the corruptor of a respectable nation.

If governors endeavoured to fulfill the obligations which the law of nature lays upon them with respect to themselves, and in their character of conductors of the state, they would be incapable of ever giving into the odious abuse just mentioned. Hitherto we have considered the obligation a nation is under to acquire knowledge and virtue, or to perfect its understanding and will;—that obligation, I say, we have considered in relation to the individuals that compose a nation: it also belongs in a proper and singular manner to the conductors of the state. A nation, while she acts in common, or in a body, is a moral person (Prelim. §2) that has an understanding and will of her own, and is not less obliged than any individual to obey the laws of nature (Book I. §5), and to improve her faculties (Book I. §21). That moral person resides in those who are invested with the public authority, and represent the entire nation.

§117. The state, or the public person, ought to perfect its understanding and will.

Whether this be the common council of the nation, an aristocratic body, or a monarch, this conductor and representative of the nation, this sovereign, of whatever kind, is therefore indispensably obliged to procure all the knowledge and information necessary to govern well, and to acquire the practice and habit of all the virtues suitable to a sovereign.

And as this obligation is imposed with a view to the public welfare, he ought to direct all his knowledge, and all his virtues, to the safety of the state, the end of civil society.

§118. And to direct the knowledge and virtues of the citizens to the welfare of the society.

He ought even to direct, as much as possible, all the abilities, the knowledge, and the virtues of the citizens to this great end; so that they may not only be useful to the individuals who possess them, but also to the state. This is one of the great secrets in the art of reigning. The state will be powerful and happy, if the good qualities of the subject, passing beyond the narrow sphere of private virtues, become civic virtues. This happy disposition raised the Roman republic to the highest pitch of power and glory.

§119. Love for their country.

The grand secret of giving to the virtues of individuals a <53> turn so advantageous to the state, is to inspire the citizens with an ardent love for their country. It will then naturally follow, that each will endeavour to serve the state, and to apply all his powers and abilities to the advantage and glory of the nation. This love of their country is natural to all men. The good and wise author of nature has taken care to bind them, by a kind of instinct, to the places where they received their first breath, and they love their own nation, as a thing with which they are intimately connected. But it often happens that some causes unhappily weaken or destroy this natural impression. The injustice or the severity of the government too easily effaces it from the hearts of the subjects: can self-love attach an individual to the affairs of a country where every thing is done with a view to a single person?—far from it:—we see, on the contrary, that free nations are passionately interested in the glory and the happiness of their country. Let us call to mind the citizens of Rome in the happy days of the republic, and consider, in modern times, the English and the Swiss.

§120. In individuals.

The love and affection a man feels for the state of which he is a member, is a necessary consequence of the wise and rational love he owes to himself, since his own happiness is connected with that of his country. This sensation ought also to flow from the engagements he has entered into with society. He has promised to procure its safety and advantage as far as in his power: and how can he serve it with zeal, fidelity, or courage, if he has not a real love for it?

The nation in a body ought doubtless to love itself, and desire its own happiness as a nation. The sensation is too natural to admit of any failure in this obligation: but this duty relates more particularly to the conductor, the sovereign, who represents the nation, and acts in its name. He ought to love it as what is most dear to him, to prefer it to every thing, for it is the only lawful object of his care, and of his actions, in every thing he does by virtue of the public authority. The monster who does not love his people is no better than an odious usurper, and deserves, no doubt, to be hurled from the throne. There is no kingdom where the statue of Codrus[32] ought not to be placed before the palace of the sovereign. That magnanimous king of Athens sacrificed his life for his people.* That great prince, and Louis XII.[33] are illustrious models of the tender love a sovereign owes to his subjects.

§121. In the nation or state itself, and in the sovereign.

The term, *country,* seems to be pretty generally known: but as it is taken in different senses, it may not be unuseful to give it here an exact definition. It commonly signifies *the state of which one is a member:* in this sense we have used it in the <54> preceding sections; and it to be thus understood in the law of nations.

§122. Definition of the term country.

In a more confined sense, and more agreeably to its etymology, this term signifies the state, or even more particularly the town or place, where our parents had their fixed residence at the moment of our birth. In this sense, it is justly said, that our country cannot be changed, and always remains the same, to whatsoever place we may afterwards remove. A man ought to preserve gratitude and affection for the state to which

---

* His country being attacked by the Heraclidae, he consulted the oracle of Apollo; and being answered, that the people whose chief should be slain, should remain victorious, Codrus disguised himself, and, rushing into the battle, was killed by one of the enemy's soldiers. [[Note added in 1773/1797 editions.]]

32. Codrus, king of Athens, r. ca. 1089–1068 B.C.

33. Louis XII, r. 1498–1515.

he is indebted for his education, and of which his parents were members when they gave him birth. But as various lawful reasons may oblige him to chuse another country,—that is, to become a member of another society; so, when we speak in general of the duty to our country, the term is to be understood as meaning the state of which a man is an actual member; since it is the latter, in preference to every other state, that he is bound to serve with his utmost efforts.

§123. How shameful and criminal to injure our country.

If every man is obliged to entertain a sincere love for his country, and to promote its welfare as far as in his power, it is a shameful and detestable crime to injure that very country. He who becomes guilty of it, violates his most sacred engagements, and sinks into base ingratitude: he dishonours himself by the blackest perfidy, since he abuses the confidence of his fellow-citizens, and treats as enemies those who had a right to expect his assistance and services. We see traitors to their country only among those men who are solely sensible to base interest, who only seek their own immediate advantage, and whose hearts are incapable of every sentiment of affection for others. They are therefore justly detested by mankind in general, as the most infamous of all villains.

§124. The glory of good citizens.

Examples.

On the contrary, those generous citizens are loaded with honour and praise, who, not content with barely avoiding a failure in duty to their country, make noble efforts in her favour, and are capable of making her the greatest sacrifices. The names of Brutus,[34] Curtius,[35] and the two Decii,[36] will live as long as that of Rome. The Swiss will never forget Arnold de Winkelried,[37] that hero, whose exploit would have deserved to be transmitted to posterity by the pen of a Livy. He truly devoted his life for his country's sake: but he devoted it as a general, as an undaunted

---

34. Marcus Junius Brutus Caepio, governor of Gaul and praetor, most famous for his role in the murder of Julius Caesar in 44 B.C.

35. Marcus Curtius, legendary hero of ancient Rome, who (Livy, *History of Rome*, I.6.1–6) managed to close a chasm that had opened in the Forum by leaping, fully armed and on horseback, into it.

36. The two Decii, father and son, sacrificed themselves to the gods for the deliverance and safe keeping of the Roman army.

37. At Sempach, Winkelried sacrificed himself to save the Swiss Confederation by creating a passage through the rows of enemy lances with his body.

warrior, not as a superstitious visionary. That nobleman, who was of the country of Underwald, seeing at the battle of Sempach[38] that his countrymen could not break through the Austrians, because the latter, armed cap-a-pie, had dismounted, and, forming a close battalion, presented a front covered with steel, and bristling with pikes and lances,—formed the generous design of sacrificing himself for his country. "My friends," said he to the Swiss, who began to be dispirited, "I will this day give my life to procure you the victory: I only recommend to you my family: follow me, and act in consequence of what <55> you see me do." At these words he ranged them in that form which the Romans called *cuneus,* and placing himself in the point of the triangle, marched to the centre of the enemy; when, embracing between his arms as many of the enemy's pikes as he could compass, he threw himself to the ground, thus opening for his followers a passage to penetrate into the midst of this thick battalion. The Austrians, once broken, were conquered, as the weight of their armour then became fatal to them, and the Swiss obtained a complete victory.*

CHAPTER XII

Of Piety and Religion.

Piety and religion have an essential influence on the happiness of a nation, and, from their importance, deserve a particular chapter. Nothing is so proper as piety to strengthen virtue, and give it its due extent. By the word *piety,* I mean a disposition of soul that leads us to direct all our

§125. Of piety.

---

* This affair happened in the year 1386. The Austrian army consisted of four thousand chosen men, among whom were a great number of princes, counts, and nobility of distinguished rank, all armed from head to foot. The Swiss were no more than thirteen hundred men, ill armed. In this battle, the duke of Austria perished with two thousand of his forces, in which number were six hundred and seventy-six noblemen of the best families in Germany. *History of the Helvetic Confederacy, by de* WATTEVILLE, *Vol.* I. *p.* 183.—TSCHUDI.—ETTERLIN.—SCHODELER.—RAEBMAN [[Rebmann]].

38. Battle of Sempach, 1386.

actions towards the Deity, and to endeavour to please him in every thing we do. To the practice of this virtue all mankind are indispensably obliged: it is the purest source of their felicity; and those who unite in civil society, are under still greater obligations to practise it. A nation ought then to be pious. The superiors intrusted with the public affairs should constantly endeavour to deserve the approbation of their divine master; and whatever they do in the name of the state, ought to be regulated by this grand view. The care of forming pious dispositions in all the people should be constantly one of the principal objects of their vigilance, and from this the state will derive very great advantages. A serious attention to merit in all our actions the approbation of an infinitely wise Being, cannot fail of producing excellent citizens. Enlightened piety in the people is the firmest support of a lawful authority; and, in the sovereign's heart, it is the pledge of the people's safety, and excites their confidence. Ye lords of the earth, who acknowledge no superior here below, what security can we have for the purity of your intentions, if we do not conceive you to be deeply impressed with respect for the common Father and Lord of men, and animated with a desire to please him?

§126. It ought to be attended with knowledge.

We have already insinuated that piety ought to be attended with knowledge. In vain would we propose to please God, if <56> we know not the means of doing it. But what a deluge of evils arises when men heated by so powerful a motive are prompted to take methods that are equally false and pernicious! A blind piety only produces superstitious bigots, fanatics and persecutors, a thousand times more dangerous and destructive to society than libertines are. There have appeared barbarous tyrants who have talked of nothing but the glory of God, while they crushed the people, and trampled under foot the most sacred laws of nature. It was from a refinement of piety, that the anabaptists of the sixteenth century refused all obedience to the powers of the earth. James Clement and Ravaillac,* those execrable parricides, thought themselves animated by the most sublime devotion.

* The former assassinated Henry III. of France [[r. 1574–89]]; the latter murdered his successor, Henry IV [[r. 1594–1610]].

Religion consists in the doctrines concerning the Deity and the things of another life, and in the worship appointed to the honour of the supreme Being. So far as it is seated in the heart, it is an affair of conscience, in which every one ought to be directed by his own understanding: but so far as it is external, and publicly established, it is an affair of state.

§127. Of religion internal and external.

Every man is obliged to endeavour to obtain just ideas of God, to know his laws, his views with respect to his creatures, and the end for which they were created. Man, doubtless, owes the most pure love, the most profound respect to his Creator; and to keep alive these dispositions, and act in consequence of them, he should honour God in all his actions, and shew, by the most suitable means, the sentiments that fill his mind. This short explanation is sufficient to prove that man is essentially and necessarily free to make use of his own choice in matters of religion. His belief is not to be commanded; and what kind of worship must that be, which is produced by force! Worship consists in certain actions performed with an immediate view to the honour of God; there can then be no worship proper for any man, which he does not believe suitable to that end. The obligation of sincerely endeavouring to know God, of serving him, and adoring him from the bottom of the heart, being imposed on man by his very nature,—it is impossible that, by his engagements with society, he should have exonerated himself from that duty, or deprived himself of the liberty which is absolutely necessary for the performance of it. It must then be concluded, that liberty of conscience is a natural and inviolable right. It is a disgrace to human nature, that a truth of this kind should stand in need of proof.

§128. Rights of individuals.

Liberty of conscience.

But we should take care not to extend this liberty beyond its just bounds. In religious affairs a citizen has only a right to be free from compulsion, but can by no means claim that of openly doing what he pleases, without regard to the consequences it may produce on society. The establishment of re-<57>ligion by law, and its public exercise, are matters of state, and are necessarily under the jurisdiction of the political authority. If all men are bound to serve God, the entire nation, in her national capacity, is doubtless obliged to serve and honour him (Prelim. §5). And as this important duty is to be discharged by the nation in whatever manner she judges best,—to the nation it belongs to determine what

§129. Public establishment of religion.

Duties and rights of the nation.

religion she will follow, and what public worship she thinks proper to establish.

§130. When there is as yet no established religion. If there be as yet no religion established by public authority, the nation ought to use the utmost care, in order to know and establish the best. That which shall have the approbation of the majority shall be received, and publicly established by law; by which means it will become the religion of the state. But if a considerable part of the nation is obstinately bent upon following another, it is asked—What does the law of nations require in such a case? Let us first remember that liberty of conscience is a natural right, and that there must be no constraint in this respect. There remain then but two methods to take,—either to permit this party of the citizens to exercise the religion they chuse to profess,—or to separate them from the society,—leaving them their property, and their share of the country that belonged to the nation in common,—and thus to form two new states instead of one. The latter method appears by no means proper:—it would weaken the nation, and thus would be inconsistent with that regard which she owes to her own preservation. It is therefore of more advantage to adopt the former method, and thus to establish two religions in the state. But if these religions are too incompatible,—if there be reason to fear that they will produce divisions among the citizens, and disorder in public affairs,—there is a third method, a wise medium between the two former, of which the Swiss have furnished examples. The cantons of Glaris and Appenzel were, in the sixteenth century, each divided into two parts: the one preserved the Romish religion, and the other embraced the reformation: each part has a distinct government of its own for domestic affairs; but on foreign affairs they unite, and form but one and the same republic, one and the same canton.

Finally, if the number of citizens who would profess a different religion from that established by the nation be inconsiderable,—and if for good and just reasons it be thought improper to allow the exercise of several religions in the state,—those citizens have a right to sell their lands, to retire with their families, and take all their property with them. For their engagements to society, and their submission to the public authority, can never oblige them to violate their consciences. If the society

will not allow me to do that to which I think myself bound by an indispensable obligation, it is obliged to allow me permission to depart.

When the choice of a religion is already made, and there is one established by law, the nation ought to protect and support <58> that religion, and preserve it as an establishment of the greatest importance,—
without, however, blindly rejecting the changes that may be proposed
to render it more pure and useful: for we ought, in all things, to aim at
perfection (§21). But as all innovations, in this case, are full of danger,
and can seldom be produced without disturbances, they ought not to be
attempted upon slight grounds, without necessity, or very important
reasons. It solely belongs to the society, the state, the entire nation, to
determine the necessity or propriety of those changes; and no private
individual has a right to attempt them by his own authority, nor consequently to preach to the people a new doctrine. Let him offer his sentiments to the conductors of the nation, and submit to the orders he
receives from them.

§131. When
there is an
established
religion.

But if a new religion spreads, and becomes fixed in the minds of the
people, as it commonly happens, independently of the public authority,
and without any deliberation in common,—it will be then necessary to
adopt the mode of reasoning we followed in the preceding section on
the case of chusing a religion,—to pay attention to the number of those
who follow the new opinions,—to remember that no earthly power has
authority over the consciences of men,—and to unite the maxims of
sound policy with those of justice and equity.

We have thus given a brief compendium of the duties and rights of
a nation with regard to religion. Let us now come to those of the sovereign. These cannot be exactly the same as those of the nation which
the sovereign represents. The nature of the subject opposes it; for in
religion nobody can give up his liberty. To give a clear and distinct view
of those rights and duties of the prince, and to establish them on a solid
basis, it is necessary here to refer to the distinction we have made in the
two preceding sections:—if there is question of establishing a religion
in a state that has not yet received one, the sovereign may doubtless favour that which to him appears the true or the best religion,—may have
it announced to the people, and, by mild and suitable means, endeavour

§132. Duties
and rights of
the sovereign
with regard
to religion.

to establish it:—he is even bound to do this, because he is obliged to attend to every thing that concerns the happiness of the nation. But in this he has no right to use authority and constraint. Since there was no religion established in the society when he received his authority, the people gave him no power in this respect; the support of the laws relating to religion is no part of his office, and does not belong to the authority with which they intrusted him. Numa was the founder of the religion of the ancient Romans: but he persuaded the people to receive it. If he had been able to command in that instance, he would not have had recourse to the revelations of the nymph Egeria.[39] Though the sovereign cannot exert any authority in order to establish a religion where there is none, he is authorised and even obliged to employ all his power to hinder the introduction of one which he judges pernicious to morality and dangerous to the state. For he ought <59> to preserve his people from every thing that may be injurious to them; and so far is a new doctrine from being an exception to this rule, that it is one of its most important objects. We shall see, in the following sections, what are the duties and rights of the prince in regard to the religion publicly established.

§133. Where there is an established religion. The prince, or the conductor, to whom the nation has intrusted the care of the government, and the exercise of the sovereign power, is obliged to watch over the preservation of the received religion, the worship established by law,—and has a right to restrain those who attempt to destroy or disturb it. But to acquit himself of this duty in a manner equally just and wise, he ought never to lose sight of the character in which he is called to act, and the reason of his being invested with it. Religion is of extreme importance to the peace and welfare of society; and the prince is obliged to have an eye to every thing in which the state is interested. This is all that calls him to interfere in religion, or to protect and defend it. It is therefore upon this footing only that he can interfere: consequently he ought to exert his authority against those alone whose conduct in religious matters is prejudicial or dangerous to the state; but

---

39. In Roman myth the water nymph was consulted by Numa concerning the establishment of the Roman calendar in a series of nocturnal interviews (Livy, *History of Rome,* I.19).

he must not extend it to pretended crimes against God, the punishment of which exclusively belongs to the Sovereign Judge, the Searcher of hearts. Let us remember that religion is no farther an affair of state, than as it is exterior and publicly established: that of the heart can only depend on the conscience. The prince has no right to punish any persons but those that disturb society; and it would be very unjust in him to inflict pains and penalties on any person whatsoever for his private opinions, when that person neither takes pains to divulge them, nor to obtain followers. It is a principle of fanaticism, a source of evils, and of the most notorious injustice, to imagine that frail mortals ought to take up the cause of God, maintain his glory by acts of violence, and avenge him on his enemies. *Let us only give to sovereigns,* said a great statesman and an excellent citizen*—let us give them, *for the common advantage, the power of punishing whatever is injurious to charity in society. It appertains not to human justice to become the avenger of what concerns the cause of God.*† Cicero, who was as able and as great in state affairs as in philosophy and eloquence, thought like the duke of Sully. In the laws he proposes relating to religion, he says, on the subject of piety and interior religion, "if any one transgresses, God will revenge it": but he declares the crime capital that should be committed against the religious ceremonies established for public affairs, and in which the whole state is concerned.‡ The wise Romans < 60 > were very far from persecuting a man for his creed; they only required that people should not disturb the public order.

The creeds or opinions of individuals, their sentiments with respect to the Deity,—in a word, interior religion—should, like piety, be the object of the prince's attention: he should neglect no means of enabling his subjects to discover the truth, and of inspiring them with good sentiments; but he should employ for this purpose only mild and paternal

§134. Objects of his care, and the means he ought to employ.

---

* The duke de Sully; see his Memoirs digested by M. de l'Ecluse, Vol. V. p. 135, 136.

† Deorum injuriae diis curae. Tacit. Ann. book I. c. 73. [["The gods must look to their own wrongs" (trans. Eds.). Tacitus, *Annales I,* chap. 23, p. 369.]]

‡ Qui secus faxit, Deus ipse vindex erit. . . . Qui non paruerit, capitale esto. [["He who acts otherwise will have God for his avenger. . . . If a person disobeys, it will be a capital offense." (trans. Eds.)]] *De Legib. Lib.* II.

methods.* Here he cannot command (§128). It is in external religion and its public exercise that his authority may be employed. His task is to preserve it, and to prevent the disorders and troubles it may occasion. To preserve religion, he ought to maintain it in the purity of its institution, to take care that it be faithfully observed in all its public acts and ceremonies, and punish those who dare to attack it openly. But he can require nothing by force except silence, and ought never to oblige any person to bear a part in external ceremonies:—by constraint, he would only produce disturbances or hypocrisy.

A diversity of opinions and worship has often produced disorders and fatal dissensions in a state: and for this reason, many will allow but one and the same religion. A prudent and equitable sovereign will, in particular conjunctures, see whether it be proper to tolerate or forbid the exercise of several different kinds of worship.

§135. Of toleration.   But, in general, we may boldly affirm that the most certain and equitable means of preventing the disorders that may be occasioned by difference of religion, is an universal toleration of all religions which contain no tenets that are dangerous either to morality or to the state. Let interested priests declaim!—they would not trample under foot the laws of humanity, and those of God himself, to make their doctrine triumph, if it were not the foundation on which are erected their opulence, luxury, and power. Do but crush the spirit of persecution,—punish severely whoever shall dare to disturb others on account of their creed,—and you will see all sects living in peace in their common country, and ambitious of producing good citizens. Holland and the states of the king of Prussia furnish a proof of this: Calvinists, Lutherans, Catholics, Pietists, Socinians, Jews, all live there in peace, because they are equally protected by the sovereign; and none are punished, but the disturbers of the tranquillity of others.

---

* Quas (religiones) non metu, sed ea conjunctione quae est homini cum deo, conservandas puto. [["Which, I believe, need to be preserved not out of fear but because of the bond which exists between human and god."]] *Cicero de Legib. Lib.* I. What a fine lesson does this pagan philosopher give to Christians!

If, in spite of the prince's care to preserve the established religion, the entire nation, or the greater part of it, should be disgusted with it, and desire to have it changed, the sovereign cannot do violence to his people, nor constrain them in an affair of this nature. The public religion was established for the safety <61> and advantage of the nation: and, besides its proving inefficacious when it ceases to influence the heart, the sovereign has here no other authority than that which results from the trust reposed in him by the people,—and they have only committed to him that of protecting whatever religion they think proper to profess.

§136. What the prince ought to do when the nation is resolved to change its religion.

But at the same time it is very just that the prince should have the liberty of continuing in the profession of his own religion, without losing his crown. Provided that he protect the religion of the state, this is all that can be required of him. In general, a difference of religion can never make any prince forfeit his claims to the sovereignty, unless a fundamental law ordain it otherwise. The pagan Romans did not cease to obey Constantine,[40] when he embraced Christianity; nor did the Christians revolt from Julian,[41] after he had quitted it.*

§137. Difference of religion does not deprive a prince of his crown.

We have established liberty of conscience for individuals (§128). However, we have also shewn that the sovereign has a right, and is even under an obligation, to protect and support the religion of the state, and not suffer any person to attempt to corrupt or destroy it,—that he may even, according to circumstances, permit only one kind of public worship throughout the whole country. Let us reconcile those different duties and rights, between which it may be thought that there is some contradiction:—let us, if possible, omit no material argument on so important and delicate a subject.

§138. Duties and rights of the sovereign reconciled with those of the subjects.

If the sovereign will allow the public exercise of only one and the

---

* When the chief part of the people in the principality of Neufchatel and Vallangin embraced the reformed religion in the sixteenth century, Joan of Hochberg, their sovereign, continued to live in the Roman Catholic faith, and nevertheless still retained all her rights. The state council enacted ecclesiastical laws and constitutions similar to those of the reformed churches in Switzerland; and the princess gave them her sanction. [[Note added in 1773/1797 editions.]]

40. Constantine I, Roman emperor, r. A.D. 306–37.
41. Julian, Roman emperor, r. A.D. 361–63.

same religion, let him oblige no body to do any thing contrary to his conscience; let no subject be forced to bear a part in a worship which he disapproves, or to profess a religion which he believes to be false; but let the subject on his part rest content with avoiding the guilt of a shameful hypocrisy; let him, according to the light of his own knowledge, serve God in private, and in his own house,—persuaded that providence does not call upon him for public worship, since it has placed him in such circumstances, that he cannot perform it without creating disturbances in the state. God would have us obey our sovereign, and avoid every thing that may be pernicious to society. These are immutable precepts of the law of nature: the precept that enjoins public worship is conditional, and dependent on the effects which that worship may produce. Interior worship is necessary in its own nature; and we ought to confine ourselves to it, in all cases in which it is most convenient. Public worship is appointed for the edification of men in glorifying God: but it counteracts that end, and ceases to be laudable, on those occasions when it only produces disturbances, and gives offence. <62> If any one believes it absolutely necessary, let him quit the country where he is not allowed to perform it according to the dictates of his own conscience,—let him go and join those who profess the same religion with himself.

§139. The sovereign ought to have the inspection of the affairs of religion, and authority over those who teach it. The prodigious influence of religion on the peace and welfare of society incontrovertibly proves that the conductor of the state ought to have the inspection of what relates to it, and an authority over the ministers who teach it. The end of society and of civil government necessarily requires that he who exercises the supreme power should be invested with all the rights without which he could not exercise it in a manner the most advantageous to the state. These are the prerogatives of majesty (§45), of which no sovereign can divest himself, without the express consent of the nation. The inspection of the affairs of religion, and the authority over its ministers, constitute therefore one of the most important of those prerogatives, since, without this power, the sovereign would never be able to prevent the disturbances that religion might occasion in the state, nor to employ that powerful engine in promoting the welfare and safety of the society. It would be certainly very strange that a multitude of men who united themselves in society for their common advantage, that each might in tranquillity labour to supply his necessities, promote his own perfection and happiness, and live as becomes a rational being,—it would be very strange, I say, that such a society should not have a right to follow their own judgment in an affair of the utmost importance,—to determine what they think most suitable with regard to religion,—and to take care that nothing dangerous or hurtful be mixed with it. Who shall dare to dispute that an independent nation has, in this respect as in all others, a right to proceed according to the light of conscience? and when once she has made choice of a particular religion and worship, may she not confer on her conductor all the power she possesses of regulating and directing that religion and worship, and enforcing their observance?

Let us not be told that the management of sacred things belongs not to a profane hand. Such discourses, when brought to the bar of reason, are found to be only vain declamations. There is nothing on earth more august and sacred than a sovereign; and why should God, who calls him by his providence to watch over the safety and happiness of a whole nation, deprive him of the direction of the most powerful spring that actuates mankind? The law of nature secures to him this right, with all others that are essential to good government; and nothing is to be found in Scripture that changes this disposition. Among the Jews, neither the king nor any other person could make any innovation in the law of Moses; but the sovereign attended to its preservation, and could check the high-priest when he deviated from his duty. Where is it asserted in the New Testament, that a Christian prince has nothing to do with religious affairs? Submission and obedience to the superior powers are <63> there clearly and expressly enjoined. It were in vain to object to us the example of the apostles, who preached the gospel in opposition to the will of sovereigns:—whoever would deviate from the ordinary rules, must have a divine mission, and establish his authority by miracles.

No person can dispute that the sovereign has a right to take care that nothing contrary to the welfare and safety of the state be introduced into religion; and consequently he must have a right to examine its doctrines, and to point out what is to be taught, and what is to be suppressed in silence.

§140. He
ought to
prevent the
abuse of the
received
religion.

The sovereign ought likewise to watch attentively, in order to prevent the established religion from being employed to sinister purposes, either by making use of its discipline to gratify hatred, avarice, or other passions, or presenting its doctrines in a light that may prove prejudicial to the state. Of wild reveries, seraphic devotions, and sublime speculations, what would be the consequences to society, if it entirely consisted of individuals whose intellects were weak, and whose hearts were easily governed?—the consequences would be a renunciation of the world, a general neglect of business and of honest labour. This society of pretended saints would become an easy and certain prey to the first ambitious neighbour; or if suffered to live in peace, it would not survive the first generation; both sexes, consecrating their chastity to God, would refuse to co-operate in the designs of their creator, and to comply with the requisitions of nature and of the state. Unluckily for the missionaries, it evidently appears, even from Father Charlevoix' History of New France, that their labours were the principal cause of the ruin of the Hurons. That author expressly says, that a great number of those converts would think of nothing but the faith,—that they forgot their activity and valour,—that divisions arose between them and the rest of the nation, &c. That nation was therefore soon destroyed by the Iroquois, whom they had before been accustomed to conquer.*

§141. The
sovereign's
authority over
the ministers
of religion.

To the prince's inspection of the affairs and concerns of religion we have joined an authority over its ministers: without the latter power, the former would be nugatory and ineffectual:—they are both derived from the same principle. It is absurd, and contrary to the first foundations of society, that any citizens should claim an independence of the sovereign authority, in offices of such importance to the repose, the happiness, and safety of the state. This is establishing two independent powers in the same society,—an unfailing source of division, disturbance, and ruin. There is but one supreme power in the state; the functions of the subordinate powers vary according to their different objects:—ecclesiastics, magistrates, and commanders of the troops, are all officers of the re-

---

* *History of New France, Books* V. VI. *and* VII.

public, each in his own department; and all are equally accountable to the sovereign. <64>

A prince cannot indeed justly oblige an ecclesiastic to preach a doctrine, or to perform a religious rite, which the latter does not think agreeable to the will of God. But if the minister cannot, in this respect, conform to the will of his sovereign, he ought to resign his station, and consider himself as a man who is not called to fill it,—two things being necessary for the discharge of the duty annexed to it, viz. to teach and behave with sincerity, according to the dictates of his own conscience, and to conform to the prince's intentions, and the laws of the state. Who can forbear being filled with indignation, at seeing a bishop audaciously resist the orders of the sovereign, and the decrees of the supreme tribunals, solemnly declaring that he thinks himself accountable to God alone, for the power with which he is intrusted?

§142. Nature of this authority.

On the other hand, if the clergy are rendered contemptible, it will be out of their power to produce the fruits for which their ministry was appointed. The rule that should be followed with respect to them may be comprised in a few words:—let them enjoy a large portion of esteem; but let them have no authority, and still less any claim to independence. In the first place, let the clergy, as well as every other order of men, be, in their functions, as in every thing else, subject to the public power, and accountable to the sovereign for their conduct. Secondly, let the prince take care to render the ministers of religion respectable in the eyes of the people; let him trust them with the degree of authority necessary to enable them to discharge their duty with success; let him, in case of need, support them with the power he possesses. Every man in office ought to be vested with an authority commensurate to his functions; otherwise he will be unable to discharge them in a proper manner. I see no reason why the clergy should be excepted from this general rule; only the prince should be more particularly watchful that they do not abuse their authority; the affair being altogether the most delicate, and the most fruitful in dangers. If he renders the character of churchmen respectable, he should take care that this respect be not carried to such a superstitious veneration, as shall arm the hand of an ambitious priest with a powerful engine with which he may force weak minds into whatever direction he

§143. Rule to be observed with respect to ecclesiastics.

pleases. When once the clergy become a separate body, they become formidable. The Romans (we shall often have occasion to recur to them)—the wise Romans elected from among the senators their pontifex-maximus,[42] and the principal ministers of the altar; they knew no distinction between *clergy* and *laity;* nor had they a set of gownsmen to constitute a separate class from the rest of the citizens.

§144. Recapitulation of the reasons which establish the sovereign's rights in matters of religion.

If the sovereign be deprived of this power in matters of religion, and this authority over the clergy, how shall he preserve the religion pure from the admixture of any thing contrary to the welfare of the state? How can he cause it to be constantly taught and practised in the manner most conducive to the pub-<65>lic welfare? And especially, how can he prevent the disorders it may occasion, either by its doctrines, or the manner in which its discipline is exerted? These cares and duties can only belong to the sovereign, and nothing can dispense with his discharging them.

Authorities and examples.

Hence we see that the prerogatives of the crown, in ecclesiastical affairs, have been constantly and faithfully defended by the parliaments of France. The wise and learned magistrates of whom those illustrious bodies are composed, are sensible of the maxims which sound reason dictates on this subject. They know how important it is not to suffer an affair of so delicate a nature, so extensive in its connections and influence, and so momentous in its consequences, to be placed beyond the reach of the public authority.—What! Shall ecclesiastics presume to propose to the people, as an article of faith, some obscure and useless dogma, which constitutes no essential part of the received religion?—shall they exclude from the church, and defame those who do not shew a blind obedience?—shall they refuse them the sacraments, and even the rites of burial?—and shall not the prince have power to protect his subjects, and preserve the kingdom from a dangerous schism?

The kings of England have asserted the prerogatives of their crown: they have caused themselves to be acknowledged heads of the church; and this regulation is equally approved by reason and sound policy, and

42. The pontifex maximus was the high priest of the ancient Roman College of Pontiffs.

is also conformable to ancient custom. The first christian emperors exercised all the functions of heads of the church; they made laws on subjects relating to it,*—summoned councils, and presided in them,—appointed and deposed bishops, &c. In Switzerland there are wise republics, whose sovereigns, knowing the full extent of the supreme authority, have rendered the ministers of religion subject to it, without offering violence to their consciences. They have prepared a formulary of the doctrines that are to be preached, and published laws of ecclesiastical discipline, such as they would have it exercised in the countries under their jurisdiction,—in order that those who will not conform to these establishments may not devote themselves to the service of the church. They keep all the ministers of religion in a lawful dependence, and suffer no exertion of church discipline but under their own authority. It is not probable that religion will ever occasion disturbances in these republics.

If Constantine and his successors had caused themselves to be formally acknowledged heads of the church,—and if Christian kings and princes had, in this instance, known how to maintain the rights of sovereignty,—would the world ever have witnessed those horrid disorders produced by the pride and ambition of some popes and ecclesiastics, emboldened by the weakness of princes, and supported by the superstition of the people,—<66>rivers of blood shed in the quarrels of monks, about speculative questions that were often unintelligible, and almost always as useless to the salvation of souls, as in themselves indifferent to the welfare of society,—citizens and even brothers armed against each other,—subjects excited to revolt, and kings hurled from their thrones? *Tantum religio potuit suadere malorum!*[43] The history of the emperors Henry IV.[44] Frederic I.[45] Frederic II.[46] and Louis of Ba-

§145. Pernicious consequences of the contrary opinion.

---

* See the *Theodosian Code.*

43. "So potent was religion in persuading to evil deeds." Lucretius, *De rerum natura* I.102.

44. Henry IV, Holy Roman Emperor, r. 1084–1105, and king of Germany, r. 1056–1105.

45. Frederic I, Holy Roman Emperor, r. 1155–90.

46. Frederic II, Holy Roman Emperor, r. 1220–50.

varia, are well known. Was it not the independence of the ecclesiastics,—was it not that system in which the affairs of religion are submitted to a foreign power,—that plunged France into the horrors of the league, and had nearly deprived her of the best and greatest of her kings? Had it not been for that strange and dangerous system, would a foreigner, pope Sixtus V. have undertaken to violate the fundamental law of the kingdom, and declared the lawful heir incapable of wearing the crown? Would the world have seen, at other times and in other places,* the succession to the crown rendered uncertain by a bare informality—the want of a dispensation, whose validity was disputed, and which a foreign prelate claimed the sole right of granting? Would that same foreigner have arrogated to himself the power of pronouncing on the legitimacy of the issue of a king? Would kings have been assassinated in consequence of a detestable doctrine?† Would a part of France have been afraid to acknowledge the best of their kings,‡ until he had received absolution from Rome? And would many other princes have been unable to give a solid peace to their people, because no decision could be formed within their own dominions on articles or conditions in which religion was interested?§

§146. The abuses particularised. 1. The power of the popes.

All we have advanced on this subject, so evidently flows from the notions of independence and sovereignty, that it will never be disputed by any honest man who endeavours to reason justly. If a state cannot finally determine every thing relating to religion, the nation is not free, and the prince is but half a sovereign. There is no medium in this case; either each state must, within its own territories, possess supreme power in this respect, as well as in all others, or we must adopt the system of Boniface VIII.[47] and consider all Roman catholic countries as forming only one state, of which the pope shall be the supreme head, and the kings

---

* In England, under Henry VIII.

† Henry III. and Henry IV. assassinated by fanatics, who thought they were serving God and the church by stabbing their king.

‡ Though Henry IV. returned to the Romish religion, a great number of Catholics did not dare to acknowledge him until he had received the pope's absolution.

§ Many kings of France in the civil wars on account of religion.

47. Pope Boniface VIII, r. 1294–1303.

subordinate administrators of temporal affairs, each in his province,—nearly as the sultans were formerly under the authority of the caliphs. We know that the above-mentioned pope had the presumption to write to Philip the Fair, king of France, *Scire te volumus, quod in spiritualibus & tempo-<67>ralibus nobis subes**—"We would have thee know that thou art subject to us as well in temporals as in spirituals." And we may see in the canon law† his famous bull *Unam sanctam*, [48] in which he attributes to the church two swords, or a double power, spiritual and temporal,—condemns those who think otherwise, as men, who, after the example of the Manicheans, establish two principles,—and finally declares, that *it is an article of faith, necessary to salvation, to believe that every human creature is subject to the Roman pontiff.*‡

---

* *Turretin. Hist. Ecclesiast. Compendium,* p. 182. Where may also be seen the resolute answer of the king of France.

† *Extravag. Commun.* Lib. I. Tit. *De Majoritate & Obedientia.*

‡ Gregory VII. endeavoured to render almost all the states of Europe tributary to him. He maintained that Hungary, Dalmatia, Russia, Spain, and Corsica, were absolutely his property, as successor to St. Peter, or were feudatory dependencies of the holy see. GREG. *Epist. Concil.* Vol. VI. Edit. Harduin [[Harduin, *Conciliorum* collection]].—He summoned the emperor Henry IV. to appear before him, and make his defence against the accusations of some of his subjects: and, on the emperor's non-compliance, he deposed him. In short, here are the expressions he made use of in addressing the council assembled at Rome on the occasion: "Agite nunc, quaeso, patres et principes sanctissimi, ut omnis mundus intelligat et cognoscat, quia si potestis in coelo ligare et solvere, potestis in terra imperia, regna, principatus, ducatus, marchias, comitatus, et omnium hominum possessiones, pro meritis tollere unicuique et concedere." [["Act now, I beseech you, fathers and most holy princes [cardinals], that all the world may understand and know that if you have power to bind and loose in heaven, you have the same power on earth over each and every one to take away and to grant, according to deserts, empires, kingdoms, dominions [or principalities], dukedoms, marches, retinues, and the possessions of all men" (trans. Eds.).]] NATAL. [[Noell]] ALEX. *Dissert. Hist. Eccl.* s. xi. and xii. p. 384.

The canon law boldly decides that the regal power is subordinate to the priesthood. "Imperium non praeest sacerdotio, sed subest, et ei obedire tenetur." [["[Royal] power is not superior to the priesthood, but is subordinate and is required to obey it." *Decretals of Pope Gregory IX,* bk. I, chap. vi, titulus 33, "De maioritate et obedienta."]] RUBRIC. ch. vi. *De Major. et Obed.* "Et est multum allegabile," [["And it is very excusable"]] is the complaisant remark of the writer of the article. [[Note added in 1773/1797 editions.]]

48. The papal bull *Unam sanctam*, 1302.

We shall consider the enormous power of the popes as the first abuse that sprung from this system, which divests sovereigns of their authority in matters of religion. This power in a foreign court directly militates against the independence of nations and the sovereignty of princes. It is capable of overturning a state; and wherever it is acknowledged, the sovereign finds it impossible to exercise his authority in such a manner as is most for the advantage of the nation. We have already, in the last section, given several remarkable instances of this; and history presents others without number. The senate of Sweden having condemned Trollius,[49] archbishop of Upsal, for the crime of rebellion, to be degraded from his see, and to end his days in a monastery, pope Leo X.[50] had the audacity to excommunicate the administrator Steno, and the whole senate, and sentenced them to rebuild at their own expense a fortress belonging to the archbishop, which they had caused to be demolished, and pay a fine of a hundred thousand ducats to the deposed prelate.* The barbarous Christiern,[51] king of Denmark, took advantage of this decree to lay waste the territories of Sweden, and to spill the blood of the most illustrious of her nobility. Paul V.[52] thundered out an interdict against Venice, on account of some very wise laws made with respect to the government of the city, but which displeased that pontiff, who thus threw the republic into an embarrassment, from which all the wisdom and firmness of the senate found it difficult to extricate it. Pius V.[53] in his < 68 > bull *In Coena Domini,* of the year 1567, declares, that all princes who shall introduce into their dominions any new taxes, of what nature soever they be, or shall increase the ancient ones, without having first obtained the approbation of the holy see, are *ipso facto* excommunicated. Is not this a direct attack on the independence of nations, and a subversion of the authority of sovereigns?

In those unhappy times, those dark ages that preceded the revival of

---

* *History of the Revolutions in Sweden* [[René-Aubert de Vertot]].
49. Trollius, archbishop of Upsal, was condemned in 1515.
50. Pope Leo X, r. 1513–21.
51. Christiern, king of Denmark, r. 1513–23.
52. Pope Paul V, r. 1605–21.
53. Pope Pius V, r. 1566–72.

literature and the reformation, the popes attempted to regulate the actions of princes, under the pretence of conscience,—to judge of the validity of their treaties,—to break their alliances, and declare them null and void. But those attempts met with a vigorous resistance, even in a country which is generally thought to have then possessed valour alone, with a very small portion of knowledge. The pope's nuncio, in order to detach the Swiss from the interests of France, published a monitory against all those cantons that favoured Charles VIII. declaring them excommunicated,[54] if within the space of fifteen days they did not abandon the cause of that prince, and enter into the confederacy which was formed against him: but the Swiss opposed this act by protesting against it as an iniquitous abuse, and caused their protest to be publicly posted up in all the places under their jurisdiction,—thus shewing their contempt for a proceeding that was equally absurd and derogatory to the rights of sovereigns.* We shall mention several other similar attempts, when we come to treat of the faith of treaties.

This power in the popes has given birth to another abuse, that deserves the utmost attention from a wise government. We see several countries in which ecclesiastical dignities, and all the higher benefices, are distributed by a foreign power,—by the pope,—who bestows them on his creatures, and very often on men who are not subjects of the state. This practice is at once a violation of the nation's rights, and of the principles of common policy. A nation ought not to suffer foreigners to dictate laws to her, to interfere in her concerns, or deprive her of her natural advantages: and yet how does it happen that so many states still tamely suffer a foreigner to dispose of posts and employments of the highest importance to their peace and happiness? The princes who consented to the introduction of so enormous an abuse, were equally wanting to themselves and their people. In our times the court of Spain has been obliged to expend immense sums in order to recover without dan-

§147.
2. Important employments conferred by a foreign power.

---

* *Vogel's Historical and Political Treatise on the Alliances between France and the Thirteen Cantons,* p. 33, and 36.

54. Pope Alexander VI, r. 1492–1503; Charles VIII of France, r. 1483–98, excommunicated in 1495.

ger the peaceable possession of a right which essentially belonged to the nation, or its head.

§148.
3. Powerful subjects dependent on a foreign court.

Even in those states whose sovereigns have preserved so important a prerogative of the crown, the abuse in a great measure subsists. The sovereign nominates indeed to bishoprics <69> and great benefices; but his authority is not sufficient to enable the persons nominated to enter on the exercise of their functions; they must also have bulls from Rome.* By this and a thousand other links of attachment, the whole body of the clergy, in those countries, still depend on the court of Rome; from it they expect dignities,—from it, that purple, which, according to the proud pretensions of those who are invested with it, renders them equal to sovereigns: from the resentment of that court, they have every thing to fear; and of course we see them almost invariably disposed to gratify it on every occasion. On the other hand, the court of Rome supports those clergy with all her might,—assists them by her politics and credit,—protects them against their enemies, and against those who would set bounds to their power,—nay, often against the just indignation of their sovereign,—and by this means attaches them to her still more strongly. Is it not doing an injury to the rights of society, and shocking the first elements of government, thus to suffer a great number of subjects, and even subjects in high posts, to be dependent on a foreign prince, and entirely devoted to him? Would a prudent sovereign receive men who preached such doctrines? There needed no more to cause all the missionaries to be driven from China.

§149.
4. The celibacy of the priests.

It was for the purpose of more firmly securing the attachment of churchmen, that the celibacy of the clergy was invented. A priest, a prelate, already bound to the see of Rome by his functions and his hopes, is further detached from his country, by the celibacy he is obliged to observe. He is not connected with civil society by a family: his grand

---

* We may see in the letters of Cardinal d'Ossat [[b. 1536–d. 1604]], what difficulties, what opposition, what long delays Henry IV. had to encounter when he wished to confer the archbishopric of Sens on Renauld de Baune, archbishop of Bourges, who had saved France, by receiving that great prince into the Roman catholic church.

interests are all centred in the church; and provided he has the pope's
favour, he has no further concern: in what country soever he was born,
Rome is his refuge, the centre of his adopted country. Every body knows
that the religious orders are a sort of papal militia, spread over the face
of the earth, to support and advance the interests of their monarch. This
is doubtless a strange abuse,—a subversion of the first laws of society.
But this is not all: if the prelates were married, they might enrich the
state with a number of good citizens; rich benefices affording them the
means of giving their legitimate children a suitable education. But what
a multitude of men are there in convents, consecrated to idleness under   Convents.
the cloak of devotion! Equally useless to society in peace and war, they
neither serve it by their labour in necessary professions, nor by their courage in arms: yet they enjoy immense revenues; and the people are
obliged, by the sweat of their brow, to furnish support for these swarms
of sluggards. What should we think of a husbandman who pro-
<70>tected useless hornets to devour the honey of his bees?* It is not
the fault of the fanatic preachers of over-strained sanctity, if all their
devotees do not imitate the celibacy of the monks. How happened it
that princes could suffer them publicly to extol, as the most sublime
virtue, a practice equally repugnant to nature, and pernicious to society?
Among the Romans, laws were made to diminish the number of those
who lived in celibacy, and to favour marriage:† but superstition soon
attacked such just and wise regulations; and the christian emperors, persuaded by churchmen, thought themselves obliged to abrogate them.‡
Several of the fathers of the church have censured those laws against
celibacy,—*doubtless,* says a great man,§ *with a laudable zeal for the things
of another life, but with very little knowledge of the affairs of this.* That
great man lived in the church of Rome:—he did not dare to assert in

---

* This reflection has no relation to the religious houses in which literature is cultivated. Establishments that afford to learned men a peaceful retreat, and that leisure
and tranquillity required in deep scientific research, are always laudable, and may
become very useful to the state.
  † The Papia-Poppaean law.
  ‡ In the Theodosian Code.
  § The president de Montesquieu, in his Spirit of Laws.

direct terms, that voluntary celibacy is to be condemned even with respect to conscience and the things of another life:—but it is certainly a conduct well becoming genuine piety, to conform ourselves to nature, to fulfil the views of the Creator, and to labour for the welfare of society. If a person is capable of rearing a family, let him marry, let him be attentive to give his children a good education:—in so doing, he will discharge his duty, and be undoubtedly in the road to salvation.

§150.
5. Enormous
pretensions of
the clergy.

Pre-eminence.

The enormous and dangerous pretensions of the clergy are also another consequence of this system which places every thing relating to religion beyond the reach of the civil power. In the first place, the ecclesiastics, under pretence of the holiness of their functions, have raised themselves above all the other citizens, even the principal magistrates: and, contrary to the express injunctions of their master, who said to his apostles *seek not the first places at feasts,* they have almost every where arrogated to themselves the first rank. Their head, in the Roman church, obliges sovereigns to kiss his feet; emperors have held the bridle of his horse; and if bishops or even simple priests do not at present raise themselves above their prince, it is because the times will not permit it: they have not always been so modest; and one of their writers has had the assurance to assert, *that a priest is as much above a king, as a man is above a beast.** How many authors, better known and more esteemed than the one just quoted, have taken a pleasure in praising and extolling that silly speech attributed to the emperor Theodosius <71> the First—*Ambrose has taught me the great distance there is between the empire and the priesthood!*

We have already observed that ecclesiastics ought to be honoured: but modesty, and even humility, should characterise them: and does it become them to forget it in their own conduct, while they preach it to others? I would not mention a vain ceremonial, were it not attended with

---

* Tantum sacerdos praestat regi, quantum homo bestiae. *Stanislaus Orichovius.*—*Vide Tribbechov. Exerc.* 1. *ad Baron. Annal. Sect.* 2. [[Adam Tribbechov, *Exercitationes ad Baronii Annales,* 1667]] & *Thomas. Nat. ad Lancell.* [[Thomasius's edition of Paolo Lancellotti's *Institutiones Juris Canonici* (Halle, 1715–17)]].

very material consequences, from the pride with which it inspires many priests, and the impressions it may make on the minds of the people. It is essentially necessary to good order, that subjects should behold none in society so respectable as their sovereign, and, next to him, those on whom he has devolved a part of his authority.

Ecclesiastics have not stopped in so fair a path. Not contented with rendering themselves independent with respect to their functions,—by the aid of the court of Rome, they have even attempted to withdraw themselves entirely, and in every respect, from all subjection to the political authority. There have been times when an ecclesiastic could not be brought before a secular tribunal for any crime whatsoever.* The canon law declares expressly, *It is indecent for laymen to judge a churchman*.† The popes Paul III. Pius V. and Urban VIII.[55] excommunicated all lay judges who should presume to undertake the trial of ecclesiastics. Even the bishops of France have not been afraid to say on several occasions, *that they did not depend on any temporal prince;* and, in 1656, the general assembly of the French clergy had the assurance to use the following expressions— *"The decree of council having been read, was disapproved by the assembly, because it leaves the king judge over the bishops, and*

§151.
6. Independence.
Immunities.

---

* The Congregation of Immunities has decided that the cognisance of causes against ecclesiastics, even for the crime of high treason, exclusively belongs to the spiritual court:—"Cognitio causae contra ecclesiasticos, etiam pro delicto laesae majestatis, fieri debet a judice ecclesiastico." RICCI *Synops. Decret. et Resol. S. Congreg. Immunit.* p. 105.—A constitution of pope Urban VI. pronounces those sovereigns or magistrates guilty of sacrilege, who shall banish an ecclesiastic from their territories, and declares them to have *ipso facto* incurred the sentence of excommunication. *Cap.* II. *De Foro Compet. in* VII.—To this immunity may be added the indulgence shewn by the ecclesiastical tribunals to the clergy, on whom they never inflicted any but slight punishments, even for the most atrocious crimes. The dreadful disorders that arose from this cause at length produced their own remedy in France, where the clergy were at length subjected to the temporal jurisdiction for all transgressions that are injurious to society. See PAPON *Arrêts Notables.* Book I. tit V. Act 34. [[Note added in 1773/1797 editions.]]

† Indecorum est laïcos homines viros ecclesiasticos judicare. *Can. in nona actione* 22. XVI. q. 7.

55. Pope Paul III, r. 1534–49; Pope Urban VIII, r. 1623–44.

*seems to subject their immunities to his judges.** There are decrees of the
popes that excommunicate whoever imprisons a bishop. According to
the principles of the church of Rome, a prince has not the power of
punishing an ecclesiastic with death, though a rebel, or a malefactor;—
he must first apply to the ecclesiastical power; and the latter will, if it
thinks proper, deliver up the culprit to the secular arm, after having degraded him.† History affords <72> us a thousand examples of bishops
who remained unpunished, or were but slightly chastised, for crimes for
which nobles of the highest rank forfeited their lives. John de Braganza,
king of Portugal, justly inflicted the penalty of death on those noblemen

---

* See *the Statement of Facts on the System of the Independence of Bishops.* [[Henri-
Philippe Chauvelin, *Tradition des faits, qui manifestent le sistème d'indépendance que
les évêques ont opposé dans les différens siècles aux principes invariables de la justice souveraine du roi sur tous ses sujets,* 1753.]]

† In the year 1725, a parish-priest, of the canton of Lucerne, having refused to
appear before the supreme council, was, for his contumacy, banished from the canton.
Hereupon, his diocesan, the bishop of Constance, had the assurance to write to the
council that they had infringed the ecclesiastical immunities,—that "it is unlawful to
subject the ministers of God to the decisions of the temporal power." In these pretensions, he was sanctioned by the approbation of the pope's nuncio and the court
of Rome. But the council of Lucerne firmly supported the rights of sovereignty,
and—without engaging with the bishop in a controversy which would have been
derogatory to their dignity,—answered him—"Your Lordship quotes various passages
from the writings of the fathers, which we, on our side, might also quote in our own
favour, if it were necessary, or if there was question of deciding the contest by dint
of quotations. But let your Lordship rest assured that we have a right to summon
before us a priest, our natural subject, who encroaches on our prerogatives,—to point
out to him his error,—to exhort him to a reform of his conduct,—and, in consequence of his obstinate disobedience after repeated citations, to banish him from our
dominions. We have not the least doubt that this right belongs to us; and we are
determined to defend it. And indeed it ought not to be proposed to any sovereign to
appear as party in a contest with a refractory subject like him,—to refer the cause to
the decision of a third party, whoever he be,—and run the risk of being condemned
to tolerate in the state a person of such character, with what dignity soever he might
be invested," &c. The bishop of Constance had proceeded so far as to assert, in his
letter to the canton, dated December 18, 1725, that "churchmen, as soon as they have
received holy orders, cease to be natural subjects, and are thus released from the bond-
age in which they lived before." *Memorial on the Dispute between the Pope and the
Canton of Lucerne,* p. 65. [[Note added in 1773/1797 editions.]]

who had conspired his destruction; but he did not dare to put to death the archbishop of Braga, the author of that detestable plot.*[56]

For an entire body of men, numerous and powerful, to stand beyond the reach of the public authority, and be dependent on a foreign court, is an entire subversion of order in the republic, and a manifest diminution of the sovereignty. This is a mortal stab given to society, whose very essence it is that every citizen should be subject to the public authority. Indeed the immunity which the clergy arrogate to themselves in this respect, is so inimical to the natural and necessary rights of a nation, that the king himself has not the power of granting it. But churchmen will tell us they derive this immunity from God himself: but till they have furnished some proof of their pretensions, let us adhere to this certain principle, that God desires the safety of states, and not that which will only be productive of disorder and destruction to them.

The same immunity is claimed for the possessions of the church. The state might, no doubt, exempt those possessions from every species of tax at a time when they were scarcely sufficient for the support of the ecclesiastics: but, for that favour, these men ought to be indebted to the public authority alone, which has always a right to revoke it, whenever the welfare of the state makes it necessary. It being one of the fundamental and essential laws of every society, that, in case of necessity, the wealth of all the members ought to contribute proportionally to <73> the common necessities,—the prince himself cannot, of his own authority, grant a total exemption to a very numerous and rich body, without being guilty of extreme injustice to the rest of his subjects, on whom, in consequence of that exemption, the whole weight of the burthen will fall.

§152.
7. Immunity
of church
possessions.

The possessions of the church are so far from being entitled to an exemption on account of their being consecrated to God, that, on the contrary, it is for that very reason they ought to be taken the first for the

* [[René-Aubert de Vertot]], Revolutions of Portugal.
56. John de Braganza, King John IV of Portugal, r. 1640–56. The plot to assassinate the king in 1641 was led by the natural son of King Peter II, José of Braganza, archbishop of Braga (1703–56).

use and safety of the state. For nothing is more agreeable to the common Father of mankind than to save a state from ruin. God himself having no need of any thing, the consecration of wealth to him is but a dedication of it to such uses as shall be agreeable to him. Besides, a great part of the revenues of the church, by the confession of the clergy themselves, is destined for the poor. When the state is in necessity, it is doubtless the first and principal pauper, and the most worthy of assistance. We may extend this principle even to the most common cases, and safely assert that to supply a part of the current expenses of the state from the revenues of the church, and thus take so much from the weight of the people's burthen, is really giving a part of those revenues to the poor, according to their original destination. But it is really contrary to religion and the intentions of the founders, to waste in pomp, luxury, and epicurism, those revenues that ought to be consecrated to the relief of the poor.*

§153.
8. Excommunication of men in office.

Not satisfied however with rendering themselves independent, the ecclesiastics undertook to bring mankind under their dominion; and indeed they had reason to despise the stupid mortals who suffered them to proceed in their plan. Excommunication was a formidable weapon among ignorant and superstitious men, who neither knew how to keep it within its proper bounds, nor to distinguish between the use and the abuse of it. Hence arose disorders, which have prevailed even in some protestant countries. Churchmen have presumed, by their own authority alone, to excommunicate men in high employments, magistrates whose functions were daily useful to society,—and have boldly asserted that those officers of the state, being struck with the thunders of the church, could no longer discharge the duty of their posts. What a perversion of order and reason! What! shall not a nation be allowed to intrust its affairs, its happiness, its repose and safety, to the hands of those whom it deems the most skilful and the most worthy of that trust? Shall the power of a churchman, whenever he pleases, deprive the state of its wisest conductors, of its firmest supports, and rob the prince of his most faithful servants? So absurd a pretension has been condemned by princes,

* See *Letters on the Pretensions of the Clergy*.

and even by prelates, respectable for their character and judgment. We read in the 171st letter of Ives de Chartres,[57] to the archbishop of Sens, that the royal capi-<74>tularies (conformably to the thirteenth canon of the twelfth council of Toledo, held in the year 681) enjoined the priests to admit to their conversation all those whom the king's majesty had received into favour, or entertained at his table, though they had been excommunicated by them, or by others,—in order that the church might not appear to reject or condemn those whom the king was pleased to employ in his service.*

The excommunications pronounced against the sovereigns themselves, and accompanied with the absolution of their subjects from their oaths of allegiance, put the finishing stroke to this enormous abuse; and it is almost incredible that nations should have suffered such odious procedures. We have slightly touched on this subject in §§145 and 146. The thirteenth century gives striking instances of it. Otho IV. for endeavouring to oblige several provinces of Italy to submit to the laws of the empire, was excommunicated and deprived of the empire by Innocent III.[58] and his subjects absolved from their oath of allegiance. Finally, this unfortunate emperor, being abandoned by the princes, was obliged to resign the crown to Frederic II. John, king of England, endeavouring to maintain the rights of his kingdom in the election of an archbishop of Canterbury,[59] found himself exposed to the audacious enterprises of the same pope. Innocent excommunicated the king,—laid the whole kingdom under an interdict,—had the presumption to declare John unworthy of the throne, and to absolve his subjects from their oath of fidelity: he stirred up the clergy against him,—excited his subjects to rebel,—solicited the king of France to take up arms to dethrone him,— publishing at the same time a crusade against him, as he would have done against the Saracens. The king of England at first appeared determined to defend himself with vigour: but soon losing courage, he suffered him-

§154.
9. And of sovereigns themselves.

* See *Letters on the Pretensions of the Clergy.*
57. Ives (Ivo) de Chartres, ca. 1040–1116, bishop of Chartres.
58. Otho IV, Holy Roman Emperor, r. 1209–15; Pope Innocent III, r. 1198–1216.
59. John de Gray, 1205.

self to be brought to such an excess of infamy, as to resign his kingdoms into the hands of the pope's legate, to receive them back from him, and hold them as a fief of the church, on condition of paying tribute.*

The popes were not the only persons guilty of such enormities: there have also been councils who bore a part in them. That of Lyons, summoned by Innocent IV.[60] in the year 1245, had the audacity to cite the emperor Frederic II. to appear before them in order to exculpate himself from the charges brought against him,—threatening him with the thunders of the church if he failed to do it. That great prince did not give himself much trouble about so irregular a proceeding. He said, "that the pope aimed at rendering himself both a judge and a sovereign; but that, from all antiquity, the emperors themselves had called councils, where the popes and prelates rendered to them, as to their sovereigns, the respect and obedience that <75> was their due."† The emperor, however, thinking it necessary to yield a little to the superstition of the times, condescended to send ambassadors to the council, to defend his cause: but this did not prevent the pope from excommunicating him, and declaring him deprived of the crown. Frederic, like a man of a superior genius, laughed at the empty thunders of the Vatican, and proved himself able to preserve the crown in spite of the election of Henry, Landgrave of Thuringia,[61] whom the ecclesiastical electors, and many bishops, had presumed to declare king of the Romans,—but who obtained little more by that election, than the ridiculous title of *king of the priests.*

I should never have done, were I to accumulate examples: but those I have already quoted are but too many for the honour of humanity. It is an humiliating sight to behold the excess of folly to which superstition had reduced the nations of Europe in those unhappy times.‡

---

60. Pope Innocent IV, r. 1243–54.

61. Henry, Landgrave of Thuringia, r. 1292–1308.

* Matthew Paris.—*Turretin. Compend. Hist. Eccles. Secul.* XIII.

† HEISS's *History of the Empire,* Book II. Chap. XVI.

‡ Sovereigns were sometimes found, who, without considering future consequences, favoured the papal encroachments when they were likely to prove advantageous to their own interests. Thus Louis VIII. [[r. 1223–26]] king of France, wishing to invade the territories of the count of Toulouse, under pretence of making war on

By means of the same spiritual arms, the clergy drew every thing to themselves, usurped the authority of the tribunals, and disturbed the course of justice. They claimed a right to take cognisance of all causes, *on account of sin, of which* (says Innocent III.)* *every man of sense must know that the cognisance belongs to our ministry.* In the year 1329, the prelates of France had the assurance to tell king Philip de Valois, that, to prevent causes of any kind from being brought before the ecclesiastical courts, was depriving the church of all its rights, *omnia ecclesiarum jura tollere.*†[62] And accordingly it was their aim to have to themselves the decision of all disputes. They boldly opposed the civil authority, and made themselves feared by proceeding in the way of excommunication. It even happened sometimes, that, as dioceses were not always confined to the extent of the <76> political territory, a bishop would summon foreigners before his tribunal, for causes purely civil, and take upon him to decide them, in manifest violation of the rights of nations. To such a height had the disorder arisen three or four centuries ago, that our wise ancestors thought themselves obliged to take serious measures to put a

---

the Albigenses, requested of the pope, among other things, "that he would issue a bull, declaring that the two Raymonds, father and son, together with all their adherents, associates, and allies, had been and were deprived of all their possessions." VELLY's *Hist. of France.* Vol IV. p. 33.—Of a similar nature to the preceding, is the following remarkable fact. Pope Martin IV. excommunicated Peter, king of Arragon,—declared that he had forfeited his kingdom, all his lands, and even the regal dignity,—and pronounced his subjects absolved from their oaths of allegiance. He even excommunicated all who should acknowledge him as king, or perform towards him any of the duties of a subject. He then offered Arragon and Catalonia to the count de Valois, second son of Philip the Bold, on condition that he and his successors should acknowledge themselves vassals of the holy see, take an oath of fealty to the pope, and pay him a yearly tribute. The king of France assembled the barons and prelates of his kingdom to deliberate on the pope's offer; and they advised him to accept it:—"Strange blindness of kings and their counsellors!" exclaims, with good reason, a modern historian: "they did not perceive, that, by thus accepting kingdoms from the hands of the pope, they strengthened and established his pretensions to the right of deposing themselves." VELLY's *Hist. of France.* Vol. VI. p. 190. [[Note added in 1773/1797 editions.]]

* *In cap. Novit. de Judiciis.*

† See Leibnitii Codex *Juris Gent. Diplomat.* Dipl. LXVII. §9.

62. "To acknowledge all ecclesiastical laws."

stop to it; and stipulated in their treaties, that *none of the confederates should be summoned before spiritual courts, for money debts, since every one ought to be contented with the ordinary modes of justice that were observed in the country.** We find in history that the Swiss on many occasions repressed the encroachments of the bishops and their judges.

Over every affair of life they extended their authority, under pretence that conscience was concerned. They obliged new-married husbands to purchase permission to lie with their wives, the first three nights after marriage.†

§156.
11. Money drawn to Rome.

This burlesque invention leads us to remark another abuse, manifestly contrary to the rules of a wise policy, and to the duty a nation owes to herself,—I mean the immense sums, which bulls, dispensations, &c. annually drew to Rome, from all the countries in communion with her. How much might be said on the scandalous trade of indulgences! but it at last became ruinous to the court of Rome, which, by endeavouring to gain too much, suffered irreparable losses.

§157.
12. Laws and customs contrary to the welfare of states.

Finally, that independent authority intrusted to ecclesiastics, who were often incapable of understanding the true maxims of government, or too careless to take the trouble of studying them, and whose minds were wholly occupied by a visionary fanaticism, by empty speculations, and notions of a chimerical and overstrained purity,—that authority, I say, produced, under the pretence of sanctity, laws and customs that were pernicious to the state. Some of these we have noticed: but a very remarkable instance is mentioned by Grotius. "In the ancient Greek church," says he, "was long observed a canon, by which those who had killed an enemy in any war whatsoever, were excommunicated for three years."‡ A fine reward decreed for the heroes who defended their country, instead of the crowns and triumphs with which pagan Rome had been

---

* *Ibid.* Alliance of Zurich with the cantons of Uri, Schweitz, and Underwald, dated May 1, 1351, §7.

† See *A Regulation of Parliament in an arret of March* 19, 1409. *Spirit of Laws.* These (says Montesquieu) were the very best nights they could pitch upon: they would have made no great profit of any other.

‡ *De Jure Belli & Pacis, Lib.* II. *Cap.* XXIV. He quotes *Basil ad Amphiloch.* X. 13. *Zonarcas in Niceph. Phoc.* Vol. III.

accustomed to honour them! Pagan Rome became mistress of the world:—she adorned her bravest warriors with crowns. The empire, having embraced christianity, soon became a prey to barbarians:—her subjects, by defending her, incurred the penalty of a degrading excommunication. By devoting themselves to an idle life, they thought themselves pursuing the path to heaven, and actually found themselves in the high road to riches and greatness. <77>

CHAPTER XIII

Of Justice and Polity.

Next to the care of religion, one of the principal duties of a nation relates to justice. They ought to employ their utmost attention in causing it to prevail in the state, and to take proper measures for having it dispensed to every one in the most certain, the most speedy, and the least burthensome manner. This obligation flows from the object proposed by uniting in civil society, and from the social compact itself. We have seen (§15) that men have bound themselves by the engagements of society, and consented to divest themselves, in its favour, of a part of their natural liberty, only with a view of peaceably enjoying what belongs to them, and obtaining justice with certainty. The nation would therefore neglect her duty to herself, and deceive the individuals, if she did not seriously endeavour to make the strictest justice prevail. This attention she owes to her own happiness, repose, and prosperity. Confusion, disorder, and despondency, will soon arise in a state, when the citizens are not sure of easily and speedily obtaining justice in all their disputes: without this, the civil virtues will become extinguished, and the society weakened.

§158. A nation ought to make justice reign.

There are two methods of making justice flourish,—good laws, and the attention of the superiors to see them executed. In treating of the constitution of a state (Chap. III.) we have already shewn, that a nation ought to establish just and wise laws, and have also pointed out the reasons, why we cannot here enter into the particulars of those laws. If men

§159. To establish good laws.

were always equally just, equitable, and enlightened, the laws of nature would doubtless be sufficient for society. But ignorance, the illusions of self-love, and the violence of the passions, too often render these sacred laws ineffectual. And we see, in consequence, that all well-governed nations have perceived the necessity of enacting positive laws. There is a necessity for general and formal regulations, that each may clearly know his own rights without being misled by self-deception: sometimes even it is necessary to deviate from natural equity, in order to prevent abuses and frauds, and to accommodate ourselves to circumstances; and since the sensation of duty has frequently so little influence on the heart of man, a penal sanction becomes necessary, to give the laws their full efficacy. Thus is the law of nature converted into civil law.* It would be dangerous to commit the interests of the citizens to the mere discretion of those who are to dispense justice. The legislator should assist the understanding of the judges, force their prejudices and inclinations, and subdue their will, by simple, fixed, and certain rules. These again are the civil laws. <78>

§160. To enforce them.

The best laws are useless, if they be not observed. The nation ought then to take pains to support them, and to cause them to be respected and punctually executed: with this view she cannot adopt measures too just, too extensive, or too effectual; for hence, in a great degree, depend her happiness, glory, and tranquillity.

§161. Functions and duties of the prince in this respect.

We have already observed (§41) that the sovereign, who represents a nation and is invested with its authority, is also charged with its duties. An attention to make justice flourish in the state must then be one of the principal functions of the prince; and nothing can be more worthy of the sovereign majesty. The emperor Justinian thus begins his book of the Institutes: *Imperatoriam majestatem non solum armis decoratam, sed etiam legibus oportet esse armatam, ut utrumque tempus, & bellorum & pacis, recte possit gubernari.*[63] The degree of power intrusted by the na-

---

* See a dissertation on this subject, in the *Loisir Philosophique,* page 71 [[by Vattel, published in 1747]].

63. "The imperial majesty should not only be decorated with arms but should also be armed with laws so that there may be good government in times both of war and of peace." Justinian, *Institutes,* prooemium.

tion to the head of the state, is then the rule of his duties and his functions in the administration of justice. As the nation may either reserve the legislative power to itself, or intrust it to a select body,—it has also a right, if it thinks proper, to establish a supreme tribunal to judge of all disputes, independently of the prince. But the conductor of the state must naturally have a considerable share in legislation, and it may even be entirely intrusted to him. In this last case, it is he who must establish salutary laws, dictated by wisdom and equity: but in all cases, he should be the guardian of the law; he should watch over those who are invested with authority, and confine each individual within the bounds of duty.

The executive power naturally belongs to the sovereign,—to every conductor of a people: he is supposed to be invested with it, in its fullest extent, when the fundamental laws do not restrict it. When the laws are established, it is the prince's province to have them put in execution. To support them with vigour, and to make a just application of them to all cases that present themselves, is what we call rendering justice. And this is the duty of the sovereign, who is naturally the judge of his people. We have seen the chiefs of some small states perform these functions themselves: but this custom becomes inconvenient, and even impossible, in a great kingdom.

§162. How he is to dispense justice.

The best and safest method of distributing justice is by establishing judges, distinguished by their integrity and knowledge, to take cognisance of all the disputes that may arise between the citizens. It is impossible for the prince to take upon himself this painful task: he cannot spare sufficient time either for the thorough investigation of all causes, or even for the acquisition of the knowledge necessary to decide them. As the sovereign cannot personally discharge all the functions of government, he should, with a just discernment, reserve to himself such as he can successfully perform, and are of most importance,—intrusting the others to officers and magistrates who shall execute them under his authority. There is no inconvenience in trusting the <79> decision of a law-suit to a body of prudent, honest, and enlightened men:—on the contrary it is the best mode the prince can possibly adopt; and he fully acquits himself of the duty he owes to his people in this particular, when he gives them judges adorned with all the qualities suitable to ministers

§163. He ought to appoint enlightened and upright judges.

of justice: he has then nothing more to do but to watch over their conduct, in order that they may not neglect their duty.

§164. The ordinary courts should determine causes relating to the revenue.

The establishment of courts of justice is particularly necessary for the decision of all fiscal causes,—that is to say, all the disputes that may arise between the subjects on the one hand, and, on the other, the persons who exert the profitable prerogatives of the prince. It would be very unbecoming, and highly improper for a prince, to take upon him to give judgment in his own cause:—he cannot be too much on his guard against the illusions of interest and self-love; and even though he were capable of resisting their influence, still he ought not to expose his character to the rash judgments of the multitude. These important reasons ought even to prevent his submitting the decision of causes in which he is concerned, to the ministers and counsellors particularly attached to his person. In all well-regulated states, in countries that are really states, and not the dominions of a despot, the ordinary tribunals decide all causes in which the sovereign is a party, with as much freedom as those between private persons.

§165. There ought to be established supreme courts of justice, wherein causes should be finally determined.

The end of all trials at law is justly to determine the disputes that arise between the citizens. If, therefore, suits are prosecuted before an inferior judge, who examines all the circumstances and proofs relating to them, it is very proper, that, for the greater safety, the party condemned should be allowed to appeal to a superior tribunal, where the sentence of the former judge may be examined, and reversed, if it appear to be ill-founded. But it is necessary that this supreme tribunal should have the authority of pronouncing a definitive sentence without appeal: otherwise the whole proceeding will be vain, and the dispute can never be determined.

The custom of having recourse to the prince himself, by laying a complaint at the foot of the throne, when the cause has been finally determined by a supreme court, appears to be subject to very great inconveniences. It is more easy to deceive the prince by specious reasons, than a number of magistrates well skilled in the knowledge of the laws; and experience too plainly shews, what powerful resources are derived from favour and intrigue in the courts of kings. If this practice be authorised by the laws of the state, the prince ought always to fear that these complaints are only formed with a view of protracting a suit, and procrastinating a just condemnation. A just and wise sovereign will not admit them without great caution; and if he reverses the sentence that is complained of, he ought not to try the cause himself, but submit it to the examination of another tribunal, as is the practice in France. The ruinous length of <80> these proceedings authorises us to say, that it is more convenient and advantageous to the state, to establish a sovereign tribunal, whose definitive decrees should not be subject to a reversal even by the prince himself. It is sufficient for the security of justice, that the sovereign keep a watchful eye over the judges and magistrates, in the same manner as he is bound to watch all the other officers in the state,— and that he have power to call to an account and to punish such as are guilty of prevarication.

When once this sovereign tribunal is established, the prince cannot meddle with its decrees; and, in general, he is absolutely obliged to preserve and maintain the forms of justice. Every attempt to violate them is an assumption of arbitrary power, to which it cannot be presumed that any nation could ever have intended to subject itself.

§166. The prince ought to preserve the forms of justice.

When those forms are defective, it is the business of the legislator to reform them. This being done or procured in a manner agreeable to the fundamental laws, will be one of the most salutary benefits the sovereign can bestow upon his people. To preserve the citizens from the danger of ruining themselves in defending their rights,—to repress and destroy that monster, chicanery,—will be an action more glorious in the eyes of the wise man, than all the exploits of a conqueror.

Justice is administered in the name of the sovereign; the prince relies on the judgment of the courts, and, with good reason, looks upon their decisions as sound law and justice. His part in this branch of the government is then to maintain the authority of the judges, and to cause their sentences to be executed; without which, they would be vain and delusive; for justice would not be rendered to the citizens.

§167. The prince ought to support the authority of the judges.

There is another kind of justice named *attributive* or *distributive*, which in general consists in treating every one according to his deserts. This virtue ought to regulate the distribution of public employments, honours, and rewards in a state. It is, in the first place, a duty the nation

§168. Of distributive justice.

The distri-
bution of
employments
and rewards.
owes to herself, to encourage good citizens, to excite every one to virtue by honours and rewards, and to intrust with employments such persons only as are capable of properly discharging them. In the next place, it is a duty the nation owes to individuals, to shew herself duly attentive to reward and honour merit. Although a sovereign has the power of distributing his favours and employments to whomsoever he pleases, and nobody has a perfect right to any post or dignity,—yet a man who by intense application has qualified himself to become useful to his country, and he who has rendered some signal service to the state, may justly complain if the prince overlooks them, in order to advance useless men without merit. This is treating them with an ingratitude that is wholly unjustifiable, and adapted only to extinguish emulation. There is hardly any fault that in a course of time can become more prejudicial to a state: it introduces into it a general relaxation; and its public affairs, being managed by incompetent hands, cannot fail to <81> be attended with ill-success. A powerful state may support itself for some time by its own weight; but at length it falls into decay; and this is perhaps one of the principal causes of those revolutions observable in great empires. The sovereign is attentive to the choice of those he employs, while he feels himself obliged to watch over his own safety, and to be on his guard: but when once he thinks himself elevated to such a pitch of greatness and power as leaves him nothing to fear, he follows his own caprice, and all public offices are distributed by favour.

§169. Punish-
ment of
transgressors.
The punishment of transgressors commonly belongs to distributive justice, of which it is really a branch; since good order requires that malefactors should be made to suffer the punishments they have deserved. But if we would clearly establish this on its true foundations, we must

Foundation of
the right of
punishing.
recur to first principles. The right of punishing, which in a state of nature belongs to each individual, is founded on the right of personal safety. Every man has a right to preserve himself from injury, and by force to provide for his own security, against those who unjustly attack him. For this purpose, he may, when injured, inflict a punishment on the aggressor, as well with the view of putting it out of his power to injure him for the future, or of reforming him, as of restraining, by his example, all those who might be tempted to imitate him. Now, when

men unite in society,—as the society is thenceforward charged with the duty of providing for the safety of its members, the individuals all resign to it their private right of punishing. To the whole body, therefore, it belongs to avenge private injuries, while it protects the citizens at large. And as it is a moral person, capable also of being injured, it has a right to provide for its own safety, by punishing those who trespass against it;—that is to say, it has a right to punish public delinquents. Hence arises the right of the sword, which belongs to a nation, or to its conductor. When the society use it against another nation, they make war; when they exert it in punishing an individual, they exercise vindictive justice. Two things are to be considered in this part of government,—the laws, and their execution.

It would be dangerous to leave the punishment of transgressors entirely to the discretion of those who are invested with authority. The passions might interfere in a business which ought to be regulated only by justice and wisdom. The punishment, pre-ordained for an evil action, lays a more effectual restraint on the wicked, than a vague fear, in which they may deceive themselves. In short, the people, who are commonly moved at the sight of a suffering wretch, are better convinced of the justice of his punishment, when it is inflicted by the laws themselves. Every well-governed state ought then to have its laws for the punishment of criminals. It belongs to the legislative power, whatever that be, to establish them with justice and wisdom. But this is not a proper place for giving a general theory of them: we shall therefore only say, that each nation ought, in this as in every <82> other instance, to chuse such laws as may best suit her peculiar circumstances.

§170. Criminal laws.

We shall only make one observation, which is connected with the subject in hand, and relates to the degree of punishment. From the foundation even of the right of punishing, and from the lawful end of inflicting penalties, arises the necessity of keeping them within just bounds. Since they are designed to procure the safety of the state and of the citizens, they ought never to be extended beyond what that safety requires. To say that any punishment is just since the transgressor knew beforehand the penalty he was about to incur, is using a barbarous language, repugnant to humanity, and to the law of nature, which forbids

§171. Degree of punishment.

our doing any ill to others, unless they lay us under the necessity of inflicting it in our own defence and for our own security. Whenever then a particular crime is not much to be feared in society, as when the opportunities of committing it are very rare, or when the subjects are not inclined to it, too rigorous punishments ought not to be used to suppress it. Attention ought also to be paid to the nature of the crime; and the punishment should be proportioned to the degree of injury done to the public tranquillity and the safety of society, and the wickedness it supposes in the criminal.

These maxims are not only dictated by justice and equity, but also as forcibly recommended by prudence and the art of government. Experience shews us, that the imagination becomes familiarised to objects which are frequently presented to it. If, therefore, terrible punishments are multiplied, the people will become daily less affected by them, and at length contract, like the Japanese, a savage and ferocious character:— these bloody spectacles will then no longer produce the effect designed; for they will cease to terrify the wicked. It is with these examples as with honours:—a prince who multiplies titles and distinctions to excess, soon depreciates them, and makes an injudicious use of one of the most powerful and convenient springs of government. When we recollect the practice of the ancient Romans with respect to criminals,—when we reflect on their scrupulous attention to spare the blood of the citizens,— we cannot fail to be struck at seeing with how little ceremony it is now-a-days shed in the generality of states. Was then the Roman republic but ill governed? Does better order and greater security reign among us?— It is not so much the cruelty of the punishments, as a strict punctuality in enforcing the penal code, that keeps mankind within the bounds of duty: and if simple robbery is punished with death, what further punishment is reserved to check the hand of the murderer?

§172. Execution of the laws.   The execution of the laws belongs to the conductor of the state: he is intrusted with the care of it, and is indispensably obliged to discharge it with wisdom. The prince then is to see that the criminal laws be put in execution; but he is not to attempt in his own person to try the guilty. Besides the reasons <83> we have already alleged in treating of civil causes, and which are of still greater weight in regard to those of a criminal nature,—to appear in the character of a judge pronouncing sentence on a wretched criminal, would ill become the majesty of the sovereign, who ought in every thing to appear as the father of his people. It is a very wise maxim commonly received in France, that the prince ought to reserve to himself all matters of favour, and leave it to the magistrates to execute the rigour of justice. But then justice ought to be exercised in his name, and under his authority. A good prince will keep a watchful eye over the conduct of the magistrates; he will oblige them to observe scrupulously the established forms, and will himself take care never to break through them. Every sovereign who neglects or violates the forms of justice in the prosecution of criminals, makes large strides towards tyranny: and the liberty of the citizens is at an end, when once they cease to be certain that they cannot be condemned, except in pursuance of the laws, according to the established forms, and by their ordinary judges. The custom of committing the trial of the accused party to commissioners chosen at the pleasure of the court, was the tyrannical invention of some ministers who abused the authority of their master. By this irregular and odious procedure, a famous minister always succeeded in destroying his enemies. A good prince will never give his consent to such a proceeding, if he has sufficient discernment to foresee the dreadful abuse his ministers may make of it. If the prince ought not to pass sentence himself,—for the same reason, he ought not to aggravate the sentence passed by the judges.

The very nature of government requires that the executor of the laws should have the power of dispensing with them, when this may be done without injury to any person, and in certain particular cases where the welfare of the state requires an exception. Hence the right of granting pardons is one of the attributes of sovereignty. But, in his whole conduct, in his severity as well as in his mercy, the sovereign ought to have no other object in view than the greater advantage of society. A wise prince knows how to reconcile justice with clemency,—the care of the public safety, with that pity which is due to the unfortunate. §173. Right of pardoning.

The internal police consists in the attention of the prince and magistrates to preserve every thing in order. Wise regulations ought to prescribe whatever will best contribute to the public safety, utility and con- §174. Internal police.

venience; and those who are invested with authority cannot be too attentive to enforce them. By a wise police, the sovereign accustoms the people to order and obedience, and preserves peace, tranquillity, and concord among the citizens. The magistrates of Holland are said to possess extraordinary talents in this respect:—a better police prevails in their cities, and even their establishments in the Indies, than in any other places in the known world. <84>

§175. Duel, or single combat.

Laws and the authority of the magistrates having been substituted in the room of private war, the conductor of a nation ought not to suffer individuals to attempt to do themselves justice, when they can have recourse to the magistrates. Duelling—that species of combat, in which the parties engage on account of a private quarrel—is a manifest disorder, repugnant to the ends of civil society. This phrenzy was unknown to the ancient Greeks and Romans, who raised to such a height the glory of their arms: we received it from barbarous nations who knew no other law but the sword. Louis XIV. deserves the greatest praise for his endeavours to abolish this savage custom.

§176. Means of putting a stop to this disorder.

But why was not that prince made sensible that the most severe punishments were incapable of curing the rage for duelling? They did not reach the source of the evil; and since a ridiculous prejudice had persuaded all the nobility and gentlemen of the army, that a man who wears a sword is bound in honour to avenge, with his own hand, the least injury he has received; this is the principle on which it is proper to proceed. We must destroy this prejudice, or restrain it by a motive of the same nature. While a nobleman, by obeying the law, shall be regarded by his equals as a coward and as a man dishonoured,—while an officer in the same case shall be forced to quit the service,—can you hinder his fighting by threatening him with death? On the contrary, he will place a part of his bravery in doubly exposing his life, in order to wash away the affront. And certainly, while the prejudice subsists, while a nobleman or an officer cannot act in opposition to it, without embittering the rest of his life, I do not know whether we can justly punish him who is forced to submit to its tyranny, or whether he be very guilty with respect to morality. That worldly honour, be it as false and chimerical as you please, is to him a substantial and necessary possession, since without it, he can neither live with his equals, nor exercise a profession that is often his only resource. When therefore any insolent fellow would unjustly ravish from him that chimera so esteemed and so necessary, why may he not defend it as he would his life and property against a robber? As the state does not permit an individual to pursue with arms in his hand the usurper of his property, because he may obtain justice from the magistrate,—so, if the sovereign will not allow him to draw his sword against the man from whom he has received an insult, he ought necessarily to take such measures that the patience and obedience of the citizen who has been insulted, shall not prove prejudicial to him. Society cannot deprive man of his natural right of making war against an aggressor, without furnishing him with some other means of securing himself from the evil his enemy would do him. On all those occasions where the public authority cannot lend us its assistance, we resume our original and natural right of self-defence. Thus a traveller may, without hesitation, kill the robber who attacks him on the highway; <85> because it would, at that moment, be in vain for him to implore the protection of the laws and of the magistrate. Thus a chaste virgin would be praised for taking away the life of a brutal ravisher who attempted to force her to his desires.

Till men have got rid of this Gothic idea, that honour obliges them, even in contempt of the laws, to avenge their personal injuries with their own hands, the most effectual method of putting a stop to the effects of this prejudice would perhaps be to make a total distinction between the offended and the aggressor,—to pardon the former without difficulty, when it appears that his honour has been really attacked,—and to exercise justice without mercy on the party who has committed the outrage. And as to those who draw the sword for trifles and punctilios, for little piques or railleries in which honour is not concerned, I would have them severely punished. By this means a restraint would be put on those peevish and insolent folks, who often reduce even the most moderate men to a necessity of chastising them. Every one would be on his guard, to avoid being considered as the aggressor; and with a view to gain the advantage of engaging in duel (if unavoidable) without incurring the penalties of the law, both parties would curb their passions; by which means the quarrel would fall of itself, and be attended with no consequences. It frequently happens that a bully is at bottom a coward; he gives himself haughty airs, and offers insult, in hopes that the rigour of the law will oblige people to put up with his insolence. And what is the consequence?—A man of spirit will run every risk, rather than submit to be insulted:—the aggressor dares not recede: and a combat ensues, which would not have taken place, if the latter could have once imagined that there was nothing to prevent the other from chastising him for his presumption,—the offended person being acquitted by the same law that condemns the aggressor.

To this first law, whose efficacy would, I doubt not, be soon proved by experience, it would be proper to add the following regulations:—1. Since it is an established custom that the nobility and military men should appear armed even in time of peace, care should be taken to enforce a rigid observance of the laws which allow the privilege of wearing swords to these two orders of men only. 2. It would be proper to establish a particular court, to determine, in a summary manner, all affairs of honour between persons of these two orders. The marshals' court in France is in possession of this power; and it might be invested with it in a more formal manner and to a greater extent. The governors of provinces and strong places, with their general officers,—the colonels and captains of each regiment,—might, in this particular, act as deputies to the marshals. These courts, each in its own department, should alone confer the right of wearing a sword. Every nobleman at sixteen or eighteen years of age, and every soldier at his entrance into the regiment, should be obliged to appear before the court to receive <86> the sword. 3. On its being there delivered to him, he should be informed, that it is intrusted to him only for the defence of his country; and care might be taken to inspire him with true ideas of honour. 4. It appears to me of great importance, to establish, for different cases, punishments of a different nature. Whoever should so far forget himself, as, either by word or deed, to insult a man who wears a sword, might be degraded from the rank of nobility, deprived of the privilege of carrying arms, and subjected to corporal punishment,—even the punishment of death, according to the grossness of the insult: and, as I before observed, no favour should be shewn to the offender in case a duel was the consequence, while at the same time the other party should stand fully acquitted. Those who fight on slight occasions, I would not have condemned to death, unless in such cases where the author of the quarrel,—he, I mean, who carried it so far as to draw his sword, or to give the challenge,—has killed his adversary. People hope to escape punishment, when it is too severe; and, besides, a capital punishment, in such cases, is not considered as infamous. But let them be ignominiously degraded from the rank of nobility and the use of arms, and for ever deprived of the right of wearing a sword, without the least hope of pardon: this would be the most proper method to restrain men of spirit, provided that due care was taken to make a distinction between different offenders, according to the degree of the offence. As to persons below the rank of nobility, and who do not belong to the army, their quarrels should be left to the cognisance of the ordinary courts, which, in case of bloodshed, should punish the offenders according to the common laws against violence and murder. It should be the same with respect to any quarrel that might arise between a commoner and a man entitled to carry arms: it is the business of the ordinary magistrate to preserve order and peace between those two classes of men, who cannot have any points of honour to settle, the one with the other. To protect the people against the violence of those who wear the sword, and to punish the former severely, if they should dare to insult the latter, should further be, as it is at present, the business of the magistrate.

I am sanguine enough to believe that these regulations, and this method of proceeding, if strictly adhered to, would extirpate that monster, duelling, which the most severe laws have been unable to restrain. They go to the source of the evil by preventing quarrels, and oppose a lively sensation of true and real honour to that false and punctilious honour which occasions the spilling of so much blood. It would be worthy a great monarch to make a trial of it: its success would immortalise his name; and by the bare attempt he would merit the love and gratitude of his people. <87>

CHAPTER XIV

The third Object of a good Government,—to fortify
itself against external Attacks.

§177. A nation ought to fortify itself against external attacks. We have treated at large of what relates to the felicity of a nation: the subject is equally copious and complicated. Let us now proceed to a third division of the duties which a nation owes to itself,—a third object of good government. One of the ends of political society is to defend itself with its combined strength against all external insult or violence (§15). If the society is not in a condition to repulse an aggressor, it is very imperfect,—it is unequal to the principal object of its destination, and cannot long subsist. The nation ought to put itself in such a state as to be able to repel and humble an unjust enemy: this is an important duty, which the care of its own perfection, and even of its preservation, imposes both on the state and its conductor.

§178. National strength. It is its strength alone that can enable a nation to repulse all aggressors, to secure its rights, and render itself every where respectable. It is called upon by every possible motive, to neglect no circumstance that can tend to place it in this happy situation. The strength of a state consists in three things,—the number of the citizens, their military virtues, and their riches. Under this last article we may comprehend fortresses, artillery, arms, horses, ammunition, and, in general, all that immense apparatus at present necessary in war, since they can all be procured with money.

§179. Increase of population. To increase the number of the citizens as far as it is possible or convenient, is then one of the first objects that claim the attentive care of the state or its conductor: and this will be successfully effected by complying with the obligation to procure the country a plenty of the necessaries of life,—by enabling the people to support their families with the fruits of their labour,—by giving proper directions that the poorer classes, and especially the husbandmen, be not harassed and oppressed by the levying of taxes,—by governing with mildness, and in a manner, which, instead of disgusting and dispersing the present subjects of the state, shall rather attract new ones,—and, finally, by encouraging marriage, after the example of the Romans. That nation, so attentive to every thing capable of increasing and supporting their power, made wise laws against celibacy (as we have already observed in §149), and granted privileges and exemptions to married men, particularly to those who had numerous families: laws that were equally wise and just, since a citizen who rears <88> subjects for the state, has a right to expect more favour from it than the man who chuses to live for himself alone.*

Every thing tending to depopulate a country is a defect in a state not overstocked with inhabitants. We have already spoken of convents and the celibacy of priests. It is strange that establishments, so directly repugnant to the duties of a man and a citizen, as well as to the advantage and safety of society, should have found such favour, and that princes, instead of opposing them as it was their duty to do, should have protected and enriched them. A system of policy, that dextrously took advantage of superstition to extend its own power, led princes and subjects astray, caused them to mistake their real duties, and blinded sovereigns even with respect to their own interest. Experience seems at length to have opened the eyes of nations and their conductors; the pope himself (let us mention it to the honour of Benedict XIV.) endeavours gradually to reform so palpable an abuse; by his orders, none in his dominions are any longer permitted to take the vow of celibacy before they are twenty-

---

* It is impossible to suppress the emotions of indignation that arise on reading what some of the fathers of the church have written against marriage and in favour of celibacy. "Videtur esse matrimonii et stupri differentia (says Tertullian): sed utrobique est communicatio.† Ergo, inquis, et primas nuptios damnas? Nec immerito, quoniam et ipsae constant ex eo quod est stuprum." [[Tertullian: "There is a difference between marriage and fornication, but in both cases there is intercommunication [defilement]. . . . Are you saying, then, that you condemn first marriages as well? Yes, and not without reason, because these too are composed of what is essentially fornication" (trans. Eds.).]] Exhort. Castit. [[PL 2, 925]]—And thus Jerome: "Hanc tantum esse differentiam inter uxorem et scortum, quod tolerabilius sit uni esse prostitutam quam pluribus." [["This is the only difference between a wife and a strumpet, that it is more endurable to be prostituted to one than to many" (trans. Eds.).]] [[Note added in 1773/1797 editions.]]

† Contaminatio? Edit.

five years of age. That wise pontiff gives the sovereigns of his communion a salutary example; he invites them to attend at length to the safety of their states,—to narrow at least, if they cannot entirely close up, the avenues of that sink that drains their dominions. Take a view of Germany; and there, in countries which are in all other respects upon an equal footing, you will see the protestant states twice as populous as the catholic ones. Compare the desert state of Spain with that of England teeming with inhabitants:—survey many fine provinces, even in France, destitute of hands to till the soil;—and then tell me, whether the many thousands of both sexes, who are now locked up in convents, would not serve God and their country infinitely better, by peopling those fertile plains with useful cultivators? It is true, indeed, that the catholic cantons of Switzerland are nevertheless very populous: but this is owing to a profound peace, and the nature of the government, which abundantly repair the losses occasioned by convents. Liberty is able to remedy the greatest evils; it is the soul of a state, and was with great justice called by the Romans *alma Libertas.*

§180. Valour.　　A cowardly and undisciplined multitude are incapable of repulsing a warlike enemy: the strength of the state consists less in the number than the military virtues of its citizens. Valour, that heroic virtue which makes us undauntedly encounter danger <89> in defence of our country, is the firmest support of the state: it renders it formidable to its enemies, and often even saves it the trouble of defending itself. A state whose reputation in this respect is once well established, will be seldom attacked, if it does not provoke other states by its enterprises. For above two centuries the Swiss have enjoyed a profound peace, while the din of arms resounded all around them, and the rest of Europe was desolated by the ravages of war. Nature gives the foundation of valour; but various causes may animate it, weaken it, and even destroy it. A nation ought then to seek after and cultivate a virtue so useful; and a prudent sovereign will take all possible measures to inspire his subjects with it:—his wisdom will point out to him the means. It is this generous flame that animates the French nobility: fired with a love of glory and of their country, they fly to battle, and cheerfully spill their blood in the field of honour. To what an extent would they not carry their conquests, if that kingdom were surrounded by nations less warlike! The Briton, generous and intrepid, resembles a lion in combat; and in general, the nations of Europe surpass in bravery all the other people upon earth.

But valour alone is not always successful in war: constant success can only be obtained by an assemblage of all the military virtues. History shews us the importance of ability in the commanders, of military discipline, frugality, bodily strength, dexterity, and being inured to fatigue and labour. These are so many distinct branches which a nation ought carefully to cultivate. It was the assemblage of all these that raised so high the glory of the Romans, and rendered them the masters of the world. It were a mistake to suppose that valour alone produced those illustrious exploits of the ancient Swiss,—the victories of Morgarten, Sempach, Laupen, Morat, and many others.[64] The Swiss not only fought with intrepidity: they studied the art of war,—they inured themselves to its toils, they accustomed themselves to the practice of all its manoeuvres,—and their very love of liberty made them submit to a discipline which could alone secure to them that treasure, and save their country. Their troops were no less celebrated for their discipline than their bravery. Mezeray, after having given an account of the behaviour of the Swiss at the battle of Dreux,[65] adds these remarkable words: "in the opinion of all the officers of both sides who were present, the Swiss, in that battle, under every trial, against infantry and cavalry, against French and against Germans, gained the palm for military discipline, and acquired the reputation of being the best infantry in the world."*

§181. Other military virtues.

Finally, the wealth of a nation constitutes a considerable part of its power, especially in modern times, when war requires such immense expenses. It is not simply in the revenues of the sovereign, or the public treasure, that the riches of a nation <90> consist: its opulence is also rated from the wealth of individuals. We commonly call a nation rich, when it contains a great number of citizens in easy and affluent circumstances. The wealth of private persons really increases the strength of

§182. Riches.

---

* *History of France,* Vol. II. p. 888.
64. Morgarten, 1315; Sempach, 1386; Laupen, 1339; Morat, 1476.
65. Battle of Dreux, 1562.

the nation; since they are capable of contributing large sums towards supplying the necessities of the state, and that, in a case of extremity, the sovereign may even employ all the riches of his subjects in the defence, and for the safety of the state, in virtue of the supreme command with which he is invested, as we shall hereafter shew. The nation then ought to endeavour to acquire those public and private riches, that are of such use to it: and this is a new reason for encouraging a commerce with other nations, which is the source from whence they flow,—and a new motive for the sovereign to keep a watchful eye over the different branches of foreign trade carried on by his subjects, in order that he may preserve and protect the profitable branches, and cut off those that occasion the exportation of gold and silver.

§183. Public revenues, and taxes.

It is requisite that the state should possess an income proportionate to its necessary expenditures. That income may be supplied by various means,—by lands reserved for that purpose, by contributions, taxes of different kinds, &c.—but of this subject we shall treat in another place.

§184. The nation ought not to increase its power by illegal means.

We have here summed up the principal ingredients that constitute that strength which a nation ought to augment and improve.—Can it be necessary to add the observation, that this desirable object is not to be pursued by any other methods than such as are just and innocent? A laudable end is not sufficient to sanctify the means; for these ought to be in their own nature lawful. The law of nature cannot contradict itself: if it forbids an action as unjust or dishonest in its own nature, it can never permit it for any purpose whatever. And therefore in those cases where that object, in itself so valuable and so praiseworthy, cannot be attained without employing unlawful means, it ought to be considered as unattainable, and consequently be relinquished. Thus we shall shew, in treating of the just causes of war, that a nation is not allowed to attack another with a view to aggrandise itself by subduing and giving law to the latter. This is just the same as if a private person should attempt to enrich himself by seizing his neighbour's property.

§185. Power is but relative.

The power of a nation is relative, and ought to be measured by that of its neighbours, or of all the nations from whom it has any thing to fear. The state is sufficiently powerful, when it is capable of causing itself to be respected, and of repelling whoever would attack it. It may be placed in this happy situation, either by keeping up its own strength equal or even superior to that of its neighbours,—or by preventing their rising to a predominant and formidable power. But we cannot shew here, in what cases, and by what means, a state may justly set bounds to the power of another: it is necessary first to explain the duties <91> of a nation towards others, in order to combine them afterwards with its duties towards itself. For the present we shall only observe that a nation, while it obeys the dictates of prudence and wise policy in this instance, ought never to lose sight of the maxims of justice.

CHAPTER XV

Of the Glory of a Nation.

The glory of a nation is intimately connected with its power, and indeed forms a considerable part of it. It is this brilliant advantage that procures it the esteem of other nations, and renders it respectable to its neighbours. A nation whose reputation is well established,—especially one whose glory is illustrious,—is courted by all sovereigns: they desire its friendship, and are afraid of offending it. Its friends, and those who wish to become so, favour its enterprises, and those who envy its prosperity are afraid to shew their ill-will. §186. Advantages of glory.

It is then of great advantage to a nation to establish its reputation and glory: hence this becomes one of the most important of the duties it owes to itself. True glory consists in the favourable opinion of men of wisdom and discernment: it is acquired by the virtues or good qualities of the head and the heart, and by great actions which are the fruits of those virtues. A nation may have a two-fold claim to it—first, by what it does in its national character, by the conduct of those who have the administration of its affairs, and are invested with its authority and government,—and, secondly, by the merit of the individuals of whom the nation is composed. §187. Duty of the nation.

How true glory is acquired.

A prince, a sovereign of whatever kind, being bound to exert every effort for the good of the nation, is doubtless obliged to extend its glory, §188. Duty of the prince.

as far as lies in his power. We have seen that his duty is to labour after the perfection of the state, and of the people who are subject to him: by that means he will make them merit a good reputation and glory. He ought always to have this object in view in every thing he undertakes, and in the use he makes of his power. Let him, in all his actions, display justice, moderation, and greatness of soul: and he will thus acquire for himself and his people a name respected by the universe, and not less useful than glorious. The glory of Henry IV.[66] saved France: in the deplorable state in which he found affairs, his virtues gave animation to the loyal part of his subjects, and encouraged foreign nations to lend him their assistance, and to enter into an alliance with him against the ambitious Spaniards. In his circumstances, a weak prince of little estimation would have been abandoned by all the world; people would have been afraid of being involved in his ruin. <92>

Besides the virtues which constitute the glory of princes as well as of private persons, there is a dignity and decorum that particularly belong to the supreme rank, and which a sovereign ought to observe with the greatest care. He cannot neglect them without degrading himself, and casting a stain upon the state. Every thing that emanates from the throne ought to bear the character of purity, nobleness, and greatness. What an idea do we conceive of a people, when we see their sovereign display in his public acts a meanness of sentiment, by which a private person would think himself disgraced! All the majesty of the nation resides in the person of the prince:—what then must become of it if he prostitutes it, or suffers it to be prostituted by those who speak and act in his name? The minister who puts into his master's mouth a language unworthy of him, deserves to be turned out of office with every mark of ignominy.

§189. Duty of the citizens.   The reputation of individuals is, by a common and natural mode of speaking and thinking, made to reflect on the whole nation. In general we attribute a virtue or a vice to a people, when that vice or that virtue is frequently observed among them. We say that a nation is warlike, when it produces a great number of brave warriors,—that it is learned, when there are many learned men among the citizens,—and that it excels in

66. King Henry IV of France, r. 1589–1610.

the arts, when it produces many able artists: on the other hand, we call it cowardly, lazy or stupid, when men of those characters are more numerous there than elsewhere. The citizens, being obliged to labour with all their might to promote the welfare and advantage of their country, not only owe to themselves the care of deserving a good reputation, but they also owe it to the nation, whose glory is so liable to be influenced by theirs. Bacon, Newton, Descartes, Leibnitz, and Bernouilli,[67] have each done honour to his native country, and essentially benefited it by the glory he acquired. Great ministers, and great generals,—an Oxenstiern,[68] a Turenne,[69] a Marlborough,[70] a Ruyter,[71]—serve their country in a double capacity, both by their actions, and by their glory. On the other hand, the fear of reflecting a disgrace on his country will furnish the good citizen with a new motive for abstaining from every dishonourable action. And the prince ought not to suffer his subjects to give themselves up to vices capable of bringing infamy on the nation, or even of simply tarnishing the brightness of its glory:—he has a right to suppress and to punish scandalous enormities, which do a real injury to the state.

The example of the Swiss is very capable of shewing how advantageous glory may prove to a nation. The high reputation they have acquired for their valour, and which they still gloriously support, has preserved them in peace for above two centuries, and rendered all the powers of Europe desirous of their assistance. Louis XI. while dauphin, was witness of the prodigies of valour they performed at the battle of St. Jaques,[72] near <93> Basle, and he immediately formed the design of closely attaching to his interest so intrepid a nation.* The twelve hundred

§190. Example of the Swiss.

---

* See *the Memoirs of Commines.*

67. Jacob Bernouilli, 1654–1705, Swiss mathematician and natural philosopher.

68. Axel Oxenstierna, 1588–1654, lord high chancellor of Sweden.

69. Henri de la Tour d'Auvergne, Vicomte de Turenne, 1611–75, military commander and marshal of France.

70. John Churchill, first duke of Marlborough, 1650–1712, military commander serving William of Orange and Queen Anne.

71. Michiel de Ruyter, 1607–76, victorious Dutch admiral in the Anglo-Dutch wars.

72. Louis XI of France, r. 1461–83; battle of St. Jacques, August 26, 1444.

gallant heroes, who on this occasion attacked an army of between fifty and sixty thousand veteran troops, first defeated the vanguard of the Armagnacs, which was eighteen thousand strong; afterwards rashly engaging the main body of the army, they perished almost to a man, without being able to complete their victory.* But besides their terrifying the enemy, and preserving Switzerland from a ruinous invasion, they rendered her essential service by the glory they acquired for her arms. A reputation for an inviolable fidelity is no less advantageous to that nation; and they have at all times been jealous of preserving it. The canton of Zug punished with death that unworthy soldier who betrayed the confidence of the duke of Milan by discovering that prince to the French, when, to escape them, he had disguised himself in the habit of the Swiss and placed himself in their ranks as they were marching out of Novara.†

§191.
Attacking the glory of a nation is doing her an injury.

Since the glory of a nation is a real and substantial advantage, she has a right to defend it, as well as her other advantages. He who attacks her glory does her an injury; and she has a right to exact of him, even by force of arms, a just reparation. We cannot then condemn those measures sometimes taken by sovereigns to support or avenge the dignity of their crown. They are equally just and necessary. If, when they do not proceed from too lofty pretensions, we attribute them to a vain pride, we only betray the grossest ignorance of the art of reigning, and despise one of the firmest supports of the greatness and safety of a state.

---

* Of this small army, "eleven hundred and fifty-eight were counted dead on the field, and thirty-two wounded. Twelve men only escaped, who were considered by their countrymen as cowards, that had preferred a life of shame to the honour of dying for their country." *History of the Helvetic Confederacy, by M. de Watteville, Vol.* I. *p.* 250.—Tschudi, p. 425.

† Vogel's Historical and Political Treatise of the Alliances between France and the Thirteen Cantons, pag. 75, 76.

CHAPTER XVI

Of the Protection sought by a Nation, and its voluntary Submission to a foreign Power.

When a nation is not capable of preserving herself from insult and op- §192. pression, she may procure the protection of a more powerful state. If Protection. she obtains this by only engaging to perform certain articles, as, to pay a tribute in return for the safety obtained,—to furnish her protector with troops,—and to embark in all his wars as a joint concern,—but still reserving to herself the right of administering her own government at pleasure,—it is a <94> simple treaty of protection, that does not at all derogate from her sovereignty, and differs not from the ordinary treaties of alliance otherwise than as it creates a difference in the dignity of the contracting parties.

But this matter is sometimes carried still farther: and although a na- §193. Volun-tion is under an obligation to preserve with the utmost care the liberty tary submis-sion of one and independence it inherits from nature,—yet, when it has not suffi- nation to cient strength of itself, and feels itself unable to resist its enemies, it may another. lawfully subject itself to a more powerful nation on certain conditions agreed to by both parties: and the compact or treaty of submission will thenceforward be the measure and rule of the rights of each. For since the people who enter into subjection resign a right which naturally belongs to them, and transfer it to the other nation, they are perfectly at liberty to annex what conditions they please to this transfer; and the other party, by accepting their submission on this footing, engages to observe religiously all the clauses of the treaty.

This submission may be varied to infinity, according to the will of §194. Several the contracting parties: it may either leave the inferior nation a part of kinds of submission. the sovereignty, restraining it only in certain respects,—or it may totally abolish it, so that the superior nation shall become the sovereign of the other,—or, finally, the lesser nation may be incorporated with the greater, in order thenceforward to form with it but one and the same state: and then the citizens of the former will have the same privileges as those with whom they are united. The Roman history furnishes examples of each of these three kinds of submission,—1. the allies of the Roman people, such as the inhabitants of Latium were for a long time, who, in several respects, depended on Rome, but, in all others, were governed according to their own laws, and by their own magistrates;—2. the countries reduced to Roman provinces, as Capua, whose inhabitants submitted absolutely to the Romans;*—3. the nations to which Rome granted the freedom of the city. In after times the emperors granted that privilege to all the nations subject to the empire, and thus transformed all their subjects into citizens.

§195. Right of the citizens when the nation submits to a foreign power.   In the case of a real subjection to a foreign power, the citizens who do not approve this change are not obliged to submit to it:—they ought to be allowed to sell their effects and retire elsewhere. For my having entered into a society does not oblige me to follow its fate, when it dissolves itself in order to submit to a foreign dominion. I submitted to the society as it then was, to live in that society as the member of a sovereign state, and not in another: I am bound to obey it, while it remains a political society: but when it divests itself of that quality in order to re-<95>ceive its laws from another state, it breaks the bond of union between its members, and releases them from their obligations.

§196. These compacts annulled by the failure of protection.   When a nation has placed itself under the protection of another that is more powerful, or has even entered into subjection to it with a view to receiving its protection,—if the latter does not effectually protect the other in case of need, it is manifest, that, by failing in its engagements, it loses all the rights it had acquired by the convention, and that the other, being disengaged from the obligation it had contracted, re-enters into the possession of all its rights, and recovers its independence, or its liberty. It is to be observed, that this takes place even in cases where the protector does not fail in his engagements through a want of good faith,

---

* Itaque populum Campanum, urbemque Capuam, agros, delubra deûm, divina humanaque omnia, in vestram, patres conscripti, populique Romani ditionem dedimus. [["Therefore we now place under your sway and jurisdiction, senators, and that of the Roman people, the people of Campania and the city of Capua, its fields, its sacred temples, all things human and divine."]] LIVY, book vii. c. 31. [[*Ab urbe condita*, VII, 31.]]

but merely through inability. For the weaker nation having submitted only for the sake of obtaining protection,—if the other proves unable to fulfil that essential condition, the compact is dissolved;—the weaker resumes its right, and may, if it thinks proper, have recourse to a more effectual protection.* Thus the dukes of Austria, who had acquired a right of protection, and in some sort a sovereignty over the city of Lucerne, being unwilling or unable to protect it effectually, that city concluded an alliance with the three first cantons; and the dukes having carried their complaint to the emperor, the inhabitants of Lucerne replied, "that they had used the natural right common to all men, by which every one is permitted to endeavour to procure his own safety when he is abandoned by those who are obliged to grant him assistance."†

The law is the same with respect to both the contracting parties: if the party protected do not fulfil their engagements with fidelity, the protector is discharged from his; he may afterwards refuse his protection, and declare the treaty broken, in case the situation of his affairs renders such a step advisable.

§197. Or by the infidelity of the party protected.

In virtue of the same principle which discharges one of the contracting parties when the other fails in his engagements, if the more powerful nation should assume a greater authority over the weaker one than the treaty of protection or submission allows, the latter may consider the treaty as broken, and provide for its safety according to its own discretion. If it were otherwise, the inferior nation would lose by a convention which it had only formed with a view to its safety; and if it were still bound by its engagements when its protector abuses them and openly violates his own, the treaty would, to the weaker party, prove a downright

§198. And by the encroachments of the protector.

---

* We speak here of a nation that has rendered itself subject to another, and not of one that has incorporated itself with another state, so as to constitute a part of it. The latter stands in the same predicament with all the other citizens. Of this case we shall treat in the following chapter.

† See [[Watteville]] *The History of Switzerland* [[the first edition is titled *Les historiens de la Suisse*]].—The United Provinces, having been obliged to rely wholly on their own efforts in defending themselves against Spain, would no longer acknowledge any dependence on the empire, from which they had received no assistance. GROTIUS, *Hist. of the Troubles in the Low Countries*, B. xvi. *p.* 627. [[Note added in 1773/1797 editions.]]

deception. However, as some people maintain, that, <96> in this case, the inferior nation has only the right of resistance and of imploring foreign aid,—and particularly as the weak cannot take too many precautions against the powerful, who are skilful in colouring over their enterprises,—the safest way is to insert in this kind of treaty a clause declaring it null and void whenever the superior power shall arrogate to itself any rights not expressly granted by the treaty.

§199. How the right of the nation protected is lost by its silence. But if the nation that is protected, or that has placed itself in subjection on certain conditions, does not resist the encroachments of that power from which it has sought support,—if it makes no opposition to them,—if it preserves a profound silence, when it might and ought to speak,—its patient acquiescence becomes in length of time a tacit consent that legitimates the rights of the usurper. There would be no stability in the affairs of men, and especially in those of nations, if long possession, accompanied by the silence of the persons concerned, did not produce a degree of right. But it must be observed, that silence, in order to shew tacit consent, ought to be voluntary. If the inferior nation proves that violence and fear prevented its giving testimonies of its opposition, nothing can be concluded from its silence, which therefore gives no right to the usurper.

CHAPTER XVII

How a Nation may separate itself from the State of which it is a Member, or renounce its Allegiance to its Sovereign when it is not protected.

§200. Difference between the present case and those in the preceding chapter. We have said that an independent nation, which, without becoming a member of another state, has voluntarily rendered itself dependent on or subject to it in order to obtain protection, is released from its engagements as soon as that protection fails, even though the failure happen through the inability of the protector. But we are not to conclude that it is precisely the same case with every nation that cannot obtain speedy and effectual protection from its natural sovereign or the state of which it is a member. The two cases are very different. In the former, a free nation becomes subject to another state,—not to partake of all the other's advantages, and form with it an absolute union of interests (for if the more powerful state were willing to confer so great a favour, the weaker one would be incorporated, not subjected),—but to obtain protection alone by the sacrifice of its liberty, without expecting any other return. When therefore the sole and indispensable condition of its subjection is (from what cause soever) not complied with, it is free from its engagements; and its duty towards itself obliges it to take fresh methods to provide for its own security. But the several members of one individual state, as they all equally participate in the advantages it procures, are bound uniformly to sup-<97>port it: they have entered into mutual engagements to continue united with each other, and to have on all occasions but one common cause. If those who are menaced or attacked might separate themselves from the others in order to avoid a present danger, every state would soon be dismembered and destroyed. It is then essentially necessary for the safety of society, and even for the welfare of all its members, that each part should with all its might resist a common enemy, rather than separate from the others; and this is consequently one of the necessary conditions of the political association. The natural subjects of a prince are bound to him without any other reserve than the observation of the fundamental laws;—it is their duty to remain faithful to him, as it is his, on the other hand, to take care to govern them well: both parties have but one common interest; the people and the prince together constitute but one complete whole, one and the same society. It is then an essential and necessary condition of the political society, that the subjects remain united to their prince, as far as in their power.

When, therefore, a city or a province is threatened or actually attacked, it must not, for the sake of escaping the danger, separate itself from the state of which it is a member, or abandon its natural prince, even when the state or the prince is unable to give it immediate and effectual assistance. Its duty, its political engagements, oblige it to make the greatest efforts, in order to maintain itself in its present state. If it is overcome by force,—necessity, that irresistible law, frees it from its former engagements, and gives it a right to treat with the conqueror, in order to obtain the best terms possible. If it must either submit to him or

§201. Duty of the members of a state, or subjects of a prince, who are in danger.

perish, who can doubt but that it may and even ought to prefer the former alternative? Modern usage is conformable to this decision:—a city submits to the enemy when it cannot expect safety from a vigorous resistance; it takes an oath of fidelity to him; and its sovereign lays the blame on fortune alone.

§202. Their right when they are abandoned.   The state is obliged to defend and preserve all its members (§17); and the prince owes the same assistance to his subjects. If, therefore, the state or the prince refuses or neglects to succour a body of people who are exposed to imminent danger, the latter, being thus abandoned, become perfectly free to provide for their own safety and preservation in whatever manner they find most convenient, without paying the least regard to those who, by abandoning them, have been the first to fail in their duty. The country of Zug, being attacked by the Swiss in 1352, sent for succour to the duke of Austria its sovereign; but that prince, being engaged in discourse concerning his hawks at the time when the deputies appeared before him, would scarcely condescend to hear them. Thus abandoned, the people of Zug entered into the Helvetic confederacy.* The city of Zurich <98> had been in the same situation the year before. Being attacked by a band of rebellious citizens who were supported by the neighbouring nobility and the house of Austria, it made application to the head of the empire: but Charles IV.[73] who was then emperor, declared to its deputies that he could not defend it;—upon which, Zurich secured its safety by an alliance with the Swiss.† The same reason has authorised the Swiss in general to separate themselves entirely from the empire, which never protected them in any emergency: they had not owned its authority for a long time before their independence was acknowledged by the emperor and the whole Germanic body, at the treaty of Westphalia.

* See Etterlin, Simler, and de Watteville.

† See the same historians, and Bullinger, Stumpf, Tschudi, and Stettler.

73. Bullinger discusses the events Vattel refers to at Zurich, including the role of Charles IV (r. 1355–78), in his famous Chronicle of Zurich ("Tigurinerchronik," pt. 1, bk. 8, chap. 5). Never published, the Chronicle was available only in several manuscript copies (see Zentralbibliothek Zürich, Ms. Car 43 and 44; for the relevant passage see Car 43, p. 371r–374v). Vattel may well have had access to the Chronicle, although there is no evidence to support such a claim.

CHAPTER XVIII

Of the Establishment of a Nation in a Country.

Hitherto we have considered the nation merely with respect to itself, without any regard to the country it possesses. Let us now see it established in a country, which becomes its own property and habitation. The earth belongs to mankind in general; destined by the creator to be their common habitation, and to supply them with food, they all possess a natural right to inhabit it, and to derive from it whatever is necessary for their subsistence, and suitable to their wants. But when the human race became extremely multiplied, the earth was no longer capable of furnishing spontaneously, and without culture, sufficient support for its inhabitants; neither could it have received proper cultivation from wandering tribes of men continuing to possess it in common. It therefore became necessary that those tribes should fix themselves somewhere, and appropriate to themselves portions of land, in order that they might, without being disturbed in their labour, or disappointed of the fruits of their industry, apply themselves to render those lands fertile, and thence derive their subsistence. Such must have been the origin of the rights of *property* and *dominion:* and it was a sufficient ground to justify their establishment. Since their introduction, the right which was common to all mankind is individually restricted to what each lawfully possesses. The country which a nation inhabits, whether that nation has emigrated thither in a body, or that the different families of which it consists were previously scattered over the country, and there uniting, formed themselves into a political society,—that country, I say, is the settlement of the nation, and it has a peculiar and exclusive right to it.

§203. Possession of a country by a nation.

This right comprehends two things: 1. The *domain,* by virtue of which the nation alone may use this country for the supply of its necessities, may dispose of it as it thinks proper, and <99> derive from it every advantage it is capable of yielding.—2. The *empire,* or the right of sovereign command, by which the nation directs and regulates at its pleasure every thing that passes in the country.

§204. Its right over the parts in its possession.

§205. Acquisition of the sovereignty in a vacant country.

When a nation takes possession of a country to which no prior owner can lay claim, it is considered as acquiring the *empire* or sovereignty of it, at the same time with the *domain*. For since the nation is free and independent, it can have no intention, in settling in a country, to leave to others the right of command, or any of those rights that constitute sovereignty. The whole space over which a nation extends its government, becomes the seat of its jurisdiction, and is called its *territory*.

§206. Another manner of acquiring the empire in a free country.

If a number of free families, scattered over an independent country, come to unite for the purpose of forming a nation or state, they all together acquire the sovereignty over the whole country they inhabit; for they were previously in possession of the domain,—a proportional share of it belonging to each individual family: and since they are willing to form together a political society, and establish a public authority which every member of the society shall be bound to obey, it is evidently their intention to attribute to that public authority the right of command over the whole country.

§207. How a nation appropriates to itself a desert country.

All mankind have an equal right to things that have not yet fallen into the possession of any one; and those things belong to the person who first takes possession of them. When therefore a nation finds a country uninhabited and without an owner, it may lawfully take possession of it: and after it has sufficiently made known its will in this respect, it cannot be deprived of it by another nation. Thus navigators going on voyages of discovery, furnished with a commission from their sovereign, and meeting with islands or other lands in a desert state, have taken possession of them in the name of their nation: and this title has been usually respected, provided it was soon after followed by a real possession.

§208. A question on this subject.

But it is questioned whether a nation can, by the bare act of taking possession, appropriate to itself countries which it does not really occupy, and thus engross a much greater extent of territory than it is able to people or cultivate. It is not difficult to determine, that such a pretension would be an absolute infringement of the natural rights of men, and repugnant to the views of nature, which, having destined the whole earth to supply the wants of mankind in general, gives no nation a right to appropriate to itself a country, except for the purpose of making use of it, and not of hindering others from deriving advantage from it. The law of nations will therefore not acknowledge the property and sovereignty of a nation over any uninhabited countries, except those of which it has really taken actual possession, in which it has formed settlements, or of which it makes actual use. In effect, when navigators have met with desert countries in which those of other nations had, in their transient visits, erected <100> some monument to shew their having taken possession of them, they have paid as little regard to that empty ceremony, as to the regulation of the popes, who divided a great part of the world between the crowns of Castile and Portugal.*

---

* Those decrees being of a very singular nature, and hardly any where to be found but in very scarce books, the reader will not be displeased with seeing here an extract of them.

The bull of Alexander VI. by which he gives to Ferdinand and Isabella, king and queen of Castile and Arragon, the New World, discovered by Christopher Columbus.

"Motu proprio," (says the pope) "non ad vestram, vel alterius pro vobis super hoc nobis oblatae petitionis instantiam, sed de nostra mera liberalitate, & ex certa scientia, ac de apostolicae potestatis plenitudine, omnes insulas & terras firmas, inventas, & inveniendas, detectas & detegendas versus occidentem & meridiem," (drawing a line from one pole to the other, at an hundred leagues to the west of the Azores) "auctoritate omnipotentis Dei nobis in beato Petro concessa, ac vicariatus Jesu Christi, qua fungimur in terris, cum omnibus illarum dominiis, civitatibus, &c. vobis, haeredibusque & successoribus vestris, Castellae & Legionis regibus, in perpetuum tenore praesentium donamus, concedimus, assignamus, vosque, & haeredes ac successores praefatos, illorum dominos, cum plena libera & omni moda potestate, auctoritate & jurisdictione, facimus, constituimus, & deputamus." [["We, of our own accord, not at your instance nor the request of anyone else in your regard, but of our own sole largesse and certain knowledge and out of the fullness of our apostolic power, by the authority of Almighty God conferred upon us in blessed Peter and of the vicarship of Jesus Christ, which we hold on earth, do by tenor of these presents, should any of said islands have been found by your envoys and captains, give, grant, and assign to you and your heirs and successors, kings of Castile and Leon, forever, together with all their dominions, cities, camps, places, and villages, and all rights, jurisdictions, and appurtenances, all islands and mainlands found and to be found, discovered and to be discovered towards the west and south." Alexander VI, *In caetera,* May 4, 1493.]] The pope excepts only what might be in the possession of some other Christian prince before the year 1493,—as if he had a greater right to give what belonged to nobody, and especially what was possessed by the American nations.— He adds: "Ac quibuscunque personis cujuscunque dignitatis, etiam imperialis & regalis, status, gradus, ordinis, vel conditionis, sub excommunicationis latae sententiae poena, quam eo ipso, si contra fecerint, incurrant, districtius inhibemus ne ad insulas

§209. Whether it be lawful to possess a part of a country inhabited only by a few wandering tribes.

There is another celebrated question, to which the discovery of the new world has principally given rise. It is asked whether a nation may lawfully take possession of some part of a vast country, in which there are none but erratic nations whose scanty population is incapable of occupying the whole? We have already observed (§81), in establishing the obligation to cultivate the earth, that those nations cannot exclusively appropriate to themselves more land than they have occasion for, or more than they are able to settle and cultivate. Their unsettled habitation in those immense regions cannot be accounted a true and legal possession; and the people of Europe, too closely pent up at home, finding land of which the savages stood in no particular need, and of which they made no actual and constant use, were lawfully entitled to take possession of it, and settle it with colonies. The earth, as we have already observed, belongs to mankind in general, and was designed to furnish them with subsistence: if each nation had from the beginning resolved to appropriate to itself a vast country, that the people might live only by hunting, fishing, and wild fruits, our globe would not be sufficient to maintain a tenth part of its present inhabitants. < 101 > We do not therefore deviate from the views of nature in confining the Indians within narrower limits. However, we cannot help praising the moderation of the English puritans who first settled in New England; who, notwith-

---

& terras firmas inventas & inveniendas, detectas & detegendas, versus occidentem & meridiem . . . pro mercibus habendis, vel quavis alia de causa, accedere praesumant absque vestra ac haeredum & successorum vestrorum praedictorum licentia speciali, &c. Datum Romae apud S. Petrum anno 1493. IV. nonas Maji, Pontific. nostri anno primo." [["Furthermore, under penalty of excommunication *late sententie* to be incurred *ipso facto,* should anyone thus contravene, we strictly forbid all persons of whatsoever rank, even imperial and royal, or of whatsoever estate, degree, order, or condition, to dare, without your special permit or that of your aforesaid heirs and successors, to go for the purpose of trade or any other reason to the islands or mainlands, found and to be found, discovered and to be discovered, towards the west and south."]] *Leibnitii Codex Juris Gent. Diplomat. Diplom.* 203.

See *ibid.* (*Diplom.* 165.) the bull by which pope Nicholas V. gave to Alphonso, king of Portugal, and to the Infant Henry, the sovereignty of Guinea, and the power of subduing the barbarous nations of those countries, forbidding any other to visit that country, without the permission of Portugal. This act is dated Rome on the 8th of January, 1454.

standing their being furnished with a charter from their sovereign, purchased of the Indians the land of which they intended to take possession.* This laudable example was followed by William Penn[74] and the
colony of quakers that he conducted to Pennsylvania.

When a nation takes possession of a distant country, and settles a
colony there, that country, though separated from the principal establishment, or mother-country, naturally becomes a part of the state,
equally with its ancient possessions. Whenever therefore the political
laws, or treaties, make no distinction between them, every thing said of
the territory of a nation, must also extend to its colonies.

§210.
Colonies.

CHAPTER XIX

Of our Native Country, and several Things
that relate to it.

The whole of the countries possessed by a nation and subject to its laws,
forms, as we have already said, its territory, and is the common country
of all the individuals of the nation. We have been obliged to anticipate
the definition of the term, *native country* (§122), because our subject led
us to treat of the love of our country,—a virtue so excellent and so necessary in a state. Supposing then this definition already known, it remains that we should explain several things that have a relation to this
subject, and answer the questions that naturally arise from it.

§211. What is
our country.

The citizens are the members of the civil society: bound to this society
by certain duties, and subject to its authority, they equally participate in
its advantages. The natives, or natural-born citizens, are those born in
the country, of parents who are citizens. As the society cannot exist and
perpetuate itself otherwise than by the children of the citizens, those
children naturally follow the condition of their fathers, and succeed to

§212. Citizens
and natives.

* History of the English Colonies in North America. [[William Burke, *An Account
of the European Settlements in the Americas.*]]
74. William Penn, 1644–1718.

all their rights. The society is supposed to desire this, in consequence of what it owes to its own preservation; and it is presumed, as matter of course, that each citizen, on entering into society, reserves to his children the right of becoming members of it. The country of the fathers is therefore that of the children; and these become true citizens merely by their tacit consent. We shall soon see, whether, on their coming to the years of discretion, they may renounce their right, and what they owe to the society in which they were born. I say, that, in order to be of the country, it is necessary that a person be born of a father who is a citizen; for if he is born there of a foreigner, it will be only the place of his birth, and not his country. <102>

§213. Inhabitants.

The inhabitants, as distinguished from citizens, are foreigners, who are permitted to settle and stay in the country. Bound to the society by their residence, they are subject to the laws of the state, while they reside in it; and they are obliged to defend it, because it grants them protection, though they do not participate in all the rights of citizens. They enjoy only the advantages which the law or custom gives them. The *perpetual inhabitants* are those who have received the right of perpetual residence. These are a kind of citizens of an inferior order, and are united to the society, without participating in all its advantages. Their children follow the condition of their fathers; and as the state has given to these the right of perpetual residence, their right passes to their posterity.

§214. Naturalisation.

A nation, or the sovereign who represents it, may grant to a foreigner the quality of citizen, by admitting him into the body of the political society. This is called *naturalisation*. There are some states in which the sovereign cannot grant to a foreigner all the rights of citizens,—for example, that of holding public offices,—and where, consequently, he has the power of granting only an imperfect naturalisation. It is here a regulation of the fundamental law, which limits the power of the prince. In other states, as in England and Poland, the prince cannot naturalise a single person, without the concurrence of the nation represented by its deputies. Finally, there are states, as, for instance, England, where the single circumstance of being born in the country naturalises the children of a foreigner.

It is asked, whether the children born of citizens in a foreign country are citizens? The laws have decided this question in several countries, and their regulations must be followed. By the law of nature alone, children follow the condition of their fathers, and enter into all their rights (§212); the place of birth produces no change in this particular, and cannot of itself furnish any reason for taking from a child what nature has given him; I say "of itself," for civil or political laws may, for particular reasons, ordain otherwise. But I suppose that the father has not entirely quitted his country in order to settle elsewhere. If he has fixed his abode in a foreign country, he is become a member of another society, at least as a perpetual inhabitant; and his children will be members of it also.

§215. Children of citizens, born in a foreign country.

As to children born at sea, if they are born in those parts of it that are possessed by their nation, they are born in the country: if it is on the open sea, there is no reason to make a distinction between them and those who are born in the country; for, naturally, it is our extraction, not the place of our birth, that gives us rights: and if the children are born in a vessel belonging to the nation, they may be reputed born in its territories; for it is natural to consider the vessels of a nation as parts of its territory, especially when they sail upon a free sea, since the state retains its jurisdiction over those vessels. And as, according to the commonly received custom, this jurisdiction is <103> preserved over the vessels, even in parts of the sea subject to a foreign dominion, all the children born in the vessels of a nation are considered as born in its territory. For the same reason, those born in a foreign vessel are reputed born in a foreign country, unless their birth took place in a port belonging to their own nation: for the port is more particularly a part of the territory; and the mother, though at that moment on board a foreign vessel, is not on that account out of the country. I suppose that she and her husband have not quitted their native country to settle elsewhere.

§216. Children born at sea.

For the same reasons also, children born out of the country in the armies of the state, or in the house of its minister at a foreign court, are reputed born in the country; for a citizen, who is absent with his family on the service of the state, but still dependent on it, and subject to its jurisdiction, cannot be considered as having quitted its territory.

§217. Children born in the armies of the state, or in the house of its minister at a foreign court.

§218.
Settlement.

Settlement is a fixed residence in any place with an intention of always staying there. A man does not then establish his settlement in any place, unless he makes sufficiently known his intention of fixing there, either tacitly, or by an express declaration. However, this declaration is no reason why, if he afterwards changes his mind, he may not transfer his settlement elsewhere. In this sense, a person who stops at a place upon business, even though he stay a long time, has only a simple habitation there, but has no settlement. Thus the envoy of a foreign prince has not his settlement at the court where he resides.

The *natural* or *original settlement* is that which we acquire by birth, in the place where our father has his; and we are considered as retaining it, till we have abandoned it, in order to chuse another. The *acquired settlement (adscititium)* is that where we settle by our own choice.

§219.
Vagrants.

Vagrants are people who have no settlement. Consequently those born of vagrant parents have no country, since a man's country is the place where, at the time of his birth, his parents had their settlement (§122), or it is the state of which his father was then a member;—which comes to the same point: for to settle for ever in a nation, is to become a member of it, at least as a perpetual inhabitant, if not with all the privileges of a citizen. We may, however, consider the country of a vagrant to be that of his child, while that vagrant is considered as not having absolutely renounced his natural or original settlement.

§220. Whether a person may quit his country.

Many distinctions will be necessary in order to give a complete solution to the celebrated question, whether a man may quit his country or the society of which he is a member. 1. The children are bound by natural ties to the society in which they were born: they are under an obligation to shew themselves grateful for the protection it has afforded to their fathers, and are in a great measure indebted to it for their birth and education. They ought therefore to love it, as we have already shewn (§122),—to express a just gratitude to it, and requite its services as far as possible by serving it in turn. We have observed above (§212), that they have a right to enter <104> into the society of which their fathers were members. But every man is born free; and the son of a citizen, when come to the years of discretion, may examine whether it be convenient for him to join the society for which he was destined by his birth. If he does not find it advantageous to remain in it, he is at liberty to quit it on making it a compensation for what it has done in his favour,* and preserving, as far as his new engagements will allow him, the sentiments of love and gratitude he owes it. A man's obligations to his natural country may, however, change, lessen, or entirely vanish, according as he shall have quitted it lawfully, and with good reason, in order to choose another, or has been banished from it deservedly or unjustly, in due form of law, or by violence.

2. As soon as the son of a citizen attains the age of manhood, and acts as a citizen, he tacitly assumes that character; his obligations, like those of others who expressly and formally enter into engagements with society, become stronger and more extensive: but the case is very different with respect to him of whom we have been speaking. When a society has not been formed for a determinate time, it is allowable to quit it, when that separation can take place without detriment to the society. A citizen may therefore quit the state of which he is a member, provided it be not in such a conjuncture when he cannot abandon it without doing it a visible injury. But we must here draw a distinction between what may in strict justice be done, and what is honourable and conformable to every duty,—in a word, between the *internal* and the *external* obligation. Every man has a right to quit his country, in order to settle in any other, when by that step he does not endanger the welfare of his country. But a good citizen will never determine on such a step without necessity, or without very strong reasons. It is taking a dishonourable advantage of our liberty, to quit our associates upon slight pretences, after having derived considerable advantages from them: and this is the case of every citizen with respect to his country.

3. As to those who have the cowardice to abandon their country in a time of danger, and seek to secure themselves instead of defending it,— they manifestly violate the social compact, by which all the contracting parties engaged to defend themselves in an united body, and in concert:

---

* This is the foundation of the tax paid on quitting a country, called, in Latin, *census emigrationis*.

they are infamous deserters whom the state has a right to punish severely.* <105>

§221. How a
person may
absent himself
for a time.

In a time of peace and tranquillity, when the country has no actual
need of all her children, the very welfare of the state, and that of the
citizens, requires that every individual be at liberty to travel on business,
provided that he be always ready to return, whenever the public interest
recalls him. It is not presumed that any man has bound himself to the
society of which he is a member, by an engagement never to leave the
country when the interest of his affairs requires it, and when he can
absent himself without injury to his country.

§222. Varia-
tion of the
political laws
in this respect.

These must be
obeyed.

The political laws of nations vary greatly in this respect. In some nations, it is at all times, except in case of actual war, allowed to every citizen
to absent himself, and even to quit the country altogether, whenever he
thinks proper, without alleging any reason for it. This liberty, contrary
in its own nature to the welfare and safety of society, can no where be
tolerated but in a country destitute of resources and incapable of supplying the wants of its inhabitants. In such a country there can only be
an imperfect society; for civil society ought to be capable of enabling all
its members to procure by their labour and industry all the necessaries
of life:—unless it effects this, it has no right to require them to devote
themselves entirely to it. In some other states, every citizen is left at liberty to travel abroad on business, but not to quit his country altogether,
without the express permission of the sovereign. Finally, there are states
where the rigour of the government will not permit any one whatsoever
to go out of the country, without passports in form, which are even not

---

* Charles XII. [[of Sweden, r. 1697–1718]] condemned to death and executed general Patkul, a native of Livonia, whom he had made prisoner in an engagement with
the Saxons. But the sentence and execution were a violation of the laws of justice.
Patkul, it is true, had been born a subject of the king of Sweden: but he had quitted
his native country at the age of twelve years, and, having been promoted in the army
of Saxony, had, with the permission of his former sovereign, sold the property he
possessed in Livonia. He had therefore quitted his own country, to chuse another (as
every free citizen is at liberty to do, except, as we have observed above, at a critical
moment when the circumstances of his country require the aid of all her sons)—and
the King of Sweden, by permitting him to sell his property, had consented to his
emigration. [[Note added in 1773/1797 editions.]]

granted without great difficulty. In all these cases it is necessary to conform to the laws, when they are made by a lawful authority. But in the
last-mentioned case, the sovereign abuses his power, and reduces his subjects to an insupportable slavery, if he refuses them permission to travel
for their own advantage, when he might grant it to them without inconvenience, and without danger to the state. Nay it will presently appear, that, on certain occasions, he cannot, under any pretext, detain
persons who wish to quit the country with the intention of abandoning
it for ever.

There are cases in which a citizen has an absolute right to renounce §223. Cases in
his country, and abandon it entirely,—a right, founded on reasons de- which a citizen
has a right
rived from the very nature of the social compact.—1. If the citizen can- to quit his
not procure subsistence in his own country, it is undoubtedly lawful for country.
him to seek it elsewhere. For political or civil society being entered into
only with a view of facilitating to each of its members the means of
supporting himself, and of living in happiness and safety, it would be
absurd to pretend that a member, whom it cannot furnish with such
things as are most necessary, has not a right to leave it.

2. If the body of the society, or he who represents it, absolutely fail
to discharge their obligations towards a citizen, the latter may withdraw
himself. For if one of the contracting parties does not observe his engagements, the other is no longer bound to fulfil his; for the contract is
reciprocal between the society and < 106 > its members. It is on the same
principle also that the society may expel a member who violates its laws.

3. If the major part of the nation, or the sovereign who represents it,
attempt to enact laws relative to matters in which the social compact
cannot oblige every citizen to submission, those who are averse to these
laws have a right to quit the society, and go settle elsewhere. For instance,
if the sovereign, or the greater part of the nation, will allow but one
religion in the state, those who believe and profess another religion have
a right to withdraw, and to take with them their families and effects. For
they cannot be supposed to have subjected themselves to the authority
of men, in affairs of conscience;* and if the society suffers and is weak-

* See, above, the chapter on religion.

ened by their departure, the blame must be imputed to the intolerant party: for it is they who fail in their observance of the social compact,— it is they who violate it, and force the others to a separation. We have elsewhere touched upon some other instances of this third case,—that of a popular state wishing to have a sovereign (§33),—and that of an independent nation taking the resolution to submit to a foreign power (§195).

§224. Emigrants. Those who quit their country for any lawful reason, with a design to settle elsewhere, are called *emigrants,* and take their families and property with them.

§225. Sources of their right. Their right to emigrate may arise from several sources. 1. In the cases we have just mentioned (§223), it is a natural right, which is certainly reserved to each individual in the very compact itself by which civil society was formed.

2. The liberty of emigration may, in certain cases, be secured to the citizens by a fundamental law of the state. The citizens of Neufchatel and Valangin in Switzerland may quit the country and carry off their effects at their own pleasure, without even paying any duties.

3. It may be voluntarily granted them by the sovereign.

4. Finally, this right may be derived from some treaty made with a foreign power, by which a sovereign has promised to leave full liberty to those of his subjects, who, for a certain reason, on account of religion for instance, desire to transplant themselves into the territories of that power. There are such treaties between the German princes, particularly for cases in which religion is concerned. In Switzerland likewise, a citizen of Bern who wishes to emigrate to Fribourg and there profess the religion of the place, and reciprocally a citizen of Fribourg who, for a similar reason, is desirous of removing to Bern, has a right to quit his native country, and carry off with him all his property.

It appears from several passages in history, particularly the history of Switzerland and the neighbouring countries, that the law of nations, established there by custom some ages back, did not permit a state to receive the subjects of another state into the number of its citizens. This vicious custom had no other <107> foundation than the slavery to which the people were then reduced. A prince, a lord, ranked his subjects under the head of his private property: he calculated their number, as he did that of his flocks; and, to the disgrace of human nature, this strange abuse is not yet every where eradicated.

If the sovereign attempts to molest those who have a right to emigrate, he does them an injury; and the injured individuals may lawfully implore the protection of the power who is willing to receive them. Thus we have seen Frederic William,[75] king of Prussia, grant his protection to the emigrant protestants of Saltzburgh.

§226. If the sovereign infringes their right, he injures them.

The name of *supplicants* is given to all fugitives who implore the protection of a sovereign against the nation or prince they have quitted. We cannot solidly establish what the law of nations determines with respect to them, until we have treated of the duties of one nation towards others.

§227. Supplicants.

Finally, *exile* is another manner of leaving our country. An *exile* is a man driven from the place of his settlement, or constrained to quit it, but without a mark of infamy. Banishment is a similar expulsion, with a mark of infamy annexed.* Both may be for a limited time, or for ever. If an exile or banished man had his settlement in his own country, he is exiled or banished from his country. It is however proper to observe that common usage applies also the terms, exile and banishment, to the expulsion of a foreigner who is driven from a country where he had no settlement, and to which he is, either for a limited time or for ever, prohibited to return.

§228. Exile and banishment.

As a man may be deprived of any right whatsoever by way of punishment,—exile, which deprives him of the right of dwelling in a certain place, may be inflicted as a punishment: banishment is always one; for a mark of infamy cannot be set on any one, but with the view of punishing him for a fault, either real or pretended.

---

* The common acceptation of these two terms is not repugnant to our application of them. The French academy says, *"Banishment* is only applied to condemnations in due course of law,—*Exile* is only an absence caused by some disgrace at court."— The reason is plain;—such a condemnation from the tribunal of justice entails infamy on the emigrant; whereas a disgrace at court does not usually involve the same consequence.

75. Frederic William I, r. 1713–40.

When the society has excluded one of its members by a perpetual banishment, he is only banished from the lands of that society, and it cannot hinder him from living wherever else he pleases; for, after having driven him out, it can no longer claim any authority over him. The contrary, however, may take place by particular conventions between two or more states. Thus every member of the Helvetic confederacy may banish its own subjects out of the territories of Switzerland in general; and in this case the banished person will not be allowed to live in any of the cantons, or in the territories of their allies.

Exile is divided into *voluntary* and *involuntary*. It is voluntary, when a man quits his settlement, to escape some punish-<108>ment, or to avoid some calamity,—and involuntary, when it is the effect of a superior order.

Sometimes a particular place is appointed, where the exiled person is to remain during his exile; or a certain space is particularised, which he is forbid to enter. These various circumstances and modifications depend on him who has the power of sending into exile.

§229. The exile and banished man have a right to live somewhere.

A man, by being exiled or banished, does not forfeit the human character, nor consequently his right to dwell somewhere on earth. He derives this right from nature, or rather from its author, who has destined the earth for the habitation of mankind; and the introduction of property cannot have impaired the right which every man has to the use of such things as are absolutely necessary,—a right which he brings with him into the world at the moment of his birth.

§230. Nature of this right.

But though this right is necessary and perfect in the general view of it, we must not forget that it is but imperfect with respect to each particular country. For, on the other hand, every nation has a right to refuse admitting a foreigner into her territory, when he cannot enter it without exposing the nation to evident danger, or doing her a manifest injury. What she owes to herself, the care of her own safety, gives her this right; and in virtue of her natural liberty, it belongs to the nation to judge, whether her circumstances will or will not justify the admission of that foreigner (Prelim. §16). He cannot then settle by a full right, and as he pleases, in the place he has chosen, but must ask permission of the chief of the place; and if it is refused, it is his duty to submit.

However, as property could not be introduced to the prejudice of the right acquired by every human creature, of not being absolutely deprived of such things as are necessary,—no nation can, without good reasons, refuse even a perpetual residence to a man driven from his country. But if particular and substantial reasons prevent her from affording him an asylum, this man has no longer any right to demand it,—because, in such a case, the country inhabited by the nation cannot, at the same time, serve for her own use, and that of this foreigner. Now, supposing even that things are still in common, nobody can arrogate to himself the use of a thing which actually serves to supply the wants of another. Thus a nation, whose lands are scarcely sufficient to supply the wants of the citizens, is not obliged to receive into its territories a company of fugitives or exiles. Thus it ought even absolutely to reject them, if they are infected with a contagious disease. Thus also it has a right to send them elsewhere, if it has just cause to fear that they will corrupt the manners of the citizens, that they will create religious disturbances, or occasion any other disorder, contrary to the public safety. In a word, it has a right, and is even obliged, to follow, in this respect, the suggestions of prudence. But this prudence should be free from unnecessary suspicion and jealousy;—it should not be carried so far as to <109> refuse a retreat to the unfortunate, for slight reasons, and on groundless and frivolous fears. The means of tempering it will be never to lose sight of that charity and commiseration which are due to the unhappy. We must not suppress those feelings even for those who have fallen into misfortune through their own fault. For we ought to hate the crime, but love the man, since all mankind ought to love each other.

§231. Duty of nations towards them.

If an exile or banished man has been driven from his country for any crime, it does not belong to the nation in which he has taken refuge, to punish him for that fault committed in a foreign country. For nature does not give to men or to nations any right to inflict punishment, except for their own defence and safety (§169); whence it follows, that we cannot punish any but those by whom we have been injured.

§232. A nation cannot punish them for faults committed out of its territories,

But this very reason shews, that, although the justice of each nation ought in general to be confined to the punishment of crimes committed in its own territories, we ought to except from this rule those villains,

§233. except such as affect the common safety of mankind.

who, by the nature and habitual frequency of their crimes, violate all
public security, and declare themselves the enemies of the human race.
Poisoners, assassins, and incendiaries by profession, may be extermi-
nated wherever they are seized; for they attack and injure all nations, by
trampling under foot the foundations of their common safety. Thus pirates are sent to the gibbet by the first into whose hands they fall. If the
sovereign of the country where crimes of that nature have been committed, reclaims the perpetrators of them in order to bring them to punishment, they ought to be surrendered to him, as being the person who
is principally interested in punishing them in an exemplary manner. And
as it is proper to have criminals regularly convicted by a trial in due form
of law, this is a second reason for delivering up malefactors of that class
to the states where their crimes have been committed.

CHAPTER XX

Of public, common, and private Property.

§234. What
the Romans
called *res
communes.*

Let us now see what is the nature of the different things contained in
the country possessed by a nation, and endeavour to establish the general
principles of the law by which they are regulated. This subject is treated
by civilians under the title *de rerum divisione.* There are things which in
their own nature cannot be possessed; there are others, of which nobody
claims the property, and which remain common, as in their primitive
state, when a nation takes possession of a country: the Roman lawyers
called these things *res communes,* things common: such were, with them,
the air, the running water, the sea, the fish, and wild beasts.

§235. Aggre-
gate wealth of
a nation, and
its divisions.

Every thing susceptible of property is considered as belonging to the
nation that possesses the country, and as forming the aggre-<110>gate
mass of its wealth. But the nation does not possess all those things in
the same manner. Those not divided between particular communities,
or among the individuals of a nation, are called *public property.* Some
are reserved for the necessities of the state, and form the demesne of the

crown, or of the republic: others remain common to all the citizens, who take advantage of them, each according to his necessities, or according to the laws which regulate their use; and these are called *common property.*—There are others that belong to some body or community, termed *joint property, res universitatis;* and these are, with respect to this body in particular, what the public property is with respect to the whole nation. As the nation may be considered as a great community, we may indifferently give the name of *common property* to those things that belong to it in common, in such a manner that all the citizens may make use of them, and to those that are possessed in the same manner by a body or community: the same rules hold good with respect to both.—Finally, the property possessed by individuals is termed *private property, res singulorum.*

When a nation in a body takes possession of a country, every thing that is not divided among its members remains common to the whole nation, and is called *public property.* There is a second way whereby a nation, and, in general, every community, may acquire possessions, viz. by the will of whosoever thinks proper to convey to it, under any title whatsoever, the domain or property of what he possesses.

§236. Two ways of acquiring public property.

As soon as the nation commits the reins of government to the hands of a prince, it is considered as committing to him, at the same time, the means of governing. Since therefore the income of the public property, of the domain of the state, is destined for the expenses of government, it is naturally at the prince's disposal, and ought always to be considered in this light, unless the nation has, in express terms, excepted it in conferring the supreme authority, and has provided in some other manner for its disposal, and for the necessary expenses of the state, and the support of the prince's person and household. Whenever therefore the prince is purely and simply invested with the sovereign authority, it includes a full discretional power to dispose of the public revenues. The duty of the sovereign indeed obliges him to apply those revenues only to the necessities of the state; but he alone is to determine the proper application of them, and is not accountable for them to any person.

§237. The revenues of the public property are naturally at the sovereign's disposal.

§238. The
nation may
grant him
the use and
property of
its common
possessions,

The nation may invest the superior with the sole use of its common possessions, and thus add them to the domain of the state. It may even cede the property of them to him. But this cession of the use or property requires an express act of the proprietor, which is the nation. It is difficult to found it on a tacit consent, because fear too often hinders the subjects from protesting against the unjust encroachments of the sovereign.

§239. or allow
him the do-
main, and
reserve to
itself the use
of them.

The people may even allow the superior the domain of the things they possess in common, and reserve to themselves the < III > use of them in the whole or in part. Thus the domain of a river, for instance, may be ceded to the prince, while the people reserve to themselves the use of it for navigation, fishing, the watering of cattle, &c. They may also allow the prince the sole right of fishing, &c. in that river. In a word, the people may cede to the superior whatever right they please over the common possessions of the nation; but all those particular rights do not naturally and of themselves flow from the sovereignty.

§240. Taxes.

If the income of the public property, or of the domain, is not sufficient for the public wants, the state supplies the deficiency by taxes. These ought to be regulated in such a manner, that all the citizens may pay their quota in proportion to their abilities, and the advantages they reap from the society. All the members of civil society being equally obliged to contribute, according to their abilities, to its advantage and safety,—they cannot refuse to furnish the subsidies necessary to its preservation, when they are demanded by lawful authority.

§241. The
nation may
reserve to itself
the right of
imposing
them.

Many nations have been unwilling to commit to the prince a trust of so delicate a nature, or to grant him a power that he may so easily abuse. In establishing a domain for the support of the sovereign and the ordinary expenses of the state, they have reserved to themselves the right of providing, by themselves or by their representatives, for extraordinary wants, in imposing taxes payable by all the inhabitants. In England, the king lays the necessities of the state before the parliament; that body, composed of the representatives of the nation, deliberates, and, with the concurrence of the king, determines the sum to be raised, and the manner of raising it. And of the use the king makes of the money thus raised, that same body oblige him to render them an account.

In other states where the sovereign possesses the full and absolute authority, it is he alone that imposes taxes, regulates the manner of raising them, and makes use of them as he thinks proper, without giving an account to any body. The French king at present enjoys this authority, with the simple formality of causing his edicts to be registered by the parliament; and that body has a right to make humble remonstrances, if it sees any inconveniences attending the imposition ordered by the prince:—a wise establishment for causing truth and the cries of the people to reach the ears of the sovereign, and for setting some bounds to his extravagance, or to the avidity of the ministers and persons concerned in the revenue.* <112>

§242. Of the sovereign who has this power.

The prince who is invested with the power of taxing his people ought by no means to consider the money thus raised as his own property. He ought never to lose sight of the end for which this power was granted

§243. Duties of the prince with respect to taxes.

---

* Too great attention cannot be used in watching the imposition of taxes, which, once introduced, not only continue, but are so easily multiplied.—Alphonso VIII. king of Castile [[r. 1158–1214]], besieging a city belonging to the Moors (Concham urbem in Celtiberis) [[the city of Concha (now Cuenca) in Celtiberia (central Spain)]], and being in want of money, applied to the states of his kingdom for permission to impose on every free inhabitant a capitation-tax of five golden maravedis. But Peter, count de Lara, vigorously opposed the measure, "contractaque nobilium manu, ex conventu discedit, armis tueri paratus partam armis et virtute a majoribus immunitatem, neque passurum affirmans nobilitatis opprimendae atque novis vectigalibus vexandae ab eo aditu initium fieri; Mauros opprimere non esse tanti, ut graviori servitute rempublicam implicari sinant. Rex, periculo permotus, ab ea cogitatione desistit. Pertrum nobiles, consilio communicato, quotannis convivio excipere decreverunt, ipsum et posteros,—navatae operae mercedem, rei gestae bonae posteritati monumentum, documentumque ne quavis occasione jus libertatis imminui patiantur." [[And having gathered the group of noblemen, he leaves the assembly, ready to defend with arms and bravery the immunity obtained by their predecessors, and affirming that he was not going to tolerate through this opportunity the beginning of the oppression of the nobility and its harassment with new taxes, and [affirming] that oppressing the Moors was not so expensive for them to allow the commonwealth to be entangled in a more degrading servitude. The king, moved by the danger, desisted from that intention. Once this decision had been communicated, the noblemen decided to celebrate Peter every year in a banquet, him and his successors, as a reward for a zealous act and a reminder and testimony of a good work, so that on no occasion would they allow the right to freedom [ius libertatis] to be diminished (trans. Eds.).]] MARIANA. [[Juan de Mariana, De rege et regis institutione.]] [[Note added in 1773/ 1797 editions.]]

him: the nation was willing to enable him to provide, as it should seem best to his wisdom, for the necessities of the state. If he diverts this money to other uses,—if he consumes it in idle luxury, to gratify his pleasures, to satiate the avarice of his mistresses and favourites,—we hesitate not to declare to those sovereigns who are still capable of listening to the voice of truth, that such a one is not less guilty, nay, that he is a thousand times more so, than a private person who makes use of his neighbours' property to gratify his irregular passions. Injustice, though screened from punishment, is not the less shameful.

§244. *Eminent domain annexed to the sovereignty.*   Every thing in the political society ought to tend to the good of the community; and since even the persons of the citizens are subject to this rule, their property cannot be excepted. The state could not subsist, or constantly administer the public affairs in the most advantageous manner, if it had not a power to dispose occasionally of all kinds of property subject to its authority. It is even to be presumed, that, when the nation takes possession of a country, the property of certain things is given up to individuals only with this reserve. The right which belongs to the society, or to the sovereign, of disposing, in case of necessity and for the public safety, of all the wealth contained in the state, is called the *eminent domain.* It is evident that this right is, in certain cases, necessary to him who governs, and consequently is a part of the empire or sovereign power, and ought to be placed in the number of the prerogatives of majesty (§45). When therefore the people confer the empire on any one, they at the same time invest him with the *eminent domain,* unless it be expressly reserved. Every prince who is truly sovereign is invested with this right when the nation has not excepted it,—however limited his authority may be in other respects.

If the sovereign disposes of the *public property* in virtue of his eminent domain, the alienation is valid, as having been made with sufficient powers.

When, in a case of necessity, he disposes in like manner of the possessions of a community or an individual, the alienation will, for the same reason, be valid. But justice requires that this community or this individual be indemnified at the public charge: and if the treasury is not able to bear the expense, all the citizens are obliged to contribute to it;

for the burthens of the state ought to be supported equally, or in a just proportion. The same rules <113> are applicable to this case as to the loss of merchandise thrown overboard to save the vessel.

Besides the *eminent domain,* the sovereignty gives a right of another nature over all public, common, and private property,—that is, the empire, or the right of command in all places of the country belonging to the nation. The supreme power extends to every thing that passes in the state, wherever it is transacted; and consequently the sovereign commands in all public places, on rivers, on highways, in deserts, &c. Every thing that happens there is subject to his authority.

§245. Government of public property.

In virtue of the same authority, the sovereign may make laws to regulate the manner in which common property is to be used,—as well the property of the nation at large, as that of distinct bodies or corporations. He cannot, indeed, take away their right from those who have a share in that property: but the care he ought to take of the public repose, and of the common advantage of the citizens, gives him doubtless a right to establish laws tending to this end, and consequently to regulate the manner in which things possessed in common are to be enjoyed. This affair might give room for abuses, and excite disturbances, which it is important to the state to prevent, and against which the prince is obliged to take just measures. Thus the sovereign may establish wise laws with respect to hunting and fishing,—forbid them in the seasons of propagation,—prohibit the use of certain nets, and of every destructive method, &c. But as it is only in the character of the common father, governor, and guardian of his people, that the sovereign has a right to make those laws, he ought never to lose sight of the ends which he is called upon to accomplish by enacting them: and if, upon those subjects, he makes any regulations with any other view than that of the public welfare, he abuses his power.

§246. The superior may make laws with respect to the use of things possessed in common.

A corporation, as well as every other proprietor, has a right to alienate and mortgage its property: but the present members ought never to lose sight of the destination of that joint property, nor dispose of it otherwise than for the advantage of the body, or in cases of necessity. If they alienate it with any other view, they abuse their power, and transgress against the duty they owe to their own corporation and their posterity; and the

§247. Alienation of the property of a corporation.

prince, in quality of common father, has a right to oppose the measure. Besides, the interest of the state requires that the property of corporations be not squandered away;—which gives the prince, intrusted with the care of watching over the public safety, a new right to prevent the alienation of such property. It is then very proper to ordain in a state, that the alienation of the property of corporations should be invalid, without the consent of the superior powers. And indeed the civil law, in this respect, gives to corporations the rights of minors. But this is strictly no more than a civil law; and the opinion of those who make the law of nature alone a sufficient authority to take from a corporation the power of alienating their property without the <114> consent of the sovereign, appears to me to be void of foundation, and contrary to the notion of property. A corporation, it is true, may have received property either from their predecessors, or from any other persons, with a clause that disables them from alienating it: but in this case they have only the perpetual use of it, not the entire and free property. If any of their property was solely given for the preservation of the body, it is evident that the corporation has not a right to alienate it, except in a case of extreme necessity:—and whatever property they may have received from the sovereign, is presumed to be of that nature.

§248. Use of common property.

All the members of a corporation have an equal right to the use of its common property. But, respecting the manner of enjoying it, the body of the corporation may make such regulations as they think proper, provided that those regulations be not inconsistent with that equality which ought to be preserved in a communion of property. Thus a corporation may determine the use of a common forest or pasture, either allowing it to all the members according to their wants, or allotting to each an equal share; but they have not a right to exclude any one of the number, or to make a distinction to his disadvantage by assigning him a less share than that of the others.

§249. How each member is to enjoy it.

All the members of a body having an equal right to its common property, each individual ought so to manage in taking advantage of it, as not in any wise to injure the common use. According to this rule, an individual is not permitted to construct upon any river that is public property, any work capable of rendering it less convenient for the use of every one else, as erecting mills, making a trench to turn the water upon his own lands, &c. If he attempts it, he arrogates to himself a private right, derogatory to the common right of the public.

The right of *anticipation* (*jus praeventionis*) ought to be faithfully observed in the use of common things which cannot be used by several persons at the same time. This name is given to the right which the first-comer acquires, to the use of things of this nature. For instance, if I am actually drawing water from a common or public well, another who comes after me cannot drive me away to draw out of it himself: and he ought to wait till I have done. For I make use of my right in drawing that water, and nobody can disturb me: a second, who has an equal right, cannot assert it to the prejudice of mine; to stop me by his arrival, would be arrogating to himself a better right than he allows me, and thereby violating the law of equality.

§250. Right of anticipation in the use of it.

The same rule ought to be observed in regard to those common things which are consumed in using them. They belong to the person who first takes possession of them with the intention of applying them to his own use; and a second, who comes after, has no right to take them from him. I repair to a common forest, and begin to fell a tree: you come in afterwards, and would wish to have the same tree: you cannot take it from me; for this would be arrogating to yourself a right superior to mine, <115> whereas our rights are equal. The rule in this case is the same as that which the law of nature prescribes in the use of the productions of the earth, before the introduction of property.

§251. The same right in another case.

The expenses necessary for the preservation or reparation of the things that belong to the public, or to a community, ought to be equally borne by all who have a share in them, whether the necessary sums be drawn from the common coffer, or that each individual contributes his quota. The nation, the corporation, and, in general, every collective body, may also establish extraordinary taxes, imposts, or annual contributions, to defray those expenses,—provided there be no oppressive exaction in the case, and that the money so levied be faithfully applied to the use for which it was raised. To this end also, as we have before observed (§103), toll-duties are lawfully established. High-ways, bridges, and causeways, are things of a public nature, from which all who pass

§252. Preservation and repairs of common possessions.

over them derive advantage: it is therefore just that all those passengers should contribute to their support.

§253. Duty and right of the sovereign in this respect.

We shall see presently that the sovereign ought to provide for the preservation of the public property. He is no less obliged, as the conductor of the whole nation, to watch over the preservation of the property of a corporation. It is the interest of the state at large that a corporation should not fall into indigence, by the ill conduct of its members for the time being. And as every obligation generates the correspondent right which is necessary to discharge it, the sovereign has here a right to oblige the corporation to conform to their duty. If therefore he perceives, for instance, that they suffer their necessary buildings to fall to ruin, or that they destroy their forests, he has a right to prescribe what they ought to do, and to put his orders in force.

§254. Private property.

We have but a few words to say with respect to private property: every proprietor has a right to make what use he pleases of his own substance, and to dispose of it as he pleases, when the rights of a third person are not involved in the business. The sovereign, however, as the father of his people, may and ought to set bounds to a prodigal, and to prevent his running to ruin, especially if this prodigal be the father of a family. But he must take care not to extend this right of inspection so far as to lay a restraint on his subjects in the administration of their affairs;—which would be no less injurious to the true welfare of the state than to the just liberty of the citizens. The particulars of this subject belong to public law and politics.

§255. The sovereign may subject it to regulations of police.

It must also be observed, that individuals are not so perfectly free in the economy or government of their affairs, as not to be subject to the laws and regulations of police made by the sovereign. For instance, if vineyards are multiplied to too great an extent in a country which is in want of corn, the sovereign may forbid the planting of the vine in fields proper for tillage; for here the public welfare and the safety of the state are concerned. When a reason of such importance requires it, the sovereign or the magistrate may oblige an individual to sell all the provisions <116> in his possession above what are necessary for the subsistence of his family, and may fix the price he shall receive for them. The public authority may and ought to hinder monopolies, and suppress all practices tending to raise the price of provisions,—to which practices the Romans applied the expressions *annonam incendere, comprimere, vexare.*[76]

Every man may naturally chuse the person to whom he would leave his property after his death, as long as his right is not limited by some indispensable obligation,—as, for instance, that of providing for the subsistence of his children. The children also have naturally a right to inherit their father's property in equal portions. But this is no reason why particular laws may not be established in a state, with regard to testaments and inheritances,—a respect being however paid to the essential laws of nature. Thus, by a rule established in many places with a view to support noble families, the eldest son is, of right, his father's principal heir. Lands, perpetually appropriated to the eldest male heir of a family, belong to him by virtue of another right, which has its source in the will of the person, who, being sole owner of those lands, has bequeathed them in that manner.

§256.
Inheritances.

CHAPTER XXI

Of the Alienation of the public Property, or the Domain, and that of a Part of the State.

The nation being the sole mistress of the property in her possession, may dispose of it as she thinks proper, and may lawfully alienate or mortgage it. This right is a necessary consequence of the full and absolute domain: the exercise of it is restrained by the law of nature, only with respect to proprietors who have not the use of reason necessary for the management of their affairs; which is not the case with a nation. Those who think otherwise cannot allege any solid reason for their opinion; and it would follow from their principles, that no safe contract can be entered into with any nation;—a conclusion, which attacks the foundation of all public treaties.

§257. The nation may alienate its public property.

76. "To increase, lower [compress], or alter the market rate [of the year's harvest]."

§258. Duties of a nation in this respect.

But it is very just to say that the nation ought carefully to preserve her public property,—to make a proper use of it,—not to dispose of it without good reasons, nor to alienate or mortgage it but for a manifest public advantage, or in case of a pressing necessity. This is an evident consequence of the duties a nation owes to herself. The public property is extremely useful and even necessary to the nation; and she cannot squander it improperly, without injuring herself, and shamefully neglecting the duty of self-preservation. I speak of the public property strictly so called, or the domain of the state. Alienating its revenues is cutting the sinews of government. As to the property common to all the citizens, the nation does an injury to those who derive advan-<117>tage from it, if she alienates it without necessity, or without cogent reasons. She has a right to do this as proprietor of these possessions; but she ought not to dispose of them except in a manner that is consistent with the duties which the body owes to its members.

§259. Duties of the prince.

The same duties lie on the prince, the director of the nation: he ought to watch over the preservation and prudent management of the public property,—to stop and prevent all waste of it,—and not suffer it to be applied to improper uses.

§260. He cannot alienate the public property.

The prince, or the superior of the society, whatever he is, being naturally no more than the administrator, and not the proprietor of the state, his authority, as sovereign or head of the nation, does not of itself give him a right to alienate or mortgage the public property. The general rule then is, that the superior cannot dispose of the public property, as to its substance,—the right to do this being reserved to the proprietor alone, since proprietorship is defined to be the right to dispose of a thing substantially. If the superior exceeds his powers with respect to this property, the alienation he makes of it will be invalid, and may at any time be revoked by his successor, or by the nation. This is the law generally received in France; and it was upon this principle that the duke of Sully* advised Henry IV. to resume the possession of all the domains of the crown alienated by his predecessors.

* See his Memoirs.

The nation having the free disposal of all the property belonging to her (§257), may convey her right to the sovereign, and consequently confer upon him that of alienating and mortgaging the public property. But this right not being necessary to the conductor of the state, to enable him to render the people happy by his government,—it is not to be presumed, that the nation have given it to him; and if they have not made an express law for that purpose, we are to conclude that the prince is not invested with it, unless he has received full, unlimited, and absolute authority.

§261. The nation may give him a right to it.

The rules we have just established relate to alienations of public property in favour of individuals. The question assumes a different aspect when it relates to alienations made by one nation to another:* it requires other principles to decide it in the different cases that may present themselves. Let us endeavour to give a general theory of them.

§262. Rules on this subject with respect to treaties between nation and nation.

I. It is necessary that nations should be able to treat and contract validly with each other, since they would otherwise find it impossible to bring their affairs to an issue, or to obtain the blessings of peace with any degree of certainty. Whence it follows, that when a nation has ceded any part of its property to another, the cession ought to be deemed valid and irrevocable, as < 118 > in fact it is, in virtue of the notion of *property.* This principle cannot be shaken by any fundamental law, by which a nation might pretend to deprive themselves of the power of alienating what belongs to them: for this would be depriving themselves of all power to form contracts with other nations, or attempting to deceive them. A nation with such a law ought never to treat concerning its property: if it is obliged to it by necessity, or determined to do it for its own

---

* Quod domania regnorum inalienabilia & semper revocabilia dicuntur, id respectu privatorum intelligitur; nam contra alias gentes divino privilegio opus foret. [["The domains of kings are said to be inalienable and always revocable [i.e., subject to forfeit], and this is understood to apply to private individuals, for against other nations there is need of special law from God" (trans. Eds.). (Kings cannot sell off their territories to private individuals and indeed are trustees rather than absolute owners of their lands, but when it comes to international relations we need different rules from God governing territorial acquisition and transfer.)]] *Leibnitz, Praefat. ad Cod. Jur. Gent. Diplomat.* [[Leibniz, *Introduction to Codex juris gentium diplomaticus.*]]

advantage, the moment it broaches a treaty on the subject, it renounces its fundamental law. It is seldom disputed that an entire nation may alienate what belongs to itself: but it is asked, whether its conductor, its sovereign, has this power? The question may be determined by the fundamental laws. But if the laws say nothing directly on this subject, then we have recourse to our second principle, viz.

2. If the nation has conferred the full sovereignty on its conductor,— if it has intrusted to him the care, and, without reserve, given him the right, of treating and contracting with other states, it is considered as having invested him with all the powers necessary to make a valid contract. The prince is then the organ of the nation; what he does is considered as the act of the nation itself; and though he is not the owner of the public property, his alienations of it are valid, as being duly authorised.

§263. Alienation of a part of the state. The question becomes more difficult, when it relates, not to the alienation of some parts of the public property, but to the dismembering of the nation or state itself,—the cession of a town or a province that constitutes a part of it. This question however admits of a sound decision on the same principles. A nation ought to preserve itself (§16),—it ought to preserve all its members,—it cannot abandon them; and it is under an engagement to support them in their rank as members of the nation (§17). It has not then a right to traffic with their rank and liberty, on account of any advantages it may expect to derive from such a negotiation. They have joined the society for the purpose of being members of it:—they submit to the authority of the state, for the purpose of promoting in concert their common welfare and safety, and not of being at its disposal, like a farm or an herd of cattle. But the nation may lawfully abandon them in a case of extreme necessity; and she has a right to cut them off from the body, if the public safety requires it. When therefore, in such a case, the state gives up a town or a province to a neighbour or to a powerful enemy, the cession ought to remain valid as to the state, since she had a right to make it: nor can she any longer lay claim to the town or province thus alienated, since she has relinquished every right she could have over them.

But this province or town, thus abandoned and dismembered from the state, is not obliged to receive the new master whom the state attempts to set over it. Being separated from the society of which it was a member, it resumes all its original rights; and if it be capable of defending its liberty against the prince who would subject it to his authority, it may lawfully resist him. <119> Francis I.[77] having engaged by the treaty of Madrid[78] to cede the duchy of Burgundy to the emperor Charles V.[79] the states of that province declared, "that, having never been subject but to the crown of France, they would die subject to it; and that if the king abandoned them, they would take up arms, and endeavour to set themselves at liberty, rather than pass into a new state of subjection."* It is true, subjects are seldom able to make resistance on such occasions; and, in general, their wisest plan will be to submit to their new master, and endeavour to obtain the best terms they can.

§264. Rights of the dismembered party.

Has the prince—or the superior, of whatever kind—a power to dismember the state?—We answer as we have done above with respect to the domain:—if the fundamental laws forbid all dismemberment by the sovereign, he cannot do it without the concurrence of the nation or its representatives. But if the laws are silent, and if the prince has received a full and absolute authority, he is then the depositary of the rights of the nation, and the organ by which it declares its will. The nation ought never to abandon its members but in a case of necessity, or with a view to the public safety, and to preserve itself from total ruin; and the prince ought not to give them up except for the same reasons. But since he has received an absolute authority, it belongs to him to judge of the necessity of the case, and of what the safety of the state requires.

§265. Whether the prince has power to dismember the state.

On occasion of the above-mentioned treaty of Madrid, the principal persons in France, assembled at Cognac[80] after the king's return, unan-

* Mezeray's History of France, vol. ii, p. 458.
77. Francis I, r. 1515–47.
78. Treaty of Madrid, 1526.
79. Charles V reigned as Holy Roman Emperor (1519–56) and also as King Carlos I of Spain (1516–56).
80. 1526.

imously resolved, "that his authority did not extend so far as to dismember the crown."* The treaty was declared void, as being contrary to the fundamental law of the kingdom: and indeed it had been concluded without sufficient powers: for as the laws in express terms refused to the king the power of dismembering the kingdom, the concurrence of the nation was necessary for that purpose; and it might give its consent by the medium of the states-general. Charles V. ought not to have released his prisoner before those very states had approved the treaty; or rather, making a more generous use of his victory, he should have imposed less rigorous conditions, such as Francis I. would have been able to comply with, and such as he could not, without dishonour, have refused to perform. But now that there are no longer any meetings of the states-general in France, the king remains the sole organ of the state, with respect to other powers: these latter have a right to take his will for that of all France; and the cessions the king might make them, would remain valid, in virtue of the tacit consent by which the nation has vested the king with unlimited powers to treat with them. Were it otherwise, no solid treaty could be entered into with the crown of France. For greater security, however, other powers have <120> often required that their treaties should be registered in the parliament of Paris: but at present even this formality seems to be laid aside.

CHAPTER XXII

Of Rivers, Streams, and Lakes.

§266. A river that separates two territories.

When a nation takes possession of a country with a view to settle there, it takes possession of every thing included in it, as lands, lakes, rivers, &c. But it may happen that the country is bounded and separated from another by a river;—in which case, it is asked, to whom this river belongs? It is manifest from the principles established in Chap. XVIII. that it ought to belong to the nation who first took possession of it. This

---

* Mezeray, ibid.

principle cannot be denied; but the difficulty is, to make the application. It is not easy to determine which of the two neighbouring nations was the first to take possession of a river that separates them.—For the decision of such questions, the rules which may be deduced from the principles of the law of nations, are as follow:—

1. When a nation takes possession of a country bounded by a river, she is considered as appropriating to herself the river also; for the utility of a river is too great to admit a supposition that the nation did not intend to reserve it to herself. Consequently, the nation that first established her dominion on one of the banks of the river, is considered as being the first possessor of all that part of the river which bounds her territory. When there is question of a very broad river, this presumption admits not of a doubt, so far at least as relates to a part of the river's breadth; and the strength of the presumption increases or diminishes in an *inverse ratio* with the breadth of the river: for the narrower the river is, the more does the safety and convenience of its use require that it should be subject entirely to the empire and property of that nation.

2. If that nation has made any use of the river, as for navigation or fishing, it is presumed with the greater certainty, that she has resolved to appropriate the river to her own use.

3. If, of two nations inhabiting the opposite banks of the river, neither party can prove that they themselves, or those whose rights they inherit, were the first settlers in those tracts, it is to be supposed that both nations came there at the same time, since neither of them can give any reason for claiming the preference: and in this case, the dominion of each will extend to the middle of the river.

4. A long and undisputed possession establishes the right of nations; otherwise there could be no peace, no stability between them: and notorious facts must be admitted to prove the possession. Thus, when, from time immemorial, a nation has without contradiction exercised the sovereignty upon a river which forms <121> her boundary, nobody can dispute with that nation the supreme dominion over the river in question.

5. Finally, if treaties determine any thing on this question, they must be observed. To decide it by accurate and express stipulations, is the safest mode: and such is, in fact, the method taken by most powers at present.

§267. Of the
bed of a river
which is dried
up or takes an-
other course.

If a river leaves its bed, whether it be dried up or takes its course elsewhere, the bed belongs to the owner of the river; for the bed is a part of the river; and he who had appropriated to himself the whole, had necessarily appropriated to himself all its parts.

§268. The
right of
alluvion.

If a territory which terminates on a river has no other boundary than that river, it is one of those territories that have natural or indeterminate bounds (*territoria arcifinia*), and it enjoys the right of *alluvion;* that is to say,—every gradual increase of soil, every addition which the current of the river may make to its bank on that side, is an addition to that territory, stands in the same predicament with it, and belongs to the same owner. For if I take possession of a piece of land, declaring that I will have for its boundary the river which washes its side,—or if it is given to me upon that footing,—I thus acquire beforehand the right of *alluvion;* and consequently I alone may appropriate to myself whatever additions the current of the river may insensibly make to my land:—I say *"insensibly,"* because in the very uncommon case, called *avulsion,* when the violence of the stream separates a considerable part from one piece of land and joins it to another, but in such manner that it can still be identified, the property of the soil so removed naturally continues vested in its former owner. The civil laws have thus provided against and decided this case when it happens between individual and individual; they ought to unite equity with the welfare of the state, and the care of preventing litigations.

In case of doubt, every territory terminating on a river is presumed to have no other boundary than the river itself; because nothing is more natural than to take a river for a boundary, when a settlement is made; and wherever there is a doubt, that is always to be presumed, which is most natural and most probable.

§269. Whether
alluvion
produces any
change in the
right to a river.

As soon as it is determined that a river constitutes the boundary-line between two territories, whether it remains common to the inhabitants on each of its banks, or whether each shares half of it,—or, finally, whether it belongs entirely to one of them,—their rights with respect to the river are in no wise changed by the alluvion. If therefore it happens that, by a natural effect of the current, one of the two territories receives an increase, while the river gradually encroaches on the opposite bank,—

the river still remains the natural boundary of the two territories, and, notwithstanding the progressive changes in its course, each retains over it the same rights which it possessed before; so that, if, for instance, it be divided in the middle between the owners of the opposite banks, that middle, though it changes its place, will continue to <122> be the line of separation between the two neighbours. The one loses, it is true, while the other gains: but nature alone produces this change: she destroys the land of the one, while she forms new land for the other. The case cannot be otherwise determined, since they have taken the river alone for their limits.

But if, instead of a gradual and progressive change of its bed, the river, by an accident merely natural, turns entirely out of its course, and runs into one of the two neighbouring states, the bed which it has abandoned becomes thenceforward their boundary, and remains the property of the former owner of the river (§267): the river itself is, as it were, anihilated in all that part, while it is reproduced in its new bed, and there belongs only to the state in which it flows. §270. What is the case when the river changes its bed.

This case is very different from that of a river which changes its course without going out of the same state. The latter, in its new course, continues to belong to its former owner, whether that owner be the state or any individual to whom the state has given it,—because rivers belong to the public, in whatever part of the country they flow. Of the bed which it has abandoned, a moiety accrues to the contiguous lands on each side, if they are lands that have natural boundaries with the right of alluvion. That bed (notwithstanding what we have said in §267) is no longer the property of the public, because of the right of alluvion vested in the owners of its banks, and because the public held possession of the bed, only on account of its containing a river. But if the adjacent lands have not natural boundaries, the public still retains the property of the bed. The new soil over which the river takes its course is lost to the proprietor, because all the rivers in the country belong to the public.

It is not allowable to raise any works on the bank of a river, which have a tendency to turn its course, and to cast it upon the opposite bank: this would be promoting our own advantage at our neighbour's expense. Each can only secure himself, and hinder the current from undermining and carrying away his land. §271. Works tending to turn the current,

§272. or, in general, prejudicial to the rights of others.

In general, no person ought to build on a river, any more than else-where, any work that is prejudicial to his neighbour's rights. If a river belongs to one nation, and another has an incontestable right to navigate it, the former cannot erect upon it a dam or a mill which might render it unfit for navigation. The right which the owners of the river possess in this case is only that of a limited property; and, in the exercise of it, they are bound to respect the rights of others.

§273. Rules in relation to interfering rights.

But when two different rights to the same thing happen to clash with each other, it is not always easy to determine which ought to yield to the other: the point cannot be satisfactorily decided, without atten-tively considering the nature of the rights, and their origin. For ex-ample, a river belongs to me, but you have a right to fish in it: and the question is, whether I may erect mills on my river, whereby the fishery will become more difficult and less advantageous? The nature of our rights seems <123> to determine the question in the affirmative.—I, as proprietor, have an essential right over the river itself:—you have only a right to make use of it,—a right which is merely accessory, and de-pendent on mine: you have but a general right to fish as you can in my river, such as you happen to find it, and in whatever state I may think fit to possess it. I do not deprive you of your right by erecting my mills: it still exists in the general view of it; and if it becomes less useful to you, it is by accident, and because it is dependent on the exercise of mine.

The case is different with respect to the right of navigation, of which we have spoken. This right necessarily supposes that the river shall re-main free and navigable, and therefore excludes every work that will en-tirely interrupt its navigation.

The antiquity and origin of the rights serve, no less than their nature, to determine the question. The more ancient right, if it be absolute, is to be exerted in its full extent, and the other only so far as it may be extended without prejudice to the former; for it could only be established on this footing, unless the possessor of the first right has expressly con-sented to its being limited.

In the same manner, rights ceded by the proprietor of any thing are considered as ceded without prejudice to the other rights that belong to him, and only so far as they are consistent with these latter, unless an express declaration, or the very nature of the right, determine it otherwise. If I have ceded to another the right of fishing in my river, it is manifest that I have ceded it without prejudice to my other rights, and that I remain free to build on that river such works as I think proper, even though they should injure the fishery, provided they do not altogether destroy it. A work of this latter kind, such as a dam that would hinder the fish from ascending it, could not be built but in a case of necessity, and on making, according to circumstances, an adequate compensation to the person who has a right to fish there.

What we have said of rivers and streams, may be easily applied to lakes. Every lake, entirely included in a country, belongs to the nation that is the proprietor of that country; for, in taking possession of a territory, a nation is considered as having appropriated to itself every thing included in it: and as it seldom happens that the property of a lake of any considerable extent falls to the share of individuals, it remains common to the nation. If this lake is situated between two states, it is presumed to be divided between them at the middle, while there is no title, no constant and manifest custom, to determine otherwise. §274. Lakes.

What has been said of the right of alluvion in speaking of rivers, is also to be understood as applying to lakes. When a lake, which bounds a state, belongs entirely to it, every increase in the extent of that lake falls under the same predicament as the lake itself; but it is necessary that the increase should be insensible, as that of land in alluvion, and moreover that it be real, constant, and complete. To explain myself more fully,—1. I speak of insensible increase: this is the reverse of alluvion: the question <124> here relates to the increase of a lake, as in the other case to an increase of soil. If this increase be not insensible,—if the lake, overflowing its banks, inundates a large tract of land, this new portion of the lake, this tract thus covered with water, still belongs to its former owner. Upon what principles can we found the acquisition of it in behalf of the owner of the lake? The space is very easily identified, though it has changed its nature: and it is too considerable to admit a presumption that the owner had no intention to preserve it to himself, notwithstanding the changes that might happen to it. §275. Increase of a lake.

But, 2. If the lake insensibly undermines a part of the opposite territory, destroys it, and renders it impossible to be known, by fixing itself
there, and adding it to its bed, that part of the territory is lost to its former
owner; it no longer exists; and the whole of the lake thus increased still
belongs to the same state as before.

3. If some of the lands bordering on the lake are only overflowed at
high water, this transient accident cannot produce any change in their
dependence. The reason why the soil, which the lake invades by little
and little, belongs to the owner of the lake, and is lost to its former
proprietor, is because the proprietor has no other boundary than the lake,
nor any other marks than its banks, to ascertain how far his possessions
extend. If the water advances insensibly, he loses; if it retires in like
manner, he gains: such must have been the intention of the nations who
have respectively appropriated to themselves the lake and the adjacent
lands:—it can scarcely be supposed that they had any other intention.
But a territory overflowed for a time, is not confounded with the rest of
the lake: it can still be recognised; and the owner may still retain his right
of property in it. Were it otherwise, a town overflowed by a lake would
become subject to a different government during the inundation, and
return to its former sovereign as soon as the waters were dried up.

4. For the same reasons, if the waters of the lake, penetrating by an
opening into the neighbouring country, there form a bay, or new lake,
joined to the first by a canal,—this new body of water, and the canal,
belong to the owner of the country in which they are formed. For the
boundaries are easily ascertained: and we are not to presume an intention
of relinquishing so considerable a tract of land in case of its happening
to be invaded by the waters of an adjoining lake.

It must be observed that we here treat the question as arising between
two states: it is to be decided by other principles when it relates to proprietors who are members of the same state. In the latter case, it is not
merely the bounds of the soil, but also its nature and use, that determine
the possession of it. An individual, who possesses a field on the borders
of a lake, cannot enjoy it as a field when it is overflowed; and a person
who has, for instance, the right of fishing in the lake, may exert his right
in this new extent: if the waters retire, the field is restored to <125> the

use of its former owner. If the lake penetrates by an opening into the low lands in its neighbourhood, and there forms a permanent inundation, this new lake belongs to the public, because all lakes belong to the public.

The same principles shew, that if the lake insensibly forms an accession of land on its banks, either by retiring or in any other manner, this increase of land belongs to the country which it joins, when that country has no other boundary than the lake. It is the same thing as alluvion on the banks of a river.

§276. Land formed on the banks of a lake.

But if the lake happened to be suddenly dried up, either totally or in a great part of it, the bed would remain in the possession of the sovereign of the lake; the nature of the soil, so easily known, sufficiently marking out the limits.

§277. Bed of a lake dried up.

The empire or jurisdiction over lakes and rivers is subject to the same rules as the property of them, in all the cases which we have examined. Each state naturally possesses it over the whole or the part, of which it possesses the domain. We have seen (§245) that the nation, or its sovereign, commands in all places in its possession.

§278. Jurisdiction over lakes and rivers.

CHAPTER XXIII

Of the Sea.

In order to complete the exposition of the principles of the law of nations with respect to the things a nation may possess, it remains to treat of the open sea. The use of the open sea consists in navigation, and in fishing; along its coasts it is moreover of use for the procuring of several things found near the shore, such as shell-fish, amber, pearls, &c. for the making of salt, and, finally, for the establishment of places of retreat and security for vessels.

§279. The sea and its use.

The open sea is not of such a nature as to admit the holding possession of it, since no settlement can be formed on it, so as to hinder others from passing. But a nation powerful at sea may forbid others to fish in it and to navigate it, declaring that she appropriates to herself the dominion

§280. Whether the sea can be possessed, and its dominion appropriated.

over it, and that she will destroy the vessels that shall dare to appear in it without her permission. Let us see whether she has right to do this.

§281. Nobody has a right to appropriate to himself the use of the open sea.

It is manifest that the use of the open sea, which consists in navigation and fishing, is innocent and inexhaustible; that is to say—he who navigates or fishes in the open sea, does no injury to any one, and the sea, in these two respects, is sufficient for all mankind. Now nature does not give to man a right of appropriating to himself things that may be innocently used, and that are inexhaustible, and sufficient for all. For since those things, while common to all, are sufficient to supply the wants of each,—whoever should, to the exclusion of all other participants, attempt to render himself sole proprietor of them, would unreasonably <126> wrest the bounteous gifts of nature from the parties excluded. The earth no longer furnishing without culture the things necessary or useful to the human race, who were extremely multiplied, it became necessary to introduce the right of property, in order that each might apply himself with more success to the cultivation of what had fallen to his share, and multiply by his labour the necessaries and conveniences of life. It is for this reason the law of nature approves the rights of dominion and property, which put an end to the primitive manner of living in common. But this reason cannot apply to things which are in themselves inexhaustible; and consequently it cannot furnish any just grounds for seizing the exclusive possession of them. If the free and common use of a thing of this nature was prejudicial or dangerous to a nation, the care of their own safety would authorise them to reduce that thing under their own dominion if possible, in order to restrict the use of it by such precautions as prudence might dictate to them. But this is not the case with the open sea, on which people may sail and fish without the least prejudice to any person whatsoever, and without putting any one in danger. No nation therefore has a right to take possession of the open sea, or claim the sole use of it, to the exclusion of other nations. The kings of Portugal formerly arrogated to themselves the empire of the seas of Guinea and the East-Indies;* but the other maritime powers gave themselves little trouble about such a pretension.

* See Grotius's Mare Liberum, and Selden's Mare Clausum, lib. i. cap. xvii.

The right of navigating and fishing in the open sea being then a right common to all men, the nation that attempts to exclude another from that advantage, does her an injury, and furnishes her with sufficient grounds for commencing hostilities, since nature authorises a nation to repel an injury,—that is, to make use of force against whoever would deprive her of her rights.

§282. The nation that attempts to exclude another, does it an injury.

Nay more,—a nation, which, without a legitimate claim, would arrogate to itself an exclusive right to the sea, and support its pretensions by force, does an injury to all nations; it infringes their common right; and they are justifiable in forming a general combination against it, in order to repress such an attempt. Nations have the greatest interest in causing the law of nations, which is the basis of their tranquillity, to be universally respected. If any one openly tramples it under foot, they all may and ought to rise up against him; and, by uniting their forces to chastise the common enemy, they will discharge their duty towards themselves, and towards human society, of which they are members (Prelim. §22).

§283. It even does an injury to all nations.

However, as every one is at liberty to renounce his right, a nation may acquire exclusive rights of navigation and fishing, by treaties, in which other nations renounce, in its favour, the rights they derive from nature. The latter are obliged to observe their treaties; and the nation they have favoured has a right to maintain by force the possession of its advantages. Thus the <127> house of Austria has renounced, in favour of England and Holland, the right of sending vessels from the Netherlands to the East-Indies. In *Grotius, de Jure Belli & Pacis, Lib.* II. *Cap.* III. §15, may be found many instances of similar treaties.

§284. It may acquire an exclusive right by treaties,

As the rights of navigation and of fishing, and other rights which may be exercised on the sea, belong to the class of those rights of mere ability (*jura merae facultatis*) which are imprescriptible (§95),—they cannot be lost for want of use. Consequently, although a nation should happen to have been, from time immemorial, in sole possession of the navigation or fishery in certain seas, it cannot, on this foundation, claim an exclusive right to those advantages. For though others have not made use of their common right to navigation and fishery in those seas, it does not thence

§285. but not by prescription and long use,

follow that they have had any intention to renounce it; and they are entitled to exert it whenever they think proper.

§286. unless by virtue of a tacit agreement. But it may happen, that the non-usage of the right may assume the nature of a consent or tacit agreement, and thus become a title in favour of one nation against another. When a nation, that is in possession of the navigation and fishery in certain tracts of sea, claims an exclusive right to them, and forbids all participation on the part of other nations,—if the others obey that prohibition with sufficient marks of acquiescence, they tacitly renounce their own right, in favour of that nation, and establish for her a new right, which she may afterwards lawfully maintain against them, especially when it is confirmed by long use.

§287. The sea near the coasts may become a property. The various uses of the sea near the coasts render it very susceptible of property. It furnishes fish, shells, pearls, amber, &c. Now in all these respects its use is not inexhaustible; wherefore the nation to whom the coasts belong may appropriate to themselves, and convert to their own profit, an advantage which nature has so placed within their reach as to enable them conveniently to take possession of it, in the same manner as they possessed themselves of the dominion of the land they inhabit. Who can doubt, that the pearl fisheries of Bahrem and Ceylon may lawfully become property? And though, where the catching of fish is the only object, the fishery appears less liable to be exhausted,—yet if a nation have on their coast a particular fishery of a profitable nature, and of which they may become masters, shall they not be permitted to appropriate to themselves that bounteous gift of nature, as an appendage to the country they possess, and to reserve to themselves the great advantages which their commerce may thence derive in case there be a sufficient abundance of fish to furnish the neighbouring nations? But if, so far from taking possession of it, the nation has once acknowledged the common right of other nations to come and fish there, it can no longer exclude them from it; it has left that fishery in its primitive freedom, at least with respect to those who have been accustomed to take advantage of it. The English not having originally taken exclusive possession of the herring-fishery on their coasts, it is become common to them with other nations. <128>

A nation may appropriate to herself those things, of which the free and common use would be prejudicial or dangerous to her. This is a second reason for which governments extend their dominion over the sea along their coasts, as far as they are able to protect their right. It is of considerable importance to the safety and welfare of the state, that a general liberty be not allowed to all comers to approach so near their possessions, especially with ships of war, as to hinder the approach of trading nations, and molest their navigation. During the war between Spain and the United Provinces,[81] James I. king of England,[82] marked out, along his coasts, certain boundaries within which he declared that he would not suffer any of the powers at war to pursue their enemies, nor even allow their armed vessels to stop and observe the ships that should enter or sail out of the ports.* These parts of the sea, thus subject to a nation, are comprehended in her territory; nor must any one navigate them without her consent. But to vessels that are not liable to suspicion, she cannot, without a breach of duty, refuse permission to approach for harmless purposes, since it is a duty incumbent on every proprietor to allow to strangers a free passage, even by land, when it may be done without damage or danger. It is true, that the state itself is sole judge of what is proper to be done in every particular case that occurs: and if it judges amiss, it is to blame; but the others are bound to submit. It is otherwise, however, in cases of necessity,—as, for instance, when a vessel is obliged to enter a road which belongs to you, in order to shelter herself from a tempest. In this case, the right of entering wherever we can, provided we cause no damage, or that we repair any damage done, is, as we shall shew more at large, a remnant of the primitive freedom, of which no man can be supposed to have divested himself; and the vessel may lawfully enter in spite of you, if you unjustly refuse her permission.

§288. Another reason for appropriating the sea bordering on the coasts.

* Selden's Mare Clausum, Lib. II.

81. 1566–1648.

82. James I of England (r. 1603–25) also ruled as James VI of Scotland (r. 1567–1625).

§289. How far
this possession
may extend.   It is not easy to determine to what distance a nation may extend its
rights over the sea by which it is surrounded. Bodinus* pretends, that,
according to the common right of all maritime nations, the prince's dominion extends to the distance of thirty leagues from the coast. But this
exact determination can only be founded on a general consent of nations, which it would be difficult to prove. Each state may, on this head,
make what regulations it pleases, so far as respects the transactions of
the citizens with each other, or their concerns with the sovereign: but
between nation and nation, all that can reasonably be said, is, that, in
general, the dominion of the state over the neigbouring sea extends as
far as her safety renders it necessary and her power is able to assert it;
since, on the one hand, she cannot appropriate to herself a thing that is
common to all mankind, such as the sea, except so far as she has need
of it for some lawful end (§281), and, on the other, it would be a vain
and ridiculous pre-<129>tension to claim a right which she were wholly
unable to assert. The fleets of England have given room to her kings to
claim the empire of the seas which surround that island, even as far as
the opposite coasts.† Selden relates a solemn act‡ by which it appears
that, in the time of Edward I.[83] that empire was acknowledged by the
greatest part of the maritime nations of Europe; and the republic of the
United Provinces acknowledged it, in some measure, by the treaty of
Breda in 1667, at least so far as related to the honours of the flag. But
solidly to establish a right of such extent, it were necessary to prove very
clearly the express or tacit consent of all the powers concerned. The
French have never agreed to this pretension of England; and in that very
treaty of Breda, just mentioned, Louis XIV. would not even suffer the
Channel to be called the English Channel, or the British Sea. The republic of Venice claims the empire of the Adriatic; and every body
knows the ceremony annually performed upon that account. In confir-

* In his Republic, Book I. Chap. X.
† See Selden's Mare Clausum.
‡ Ibid. lib. ii, cap. xxviii.
83. Edward I, king of England, r. 1272–1307.

mation of this right, we are referred to the examples of Uladislaus,[84] king of Naples, of the emperor Frederic III.[85] and of some of the kings of Hungary, who asked permission of the Venetians for their vessels to pass through that sea.* That the empire of the Adriatic belongs to the republic to a certain distance from her own coasts, in the places of which she can keep possession, and of which the possession is important to her own safety,—appears to me incontestable: but I doubt very much whether any power is at present disposed to acknowledge her sovereignty over the whole Adriatic sea. Such pretensions to empire are respected as long as the nation that makes them is able to assert them by force; but they vanish of course on the decline of her power. At present the whole space of the sea within cannon-shot of the coast is considered as making a part of the territory; and for that reason a vessel taken under the cannon of a neutral fortress is not a lawful prize.

The shores of the sea incontestably belong to the nation that possesses the country of which they are a part; and they belong to the class of public things. If civilians have set them down as things common to all mankind (*res communes*), it is only in regard to their use; and we are not thence to conclude that they considered them as independent of the empire: the very contrary appears from a great number of laws. Ports and harbours are manifestly an appendage to and even a part of the country, and consequently are the property of the nation. Whatever is said of the land itself, will equally apply to them, so far as respects the consequences of the domain and of the empire.

§290. Shores and ports.

All we have said of the parts of the sea near the coast, may be said more particularly, and with much greater reason, of roads, bays, and straits, as still more capable of being possessed, and of greater importance to the safety of the country. But I speak of <130> bays and straits of small extent, and not of those great tracts of sea to which these names are sometimes given, as Hudson's Bay and the Straits of Magellan, over which the empire cannot extend, and still less a right of property. A bay whose entrance can

§291. Bays and straits.

---

* Ibid. lib. i. cap. xvi.
84. Uladislaus (Ladislaus), king of Naples, r. 1386–1414.
85. Frederic III, Holy Roman Emperor, r. 1452–93.

be defended, may be possessed and rendered subject to the laws of the sovereign; and it is of importance that it should be so, since the country might be much more easily insulted in such a place, than on a coast that lies exposed to the winds and the impetuosity of the waves.

§292. Straits in particular.   It must be remarked with regard to straits, that, when they serve for a communication between two seas, the navigation of which is common to all or several nations, the nation which possesses the strait, cannot refuse the others a passage through it, provided that passage be innocent, and attended with no danger to herself. By refusing it without just reasons, she would deprive those nations of an advantage granted them by nature; and indeed the right to such a passage is a remnant of the primitive liberty enjoyed by all mankind. Nothing but the care of his own safety can authorise the owner of the strait to make use of certain precautions, and to require certain formalities, commonly established by the custom of nations. He has a right to levy a moderate tax on the vessels that pass, partly on account of the inconvenience they give him by obliging him to be on his guard,—partly as a return for the safety he procures them by protecting them from their enemies, by keeping pirates at a distance, and by defraying the expense attendant on the support of lighthouses, sea-marks, and other things necessary to the safety of mariners. Thus the king of Denmark requires a custom at the straits of the Sound. Such right ought to be founded on the same reasons, and subject to the same rules, as the tolls established on land or on a river. (See §§103 and 104.)

§293. Right to wrecks.   It is necessary to mention the right to wrecks,—a right which was the wretched offspring of barbarism, and which has almost every-where fortunately disappeared with its parent. Justice and humanity cannot allow of it except in those cases only where the proprietors of the effects saved from a wreck cannot possibly be discovered. In such cases, those effects belong to the person who is the first to take possession of them, or to the sovereign, if the law reserves them for him.

§294. A sea inclosed within the territories of a nation.   If a sea is entirely inclosed by the territories of a nation, and has no other communication with the ocean than by a channel of which that nation may take possession, it appears that such a sea is no less capable of being occupied, and becoming property, than the land; and it ought to follow the fate of the country that surrounds it. The Mediterranean, in former times, was absolutely inclosed within the territories of the Romans; and that people, by rendering themselves masters of the strait which joins it to the ocean, might subject the Mediterranean to their empire, and assume the dominion over it. They did not, by such procedure, injure the rights of other nations; a particular sea being mani- <131>festly designed by nature for the use of the countries and nations that surround it. Besides, by barring the entrance of the Mediterranean against all suspected vessels, the Romans, by one single stroke, secured the immense extent of their coasts: and this reason was sufficient to authorise them to take possession of it. And as it had absolutely no communication but with the states which belonged to them, they were at liberty to permit or prohibit the entrance into it, in the same manner as into any of their towns or provinces.

When a nation takes possession of certain parts of the sea, it takes possession of the empire over them, as well as of the domain, on the same principle which we advanced in treating of the land (§205). These parts of the sea are within the jurisdiction of the nation, and a part of its territory: the sovereign commands there; he makes laws, and may punish those who violate them: in a word, he has the same rights there as on land, and, in general, every right which the laws of the state allow him.

§295. The parts of the sea possessed by a power are within its jurisdiction.

It is however true that the *empire,* and the *domain* or *property,* are not inseparable in their own nature, even in a sovereign state.* As a nation may possess the domain or property of a tract of land or sea without having the sovereignty of it, so it may likewise happen that she shall possess the sovereignty of a place, of which the property or the domain, with respect to use, belongs to some other nation. But it is always presumed, that when a nation possesses the useful domain of any place whatsoever, she has also the higher domain and empire, or the sovereignty (§205). We cannot, however, from the possession of the empire, infer with equal probability a co-existent possession of the useful domain; for a nation may have good reasons for claiming the empire over

* See Book II. §83.

a country, and particularly over a tract of sea, without pretending to have any property in it, or any useful domain. The English have never claimed the property of all the seas over which they have claimed the empire.

This is all we have to say in this first book. A more minute detail of the duties and rights of a nation, considered in herself would lead us too far. Such detail must, as we have already observed, be sought for in particular treatises on the public and political law. We are very far from flattering ourselves that we have omitted no important article: this is a slight sketch of an immense picture: but an intelligent reader will without difficulty supply all our omissions by making a proper application of the general principles: we have taken the utmost care solidly to establish those principles, and to develop them with precision and perspicuity. <132> <133>

THE
LAW
OF
NATIONS

ɷɷ **BOOK II** ɷɷ

Of a Nation considered in
its Relations to others

CHAPTER I

Of the Common Duties of a Nation towards others,
or of the Offices of Humanity between Nations.

The following maxims will appear very strange to cabinet politicians: §1. Founda-
and such is the misfortune of mankind, that, to many of those refined tion of the
conductors of nations, the doctrine of this chapter will be a subject of common and
mutual duties
ridicule. Be it so!—but we will nevertheless boldly lay down what the of nations.
law of nature prescribes to nations. Shall we be intimidated by ridicule,
when we speak after Cicero? That great man held the reins of the most
powerful state that ever existed; and in that station he appeared no less
eminent than at the bar. The punctual observance of the law of nature
he considered as the most salutary policy to the state. In my preface, I
have already quoted this fine passage: *Nihil est quod adhuc de republica*
putem dictum, & quo possim longius progredi, nisi sit confirmatum, non
modo falsum esse illud, sine injuria non posse, sed hoc verissimum, sine

259

summa justitia rempublicam regi non posse.*¹ I might say on good grounds, that, by the words, *summa justitia,* Cicero means that universal justice which consists in completely fulfilling the law of nature. But in another place he explains himself more clearly on this head, and gives us sufficiently to understand that he does not confine <134> the mutual duties of men to the observance of justice, properly so called. "Nothing," says he, "is more agreeable to nature, more capable of affording true satisfaction, than, in imitation of Hercules, to undertake even the most arduous and painful labours for the benefit and preservation of all nations." *Magis est secundum naturam, pro omnibus gentibus, si fieri possit, conservandis aut juvandis, maximos labores molestiasque suscipere, imitantem Herculem illum, quem hominum fama, beneficiorum memor, in concilium coelestium collocavit, quam vivere in solitudine, non modo sine ullis molestiis, sed etiam in maximis voluptatibus, abundantem omnibus copiis, ut excellas etiam pulchritudine & viribus. Quocirca optimo quisque & splendidissimo ingenio longe illam vitam huic anteponit.*†² In the same chapter, Cicero expressly refutes those who are for excluding foreigners from the benefit of those duties to which they acknowledge themselves bound towards their fellow citizens. *Qui autem civium rationem dicunt habendam, externorum negant, hi dirimunt communem humani generis societatem; qua sublata, beneficentia, liberalitas, bonitas, justitia, funditus tollitur: quae qui tollunt, etiam adversus Deos immor-*

---

* Fragm. ex lib. ii. De Republica.

† De Officiis lib. iii. cap. 5.

1. "A state cannot be happily governed without committing injustice; without a strict attention to the most rigid justice, public affairs cannot be advantageously administered." Cicero, Fragment. Ex lib. ii *De republica* (see also preface, p. 19).

2. "It is more in accord with Nature to emulate the great Hercules and undergo the greatest toil and trouble for the sake of aiding or saving the world, if possible, than to live in seclusion, not only free from all care but also reveling in pleasures and abounding in wealth, while excelling others also in beauty and strength. Thus Hercules denied himself and underwent toil and tribulation for the world, and, out of gratitude for his services, popular belief has given him a place in the council of gods. The better and more noble therefore the character with which a man is endowed, the more does he prefer the life of service to the life of pleasure." Cicero, *De officiis* III.v.25.

tales impii judicandi sunt; ab iis enim constitutam inter homines socie-
tatem evertunt. [3]

And why should we not hope still to find, among those who are at
the head of affairs, some wise individuals, who are convinced of this
great truth, that virtue is, even for sovereigns and political bodies, the
most certain road to prosperity and happiness? There is at least one benefit to be expected from the open assertion and publication of sound
maxims, which is, that even those who relish them the least, are thereby
laid under a necessity of keeping within some bounds, lest they should
forfeit their characters altogether. To flatter ourselves with the vain expectation that men, and especially men in power, will be inclined strictly
to conform to the laws of nature, would be a gross mistake; and to renounce all hope of making impression on some of them, would be to
give up mankind for lost.

Nations being obliged by nature reciprocally to cultivate human society (Prelim. §11), are bound to observe towards each other all the duties
which the safety and advantage of that society require.

The offices of humanity are those succours, those duties, which men
owe to each other, as men, that is, as social beings formed to live in
society, and standing in need of mutual assistance for their preservation
and happiness, and to enable them to live in a manner conformable to
their nature. Now the laws of nature being no less obligatory on nations
than on individuals (Prelim. §5), whatever duties each man owes to other
men, the same does each nation, in its way, owe to other nations (Prelim.
§10, &c.). Such is the foundation of those common duties,—of those
offices of humanity,—to which nations are reciprocally bound towards
each other. They consist, generally, in do-<135>ing every thing in our
power for the preservation and happiness of others, as far as such conduct is reconcilable with our duties towards ourselves.

§2. Offices
of humanity,
and their
foundation.

3. "Others again who say that regard should be had for the rights of fellow citizens,
but not for foreigners, would destroy the universal brotherhood of mankind; and,
when this is annihilated, kindness, generosity, goodness, and justice must utterly perish; and those who work all this destruction must be considered as wickedly rebelling
against the immortal gods. For they uproot the fellowship between humans." Cicero,
De officiis III.vi.28.

§3. General
principle of all
the mutual
duties of
nations.

The nature and essence of man—who, without the assistance of his fellow men, is unable to supply all his wants, to preserve himself, to render himself perfect, and to live happily—plainly shews us that he is destined to live in society, in the interchange of mutual aid,—and, consequently, that all men are, by their very nature and essence, obliged to unite their common efforts for the perfection of their own being and that of their condition. The surest method of succeeding in this pursuit is, that each individual should exert his efforts, first for himself, and then for others. Hence it follows that whatever we owe to ourselves, we likewise owe to others, so far as they stand in need of assistance, and we can grant it to them without being wanting to ourselves. Since then one nation, in its way, owes to another nation every duty that one man owes to another man, we may confidently lay down this general principle:— One state owes to another state whatever it owes to itself, so far as that other stands in real need of its assistance, and the former can grant it without neglecting the duties it owes to itself. Such is the eternal and immutable law of nature. Those who might be alarmed at this doctrine, as totally subversive of the maxims of sound policy, will be relieved from their apprehensions by the two following considerations—

1. Social bodies or sovereign states are much more capable of supplying all their wants than individual men are; and mutual assistance is not so necessary among them, nor so frequently required. Now, in those particulars which a nation can itself perform, no succour is due to it from others.

2. The duties of a nation towards itself, and chiefly the care of its own safety, require much more circumspection and reserve, than need be observed by an individual in giving assistance to others. This remark we shall soon illustrate.

§4. Duties of a
nation for the
preservation
of others.

Of all the duties of a nation towards itself the chief object is its preservation and perfection, together with that of its state. The detail given of them in the first book of this work may serve to point out the several objects in relation to which a state may and should assist another state. Every nation ought, on occasion, to labour for the preservation of others, and for securing them from ruin and destruction, as far as it can do this, without exposing itself too much. Thus, when a neighbouring nation is unjustly attacked by a powerful enemy who threatens to oppress it,—if you can defend it without exposing yourself to great danger, unquestionably it is your duty to do so. Let it not be said, in objection to this, that a sovereign is not to expose the lives of his soldiers, for the safety of a foreign nation with which he has not contracted a defensive alliance. It may be his own case to stand in need of assistance; and consequently he is acting for the safety of his own nation, in giving energy to the spirit <136> and disposition to afford mutual aid. Accordingly, policy here coincides with and enforces obligation and duty. It is the interest of princes to stop the progress of an ambitious monarch who aims at aggrandising himself by subjugating his neighbours. A powerful league was formed in favour of the United Provinces, when threatened with the yoke of Lewis XIV.* When the Turks laid siege to Vienna, the brave Sobieski king of Poland saved the house of Austria,† and possibly all Germany, and his own kingdom.⁴

For the same reason, if a nation is afflicted with famine, all those who have provisions to spare ought to relieve her distress, without however exposing themselves to want. But if that nation is able to pay for the provisions thus furnished, it is perfectly lawful to sell them to her at a reasonable rate; for they are not bound to furnish her with what she is herself capable of procuring; and consequently there is no obligation of gratuitously bestowing on her such things as she is able to purchase. To give assistance in such extreme necessity is so essentially conformable to humanity, that the duty is seldom neglected by any nation that has received the slightest polish of civilisation. The great Henry the Fourth⁵ could not forbear to comply with it in favour of obstinate rebels who were bent on his destruction.‡

§5. It ought to assist a nation afflicted with famine or any other calamities.

Whatever be the calamity with which a nation is afflicted, the like assistance is due to it. We have seen little states in Switzerland order

* In 1672.
† He defeated the Turks, and obliged them to raise the siege of Vienna, in 1683.
‡ At the famous siege of Paris [[1590]].
4. Jan III Sobieski (r. 1674–99) defeated the Turks in 1683 at the battle of Vienna, ending a two-month seige by the Ottoman Empire army.
5. Henry IV, king of France, r. 1589–1610.

public collections to be made in behalf of towns or villages of the neighbouring countries, which had been ruined by fire, and remit them liberal succours; the difference of religion proving no bar to the performance of so humane a deed. The calamities of Portugal have given England an opportunity of fulfilling the duties of humanity with that noble generosity which characterises a great nation. On the first intelligence of the disastrous fate of Lisbon,*[6] the parliament voted a hundred thousand pounds sterling for the relief of an unfortunate people; the king also added considerable sums: ships, laden with provisions and all kinds of succours, were sent away with the utmost dispatch; and their arrival convinced the Portuguese, that an opposition in belief and worship does not restrain the beneficence of those who understand the claims of humanity. On the same occasion likewise the king of Spain signally displayed his tenderness for a near ally, and exerted in a conspicuous manner his humanity and generosity.

§6. It ought to contribute to the perfection of other states.   A nation must not simply confine itself to the preservation of other states; it should likewise, according to its power and their want of its assistance, contribute to their perfection. We have already shewn (Prelim. §13) that natural society imposes on it this general obligation. We are now come to the proper place <137> for treating of the obligation somewhat more in detail. A state is more or less perfect, as it is more or less adapted to attain the end of civil society, which consists in procuring for its members every thing of which they stand in need, for the necessities, the conveniences and enjoyments of life, and for their happiness in general,—in providing for the peaceful enjoyment of property, and the safe and easy administration of justice,—and, finally, in defending itself against all foreign violence (Book I. §15). Every nation therefore should occasionally, and according to its power, contribute, not only to put another nation in possession of these advantages, but likewise to render it capable of procuring them itself. Accordingly, a learned nation, if applied to for masters and teachers in the sciences, by another nation desirous of shaking off its native barbarism, ought not to refuse such a

---

* The earthquake by which a great part of that city was destroyed.
6. The Lisbon earthquake struck on November 1, All Saints' Day, 1755.

request. A nation whose happiness it is to live under wise laws, should, on occasion, make it a point of duty to communicate them. Thus when the wise and virtuous Romans sent ambassadors to Greece to collect good laws, the Greeks were far from rejecting so reasonable and so laudable a request.

But though a nation be obliged to promote, as far as lies in its power, the perfection of others, it is not entitled forcibly to obtrude these good offices on them. Such an attempt would be a violation of their natural liberty. In order to compel any one to receive a kindness, we must have an authority over him; but nations are absolutely free and independent (Prelim. §4). Those ambitious Europeans who attacked the American nations, and subjected them to their greedy dominion, in order, as they pretended, to civilise them, and cause them to be instructed in the true religion,—those usurpers, I say, grounded themselves on a pretext equally unjust and ridiculous. It is strange to hear the learned and judicious Grotius assert, that a sovereign may justly take up arms to chastise nations which are guilty of enormous transgressions of the law of nature, *which treat their parents with inhumanity like the Sogdians, which eat human flesh as the ancient Gauls, &c.** What led him into this error, was his attributing to every independent man, and of course to every sovereign, an odd kind of right to punish faults which involve an enormous violation of the laws of nature, though they do not affect either his rights or his safety. But we have shewn (Book I. §169) that men derive the right of punishment solely from their right to provide for their own safety; and consequently they cannot claim it except against those by whom they have been injured. Could it escape Grotius, that, notwithstanding all the precautions added by him in the following paragraphs, his opinion opens a door to all the ravages of enthusiasm and fanaticism, and furnishes ambition with numberless pretexts? Mahomet and his successors have desolated and subdued Asia, to avenge the indignity done to the unity of the Godhead; all whom they termed associators or idolaters fell victims to their devout fury. <138>

§7. But not by force.

---

* De Jure Belli et Pacis, lib. ii. cap. xx. §11.

§8. The right
to require the
offices of
humanity.

Since nations ought to perform these duties or offices of humanity towards each other, according as one stands in need, and the other can reasonably comply with them,—every nation being free, independent, and sole arbitress of her own actions, it belongs to each to consider whether her situation warrants her in asking or granting any thing on this head. Thus 1. Every nation has a perfect right to ask of another that assistance and those kind offices which she conceives herself to stand in need of. To prevent her, would be doing her an injury. If she makes the application without necessity, she is guilty of a breach of duty; but in this respect, she is wholly independent of the judgment of others. A nation has a right to ask for these kind offices, but not to demand them.

§9. The right
of judging
whether they
are to be
granted.

For, 2. These offices being due only in necessity, and by a nation which can comply with them without being wanting to itself; the nation that is applied to has, on the other hand, a right of judging whether the case really demands them, and whether circumstances will allow her to grant them consistently with that regard which she ought to pay to her own safety and interests: for instance, a nation is in want of corn, and applies to another nation to sell her a quantity of it:—in this case it rests with the latter party to judge whether, by a compliance with the request, they will not expose themselves to the danger of a scarcity: and if they refuse to comply, their determination is to be patiently acquiesced in. We have very lately seen a prudent performance of this duty on the part of Russia: she generously assisted Sweden when threatened with a famine,[7] but refused to other powers the liberty of purchasing corn in Livonia, from the circumstance of standing herself in need of it, and, no doubt, from weighty political motives likewise.

§10. A nation
is not to com-
pel another
to perform
those offices
of which the
refusal is no
wrong.

Thus the right which a nation has to the offices of humanity is but an imperfect one: she cannot compel another nation to the performance of them. The nation that unreasonably refuses them, offends against equity, which consists in acting conformably to the imperfect right of another: but thereby no injury is done; injury or injustice being a trespass against the perfect right of another.

7. 1740–63.

It is impossible that nations should mutually discharge all these several duties if they do not love each other. This is the pure source from which the offices of humanity should proceed; they will retain the character and perfection of it. Then nations will be seen sincerely and cheerfully to help each other, earnestly to promote their common welfare, and cultivate peace without jealousy or distrust.

§11. Mutual love of nations.

A real friendship will be seen to reign among them; and this happy state consists in a mutual affection. Every nation is obliged to cultivate the friendship of other nations, and carefully to avoid whatever might kindle their enmity against her. Wise and prudent nations often pursue this line of conduct from views of direct and present interest: a more noble, more general, and <139> less direct interest, is too rarely the motive of politicians. If it be incontestable that men must love each other in order to answer the views of nature and discharge the duties which she prescribes them, as well as for their own private advantage,—can it be doubted that nations are under the like reciprocal obligation? Is it in the power of men, on dividing themselves into different political bodies, to break the ties of that universal society which nature has established amongst them?

§12. Each nation ought to cultivate the friendship of others.

If a man ought to qualify himself for becoming useful to other men,—and a citizen, for rendering useful services to his country and fellow citizens,—a nation likewise, in perfecting herself, ought to have in view the acquisition of a greater degree of ability to promote the perfection and happiness of other nations: she should be careful to set them good examples, and avoid setting them a pattern of any thing evil. Imitation is natural to mankind: the virtues of a celebrated nation are sometimes imitated, and much more frequently its vices and defects.

§13. To perfect itself with a view to the advantage of others, and set them good examples.

Glory being a possession of great importance to a nation, as we have shewn in a particular chapter expressly devoted to the subject,*—the duty of a nation extends even to the care of the glory of other nations. In the first place, she should, on occasion, contribute to enable them to merit true glory: secondly, she should do them in this respect all the justice due to them, and use all proper endeavours that such justice be

§14. To take care of their glory.

* Book i. chap. xv.

universally done them: finally, instead of irritating, she should kindly extenuate the bad effect which some slight blemishes may produce.

§15. Difference of religion ought not to preclude the offices of humanity.

From the manner in which we have established the obligation of performing the offices of humanity, it plainly appears to be solely founded on the nature of man. Wherefore no nation can refuse them to another, under pretence of its professing a different religion: to be entitled to them, it is sufficient that the claimant is our fellow-creature. A conformity of belief and worship may become a new tie of friendship between nations; but no difference in these respects can warrant us in laying aside the character of men, or the sentiments annexed to it. As we have already related (§5) some instances well worthy of imitation, let us here do justice to the pontiff who at present fills the see of Rome, and has recently given a very remarkable example, and which cannot be too highly commended. Information being given to that prince, that several Dutch ships remained at Civita Vecchia, not daring to put to sea for fear of the Algerine corsairs, he immediately issued orders that the frigates of the ecclesiastical state should convoy those ships out of danger; and his nuncio at Brussels received instructions to signify to the ministers of the states-general, that his holiness made it a rule to protect commerce and perform the duties of humanity, without regarding any difference of religion. Such exalted sentiments cannot fail of raising a veneration for Benedict XIV.[8] even amongst protestants. <140>

§16. Rule and measure the offices of humanity.

How happy would mankind be, were these amiable precepts of nature every where observed! Nations would communicate to each other their products and their knowledge; a profound peace would prevail all over the earth, and enrich it with its invaluable fruits; industry, the sciences, and the arts, would be employed in promoting our happiness, no less than in relieving our wants; violent methods of deciding contests would be no more heard of: all differences would be terminated by moderation, justice, and equity; the world would have the appearance of a large republic; men would live every-where like brothers, and each individual be a citizen of the universe. That this idea should be but a delightful

8. Pope Benedict XIV, r. 1740–58.

dream! yet it flows from the nature and essence of man.* But disorderly passions, and private and mistaken interest, will forever prevent its being realised. Let us then consider what limitations the present state of men, and the ordinary maxims and conduct of nations, may render necessary in the practice of these precepts of nature, which are in themselves so noble and excellent.

The law of nature cannot condemn the good to become the dupes and prey of the wicked, and the victims of their injustice and ingratitude. Melancholy experience shews that most nations aim only to strengthen and enrich themselves at the expense of others,—to domineer over them, and even, if an opportunity offers, to oppress and bring them under the yoke. Prudence does not allow us to strengthen an enemy, or one in whom we discover a desire of plundering and oppressing us; and the care of our own safety forbids it. We have seen (§3, &c.) that a nation does not owe her assistance and the offices of humanity to other nations, except so far as the grant of them is reconcilable with her duties to herself. Hence it evidently follows, that, though the universal love of mankind obliges us to grant at all times, and to all, even to our enemies,

---

* Here again let us call in the authority of Cicero to our support. "All mankind (says that excellent philosopher) should lay it down as their constant rule of action, that individual and general advantage should be the same; for if each man strives to grasp every advantage for himself, all the ties of human society will be broken. And if nature ordains that man should feel interested in the welfare of his fellow man, whoever he be, and for the single reason that he is a man,—it necessarily follows, that, according to the intentions of nature, all mankind must have one common interest.—Ergo unum debet esse omnibus propositum, ut eadem sit utilitas unius-cujusque et universorum: quam si ad se quisque rapiat, dissolvetur omnis humana consociatio. Atque si etiam hoc natura praescribit, ut homo homini, quicunque sit, ob eam ipsam causam, quod is homo sit, consultum velit, necesse est, secundum eandem naturam, omnium utilitatem esse communem. [["This, then, ought to be the chief end of all men, to make the interest of each individual and of the whole body political identical. For, if the individual appropriates to selfish ends what should be devoted to the common good, all human fellowship will be destroyed. And further, if Nature ordains that one man shall desire to promote the interest of a fellow man, whoever he may be, just because he is a fellow man, then it follows, in accordance with that same Nature, that there are interests which all men have in common."]] *De Offic.* lib. iii. cap. vi.

those offices which can only tend to render them more moderate and virtuous, because no inconvenience is to be apprehended from granting them,—we are not obliged to give them such succours as probably may become destructive to ourselves. Thus, 1. the exceeding importance of trade not only to the wants and conveniences of life, but likewise to the strength of a state, and furnishing it with the means of defending itself against its enemies,—and the insatiable <141> avidity of those nations which seek wholly and exclusively to engross it,—thus, I say, these circumstances authorise a nation possessed of a branch of trade, or the secret of some important manufacture or fabric, to reserve to herself those sources of wealth, and, instead of communicating them to foreign nations, to take measures against it. But where the necessaries or conveniences of life are in question, the nation ought to sell them to others at a reasonable price, and not convert her monopoly into a system of odious extortion. To commerce England chiefly owes her greatness, her power, and her safety: who then will presume to blame her for endeavouring, by every fair and just method, to retain the several branches of it in her own hand?

2. As to things directly and more particularly useful for war, a nation is under no obligation to sell them to others, of whom it has the smallest suspicion; and prudence even declares against it. Thus, by the Roman laws, people were very justly prohibited to instruct the barbarous nations in building gallies. Thus, in England laws have been enacted, to prevent the best method of ship-building from being carried out of the kingdom.

This caution is to be carried farther, with respect to nations more justly suspected. Thus, when the Turks were successfully pursuing their victorious career, and rapidly advancing to the zenith of power, all christian nations ought, independent of every bigotted consideration, to have considered them as enemies; even the most distant of those nations, though not engaged in any contest with them, would have been justifiable in breaking off all commerce with a people who made it their profession to subdue by force of arms all who would not acknowledge the authority of their prophet.

Let us farther observe, with regard to the prince in particular, that he ought not, in affairs of this nature, to obey without reserve all the suggestions of a noble and generous heart impelling him to sacrifice his own interests to the advantage of others or to motives of generosity; because it is not his private interest that is in question, but that of the state,—that of the nation who has committed herself to his care. Cicero says that a great and elevated soul despises pleasures, wealth, life itself, and makes no account of them, when the common utility lies at stake.* He is right, and such sentiments are to be admired in a private person; but generosity is not to be exerted at the expense of others. The head or conductor of a nation ought not to practise that virtue in public affairs without great circumspection, nor to a greater extent than will redound to the glory and real advantage of the state. As to the common good of human society, he ought to pay the same attention to it, as the nation he represents would be obliged to pay, were the government of her affairs in her own hand.

§17. Particular limitation with regard to the prince.

But though the duties of a nation towards herself set bounds to the obligation of performing the offices of humanity, they <142> cannot in the least affect the prohibition of doing any harm to others, of causing them any prejudice,—in a word, of injuring them.† ... If every man is, by his very nature, obliged to assist in promoting the perfection of others, much more cogent are the reasons which forbid him to increase their imperfection and that of their condition. The same duties are incumbent on nations (Prelim. §§5, 6). No nation therefore ought to commit any actions tending to impair the perfection of other nations, and that of their condition, or to impede their progress,—in other words, to injure them. And since the perfection of a nation consists in her ap-

§18. No nation ought to injure others.

* De Offic. lib. iii. cap. v.

† *Lézer* (professedly borrowed from the Latin *laedo*) is the term used by the author, who, in order the better to explain his meaning, proceeds to inform us, that *"nuire* (to hurt), *offenser* (to offend), *faire tort* (to wrong), *porter dommage* (to cause detriment), *porter prejudice* (to prejudice), *blesser* (to wound or hurt), are not of precisely the same import," and that by the word *lézer* (which is here rendered *injure*) he means, "in general, causing imperfection in the injured party, or in his condition,—rendering his person or his condition less perfect." [[Note added in 1797 edition.]]

titude to attain the end of civil society,—and the perfection of her condition, in not wanting any of the things necessary to that end (Book I. §14)—no one nation ought to hinder another from attaining the end of civil society, or to render her incapable of attaining it. This general principle forbids nations to practise any evil manoeuvres tending to create disturbance in another state, to foment discord, to corrupt its citizens, to alienate its allies, to raise enemies against it, to tarnish its glory, and to deprive it of its natural advantages.

However, it will be easily conceived that negligence in fulfilling the common duties of humanity, and even the refusal of these duties or offices, is not an injury. To neglect or refuse contributing to the perfection of a nation, is not impairing that perfection.

It must be further observed, that when we are making use of our right, when we are doing what we owe to ourselves or to others, if, from this action of ours, any prejudice results to the perfection of another,—any detriment to his exterior condition,—we are not guilty of an injury: we are doing what is lawful, or even what we ought to do. The damage which accrues to the other, is no part of our intention: it is merely an accident, the imputability of which must be determined by the particular circumstances. For instance, in case of a lawful defence, the harm we do to the aggressor is not the object we aim at:—we act only with a view to our own safety: we make use of our right; and the aggressor alone is chargeable with the mischief which he brings on himself.

§19. Offences.   Nothing is more opposite to the duties of humanity, nor more contrary to that society which should be cultivated by nations, than offences, or actions which give a just displeasure to others: every nation therefore should carefully avoid giving any other nation real offence: I say, *real;* for, should others take offence at our behaviour when we are only using our rights or fulfilling our duties, the fault lies with them, not with us. Offences ex-<143>cite such asperity and rancour between nations, that we should avoid giving any room even for ill-grounded picques, when it can be done without any inconveniency, or failure in our duty. It is said that certain medals and dull jests irritated Lewis XIV. against the United Provinces, to such a degree, as to induce him, in 1672, to undertake the destruction of that republic.

The maxims laid down in this chapter,—those sacred precepts of nature,—were for a long time unknown to nations. The ancients had no notion of any duty they owed to nations with whom they were not united by treaties of friendship.* The Jews especially placed a great part of their zeal in hating all nations; and, as a natural consequence, they were detested and despised by them in turn. At length the voice of nature came to be heard among civilised nations; they perceived that all men are brethren.† When will the happy time come that they shall behave as such?

§20. Bad custom of the ancients.

CHAPTER II

Of the Mutual Commerce between Nations.

All men ought to find on earth the things they stand in need of. In the primitive state of communion, they took them wherever they happened to meet with them, if another had not before appropriated them to his own use. The introduction of dominion and property could not deprive men of so essential a right, and consequently it cannot take place without leaving them, in general, some mean of procuring what is useful or necessary to them. This mean is commerce: by it every man may still supply his wants. Things being now become property, there is no obtaining them without the owner's consent; nor are they usually to be had for nothing; but they may be bought, or exchanged for other things of equal value. Men are therefore under an obligation to carry on that commerce with each other, if they wish not to deviate from the views of nature; and this obligation extends also to whole nations or states (Prelim. §5).

§21. General obligation of nations to carry on mutual commerce.

---

* To the example of the Romans may be added that of the English in former days,—since, on the occasion of a navigator being accused of having committed some depredations on the natives of India, "this act of injustice" (according to Grotius) "was not without advocates, who maintained, that, by the ancient laws of England, crimes committed against foreign nations, with whom there existed no public treaty of alliance, were not punishable in that kingdom." HIST. *of the Disturbances in the Low Countries,* Book xvi. [[Note added in 1773/1797 editions.]]

† See (§1) a fine passage of Cicero.

It is seldom that nature is seen in one place to produce every thing necessary for the use of man: one country abounds in corn, another in pastures and cattle, a third in timber and metals, &c. If all those countries trade together, as is agreeable to human nature, no one of them will be without such things as are useful <144> and necessary; and the views of nature, our common mother, will be fulfilled. Further, one country is fitter for some kind of products than another, as, for instance, fitter for the vine than for tillage. If trade and barter take place, every nation, on the certainty of procuring what it wants, will employ its land and its industry in the most advantageous manner; and mankind in general prove gainers by it. Such are the foundations of the general obligation incumbent on nations reciprocally to cultivate commerce.

§22. They should favour trade.

Every nation ought, therefore, not only to countenance trade, as far as it reasonably can, but even to protect and favour it. The care of the public roads,—the safety of travellers,—the establishment of ports, of places of sale, of well-regulated fairs,—all contribute to this end. And where these are attended with expense, the nation, as we have already observed (Book I. §103), may, by tolls and other duties equitably proportioned, indemnify itself for its disbursements.

§23. Freedom of trade.

Freedom being very favourable to commerce, it is implied in the duties of nations, that they should support it as far as possible, instead of cramping it by unnecessary burdens or restrictions. Wherefore those private privileges and tolls, which obtain in many places, and press so heavily on commerce, are deservedly to be reprobated, unless founded on very important reasons arising from the public good.

§24. Right of trading, belonging to nations.

Every nation, in virtue of her natural liberty, has a right to trade with those who are willing to correspond with such intentions; and to molest her in the exercise of her right is doing her an injury. The Portuguese, at the time of their great power in the East Indies, were for excluding all other European nations from any commerce with the Indians: but such a pretension, no less iniquitous than chimerical, was treated with contempt; and the other nations agreed to consider any acts of violence in support of it, as just grounds for making war against the Portuguese. This common right of all nations is, at present, generally acknowledged under the appellation of freedom of trade.

But although it be in general the duty of a nation to carry on commerce with others, and though each nation has a right to trade with those countries that are willing to encourage her,—on the other hand, a nation ought to decline a commerce which is disadvantageous or dangerous (Book I. §98); and since, in case of collision, her duties to herself are paramount to her duties to others, she has a full and clear right to regulate her conduct, in this respect, by the consideration of what her advantage or safety requires. We have already seen (Book I. §92) that each nation is, on her own part, the sole judge, whether or not it be convenient for her to cultivate such or such branch of commerce: she may therefore either embrace or reject any commercial proposals from foreign nations, without affording them any just grounds to accuse her of injustice, or to demand a reason for such refusal, much less to make use of compulsion. She is free in the administration <145> of her affairs, without being accountable to any other. The obligation of trading with other nations is in itself an imperfect obligation (Prelim. §17), and gives them only an imperfect right; so that, in cases where the commerce would be detrimental, that obligation is entirely void. When the Spaniards attacked the Americans under a pretence that those people refused to traffic with them, they only endeavoured to throw a colourable veil over their own insatiable avarice.

§25. Each nation is sole judge of the propriety of commerce on her own part.

These few remarks, together with what we have already said on the subject (Book I. Chap. VIII.) may suffice to establish the principles of the natural law of nations respecting the mutual commerce of states. It is not difficult to point out, in general, what are the duties of nations in this respect, and what the law of nature prescribes to them for the good of the great society of mankind. But as each nation is only so far obliged to carry on commerce with others, as she can do it without being wanting to herself,—and as the whole ultimately depends on the judgment that each state may form of what it can and ought to do in particular cases,—nations cannot count on any thing more than generalities, such as the inherent liberty of each to carry on trade,—and, moreover, on imperfect rights, which depend on the judgment of others, and, consequently, are ever uncertain. Wherefore, if they wish to secure to themselves any definite and constant advantages, they must procure them by treaties.

§26. Necessity of commercial treaties.

§27. General rule concerning those treaties.   Since a nation has a full right to regulate herself in commercial affairs by what is useful or advantageous to her, she may make such commercial treaties as she thinks proper; and no other nation has a right to take offence, provided those treaties do not affect the perfect rights of others. If, by the engagements contracted, a nation, unnecessarily, or without powerful reasons, renders herself incapable of joining in the general trade which nature recommends between nations, she trespasses against her duty. But the nation being the sole judge in this case (Prelim. §16), other nations are bound to respect her natural liberty,—to acquiesce in her determination, and even to suppose that she is actuated by substantial reasons. Every commercial treaty, therefore, which does not impair the perfect right of others, is allowable between nations; nor can the execution of it be lawfully opposed. But those commercial treaties alone are in themselves just and commendable, which pay to the general interest of mankind as great a degree of respect as is possible and reasonable in the particular case.

§28. Duty of nations in making those treaties.   As express promises and engagements should be inviolable, every wise and virtuous nation will be attentive to examine and weigh a commercial treaty before she concludes it, and to take care that she be not thereby engaged to any thing contrary to the duties which she owes to herself and others.

§29. Perpetual or temporary treaties, or treaties revocable at pleasure.   Nations may in their treaties insert such clauses and conditions as they think proper: they are at liberty to make them perpetual, or temporary, or dependent on certain events. It is usually most <146> prudent not to engage forever, as circumstances may afterwards intervene, by which the treaty might become very oppressive to one of the contracting parties. A nation may confine a treaty to the grant of only a precarious right,— reserving to herself the liberty of revoking it at pleasure. We have already observed (Book I. §94), that a simple permission does not, any more than long custom (ibid. §95), give any perfect right to a trade. These things are therefore not to be confounded with treaties,—not even with those which give only a precarious right.

§30. Nothing contrary to   When once a nation has entered into engagements by treaty, she is no longer at liberty to do, in favour of others, contrary to the tenor of the treaty, what she might otherwise have granted to them agreeably to the duties of humanity or the general obligation of mutual commerce: for she is to do for others no more than what is in her power; and having deprived herself of the liberty of disposing of a thing, that thing is no longer in her power. Therefore when a nation has engaged to another that she will sell certain merchandise or produce to the latter only,—as, for instance, corn,—she can no longer sell it to any other. The case is the same in a contract to purchase certain goods of that nation alone.

But it will be asked, how and on what occasions a nation may enter into engagements which deprive her of the liberty to fulfil her duties to others. As the duties we owe to ourselves are paramount to those we owe to others,—if a nation finds her safety and substantial advantage in a treaty of this nature, she is unquestionably justifiable in contracting it,—especially as she does not thereby interrupt the general commerce of nations, but simply causes one particular branch of her own commerce to pass through other hands, or ensures to a particular people certain things of which they stand in need. If a state which stands in need of salt can secure a supply of it from another, by engaging to sell her corn and cattle only to that other nation, who will doubt but she has a right to conclude so salutary a treaty? In this case, her corn or cattle are goods which she disposes of for supplying her own wants. But, from what we have observed (§28), engagements of this kind are not to be entered into, without very good reasons. However, be the reasons good or bad, the treaty is still valid, and other nations have no right to oppose it (§27).

Every one is at liberty to renounce his right: a nation therefore may lay a restriction on her commerce in favour of another nation, and engage not to traffic in a certain kind of goods, or to forbear trading with such and such a country, &c. And in departing from such engagements, she acts against the perfect right of the nation with which she has contracted; and the latter has a right to restrain her. The natural liberty of trade is not hurt by treaties of this nature: for that liberty consists only in every nation being unmolested in her right to carry on commerce with those that consent to traffic with her; each one remaining free <147> to

> the tenor of a treaty can be granted to a third party.

> §31. How far lawful to give up by treaty the liberty of trading with other nations.

> §32. A nation may abridge its commerce in favour of another.

embrace or decline a particular branch of commerce, as she shall judge most advantageous to the state.

§33. A nation may appropriate to itself a particular branch of trade.

Nations not only carry on trade for the sake of procuring necessary or useful articles, but also with a view to make it a source of opulence. Now, wherever a profit is to be made, it is equally lawful for every one to participate in it: but the most diligent may lawfully anticipate the others by taking possession of an advantage which lies open to the first occupier;—he may even secure the whole entirely to himself, if he has any lawful means of appropriating it. When therefore a particular nation is in sole possession of certain articles, another nation may lawfully procure to herself by treaty the advantage of being the only buyer, and then sell them again all over the world. And as it is indifferent to nations from what hand they receive the commodities they want, provided they obtain them at a reasonable price, the monopoly of this nation does not clash with the general duties of humanity, provided that she do not take advantage of it to set an unreasonable and exorbitant price on her goods. Should she, by an abuse of her monopoly, exact an immoderate profit, this would be an offence against the law of nature, as by such an exaction she either deprives other nations of a necessary or agreeable article which nature designed for all men, or obliges them to purchase it at too dear a rate: nevertheless she does not do them any positive wrong, because, strictly speaking, and according to external right, the owner of a commodity may either keep it, or set what price he pleases on it. Thus the Dutch, by a treaty with the king of Ceylon,[9] have wholly engrossed the cinnamon trade: yet, whilst they keep their profits within just limits, other nations have no right to complain.

But, were the necessaries of life in question,—were the monopolist inclined to raise them to an excessive price,—other nations would be authorised by the care of their own safety, and for the advantage of human society, to form a general combination in order to reduce a greedy oppressor to reasonable terms. The right to necessaries is very different

9. By the Kandyan Treaty of 1638, the Dutch allied themselves with the king of Kandy (Ceylon) against the Portuguese. In return for military assistance, the Dutch East India Company gained numerous commercial privileges.

from that to things adapted only to convenience and pleasure, which we may dispense with, if they be too dear. It would be absurd that the subsistence and being of other nations should depend on the caprice or avidity of one.

Among the modern institutions for the advantage of commerce, one of the most useful is that of consuls, or persons residing in the large trading cities, and especially the seaports, of foreign countries, with a commission to watch over the rights and privileges of their nation, and to decide disputes between her merchants there. When a nation trades largely with a country, it is requisite to have there a person charged with such a commission: and as the state which allows of this commerce must naturally favour it,—for the same reason also, it must admit the consul. But there being no absolute and perfect obligation to this, the nation <148> that wishes to have a consul, must procure this right by the commercial treaty itself. §34. Consuls.

The consul being charged with the affairs of his sovereign, and receiving his orders, continues his subject, and accountable to him for his actions.

The consul is no public minister (as will appear by what we shall say of the character of ministers, in our fourth book), and cannot pretend to the privileges annexed to such character. Yet, bearing his sovereign's commission, and being in this quality received by the prince in whose dominions he resides, he is, in a certain degree, entitled to the protection of the law of nations. This sovereign, by the very act of receiving him, tacitly engages to allow him all the liberty and safety necessary to the proper discharge of his functions, without which the admission of the consul would be nugatory and delusive.

The functions of a consul require, in the first place, that he be not a subject of the state where he resides; as, in this case, he would be obliged in all things to conform to its orders, and thus not be at liberty to acquit himself of the duties of his office.

They seem even to require that the consul should be independent of the ordinary criminal justice of the place where he resides, so as not to be molested or imprisoned, unless he himself violate the law of nations by some enormous crime.

And though the importance of the consular functions be not so great as to procure to the consul's person the inviolability and absolute independence enjoyed by public ministers,—yet, being under the particular protection of the sovereign who employs him, and intrusted with the care of his concerns,—if he commits any crime, the respect due to his master requires that he should be sent home to be punished. Such is the mode pursued by states that are inclined to preserve a good understanding with each other. But the surest way is, expressly to settle all these matters, as far as is practicable, by the commercial treaty.

Wicquefort, in his treatise of *The Ambassador,* Book I. §5, says *that consuls do not enjoy the protection of the law of nations, and that, both in civil and criminal cases, they are subject to the justice of the place where they reside.* But the very instances he quotes contradict his proposition. The states-general of the United Provinces, whose consul had been affronted and put under arrest by the governor of Cadiz, *complained of it to the court of Madrid as a breach of the law of nations.* And in the *year* 1634 *the republic of Venice was near coming to a rupture with pope Urban VIII. on account of the violence offered to the Venetian consul by the governor of Ancona.* The governor, suspecting this consul to have given information detrimental to the commerce of Ancona, had persecuted him, seized his furniture and papers, and caused him to be summoned, declared guilty of contumacy, and banished, *under pretence that, contrary to public prohibition, he had caused goods to be unloaded in a time of contagion.* This consul's suc-<149>cessor he likewise imprisoned. The Venetian senate warmly insisted on having due satisfaction: and, on the interposition of the ministers of France, who were apprehensive of an open rupture, the pope obliged the governor of Ancona to give the republic satisfaction accordingly.

In default of treaties, custom is to be the rule on these occasions; for a prince who receives a consul without express conditions, is supposed to receive him on the footing established by custom.

CHAPTER III

Of the Dignity and Equality of Nations,—
of Titles,—and other Marks of Honour.

Every nation, every sovereign and independent state, deserves consideration and respect, because it makes an immediate figure in the grand society of the human race, is independent of all earthly power, and is an assemblage of a great number of men, which is, doubtless, more considerable than any individual. The sovereign represents his whole nation; he unites in his person all its majesty. No individual, though ever so free and independent, can be placed in competition with a sovereign; this would be putting a single person upon an equality with an united multitude of his equals. Nations and sovereigns are therefore under an obligation, and at the same time have a right, to maintain their dignity, and to cause it to be respected, as being of the utmost importance to their safety and tranquillity.

§35. Dignity of nations or sovereign states.

We have already observed (Prelim. §18) that nature has established a perfect equality of rights between independent nations. Consequently none can naturally lay claim to any superior prerogative: for, whatever privileges any one of them derives from freedom and sovereignty, the others equally derive the same from the same source.

§36. Their equality.

And since precedency or pre-eminence of rank is a prerogative, no nation, no sovereign, can naturally claim it as a right. Why should nations, that are not dependent on him, give up any point to him against their will? However, as a powerful and extensive state is much more considerable in universal society, than a small state, it is reasonable that the latter should yield to the former, on occasions where one must necessarily yield to the other, as in an assembly,—and should pay it those mere ceremonial deferences, which do not in fact destroy their equality, and only shew a priority of order, a first place among equals. Other nations will naturally assign the first place to the more powerful state; and it would be equally useless as ridiculous for the weaker one obstinately to contend about it. The antiquity of the state enters also into consideration on these

§37. Precedency,

occasions: a new-comer cannot dispossess <150> any one of the honours he has enjoyed; and he must produce very strong reasons, before he can obtain a preference.

§38. The form of government is foreign to this question. The form of government is naturally foreign to this question. The dignity, the majesty, resides originally in the body of the state; that of the sovereign is derived from his representing the nation. And can it be imagined that a state possesses more or less dignity according as it is governed by a single person, or by many? At present kings claim a superiority of rank over republics: but this pretension has no other support than the superiority of their strength. Formerly, the Roman republic considered all kings as very far beneath them: but the monarchs of Europe, finding none but feeble republics to oppose them, have disdained to admit them to an equality. The republic of Venice, and that of the United Provinces, have obtained the honours of crowned heads; but their ambassadors yield precedency to those of kings.

§39. A state ought to keep its rank, notwithstanding any changes in the form of its government. In consequence of what we have just established, if the form of government in a nation happens to be changed, she will still preserve the same honours and rank of which she was before in possession. When England had abolished royalty,[10] Cromwell would suffer no abatement of the honours that had been paid to the crown, or to the nation; and he every-where maintained the English ambassadors in the rank they had always possessed.

§40. In this respect, treaties and established customs ought to be observed. If the grades of precedency have been settled by treaties, or by long custom founded on tacit consent, it is necessary to conform to the established rule. To dispute with a prince the rank he has acquired in this manner, is doing him an injury, inasmuch as it is an expression of contempt for him, or a violation of engagements that secure to him a right. Thus, by the injudicious partition between the sons of Charlemagne,[11] the elder having obtained the empire, the younger, who received the

10. Charles I of England was beheaded on January 30, 1649, after which the state was governed by the Rump Parliament and Oliver Cromwell's Protectorate (1653–58).

11. *Divisio Regnorum*, 806.

kingdom of France, yielded precedency to him the more readily, as there still remained at that time a recent idea of the majesty of the real Roman empire. His successors followed the rule they found established:—they were imitated by the other kings of Europe; and thus the imperial crown continues to possess, without opposition, the first rank in Christendom. With most of the other crowns, the point of precedency remains yet undetermined.

Some people would have us to look upon the precedency of the emperor as something more than the first place among equals: they would fain attribute to him a superiority over all kings, and in a word make him the temporal head of Christendom.* And it in fact appears, that many emperors entertained ideas of such pretensions,—as if, by reviving the name of the Roman empire, they could also revive its rights. Other states have been on their guard against these pretensions. We may see in Mezeray† the precautions taken by king Charles V.[12] when the emperor <151> Charles IV. visited France,[13] "for fear," says the historian, "lest that prince, and his son the king of the Romans, should found any right of superiority on his courtesy." Bodinus relates,‡ that "the French took great offence at the emperor Sigismund's placing himself in the royal seat in full parliament, and at his having knighted the senechal de Beaucaire,"[14]—adding, that, "to repair the egregious error they had committed in suffering it, they would not allow the same emperor, when at Lyons, to make the count of Savoy a duke." At present a king of France would doubtless think it a degradation of his dignity, were he to intimate

---

* Bartolus went so far as to say, that "all those were heretics, who did not believe that the emperor was lord of the whole earth." See Bodinus's Republic, Book i. Chap. ix. p. m. 139.

† History of France, explanation of the medals of Charles V.

‡ In his Republic, p. 138.

12. Charles V, king of France, r. 1366–80.

13. Charles IV, Holy Roman Emperor (r. 1355–78), visited his nephew Charles V of France in 1378. He died in November of that same year.

14. Sigismund, son of Charles IV, was Holy Roman Emperor from 1410 to 1437.

the most distant idea that another might claim any authority in his kingdom.*

§41. Of the name and honours given by the nation to its conductor.

As a nation may confer on her conductor what degree of authority, and what rights she thinks proper, she is equally free in regard to the name, the titles, and honours, with which she may choose to decorate him. But discretion and the care of her reputation require that she should not, in this respect, deviate too far from the customs commonly established among civilised nations. Let us further observe, that, in this point, she ought to be guided by prudence, and inclined to proportion the titles and honours of her chief to the power he possesses, and to the degree of authority with which she chooses to invest him. Titles and honours, it is true, determine nothing: they are but empty names, and vain ceremonies, when they are mis-placed: yet who does not know how powerful an influence they have on the minds of mankind? This is then a more serious affair than it appears at the first glance. The nation ought to take care not to debase herself before other states, and not to degrade her chief by too humble a title: she ought to be still more careful not to swell his heart by a vain name, by unbounded honours, so as to inspire him with the idea of arrogating to himself a commensurate authority over her, or of acquiring a proportionate power by unjust conquests. On the other hand, an exalted title may engage the chief to support with greater firmness the dignity of the nation. Prudence is guided by circumstances, and, on every occasion, keeps within due bounds. "Royalty," says a respectable author,[15] who may be believed on this subject, "rescued the house of Brandenburg from that yoke of servitude under which the

* Pentherrieder, minister plenipotentiary of the emperor at the congress of Cambray [[1722]], made an attempt to insure to his master an incontestable superiority and pre-eminence over all the other crowned heads. He induced count Provana, the king of Sardinia's minister, to sign a deed, in which he declared that neither his own sovereign nor any other prince had a right to dispute pre-eminence with the emperor. Its contents being made public, the kings made such heavy complaints on the occasion, that Provana was recalled, and the emperor ordered his minister to suppress the deed,—affecting at the same time a profound ignorance of the whole transaction:—and thus the affair was dropped. Memoirs of Mons. de St. Philippe [[San Felipe]]. Vol. iv. p. 194. [[Note added in 1773/1797 editions.]]

15. Frederick II of Prussia, in his *Memoirs of the House of Brandenburg,* 1748.

house of Austria then kept all the German princes. This was a bait which Frederic I. threw out to all his posterity, saying to them as it were, I have acquired a title for you: do you render <152> yourselves worthy of it: I have laid the foundations of your greatness; it is you who are to finish the work."*

If the conductor of the state is sovereign, he has in his hands the rights and authority of the political society; and consequently he may himself determine what title he will assume, and what honours shall be paid to him, unless these have been already determined by the fundamental laws, or that the limits which have been set to his power manifestly oppose such as he wishes to assume. His subjects are equally obliged to obey him in this, as in whatever he commands by virtue of a lawful authority. Thus the czar Peter I. grounding his pretensions on the vast extent of his dominions, took upon himself the title of emperor.

§42. Whether a sovereign may assume what title and honours he pleases.

But foreign nations are not obliged to give way to the will of a sovereign who assumes a new title, or of a people who call their chief by what name they please.†

§43. Right of other nations in this respect.

However, if this title has nothing unreasonable, or contrary to received customs, it is altogether agreeable to the mutual duties which bind nations together, to give to a sovereign or conductor of a state the same title that is given him by his people. But if this title is contrary to custom, if it implies attributes which do not belong to him who affects it, foreign nations may refuse it without his having reason to complain. The title of "Majesty" is consecrated by custom to monarchs who command great

§44. Their duty.

---

* Memoirs of the House of Brandenburg.

† Cromwell, in writing to Louis the Fourteenth, used the following style—"Olivarius, Dominus Protector Angliae, Scotiae, et Hiberniae, Ludovico XIV. Francorum Regi Christianissime Rex." [["Oliver, Lord Protector of England, Scotland, and Ireland, to Louis XIV, ruler of the French and Most Christian King."]]—And the subscription was,—"In Aula nostra Alba. Vester bonus amicus." [["In our English Court. Your good friend."]] The court of France was highly offended at this form of address.—The ambassador Boreel, in a letter to the Pensionary De Witt, dated May 25, 1655, said that Cromwell's letter had not been presented, and that those who were charged with the delivery of it, had with-held it, through an apprehension of its giving rise to some misunderstanding between the two countries. [[Note added in 1773/1797 editions.]]

nations. The emperors of Germany have long affected to reserve it to themselves, as belonging solely to the imperial crown. But the kings asserted with reason, that there was nothing on earth more eminent or more august than their dignity: they therefore refused the title of majesty to him who refused it to them;* and at present, except in a few instances founded on particular reasons, the title of majesty is a peculiar attribute of the royal character.

As it would be ridiculous for a petty prince to take the title of king, and assume the style of "Majesty," foreign nations, by refusing to comply with this whim, do nothing but what is conformable to reason and their duty. However, if there reigns anywhere a sovereign, who, notwithstanding the small extent of his power, is accustomed to receive from his neighbours the title <153> of king, distant nations who would carry on an intercourse with him, cannot refuse him that title. It belongs not to them to reform the customs of distant countries.

§45. How titles and honours may be secured.　The sovereign who wishes constantly to receive certain titles and honours from other powers, must secure them by treaties. Those who have entered into engagements in this way are obliged to conform to them, and cannot deviate from the treaties without doing him an injury. Thus, in the examples we have produced (§§41 and 42), the czar and the king of Prussia took care to negotiate before-hand with the courts in friendship with them, to secure their being acknowledged under the new titles they intended to assume.

The popes have formerly pretended that it belonged to the tiara alone to create new crowns; they had the confidence to expect that the superstition of princes and nations would allow them so sublime a prerogative. But it was eclipsed at the revival of letters.† The emperors of Ger-

---

* At the famous treaty of Westphalia, the plenipotentiaries of France agreed with those of the emperor, "that the king and queen writing with their own hand to the emperor, and giving him the title of majesty, he should answer them, with his own hand, and give them the same title." Letter of the plenipotentiaries to M. de Brienne, Oct. 15, 1646.

† Catholic princes receive still from the pope titles that relate to religion. Benedict XIV. gave that of "Most Faithful" to the king of Portugal; and the condescension of other princes connived at the imperative style in which the bull is couched.—It is dated December 23, 1748.

many, who formed the same pretensions, were at least countenanced by the example of the ancient Roman emperors. They only want the same power in order to have the same right.

In default of treaties, we ought, with respect to titles, and, in general, every other mark of honour, to conform to the rule established by general custom. To attempt a deviation from it with respect to a nation or sovereign, when there is no particular reason for such innovation, is expressing either contempt or ill-will towards them;—a conduct equally inconsistent with sound policy and with the duties that nations owe to each other.

§46. We must conform to general custom.

The greatest monarch ought to respect in every sovereign the eminent character with which he is invested. The independence, the equality of nations,—the reciprocal duties of humanity,—all these circumstances should induce him to pay even to the chief of a petty state the respect due to the station which he fills. The weakest state is composed of men as well as the most powerful; and our duties are the same towards all those who do not depend on us.

§47. Mutual respect, which sovereigns owe to each other.

But this precept of the law of nature does not extend beyond what is essential to the respect which independent nations owe to each other, or that conduct, in a word, which shews that we acknowledge a state or its chief to be truly independent and sovereign, and consequently entitled to every thing due to the quality of sovereignty. But, on the other hand, a great monarch being, as we have already observed, a very important personage in human society, it is natural, that, in matters merely ceremonial, and not derogatory to the equality of rights between nations, he should receive honours to which a petty prince can <154> have no pretensions: and the latter cannot refuse to pay the former every mark of respect which is not inconsistent with his own independence and sovereignty.

Every nation, every sovereign, ought to maintain their dignity (§35) by causing due respect to be paid to them; and especially they ought not to suffer that dignity to be impaired. If then there are titles and honours which by constant custom belong to a prince, he may insist upon them; and he ought to do it on occasions where his glory is concerned.

§48. How a sovereign ought to maintain his dignity.

But it is proper to distinguish between neglect or the omission of what the established usage requires, and positive acts of disrespect and insult. The prince may complain of an instance of neglect, and, if it be not repaired, may consider it as an indication of ill-will: he has a right to demand, even by force of arms, the reparation of an insult. The czar Peter the First,[16] in his manifesto against Sweden, complained that the cannon had not been fired on his passing at Riga. He might think it strange that they did not pay him this mark of respect, and he might complain of it; but to have made this the subject of a war, must have indicated a preposterous prodigality of human blood.

CHAPTER IV

Of the Right to Security, and the Effects of the Sovereignty and Independence of nations.

§49. Right to security. In vain does nature prescribe to nations, as well as to individuals, the care of self-preservation, and of advancing their own perfection and happiness, if she does not give them a right to preserve themselves from every thing that might render this care ineffectual. This *right* is nothing more than a *moral power of acting,* that is, the power of doing what is morally possible,—what is proper and conformable to our duties. We have then in general a right to do whatever is necessary to the discharge of our duties. Every nation, as well as every man, has therefore a right to prevent other nations from obstructing her preservation, her perfection, and happiness,—that is, to preserve herself from all injuries (§18): and this right is a perfect one, since it is given to satisfy a natural and indispensable obligation: for when we cannot use constraint in order to cause our rights to be respected, their effects are very uncertain. It is this right to preserve herself from all injury that is called the *right to security.*

§50. It produces the right of resistance; It is safest to prevent the evil, when it can be prevented. A nation has a right to resist an injurious attempt, and to make use of force and every honourable expedient against whosoever is actually engaged in

16. Czar Peter I (r. 1682–1725) joined an alliance in 1700 with Denmark-Norway and Saxony against Sweden, inaugurating the Great Northern War (1700–1721).

opposition to her, and even to anticipate his machinations, observing, however, not to attack him upon vague and uncertain suspicions, lest she should incur the imputation of becoming herself an unjust aggressor. <155>

When the evil is done, the same right to security authorises the offended party to endeavour to obtain a complete reparation, and to employ force for that purpose, if necessary.

§51. and that of obtaining reparation;

Finally, the offended party have a right to provide for their future security, and to chastise the offender, by inflicting upon him a punishment capable of deterring him thenceforward from similar aggressions, and of intimidating those who might be tempted to imitate him. They may even, if necessary, disable the aggressor from doing further injury. They only make use of their right in all these measures, which they adopt with good reason: and if evil thence results to him who has reduced them to the necessity of taking such steps, he must impute the consequences only to his own injustice.

§52. and the right of punishing.

If then there is any-where a nation of a restless and mischievous disposition, ever ready to injure others, to traverse their designs, and to excite domestic disturbances in their dominions,—it is not to be doubted that all the others have a right to form a coalition in order to repress and chastise that nation, and to put it forever after out of her power to injure them. Such would be the just fruits of the policy which Machiavel praises in Caesar Borgia. The conduct followed by Philip II. king of Spain, was calculated to unite all Europe against him; and it was from just reasons that Henry the Great formed the design of humbling a power, whose strength was formidable, and whose maxims were pernicious.

§53. Right of all nations against a mischievous people.

The three preceding propositions are so many principles, that furnish the various foundations for a just war, as we shall see in the proper place.

It is an evident consequence of the liberty and independence of nations, that all have a right to be governed as they think proper, and that no state has the smallest right to interfere in the government of another. Of all the rights that can belong to a nation, sovereignty is, doubtless, the most precious, and that which other nations ought the most scrupulously to respect, if they would not do her an injury.

§54. No nation has a right to interfere in the government of another state.

§55. One sovereign cannot make himself the judge of the conduct of another.

The sovereign is he to whom the nation has intrusted the empire, and the care of the government: she has invested him with her rights; she alone is directly interested in the manner in which the conductor she has chosen makes use of his power. It does not then belong to any foreign power to take cognisance of the administration of that sovereign, to set himself up for a judge of his conduct, and to oblige him to alter it. If he loads his subjects with taxes, and if he treats them with severity, the nation alone is concerned in the business; and no other is called upon to oblige him to amend his conduct, and follow more wise and equitable maxims. It is the part of prudence to point out the occasions when officious and amicable representations may be made to him. The Spaniards violated all rules, when they set themselves up as judges of the Inca Athualpa.[17] If that prince had violated the law of nations with respect to them, they would <156> have had a right to punish him. But they accused him of having put some of his subjects to death, of having had several wives, &c.—things, for which he was not at all accountable to them; and, to fill up the measure of their extravagant injustice, they condemned him by the laws of Spain.*

§56. How far lawful to interfere in a quarrel between a sovereign and his subjects.

But if the prince, by violating the fundamental laws, gives his subjects a legal right to resist him,—if tyranny becoming insupportable obliges the nation to rise in their own defence,—every foreign power has a right to succour an oppressed people who implore their assistance. The English justly complained of James II. The nobility and the most distinguished patriots, having determined to check him in the prosecution of his schemes, which manifestly tended to overthrow the constitution, and to destroy the liberties and the religion of the people,—applied for assistance to the United Provinces. The authority of the prince of Orange had, doubtless, an influence on the deliberations of the states-general; but it did not lead them to the commission of an act of injustice: for when a people from good reasons take up arms against an oppressor, it is but an act of justice and generosity to assist brave men in the defence of their liberties. Whenever therefore matters are carried so far as to pro-

* Garcillasso de la Vega.
17. Atahualpa, the last of the Incan emperors, was executed in 1533.

duce a civil war, foreign powers may assist that party which appears to them to have justice on its side. He who assists an odious tyrant,—he who declares for an unjust and rebellious people,—violates his duty. But when the bands of the political society are broken, or at least suspended, between the sovereign and his people, the contending parties may then be considered as two distinct powers; and since they are both equally independent of all foreign authority, nobody has a right to judge them. Either may be in the right; and each of those who grant their assistance may imagine that he is acting in support of the better cause. It follows then, in virtue of the voluntary law of nations (see Prelim. §21), that the two parties may act as having an equal right, and behave to each other accordingly, till the decision of the affair.

But we ought not to abuse this maxim, and make a handle of it to authorise odious machinations against the internal tranquillity of states. It is a violation of the law of nations to invite those subjects to revolt who actually pay obedience to their sovereign, though they complain of his government.

The practice of nations is conformable to our maxims. When the German protestants came to the assistance of the reformed party in France, the court never attempted to treat them otherwise than on the usual footing of enemies in general, and according to the laws of war. France was at the same time engaged in assisting the Netherlands then in arms against Spain,—and expected that her troops should be considered in no other light than as auxiliaries in a regular war. But no power ever fails to complain, as of an atrocious wrong, if any one attempts by his emissaries to excite his subjects to revolt. <157>

As to those monsters who, under the title of sovereigns, render themselves the scourges and horror of the human race, they are savage beasts, whom every brave man may justly exterminate from the face of the earth. All antiquity has praised Hercules for delivering the world from an Antaeus, a Busiris, and a Diomede.[18]

---

18. Antaeus, Libyan giant and son of Poseidon; Busiris, king of Egypt and son of Poseidon; and Diomede, king of Thrace, known for owning man-eating horses.

§57. Right of opposing the interference of foreign powers in the affairs of government.

After having established the position that foreign nations have no right to interfere in the government of an independent state, it is not difficult to prove that the latter has a right to oppose such interference. To govern herself according to her own pleasure, is a necessary part of her independence. A sovereign state cannot be constrained in this respect, except it be from a particular right which she has herself given to other states by her treaties; and even if she has given them such a right, yet it cannot, in an affair of so delicate a nature as that of government, be extended beyond the clear and express terms of the treaties. In every other case a sovereign has a right to treat those as enemies, who attempt to interfere in his domestic affairs otherwise than by their good offices.

§58. The same rights with respect to religion.

Religion is in every sense an object of great importance to a nation, and one of the most interesting subjects on which the government can be employed. An independent people are accountable for their religion to God alone: in this particular, as in every other, they have a right to regulate their conduct according to the dictates of their own conscience, and to prevent all foreign interference in an affair of so delicate a nature.* The custom, long kept up in Christendom, of causing all the affairs of religion to be decided and regulated in a general council, could only have been introduced by the singular circumstance of the submission of the whole church to the same civil government,—the Roman empire. When that empire was overthrown, and gave place to many independent kingdoms, this custom was found contrary to the first principles of government, to the very idea of independent states, and political societies. It was, however, long supported by prejudice, ignorance and superstition, by the authority of the popes, and the power of the clergy, and still respected even at the time of the reformation. The states who had em-

---

* When, however, we see a party inflamed with deadly hatred against the religion we profess, and a neighbouring prince persecuting in consequence the professors of that religion, it is lawful for us to give assistance to the sufferers,—as it was well remarked by James I. of England [[1603–25]] to Bouillon the ambassador of Mary de Medici, queen regent of France [[1600–1610]],—"When my neighbours are attacked in a quarrel in which I am interested, the law of nature requires that I should anticipate and prevent the evil which may thence result to myself." Le Vassor, Hist. of Louis XIII. [[Note added in 1773/1797 editions.]]

braced the reformed religion offered to submit to the decisions of an impartial council lawfully assembled. At present they would not hesitate to declare, that, in matters of religion, they are equally independent of every power on earth, as they are in the affairs of civil government. The general and absolute authority of the pope and council is absurd in every other system <158> than that of those popes who strove to unite all Christendom in a single body, of which they pretended to be the supreme monarchs.* But even catholic sovereigns have endeavoured to restrain that authority within such limits as are consistent with their supreme power: they do not receive the decrees of council or the popes' bulls, till they have caused them to be examined; and these ecclesiastical laws are of no force in their dominions unless confirmed by the prince. In the first book of this work, Chap. XII. we have sufficiently established the rights of a state in matters of religion; and we introduce them here again, only to draw just consequences from them with respect to the conduct which nations ought to observe towards each other.

It is then certain, that we cannot, in opposition to the will of a nation, interfere in her religious concerns, without violating her rights, and doing her an injury. Much less are we allowed to employ force of arms to oblige her to receive a doctrine and a worship which we consider as divine. What right have men to set themselves up as the defenders and protectors of the cause of God? He can, whenever he pleases, lead nations to the knowledge of himself, by more effectual means than those of violence. Persecutors make no true converts. The monstrous maxim of extending religion by the sword is a subversion of the rights of mankind, and the most terrible scourge of nations. Every madman will fancy he is fighting in the cause of God, and every aspiring spirit will use that pretext as a cloak for his ambition. While Charlemagne was ravaging Saxony with fire and sword in order to plant christianity there, the successors of Mahomet were ravaging Asia and Africa, to establish the Koran in those parts.

§59. No nation can be constrained with respect to religion.

* See, above, §146, and Bodinus's Republic, book i. chap. ix. with his quotations, p. m. 139.

§60. Offices of humanity in these matters.

Missionaries.

But it is an office of humanity to labour by mild and lawful means to persuade a nation to receive a religion which we believe to be the only one that is true and salutary. Missionaries may be sent to instruct the people; and this care is altogether conformable to the attention which every nation owes to the perfection and happiness of others. But it must be observed, that, in order to avoid doing an injury to the rights of a sovereign, the missionaries ought to abstain from preaching clandestinely, or without his permission, a new doctrine to his people. He may refuse to accept their proffered services; and if he orders them to leave his dominions, they ought to obey. They should have a very express order from the King of kings, before they can lawfully disobey a sovereign who commands according to the extent of his power: and the prince who is not convinced of that extraordinary order of the Deity, will do no more than exert his lawful rights, in punishing a missionary for disobedience. But what if the nation, or a considerable part of the people, are desirous of retaining the missionary, and following his doctrine?—In a former part of this work (Book I. §§128–136) we have established the rights of the nation and those of <159> the citizens: and thither we refer for an answer to this question.

§61. Circumspection to be used.

This is a very delicate subject; and we cannot authorise an inconsiderate zeal for making proselytes, without endangering the tranquillity of all nations, and even exposing those who are engaged in making converts, to act inconsistently with their duty, at the very time they imagine they are accomplishing the most meritorious work. For it is certainly performing a very bad office to a nation, and doing her an essential injury, to spread a false and dangerous religion among the inhabitants. Now there is no person who does not believe his own religion to be the only true and safe one. Recommend, kindle in all hearts the ardent zeal of the missionaries, and you will see Europe inundated with Lamas, Bonzes and Dervises, while monks of all kinds will over-run Asia and Africa. Protestant ministers will crowd to Spain and Italy, in defiance of the inquisition, while the jesuits will spread themselves among the protestants in order to bring them back into the pale of the church. Let the catholics reproach the protestants as much as they please with their lukewarmness, the conduct of the latter is undoubtedly more agreeable to reason and the law of nations. True zeal applies itself to the task of making a holy religion flourish in the countries where it is received, and of rendering it useful to the manners of the people and to the state: and, without forestalling the dispositions of providence, it can find sufficient employment at home, until an invitation come from foreign nations, or a very evident commission be given from heaven, to preach that religion abroad. Finally, let us add, that, before we can lawfully undertake to preach a particular religion to the various nations of the earth, we must ourselves be thoroughly convinced of its truth by the most serious examination.—"What! can christians doubt of their religion?"—The Mahometan entertains no doubt of his. Be ever ready to impart your knowledge,—simply and sincerely expose the principles of your belief to those who are desirous of hearing you: instruct them, convince them by evidence, but seek not to hurry them away with the fire of enthusiasm. It is a sufficient charge on each of us, to be responsible for his own conscience.—Thus neither will the light of knowledge be refused to any who wish to receive it, nor will a turbulent zeal disturb the peace of nations.

When a religion is persecuted in one country, foreign nations who profess it may intercede for their brethren: but this is all they can lawfully do, unless the persecution be carried to an intolerable excess: then indeed it becomes a case of manifest tyranny, in opposition to which all nations are allowed to assist an unhappy people (§56). A regard to their own safety may also authorise them to undertake the defence of the persecuted sufferers. A king of France replied to the ambassadors who solicited him to suffer his subjects of the reformed religion to live in peace, "that he was master in his own kingdom." But the <160> protestant sovereigns, who saw a general conspiracy of the catholics obstinately bent on their destruction, were so far masters on their side as to be at liberty to give assistance to a body of men who might strengthen their party, and help them to preserve themselves from the ruin with which they were threatened. All distinctions of states and nations are to be disregarded, when there is question of forming a coalition against a set of madmen, who would exterminate all those that do not implicitly receive their doctrines.

§62. What a sovereign may do in favour of those who profess his religion in another state.

CHAPTER V

Of the Observance of Justice between Nations.

§63. Necessity of the observance of justice in human society.
Justice is the basis of all society, the sure bond of all commerce. Human society, far from being an intercourse of assistance and good offices, would be no longer any thing but a vast scene of robbery, if no respect were paid to this virtue, which secures to every one his own. It is still more necessary between nations, than between individuals; because injustice produces more dreadful consequences in the quarrels of these powerful bodies politic, and it is more difficult to obtain redress. The obligation imposed on all men to be just is easily demonstrated from the law of nature. We here take that obligation for granted (as being sufficiently known), and content ourselves with observing, that it is not only indispensably binding on nations (Prelim. §5), but even still more sacred with respect to them, from the importance of its consequences.

§64. Obligation of all nations to cultivate and observe justice.
All nations are therefore under a strict obligation to cultivate justice towards each other, to observe it scrupulously, and carefully to abstain from every thing that may violate it. Each ought to render to the others what belongs to them, to respect their rights, and to leave them in the peaceable enjoyment of them.*

§65. Right of refusing to submit to injustice.
From this indispensable obligation which nature imposes on nations, as well as from those obligations which each nation owes to herself, results the right of every state, not to suffer any of her rights to be taken away, or any thing which lawfully be-<161>longs to her: for in opposing

* Might not this duty be extended to the execution of sentences passed in other countries according to the necessary and usual forms?—On this subject, M. Van Beuningen wrote as follows to M. De Witt, Oct. 15, 1666. "By what the courts of Holland have decreed in the affair of one Koningh of Rotterdam, I see they suppose that every judgment pronounced by the parliaments of France against the inhabitants of Holland *in judicio contradictorio,* ought to be executed on requisition made by those parliaments. But I do not know that the tribunals of this country act in the same manner with respect to sentences passed in Holland: and if they do not, an agreement might be made, that sentences passed on either side against subjects of the other state shall only take effect on such property as the condemned party is found to possess in the state where the sentence has been given." [[Note added in 1773/1797 editions.]]

this, she only acts in conformity to all her duties; and therein consists the right (§49).

This right is a perfect one,—that is to say, it is accompanied with the right of using force in order to assert it. In vain would nature give us a right to refuse submitting to injustice,—in vain would she oblige others to be just in their dealings with us, if we could not lawfully make use of force, when they refused to discharge this duty. The just would lie at the mercy of avarice and injustice, and all their rights would soon become useless.

§66. This right is a perfect one.

From the foregoing right arise, as distinct branches, first, the right of a just defence, which belongs to every nation,—or the right of making use of force against whoever attacks her and her rights. This is the foundation of defensive war.

§67. It produces 1. The right of defence.

Secondly, the right to obtain justice by force, if we cannot obtain it otherwise, or to pursue our right by force of arms. This is the foundation of offensive war.

§68. 2. The right of doing ourselves justice.

An intentional act of injustice is undoubtedly an injury. We have then a right to punish it, as we have shewn above, in speaking of injuries in general (§52). The right of refusing to suffer injustice is a branch of the right to security.

§69. The right of punishing injustice.

Let us apply to the unjust what we have said above (§53) of a mischievous nation. If there were a people who made open profession of trampling justice under foot,—who despised and violated the rights of others whenever they found an opportunity,—the interest of human society would authorise all the other nations to form a confederacy in order to humble and chastise the delinquents. We do not here forget the maxim established in our Preliminaries, that it does not belong to nations to usurp the power of being judges of each other. In particular cases, where there is room for the smallest doubt, it ought to be supposed that each of the parties may have some right: and the injustice of the party that has committed the injury may proceed from error, and not from a general contempt of justice. But if, by her constant maxims, and by the whole tenor of her conduct, a nation evidently proves herself to be actuated by that mischievous disposition,—if she regards no right as sacred,—the safety of the human race requires that she should be re-

§70. Right of all nations against one that openly despises justice.

pressed. To form and support an unjust pretension, is only doing an injury to the party whose interests are affected by that pretension; but to despise justice in general, is doing an injury to all nations.

CHAPTER VI

Of the Concern a Nation may have in the Actions of her Citizens.

§71. The sovereign ought to revenge the injuries of the state, and to protect the citizens.

We have seen in the preceding chapters what are the common duties of nations towards each other,—how they ought mutually to respect each other, and to abstain from all injury, <162> and all offence,—and how justice and equity ought to reign between them in their whole conduct. But hitherto we have only considered the actions of the body of the nation, of the state, of the sovereign. Private persons, who are members of one nation, may offend and ill-treat the citizens of another, and may injure a foreign sovereign:—it remains for us to examine, what share a state may have in the actions of her citizens, and what are the rights and obligations of sovereigns in this respect.

Whoever offends the state, injures its rights, disturbs its tranquillity, or does it a prejudice in any manner whatsoever, declares himself its enemy, and exposes himself to be justly punished for it. Whoever uses a citizen ill, indirectly offends the state, which is bound to protect this citizen; and the sovereign of the latter should avenge his wrongs, punish the aggressor, and, if possible, oblige him to make full reparation; since otherwise the citizen would not obtain the great end of the civil association, which is safety.

§72. He ought not to suffer his subjects to offend other nations or their citizens.

But, on the other hand, the nation or the sovereign ought not to suffer the citizens to do an injury to the subjects of another state, much less to offend that state itself:—and this, not only because no sovereign ought to permit those who are under his command to violate the precepts of the law of nature, which forbids all injuries,—but also because nations ought mutually to respect each other, to abstain from all offence, from all injury, from all wrong,—in a word, from every thing that may be of prejudice to others. If a sovereign, who might keep his subjects within the rules of justice and peace, suffers them to injure a foreign nation either in its body or its members, he does no less injury to that nation, than if he injured it himself. In short, the safety of the state, and that of human society, requires this attention from every sovereign. If you let loose the reins to your subjects against foreign nations, these will behave in the same manner to you; and, instead of that friendly intercourse which nature has established between all men, we shall see nothing but one vast and dreadful scene of plunder between nation and nation.

However, as it is impossible for the best regulated state, or for the most vigilant and absolute sovereign, to model at his pleasure all the actions of his subjects, and to confine them on every occasion to the most exact obedience, it would be unjust to impute to the nation or the sovereign every fault committed by the citizens. We ought not then to say in general, that we have received an injury from a nation, because we have received it from one of its members. §73. The acts of individuals are not to be imputed to the nation,

But if a nation or its chief approves and ratifies the act of the individual, it then becomes a public concern; and the injured party is to consider the nation as the real author of the injury, of which the citizen was perhaps only the instrument. §74. unless it approves or ratifies them.

If the offended state has in her power the individual who has done the injury, she may without scruple bring him to justice and punish him. If he has escaped and returned to his own <163> country, she ought to apply to his sovereign to have justice done in the case. §75. Conduct to be observed by the offended party.

And since the latter ought not to suffer his subjects to molest the subjects of other states, or to do them an injury, much less to give open, audacious offence to foreign powers,—he ought to compel the transgressor to make reparation for the damage or injury, if possible, or to inflict on him an exemplary punishment, or, finally, according to the nature and circumstances of the case, to deliver him up to the offended state, to be there brought to justice. This is pretty generally observed with respect to great crimes, which are equally contrary to the laws and safety of all nations. Assassins, incendiaries, and robbers, are seized every where, at the desire of the sovereign in whose territories the crime was committed, and are delivered up to his justice. The matter is carried still §76. Duty of the aggressor's sovereign.

farther in states that are more closely connected by friendship and good neighbourhood. Even in cases of ordinary transgressions which are only subjects of civil prosecution either with a view to the recovery of damages or the infliction of a slight civil punishment, the subjects of two neighbouring states are reciprocally obliged to appear before the magistrate of the place where they are accused of having failed in their duty. Upon a requisition of that magistrate, called Letters Rogatory, they are summoned in due form by their own magistrates, and obliged to appear. An admirable institution, by means of which many neighbouring states live together in peace, and seem to form only one republic! This is in force throughout all Switzerland. As soon as the Letters Rogatory are issued in form, the superior of the accused is bound to enforce them. It belongs not to him to examine whether the accusation be true or false; he is to presume on the justice of his neighbour, and not suffer any doubts on his own part to impair an institution so well calculated to preserve harmony and good understanding between the states: however, if by constant experience he should find that his subjects are oppressed by the neighbouring magistrates who summon them before their tribunals, it would undoubtedly be right in him to reflect on the protection due to his people, and to refuse the rogatories till satisfaction were given for the abuses committed, and proper steps taken to prevent a repetition of them. But in such case it would be his duty to allege his reasons, and set them forth in the clearest point of view.

§77. If he refuses justice, he becomes a party in the fault and offence.   The sovereign who refuses to cause reparation to be made for the damage done by his subject, or to punish the offender, or, finally, to deliver him up, renders himself in some measure an accomplice in the injury, and becomes responsible for it. But if he delivers up either the property of the offender as an indemnification in cases that will admit of pecuniary compensation,—or his person, in order that he may suffer the punishment due to his crime,—the offended party has no further demand on him. King Demetrius[19] having delivered to the Romans those <164> who had killed their ambassador, the senate sent them back, resolving to reserve to themselves the liberty of punishing that crime by avenging

19. Greco-Bactrian king, r. ca. 200–180 B.C.

it on the king himself, or on his dominions.* If this was really the case, and if the king had no share in the murder of the Roman ambassador, the conduct of the senate was highly unjust, and only worthy of men who sought but a pretext to cover their ambitious enterprises.

Finally, there is another case where the nation in general is guilty of the crimes of its members. That is when by its manners and by the maxims of its government it accustoms and authorises its citizens indiscriminately to plunder and maltreat foreigners, to make inroads into the neighbouring countries, &c. Thus the nation of the Usbecks is guilty of all the robberies committed by the individuals of which it is composed. The princes whose subjects are robbed and massacred, and whose lands are infested by those robbers, may justly level their vengeance against the nation at large. Nay more, all nations have a right to enter into a league against such a people, to repress them, and to treat them as the common enemies of the human race. The christian nations would be no less justifiable in forming a confederacy against the states of Barbary, in order to destroy those haunts of pirates, with whom the love of plunder, or the fear of just punishment, is the only rule of peace and war. But these piratical adventurers are wise enough to respect those who are most able to chastise them; and the nations that are able to keep the avenues of a rich branch of commerce open for themselves, are not sorry to see them shut against others.

§78. Another case in which the nation is guilty of the crimes of the citizens.

CHAPTER VII

Effects of the Domain, between Nations.

We have explained in Chap. XVIII. Book I. how a nation takes possession of a country, and at the same time gains possession of the domain and government thereof. That country, with every thing included in it, becomes the property of the nation in general. Let us now see what are the effects of this property, with respect to other nations. The full do-

§79. General effect of the domain.

* See Polybius, quoted by Barbeyrac, in his notes on Grotius, book iii. chap. xxiv. §vii.

main is necessarily a peculiar and exclusive right: for if I have a full right to dispose of a thing as I please, it thence follows that others have no right to it at all, since, if they had any, I could not freely dispose of it. The private domain of the citizens may be limited and restrained in several ways by the laws of the state, and it always is so by the eminent domain of the sovereign; but the general domain of the nation is full and absolute, since there exists no authority upon earth by which it can be limited: it therefore excludes all right on the part of foreigners. And as the rights of a nation ought to <165> be respected by all others (§64), none can form any pretensions to the country which belongs to that nation, nor ought to dispose of it, without her consent, any more than of the things contained in the country.

§80. What is comprehended in the domain of a nation.

The domain of the nation extends to every thing she possesses by a just title: it comprehends her ancient and original possessions and all her acquisitions made by means which are just in themselves, or admitted as such among nations,—concessions, purchases, conquests made in regular war, &c. And by her possessions, we ought not only to understand her territories, but all the rights she enjoys.

§81. The property of the citizens is the property of the nation, with respect to foreign nations.

Even the property of the individuals is in the aggregate, to be considered as the property of the nation, with respect to other states. It, in some sort, really belongs to her from the right she has over the property of her citizens, because it constitutes a part of the sum total of her riches, and augments her power. She is interested in that property by her obligation to protect all her members. In short, it cannot be otherwise, since nations act and treat together as bodies, in their quality of political societies, and are considered as so many moral persons. All those who form a society, a nation, being considered by foreign nations as constituting only one whole, one single person,—all their wealth together can only be considered as the wealth of that same person. And this is so true, that each political society may, if it pleases, establish within itself a community of goods, as Campanella[20] did in his republic of the sun. Others

20. Tommaso Campanella, 1568–1639, unorthodox natural philosopher and theologian, wrote *The City of the Sun* (*La città des sole*, 1623) while imprisoned by the Inquisition.

will not inquire what it does in this respect: its domestic regulations make no change in its rights with respect to foreigners, nor in the manner in which they ought to consider the aggregate of its property, in what way soever it is possessed.

By an immediate consequence of this principle, if one nation has a right to any part of the property of another, she has an indiscriminate right to the property of the citizens of the latter nation, until the debt be discharged. This maxim is of great use, as shall hereafter be shewn.

§82. A consequence of this principle.

The general domain of the nation over the lands she inhabits is naturally connected with the empire: for in establishing herself in a vacant country, the nation certainly does not intend to possess it in subjection to any other power: and can we suppose an independent nation not vested with the absolute command in her domestic concerns? Thus we have already observed (Book I. §205) that in taking possession of a country the nation is presumed to take possession of its government at the same time. We shall here proceed farther, and shew the natural connection of these two rights in an independent nation. How could she govern herself at her own pleasure in the country she inhabits, if she cannot truly and absolutely dispose of it? And how could she have the full and absolute domain of a place where she has not the command? Another's sovereignty, and the rights it comprehends, must deprive her of the free disposal of that place. Add <166> to this the eminent domain which constitutes a part of the sovereignty (Book I. §244), and you will the better perceive the intimate connection existing between the domain and the sovereignty of the nation. And, accordingly, what is called the *high domain,* which is nothing but the domain of the body of the nation, or of the sovereign who represents it, is every where considered as inseparable from the sovereignty. The *useful domain,* or the domain confined to the rights that may belong to an individual in the state, may be separated from the sovereignty: and nothing prevents the possibility of its belonging to a nation, in places that are not under her jurisdiction. Thus many sovereigns have fiefs, and other possessions, in the territories of another prince: in these cases they possess them in the manner of private individuals.

§83. Connection of the domain of the nation with the sovereignty.

The sovereignty united to the domain establishes the jurisdiction of the nation in her territories, or the country that belongs to her. It is her

§84. Jurisdiction.

province, or that of her sovereign, to exercise justice in all the places under her jurisdiction, to take cognisance of the crimes committed, and the differences that arise in the country.

Other nations ought to respect this right. And as the administration of justice necessarily requires that every definitive sentence, regularly pronounced, be esteemed just, and executed as such,—when once a cause in which foreigners are interested, has been decided in form, the sovereign of the defendants cannot hear their complaints. To undertake to examine the justice of a definitive sentence, is an attack on the jurisdiction of him who has passed it. The prince therefore ought not to interfere in the causes of his subjects in foreign countries, and grant them his protection, excepting in cases where justice is refused, or palpable and evident injustice done, or rules and forms openly violated, or, finally, an odious distinction made to the prejudice of his subjects, or of foreigners in general. The British court established this maxim, with great strength of evidence, on occasion of the Prussian vessels seized and declared lawful prizes during the last war.* What is here said has no relation to the merits of that particular cause, since they must depend on facts.

§85. Effects of the jurisdiction in foreign countries.   In consequence of these rights of jurisdiction, the decisions made by the judge of the place within the extent of his power, ought to be respected, and to take effect even in foreign countries. For instance, it belongs to the domestic judge to nominate tutors and guardians for minors and idiots. The law of nations, which has an eye to the common ad-

---

* See the report made to the king of Great Britain by Sir George Lee, Dr. Paul, Sir Dudley Ryder and Mr. Murray. It is an excellent piece on the law of nations. [[In his lectures on international law at Cambridge in 1887, Henry Summer Maine mentions this report: "The English Secretary of State at once addressed to him, for Prussia was a friendly Power at the time, a letter dated February 8, 1753, in which he dwells upon the unprecedented nature of the proceeding, and states that he has the King's orders to send to the King of Prussia a report made to his Majesty by Sir George Lee, Judge of the Prerogative Court; Dr. Paul, his Majesty's Advocate-General; Sir Dudley Ryder, and Mr. Murray—the Mr. Murray who afterwards became Lord Mansfield. The report in question is one of which British lawyers and the British Foreign Office have always been exceedingly proud. It is praised by two great foreign authorities of the time—Vattel and Montesquieu; they both of them speak of it as admirable; it is, in fact, a most excellent example of the method of reasoning of which International Law admits; and in the end the King of Prussia gave way to its arguments, and the interest on the Silesian loan was ever afterwards punctually paid."]]

vantage and the good harmony of nations, requires therefore that such nomination of a tutor or guardian be valid and acknowledged in all countries where the pupil may have any concerns. Use was made of this maxim in the year 1672, even with respect to a sovereign. The abbé D'Orléans, sovereign prince of Neufchatel in Switzerland, <167> being incapable of managing his own affairs, the king of France appointed, as his guardian, his mother, the duchess dowager of Longueville. The duchess of Nemours, sister to that prince, laid claim to the guardianship for the principality of Neufchatel: but the title of the duchess of Longueville was acknowledged by the three estates of the country. Her counsel rested her cause on the circumstance of her having been nominated guardian by the domestic judge.* This was a very wrong application of a just principle: for the prince's domestic residence could be no where but in his state: and it was only by the degree of the three estates, who alone had a right to chuse a guardian for their sovereign, that the authority of the duchess of Longueville became firm and lawful at Neufchatel.

In the same manner the validity of a testament, as to its form, can only be decided by the domestic judge, whose sentence delivered in form ought to be every where acknowledged. But, without affecting the validity of the testament itself, the bequests contained in it may be disputed before the judge of the place where the effects are situated, because those effects can only be disposed of conformably to the laws of the country. Thus the abbé D'Orléans above mentioned having appointed the prince of Conti[21] his universal legatee,—the three estates of Neufchatel, without waiting till the parliament of Paris should pronounce their decision on the question of two contradictory wills made by the abbé D'Orléans, gave the investiture of the principality to the duchess of Nemours,— declaring that the sovereignty was unalienable. Besides, it might have been said on this occasion also, that the domestic residence of the prince could be no where but in the state.

* Memorial in behalf of the Duchess of Longueville, 1672.

21. Armand de Bourbon, prince of Conti (1629–66). He was the second son of Henry II, prince of Condé (1588–1646), and the brother of both Louis II de Bourbon, prince of Condé (1621–86) and Anne Geneviève Bourbon Condé (1619–79).

§86. Desert and uncultivated places.

As every thing included in the country belongs to the nation,—and as none but the nation, or the person on whom she has devolved her right, is authorised to dispose of those things (§79),—if she has left uncultivated and desert places in the country, no person whatever has a right to take possession of them without her consent. Though she does not make actual use of them, those places still belong to her: she has an interest in preserving them for future use, and is not accountable to any person for the manner in which she makes use of her property. It is, however, necessary to recollect here what we have observed above (Book I. §81). No nation can lawfully appropriate to herself a too disproportionate extent of country, and reduce other nations to want subsistence, and a place of abode. A German chief, in the time of Nero, said to the Romans, "As heaven belongs to the gods, so the earth is given to the human race; and desert countries are common to all,"*—giving those proud conquerors to understand that they had no right to reserve and appropriate to themselves a country which they left desert. The <168> Romans had laid waste a chain of country along the Rhine, to cover their provinces from the incursions of the barbarians. The German's remonstrance would have had a good foundation, had the Romans pretended to keep without reason a vast country which was of no use to them: but those lands which they would not suffer to be inhabited, serving as a rampart against savage nations, were of considerable use to the empire.

§87. Duty of the nation in this respect.

When there is not this singular circumstance, it is equally agreeable to the dictates of humanity, and to the particular advantage of the state, to give those desert tracts to foreigners who are willing to clear the land and to render it valuable. The beneficence of the state thus turns to her own advantage; she acquires new subjects, and augments her riches and power. This is the practice in America; and, by this wise method, the English have carried their settlements in the new world to a degree of power, which has considerably increased that of the nation. Thus also

---

* Sicut coelum diis, ita terras generi mortalium datas; quaeque vacuae, eas publicas esse. Tacit. [["As heaven is for the gods, so the earth has been given to mankind, and lands uninhabited are common to all." *Annales XIII*]]

the king of Prussia endeavours to repeople his states laid waste by the calamities of former wars.

The nation that possesses a country is at liberty to leave in the primitive state of communion certain things that have as yet no owner, or to appropriate to herself the right of possessing those things, as well as every other advantage which that country is capable of affording. And as such a right is of use, it is, in case of doubt, presumed that the nation has reserved it to herself. It belongs to her then, to the exclusion of foreigners, unless her laws expressly declare otherwise, as those of the Romans, which left wild beasts, fish, &c. in the primitive state of communion. No foreigner, therefore, has a natural right to hunt or fish in the territories of a state, to appropriate to himself a treasure found there, &c.

§88. Right of possessing things that have no owner.

There exists no reason why a nation, or a sovereign if authorised by the laws, may not grant various privileges in their territories to another nation, or to foreigners in general, since every one may dispose of his own property as he thinks fit. Thus several sovereigns in the Indies have granted to the trading nations of Europe the privilege of having factories, ports, and even fortresses and garrisons in certain places within their dominions. We may in the same manner grant the right of fishing in a river, or on the coast, that of hunting in the forests, &c. and when once these rights have been validly ceded, they constitute a part of the possessions of him who has acquired them, and ought to be respected in the same manner as his former possessions.

§89. Rights granted to another nation.

Whoever agrees that robbery is a crime, and that we are not allowed to take forcible possession of our neighbour's property, will acknowledge, without any other proof, that no nation has a right to expel another people from the country they inhabit, in order to settle in it herself. Notwithstanding the extreme inequality of climates and soils, every people ought to be contented with that which has fallen to their share. Will the conductors of nations despise a rule that constitutes all their safety in civil society? Let <169> this sacred rule be entirely forgotten, and the peasant will quit his thatched cottage to invade the palaces of the great, or the delightful possessions of the rich. The antient Helvetians, discontented with their native soil, burned all their habitations, and commenced their march, in order to establish themselves, sword in hand, in

§90. It is not allowable to drive a nation out of a country which it inhabits;

the fertile plains of southern Gaul. But they received a terrible lesson from a conqueror of superior abilities to themselves, and who paid still less regard to the laws of justice. Caesar defeated them, and drove them back into their own country. Their posterity, however, more wise than they, confine their views to the preservation of the lands and the independence they have received from nature: they live contented; and the labour of free hands counter-balances the sterility of the soil.

§91. nor to extend by violence the bounds of empire. There are conquerors, who, aspiring after nothing more than the extension of the boundaries of their dominions, without expelling the inhabitants from a country, content themselves with subduing them;—a violence less barbarous, but not less unjust: while they spare the property of individuals, they seize all the rights of the nation, and of the sovereign.

§92. The limits of territories ought to be carefully settled. Since the least encroachment on the territory of another is an act of injustice,—in order to avoid the commission of any such act, and to prevent every subject of discord, every occasion of quarrel, the limits of territories ought to be marked out with clearness and precision. If those who drew up the treaty of Utrecht[22] had bestowed on so important a subject all the attention it deserved, we should not see France and England in arms, in order to decide by a bloody war what are to be the boundaries of their possessions in America. But the makers of treaties often designedly leave in them some obscurity, some uncertainty, in order to reserve for their nation a pretext for a rupture:—an unworthy artifice in a transaction wherein good-faith alone ought to preside! We have also seen commissioners endeavouring to overreach or corrupt those of a neighbouring state, in order to gain for their master an unjust acquisition of a few leagues of territory. How can princes or ministers stoop to dirty tricks that would dishonour a private man?

§93. Violation of territory. We should not only refrain from usurping the territory of others; we should also respect it, and abstain from every act contrary to the rights of the sovereign: for a foreign nation can claim no right in it (§79). We cannot then, without doing an injury to a state, enter its territories with

22. The Treaty of Utrecht, actually a series of separate treaties, was signed in 1713/14.

force and arms in pursuit of a criminal, and take him from thence. This would at once be a violation of the safety of the state, and a trespass on the rights of empire or supreme authority vested in the sovereign. This is what is called a violation of territory; and among nations there is nothing more generally acknowledged as an injury that ought to be vigorously repelled by every state that would not suffer itself to be oppressed. We shall make use of this principle in speaking of war, which gives occasion for many questions on the rights of territory. <170>

The sovereign may forbid the entrance of his territory either to foreigners in general, or in particular cases, or to certain persons, or for certain particular purposes, according as he may think it advantageous to the state. There is nothing in all this, that does not flow from the rights of domain and sovereignty: every one is obliged to pay respect to the prohibition; and whoever dares to violate it, incurs the penalty decreed to render it effectual. But the prohibition ought to be known, as well as the penalty annexed to disobedience: those who are ignorant of it, ought to be informed of it when they approach to enter the country. Formerly the Chinese, fearing lest the intercourse of strangers should corrupt the manners of the nation, and impair the maxims of a wise but singular government, forbade all people entering the empire: a prohibition that was not at all inconsistent with justice, provided they did not refuse humane assistance to those whom tempest or necessity obliged to approach their frontiers. It was salutary to the nation, without violating the rights of any individual, or even the duties of humanity, which permit us, in case of competition, to prefer ourselves to others. §94. Prohibition to enter the territory.

If at the same time two or more nations discover and take possession of an island or any other desert land without an owner, they ought to agree between themselves, and make an equitable partition; but if they cannot agree, each will have the right of empire and the domain in the parts in which they first settled. §95. A country possessed by several nations at the same time.

An independent individual, whether he has been driven from his country, or has legally quitted it of his own accord, may settle in a country which he finds without an owner, and there possess an independent domain. Whoever would afterwards make himself master of the entire country, could not do it with justice without respecting the rights and §96. A country possessed by a private person.

independence of this person. But if he himself finds a sufficient number of men who are willing to live under his laws, he may form a new state within the country he has discovered, and possess there both the domain and the empire. But if this individual should arrogate to himself alone an exclusive right to a country, there to reign monarch without subjects, his vain pretensions would be justly held in contempt:—a rash and ridiculous possession can produce no real right.

There are also other means by which a private person may found a new state. Thus, in the eleventh century, some Norman noblemen founded a new empire in Sicily, after having wrested that island by conquest from the common enemies of the christian name. The custom of the nation permitted the citizens to quit their country, in order to seek their fortune elsewhere.

§97. Indepen-
dent families
in a country.

When several independent families are settled in a country, they possess the free domain, but without sovereignty, since they do not form a political society. Nobody can seize the empire of that country; since this would be reducing those families to subjection against their will; and no man has a right to command men who are born free, unless they voluntarily submit to him. <171>

If those families have fixed settlements, the place possessed by each is the peculiar property of that family: the rest of the country, of which they make no use, being left in the primitive state of communion, belongs to the first occupant. Whoever chooses to settle there, may lawfully take possession of it.

Families wandering in a country, as the nations of shepherds, and ranging through it as their wants require, possess it in common: it belongs to them, to the exclusion of all other nations; and we cannot without injustice deprive them of the tracts of country of which they make use. But let us here recollect what we have said more than once (Book I. §§81 and 209, Book II. §69). The savages of North America had no right to appropriate all that vast continent to themselves: and since they were unable to inhabit the whole of those regions, other nations might without injustice settle in some parts of them, provided they left the natives a sufficiency of land. If the pastoral Arabs would carefully cultivate the soil, a less space might be sufficient for them. Nevertheless, no other nation has a right to narrow their boundaries, unless she be under an absolute want of land. For, in short, they possess their country; they make use of it after their manner; they reap from it an advantage suitable to their manner of life, respecting which, they have no laws to receive from any one. In a case of pressing necessity, I think people might without injustice settle in a part of that country, on teaching the Arabs the means of rendering it, by the cultivation of the earth, sufficient for their own wants and those of the new inhabitants.

It may happen that a nation is contented with possessing only certain places, or appropriating to itself certain rights, in a country that has not an owner,—without being solicitous to take possession of the whole country. In this case, another nation may take possession of what the first has neglected; but this cannot be done without allowing all the rights acquired by the first to subsist in their full and absolute independence. In such cases it is proper that regulations should be made by treaty; and this precaution is seldom neglected among civilised nations.

§98. Possession of certain places only, or of certain rights, in a vacant country.

CHAPTER VIII

Rules with respect to Foreigners.

We have already treated (Book I. §213) of the inhabitants, or persons who reside in a country where they are not citizens. We shall here treat only of those foreigners who pass through or sojourn in a country, either on business, or merely as travellers. The relation that subsists between them and the society in which they now live,—the objects of their journey and of their temporary residence,—the duties of humanity,—the rights, the interest, and the safety of the state which harbours them,—the rights of that to which they belong,—all these prin-<172>ciples, combined and applied according to cases and circumstances, serve to determine the conduct that ought to be observed towards them, and to point out our right and our duty with respect to them. But the intention of this chapter is not so much to shew what humanity and justice require towards foreigners, as to establish the rules of the law of nations on this

§99. General idea of the conduct the state ought to observe towards foreigners.

subject,—rules tending to secure the rights of all parties, and to prevent the repose of nations being disturbed by the quarrels of individuals.

§100. Entering the territory.

Since the lord of the territory may, whenever he thinks proper, forbid its being entered (§94), he has no doubt a power to annex what conditions he pleases to the permission to enter. This, as we have already said, is a consequence of the right of domain. Can it be necessary to add, that the owner of the territory ought in this instance to respect the duties of humanity? The case is the same with all rights whatever: the proprietor may use them at his discretion; and, in so doing, he does not injure any person: but if he would be free from guilt, and keep his conscience pure, he will never use them but in such manner as is most conformable to his duty. We speak here in general of the rights which belong to the lord of the country, reserving for the following chapter the examination of the cases in which he cannot refuse an entrance into his territory; and we shall see in Chap. X. how his duty towards all mankind obliges him on other occasions to allow a free passage through, and a residence in, his state.

If the sovereign annexes any particular condition to the permission to enter his territories, he ought to have measures taken to make foreigners acquainted with it, when they present themselves on the frontier. There are states, such as China, and Japan, into which all foreigners are forbid to penetrate without an express permission: but in Europe the access is every where free to every person who is not an enemy of the state, except, in some countries, to vagabonds and outcasts.

§101. Foreigners are subject to the laws.

But even in those countries which every foreigner may freely enter, the sovereign is supposed to allow him access only upon this tacit condition, that he be subject to the laws,—I mean the general laws made to maintain good order, and which have no relation to the title of citizen, or of subject of the state. The public safety, the rights of the nation and of the prince, necessarily require this condition; and the foreigner tacitly submits to it, as soon as he enters the country, as he cannot presume that he has access upon any other footing. The sovereignty is the right to command in the whole country; and the laws are not simply confined to regulating the conduct of the citizens towards each other, but also determine what is to be observed by all orders of people throughout the whole extent of the state.

In virtue of this submission, foreigners who commit faults, are to be punished according to the laws of the country. The object of punishment is to cause the laws to be respected, and to maintain order and safety. <173>

§102. And punishable according to the laws.

For the same reason, disputes that may arise between foreigners, or between a foreigner and a citizen, are to be determined by the judge of the place, and according to the laws of the place. And as the dispute properly arises from the refusal of the defendant, who maintains that he is not bound to perform what is required of him, it follows from the same principle, that every defendant ought to be prosecuted before his own judge, who alone has a right to condemn him, and compel him to the performance. The Swiss have wisely made this rule one of the articles of their alliance, in order to prevent the quarrels that might arise from abuses that were formerly too frequent in relation to this subject. The defendant's judge is the judge of the place where that defendant has his settled abode, or the judge of the place where the defendant is, when any sudden difficulty arises, provided it does not relate to an estate in land, or to a right annexed to such an estate. In this last case, as property of that kind is to be held according to the laws of the country where it is situated, and as the right of granting possession is vested in the ruler of the country,—disputes relating to such property can only be decided in the state on which it depends.

§103. Who is the judge of their disputes.

We have already shewn (§84) how the jurisdiction of a nation ought to be respected by other sovereigns, and in what cases alone they may interfere in the causes of their subjects in foreign countries.

The sovereign ought not to grant an entrance into his state for the purpose of drawing foreigners into a snare: as soon as he admits them, he engages to protect them as his own subjects, and to afford them perfect security, as far as depends on him. Accordingly we see that every sovereign who has given an asylum to a foreigner, considers himself no less offended by an injury done to the latter, than he would be by an act of violence committed on his own subject. Hospitality was in great honour

§104. Protection due to foreigners.

among the ancients, and even among barbarous nations, such as the Germans. Those savage nations who treated strangers ill, that Scythian tribe who sacrificed them to Diana,* were universally held in abhorrence; and Grotius justly says† that their extreme ferocity excluded them from the great society of mankind. All other nations had a right to unite their forces in order to chastise them.

§105. Their duties. From a sense of gratitude for the protection granted to him, and the other advantages he enjoys, the foreigner ought not to content himself with barely respecting the laws of the country; he ought to assist it upon occasion, and contribute to its defence, as far as is consistent with his duty as citizen of another state. We shall see elsewhere what he can and ought to do, when the country is engaged in a war. But there is nothing to hinder him from defending it against pirates or robbers, against the ravages of an inundation, or the devastations of fire. Can he pretend to <174> live under the protection of a state, to participate in a variety of advantages that it affords, and yet make no exertion for its defence, but remain an unconcerned spectator of the dangers to which the citizens are exposed?

§106. To what burdens they are subject. He cannot indeed be subject to those burdens that have only a relation to the quality of citizens; but he ought to bear his share of all the others. Being exempted from serving in the militia, and from paying those taxes destined for the support of the rights of the nation, he will pay the duties imposed upon provisions, merchandise, &c. and, in a word, every thing that has only a relation to his residence in the country, or to the affairs which brought him thither.

§107. Foreigners continue members of their own nation. The citizen or the subject of a state who absents himself for a time without any intention to abandon the society of which he is a member, does not lose his privilege by his absence: he preserves his rights, and remains bound by the same obligations. Being received in a foreign country, in virtue of the natural society, the communication, and commerce, which nations are obliged to cultivate with each other (Prelim.

---

* The Taurians. See Grotius de Jure Belli et Pacis, lib. ii. cap. xx. §xl. n. 7.
† Ibid.

§§11 and 12; Book II. §21), he ought to be considered there as a member of his own nation, and treated as such.

The state, which ought to respect the rights of other nations, and in general those of all mankind, cannot arrogate to herself any power over the person of a foreigner, who, though he has entered her territory, has not become her subject. The foreigner cannot pretend to enjoy the liberty of living in the country without respecting the laws: if he violates them, he is punishable as a disturber of the public peace, and guilty of a crime against the society in which he lives: but he is not obliged to submit, like the subjects, to all the commands of the sovereign: and if such things are required of him as he is unwilling to perform, he may quit the country. He is free at all times to leave it; nor have we a right to detain him, except for a time, and for very particular reasons, as, for instance, an apprehension, in war time, lest such foreigner, acquainted with the state of the country and of the fortified places, should communicate his knowledge to the enemy. From the voyages of the Dutch to the East Indies, we learn that the kings of Corea forcibly detain foreigners who are ship-wrecked on their coast; and Bodinus assures us,* that a custom so contrary to the law of nations was practised in his time in Aethiopia, and even in Muscovy. This is at once a violation of the rights of individuals, and of those of the state to which they belong. Things have been greatly changed in Russia; a single reign—that of Peter the Great—has placed that vast empire in the rank of civilised nations.

§108. The state has no right over the person of a foreigner;

The property of an individual does not cease to belong to him on account of his being in a foreign country; it still constitutes a part of the aggregate wealth of his nation (§81). Any power, <175> therefore, which the lord of the territory might claim over the property of a foreigner, would be equally derogatory to the rights of the individual owner, and to those of the nation of which he is a member.

§109. nor over his property.

Since the foreigner still continues to be a citizen of his own country, and a member of his own nation (§107), the property he leaves at his death in a foreign country ought naturally to devolve to those who are his heirs according to the laws of the state of which he is a member. But,

§110. Who are the heirs of a foreigner.

* In his Republic, book i. chap. vi.

notwithstanding this general rule, his immovable effects are to be disposed of according to the laws of the country where they are situated (see §103).

§111. Will of
a foreigner.

As the right of making a will, or of disposing of his fortune in case of death, is a right resulting from property, it cannot, without injustice, be taken from a foreigner. The foreigner therefore, by natural right, has the liberty of making a will. But it is asked by what laws he is obliged to regulate himself either in the form of his testament or in the disposal of his property? 1. As to the form or solemnities appointed to settle the validity of a will, it appears that the testator ought to observe those that are established in the country where he makes it, unless it be otherwise ordained by the laws of the state of which he is a member; in which case he will be obliged to observe the forms which they prescribe, if he would validly dispose of the property he possesses in his own country. I speak here of a will which is to be opened in the place where the person dies: for if a traveller makes his will, and sends it home under seal, it is the same thing as if it had been written at home; and in this case it is subject to the laws of his own country. 2. As to the bequests themselves, we have already observed that those which relate to immovables ought to be conformable to the laws of the country where those immovables are situated. The foreign testator cannot dispose of the goods, movable or immovable, which he possesses in his own country, otherwise than in a manner conformable to the laws of that country. But as to movable goods, specie, and other effects which he possesses elsewhere, which he has with him, or which follow his person, we ought to distinguish between the local laws whose effect cannot extend beyond the territory, and those laws which peculiarly affect the character of citizen. The foreigner remaining a citizen of his own country, is still bound by those last-mentioned laws, wherever he happens to be, and is obliged to conform to them in the disposal of his personal property, and all his movables whatsoever. The laws of this kind made in the country where he resides at the time, but of which he is not a citizen, are not obligatory with respect to him. Thus, a man who makes his will and dies in a foreign country, cannot deprive his widow of the part of his movable effects assigned to that widow by the laws of his own country. A Genevan, obliged by the law of Geneva to leave a dividend of his personal property to his brothers or his cousins, if they be his next heirs, cannot deprive them of it by making his <176> will in a foreign country, while he continues a citizen of Geneva: but a foreigner dying at Geneva is not obliged, in this respect, to conform to the laws of the republic. The case is quite otherwise with respect to local laws: they regulate what may be done in the territory, and do not extend beyond it. The testator is no longer subject to them when he is out of the territory; and they do not affect that part of his property which is also out of it. The foreigner is obliged to observe those laws in the country where he makes his will, with respect to the goods he possesses there. Thus, an inhabitant of Neufchatel, to whom entails are forbidden in his own country with respect to the property he possesses there, freely makes an entail of the estate he possesses out of the jurisdiction of the country, if he dies in a place where entails are allowed; and a foreigner making a will at Neufchatel cannot make an entail of even the movable property he possesses there,—unless indeed we may suppose that his movable property is excepted by the spirit of the law.

What we have established in the three preceding sections is sufficient to shew with how little justice the crown, in some states, lays claim to the effects left there by a foreigner at his death. This practice is founded on what is called *Escheatage,* by which foreigners are excluded from all inheritances in the state, either of the property of a citizen or that of an alien, and consequently cannot be appointed heirs by will, nor receive any legacy. Grotius justly observes that this law has descended to us from those ages when foreigners were almost considered as enemies.* Even after the Romans were become a very polite and learned people, they could not accustom themselves to consider foreigners as men entitled to any right in common with them. "Those nations," says Pomponius the civilian,[23] "with whom we have neither friendship, nor hospitality, nor alliance, are not therefore our enemies: yet if any thing belonging to us falls into their hands, it becomes their property; our free citizens become

§112.
Escheatage.

---

* De Jure Belli et Pacis, lib. ii. cap. vi. §14.
23. Titus Pomponius Atticus, ca. 110–32 B.C., Roman nobleman and patron of letters, close friend of Cicero.

slaves to them: and they are on the same terms with respect to us."* We cannot suppose that so wise a people retained such inhuman laws with any other view than that of a necessary retaliation, as they could not otherwise obtain satisfaction from barbarous nations with whom they had no connection or treaties existing. Bodinus shews† that *Escheatage* is derived from these worthy sources! It has been successively mitigated, or even abolished in most civilised states. The emperor Frederic II. first abolished it by an edict, which permitted *all foreigners dying within the limits of the empire to dispose of their substance by will, or, if they died intestate, to have their nearest relations for heirs.*‡ But Bodinus complains that this edict is but ill executed. Why does there still remain any vestige of so barbarous <177> a law in Europe, which is now so enlightened and so full of humanity? The law of nature cannot suffer it to be put in practice, except by way of retaliation. This is the use made of it by the king of Poland in his hereditary states. *Escheatage* is established in Saxony: but the sovereign is so just and equitable, that he enforces it only against those nations which subject the Saxons to a similar law.

§113. The right of *traite foraine*.   The right of *traite foraine* (called in Latin *jus detractûs*) is more conformable to justice, and the mutual obligation of nations. We give this name to the right by virtue of which the sovereign retains a moderate portion of the property either of citizens or aliens which is sent out of his territories to pass into the hands of foreigners. As the exportation of that property is a loss to the state, she may fairly receive an equitable compensation for it.

§114. Immovable property possessed by an alien.   Every state has the liberty of granting or refusing to foreigners the power of possessing lands or other immovable property within her territory. If she grants them that privilege, all such property, possessed by aliens, remains subject to the jurisdiction and laws of the country, and to the same taxes as other property of the same kind. The authority of the sovereign extends over the whole territory; and it would be absurd to except some parts of it, on account of their being possessed by for-

---

* Digest [[of Justinian]], lib. xix. tit xv. De Captivis & Postlimin.
† His Republic, book i. chap. vi.
‡ Ibid.

eigners. If the sovereign does not permit aliens to possess immovable property, nobody has a right to complain of such prohibition; for he may have very good reasons for acting in this manner: and as foreigners cannot claim any right in his territories (§79), they ought not to take it amiss that he makes use of his power and of his rights in the manner which he thinks most for the advantage of the state. And as the sovereign may refuse to foreigners the privilege of possessing immovable property, he is doubtless at liberty to forbear granting it except with certain conditions annexed.

There exists no natural impediment to prevent foreigners from contracting marriages in the state. But if these marriages are found prejudicial or dangerous to a nation, she has a right, and is even in duty bound to prohibit them, or to subject to certain conditions the permission to contract them: and as it belongs to the nation or to her sovereign to determine what appears most conducive to the welfare of the state, other nations ought to acquiesce in the regulations which any sovereign state has made on this head. Citizens are almost every-where forbid to marry foreign wives of a different religion; and in many parts of Switzerland a citizen cannot marry a foreign woman, unless he prove that she brings him in marriage a certain sum fixed by the law. <178>

§115.
Marriages
of aliens.

CHAPTER IX

Of the Rights retained by all Nations after the Introduction of Domain and Property.

If an obligation, as we have before observed, gives a right to those things without which it cannot be fulfilled, every absolute, necessary, and indispensable obligation produces in this manner rights equally absolute, necessary, and indefeasible. Nature imposes no obligations on men, without giving them the means of fulfilling them. They have an absolute right to the necessary use of those means: nothing can deprive them of that right, as nothing can dispense with their fulfilling their natural obligations.

§116. What
are the rights
of which men
cannot be
deprived.

§117. Right still remaining from the primitive state of communion.

In the primitive state of communion, men had, without distinction, a right to the use of every thing, as far as was necessary to the discharge of their natural obligations. And as nothing could deprive them of this right, the introduction of domain and property could not take place without leaving to every man the necessary use of things,—that is to say, the use absolutely required for the fulfilment of his natural obligations. We cannot then suppose the introduction to have taken place without this tacit restriction, that every man should still preserve some right to the things subjected to property, in those cases, where, without this right, he would remain absolutely deprived of the necessary use of things of this nature. This right is a necessary remnant of the primitive state of communion.

§118. Right retained by each nation over the property others.

Notwithstanding the domain of nations, therefore, each nation still retains some right to what is possessed by others, in those cases where she would find herself deprived of the necessary use of certain things if she were to be absolutely debarred from using them by the consideration of their being other people's property. We ought carefully to weigh every circumstance in order to make a just application of this principle.

§119. Right of necessity.

I say the same of the *right of necessity*. We thus call the right which necessity alone gives to the performance of certain actions that are otherwise unlawful, when, without these actions, it is impossible to fulfil an indispensable obligation. But it is carefully to be noted, that, in such a case, the obligation must really be an indispensable one, and the act in question the only means of fulfilling that obligation. If either of these conditions be wanting, the right of necessity does not exist on the occasion. We may see these subjects discussed in treatises on the law of nature, and particularly in that of Mr. Wolf. I confine myself here to a brief summary of those principles whose aid is necessary to us in developing the rights of nations. <179>

§120. Right of procuring provisions by force.

The earth was designed to feed its inhabitants; and he who is in want of every thing is not obliged to starve because all property is vested in others. When, therefore, a nation is in absolute want of provisions, she may compel her neighbours, who have more than they want for themselves, to supply her with a share of them at a fair price: she may even take it by force, if they will not sell it. Extreme necessity revives the primitive communion, the abolition of which ought to deprive no person of the necessaries of life (§117). The same right belongs to individuals when a foreign nation refuses them a just assistance. Captain Bontekoe, a Dutchman, having lost his vessel at sea, escaped in his boat with a part of his crew, and landed on an Indian coast, where the barbarous inhabitants refusing him provisions, the Dutch obtained them sword in hand.*

In the same manner, if a nation has a pressing want of the ships, waggons, horses, or even the personal labour of foreigners, she may make use of them either by free consent or by force, provided that the proprietors be not under the same necessity. But as she has no more right to these things than necessity gives her, she ought to pay for the use she makes of them, if she has the means of paying. The practice of Europe is conformable to this maxim. In cases of necessity, a nation sometimes presses foreign vessels which happen to be in her ports; but she pays a compensation for the services performed by them.

§121. Right of making use of the things that belong to others.

Let us say a few words on a more singular case, since authors have treated of it,—a case in which at present people are never reduced to employ force. A nation cannot preserve and perpetuate itself except by propagation. A nation of men has therefore a right to procure women, who are absolutely necessary to its preservation: and if its neighbours, who have a redundancy of females, refuse to give some of them in marriage to those men, the latter may justly have recourse to force. We have a famous example of this in the rape of the Sabine women.† But though a nation is allowed to procure for itself, even by force of arms, the liberty of obtaining women in marriage, no woman in particular can be constrained in her choice, nor become, by right, the wife of a man who carries her off by force;—a circumstance which has not been attended to by those who have decided, without restriction, that the Romans did not commit an act of injustice on that occasion.‡ It is true, that the Sabine women submitted to their fate with a good grace; and when their nation took up arms to avenge them, it sufficiently appeared from the

§122. Right of carrying off women.

---

* Bontekoe's voyage, in the Voyages of the Dutch to the East-Indies.
† Livy, book i.
‡ Wolfii Jus Gent. §341.

ardor with which those women rushed between the combatants, that they willingly acknowledged the Romans for their lawful husbands.

We may further add, that if the Romans, as many pretend, were originally only a band of robbers united under Romulus, they did not form a true nation, or a legitimate state: the neighbour-<180>ing nations had a just right to refuse them women; and the law of nature, which approves no civil society but such as is legitimate, did not require them to furnish that society of vagabonds and robbers with the means of perpetuating itself: much less did it authorise the latter to procure those means by force. In the same manner, no nation was obliged to furnish the Amazons with males. That nation of women, if it ever existed, put itself, by its own fault, out of a condition to support itself without foreign assistance.

§123. Right of passage; The right of passage is also a remnant of the primitive state of communion, in which the entire earth was common to all mankind, and the passage was every-where free to each individual according to his necessities. Nobody can be entirely deprived of this right (§117); but the exercise of it is limited by the introduction of domain and property: since they have been introduced, we cannot exert that right without paying due regard to the private rights of others. The effect of property is to give the proprietor's advantage a preference over that of all others. When, therefore, the owner of a territory thinks proper to refuse you admission into it, you must, in order to enter it in spite of him, have some reason more cogent than all his reasons to the contrary. Such is the right of necessity: this authorises an act on your part, which on other occasions would be unlawful, viz. an infringement of the right of domain. When a real necessity obliges you to enter into the territory of others,—for instance, if you cannot otherwise escape from imminent danger, or if you have no other passage for procuring the means of subsistence, or those of satisfying some other indispensable obligation,— you may force a passage when it is unjustly refused. But if an equal necessity obliges the proprietor to refuse you entrance, he refuses it justly; and his right is paramount to yours. Thus a vessel driven by stress of weather has a right to enter, even by force, into a foreign port. But if that vessel is infected with the plague, the owner of the port may fire upon it and beat it off, without any violation either of justice, or even of charity, which, in such a case, ought doubtless to begin at home.

The right of passage through a country would in most cases be useless, without that of procuring necessaries at a fair price: and we have already shewn (§120) that in case of necessity it is lawful to take provisions even by force.

§124. and of procuring necessaries.

In speaking of exile and banishment, we have observed (Book I. §§229–231) that every man has a right to dwell some-where upon earth. What we have shewn with respect to individuals, may be applied to whole nations. If a people are driven from the place of their abode, they have a right to seek a retreat: the nation to which they make application ought then to grant them a place of habitation, at least for a time, if she has not very important reasons for a refusal. But if the country inhabited by this nation is scarcely sufficient for herself, she is under no obligation to allow a band of foreigners to settle in it for ever: she <181> may even dismiss them at once, if it be not convenient to her to grant them a permanent settlement. As they have the resource of seeking an establishment elsewhere, they cannot claim any authority from the right of necessity, to stay in spite of the owners of the country. But it is necessary, in short, that these fugitives should find a retreat; and if every body rejects them, they will be justifiable in making a settlement in the first country where they find land enough for themselves, without depriving the inhabitants of what is sufficient for them. But, even in this case, their necessity gives them only the right of habitation; and they are bound to submit to all the conditions, not absolutely intolerable, which may be imposed on them by the master of the country,—such as paying him tribute, becoming his subjects, or at least living under his protection, and, in certain respects, depending on him. This right, as well as the two preceding, is a remnant of the primitive state of communion.

§125. Right of dwelling in a foreign country.

We have been occasionally obliged to anticipate the subject of the present chapter in order to follow the order of the different subjects that presented themselves. Thus, in speaking of the open sea, we have remarked (Book I. §281) that those things, the use of which is inexhaustible, cannot fall under the domain or property of any one; because, in that free and independent state in which nature has produced them, they may be equally useful to all men. And as to those things even, which in other respects are subject to domain,—if their use is inexhaustible, they remain common with respect to that use. Thus a river may be subject

§126. Things, of which the use is inexhaustible.

both to domain and empire; but in quality of running water it remains common,—that is to say, the owner of the river cannot hinder any one from drinking and drawing water out of it. Thus the sea, even in those parts that are held in possession, being sufficient for the navigation of all mankind, he who has the domain cannot refuse a passage through it to any vessel from which he has nothing to fear. But it may happen, by accident, that this inexhaustible use of the thing may be justly refused by the owner, when people cannot take advantage of it without incommoding him or doing him a prejudice. For instance, if you cannot come to my river for water without passing over my land and damaging the crop it bears, I may for that reason debar you from the inexhaustible use of the running water: in which case, it is but through accident you are deprived of it. This leads us to speak of another right which has a great connection with that just mentioned, and is even derived from it; that is the right of *innocent use.*

§127. Right of innocent use.

We call *innocent use,* or *innocent advantage,* that which may be derived from a thing without causing either loss or inconvenience to the proprietor; and the *right* of *innocent use* is the right we have to that advantage or use which may be made of things belonging to another, without causing him either loss or inconvenience. I have said that this right is derived from the right to things of which the use is inexhaustible. In fact, a thing that <182> may be useful to any one without loss or inconvenience to the owner, is, in this respect, inexhaustible in the use; and that is the reason why the law of nature still allows all men a right to it notwithstanding the introduction of domain and property. Nature, who designs her gifts for the common advantage of mankind, does not allow us to prevent the application of those gifts to an useful purpose which they may be made to serve without any prejudice to the proprietor, and without any diminution of the utility and advantages he is capable of deriving from his rights.

§128. Nature of this right in general;

This right of innocent use is not a perfect right like that of necessity; for it belongs to the owner to judge whether the use we wish to make of a thing that belongs to him will not be attended with damage or inconvenience. If others should presume to decide on the occasion, and, in case of refusal, to compel the proprietor, he would be no longer master of his own property. It may frequently happen that the person who wishes to derive advantage from a thing shall deem the use of it perfectly innocent, though it is not so in fact: and if, in such case, he attempts to force the proprietor, he exposes himself to the risk of committing an act of injustice; nay he actually commits one, since he infringes the owner's right to judge of what is proper to be done on the occasion. In all cases, therefore, which admit of any doubt, we have only an imperfect right to the innocent use of things that belong to others.

But when the innocence of the use is evident, and absolutely indubitable, the refusal is an injury. For, in addition to a manifest violation of the rights of the party by whom that innocent use is required, such refusal is moreover a testimony of an injurious disposition of hatred or contempt for him. To refuse a merchant-ship the liberty of passing through a strait, to fishermen that of drying their nets on the sea-shore or of watering at a river, is an evident infringement of the right they have to the innocent use of things in those cases. But in every case, if we are not pressed by necessity, we may ask the owner his reasons for the refusal; and if he gives none, we may consider him as an unjust man, or an enemy, with whom we are to act according to the rules of prudence. In general we should regulate our sentiments and conduct towards him, according to the greater or lesser weight of the reasons on which he acts. §129. and in cases not doubtful.

All nations do therefore still retain a general right to the innocent use of things that are under the domain of any one individual nation. But, in the particular application of this right, it is the nation in whom the property is vested, that is to determine whether the use which others wish to make of what belongs to her be really innocent: and if she gives them a denial, she ought to allege her reasons; as she must not deprive others of their right from mere caprice. All this is founded in justice: for it must be remembered that the innocent use of things is not comprehended in the domain or the exclusive property. The do-<183>main gives only the right of judging, in particular cases, whether the use be really innocent. Now he who judges ought to have his reasons; and he should mention them, if he would have us think that he forms any judgment, and not that he acts from caprice or ill-nature. All this, I say, is founded in justice. In the next chapter we shall see the line of conduct which a §130. Exercise of this right between nations.

nation is, by her duty to other nations, bound to observe in the exercise of her rights.

CHAPTER X

How a Nation is to use her Right of Domain, in order to discharge her Duties towards other Nations, with respect to the Innocent Use of Things.

§131. General duty of the proprietor. Since the law of nations treats as well of the duties of states as of their rights, it is not sufficient that we have explained, on the subject of innocent use, what all nations have a right to require from the proprietor: we are now to consider what influence his duties to others ought to have on the proprietor's conduct. As it belongs to him to judge whether the use be really innocent, and not productive of any detriment or inconvenience to himself, he ought not to give a refusal unless it be grounded upon real and substantial reasons: this is a maxim of equity: he ought not even to stop at trifles,—a slight loss, or any little inconvenience: humanity forbids this; and the mutual love which men owe to each other, requires greater sacrifices. It would certainly be too great a deviation from that universal benevolence which ought to unite the human race, to refuse a considerable advantage to an individual, or to a whole nation, whenever the grant of it might happen to be productive of the most trifling loss or the slightest inconvenience to ourselves. In this respect, therefore, a nation ought on all occasions to regulate her conduct by reasons proportioned to the advantages and necessities of others, and to reckon as nothing a small expense or a supportable inconvenience, when great good will thence result to another nation. But she is under no obligation to incur heavy expenses or embarrassments, for the sake of furnishing others with the use of any thing, when such use is neither necessary nor of any great utility to them. The sacrifice we here require is not contrary to the interests of the nation:—it is natural to think that the others will behave in the same manner in return; and how great the advantages that will result to all states from such a line of conduct!

The introduction of property cannot be supposed to have deprived nations of the general right of traversing the earth for the purposes of mutual intercourse, of carrying on commerce with each other, and for other just reasons. It is only on particular occasions when the owner of a country thinks it would be prejudicial or dangerous to allow a passage through it, that he ought to refuse <184> permission to pass. He is therefore bound to grant a passage for lawful purposes, whenever he can do it without inconvenience to himself. And he cannot lawfully annex burthensome conditions to a permission which he is obliged to grant, and which he cannot refuse if he wishes to discharge his duty, and not abuse his right of property. The count of Lupfen having improperly stopped some merchandise in Alsace, and complaints being made on the subject to the emperor Sigismund who was then at the council of Constance,[24] that prince assembled the electors, princes, and deputies of towns, to examine the affair. The opinion of the burgrave of Nuremberg deserves to be mentioned: "God," said he, "has created heaven for himself and his saints, and has given the earth to mankind, intending it for the advantage of the poor as well as of the rich. The roads are for their use, and God has not subjected them to any taxes." He condemned the count of Lupfen to restore the merchandise, and to pay costs and damages, because he could not justify his seizure by any peculiar right. The emperor approved this opinion, and passed sentence accordingly.*

§132. Innocent passage.

But if any apprehension of danger arise from the grant of liberty to pass through a country, the state has a right to require sureties: the party who wishes to pass cannot refuse them, a passage being only so far due to him as it is attended with no inconvenience.

§133. Sureties may be required.

In like manner, a passage ought also to be granted for merchandise: and as this is in general productive of no inconvenience, to refuse it without just reason, is injuring a nation, and endeavouring to deprive her of the means of carrying on a trade with other states. If this passage occasions any inconvenience, any expense for the preservation of canals

§134. Passage of merchandise.

* Stettler, vol. i. p. 114.—Tschudi, vol. ii. pp. 27, 28.
24. Council of Constance, 1414–18.

and highways, we may exact a compensation for it by toll duties (Book I. §103).

§135. Residence in the country.

In explaining the effects of domain we have said above (§§64 and 100) that the owner of the territory may forbid the entrance into it, or permit it on such conditions as he thinks proper. We were then treating of his external right,—that right which foreigners are bound to respect. But now that we are considering the matter in another view, and as it relates to his duties and to his internal right, we may venture to assert that he cannot, without particular and important reasons, refuse permission, either to pass through or reside in the country, to foreigners who desire it for lawful purposes. For, their passage or their residence being in this case an innocent advantage, the law of nature does not give him a right to refuse it: and though other nations and other men in general are obliged to submit to his judgment (§§128 and 130), he does not the less offend against his duty, if he refuses without sufficient reason: he then acts without any true right; he only abuses his external right. He cannot therefore, without some particular and cogent reason, refuse the liberty of residence to a <185> foreigner who comes into the country with the hope of recovering his health, or for the sake of acquiring instruction in the schools and academies. A difference in religion is not a sufficient reason to exclude him, provided he do not engage in controversial disputes with a view to disseminate his tenets: for that difference does not deprive him of the rights of humanity.

§136. How we are to act towards foreigners who desire a perpetual residence.

We have seen (§125) how the right of necessity may in certain cases authorise a people, who are driven from the place of their residence, to settle in the territory of another nation. Every state ought, doubtless, to grant to so unfortunate a people every aid and assistance which she can bestow without being wanting to herself: but to grant them an establishment in the territories of the nation, is a very delicate step, the consequences of which should be maturely considered by the conductor of the state. The emperors Probus and Valens[25] experienced the evil effects of their conduct in having admitted into the territories of the empire

25. Marcus Aurelius Probus, Roman emperor, r. A.D. 276–282; Flavius Julius Valens, Roman emperor, r. A.D. 364–78.

numerous bands of Gepidae, Vandals, Goths, and other barbarians.* If
the sovereign finds that such a step would be attended with too great an
inconvenience or danger, he has a right to refuse an establishment to
those fugitive people, or to adopt, on their admission, every precaution
that prudence can dictate to him. One of the safest will be, not to permit
those foreigners to reside together in the same part of the country, there
to keep up the form of a separate nation. Men who have not been able
to defend their own country, cannot pretend to any right to establish
themselves in the territory of another, in order to maintain themselves
there as a nation in a body.† The sovereign who harbours them may
therefore disperse them, and distribute them into the towns and provinces that are in want of inhabitants. In this manner his charity will turn
to his own advantage, to the increase of his power, and to the greater
benefit of the state. What a difference is observable in Brandenburg since
the settlement of the French refugees! The great elector, Frederic William,[26] offered an asylum to those unfortunate people; he provided for
their expenses on the road, and with truly regal munificence established
them in his states; by which conduct that beneficent and generous prince
merited the title of a wise and able politician.

When, by the laws or the custom of a state, certain actions are generally permitted to foreigners, as, for instance, travelling freely through
the country without any express permission, marrying there, buying or
selling merchandise, hunting, fishing, &c. we cannot exclude any one
nation from the benefit of the general permission, without doing her an
injury, unless there be <186> some particular and lawful reason for refusing to that nation what is granted indiscriminately to others. The

§137. Right
accruing from
a general
permission.

---

* Vopiscus, Prob. c. xviii.—Ammian. Marcell. lib. xxxi. [[*Roman History*]]—So-
crat. Hist. Eccles. lib. iv. c. 28.

† Caesar replied to the Tenchtheri and Usipetes, who wanted to retain possession
of the territories they had seized, that it was not just for them to invade the territories
of others, since they had not been able to defend their own.—*Neque verum esse, qui
suos fines tueri non potuerint, alienos occupare.* [["It was not probable that they who
were not able to defend their own territories, should get possession of those of
others." IV.8 (not chapter 6 as Vattel writes).]] De Bello Gallico, lib. iv. cap. vi.

26. Friedrich Wilhelm, elector of Brandenburg, r. 1640–88.

question here, it is to be observed, only relates to those actions which are productive of innocent advantage: and as the nation allows them to foreigners without distinction, she, by the very nature of that general permission, affords a sufficient proof that she deems them innocent with respect to herself; which amounts to a declaration that foreigners have a right to them (§127): the innocence of such acts is manifested by the confession of the state; and the refusal of an advantage that is manifestly innocent, is an injury (§129). Besides, to attempt without any reason to lay one nation under a prohibition where an indiscriminate permission is enjoyed by all others, is an injurious distinction, since it can only proceed from hatred or contempt. If there be any particular and well-founded reason for the exception, the advantage resulting from the act in question can no longer be deemed an innocent one with respect to the excepted nation; consequently no injury is done to them. The state may also, by way of punishment, except from the general permission a people who have given her just cause of complaint.

§138. A right granted as a favour.

As to rights of this nature granted to one or more nations for particular reasons, they are conferred on them as favours, either by treaty, or through gratitude for some particular service: those to whom the same rights are refused cannot consider themselves as offended. The nation does not esteem the advantage accruing from those acts to be an innocent one, since she does not indiscriminately allow them to all nations: and she may confer on whom she pleases any rights over her own property, without affording just grounds to any body else, either for uttering a complaint, or forming pretensions to the same favour.

§139. The nation ought to be courteous.

Humanity is not confined to the bare grant of a permission to foreign nations to make an innocent use of what belongs to us: it moreover requires that we should even facilitate to them the means of deriving advantage from it, so far as we can do this without injury to ourselves. Thus it becomes a well-regulated state to promote the general establishment of inns where travellers may procure lodging and food at a fair price,—to watch over their safety,—and to see that they be treated with equity and humanity. A polite nation should give the kindest reception to foreigners, receive them with politeness, and on every occasion shew a disposition to oblige them. By these means every citizen, while he discharges his duty to mankind in general, will at the same time render essential services to his country. Glory is the certain reward of virtue; and the good-will which is gained by an amiable character, is often productive of consequences highly important to the state. No nation is entitled to greater praise in this respect than the French: foreigners nowhere meet a reception more agreeable, or better calculated to prevent their regretting the immense sums they annually spend at Paris. <187>

CHAPTER XI

Of Usucaption and Prescription among Nations.

Let us conclude what relates to domain and property with an examination of a celebrated question on which the learned are much divided. It is asked whether *usucaption* and *prescription* can take place between independent nations and states?

Usucaption is the acquisition of domain founded on a long possession, uninterrupted and undisputed,—that is to say, an acquisition solely proved by this possession. Wolf defines it, an acquisition of domain founded on a presumed desertion. His definition explains the manner in which a long and peaceable possession may serve to establish the acquisition of domain. Modestinus,[27] *Digest. lib. 3. de Usurp. & Usucap.* says, in conformity to the principles of the Roman law, that *usucaption* is the acquisition of domain by possession continued during a certain period prescribed by law. These three definitions are by no means incompatible with each other; and it is easy to reconcile them by setting aside what relates to the civil law in the last of the three. In the first of them, we have endeavoured clearly to express the idea commonly affixed to the term *usucaption.*

§140. Definition of usucaption and prescription.

Prescription is the exclusion of all pretensions to a right,—an exclusion founded on the length of time during which that right has been neglected; or, according to Wolf's definition, it is the loss of an inherent

27. Herennius Modestinus, ca. A.D. 250, jurist and significant contributor to the *Corpus Juris Civilis.*

right by virtue of a presumed consent. This definition, too, is just; that is, it explains how a right may be forfeited by long neglect; and it agrees with the nominal definition we give of the term, *prescription,* in which we confine ourselves to the meaning usually annexed to the word. As to the rest, the term *usucaption* is but little used in French; and the word *prescription* implies, in that language, every thing expressed by the Latin terms *usucapio* and *praescriptio:* wherefore we shall make use of the word *prescription* wherever we have not particular reasons for employing the other.

§141. Usucaption and prescription derived from the law of nature.

Now, to decide the question we have proposed, we must first see whether usucaption and prescription are derived from the law of nature. Many illustrious authors have asserted and proved them to be so.* Though in this treatise we frequently suppose the reader acquainted with the law of nature, it is proper in this place to establish the decision, since the affair is disputed.

Nature has not herself established a private property over any of her gifts, and particularly over land: she only approves its establishment, for the advantage of the human race. On this <188> ground, then, it would be absurd to suppose, that, after the introduction of domain and property, the law of nature can secure to a proprietor any right capable of introducing disorder into human society. Such would be the right of entirely neglecting a thing that belongs to him,—of leaving it during a long space of time, under all the appearances of a thing utterly abandoned or not belonging to him,—and of coming at length to wrest it from a *bona-fide* possessor, who has perhaps dearly purchased his title to it,—who has received it as an inheritance from his progenitors, or as a portion with his wife,—and who might have made other acquisitions, had he been able to discover that the one in question was neither solid nor lawful. Far from giving such a right, the law of nature lays an injunction on the proprietor to take care of his property, and imposes on him an obligation to make known his rights, that others may not be led into error: it is on these conditions alone that she approves of the prop-

---

* See Grotius de Jure Belli & Pacis, lib. ii. cap. iv.—Puffendorf, Jus Nat. & Gent. lib. iv. cap. xii.—and especially Wolfius [[Wolff]], Jus Nat. part iii. cap. vii.

erty vested in him, and secures him in the possession. If he has neglected it for such a length of time that he cannot now be admitted to reclaim it without endangering the rights of others, the law of nature will no longer allow him to revive and assert his claims. We must not therefore conceive the right of private property to be a right of so extensive and imprescriptible a nature, that the proprietor may, at the risk of every inconvenience thence resulting to human society, absolutely neglect it for a length of time, and afterwards reclaim it, according to his caprice. With what other view than that of the peace, the safety, and the advantage of human society, does the law of nature ordain that all men should respect the right of private property in him who makes use of it? For the same reason therefore, the same law requires that every proprietor, who for a long time and without any just reason neglects his right, should be presumed to have entirely renounced and abandoned it. This is what forms the absolute presumption (*juris & de jure*) of its abandonment,— a presumption, upon which another person is legally entitled to appropriate to himself the thing so abandoned. The absolute presumption does not here signify a conjecture of the secret intentions of the proprietor, but a maxim which the law of nature ordains should be considered as true and invariable,—and this with a view of maintaining peace and order among men. Such presumption therefore confers a title as firm and just as that of property itself, and established and supported by the same reasons. The *bona-fide* possessor, resting his title on a presumption of this kind, has then a right which is approved by the law of nature; and that law, which requires that the rights of each individual should be stable and certain, does not allow any man to disturb him in his possession.

The right of *usucaption* properly signifies, that the *bona-fide* possessor is not obliged to suffer his right of property to be disputed after a long-continued and peaceable possession on his part: he proves that right by the very circumstance of possession, and sets up the plea of prescription in bar to the claims of the pretended <189> proprietor. Nothing can be more equitable than this rule. If the claimant were permitted to prove his property, he might happen to bring proofs very convincing indeed in appearance, but, in fact, deriving all their force only from the loss or destruction of some document or deed which would have proved how he had either lost or transferred his right. Would it be reasonable that he should be allowed to call in question the rights of the possessor, when by his own fault he has suffered matters to proceed to such a state, that there would be danger of mistaking the truth? If it be necessary that one of the two should be exposed to lose his property, it is just it should be the party who is in fault.

It is true, that if the *bona-fide* possessor should discover with perfect certainty, that the claimant is the real proprietor, and has never abandoned his right, he is bound in conscience, and by the internal principles of justice, to make restitution of whatever accession of wealth he has derived from the property of the claimant. But this estimation is not easily made; and it depends on circumstances.

§142. What foundation is required for ordinary prescription.

As prescription cannot be grounded on any but an absolute or lawful presumption, it has no foundation, if the proprietor has not really neglected his right. This condition implies three particulars: 1, that the proprietor cannot allege an invincible ignorance, either on his own part, or on that of the persons from whom he derives his right;—2, that he cannot justify his silence by lawful and substantial reasons;—3, that he has neglected his right, or kept silence during a considerable number of years: for the negligence of a few years, being incapable of producing confusion, and rendering doubtful the respective rights of the parties, is not sufficient to found or authorise a presumption of relinquishment. It is impossible to determine by the law of nature the number of years required to found a prescription: this depends on the nature of the property disputed, and the circumstances of the case.

§143. Immemorial prescription.

What we have remarked in the preceding section, relates to ordinary prescription. There is another called *immemorial,* because it is founded on immemorial possession,—that is, on a possession, the origin of which is unknown, or so deeply involved in obscurity, as to allow no possibility of proving whether the possessor has really derived his right from the original proprietor, or received the possession from another. This *immemorial* prescription secures the possessor's right, beyond the power of recovery: for it affords a legal presumption that he is the proprietor, as long as the adverse party fails to adduce substantial reasons in support of his claim: and, indeed, whence could these reasons be derived, since the origin of the possession is lost in the obscurity of time? It ought even to secure the possessor against every pretension contrary to his right. What would be the case were it permitted to call in question a right acknowledged time immemorial, when the means of proving it were destroyed by time? Immemorial possession therefore is an irrefragable title, and immemorial prescription admits of no exception: both are founded on a pre-<190>sumption which the law of nature directs us to receive as an incontestable truth.

In cases of ordinary prescription, the same argument cannot be used against a claimant who alleges just reasons for his silence, as the impossibility of speaking, or a well-founded fear, &c. because there is then no longer any room for a presumption that he has abandoned his right. It is not his fault if people have thought themselves authorised to form such a presumption; nor ought he to suffer in consequence: he cannot therefore be debarred the liberty of clearly proving his property. This method of defence in bar of prescription has been often employed against princes whose formidable power had long silenced the feeble victims of their usurpations.

§144. Claimant alleging reasons for his silence.

It is also very evident that we cannot plead prescription in opposition to a proprietor who, being for the present unable to prosecute his right, confines himself to a notification, by any token whatever, sufficient to shew that it is not his intention to abandon it. Protests answer this purpose. With sovereigns it is usual to retain the title and arms of a sovereignty or a province, as an evidence that they do not relinquish their claims to it.

§145. Proprietor sufficiently shewing that he does not mean to abandon his right.

Every proprietor, who expressly commits or omits certain acts which he cannot commit or omit without renouncing his right, sufficiently indicates by such commission or omission that it is not his intention to preserve it, unless, by an express reservation, he declare the contrary. We are undoubtedly authorised to consider as true what he sufficiently manifests on occasions where he ought to declare the truth: consequently, we may lawfully presume that he abandons his right; and if he would afterwards resume it, we can plead prescription in bar to his claim.

§146. Prescription founded on the actions of the proprietor.

§147. Usucaption and prescription take place between nations.

After having shewn that *usucaption* and *prescription* are founded in the law of nature, it is easy to prove that they are equally a part of the law of nations, and ought to take place between different states. For the law of nations is but the law of nature applied to nations in a manner suitable to the parties concerned (Prelim. §6). And so far is the nature of the parties from affording them an exemption in the case, that usucaption and prescription are much more necessary between sovereign states than between individuals. Their quarrels are of much greater consequence; their disputes are usually terminated only by bloody wars; and consequently the peace and happiness of mankind much more powerfully require that possession on the part of sovereigns should not be easily disturbed,—and that, if it has for a considerable length of time continued uncontested, it should be deemed just and indisputable. Were we allowed to recur to antiquity on every occasion, there are few sovereigns who could enjoy their rights in security, and there would be no peace to be hoped for on earth.

§148. More difficult, between nations, to found them on a presumptive desertion.

It must however be confessed, that, between nations, the rights of usucaption and prescription are often more difficult in their application, so far as they are founded on a presumption <191> drawn from long silence. Nobody is ignorant how dangerous it commonly is for a weak state even to hint a claim to the possessions of a powerful monarch. In such a case, therefore, it is not easy to deduce from long silence a legal presumption of abandonment. To this we may add, that, as the ruler of the society has usually no power to alienate what belongs to the state, his silence, even though sufficient to afford a presumption of abandonment on his own part, cannot impair the national right or that of his successors. The question then will be, whether the nation has neglected to supply the omission caused by the silence of her ruler, or has participated in it by a tacit approbation.

§149. Other principles that enforce prescription.

But there are other principles that establish the use and force of prescription between nations. The tranquillity of the people, the safety of states, the happiness of the human race, do not allow that the possessions, empire, and other rights of nations should remain uncertain, subject to dispute, and ever ready to occasion bloody wars. Between nations therefore it becomes necessary to admit prescription founded on length of time, as a valid and incontestable title. If any nation has kept silence through fear, and as it were through necessity, the loss of her right is a misfortune which she ought patiently to bear, since she could not avoid it: and why should she not submit to this as well as to have her towns and provinces taken from her by an unjust conqueror, and to be forced to cede them to him by treaty? It is however only in cases of long-continued, undisputed, and uninterrupted possession, that prescription is established on these grounds, because it is necessary that affairs should some time or other be brought to a conclusion, and settled on a firm and solid foundation. But the case is different with a possession of only a few years' continuance, during which the party whose rights are invaded may from prudential reasons find it expedient to keep silence, without at the same time affording room to accuse him of suffering things to become uncertain, and of renewing quarrels without end.

As to immemorial prescription, what we have said respecting it (§143) is sufficient to convince every one that it ought necessarily to take place between nations.

Usucaption and prescription being so necessary to the tranquillity and happiness of human society, it is justly presumed that all nations have consented to admit the lawful and reasonable use of them, with a view to the general advantage, and even to the private interest of each individual nation. §150. Effects of the voluntary law of nations on this subject.

Prescription of many years' standing, as well as usucaption, is then established by the voluntary law of nations (Prelim. §21).

Nay more, as by virtue of that law nations are, in all doubtful cases, supposed to stand on a footing of equal right in treating with each other (ibid.), prescription, when founded on long undisputed possession, ought to have its full effect between nations, without admitting any allegation of the possession being unjust, <192> unless the evidence to prove it be very clear and convincing indeed. For, without such evidence, every nation is to be considered as a *bona-fide* possessor. Such is the right that a sovereign state ought to allow to other states; but to herself she should only allow the use of the internal and necessary right (Prelim. §28). It is the *bona-fide* possessor alone, whose prescription will stand the test of conscience.

§151. Law of treaties or of custom in this matter.   Since prescription is subject to so many difficulties, it would be very proper that adjoining nations should by treaty adopt some rule on this subject, particularly with respect to the number of years required to found a lawful prescription, since this latter point cannot in general be determined by the law of nature alone. If, in default of treaties, custom has determined any thing in this matter, the nations between whom this custom is in force, ought to conform to it (Prelim. §26).

CHAPTER XII

Of Treaties of Alliance, and other public Treaties.

§152. Nature of treaties.   The subject of treaties is undoubtedly one of the most important that the mutual relations and affairs of nations can present us with. Having but too much reason to be convinced of the little dependence that is to be placed on the natural obligations of bodies politic, and on the reciprocal duties imposed upon them by humanity,—the most prudent nations endeavour to procure by treaties those succours and advantages which the law of nature would insure to them, if it were not rendered ineffectual by the pernicious counsels of a false policy.

A treaty, in Latin *foedus,* is a compact made with a view to the public welfare by the superior power, either for perpetuity, or for a considerable time.

§153. Pactions, agreements, or conventions.   The compacts which have temporary matters for their object are called agreements, conventions, and pactions. They are accomplished by one single act, and not by repeated acts. These compacts are perfected in their execution once for all: treaties receive a successive execution whose duration equals that of the treaty.

§154. By whom treaties are made.   Public treaties can only be made by the superior powers, by sovereigns who contract in the name of the state. Thus conventions made between sovereigns respecting their own private affairs, and those between a sovereign and a private person, are not public treaties.

The sovereign who possesses the full and absolute authority, has, doubtless, a right to treat in the name of the state he represents; and his engagements are binding on the whole nation. But all rulers of states have not a power to make public treaties by their own authority alone: some are obliged to take the advice of a senate, or of the representatives of the nation. It is from the <193> fundamental laws of each state that we must learn where resides the authority that is capable of contracting with validity in the name of the state.

Notwithstanding our assertion above, that public treaties are made only by the superior powers, treaties of that nature may nevertheless be entered into by princes or communities who have a right to contract them, either by the concession of the sovereign, or by the fundamental laws of the state, by particular reservations, or by custom. Thus the princes and free cities of Germany, though dependent on the emperor and the empire, have the right of forming alliances with foreign powers. The constitutions of the empire give them, in this as in many other respects, the rights of sovereignty. Some cities of Switzerland, though subject to a prince, have made alliances with the cantons: the permission or toleration of the sovereign has given birth to such treaties, and long custom has established the right to contract them.

As a state that has put herself under the protection of another, has not on that account forfeited her character of sovereignty (Book I. §192), she may make treaties and contract alliances, unless she has, in the treaty of protection, expressly renounced that right. But she continues for ever after bound by this treaty of protection, so that she cannot enter into any engagements contrary to it,—that is to say, engagements which violate the express conditions of the protection, or that are in their own nature repugnant to every treaty of protection. Thus the protected state cannot promise assistance to the enemies of her protector, nor grant them a passage. §155. Whether a state under protection may make treaties.

Sovereigns treat with each other through the medium of agents or proxies who are invested with sufficient powers for the purpose, and are commonly called plenipotentiaries. To their office we may apply all the rules of natural law which respect things done by commission. The rights of the proxy are determined by the instructions that are given him: he must not deviate from them; but every promise which he makes in the terms of his commission, and within the extent of his powers, is binding on his constituent. §156. Treaties concluded by proxies or plenipotentiaries.

At present, in order to avoid all danger and difficulty, princes reserve to themselves the power of ratifying what has been concluded upon in their name by their ministers. The plenipotentiary commission is but a procuration *cum libera*. If this commission were to have its full effect, they could not be too circumspect in giving it. But as princes cannot otherwise than by force of arms be compelled to fulfil their engagements, it is customary to place no dependence on their treaties, till they have agreed to and ratified them. Thus, as every agreement made by the minister remains invalid till sanctioned by the prince's ratification, there is less danger in vesting him with unlimited powers. But before a prince can honourably refuse to ratify a compact made in virtue of such plenipotentiary commission, he <194> should be able to allege strong and substantial reasons, and, in particular, to prove that his minister has deviated from his instructions.

§157. Validity of treaties.

A treaty is valid if there be no defect in the manner in which it has been concluded: and for this purpose nothing more can be required, than a sufficient power in the contracting parties, and their mutual consent sufficiently declared.

§158. Injury does not render them void.

An injury cannot then render a treaty invalid. He who enters into engagements ought carefully to weigh every thing before he concludes them; he may do what he pleases with his own property, forego his rights, and renounce his advantages, as he thinks proper; the acceptor is not obliged to inquire into his motives, and to estimate their due weight. If we might recede from a treaty because we found ourselves injured by it, there would be no stability in the contracts of nations. Civil laws may set bounds to injury, and determine what degree of it shall be capable of invalidating a contract. But sovereigns are subject to no superior judge. How shall they be able to prove the injury to each other's satisfaction? Who shall determine the degree of it sufficient to invalidate a treaty? The peace and happiness of nations manifestly require that their treaties should not depend on so vague and dangerous a plea of invalidity.

§159. Duty of nations in this respect.

A sovereign nevertheless is in conscience bound to pay a regard to equity, and to observe it as much as possible, in all his treaties. And if it happens that a treaty which he has concluded with upright intentions, and without perceiving any unfairness in it, should eventually prove disadvantageous to an ally, nothing can be more honourable, more praiseworthy, more conformable to the reciprocal duties of nations, than to relax the terms of such treaty as far as he can do it consistently with his duty to himself, and without exposing himself to danger, or incurring a considerable loss.

Though a simple injury, or some disadvantage in a treaty, be not sufficient to invalidate it, the case is not the same with those inconveniences that would lead to the ruin of the nation. Since, in the formation of every treaty, the contracting parties must be vested with sufficient powers for the purpose, a treaty pernicious to the state is null, and not at all obligatory, as no conductor of a nation has the power to enter into engagements to do such things as are capable of destroying the state, for whose safety the government is intrusted to him. The nation itself, being necessarily obliged to perform every thing required for its preservation and safety (Book I. §16, &c.), cannot enter into engagements contrary to its indispensable obligations. In the year 1506, the states-general of the kingdom of France, assembled at Tours, engaged Louis XII. to break the treaty he had concluded with the emperor Maximilian,[28] and the archduke Philip, his son, because that treaty was pernicious to the kingdom. They also decided, that neither the treaty, nor the oath that had accompanied it, could be binding on the king, who had no right to <195> alienate the property of the crown.* We have treated of this latter source of invalidity in the twenty-first chapter of Book I.

§160. Nullity of treaties which are pernicious to the state.

For the same reason—the want of sufficient powers—a treaty concluded for an unjust or dishonest purpose is absolutely null and void,—nobody having a right to engage to do things contrary to the law of nature. Thus, an offensive alliance, made for the purpose of plundering a nation from whom no injury has been received, may or rather ought to be broken.

§161. Nullity of treaties made for an unjust or dishonest purpose.

---

* See the French historians [[Choisy, Daniel, Mézeray, Pineau-Duclos, and Velly]].
28. King Louis XII of France, r. 1498–1515; Emperor Maximilian I, r. 1508–19. The treaty referred to was the Treaty of Trente, signed in October 1501 between Maximilian of Austria, the future emperor, who was then "king of the Romans," and Louis XII.

§162. Whether an alliance may be contracted with those who do not profess the true religion.

It is asked, whether it be allowable to contract an alliance with a nation that does not profess the true religion, and whether treaties made with the enemies of the faith are valid? Grotius has treated this subject at large:* and the discussion might have been necessary at a time when party-rage still obscured those principles which it had long caused to be forgotten: but we may venture to believe that it would be superfluous in the present age. The law of nature alone regulates the treaties of nations: the difference of religion is a thing absolutely foreign to them. Different people treat with each other in quality of men, and not under the character of Christians, or of Mahommedans. Their common safety requires that they should be capable of treating with each other, and of treating with security. Any religion that should in this case clash with the law of nature, would, on the very face of it, wear the stamp of reprobation, and could not pretend to derive its origin from the great author of nature, who is ever steady, ever consistent with himself. But if the maxims of a religion tend to establish it by violence, and to oppress all those who will not embrace it, the law of nature forbids us to favour that religion, or to contract any unnecessary alliances with its inhuman followers; and the common safety of mankind invites them rather to enter into an alliance against such a people,—to repress such outrageous fanatics, who disturb the public repose, and threaten all nations.

§163. Obligation of observing treaties.

It is a settled point in natural law, that he who has made a promise to any one, has conferred upon him a real right to require the thing promised,—and consequently, that the breach of a perfect promise is a violation of another person's right, and as evidently an act of injustice, as it would be to rob a man of his property. The tranquillity, the happiness, the security of the human race, wholly depend on justice,—on the obligation of paying a regard to the rights of others. The respect which others pay to our rights of domain and property constitutes the security of our actual possessions; the faith of promises is our security for things that cannot be delivered or executed upon the spot. There would no longer be any security, no longer any commerce between mankind, if

* De Jure Belli et Pacis, lib. ii. cap. xv. §8. et seq.

they did not think themselves obliged to keep faith with each other, and to perform their promises. This obligation is then as necessary, as it is natural and indubitable, between na-<196>tions that live together in a state of nature, and acknowledge no superior upon earth, to maintain order and peace in their society. Nations, therefore, and their conductors, ought inviolably to observe their promises and their treaties. This great truth, though too often neglected in practice, is generally acknowledged by all nations:* the reproach of perfidy is esteemed by sovereigns a most atrocious affront; yet he who does not observe a treaty, is certainly perfidious, since he violates his faith. On the contrary, nothing adds so great a glory to a prince, and to the nation he governs, as the reputation of an inviolable fidelity in the performance of promises. By such honourable conduct, as much or even more than by her valour, the Swiss nation has rendered herself respectable throughout Europe, and is deservedly courted by the greatest monarchs, who intrust their personal safety to a body-guard of her citizens. The parliament of England has more than once thanked the king for his fidelity and zeal in succouring the allies of his crown. This national magnanimity is the source of immortal glory; it presents a firm basis on which nations may build their confidence; and thus it becomes an unfailing source of power and splendor.

As the engagements of a treaty impose on the one hand a perfect obligation, they produce on the other a perfect right. The breach of a treaty is therefore a violation of the perfect right of the party with whom we have contracted; and this is an act of injustice against him.

§164. The violation of a treaty is an act of injustice.

A sovereign already bound by a treaty, cannot enter into others contrary to the first. The things, respecting which he has entered into engagements, are no longer at his disposal. If it happens that a posterior treaty be found, in any particular point, to clash with one of more ancient date, the new treaty is null and void with respect to that point, inasmuch as it tends to dispose of a thing that is no longer in the power

§165. Treaties cannot be made, contrary to those already existing.

* Mahommed warmly recommended to his disciples the observance of treaties. Ockley's History of the Saracens, vol. i.

of him who appears to dispose of it. (We are here to be understood as speaking of treaties made with different powers.) If the prior treaty is kept secret, it would be an act of consummate perfidy to conclude a contrary one, which may be rendered void whenever occasion serves. Nay, even to enter into engagements, which, from the eventual turn of affairs, may chance at a future day to militate against the secret treaty, and from that very circumstance to prove ineffectual and nugatory, is by no means justifiable, unless we have the ability to make ample compensation to our new ally: otherwise it would be practising a deception on him, to promise him a thing without informing him that cases may possibly occur, which will not allow us to substantiate our promise. The ally thus deceived is undoubtedly at liberty to renounce the treaty; but if he chuses rather to adhere to it, it will hold good <197> with respect to all the articles that do not clash with the prior treaty.

§166. How treaties may be concluded with several nations with the same view.
There is nothing to prevent a sovereign from entering into engagements of the same nature with two or more nations, if he be able to fulfil those several engagements to his different allies at the same time. For instance, a commercial treaty with one nation does not deprive us of the liberty of afterwards contracting similar engagements with other states, unless we have, in the former treaty, bound ourselves by a promise not to grant the same advantages to any other nation. We may in the same manner promise to assist two different allies with troops, if we are able to furnish them, or if there is no probability that both will have occasion for them at the same time.

§167. The more ancient ally entitled to a preference.
If nevertheless the contrary happens, the more ancient ally is entitled to a preference: for the engagement was pure and absolute with respect to him; whereas we could not contract with the more recent ally, without a reservation of the rights of the former. Such reservation is founded in justice, and is tacitly understood, even if not expressly made.

§168. We owe no assistance in an unjust war.
The justice of the cause is another ground of preference between two allies. We ought even to refuse assistance to the one whose cause is unjust, whether he be at war with one of our allies, or with another state: to assist him on such an occasion, would in the event be the same thing as if we had contracted an alliance for an unjust purpose; which we are not allowed to do (§161). No one can be validly engaged to support injustice.

Grotius divides treaties into two general classes,—first, *those which turn merely on things to which the parties were already bound by the law of nature,*—secondly, *those by which they enter into further engagements.** By the former we acquire a perfect right to things to which we before had only an imperfect right, so that we may thenceforward demand as our due what before we could only request as an office of humanity. Such treaties became very necessary between the nations of antiquity, who, as we have already observed, did not think themselves bound to any duty towards people who were not in the number of their allies. They are useful even between the most polished nations, in order the better to secure the succours they may expect,—to determine the measure and degree of those succours, and to shew on what they have to depend,—to regulate what cannot in general be determined by the law of nature,—and thus to obviate all difficulties, by providing against the various interpretations of that law. Finally, as no nation possesses inexhaustible means of assistance, it is prudent to secure to ourselves a peculiar right to that assistance which cannot be granted to all the world.

§169. General division of treaties.

1. Those that relate to things already due by the law of nature.

To this first class belong all simple treaties of peace and friendship, when the engagements which we thereby contract, make no <198> addition to those duties that men owe to each other as brethren, and as members of the human society: such are those treaties that permit commerce, passage, &c.

If the assistance and offices that are due by virtue of such a treaty, should on any occasion prove incompatible with the duties a nation owes to herself, or with what the sovereign owes to his own nation, the case is tacitly and necessarily excepted in the treaty. For neither the nation nor the sovereign could enter into an engagement to neglect the care of their own safety or the safety of the state, in order to contribute to that of their ally. If the sovereign, in order to preserve his own nation, has occasion for the things he has promised in the treaty,—if, for instance, he has engaged to furnish corn, and in a time of dearth he has scarcely sufficient for the subsistence of his subjects, he ought without hesitation to give a preference to his own nation: for it is only so far as he has it in

§170. Collision of these treaties with the duties we owe to ourselves.

* De Jure Belli et Pacis, lib. ii. cap. xv. §5.

his power to give assistance to a foreign nation, that he naturally owes such assistance; and it was upon that footing alone that he could promise it in a treaty. Now it is not in his power to deprive his own nation of the means of subsistence in order to assist another nation at their expense. Necessity here forms an exception, and he does not violate the treaty, because he cannot fulfil it.

§171. Treaties in which we barely promise to do no injury. The treaties by which we simply engage not to do any evil to an ally, to abstain, with respect to him, from all harm, offence, and injury, are not necessary, and produce no new right, since every individual already possesses a perfect natural right to be exempt from harm, injury, and real offence. Such treaties, however, become very useful, and accidentally necessary, among those barbarous nations who think they have a right to act as they please towards foreigners. They are not wholly useless with nations less savage, who, without so far divesting themselves of humanity, entertain a much less powerful sense of a natural obligation, than of one which they have themselves contracted by solemn engagements: and would to God that this manner of thinking were entirely confined to barbarians! We see too frequent effects of it among those who boast of a perfection much superior to the law of nature. But the imputation of perfidy is prejudicial to the rulers of nations, and thus becomes formidable even to those who are little solicitous to merit the appellation of virtuous men, and who feel no scruple in silencing the reproaches of conscience.

§172. Treaties concerning things that are not naturally due. Equal treaties. Treaties by which we contract engagements that were not imposed on us by the law of nature, are either *equal* or *unequal*.

Equal treaties are those in which the contracting parties promise the same things, or things that are equivalent, or, finally, things that are equitably proportioned, so that the condition of the parties is equal. Such is, for example, a defensive alliance, in which the parties reciprocally stipulate for the same succours. Such is an offensive alliance, in which it is agreed that each of <199> the allies shall furnish the same number of vessels, the same number of troops, of cavalry and infantry, or an equivalent in vessels, in troops, in artillery, or in money. Such is also a league in which the quota of each of the allies is regulated in proportion to the interest he takes or may have in the design of the league. Thus the emperor and the king of England,[29] in order to induce the states-general of the United Provinces to accede to the treaty of Vienna of the 16th of March 1731, consented that the republic should only promise to her allies the assistance of four thousand foot and a thousand horse, though they engaged, in case of an attack upon the republic, to furnish her, each, with eight thousand foot and four thousand horse. We are also to place in the class of equal treaties those which stipulate that the allies shall consider themselves as embarked in a common cause, and shall act with all their strength. Notwithstanding a real inequality in their strength, they are nevertheless willing in this instance to consider it as equal.

Equal treaties may be subdivided into as many species as there are of different transactions between sovereigns. Thus they treat of the conditions of commerce, of their mutual defence, of associations in war, of reciprocally granting each other a passage, or refusing it to the enemies of their ally; they engage not to build fortresses in certain places, &c. But it would be needless to enter into these particulars: generals are sufficient, and are easily applied to particular cases.

Nations being no less obliged than individuals to pay a regard to equity, they ought, as much as possible, to preserve equality in their treaties. When, therefore, the parties are able reciprocally to afford each other equal advantages, the law of nature requires that their treaties should be equal, unless there exist some particular reason for deviating from that equality,—such, for instance, as gratitude for a former benefit,—the hope of gaining the inviolable attachment of a nation,—some private motive which renders one of the contracting parties particularly anxious to have the treaty concluded, &c. Nay, viewing the transaction in its proper point of light, the consideration of that particular reason restores to the treaty that equality which seems to be destroyed by the difference of the things promised. §173. Obligation of preserving equality in treaties.

I see those pretended great politicians smile, who employ all their subtilty in circumventing those with whom they treat, and in so managing the conditions of the treaty, that all the advantage shall accrue to

29. Emperor Charles VI, r. 1711–40; King George II, r. 1727–60.

their masters. Far from blushing at a conduct so contrary to equity, to rectitude, and natural honesty, they glory in it, and think themselves entitled to the appellation of able negotiators. How long shall we continue to see men in public characters take a pride in practices that would disgrace a private individual? The private man, if he is void of conscience, laughs also at the rules of morality and justice; but he laughs in secret: it would be dangerous and prejudicial to him <200> to make a public mockery of them. Men in power more openly sacrifice honour and honesty to present advantage: but, fortunately for mankind, it often happens that such seeming advantage proves fatal to them; and even between sovereigns, candour and rectitude are found to be the safest policy. All the subtilties, all the tergiversations of a famous minister,[30] on the occasion of a treaty in which Spain was deeply interested, turned at length to his own confusion, and to the detriment of his master; while England, by her good faith and generosity to her allies, gained immense credit, and rose to the highest pitch of influence and respectability.

§174. Difference between equal treaties and equal alliances.   When people speak of equal treaties, they have commonly in their minds a double idea of equality, viz. equality in the engagements, and equality in the dignity of the contracting parties. It becomes therefore necessary to remove all ambiguity; and for that purpose, we may make a distinction between *equal treaties* and *equal alliances. Equal treaties* are those in which there is an equality in the promises made, as we have above explained (§172); and *equal alliances,* those in which equal treats with equal, making no difference in the dignity of the contracting parties, or, at least, admitting no too glaring superiority, but merely a preeminence of honour and rank. Thus kings treat with the emperor on a footing of equality, though they do not hesitate to allow him precedency; thus great republics treat with kings on the same footing, notwithstanding the pre-eminence which the former now-a-days yield to the latter. Thus all true sovereigns ought to treat with the most powerful monarch, since they are as really sovereigns, and as independent as himself. (See §37 of this Book.)

---

30. Cardinal Richelieu, chief minister (1624–42) to King Louis XIII of France.

Unequal treaties are those in which the allies do not reciprocally promise to each other the same things, or things equivalent; and an *alliance*
is *unequal* when it makes a difference in the dignity of the contracting
parties. It is true, that most commonly an unequal treaty will be at the
same time an unequal alliance; as great potentates are seldom accustomed to give or to promise more than is given or promised to them,
unless such concessions be fully compensated in the article of honour
and glory; and, on the other hand, a weak state does not submit to burthensome conditions without being obliged also to acknowledge the superiority of her ally.

§175. Unequal
treaties and
unequal
alliances.

Those unequal treaties that are at the same time unequal alliances, are
divided into two classes,—the first consisting of those where *the inequality prevails on the side of the more considerable power,*—the second
comprehending treaties where *the inequality is on the side of the inferior
power.*

Treaties of the former class, without attributing to the more powerful
of the contracting parties any right over the weaker, simply allow him a
superiority of honours and respect. We have treated of this in Book I.
§5. Frequently a great monarch, wishing to engage a weaker state in his
interest, offers her <201> advantageous conditions,—promises her gratuitous succours, or greater than he stipulates for himself: but at the same
time he claims a superiority of dignity, and requires respect from his ally.
It is this last particular which renders *the alliance unequal:* and to this
circumstance we must attentively advert; for with alliances of this nature
we are not to confound those in which the parties treat on a footing of
equality, though the more powerful of the allies, for particular reasons,
gives more than he receives, promises his assistance gratis, without requiring gratuitous assistance in his turn, or promises more considerable
succours, or even the assistance of all his forces:—here the alliance is
equal, but the treaty is unequal, unless indeed we may be allowed to say,
that, as the party who makes the greater concessions has a greater interest
in concluding the treaty, this consideration restores the equality. Thus,
at a time when France found herself embarrassed in a momentous war
with the house of Austria, and the cardinal de Richelieu wished to humble that formidable power, he, like an able minister, concluded a treaty

with Gustavus Adolphus,[31] in which all the advantage appeared to be on the side of Sweden. From a bare consideration of the stipulations of that treaty, it would have been pronounced an unequal one; but the advantages which France derived from it, amply compensated for that inequality. The alliance of France with the Swiss, if we regard the stipulations alone, is an unequal treaty; but the valour of the Swiss troops has long since counterbalanced that inequality; and the difference in the interests and wants of the parties serves still further to preserve the equilibrium. France, often involved in bloody wars, has received essential services from the Swiss: the Helvetic body, void of ambition, and untainted with the spirit of conquest, may live in peace with the whole world; they have nothing to fear, since they have feelingly convinced the ambitious, that the love of liberty gives the nation sufficient strength to defend her frontiers. This alliance may at certain times have appeared unequal:—our forefathers* paid little attention to ceremony:—but in reality, and especially since the absolute independence of the Swiss is acknowledged by the empire itself, the alliance is certainly equal, although the Helvetic body do not hesitate to yield to the king of France all that pre-eminence which the established usage of modern Europe attributes to crowned heads, and especially to great monarchs.

Treaties *in which the inequality prevails on the side of the inferior power,*—that is to say, those which impose on the weaker party more extensive obligations or greater burthens, or bind him down to oppressive and disagreeable conditions,—these unequal treaties, I say, are always at the same time unequal alliances; for the weaker party never submits to burthensome conditions, without being obliged also to acknowledge the superiority of his ally. These conditions are commonly imposed by the conqueror, or dictated by necessity, which obliges a weak state to seek <202> the protection or assistance of another more powerful; and by this very step, the weaker state acknowledges her own inferiority. Besides, this forced inequality in a treaty of alliance is a disparagement to her, and lowers her dignity, at the same time that it exalts that of her more powerful ally. Sometimes also, the weaker state not

---

* The author was a native of Switzerland. [[Note added in 1797 edition.]]
31. Gustavus Adolphus, king of Sweden, r. 1611–32.

being in a condition to promise the same succours as the more powerful one, it becomes necessary that she should compensate for her inability in this point, by engagements which degrade her below her ally, and often even subject her, in various respects, to his will. Of this kind are all those treaties in which the weaker party alone engages not to make war without the consent of her more powerful ally,—to have the same friends and the same enemies with him,—to support and respect his dignity,—to have no fortresses in certain places,—not to trade or raise soldiers in certain free countries,—to deliver up her vessels of war, and not to build others, as was the case of the Carthaginians when treating with their Roman conquerors,—to keep up only a certain number of troops, &c.

These *unequal alliances* are subdivided into two kinds; they *either impair the sovereignty,* or *they do not.* We have slightly touched on this, in Book I. Ch. I. and XVI.

The sovereignty subsists entire and unimpaired when none of its constituent rights are transferred to the superior ally, or rendered, as to the exertion of them, dependent on his will. But the sovereignty is impaired when any of its rights are ceded to an ally, or even if the use of them be merely rendered dependent on the will of that ally. For example, the treaty does not impair the sovereignty, if the weaker state only promises not to attack a certain nation without the consent of her ally. By such an engagement she neither divests herself of her right, nor subjects the exertion of it to another's will; she only consents to a restriction in favour of her ally: and thus she incurs no greater diminution of liberty than is incurred by promises of every kind. Such reservations are every day stipulated in alliances that are perfectly equal. But if either of the contracting parties engages not to make war against any one whatsoever without the consent or permission of an ally who on his side does not make the same promise, the former contracts an unequal alliance with diminution of sovereignty; for he deprives himself of one of the most important branches of the sovereign power, or renders the exertion of it dependent on another's will. The Carthaginians having, in the treaty that terminated the second Punic war,[32] promised not to make war on any state

32. Second Punic War, 218–202 B.C.

without the consent of the Roman people, were thenceforward, and for that reason, considered as dependent on the Romans.

§176. How an alliance with diminution of sovereignty may annul preceding treaties.

When a nation is forced to submit to the will of a superior power, she may lawfully renounce her former treaties, if the party with whom she is obliged to enter into an alliance requires it of her. As she then loses a part of her sovereignty, her ancient treaties fall to the ground together with the power that had concluded them. This is a necessity that cannot be imputed <203> to her as a crime: and since she would have a right to place herself in a state of absolute subjection, and to renounce her own sovereign, if she found such measures necessary for her preservation,—by a much stronger reason, she has a right, under the same necessity, to abandon her allies. But a generous people will exhaust every resource before they will submit to terms so severe and so humiliating.

§177. We ought to avoid as much as possible making unequal alliances.

In general, as every nation ought to be jealous of her glory, careful of maintaining her dignity, and preserving her independence, nothing short of the last extremity, or motives the most weighty and substantial, ought ever to induce a people to contract an unequal alliance. This observation is particularly meant to apply to treaties where the inequality prevails on the side of the weaker ally, and still more particularly to those unequal alliances that degrade the sovereignty. Men of courage and spirit will accept such treaties from no other hands but those of imperious necessity.

§178. Mutual duties of nations with respect to unequal alliances.

Notwithstanding every argument which selfish policy may suggest to the contrary, we must either pronounce sovereigns to be absolutely emancipated from all subjection to the law of nature, or agree that it is not lawful for them, without just reasons, to compel weaker states to sacrifice their dignity, much less their liberty, by unequal alliances. Nations owe to each other the same assistance, the same respect, the same friendship, as individuals living in a state of nature. Far from seeking to humble a weaker neighbour, and to despoil her of her most valuable advantages, they will respect and maintain her dignity and her liberty, if they are inspired by virtue more than by pride,—if they are actuated by principles of honour more than by the meaner views of sordid interest,—nay, if they have but sufficient discernment to distinguish their real interests. Nothing more firmly secures the power of a great monarch than his attention and respect to all other sovereigns. The more cautious he is to avoid offending his weaker brethren,—the greater esteem he testifies for them,—the more will they revere him in turn: they feel an affection for a power whose superiority over them is displayed only by the conferring of favours: they cling to such a monarch as their prop and support; and he becomes the arbiter of nations. Had his demeanour been stamped with arrogance, he would have been the object of their jealousy and fear, and might perhaps have one day sunk under their united efforts.

But as the weaker party ought, in his necessity, to accept with gratitude the assistance of the more powerful, and not to refuse him such honours and respect as are flattering to the person who receives them, without degrading him by whom they are rendered,—so, on the other hand, nothing is more conformable to the law of nature, than a generous grant of assistance from the more powerful state, unaccompanied by any demand of a return, or, at least, of an equivalent. And in this instance also, there exists an inseparable connection between interest and duty. <204> Sound policy holds out a caution to a powerful nation not to suffer the lesser states in her neighbourhood to be oppressed. If she abandon them to the ambition of a conqueror, he will soon become formidable to herself. Accordingly, sovereigns, who are in general sufficiently attentive to their own interests, seldom fail to reduce this maxim to practice. Hence those alliances, sometimes against the house of Austria, sometimes against its rival, according as the power of the one or the other preponderates. Hence that balance of power, the object of perpetual negotiations and wars.

§179. In alliances where the inequality is on the side of the more powerful party.

When a weak and poor nation has occasion for assistance of another kind,—when she is afflicted by famine,—we have seen (§5), that those nations who have provisions ought to supply her at a fair price. It were noble and generous to furnish them at an under price, or to make her a present of them, if she be incapable of paying their value. To oblige her to purchase them by an unequal alliance, and especially at the expense of her liberty,—to treat her as Joseph formerly treated the Egyptians,—would be a cruelty almost as dreadful, as suffering her to perish with famine.

§180. How
inequality of
treaties and
alliances may
be conform-
able to the law
of nature.

But there are cases where the inequality of treaties and alliances, dictated by some particular reasons, is not contrary to equity, nor, consequently, to the law of nature. Such, in general, are all those cases in which
the duties that a nation owes to herself, or those which she owes to other
nations, prescribe to her a departure from the line of equality. If, for instance, a weak state attempts, without necessity, to erect a fortress, which
she is incapable of defending, in a place where it might become very dangerous to her neighbour if ever it should fall into the hands of a powerful
enemy, that neighbour may oppose the construction of the fortress; and
if he does not find it convenient to pay the lesser state a compensation
for complying with his desire, he may force her compliance, by threatening to block up the roads and avenues of communication, to prohibit
all intercourse between the two nations, to build fortresses, or to keep an
army on the frontier, to consider that little state in a suspicious light, &c.
He thus indeed imposes an unequal condition; but his conduct is authorised by the care of his own safety. In the same manner he may oppose
the forming of a highway, that would open to an enemy an entrance into
his state. War might furnish us with a multitude of other examples. But
rights of this nature are frequently abused; and it requires no less moderation than prudence to avoid turning them into oppression.

Sometimes those duties to which other nations have a claim, recommend and authorise inequality in a contrary sense, without affording
any ground of imputation against a sovereign, of having neglected the
duty which he owes to himself or to his people. Thus gratitude,—the
desire of shewing his deep sense of a favour received,—may induce a
generous sovereign to enter into <205> an alliance with joy, and to give
in the treaty more than he receives.

§181. Inequal-
ity imposed by
way of pun-
ishment.

It is also consistent with justice to impose the conditions of an unequal treaty, or even an unequal alliance, by way of penalty, in order to
punish an unjust aggressor, and render him incapable of easily injuring
us for the time to come. Such was the treaty to which the elder Scipio
Africanus[33] forced the Carthaginians to submit, after he had defeated

33. Publius Cornelius Scipio Africanus Major, 236–183 B.C., defeated Hannibal at
Zama and thereby ended the Second Punic War (218–202 B.C.).

Hannibal.[34] The conqueror often dictates such terms: and his conduct in this instance is no violation of the laws of justice or equity, provided he do not transgress the bounds of moderation, after he has been crowned with success in a just and necessary war.

The different treaties of protection,—those by which a state renders itself tributary or feudatory to another,—form so many different kinds of unequal alliances. But we shall not repeat here what we have said respecting them in Book I. Chap. I. and XVI.

§182. Other kinds of which we have spoken elsewhere.

By another general division of treaties or alliances, they are distinguished into *personal* and *real:* the former are those that relate to the persons of the contracting parties, and are confined and in a manner attached to them. *Real alliances* relate only to the matters in negotiation between the contracting parties, and are wholly independent of their persons.

§183. Personal and real treaties.

A *personal alliance* expires with him who contracted it.

A *real alliance* attaches to the body of the state, and subsists as long as the state, unless the period of its duration has been limited.

It is of considerable importance not to confound these two sorts of alliances. Accordingly, sovereigns are at present accustomed to express themselves in their treaties in such a manner as to leave no uncertainty in this respect: and this is doubtless the best and safest method. In default of this precaution, the very subject of the treaty, or the expressions in which it is couched, may furnish a clue to discover whether it be real or personal.—On this head we shall lay down some general rules.

In the first place, we are not to conclude that a treaty is a personal one from the bare circumstance of its naming the contracting sovereigns: for the name of the reigning sovereign is often inserted with the sole view of shewing with whom the treaty has been concluded, without meaning thereby to intimate that it has been made with himself personally. This

§184. Naming the contracting parties in the treaty does not render it personal.

34. Hannibal Barca, 247–183 B.C., Carthaginian general who proved a threat to Roman miitary supremacy.

is an observation of the civilians Pedius[35] and Ulpian,[*][36] repeated by all writers who have treated of these subjects.

§185. An alliance made by a republic is real.   Every alliance made by a republic is in its own nature real, for it relates only to the body of the state. When a free people, a popular state, or an aristocratical republic, concludes a treaty, it is the state herself that contracts; and her engagements <206> do not depend on the lives of those who were only the instruments in forming them: the members of the people, or of the governing body, change and succeed each other; but the state still continues the same.

Since, therefore, such a treaty directly relates to the body of the state, it subsists, though the form of the republic should happen to be changed,—even though it should be transformed into a monarchy. For the state and the nation are still the same, notwithstanding every change that may take place in the form of the government; and the treaty concluded with the nation remains in force as long as the nation exists. But it is manifest that all treaties relating to the form of government are exceptions to this rule. Thus two popular states, that have treated expressly, or that evidently appear to have treated, with the view of maintaining themselves in concert in their state of liberty and popular government, cease to be allies from the very moment that one of them has submitted to be governed by a single person.

§186. Treaties concluded by kings or other monarchs.   Every public treaty, concluded by a king or by any other monarch, is a treaty of the state; it is obligatory on the whole state, on the entire nation which the king represents, and whose power and rights he exercises. It seems then at first view, that every public treaty ought to be presumed real, as concerning the state itself. There can be no doubt with respect to the obligation to observe the treaty: the only question that arises, is respecting its duration. Now there is often room to doubt whether the contracting parties have intended to extend their reciprocal

* Digest. [[of Justinian]] lib. ii. tit. xiv. de Pactis, leg. vii. §8.

35. Quintus Pedius, nephew of Julius Caesar, served as a Roman general in Gaul and became consul in 43 B.C.

36. Domitius Ulpianus (Ulpian), d. A.D. 228. Roman jurist and major contributor to the *Corpus Juris Civilis*.

engagements beyond the term of their own lives, and to bind their successors. Conjunctures change; a burthen that is at present light, may in other circumstances become insupportable or at least oppressive: the manner of thinking among sovereigns is no less variable; and there are certain things of which it is proper that each prince should be at liberty to dispose according to his own system. There are others that are freely granted to one king, and would not be allowed to his successor. It therefore becomes necessary to consider the terms of the treaty, or the matter which forms the subject of it, in order to discover the intentions of the contracting powers.

Perpetual treaties, and those made for a determinate period, are real ones, since their duration cannot depend on the lives of the contracting parties.

§187. Perpetual treaties, and those for a certain time.

In the same manner, when a king declares in the treaty that it is made "for himself and his successors," it is manifest that this is a real treaty. It attaches to the state, and is intended to last as long as the kingdom itself.

§188. Treaties made for the king and his successors.

When a treaty expressly declares that it is made for the good of the kingdom, it thus furnishes an evident proof that the contracting powers did not mean that its duration should depend on that of their own lives, but on that of the kingdom itself. Such treaty is therefore a real one.

§189. Treaties made for the good of the kingdom.

<207>

Independently even of this express declaration, when a treaty is made for the purpose of procuring to the state a certain advantage which is in its own nature permanent and unfailing, there is no reason to suppose that the prince by whom the treaty has been concluded, intended to limit it to the duration of his own life. Such a treaty ought therefore to be considered as a real one, unless there exist very powerful evidence to prove that the party with whom it was made, granted the advantage in question only out of regard to the prince then reigning, and as a personal favour: in which case the treaty terminates with the life of the prince, as the motive for the concession expires with him. But such a reservation is not to be presumed on slight grounds: for it would seem that if the contracting parties had had it in contemplation, they should have expressed it in the treaty.

§190. How presumption ought to be founded in doubtful cases.

In case of doubt, where there exists no circumstance by which we can clearly prove either the personality or the reality of a treaty, it ought to be presumed a real treaty if it chiefly consists of favourable articles,—if of odious ones, a personal treaty. By favourable articles we mean those which tend to the mutual advantage of the contracting powers, and which equally favour both parties; by odious articles, we understand those which onerate one of the parties only, or which impose a much heavier burthen upon the one than upon the other. We shall treat this subject more at large in the chapter on the "Interpretation of Treaties." Nothing is more conformable to reason and equity than this rule. Whenever absolute certainty is unattainable in the affairs of men, we must have recourse to presumption. Now, if the contracting powers have not explained themselves, it is natural, when the question relates to things favourable, and equally advantageous to the two allies, to presume that it was their intention to make a real treaty, as being the more advantageous to their respective kingdoms: and if we are mistaken in this presumption, we do no injury to either party. But if there be any thing odious in the engagements,—if one of the contracting states finds itself overburthened by them,—how can it be presumed that the prince who entered into such engagements, intended to lay that burthen upon his kingdom in perpetuity? Every sovereign is presumed to desire the safety and advantage of the state with which he is intrusted: wherefore it cannot be supposed that he has consented to load it forever with a burthensome obligation. If necessity rendered such a measure unavoidable, it was incumbent on his ally to have the matter explicitly ascertained at the time; and it is probable that he would not have neglected this precaution, well knowing that mankind in general, and sovereigns in particular, seldom submit to heavy and disagreeable burthens, unless bound to do so by formal obligations. If it happens then that the presumption is a mistake, and makes him lose something of his right, it is a consequence of his own negligence. To this we may add, that if either the one or the other must sacrifice a part of his right, it will be a <208> less grievous violation of the laws of equity that the latter should forego an expected advantage, than that the former should suffer a positive loss and detriment. This is the famous distinction *de lucro captando,* and *de damno vitando.*

We do not hesitate to include equal treaties of commerce in the number of those that are favourable, since they are in general advantageous, and perfectly conformable to the law of nature. As to alliances made on account of war, Grotius says with reason, that "defensive alliances are more of a favourable nature,—offensive alliances have something in them that approaches nearer to what is burthensome or odious."*

We could not dispense with the preceding brief summary of those discussions, lest we should in this part of our treatise leave a disgusting chasm. They are however but seldom resorted to in modern practice, as sovereigns at present generally take the prudent precaution of explicitly ascertaining the duration of their treaties. They treat for themselves and their successors,—for themselves and their kingdoms,—for perpetuity,—for a certain number of years, &c.—or they treat only for the time of their own reign,—for an affair peculiar to themselves,—for their families, &c.

Since public treaties, even those of a personal nature, concluded by a king or by any other sovereign who is invested with sufficient power, are treaties of state, and obligatory on the whole nation (§186), real treaties, which were intended to subsist independently of the person who has concluded them, are undoubtedly binding on his successors; and the obligation which such treaties impose on the state, passes successively to all her rulers as soon as they assume the public authority. The case is the same with respect to the rights acquired by those treaties: they are acquired for the state, and successively pass to her conductors.

§191. The obligations and rights resulting from a real treaty pass to the successors.

It is at present a pretty general custom for the successor to confirm or renew even real alliances concluded by his predecessors: and prudence requires that this precaution should not be neglected, since men pay greater respect to an obligation which they have themselves contracted, than to one which devolves on them from another quarter, or to which they have only tacitly subjected themselves. The reason is, that, in the former case, they consider their word to be engaged, and, in the latter, their conscience alone.

* De Jure Belli et Pacis, lib. ii. cap. xvi. §16.

§192. Treaties accomplished once for-all, and perfected.   The treaties that have no relation to the performance of reiterated acts, but merely relate to transient and single acts which are concluded at once,—those treaties (unless indeed it be more proper to call them by another name)*—those conventions, those compacts, which are accomplished once for all, and not by successive acts,—are no sooner executed than they are <209> completed and perfected. If they are valid, they have in their own nature a perpetual and irrevocable effect: nor have we them in view when we inquire whether a treaty be real or personal. Puffendorf† gives us the following rules to direct us in this inquiry—"1. That the successors are bound to observe the treaties of peace concluded by their predecessors. 2. That a successor should observe all the lawful conventions by which his predecessor has transferred any right to a third party." This is evidently wandering from the point in question: it is only saying that what is done with validity by a prince, cannot be annulled by his successors.—And who doubts it? A treaty of peace is in its own nature made with a view to its perpetual duration: and as soon as it is once duly concluded and ratified, the affair is at an end; the treaty must be accomplished on both sides, and observed according to its tenour. If it is executed upon the spot, there ends the business at once. But if the treaty contains engagements for the performance of successive and reiterated acts, it will still be necessary to examine, according to the rules we have laid down, whether it be in this respect real or personal,—whether the contracting parties intended to bind their successors to the performance of those acts, or only promised them for the time of their own reign. In the same manner, as soon as a right is transferred by a lawful convention, it no longer belongs to the state that has ceded it; the affair is concluded and terminated. But if the successor discovers any flaw in the deed of transfer, and proves it, he is not to be accused of maintaining that the convention is not obligatory on him, and refusing to fulfil it;—he only shews that such convention has not taken place: for a defective and invalid deed is a nullity, and to be considered as having never existed.

* See chap. xii. §153, of this book.
† Law of Nature and Nations, book viii. chap. ix. §8.

The third rule given by Puffendorf is no less useless with respect to this question. It is, "that if, after the other ally has already executed something to which he was bound by virtue of the treaty, the king happens to die before he has accomplished in his turn what he had engaged to perform, his successor is indispensably obliged to perform it. For, what the other ally has executed under the condition of receiving an equivalent, having turned to the advantage of the state, or at least having been done with that view, it is clear, that if he does not receive the return for which he had stipulated, he then acquires the same right as a man who has paid what he did not owe; and therefore the successor is obliged to allow him a complete indemnification for what he has done or given, or to make good, on his own part, what his predecessor had engaged to perform." All this, I say, is foreign to our question. If the alliance is real, it still subsists notwithstanding the death of one of the contracting parties; if it is personal, it expires with them, or either of them (§183). But when a personal alliance comes to be dissolved in this manner, it is quite a different ques-<210>tion to ascertain what one of the allied states is bound to perform, in case the other has already executed something in pursuance of the treaty; and this question is to be determined on very different principles. It is necessary to distinguish the nature of what has been done pursuant to the treaty. If it has been any of those determinate and substantial acts which it is usual with contracting parties mutually to promise to each other in exchange or by way of equivalent, there can be no doubt that he who has received, ought to give what he has promised in return, if he would adhere to the agreement, and is obliged to adhere to it: if he is not bound, and is unwilling to adhere to it, he ought to restore what he has received, to replace things in their former state, or to indemnify the ally from whom he has received the advantage in question. To act otherwise, would be keeping possession of another's property. In this case, the ally is in the situation, not of a man who has paid what he did not owe, but of one who has paid before-hand for a thing that has not been delivered to him. But if the personal treaty related to any of those uncertain and contingent acts which are to be performed as occasions offer,—of those promises which are not obligatory if an opportunity of fulfilling them does not occur,—it is only on oc-

§193. Treaties already accomplished on the one part.

casion likewise that the performance of similar acts is due in return: and when the term of the alliance is expired, neither of the parties remains bound by any obligation. In a defensive alliance, for instance, two kings have reciprocally promised each other a gratuitous assistance during the term of their lives: one of them is attacked: he is succoured by his ally, and dies before he has an opportunity to succour him in his turn: the alliance is at an end, and no obligation thence devolves on the successor of the deceased, except indeed that he certainly owes a debt of gratitude to the sovereign who has given a salutary assistance to his state. And we must not pronounce such an alliance an injurious one to the ally who has given assistance without receiving any. His treaty was one of those speculating contracts in which the advantages or disadvantages wholly depend on chance: he might have gained by it, though it has been his fate to lose.

We might here propose another question. The personal alliance expiring at the death of one of the allies, if the survivor, under an idea that it is to subsist with the successor, fulfils the treaty on his part in favour of the latter, defends his country, saves some of his towns, or furnishes provisions for his army,—what ought the sovereign to do, who is thus succoured? He ought, doubtless, either to suffer the alliance to subsist, as the ally of his predecessor has conceived that it was to subsist (and this will be a tacit renewal and extension of the treaty)—or to pay for the real service he has received, according to a just estimate of its importance, if he does not chuse to continue that alliance. It would be in such a case as this that we might say with Puffendorf, that he who has rendered such a service <211> has acquired the right of a man who has paid what he did not owe.

§194. The personal alliance expires if one of the contracting powers ceases to reign. The duration of a personal alliance being restricted to the persons of the contracting sovereigns,—if, from any cause whatsoever, one of them ceases to reign, the alliance expires: for they have contracted in quality of sovereigns; and he who ceases to reign, no longer exists as a sovereign, though he still lives as a man.

§195. Treaties in their own nature personal. Kings do not always treat solely and directly for their kingdoms; sometimes by virtue of the power they have in their hands, they make treaties relative to their own persons, or their families; and this they may lawfully do, as the welfare of the state is interested in the safety and advantage of the sovereign, properly understood. These treaties are personal in their own nature, and expire of course on the death of the king or the extinction of his family. Such is an alliance made for the defence of a king and his family.

It is asked, whether such an alliance subsists with the king and the royal family, when by some revolution they are deprived of the crown? We have remarked above (§194), that a personal alliance expires with the reign of him who contracted it: but that is to be understood of an alliance formed with the state, and restricted, in its duration, to the reign of the contracting king. But the alliance of which we are now to treat is of another nature. Although obligatory on the state, since she is bound by all the public acts of her sovereign, it is made directly in favour of the king and his family; it would therefore be absurd that it should be dissolved at the moment when they stand in need of it, and by the very event which it was intended to guard against. Besides, the king does not forfeit the character of royalty merely by the loss of his kingdom. If he is unjustly despoiled of it by an usurper, or by rebels, he still preserves his rights, among which are to be reckoned his alliances.

But who shall judge whether a king has been dethroned lawfully or by violence? An independent nation acknowledges no judge. If the body of the nation declare that the king has forfeited his right by the abuse he has made of it, and depose him, they may justly do it when their grievances are well founded; and no other power has a right to censure their conduct. The personal ally of this king ought not therefore to assist him against the nation who have made use of their right in deposing him: if he attempts it, he injures that nation. England declared war against Louis XIV. in the year 1688, for supporting the interests of James II.[37] who had been formally deposed by the nation. The same country declared war against him a second time at the beginning of the present century, because that prince acknowledged the son of the de-

§196. Alliance concluded for the defence of the king and the royal family.

37. James II of England, r. 1685–88.

posed monarch, under the title of James III.[38] In doubtful cases, and
when the body of the nation has not pronounced, or has not pronounced
freely, a sovereign ought naturally to support and defend an ally; and it
is then that the <212> voluntary law of nations subsists between different
states. The party who have expelled the king, maintain that they have
right on their side: the unfortunate prince and his allies flatter themselves
with having the same advantage; and as they have no common judge
upon earth, there remains no other mode of deciding the contest, than
an appeal to arms: they therefore engage in a formal war.

Finally, when the foreign prince has faithfully fulfilled his engagements towards an unfortunate monarch, when he has done, in his defence, or to procure his restoration, every thing which, by the terms of
the alliance, he was bound to do,—if his efforts have proved ineffectual,
it cannot be expected by the dethroned prince that he shall support an
endless war in his favour,—that he shall forever continue at enmity with
the nation or the sovereign who has deprived him of the throne. He
must at length think of peace, abandon his unfortunate ally, and consider him as having himself abandoned his right through necessity. Thus
Louis XIV. was obliged to abandon James II. and to acknowledge king
William,[39] though he had at first treated him as an usurper.

§197. Obliga-
tion of a real
alliance, when
the allied king
is deposed.
The same question presents itself in real alliances, and, in general, in
all alliances made with a state, and not in particular with a king, for the
defence of his person. An ally ought doubtless to be defended against
every invasion, against every foreign violence, and even against his rebellious subjects; in the same manner a republic ought to be defended
against the enterprises of one who attempts to destroy the public liberty.
But the other party in the alliance ought to recollect that he is the ally
and not the judge of the state or the nation. If the nation has deposed
her king in form, if the people of a republic have expelled their magistrates, and set themselves at liberty, or, either expressly or tacitly, ac-

---

38. Prince James Francis Edward Stuart ("the Young Pretender"), 1688–1766, son
of James II and Jacobite claimant to the British crown as James III of England and
James VIII of Scotland.

39. William III, r. 1689–1702.

knowledged the authority of an usurper,—to oppose these domestic regulations, or to dispute their justice or validity, would be interfering in the government of the nation, and doing her an injury (see §§54, &c. of this book). The ally remains the ally of the state, notwithstanding the change that has happened in it. However, if this change renders the alliance useless, dangerous, or disagreeable to him, he is at liberty to renounce it: for he may upon good grounds assert that he would not have entered into an alliance with that nation, had she been under her present form of government.

To this case we may also apply what we have said above respecting a personal ally. However just the cause of that king may be, who is expelled from the throne either by his subjects or by a foreign usurper, his allies are not obliged to support an eternal war in his favour. After having made ineffectual efforts to reinstate him, they must at length restore to their people the blessings of peace; they must come to an accommodation with the usurper, and for that purpose treat with him as with a lawful sovereign. Louis the Fourteenth, finding himself exhausted by a bloody and unsuccessful war, made an offer at Gertruyden-<213>berg, to abandon his grandson, whom he had placed on the throne of Spain: and afterwards, when the aspect of affairs was changed, Charles of Austria, the rival of Philip, saw himself, in his turn, abandoned by his allies.[40] They grew weary of exhausting their states in order to put him in possession of a crown to which they thought him justly entitled, but which they no longer saw any probability of being able to procure for him.

40. King Charles II of Spain died without a direct heir in 1700 but was succeeded by Philip of Anjou (as Philip V, r. 1700–1746), thereby raising the possibility of a union of the French and Spanish crowns. The ensuing War of the Spanish Succession (1700–1714) was fought to prevent French dominion on mainland Europe, with the Austrians, English, and Dutch favoring Archduke Charles of Austria (Holy Roman Emperor 1711–40) as the alternative to succeed Charles II.

CHAPTER XIII

Of the Dissolution and Renewal of Treaties.

§198. Expiration of alliances made for a limited time. An alliance is dissolved at the expiration of the term for which it had been concluded. This term is sometimes fixed, as when an alliance is made for a certain number of years; sometimes it is uncertain, as in personal alliances, whose duration depends on the lives of the contracting powers. The term is likewise uncertain, when two or more sovereigns form an alliance with a view to some particular object, as, for instance, that of expelling a horde of barbarous invaders from a neighbouring country,—of reinstating a sovereign on his throne, &c. The duration of such an alliance depends on the completion of the enterprise for which it was formed. Thus, in the last-mentioned instance, when the sovereign is restored, and so firmly seated on his throne, as to be able to retain the undisturbed possession of it, the alliance, which was formed with a sole view to his restoration, is now at an end. But, on the other hand, if the enterprise prove unsuccessful,—the moment his allies are convinced of the impossibility of carrying it into effect, the alliance is likewise at an end: for it is time to renounce an undertaking when it is acknowledged to be impracticable.

§199. Renewal of treaties. A treaty, entered into for a limited time, may be renewed by the common consent of the allies,—which consent may be either expressly or tacitly made known. When the treaty is expressly renewed, it is the same as if a new one were concluded, in all respects similar to the former.

The tacit renewal of a treaty is not to be presumed upon slight grounds: for engagements of so high importance are well entitled to the formality of an express consent. The presumption, therefore, of a tacit renewal must be founded on acts of such a nature as not to admit a doubt of their having been performed in pursuance of the treaty. But, even in this case, still another difficulty arises: for, according to the circumstances and nature of the acts in question, they may prove nothing more than a simple continuation or extension of the treaty,—which is very different from a renewal, especially as to the term of duration. For instance, England has entered into a subsidiary <214> treaty with a German prince, who is to keep on foot, during ten years, a stated number of troops at the disposal of that country, on condition of receiving from her a certain yearly sum. The ten years being expired, the king of England causes the sum stipulated for one year to be paid: the ally receives it: thus the treaty is indeed tacitly continued for one year; but it cannot be said to be renewed; for the transaction of that year does not impose an obligation of doing the same thing for ten years successively. But supposing a sovereign has, in consequence of an agreement with a neighbouring state, paid her a million of money for permission to keep a garrison in one of her strongholds during ten years,—if, at the expiration of that term, the sovereign, instead of withdrawing his garrison, makes his ally a tender of another million, and the latter accepts it, the treaty is, in this case, tacitly renewed.

When the term for which the treaty was made is expired, each of the allies is perfectly free, and may consent or refuse to renew it, as he thinks proper. It must, however, be confessed, that, if one of the parties, who has almost singly reaped all the advantages of the treaty, should, without just and substantial reasons, refuse to renew it now that he thinks he will no longer stand in need of it, and foresees the time approaching when his ally may derive advantage from it in turn,—such conduct would be dishonourable, inconsistent with that generosity which should characterise sovereigns, and widely distant from those sentiments of gratitude and friendship that are due to an old and faithful ally. It is but too common to see great potentates, when arrived at the summit of power, neglect those who have assisted them in attaining it.

Treaties contain promises that are perfect and reciprocal. If one of the allies fails in his engagements, the other may compel him to fulfil them:—a perfect promise confers a right to do so. But if the latter has no other expedient than that of arms to force his ally to the performance of his promises, he will sometimes find it more eligible to cancel the promises on his own side also, and to dissolve the treaty. He has undoubtedly a right to do this, since his promises were made only on condition that the ally should on his part execute every thing which he had engaged to perform. The party, therefore, who is offended or injured in those particulars which constitute the basis of the treaty, is at liberty to

§200. How a treaty is dissolved, when violated by one of the contracting parties.

chuse the alternative of either compelling a faithless ally to fulfil his engagements, or of declaring the treaty dissolved by his violation of it. On such an occasion, prudence and wise policy will point out the line of conduct to be pursued.

§201. The violation of one treaty does not cancel another.

But when there exist between allies two or more treaties, different from and independent of each other, the violation of one of those treaties does not directly disengage the injured party from the obligations he has contracted in the others: for the promises contained in these, do not depend on those included in the violated treaty. But the offended ally may, on the breach of <215> one treaty by the other party, threaten him with a renunciation, on his own part, of all the other treaties by which they are united,—and may put his threats in execution if the other disregards them. For if any one wrests or with-holds from me my right, I may, in the state of nature, in order to oblige him to do me justice, to punish him, or to indemnify myself, deprive him also of some of his rights, or seize and detain them till I have obtained complete satisfaction. And if recourse is had to arms in order to obtain satisfaction for the infringement of that treaty, the offended party begins by stripping his enemy of all the rights which had accrued to him from the different treaties subsisting between them: and we shall see, in treating of war, that he may do this with justice.

§202. The violation of one article in a treaty may cancel the whole.

Some writers* would extend what we have just said to the different articles of a treaty which have no connection with the article that has been violated,—saying we ought to consider those several articles as so many distinct treaties concluded at the same time. They maintain therefore, that if either of the allies violates one article of the treaty, the other has not immediately a right to cancel the entire treaty, but that he may either refuse, in his turn, what he had promised with a view to the violated article, or compel his ally to fulfil his promises if there still remains a possibility of fulfilling them,—if not, to repair the damage; and that for this purpose he may threaten to renounce the entire treaty,—a menace which he may lawfully put in execution, if it be disregarded by the other. Such undoubtedly is the conduct which prudence, moderation,

* See Wolfius, Jus Gent. §432.

the love of peace, and charity would commonly prescribe to nations. Who will deny this, and madly assert that sovereigns are allowed to have immediate recourse to arms, or even to break every treaty of alliance and friendship, for the least subject of complaint? But the question here turns on the simple right, and not on the measures which are to be pursued in order to obtain justice; and the principle upon which those writers ground their decision, appears to me utterly indefensible. We cannot consider the several articles of the same treaty as so many distinct and independent treaties: for though we do not see any immediate connection between some of those articles, they are all connected by this common relation, viz. that the contracting powers have agreed to some of them in consideration of the others, and by way of compensation. I would perhaps never have consented to this article, if my ally had not granted me another, which in its own nature has no relation to it. Every thing, therefore, which is comprehended in the same treaty, is of the same force and nature as a reciprocal promise, unless where a formal exception is made to the contrary. Grotius very properly observes that "every article of a treaty carries with it a condition, by the non-performance of which, the treaty is wholly cancelled."* He adds that a clause is some-< 216 >times inserted to the following effect, viz. "that the violation of any one of the articles shall not cancel the whole treaty," in order that one of the parties may not have, in every slight offence, a pretext for receding from his engagements. This precaution is extremely prudent, and very conformable to the care which nations ought to take of preserving peace, and rendering their alliances durable.

In the same manner as a personal treaty expires at the death of the king who has contracted it, a real treaty is dissolved, if one of the allied nations is destroyed,—that is to say, not only if the men who compose it happen all to perish, but also if, from any cause whatsoever, it loses its national quality, or that of a political and independent society. Thus when a state is destroyed and the people are dispersed, or when they are subdued by a conqueror, all their alliances and treaties fall to the ground with the public power that had contracted them. But it is here to be

§203. The treaty is void by the destruction of one of the contracting powers.

* Grotius de Jure Belli et Pacis, lib. ii. cap. xv. §15.

observed, that treaties or alliances which impose a mutual obligation to perform certain acts, and whose existence consequently depends on that of the contracting powers, are not to be confounded with those contracts by which a perfect right is once for all acquired, independent of any mutual performance of subsequent acts. If, for instance, a nation has forever ceded to a neighbouring prince the right of fishing in a certain river, or that of keeping a garrison in a particular fortress, that prince does not lose his rights, even though the nation, from whom he has received them, happens to be subdued, or in any other manner subjected to a foreign dominion. His rights do not depend on the preservation of that nation: she had alienated them; and the conqueror by whom she has been subjugated can only take what belonged to her. In the same manner, the debts of a nation, or those for which the sovereign has mortgaged any of his towns or provinces, are not cancelled by conquest. The king of Prussia,[41] on acquiring Silesia by conquest and by the treaty of Breslau,[42] took upon himself the debts for which that province stood mortgaged to some English merchants. In fact, his conquest extended no further than the acquisition of those rights which the house of Austria had possessed over the country; and he could only take possession of Silesia, such as he found it at the time of the conquest, with all its rights and all its burthens. For a conqueror to refuse to pay the debts of a country he has subdued, would be robbing the creditors, with whom he is not at war.

§204. Alliances of a state that has afterwards put herself under the protection of another. Since a nation or a state, of whatever kind, cannot make any treaty contrary to those by which she is actually bound (§165), she cannot put herself under the protection of another state, without reserving all her alliances, and all her existing treaties. For the convention by which a state places herself under the protection of another sovereign, is a treaty (§175); if she does it of her own accord, she ought to do it in such a manner, that the new treaty may involve no in-<217>fringement of her pre-existing ones. We have seen (§176) what rights a nation derives, in a case of necessity, from the duty of self-preservation.

41. Frederick II (r. 1740–86), king of Prussia, known as Frederick the Great.
42. The Treaty of Breslau, 1742.

The alliances of a nation are therefore not dissolved when she puts herself under the protection of another state, unless they be incompatible with the conditions of that protection. The ties by which she was bound to her former allies still subsist, and those allies still remain bound by their engagements to her, as long as she has not put it out of her power to fulfil her engagements to them.

When necessity obliges a people to put themselves under the protection of a foreign power, and to promise him the assistance of their whole force against all opponents whatsoever, without excepting their allies,— their former alliances do indeed subsist, so far as they are not incompatible with the new treaty of protection. But if the case should happen, that a former ally enters into a war with the protector, the protected state will be obliged to declare for the latter, to whom she is bound by closer ties, and by a treaty which, in case of collision, is paramount to all the others. Thus the Nepesinians having been obliged to submit to the Etrurians, thought themselves afterwards bound to adhere to their treaty of submission or capitulation, preferably to the alliance which had subsisted between them and the Romans: *postquam deditionis, quam societatis, fides sanctior erat,* says Livy.*

Finally, as treaties are made by the mutual agreement of the parties, they may also be dissolved by mutual consent, at the free will of the contracting powers. And even though a third party should find himself interested in the preservation of the treaty, and should suffer by its dissolution,—yet, if he had no share in making such treaty, and no direct promise had been made to him, those who have reciprocally made promises to each other, which eventually prove advantageous to that third party, may also reciprocally release each other from them, without consulting him, or without his having a right to oppose them. Two monarchs have bound themselves by a mutual promise to unite their forces for the defence of a neighbouring city: that city derives advantage from their assistance; but she has no right to it; and as soon as the two monarchs think proper mutually to dispense with their engagements, she will be

§205. Treaties dissolved by mutual consent.

---

* Lib. vi. cap. x. [["When the sanctity of their surrender proved to be more binding on them than that of their alliance." *Ab urbe condita* VI.10.]]

deprived of their aid, but can have no reason to complain on the occasion, since no promise had been made to her. <218>

CHAPTER XIV

Of other public Conventions,—of those that are made by subordinate Powers,—particularly of the Agreement called in Latin Sponsio,—*and of Conventions of Sovereigns with private Persons.*

§206. Conventions made by sovereigns.

The public compacts, called conventions, articles of agreement, &c. when they are made between sovereigns, differ from treaties only in their object (§153). What we have said of the validity of treaties, of their execution, of their dissolution, and of the obligations and rights that flow from them, is all applicable to the various conventions which sovereigns may conclude with each other. Treaties, conventions, and agreements, are all public engagements, in regard to which there is but one and the same right, and the same rules. We do not here wish to disgust the reader by unnecessary repetitions: and it were equally unnecessary to enter into an enumeration of the various kinds of these conventions, which are always of the same nature, and differ only in the matter which constitutes their object.

§207. Those made by subordinate powers.

But there are public conventions made by subordinate powers, in virtue either of an express mandate from the sovereign, or of the authority with which they are invested by the terms of their commission, and according as the nature of the affairs with which they are intrusted, may admit or require the exercise of that authority.

The appellation of *inferior* or *subordinate powers* is given to public persons who exercise some portion of the sovereignty in the name and under the authority of the sovereign: such are magistrates established for the administration of justice, generals of armies, and ministers of state.

When, by an express order from their sovereign on the particular occasion, and with sufficient powers derived from him for the purpose, those persons form a convention, such convention is made in the name of the sovereign himself, who contracts by the mediation and ministry of his delegate or proxy: this is the case we have mentioned in §156.

But public persons, by virtue of their office, or of the commission given to them, have also themselves the power of making conventions on public affairs, exercising on those occasions the right and authority of the sovereign by whom they are commissioned. There are two modes in which they acquire that power:—it is given to them in express terms by the sovereign; or it is naturally derived from their commission it-self,—the nature of the affairs with which these persons are intrusted, requiring that they should have a power to make such conventions, especially in cases where they cannot await the or-<219>ders of their sovereign. Thus the governor of a town, and the general who besieges it, have a power to fettle the terms of capitulation: and whatever agreement they thus form within the terms of their commission, is obligatory on the state or sovereign who has invested them with the power by which they conclude it. As conventions of this nature take place principally in war, we shall treat of them more at large in Book III.

If a public person, an embassador, or a general of an army, exceeding the bounds of his commission, concludes a treaty or a convention without orders from the sovereign, or without being authorised to do it by virtue of his office, the treaty is null, as being made without sufficient powers (§157): it cannot become valid without the express or tacit ratification of the sovereign. The express ratification is a written deed by which the sovereign approves the treaty, and engages to observe it. The tacit ratification is implied by certain steps which the sovereign is justly presumed to take only in pursuance of the treaty, and which he could not be supposed to take without considering it as concluded and agreed upon. Thus, on a treaty of peace being signed by public ministers who have even exceeded the orders of their sovereigns, if one of the sovereigns causes troops to pass on the footing of friends through the territories of his reconciled enemy, he tacitly ratifies the treaty of peace. But if, by a reservatory clause of the treaty, the ratification of the sovereign be required,—as such reservation is usually understood to imply an express ratification, it is absolutely requisite that the treaty be thus expressly ratified before it can acquire its full force.

§208. Treaties concluded by a public person, without orders from the sovereign, or without sufficient powers.

By the Latin term, *sponsio,* we express an agreement relating to affairs of state, made by a public person, who exceeds the bounds of his commission, and acts without the orders or command of the sovereign. The person who treats for the state in this manner without being commissioned for the purpose, promises of course to use his endeavours for prevailing on the state or sovereign to ratify the articles he has agreed to: otherwise his engagement would be nugatory and illusive. The foundation of this agreement can be no other, on either side, than the hope of such ratification.

The Roman history furnishes us with various instances of such agreements:—the one that first arrests our attention is that which was concluded at the Furcae Caudinae,—the most famous instance on record, and one that had been discussed by the most celebrated writers. The consuls Titus Veturius Calvinus and Spurius Postumius, with the Roman army, being inclosed in the defiles of the Furcae Caudinae without hope of escaping, concluded a shameful agreement with the Samnites,[43]—informing them, however, that they could not make a real public treaty (*foedus*) without orders from the Roman people, without the *feciales,* and the ceremonies consecrated by custom. The Samnite general contented himself with exacting a promise from the consuls and <220> principal officers of the army, and obliging them to deliver him six hundred hostages; after which, having made the Roman troops lay down their arms, and obliged them to pass under the yoke, he dismissed them. The senate, however, refused to accede to the treaty,—delivered up those who had concluded it to the Samnites, who refused to receive them,—and then thought themselves free from all obligation, and screened from all reproach.* Authors have entertained very different sentiments of this conduct. Some assert, that if Rome did not chuse to ratify the treaty, she ought to have replaced things in the same situation they were in before the agreement, by sending back the whole army to their encampment at the Furcae Caudinae; and this the Samnites also insisted

* Livy, lib. ix.
43. Battle at the Caudine Forks (321 B.C.) as described in the ninth book of Livy's *History of Rome* (the Second Samnite War 321–304 B.C.).

upon. I confess that I am not entirely satisfied with the reasonings I have found on this question, even in authors whose eminent superiority I am in other respects fully inclined to acknowledge. Let us therefore endeavour, with the aid of their observations, to set the affair in a new light.

It presents two questions,—first, what is the person bound to do, who has made an agreement (*sponsor*), if the state disavows it?—Secondly, what is the state bound to do?—But, previous to the discussion of these questions, it is necessary to observe, with Grotius,* that the state is not bound by an agreement of that nature. This is manifest, even from the definition of the agreement called *sponsio*. The state has not given orders to conclude it: neither has she in any manner whatever conferred the necessary powers for the purpose: she has neither expressly given them by her injunctions or by a plenipotentiary commission, nor tacitly, by a natural or necessary consequence of the authority intrusted to him who makes the agreement (*sponsori*). The general of an army has, indeed, by virtue of his commission, a power to enter, as circumstances may require, into a private convention,—a compact relative to himself, to his troops, or to the occurrences of war: but he has no power to conclude a treaty of peace. He may bind himself, and the troops under his command, on all the occasions where his functions require that he should have the power of treating; but he cannot bind the state beyond the extent of his commission.

§210. The state is not bound by such an agreement.

Let us now see to what the person promising (*sponsor*) is bound, when the state disavows the agreement. We ought not here to deduce our arguments from the rules which obtain between private individuals under the law of nature: for the nature of the things in question, and the situation of the contracting parties, necessarily make a difference between the two cases. It is certain that, between individuals, he who purely and simply promises what depends on the will of another, without being authorised to make such promise, is obliged, if the other disavows the transaction, to accomplish himself what he has promised,—<221>to give an equivalent,—to restore things to their former state,—or, finally, to make full compensation to the person with whom he has treated,

§211. To what the promiser is bound when it is disavowed.

* De Jure Belli & Pacis, lib. ii. cap. xv. §16.

according to the various circumstances of the case. His promise (*sponsio*) can be understood in no other light. But this is not the case with respect to a public person, who, without orders and without authority, engages for the performance of his sovereign. The question in such case relates to things that infinitely surpass his power and all his faculties,—things which he can neither execute himself, nor cause to be executed, and for which he cannot offer either an equivalent or a compensation in any wise adequate: he is not even at liberty to give the enemy what he has promised, without authority: finally, it is equally out of his power to restore things entirely to their former state. The party who treats with him cannot expect any thing of this nature. If the promiser has deceived him by saying he was sufficiently authorised, he has a right to punish him. But if, like the Roman consuls at the Furcae Caudinae, the promiser has acted with sincerity, informing him that he had not a power to bind the state by a treaty,—nothing else can be presumed, but that the other party was willing to run the risk of making a treaty that must become void, if not ratified,—hoping that a regard for him who had promised, and for the hostages, would induce the sovereign to ratify what had been thus concluded. If the event deceives his hopes, he can only blame his own imprudence. An eager desire of obtaining peace on advantageous conditions, and the temptation of some present advantages, may have been his only inducements to make so hazardous an agreement. This was judiciously observed by the consul Postumius himself, after his return to Rome. In his speech to the senate, as given to us by Livy,[44] "Your generals," said he, "and those of the enemy, were equally guilty of imprudence,—we, in incautiously involving ourselves in a dangerous situation,—they, in suffering a victory to escape them, of which the nature of the ground gave them a certainty,—still distrusting their own advantages, and hasting, at any price, to disarm men who were ever formidable while they had arms in their hands. Why did they not keep us shut up in our camp? Why did they not send to Rome, in order to treat for peace, on sure grounds, with the senate and the people?"

It is manifest that the Samnites contented themselves with the hope

44. Livy, *History of Rome*, ii, 16.

that the engagement which the consuls and principal officers had entered into, and the desire of saving six hundred knights, left as hostages, would induce the Romans to ratify the agreement,—considering, that, at all events, they should still have those six hundred hostages, with the arms and baggage of the army, and the vain, or rather, as it is proved by its consequences, the fatal glory, of having made them pass under the yoke.

Under what obligation then were the consuls, and all the others who had joined with them in the promise (*sponsores*)? They themselves judged that they ought to be delivered up to <222> the Samnites. This was not a natural consequence of the agreement (*sponsionis*); and from the observations above made, it does not appear that a general in such circumstances, having promised things which the promisee well knew to be out of his power, is obliged, on his promise being disavowed, to surrender his own person by way of compensation. But as he has a power expressly to enter into such an engagement, which lies fairly within the bounds of his commission, the custom of those times had doubtless rendered such engagement a tacit clause of the agreement called *sponsio*, since the Romans delivered up all the *sponsores*, all those who had promised:—this was a maxim of their *fecial law.**

If the *sponsor* has not expressly engaged to deliver himself up, and if established custom does not lay him under an obligation to do so, it would seem that he is bound to nothing further by his promise than honestly to endeavour by every lawful means to induce the sovereign to ratify what he has promised: and there cannot exist a doubt in the case, provided the treaty be at all equitable, advantageous to the state, or supportable in consideration of the misfortune from which it has preserved her. But to set out with the intention of making a treaty the instrument to ward off a deadly blow from the state, and soon after to advise the sovereign to refuse his ratification, not because the treaty is insupport-

---

* I have said in my preface, that the fecial law of the Romans was their law of war. The college of the feciales were consulted on the causes that might authorise the nation to engage in a war, and on the questions to which it gave rise. They had also the care of the ceremonies on the declaration of war, and on concluding treaties of peace. The feciales were likewise consulted, and their agency employed, in all public treaties.

able, but because an advantage may be taken of its having been concluded without authority,—such a proceeding would undoubtedly be a
fraudulent and shameful abuse of the faith of treaties. But what must
the general do, who, in order to save his army, has been forced to conclude a treaty that is detrimental or dishonourable to the state? Must he
advise the sovereign to ratify it?—He will content himself with laying
open the motives of his conduct, and the necessity that obliged him to
treat; he will shew, as Postumius did, that he alone is bound, and that
he consents to be disowned and delivered up for the public safety. If the
enemy are deceived, it is through their own folly. Was the general bound
to inform them, that, in all probability, his promises would not be ratified? It would be too much to require this of him. In such a case, it is
sufficient that he does not impose on the enemy by pretending to more
extensive powers than he really possesses, but contents himself with embracing the overtures which they make to him, without on his side holding forth any delusive hopes to decoy them into a treaty. It is the enemy's
business to take all possible precautions for their own security: if they
neglect them, why should not the general avail himself of their imprudence, as of an advantage presented to him by the hand of fortune? "It
is she," said Postumius, "who has <223> saved our army after having put
it in danger. The enemy's head was turned in his prosperity; and his
advantages have been no more to him than a pleasant dream."

If the Samnites had only required of the Roman generals and army
such engagements as the nature of their situation, and their commission,
empowered them to enter into,—if they had obliged them to surrender
themselves prisoners of war,—or if, from their inability to hold them all
prisoners, they had dismissed them upon their promise not to bear arms
against them for some years, in case Rome should refuse to ratify the
peace,—the agreement would have been valid, as being made with sufficient powers; and the whole army would have been bound to observe
it; for it is absolutely necessary that the troops, or their officers, should
have a power of entering into a contract on those occasions, and upon
that footing. This is the case of capitulations, of which we shall speak
in treating of war.

If the promiser has made an equitable and honourable convention, on an affair of such a nature, that, in case the convention be disallowed, he still has it in his own power to indemnify the party with whom he has treated,—he is presumed to have personally pledged himself for such indemnification; and he is bound to make it, in order to discharge his promise, as did Fabius Maximus[45] in the instance mentioned by Grotius.* But there are occasions when the sovereign may forbid him to act in that manner, or to give any thing to the enemies of the state.

We have shewn, that a state cannot be bound by an agreement made without her orders, and without her having granted any power for that purpose. But is she absolutely free from all obligation? That is the point which now remains for us to examine. If matters as yet continue in their original situation, the state or the sovereign may simply disavow the treaty, which is of course done away by such disavowal, and becomes as perfect a nullity as if it had never existed. But the sovereign ought to make known his intentions as soon as the treaty comes to his knowledge; not indeed that his silence alone can give validity to a convention which the contracting parties have agreed not to consider as valid without his approbation; but it would be a breach of good-faith in him to suffer a sufficient time to elapse for the other party to execute on his side an agreement which he himself is determined not to ratify.

§212. To what the sovereign is bound.

If any thing has already been done in consequence of the agreement,—if the party, who has treated with the *sponsor*, has on his side fulfilled his engagements either in the whole or in part,—is the other party, on disavowing the treaty, bound to indemnify him, or restore things to their former situation,—or is he allowed to reap the fruits of the treaty, at the same time that he refuses <224> to ratify it? We should here distinguish the nature of the things that have been executed, and that of the advantages which have thence accrued to the state. He who,

---

* Lib. ii. chap. xv. §16 [[Grotius, *Law of War and Peace*]]. Fabius Maximus having concluded an agreement with the enemy which the senate disapproved, sold a piece of land for which he received two hundred thousand sesterces, in order to make good his promise. It related to the ransom of the prisoners. Aurel. Victor [[Sextus Aurelius Victor]], de Viris Illustr. Plutarch's life of Fabius Maximus.

45. Quintus Fabius Maximus Verrucosus, ca. 275–203 B.C., served as consul, dictator, and censor at Rome and fought in the Second Punic War.

having treated with a public person not furnished with sufficient powers, executes the agreement on his side without waiting for its ratification, is guilty of imprudence, and commits an egregious error, into which he has not been led by the state with which he supposes he has contracted. If he has given up any part of his property, the other party is not justifiable in taking advantage of his folly, and retaining possession of what he has so given. Thus, when a state, thinking she has concluded a peace with the enemy's general, has in consequence delivered up one of her strong places, or given a sum of money, the sovereign of that general is undoubtedly bound to restore what he has received, if he does not chuse to ratify the agreement. To act otherwise would be enriching himself with another's property, and retaining that property without having any title to it.

But if the agreement has given nothing to the state which she did not before possess,—if, as in that of the Furcae Caudinae, the advantage simply consists in her escape from an impending danger, her preservation from a threatened loss,—such advantage is a boon of fortune, which she may enjoy without scruple. Who would refuse to be saved by the folly of his enemy? And who would think himself obliged to indemnify that enemy for the advantage he had suffered to escape him, when no fraud had been used to induce him to forego that advantage? The Samnites pretended, that if the Romans would not ratify the treaty made by their consuls, they ought to send back the army to the Furcae Caudinae, and restore every thing to its former state. Two tribunes of the people, who had been in the number of the *sponsores,* and wished to avoid being delivered up, had the assurance to maintain the same doctrine; and some authors have declared themselves of their opinion. What! the Samnites take advantage of conjunctures in order to give law to the Romans, and to wrest from them a shameful treaty,—they are so imprudent as to treat with the consuls who expressly declare themselves unauthorised to contract for the state,—they suffer the Roman army to escape, after having covered them with infamy,—and shall not the Romans take advantage of the folly of an enemy so void of generosity? Must they either ratify a shameful treaty, or restore to that enemy all those advantages which the situation of the ground had given him, but which he had lost merely through his own folly? Upon what principle can such a decision be founded? Had Rome promised any thing to the Samnites? had she prevailed upon them to let her army go, previous to the ratification of the agreement made by the consuls?—If she had received any thing in consequence of that agreement, she would have been bound to restore it, as we have already said, because she would have possessed it without a title, on declaring the treaty null. But she had no share in the conduct of her enemies: she did not contribute to the egregious blunder they had committed; <225> and she might as justly take advantage of it, as generals in war do of the mistakes of an unskilful opponent. Suppose a conqueror, after having concluded a treaty with ministers who have expressly reserved the ratification to their master, should have the imprudence to abandon all his conquests without waiting for such ratification,—must the other, with a foolish generosity, invite him back to take possession of them again, in case the treaty be not ratified?

I confess, however, and freely acknowledge, that if the enemy who suffer an entire army to escape on the faith of an agreement concluded with the general, who is unprovided with sufficient powers, and a simple *sponsor,*—I confess, I say, that if the enemy have behaved generously,—if they had not availed themselves of their advantages to dictate shameful or too severe conditions,—equity requires that the state should either ratify the agreement, or conclude a new treaty on just and reasonable conditions, abating even of her pretensions as far as the public welfare will allow. For we ought never to abuse the generosity and noble confidence even of an enemy. Puffendorf* thinks that the treaty at the Furcae Caudinae contained nothing that was too severe or insupportable. That author seems to make no great account of the shame and ignominy with which it would have branded the whole republic. He did not see the full extent of the Roman policy, which would never permit them, in their greatest distresses, to accept a shameful treaty, or even to make peace on the footing of a conquered nation:—a sublime policy, to which Rome was indebted for all her greatness.

Finally, let us observe, that, when the inferior power has, without or-

* Jus Nat. et Gent. lib. viii. cap. ix. §12.

ders, and without authority, concluded an equitable and honourable treaty, to rescue the state from an imminent danger,—if the sovereign afterwards, on seeing himself thus delivered, should refuse to ratify the treaty, not because he thinks it a disadvantageous one, but merely through a wish to avoid performing those conditions which were annexed as the price of his deliverance, he would certainly act in opposition to all the rules of honour and equity. This would be a case in which we might apply the maxim, *summum jus, summa injuria.*[46]

To the example we have drawn from the Roman history, let us add a famous one taken from modern history. The Swiss, dissatisfied with France, entered into an alliance with the emperor[47] against Louis XII. and made an irruption into Burgundy, in the year 1513. They laid siege to Dijon. La Trimouille, who commanded in the place, fearing that he should be unable to save it, treated with the Swiss, and, without waiting for a commission from the king, concluded an agreement, by virtue of which the king of France was to renounce his pretensions to the duchy of Milan, and to pay the Swiss, by settled instalments, the sum of six hundred thousand crowns; whereas the Swiss, on their side, <226> promised nothing further than to return home to their own country,— thus remaining at liberty to attack France again, if they thought proper. They received hostages, and departed. The king was very much dissatisfied with the treaty, though it had saved Dijon, and rescued the kingdom from an imminent and alarming danger; and he refused to ratify it.* It is certain that La Trimouille had exceeded the powers he derived from his commission, especially in promising that the king should renounce the duchy of Milan. It is probable indeed that his only view was to rid himself of an enemy whom it was less difficult to over-reach in negotiation than to subdue in battle. Louis was not obliged to ratify and execute a treaty concluded without orders and without authority; and if the Swiss were deceived, they could only blame their own imprudence.

* Guicciardini, book xii. chap. ii.—De Watteville's Hist. of the Helvetic Confederacy, part ii. p. 185, &c. [[Note added in 1773/1797 editions.]]

46. "The rigor of the law is the greatest injury."

47. Maximilian I, Holy Roman Emperor, r. 1508–19; Louis II de la Trémoille, 1460–1525.

But as it manifestly appeared that La Trimouille did not behave towards them with candor and honesty, since he had deceived them on the subject of the hostages, by giving, in that character, men of the meanest rank, instead of four of the most distinguished citizens, as he had promised,*—the Swiss would have been justifiable in refusing to make peace without obtaining satisfaction for that act of perfidy, either by the surrender of him who was the author of it, or in some other manner.

The promises, the conventions, all the private contracts of the sovereign, are naturally subject to the same rules as those of private persons. If any difficulties arise on the subject, it is equally conformable to the rules of decorum, to that delicacy of sentiment which ought to be particularly conspicuous in a sovereign, and to the love of justice, to cause them to be decided by the tribunals of the state. And such indeed is the practice of all civilised states that are governed by settled laws. §213. Private contracts of the sovereign.

The conventions and contracts which the sovereign, in his sovereign character and in the name of the state, forms with private individuals of a foreign nation, fall under the rules we have laid down with respect to public treaties. In fact, when a sovereign enters into a contract with one who is wholly independent of him and of the state, whether it be with a private person, or with a nation or sovereign, this circumstance does not produce any difference in the rights of the parties. If the private person who has treated with a sovereign is his subject, the rights of each party in this case also are the same: but there is a difference in the manner of deciding the controversies which may arise from the contract. That private person, being a subject of the state, is obliged to submit his pretensions to the established courts of justice. It is added by some writers on this subject, that the sovereign may rescind those contracts, if they prove inimical to the public welfare. Undoubtedly he may do so, but not upon any principle derived from the peculiar nature of such con-<227>tracts:—it must be either upon the same principle which invalidates even a public treaty when it is ruinous to the state and inconsistent with the public safety,—or by virtue of the *eminent domain,* which gives §214. Contracts made by him with private persons in the name of the state.

* See De Watteville's Hist. of the Helvetic Confederacy, p. 190. [[Note added in 1773/1797 editions.]]

the sovereign a right to dispose of the property of the citizens with a view to the common safety. We speak here of an absolute sovereign. It is from the constitution of each state that we are to learn who are the persons, and what is the power, entitled to contract in the name of the state, to exercise the supreme authority, and to pronounce on what the public welfare requires.

§215. They are binding on the nation, and on his successors.   When a lawful power contracts in the name of the state, it lays an obligation on the nation itself, and consequently on all the future rulers of the society. When therefore a prince has the power to form a contract in the name of the state, he lays an obligation on all his successors; and these are not less bound than himself to fulfil his engagements.

§216. Debts of the sovereign and the state.   The conductor of the nation may have dealings of his own, and private debts; and his private property alone is liable for the discharge of such debts. But loans contracted for the service of the state, debts incurred in the administration of public affairs, are contracts in all the strictness of law, and obligatory on the state and the whole nation, which is indispensably bound to discharge those debts.* When once they have been contracted by lawful authority, the right of the creditor is indefeasible. Whether the money borrowed has been turned to the advantage of the state, or squandered in foolish expenses, is no concern of the person who has lent it: he has intrusted the nation with his property; and the nation is bound to restore it to him again: it is so much the worse for her if she has committed the management of her affairs to improper hands.

This maxim, however, has its bounds, founded even on the nature of the thing. The sovereign has not, in general, a power to render the state

* In 1596, Philip II. [[King of Spain]] declared himself a bankrupt, under pretence that an unfair advantage had been taken of his necessities. His creditors loudly exclaimed against his conduct, and asserted that no confidence could thenceforward be placed either in his word or his treaties, since he interposed the royal authority to supercede them. He could no longer find any one who was willing to lend him money; and his affairs suffered so severely in consequence, that he was obliged to replace things on their former footing, and to heal the wound which he had given to the public faith. Grotius, Hist. of the Disturbances in the Netherlands, book v. [[Note added in 1773/1797 editions.]]

or body corporate liable for the debts he contracts, unless they be incurred with a view to the national advantage, and in order to enable him to provide for all occurrences. If he is absolute, it belongs to him alone to decide, in all doubtful cases, what the welfare and safety of the state require. But if he should, without necessity, contract debts of immense magnitude and capable of ruining the nation for ever, there could not then exist any doubt in the case: the sovereign has evidently acted without authority; and those who have lent him their money, have imprudently risked it. It cannot be pre-<228>sumed that a nation has ever consented to submit to utter ruin through the caprice and foolish prodigality of her ruler.

As the national debts can only be paid by contributions and taxes,— wherever the sovereign has not been intrusted by the nation with a power to levy taxes and contributions, or, in short, to raise supplies by his own authority,—neither has he a power to render her liable for what he borrows, or to involve the state in debt. Thus the king of England, who has the right of making peace and war, has not that of contracting national debts, without the concurrence of parliament, because he cannot, without their concurrence, levy any money on his people.

The case is not the same with the donations of the sovereign as with his debts. When a sovereign has borrowed without necessity, or for an unwise purpose, the creditor has intrusted the state with his property; and it is just that the state should restore it to him, if, at the time of the transaction, he could entertain a reasonable presumption that it was to the state he was lending it. But when the sovereign gives away any of the property of the state,—a part of the national domain,—a considerable fief,—he has no right to make such grant except with a view to the public welfare, as a reward for services rendered to the state, or for some other reasonable cause, in which the nation is concerned: if he has made the donation without reason and without a lawful cause, he has made it without authority. His successor, or the state, may at any time revoke such a grant: nor would the revocation be a wrong done to the grantee, since it does not deprive him of any thing which he could justly call his own. What we here advance holds true of every sovereign whom the law does not expressly invest with the free and absolute disposal of

§217. Donations of the sovereign.

the national property: so dangerous a power is never to be founded on presumption.

Immunities and privileges conferred by the mere liberality of the sovereign are a kind of donations, and may be revoked in the same manner, if they prove detrimental to the state. But a sovereign cannot revoke them by his bare authority, unless he be absolute: and even in this case, he ought to be cautious and moderate in the exertion of his power, uniting an equal share of prudence and equity on the occasion. Immunities granted for particular reasons, or with a view to some return, partake of the nature of a burthensome contract, and can only be revoked in case of abuse, or when they become incompatible with the safety of the state. And if they be suppressed on this latter account, an indemnification is due to those who enjoyed them. <229>

CHAPTER XV

Of the Faith of Treaties.

§218. What is sacred among nations.

Though we have sufficiently established (§§163 and 164) the indispensable necessity of keeping promises, and observing treaties, the subject is of such importance, that we cannot forbear considering it here in a more general view, as interesting, not only to the contracting parties, but likewise to all nations, and to the universal society of mankind.

Every thing which the public safety renders inviolable is sacred in society. Thus the person of the sovereign is sacred, because the safety of the state requires that he should be in perfect security, and above the reach of violence: thus the people of Rome declared the persons of their tribunes sacred,—considering it as essential to their own safety that their defenders should be screened from all violence, and even exempt from fear. Every thing, therefore, which the common safety of mankind and the peace and security of human society require to be held inviolable, is a thing that should be sacred among nations.

§219. Treaties are sacred between nations.

Who can doubt that treaties are in the number of those things that are to be held sacred by nations? By treaties the most important affairs are determined; by them the pretensions of sovereigns are regulated; on them nations are to depend for the acknowledgement of their rights, and the security of their dearest interests. Between bodies politic,—between sovereigns who acknowledge no superior on earth,—treaties are the only means of adjusting their various pretensions,—of establishing fixed rules of conduct,—of ascertaining what they are entitled to expect, and what they have to depend on. But treaties are no better than empty words, if nations do not consider them as respectable engagements,—as rules which are to be inviolably observed by sovereigns, and held sacred throughout the whole earth.

The faith of treaties,—that firm and sincere resolution,—that invariable constancy in fulfilling our engagements,—of which we make profession in a treaty, is therefore to be held sacred and inviolable between the nations of the earth, whose safety and repose it secures: and if mankind be not wilfully deficient in their duty to themselves, infamy must ever be the portion of him who violates his faith. §220. The faith of treaties is sacred.

He who violates his treaties, violates at the same time the law of nations; for he disregards the faith of treaties,—that faith which the law of nations declares sacred; and, so far as depends on him, he renders it vain and ineffectual. Doubly guilty, he does an injury to his ally, he does an injury to all nations, and inflicts a wound on the great society of mankind. "On the ob-<230>servance and execution of treaties," said a respectable sovereign, "depends all the security which princes and states have with respect to each other: and no dependence could henceforward be placed in future conventions, if the existing ones were not to be observed."* §221. He who violates his treaties, violates the law of nations.

As all nations are interested in maintaining the faith of treaties, and causing it to be every-where considered as sacred and inviolable, so likewise they are justifiable in forming a confederacy for the purpose of repressing him who testifies a disregard for it,—who openly sports with it,—who violates and tramples it under foot. Such a man is a public enemy who saps the foundations of the peace and common safety of nations. But we should be careful not to extend this maxim to the prej- §222. Right of nations against him who disregards the faith of treaties.

* Resolution of the States-General, of the 15th of March 1726, in answer to the Memorial of the Marquis de St Philip, Embassador of Spain.

udice of that liberty and independence to which every nation has a claim. When a sovereign breaks his treaties, or refuses to fulfil them, this does not immediately imply that he considers them as empty names, and that he disregards the faith of treaties: he may have good reasons for thinking himself liberated from his engagements; and other sovereigns have not a right to judge him. It is the sovereign who violates his engagements on pretences that are evidently frivolous, or who does not even think it worth his while to allege any pretence whatever, to give a colourable gloss to his conduct, and cast a veil over his want of faith,—it is such a sovereign, who deserves to be treated as an enemy of the human race.

§223. The law of nations violated by the pope.   In treating of religion, in the first book of this work, we could not avoid giving several instances of the enormous abuses which the popes formerly made of their authority. There was one in particular, which was equally injurious to all states, and subversive of the law of nations. Several popes have undertaken to break the treaties of sovereigns; they carried their daring audacity so far as to release a contracting power from his engagements, and to absolve him from the oaths by which he had confirmed them. Cesarini, legate of pope Eugenius the Fourth, wishing to break the treaty which Uladislaus king of Poland and Hungary had concluded with the sultan Amurath,[48] pronounced, in the pope's name, the king's absolution from his oaths.* In those times of ignorance, people thought themselves really bound by nothing but their oaths, and they attributed to the pope the power of absolving them from oaths of every kind. Uladislaus renewed hostilities against the Turks: but that prince, in other respects worthy of a better fate, paid dearly for his perfidy, or rather for his superstitious weakness: he perished, with his army, near Varna:[49]—a loss which was fatal to Christendom, and brought on her by her spiritual head. The following epitaph was written on Uladislaus: <231>

* History of Poland by the Chevalier de Solignac [[La Pimpie Solignac]], vol. iv. 112. He quotes Dlugoss, Neugebauer, Sarnicki, Herburt, De Fulstin, &c.
48. Pope Eugene IV, r. 1431–47; King Vladislaus III of Poland, r. 1434–44; Sultan Amurath (Murad) II, r. 1421–51.
49. In 1444.

Romulidae Cannas, ego Varnam clade notavi.
Discite, mortales, non temerare fidem.
Me nisi pontifices jussissent rumpere foedus,
Non ferret Scythicum Pannonis ora jugum.[50]

Pope John XII.[51] declared null the oath which the emperor Louis of Bavaria, and his competitor Frederic of Austria, had mutually taken when the emperor set the latter at liberty.[52] Philip duke of Burgundy, abandoning the alliance of the English, procured from the pope and the council of Basil an absolution from his oath. And at a time when the revival of letters and the establishment of the reformation should have rendered the popes more circumspect, the legate Caraffa, in order to induce Henry II.[53] of France to a renewal of hostilities, had the audacity to absolve him, in 1556, from the oath he had made to observe the truce of Vaucelles.* The famous peace of Westphalia displeasing the pope[54] on many accounts, he did not confine himself to protesting against the articles of a treaty in which all Europe was interested: he published a bull in which, *from his own certain knowledge, and full ecclesiastical power,* he declared several articles of the treaty *null, vain, invalid, iniquitous,*

---

* On these facts, see the French and German historians.—"Thus war was determined on in favour of the pope: and after cardinal Caraffa, by virtue of the powers vested in him by his holiness, had absolved the king from the oaths he had taken in ratification of the truce, he even permitted him to attack the emperor and his son without a previous declaration of hostilities." De Thou [[Jacques Auguste de Thou]], lib. xvii. [[The quoted material and the source were added in the 1773/1797 editions.]]

50. "The sons of Romulus mark Cannae by its disaster, and so I mark Varna. / Learn, ye mortals, not to violate faith. / If the bishops had not ordered me to break the treaty, / the shores of Pannonia would not have to bear the Scythian yoke" (trans. Eds.).

51. The text is in error here. It should read: Pope John XXII.

52. Frederick of Austria promised to recognize Louis IV of Bavaria as Holy Roman Emperor in return for his freedom, having been defeated at the battle of Mühldorf (1322). He returned to prison having failed to persuade his brothers to also recognize Louis IV. Pope John XXII (r. 1316–34) declared the oath invalid, and Frederick was given the title "King of the Romans."

53. Henry II, king of France, r. 1547–59.

54. Pope Innocent X (r. 1644–55) condemned the Treaty of Westphalia (1648) in his bull *Zelo Domus Dei.*

unjust, condemned, reprobated, frivolous, void of force and effect, and that nobody was bound to observe them or any of them, though they were confirmed by oath.—Nor was this all:—his holiness, assuming the tone of an absolute master, proceeds thus—*And nevertheless, for the greater precaution, and as much as need be, from the same motions, knowledge, deliberations, and plenitude of power, we condemn, reprobate, break, annul, and deprive of all force and effect, the said articles, and all the other things prejudicial to the above,* &c.* Who does not see, that these daring acts of the popes, which were formerly very frequent, were violations of the law of nations, and directly tended to destroy all the bands that could unite mankind, and to sap the foundations of their tranquillity, or to render the pope sole arbiter of their affairs?

§224. This abuse authorised by princes. But who can restrain his indignation at seeing this strange abuse authorised by princes themselves? In the treaty concluded at Vincennes, between Charles V. king of France, and Robert Stuart[55] king of Scotland, in 1371, it was agreed, *that the pope should absolve the Scots from all the oaths they had taken in swearing to a truce with the English, and that he should promise never to absolve the French or Scots from the oaths they were about to make in swearing to the new treaty.*† <232>

§225. Use of an oath in treaties. The custom, generally received in former times, of swearing to the observance of treaties, had furnished the popes with a pretext for claiming the power of breaking them, by absolving the contracting parties from their oaths. But in the present day, even children know

It does not constitute the obligation. that an oath does not constitute the obligation to keep a promise or a treaty: it only gives an additional strength to that obligation, by calling God to bear witness. A man of sense, a man of honour, does not think himself less bound by his word alone, by his faith once pledged, than if he had added the sanction of an oath. Cicero would not have us to make much difference between a perjurer and a liar. "The habit of lying (says that great man) paves the way to perjury. Whoever can be prevailed on to utter a falsehood, may be easily won over to commit per-

---

* History of the Treaty of Westphalia by Father Bougeant, in 12mo, vol. vi. p. 413.
† Choisy's History of Charles V. p. 282.
55. Charles V, king of France, r. 1364–80; Robert II, king of Scotland, r. 1371–90.

jury: for the man who has once deviated from the line of truth, generally feels as little scruple in consenting to a perjury as to a lie. For, what influence can the invocation of the gods have on the mind of him who is deaf to the voice of conscience? The same punishment, therefore, which heaven has ordained for the perjurer, awaits also the liar: for it is not on account of the formula of words in which the oath is couched, but of the perfidy and villany displayed by the perjurer in plotting harm against his neighbour, that the anger and indignation of the gods is roused."*

The oath does not then produce a new obligation: it only gives additional force to the obligation imposed by the treaty, and in every thing shares the same fate with it. Where the treaty is of its own nature valid and obligatory, the oath (in itself a supererogatory obligation) is so too: but where the treaty is void, the oath is void likewise.

The oath is a personal act; it can therefore only regard the person of him who swears, whether he swears himself, or deputes another to swear in his name. However, as this act does not produce a new obligation, it makes no change in the nature of a treaty. Thus an alliance confirmed by oath is so confirmed only with respect to him who has contracted it: but if it be a *real* alliance, it survives him, and passes to his successors as an alliance not confirmed by oath.

§226. It does not change the nature of obligations.

For the same reason, since the oath can impose no other obligation than that which results from the treaty itself, it gives no pre-eminence to one treaty, to the prejudice of those that are not sworn to. And as, in case of two treaties clashing with each other, the more ancient ally is to be preferred (§167), the same <233> rule should be observed, even though

§227. It gives no pre-eminence to one treaty above another.

---

* At quid interest inter perjurum et mendacem? Qui mentiri solet, pejerare consuevit. Quem ego, ut mentiatur, inducere possum, ut pejeret, exorare facile potero: nam qui semel a veritate deflexit, hic non majori religione ad perjurium quam ad mendacium perduci consuevit. Quis enim deprecatione deorum, non conscientiae fide commovetur? Propterea, quae poena ab diis immortalibus perjuro, haec eadem mendaci constituta est. Non enim ex pactione verborum quibus jusjurandum comprehenditur, sed ex perfidia et malitia per quam insidiae tenduntur alicui, dii immortales hominibus irasci et succensere consuêrunt. Cicer. Orat. pro Q. Roscio, comoedo.

the more recent treaty has been confirmed by an oath. In the same manner, since it is not allowable to engage in treaties inconsistent with existing ones (§165), the circumstance of an oath will not justify such treaties, nor give them sufficient validity to supercede those which are incompatible with them:—if it had such an effect, this would be a convenient mode for princes to rid themselves of their engagements.

§228. It cannot give force to a treaty that is invalid.

Thus also an oath cannot give validity to a treaty that is of its own nature invalid,—justify a treaty which is in itself unjust,—or impose any obligation to fulfil a treaty, however lawfully concluded, when an occasion occurs in which the observance of it would be unlawful,—as, for instance, if the ally to whom succours have been promised, undertakes a war that is manifestly unjust. In short, every treaty made for a dishonourable purpose (§161), every treaty prejudicial to the state (§160), or contrary to her fundamental laws (Book I. §265), being in its own nature void,—the oath that may have been added to such a treaty, is void likewise, and falls to the ground together with the covenant which it was intended to confirm.

§229. Asseverations.

The asseverations used in entering into engagements are forms of expression intended to give the greater force to promises. Thus, kings promise in *the most sacred manner, with good faith, solemnly, irrevocably,* and engage their *royal word,* &c. A man of honour thinks himself sufficiently bound by his word alone: yet these asseverations are not useless, inasmuch as they tend to prove that the contracting parties form their engagements deliberately, and with a knowledge of what they are about. Hence, consequently, the violation of such engagements becomes the more disgraceful. With mankind, whose faith is so uncertain, every circumstance is to be turned to advantage: and since the sense of shame operates more powerfully on their minds than the sentiment of duty, it would be imprudent to neglect this method.

§230. The faith of treaties does not depend on the difference of religion.

After what we have said above (§162), it were unnecessary to undertake in this place to prove that the faith of treaties has no relation to the difference of religion, and cannot in any manner depend upon it. The monstrous maxim, that *no faith is to be kept with heretics,* might formerly raise its head amidst the madness of party, and the fury of superstition: but it is at present generally detested.

If the security of him who stipulates for any thing in his own favour prompts him to require precision, fulness, and the greatest clearness in the expressions,—good faith demands, on the other hand, that each party should express his promises clearly, and without the least ambiguity. The faith of treaties is basely prostituted by studying to couch them in vague or equivocal terms, to introduce ambiguous expressions, to reserve subjects of dispute, to over-reach those with whom we treat, and outdo them in cunning and duplicity. Let the man who excels in these arts boast of his happy talents, and esteem himself a keen nego-<234>tiator: but reason and the sacred law of nature will class him as far beneath a vulgar cheat, as the majesty of kings is exalted above private persons. True diplomatic skill consists in guarding against imposition, not in practising it.

§231. Precautions to be taken in wording treaties.

Subterfuges in a treaty are not less contrary to good faith. His catholic majesty Ferdinand, having concluded a treaty with the archduke his son-in-law,[56] thought he could evade it by privately protesting against the treaty:—a puerile finesse! which, without giving any right to that prince, only exposed his weakness and duplicity.

§232. Subterfuges in treaties.

The rules that establish a lawful interpretation of treaties are sufficiently important to be made the subject of a distinct chapter. For the present let us simply observe that an evidently false interpretation is the grossest imaginable violation of the faith of treaties. He that resorts to such an expedient, either impudently sports with that sacred faith, or sufficiently evinces his inward conviction of the degree of moral turpitude annexed to the violation of it: he wishes to act a dishonest part, and yet preserve the character of an honest man: he is a puritanical impostor who aggravates his crime by the addition of a detestable hypocrisy. Grotius quotes several instances of evidently false interpretations put upon treaties:*—the Plateans having promised the Thebans to restore their prisoners, restored them after they had put them to death.

§233. An evidently false interpretation inconsistent with the faith of treaties.

---

* De Jure Belli et Pacis, lib. ii. cap xvi. §5.
56. Ferdinand II, king of Spain, r. 1479–1516; Philip I of Castile, son-in-law of Ferdinand, r. 1478–1506.

Pericles[57] having promised to spare the lives of such of the enemy as laid down their arms,* ordered all those to be killed who had iron clasps to their cloaks. A Roman general† having agreed with Antiochus[58] to restore him half of his fleet, caused each of the ships to be sawed in two. All these interpretations are as fraudulent as that of Rhadamistus,[59] who, according to Tacitus's account,‡ having sworn to Mithridates[60] that he would not employ either poison or the steel against him, caused him to be smothered under a heap of clothes.

§234. Faith tacitly pledged.   Our faith may be tacitly pledged, as well as expressly: it is sufficient that it be pledged, in order to become obligatory: the manner can make no difference in the case. The tacit pledging of faith is founded on a tacit consent; and a tacit consent is that which is, by fair deduction, inferred from our actions. Thus, as Grotius observes,§ whatever is included in the nature of certain acts which are agreed upon, is tacitly comprehended in the agreement: or, in other words, every thing which is indispensably necessary to give effect to the articles agreed on, is tacitly granted. If, for instance, a promise is made to a hostile army who have advanced far into the country, that they shall be allowed to return home in safety, it is manifest that they cannot <235> be refused provisions; for they cannot return without them. In the same manner, in demanding or accepting an interview, full security is tacitly promised. Livy justly says, that the Gallo-Greeks violated the law of nations in attacking the consul Manlius at the time when he was repairing to the place of interview to which they had invited him.¶ The emperor Valerian having been defeated by Sapor

---

* Literally, "laid down their *iron* or *steel*": hence the perfidious quibble on the word *iron,* which cannot be so well rendered in English.

† Q. Fabius Labeo [[Quintus Fabius Labeo, Roman consul ca. 183 B.C.]], according to Valerius Maximus. Livy makes no mention of the transaction.

‡ Annal. lib. xii.

§ Lib. iii. cap. xxiv. §1 [[*Law of War and Peace*]].

¶ Livy, lib. xxxviii. cap. xxv.

57. Pericles, 495–429 B.C., Athenian statesman, orator, and general.

58. Antiochus IV Epiphanes, ruler of the Seleucid Empire 215–163 B.C.

59. Rhadamistus, ruler of Iberia A.D. 51–55, became king of Armenia, having killed his uncle and married the uncle's daughter, Zenobia.

60. Mithridates, king of Armenia A.D. 42–55, uncle of Rhadamistus.

king of Persia,[61] sent to him to sue for peace. Sapor declared that he wished to treat with the emperor in person; and Valerian having consented to the interview without any suspicion of fraud, was carried off by the perfidious enemy, who kept him a prisoner till his death, and treated him with the most brutal cruelty.*

Grotius, in treating of tacit conventions, speaks of those in which the parties pledge their faith by mute signs.† But we ought not to confound these two kinds of tacit conventions: for that consent which is sufficiently notified by a sign, is an express consent, as clearly as if it had been signified by the voice. Words themselves are but signs established by custom: and there are mute signs which established custom renders as clear and as express as words. Thus, at the present day, by displaying a white flag, a parley is demanded, as expressly as it could be done by the use of speech. Security is tacitly promised to the enemy who advances upon this invitation.

CHAPTER XVI

Of Securities given for the Observance of Treaties.

Convinced by unhappy experience, that the faith of treaties, sacred and inviolable as it ought to be, does not always afford a sufficient assurance that they shall be punctually observed,—mankind have sought for securities against perfidy,—for methods, whose efficacy should not depend on the good-faith of the contracting parties. A *guaranty* is one of these means. When those who make a treaty of peace, or any other treaty, are not perfectly easy with respect to its observance, they require the guaranty of a powerful sovereign. The *guarantee* promises to maintain the conditions of the treaty, and to cause it to be observed. As he may find himself obliged to make use of force against the party who attempts to

§235.
Guaranty.

---

* The Life of Valerian in Crevier's History of the Emperors.
† Lib. iii. cap. xxiv. §5 [[*Law of War and Peace*]].
61. Valerian, emperor of Rome, r. A.D. 253–60; Sapor I, king of Persia, r. A.D. 241–71.

violate his promises, it is an engagement that no sovereign ought to enter into lightly, and without good reason. Princes indeed seldom enter into it unless when they have an indirect interest in the observance of the treaty, or are induced by particular relations of friendship. The <236> guaranty may be promised equally to all the contracting parties, to some of them, or even to one alone: but it is commonly promised to all in general. It may also happen, when several sovereigns enter into a common alliance, that they all reciprocally pledge themselves to each other, as guarantees for its observance. The guaranty is a kind of treaty, by which assistance and succours are promised to any one, in case he has need of them, in order to compel a faithless ally to fulfil his engagements.

§236. It gives the guarantee no right to interfere unasked in the execution of a treaty.

Guaranty being given in favour of the contracting powers, or of one of them, it does not authorise the guarantee to interfere in the execution of the treaty, or to enforce the observance of it, unasked, and of his own accord. If, by mutual consent, the parties think proper to deviate from the tenor of the treaty, to alter some of the articles, or to cancel it altogether,—or if one party be willing to favour the other by a relaxation of any claim,—they have a right to do this, and the guarantee cannot oppose it. Simply bound by his promise to support the party who should have reason to complain of the infraction of the treaty, he has acquired no rights for himself. The treaty was not made for him; for, had that been the case, he would have been concerned, not merely as a guarantee, but as a principal in the contract. This observation is of great importance: for care should be taken, lest, under colour of being a guarantee, a powerful sovereign should render himself the arbiter of the affairs of his neighbours, and pretend to give them laws.

But it is true, that if the parties make any change in the articles of the treaty without the consent and concurrence of the guarantee, the latter is no longer bound to adhere to the guaranty; for the treaty thus changed is no longer that which he guarantied.

§237. Nature of the obligation it imposes.

As no nation is obliged to do any thing for another nation, which that other is herself capable of doing, it naturally follows that the guarantee is not bound to give his assistance except where the party to whom he has granted his guaranty is of himself unable to obtain justice.

If there arises any dispute between the contracting parties respecting the sense of any article of the treaty, the guarantee is not immediately obliged to assist him in favour of whom he has given his guaranty. As he cannot engage to support injustice, he is to examine, and to search for the true sense of the treaty, to weigh the pretensions of him who claims his guaranty; and if he finds them ill founded, he may refuse to support them, without failing in his engagements.

It is no less evident that the guaranty cannot impair the rights of any one who is not a party to the treaty. If, therefore, it happens that the guarantied treaty proves derogatory to the rights of those who are not concerned in it,—the treaty being unjust in this point, the guarantee is in no wise bound to procure the performance of it; for, as we have shewn above, he can never have incurred an obligation to support injustice. This was the reason alleged by France, when, notwithstanding her having guarantied <237> the famous *pragmatic* sanction of Charles VI. she declared for the house of Bavaria, in opposition to the heiress of that emperor.[62] This reason is incontestably a good one, in the general view of it: and the only question to be decided at that time, was, whether the court of France made a just application of it.

§238. The guaranty cannot impair the rights of a third party.

Non nostrum inter vos tantas componere lites.[63]

I shall observe on this occasion, that, according to common usage, the term *guaranty* is often taken in a sense somewhat different from that we have given to it. For instance, most of the powers of Europe *guarantied* the act by which Charles VI. had regulated the succession to his dominions;—sovereigns sometimes reciprocally *guaranty* their respective states. But we should rather denominate those transactions treaties of alliance, for the purpose, in the former case, of maintaining that rule of succession,—and, in the latter, of supporting the possession of those states.

62. The Pragmatic Sanction was issued as a decree on April 19, 1713, by the Holy Roman Emperor Charles VI, with the intent that all of his Hapsburg kingdoms would descend without partition to his eldest daughter, Maria-Theresa.

63. "It is not for us to end such great disputes" Virgil, *Eclogues,* III (trans. Eds.).

§239. Duration of the guaranty.

The guaranty naturally subsists as long as the treaty that is the object of it; and in case of doubt, this ought always to be presumed, since it is required, and given, for the security of the treaty. But there is no reason which can naturally prevent its limitation to a certain period,—to the lives of the contracting powers, to that of the guarantee, &c. In a word, whatever we have said of treaties in general, is equally applicable to a treaty of guaranty.

§240. Treaties with surety.

When there is question of things which another may do or give as well as he who promises, as for instance, the payment of a sum of money, it is safer to demand a *security* than a *guaranty;* for the *surety* is bound to make good the promise in default of the principal,—whereas the guarantee is only obliged to use his best endeavours to obtain a performance of the promise from him who has made it.

§241. Pawns, securities, and mortgages.

A nation may put some of her possessions into the hands of another, for the security of her promises, debts, or engagements. If she thus deposits movable property, she gives *pledges.* Poland formerly pledged a crown and other jewels to the sovereigns of Prussia. But sometimes towns and provinces are given in pawn. If they are only pledged by a deed which assigns them as security for a debt, they serve as a *mortgage:* if they are actually put into the hands of the creditor, or of him with whom the affair has been transacted, he holds them as pledges: and if the revenues are ceded to him as an equivalent for the interest of the debt, the transaction is called a compact of *antichresis.*

§242. A nation's right over what she holds as a pledge.

The right which the possession of a town or province confers upon him who holds it in pledge, extends no further than to secure the payment of what is due to him, or the performance of the promise that has been made to him. He may therefore retain the town or the province in his hands, till he is satisfied; but he has no right to make any change in it; for that town, or <238> that country, does not belong to him as proprietor. He cannot even interfere in the government of it, beyond what is required for his own security, unless the empire, or the exercise of sovereignty, has been expressly made over to him. This last point is not naturally to be presumed, since it is sufficient for the security of the mortgagee, that the country is put into his hands, and under his power. Further, he is obliged, like every other person who has received a pledge, to preserve the country he holds as a security, and, as far as in his power, to prevent its suffering any damage or dilapidation: he is responsible for it; and if the country is ruined through his fault, he is bound to indemnify the state that intrusted him with the possession of it. If the sovereignty is deposited in his hands together with the country itself, he ought to govern it according to its constitution, and precisely in the same manner as the sovereign of the country was obliged to govern it; for the latter could only pledge his lawful right.

As soon as the debt is paid, or the treaty is fulfilled, the term of the security expires, and he who holds a town or a province by this title, is bound to restore it faithfully, in the same state in which he received it, so far as this depends on him. §243. How she is obliged to restore it.

But to those who have no law but their avarice, or their ambition,— who, like Achilles, place all their right in the point of their sword,*—a tempting allurement now presents itself: they have recourse to a thousand quibbles, a thousand pretences, to retain an important place, or a country which is conveniently situated for their purposes. The subject is too odious for us to allege examples: they are well enough known, and sufficiently numerous to convince every sensible nation, that it is very imprudent to make over such securities.

But if the debt be not paid at the appointed time, or if the treaty be not fulfilled, what has been given in security, may be retained and appropriated, or the mortgage seized, at least until the debt be discharged, or a just compensation made. The house of Savoy had mortgaged the country of Vaud to the cantons of Bern and Fribourg; and those two cantons, finding that no payments were made, had recourse to arms, and took possession of the country. The duke of Savoy, instead of immediately satisfying their just demands, opposed force to force, and gave them still further grounds of complaint: wherefore the cantons, finally successful in the contest, have since retained possession of that fine coun- §244. How she may appropriate it to herself.

---

* Jura negat sibi nata, nihil non arrogat armis. HORAT. [["He denies that laws were made for him, and thinks that everything should yield to arms" (said of Achilles). Horace, *Ars poetica,* 121.]]

try, as well for the payment of the debt, as to defray the expenses of the war, and to obtain a just indemnification.

§245.
Hostages.

Finally, there is, in the way of security, another precaution, of very ancient institution, and much used among nations,—which is, to require hostages. These are persons of consequence, delivered up by the promising party, to him with whom he enters into an engagement, and to be detained by the latter until the performance of the promises which are made to him. In this <239> case, as well as in those above mentioned, the transaction is a pignorary contract, in which free men are delivered up, instead of towns, countries, or jewels. With respect to this contract, therefore, we may confine ourselves to those particular observations which the difference of the things pledged renders necessary.

§246. What right we have over hostages.

The sovereign who receives hostages, has no other right over them, than that of securing their persons, in order to detain them till the entire accomplishment of the promises of which they are the pledge. He may therefore take precautions to prevent their escaping from him: but those precautions should be moderated by humanity, towards men whom he has no right to use ill; and they ought not to be extended beyond what prudence requires.

It is pleasing to behold the European nations in the present age content themselves with the bare parole of their hostages. The English noblemen who were sent to France in that character in pursuance of the treaty of Aix-la-Chapelle, in 1748, to stay till the restitution of Cape Breton, were solely bound by their word of honour, and lived at court, and at Paris, rather as ministers of their nation, than as hostages.

§247. Their liberty alone is pledged.

The liberty of the hostages is the only thing pledged: and if he who has given them breaks his promise, they may be detained in captivity. Formerly they were in such cases put to death;—an inhuman cruelty, founded on an error. It was imagined that the sovereign might arbitrarily dispose of the lives of his subjects, or that every man was the master of his own life, and had a right to stake it as a pledge when he delivered himself up as an hostage.

§248. When they are to be sent back.

As soon as the engagements are fulfilled, the cause for which the hostages were delivered no longer subsists: they then immediately become free, and ought to be restored without delay. They ought also to be restored, if the reason for which they were demanded does not take place: to detain them then, would be to abuse the sacred faith upon which they were delivered. The perfidious Christiern II. king of Denmark,[64] being delayed by contrary winds before Stockholm, and, together with his whole fleet, ready to perish with famine, made proposals of peace: whereupon, the administrator, Steno,[65] imprudently trusting to his promises, furnished the Danes with provisions, and even gave Gustavus and six other noblemen as hostages for the safety of the king, who pretended to have a desire to come on shore: but, with the first fair wind, Christiern weighed anchor, and carried off the hostages; thus repaying the generosity of his enemy by an infamous act of treachery.*

Hostages being delivered on the faith of treaties, and he who receives them, promising to restore them, as soon as the promise, of which they are the surety, shall be fulfilled,—such engagements ought to be literally accomplished: and the hostages should be really and faithfully restored to their former condition, as soon as the accomplishment of the promise has disengaged <240> them. It is therefore not allowable to detain them for any other cause; and I am astonished to find that some learned writers teach a contrary doctrine.† They ground their opinion upon the principle which authorises a sovereign to seize and detain the subjects of another state in order to compel their rulers to do him justice. The principle is true; but the application is not just. These authors seem to have overlooked the circumstance, that, were it not for the faith of the treaty by virtue of which the hostage has been delivered, he would not be in the power of that sovereign, nor exposed to be so easily seized; and that the faith of such a treaty does not allow the sovereign to make any other use of his hostage than that for which he was intended, or to take advantage of his detention beyond what has been expressly stipulated. The

§249. Whether they may be detained on any other account.

---

* History of the Revolutions of Sweden. [[René-Aubert de Vertot, *History of the Revolutions in Sweden.*]]

† Grotius, lib. iii. cap. xx. §55 [[*Law of War and Peace*]].—Wolfius, Jus Gent. §503.

64. Christiern (Christian) II, king of Denmark and Norway, r. 1513–23.

65. Regent Sten Sture (the Younger), r. 1512–20.

hostage is delivered for the security of a promise, and for that alone. As soon, therefore, as the promise is fulfilled, the hostage, as we have just observed, ought to be restored to his former condition. To tell him that he is released as a hostage, but detained as a pledge for the security of any other pretension, would be taking advantage of his situation as a hostage, in evident violation of the spirit and even the letter of the convention, according to which, as soon as the promise is accomplished, the hostage is to be restored to himself and his country, and reinstated in his pristine rank, as if he had never been a hostage. Without a rigid adherence to this principle, it would no longer be safe to give hostages, since princes might on every occasion easily devise some pretext for detaining them. Albert the Wise,[66] duke of Austria, making war against the city of Zurich in the year 1351, the two parties referred the decision of their disputes to arbitrators, and Zurich gave hostages. The arbitrators passed an unjust sentence, dictated by partiality. Zurich, nevertheless, after having made a well-grounded complaint on the subject, determined to submit to their decision. But the duke formed new pretensions, and detained the hostages,* contrary to the faith of the compromise, and in evident contempt of the law of nations.

§250. They may be detained for their own actions. But a hostage may be detained for his own actions, for crimes committed, or debts contracted in the country while he is in hostage there. This is no violation of the faith of the treaty. In order to be sure of recovering his liberty according to the terms of the treaty, the hostage must not claim a right to commit, with impunity, any outrages against the nation by which he is kept; and when he is about to depart, it is just that he should pay his debts.

§251. Of the support of hostages. It is the party who gives the hostages, that is to provide for their support; for it is by his order, and for his service, that they are in hostage. He who receives them for his own security is not bound to defray the expense of their subsistence, but simply <241> that of their custody if he thinks proper to set a guard over them.

* Tschudi, vol. i. p. 421.
66. Albert II, king of Austria, r. 1298–1358.

The sovereign may dispose of his subjects for the service of the state; he may therefore give them also as hostages; and the person who is nominated for that purpose, is bound to obey, as he is on every other occasion when commanded for the service of his country. But as the expenses ought to be borne equally by the citizens, the hostage is entitled to be defrayed and indemnified at the public charge.

§252. A subject cannot refuse to be a hostage.

It is, evidently, a subject alone, who can be given as a hostage against his will. With a vassal, the case is otherwise. What he owes to the sovereign, is determined by the conditions of his fief; and he is bound to nothing more. Accordingly, it is a decided point that a vassal cannot be constrained to go as a hostage, unless he be at the same time a subject.

Whoever has a power to make treaties or conventions, may give and receive hostages. For this reason, not only the sovereign, but also the subordinate authorities, have a right to give hostages in the agreements they make, according to the powers annexed to their office, and the extent of their commission. The governor of a town, and the besieging general, give and receive hostages for the security of the capitulation: whoever is under their command, is bound to obey, if he is nominated for that purpose.

Hostages ought naturally to be persons of consequence, since they are required as a security. Persons of mean condition would furnish but a feeble security, unless they were given in great numbers. Care is commonly taken to settle the rank of the hostages that are to be delivered; and the violation of a compact in this particular is a flagrant dereliction of good-faith and honour. It was a shameful act of perfidy in La Trimouille to give the Swiss only hostages from the dregs of the people, instead of four of the principle citizens of Dijon, as had been stipulated in the famous treaty we have mentioned above (§212). Sometimes the principal persons of the state, and even princes, are given in hostage. Francis I. gave his own sons as security for the treaty of Madrid.[67]

§253. Rank of the hostages.

The sovereign who gives hostages ought to act ingenuously in the affair,—giving them in reality as pledges of his word, and consequently with the intention that they should be kept till the entire accomplish-

§254. They ought not to make their escape.

67. King Francis I of France (r. 1515–47) signed the Treaty of Madrid in 1526.

ment of his promise. He cannot therefore approve of their making their escape: and if they take such a step, so far from harbouring them, he is bound to send them back. The hostage, on his side, conformably to the presumed intention of his sovereign, ought faithfully to remain with him to whom he is delivered, without endeavouring to escape. Cloelia made her escape from the hands of Porsenna,[68] to whom she had been delivered as a hostage: but the Romans sent her back, that they might not incur the guilt of violating the treaty.* <242>

§255. Whether a hostage who dies is to be replaced.

If the hostage happens to die, he who has given him is not obliged to replace him, unless this was made a part of the agreement. The hostage was a security required of him: that security is lost without any fault on his side; and there exists no reason why he should be obliged to give another.

§256. Of him who takes the place of a hostage.

If any one substitutes himself for a time in the place of a hostage, and the hostage happens in the interim to die a natural death, the substitute is free: for in this case, things are to be replaced in the same situation in which they would have been if the hostage had not been permitted to absent himself, and substitute another in his stead: and for the same reason, the hostage is not free by the death of him who has taken his place only for a time. It would be quite the contrary, if the hostage had been exchanged for another: the former would be absolutely free from all engagement; and the person who had taken his place would alone be bound.

§257. A hostage succeeding to the crown.

If a prince, who has been given in hostage, succeeds to the crown, he ought to be released on the delivery of another sufficient hostage, or a number of others, who shall together constitute an aggregate security equivalent to that which he himself afforded when he was originally given. This is evident from the treaty itself, which did not import that the king should be a hostage. The detention of the king's person by a foreign power is a thing of too interesting a nature to admit a presump-

---

* Et Romani pignus pacis ex foedere restituerunt. [["And the Romans returned the pledge of peace, as the treaty required."]] Tit. Liv. [[*History of Rome*]] lib. ii. cap. xiii.

68. Lars Porsenna of Clusium, king of the Etruscans, ca. 500 B.C.

tion that the state had intended to expose herself to the consequences of such an event. Good-faith ought to preside in all conventions; and the manifest or justly presumed intention of the contracting parties ought to be adhered to. If Francis I. had died after having given his sons as hostages, certainly the dauphin should have been released: for he had been delivered only with a view of restoring the king to his kingdom; and if the emperor had detained him, that view would have been frustrated, since the king of France would still have been a captive. It is evident that, in this reasoning, I proceed on the supposition that no violation of the treaty has taken place on the part of the state which has given a prince in hostage. In case that state had broken its promise, advantage might reasonably be taken of an event which rendered the hostage still more valuable, and his release the more necessary.

The liability of a hostage, as that of a city or a country, expires with the treaty which it was intended to secure (§§243, 248): and consequently if the treaty is personal, the hostage is free at the moment when one of the contracting powers happens to die.

§258. The liability of the hostage ends with the treaty.

The sovereign who breaks his word after having given hostages, does an injury not only to the other contracting power, but also to the hostages themselves. For though subjects are indeed bound to obey their sovereign who gives them in hostage, that sovereign has not a right wantonly to sacrifice their liberty, and expose their lives to danger without just reasons. Delivered <243> up as a security for their sovereign's promise, not for the purpose of suffering any harm,—if he entails misfortune on them by violating his faith, he covers himself with double infamy. Pawns and mortgages serve as securities for what is due; and their acquisition indemnifies the party to whom the other fails in his engagements. Hostages are rather pledges of the faith of him who gives them; and it is supposed that he would abhor the idea of sacrificing innocent persons. But if particular conjunctures oblige a sovereign to abandon the hostages,—if, for example, the party who has received them violates his engagements in the first instance, and, in consequence of his violation, the treaty can no longer be accomplished without exposing the state to danger,—no measure should be left untried for the delivery of those unfortunate hostages; and the state cannot refuse to compensate them for

§259. The violation of the treaty is an injury done to the hostages.

their sufferings, and to make them amends, either in their own persons, or in those of their relatives.

§260. The fate of the hostage, when he who has given him fails in his engagements.

At the moment when the sovereign, who has given the hostage, has violated his faith, the latter ceases to retain the character of a hostage, and becomes a prisoner to the party who had received him, and who has now a right to detain him in perpetual captivity. But it becomes a generous prince to refrain from an exertion of his rights at the expense of an innocent individual. And as the hostage is no longer bound by any tie to his own sovereign who has perfidiously abandoned him,—if he chooses to transfer his allegiance to the prince who is now the arbiter of his fate, the latter may acquire a useful subject, instead of a wretched prisoner, the troublesome object of his commiseration. Or he may liberate and dismiss him, on settling with him the conditions.

§261. Of the right founded on custom.

We have already observed that the life of a hostage cannot be lawfully taken away on account of the perfidy of the party who has delivered him. The custom of nations, the most constant practice, cannot justify such an instance of barbarous cruelty, repugnant to the law of nature. Even at a time when that dreadful custom was but too much authorised, the great Scipio publicly declared that he would not suffer his vengeance to fail on innocent hostages, but on the persons themselves who had incurred the guilt of perfidy, and that he was incapable of punishing any but armed enemies.* The emperor Julian made the same declaration.† All that such a custom can produce, is impunity among the nations who practise it. Whoever is guilty of it cannot complain that another is so too: but every nation may and ought to declare, that she considers the action as a barbarity injurious to human nature. <244>

* Tit. Liv. [[*History of Rome*]] lib. xxviii. cap. xxxiv.
† See Grotius, lib. iii. cap. xi. §18, not. 2 [[*Law of War and Peace*]].

CHAPTER XVII

Of the Interpretation of Treaties.

If the ideas of men were always distinct and perfectly determinate,—if, for the expression of those ideas, they had none but proper words, no terms but such as were clear, precise, and susceptible only of one sense,—there would never be any difficulty in discovering their meaning in the words by which they intended to express it: nothing more would be necessary, than to understand the language. But, even on this supposition, the art of interpretation would still not be useless. In concessions, conventions, and treaties, in all contracts, as well as in the laws, it is impossible to foresee and point out all the particular cases that may arise: we decree, we ordain, we agree upon certain things, and express them in general terms; and though all the expressions of a treaty should be perfectly clear, plain, and determinate, the true interpretation would still consist in making, in all the particular cases that present themselves, a just application of what has been decreed in a general manner. But this is not all:—conjunctures vary, and produce new kinds of cases, that cannot be brought within the terms of the treaty or the law, except by inferences drawn from the general views of the contracting parties, or of the legislature. Between different clauses, there will be found contradictions and inconsistencies, real or apparent; and the question is, to reconcile such clauses, and point out the path to be pursued. But the case is much worse if we consider that fraud seeks to take advantage even of the imperfection of language, and that men designedly throw obscurity and ambiguity into their treaties, in order to be provided with a pretence for eluding them upon occasion. It is therefore necessary to establish rules founded on reason, and authorised by the law of nature, capable of diffusing light over what is obscure, of determining what is uncertain, and of frustrating the views of him who acts with duplicity in forming the compact. Let us begin with those that tend particularly to this last end,—with those maxims of justice and equity which are calculated to repress fraud, and to prevent the effect of its artifices.

§262. Necessity of establishing rules of interpretation.

§263.
1st General
maxim: it is
not allowable
to interpret
what has no
need of inter-
pretation.

The first general maxim of interpretation is, that *It is not allowable to interpret what has no need of interpretation.* When a deed is worded in clear and precise terms,—when its meaning is evident, and leads to no absurd conclusion,—there can be no reason for refusing to admit the meaning which such deed naturally presents. To go elsewhere in search of conjectures in order to restrict or extend it, is but an attempt to elude it. If this dangerous method be once admitted, there will be no deed which it will not render useless. However luminous each clause may <245> be,—however clear and precise the terms in which the deed is couched,—all this will be of no avail, if it be allowed to go in quest of extraneous arguments to prove that it is not to be understood in the sense which it naturally presents.*

§264.
2d General
maxim: if he
who could and
ought to have
explained
himself, has
not done it, it
is to his own
detriment.

Those cavillers, who dispute the sense of a clear and determinate article, are accustomed to seek their frivolous subterfuges in the pretended intentions and views which they attribute to its author. It would be very often dangerous to enter with them into the discussion of those supposed views, that are not pointed out in the piece itself. The following rule is better calculated to foil such cavillers, and will at once cut short all chicanery:—*If he who could and ought to have explained himself clearly and fully, has not done it, it is the worse for him: he cannot be allowed to introduce subsequent restrictions which he has not expressed.* This is a maxim of the Roman law: *Pactionem obscuram iis nocere, in quorum fuit potesiate legem apertius conscribere.*†[69] The equity of this rule is glaringly obvious, and its necessity is not less evident. There will be no security in conventions, no stability in grants or concessions, if they may be ren-

---

* Standum omnino est iis, quae verbis expressis, quorum manifestus est significatus, indicata fuerunt, nisi omnem a negotiis humanis certitudinem removere volueris. WOLF. Jus Nat. par. vii. n. 822. [[Note added in 1773/1797 editions.]]

† [[Justinian's]] Digest. lib. ii. tit. xiv. de Pactis, leg. 39.—See likewise Digest. lib. xviii. tit. i. de Contrahenda Emptione, leg. 21. Labeo scripsit obscuritatem pacti nocere potius debere venditori, qui id dixerit, quam emptori; quia potuit re integra apertius dicere. [["Labeo wrote that obscurity in a contract should harm the vendor who had spoken it rather than the purchaser, because he could have spoken more clearly in the whole matter" (trans. Eds.).]]

69. "An obscure contract [should] injure those in whose power it was to write the law more clearly." *Digesta Justiniana,* liber 18.1.21.

dered nugatory by subsequent limitations, which ought to have been originally specified in the deed, if they were in the contemplation of the contracting parties.

The third general maxim, or principle, on the subject of interpretation is, that *Neither the one nor the other of the parties interested in the contract has a right to interpret the deed or treaty according to his own fancy.* For if you are at liberty to affix whatever meaning you please to my promise, you will have the power of obliging me to do whatever you choose, contrary to my intention, and beyond my real engagements: and on the other hand, if I am allowed to explain my promises as I please, I may render them vain and illusory, by giving them a meaning quite different from that which they presented to you, and in which you must have understood them at the time of your accepting them.

§265. 3d General maxim: neither of the contracting parties has a right to interpret the treaty according to his own fancy.

On every occasion when a person could and ought to have made known his intention, we assume for true against him what he has sufficiently declared. This is an incontestable principle, applied to treaties; for if they are not a vain play of words, the contracting parties ought to express themselves in them with truth, and according to their real intentions. If the intention which is sufficiently declared were not to be taken of course as the true intention of him who speaks and enters into engagements, it would be perfectly useless to form contracts or treaties.

§266. 4th General maxim: what is sufficiently declared, is to be taken for true.

But it is here asked, which of the contracting parties ought to have his expressions considered as the more decisive, with respect to the true meaning of the contract,—whether we should lay a < 246 > greater stress on the words of him who makes the promise than on those of the party who stipulates for its performance?—As the force and obligation of every contract arises from a perfect promise,—and the person who makes the promise is no further engaged than his will is sufficiently declared,—it is very certain, that, in order to discover the true meaning of the contract, attention ought principally to be paid to the words of the promising party. For he voluntarily binds himself by his words; and we take for true against him, what he has sufficiently declared. This question seems to have originated from the manner in which conventions are sometimes made: the one party offers the conditions, and the other accepts them; that is to say, the former proposes what he requires that the

§267. We ought to attend rather to the words of the person promising, than to those of the party stipulating.

other shall oblige himself to perform, and the latter declares the obligations into which he really enters. If the words of him who accepts the conditions bear relation to the words of him who offers them, it is certainly true that we ought to lay our principal stress on the expressions of the latter; but this is because the person promising is considered as merely repeating them in order to form his promise. The capitulations of besieged towns may here serve us for an example. The besieged party proposes the conditions on which he is willing to surrender the place: the besieger accepts them: the expressions of the former lay no obligation on the latter, unless so far as he adopts them. He who accepts the conditions is in reality the promising party; and it is in his words that we ought to seek for the true meaning of the articles, whether he has himself chosen and formed his expressions, or adopted those of the other party by referring to them in his promise. But still we must bear in mind the maxim above laid down, viz. that what he has sufficiently declared, is to be taken as true against him. I proceed to explain myself more particularly on this subject.

§268.
5th General
maxim: the
interpretation
ought to be
made according to certain
rules.
In the interpretation of a treaty, or of any other deed whatsoever, the question is, to discover what the contracting parties have agreed upon,—to determine precisely, on any particular occasion, what has been promised and accepted,—that is to say, not only what one of the parties intended to promise, but also what the other must reasonably and candidly have supposed to be promised to him,—what has been sufficiently declared to him, and what must have influenced him in his acceptance. *Every deed,* therefore, *and every treaty, must be interpreted by certain fixed rules calculated to determine its meaning, as naturally understood by the parties concerned, at the time when the deed was drawn up and accepted.* This is a fifth principle.

As these rules are founded on right reason, and are consequently approved and prescribed by the law of nature, every man, every sovereign, is obliged to admit and to follow them. Unless certain rules be admitted for determining the sense in which the expressions are to be taken, treaties will be only empty words; nothing can be agreed upon with security, and it will be <247> almost ridiculous to place any dependence on the effect of conventions.

But as sovereigns acknowledge no common judge, no superior that can oblige them to adopt an interpretation founded on just rules, the faith of treaties constitutes, in this respect, all the security of the contracting powers. That faith is no less violated by a refusal to admit an evidently fair interpretation, than by an open infraction. It is the same injustice, the same want of good-faith; nor is its turpitude rendered less odious by being cloaked up in the subtilties of fraud.

§269. The faith of treaties lays an obligation to follow these rules.

Let us now enter into the particular rules on which the interpretation ought to be formed, in order to be just and fair. Since the sole object of the lawful interpretation of a deed ought to be the discovery of the thoughts of the author or authors of that deed,—*whenever we meet with any obscurity in it, we are to consider what probably were the ideas of those who drew up the deed, and to interpret it accordingly.* This is the general rule for all interpretations. It particularly serves to ascertain the meaning of particular expressions whose signification is not sufficiently determinate. Pursuant to this rule, we should take those expressions in their utmost latitude when it seems probable that the person speaking had in contemplation every thing which, in that extensive sense, they are capable of designating: and, on the other hand, we ought to restrict their meaning, if the author appears to have confined his idea to what they comprehend in their more limited signification. Let us suppose that a husband has bequeathed to his wife all his money. It is required to know whether this expression means only his ready money, or whether it extends also to that which is lent out, and is due on notes and other securities. If the wife is poor,—if she was beloved by her husband,—if the amount of the ready money be inconsiderable, and the value of the other property greatly superior to that of the money both in specie and in paper,—there is every reason to presume that the husband meant to bequeath to her as well the money due to him as that actually contained in his coffers. On the other hand, if the woman be rich,—if the amount of the ready specie be very considerable, and the money due greatly exceeds in value all the other property,—the probability is, that the husband meant to bequeath to his wife his ready money only.

§270. General rule of interpretation.

By the same rule, we are to interpret a clause in the utmost latitude that the strict and appropriate meaning of the words will admit, if it appears that the author had in view every thing which that strict and appropriate meaning comprehends: but we must interpret it in a more limited sense when it appears probable that the author of the clause did not mean to extend it to every thing which the strict propriety of the terms might be made to include. As for instance, a father, who has an only son, bequeaths to the daughter of his friend *all his jewels*. He has a sword enriched with diamonds, given him by a sovereign <248> prince. In this case it is certainly very improbable that the testator had any intention of making over that honourable badge of distinction to a family of aliens. That sword, therefore, together with the jewels with which it is ornamented, must be excepted from the legacy, and the meaning of the words be restricted to his other jewels. But if the testator has neither son nor heir of his own name, and bequeaths his property to a stranger, there is no reason to limit the signification of the terms; they should be taken in their full import, it being probable that the testator used them in that sense.

§271. The terms are to be explained conformably to common usage.

The contracting parties are obliged to express themselves in such manner that they may mutually understand each other. This is evident from the very nature of the transaction. Those who form the contract, concur in the same intentions; they agree in desiring the same thing; and how shall they agree in this instance, if they do not perfectly understand each other? Without this, their contract will be no better than a mockery or a snare. If then they ought to speak in such a manner as to be understood, it is necessary that they should employ the words in their proper signification,—the signification which common usage has affixed to them,— and that they annex an established meaning to every term, every expression, they make use of. They must not, designedly and without mentioning it, deviate from the common usage and the appropriate meaning of words: and it is presumed that they have conformed to established custom in this particular, as long as no cogent reasons can be adduced to authorise a presumption to the contrary; for the presumption is, in general, that things have been done as they ought. From all these incontestable truths, results this rule: *In the interpretation of treaties, compacts, and promises, we ought not to deviate from the common use of the language, unless we have very strong reasons for it.* In all human affairs, where absolute certainty is not at hand to point out the way, we must take probability for our guide. In most cases, it is extremely probable that the parties have expressed themselves conformably to the established usage: and such probability ever affords a strong presumption, which cannot be over-ruled but by a still stronger presumption to the contrary. Camden* gives us a treaty, in which it is expressly said that the treaty shall be precisely understood according to the force and appropriate signification of the terms. After such a clause, we cannot, under any pretence, deviate from the proper meaning which custom has affixed to the terms,—the will of the contracting parties being thereby formally declared in the most unambiguous manner.

The usage we here speak of, is that of the time when the treaty, or the deed, of whatever kind, was drawn up and concluded. Languages incessantly vary, and the signification and force of words changes with time. When, therefore, an ancient deed is to be interpreted, we should be acquainted with the com-<249>mon use of the terms at the time when it was written; and that knowledge is to be acquired from deeds of the same period, and from contemporary writers, by diligently comparing them with each other. This is the only source from which to derive any information that can be depended on. The use of the vulgar languages being, as every one knows, very arbitrary,—etymological and grammatical investigations, pursued with a view to discover the true import of a word in common usage, would furnish but a vain theory, equally useless and destitute of proof. §272. Interpretation of ancient treaties.

Words are only designed to express the thoughts; thus the true signification of an expression, in common use, is the idea which custom has affixed to that expression. It is then a gross quibble to affix a particular sense to a word, in order to elude the true sense of the entire expression. Mahomet,[70] emperor of the Turks, at the taking of Negropont,[71] having promised a man to spare his head, caused him to be cut in two through the middle of the body. Tamerlane, after having engaged the city of §273. Of quibbles on words.

* History of Queen Elizabeth.
70. Muhammad II, sultan of the Ottoman Empire, r. 1451–81.
71. Negropont, an island in the Aegean Sea, was conquered by the Turks in 1470.

Sebastia to capitulate[72] under his promise of shedding no blood, caused all the soldiers of the garrison to be buried alive:* gross subterfuges which, as Cicero remarks,† only serve to aggravate the guilt of the perfidious wretch who has recourse to them. *To spare the head of any one,* and *to shed no blood,* are expressions, which, according to common custom, and especially on such an occasion, manifestly imply *to spare the lives of the parties.*

§274. A rule on this subject.   All these pitiful subtilties are overthrown by this unerring rule: *When we evidently see what is the sense that agrees with the intention of the contracting parties, it is not allowable to wrest their words to a contrary meaning.* The intention, sufficiently known, furnishes the true matter of the convention,—what is promised and accepted, demanded and granted. A violation of the treaty is rather a deviation from the intention which it sufficiently manifests, than from the terms in which it is worded: for the terms are nothing without the intention by which they must be dictated.

§275. Mental reservations.   Is it necessary, in an enlightened age, to say that mental reservations cannot be admitted in treaties? This is manifest, since, by the very nature of the treaty, the parties are bound to express themselves in such manner that they may mutually understand each other (§271). There is scarcely an individual now to be found, who would not be ashamed of building upon a mental reservation. What can be the use of such an artifice, unless to lull the opposite party into a false security, under the vain appearance of a contract? It is then a real piece of knavery.

§276. Interpretation of technical terms.   Technical terms, or terms peculiar to the arts and sciences, ought commonly to be interpreted according to the definition given of them by masters of the art, or persons versed in the <250> knowledge of the art or science to which the terms belong. I say *commonly;* for this rule is not so absolute, but that we may and even ought to deviate from it, when

---

* See Puffendorf's Law of Nature and Nations, book v. chap xii. §3.—La Croix, in his Hist. of Timurbec, book v. ch. xv. speaks of this cruelty of Timurbec or Tamerlane towards 4,000 Armenian horsemen, but says nothing of the perfidy which others attribute to him.

† Fraus enim adstringit, non dissolvit perjurium. De Offic. lib. iii. cap. xxxii.

72. In 1400.

we have good reasons for such deviation; as, for instance, if it were proved that he who speaks in a treaty, or in any other deed, did not understand the art or science from which he borrowed the term,—that he was unacquainted with its import as a technical word,—that he employed it in a vulgar acceptation, &c.

If, however, the technical or other terms relate to things that admit of different degrees, we ought not scrupulously to adhere to definitions, but rather to take the terms in a sense agreeable to the context: for, a regular definition describes a thing in its most perfect state; and yet it is certain that we do not always mean it in that state of its utmost perfection, whenever we speak of it. Now the interpretation should only tend to the discovery of the will of the contracting parties (§268): to each term, therefore, we should affix that meaning, which the party whose words we interpret, probably had in contemplation. Thus, when the parties in a treaty have agreed to submit their pretensions to the decision of two or three able civilians, it would be ridiculous to endeavour to elude the compromise, under the pretence that we can find no civilian accomplished in every point, or to strain the terms so far as to reject all who do not equal Cujas[73] or Grotius. Would he who had stipulated for the assistance of ten thousand good troops have any reason to insist upon soldiers of whom the very worst should be comparable to the veterans of Julius Caesar? And if a prince had promised his ally a good general, must he send him none but a Marlborough or a Turenne?

§277. Of terms whose signification admits of degrees.

There are figurative expressions that are become so familiar in the common use of language, that, in numberless instances, they supply the place of proper terms, so that we ought to take them in a figurative sense, without paying any attention to their original, proper, and direct signification: the subject of the discourse sufficiently indicates the meaning that should be affixed to them. To *hatch a plot,* to *carry fire and sword into a country,** are expressions of this sort; and there scarcely can occur

§278. Of figurative expressions.

* The French expression, *"ourdir une trame,"* which is here rendered *"hatch a plot,"* literally signifies *"to lay the warp of a web"*;— *"fire and sword,"* literally, *"fire and steel"* (or iron). [[Note added in 1797 edition.]]

73. Jacques Cujas, 1520–90, French jurist, professor at Toulouse, and counsellor to the Parlement of Grenoble.

an instance where it would not be absurd to take them in their direct and literal sense.

§279. Of equivocal expressions.

There is not perhaps any language that does not also contain words which signify two or more different things, and phrases which are susceptible of more than one sense. Thence arises ambiguity in discourse. The contracting parties ought carefully to avoid it. Designedly to use it with a view to elude their engagements in the sequel, is downright perfidy, since the faith of treaties obliges the contracting parties to express their intentions clearly (§271). But if an ambiguous expression has found its <251> way into a deed, it is the part of the interpreter to clear up any doubt thereby occasioned.

§280. The rule for these two cases.

The following is the rule that ought to direct the interpretation in this as well as in the preceding case: *We ought always to affix such meaning to the expressions, as is most suitable to the subject or matter in question.* For, by a true interpretation, we endeavour to discover the thoughts of the persons speaking, or of the contracting parties in a treaty. Now it ought to be presumed that he who has employed a word which is susceptible of many different significations, has taken it in that which agrees with his subject. In proportion as he employs his attention on the matter in question, the terms proper to express his thoughts present themselves to his mind; this equivocal word could therefore only present itself in the sense proper to express the thought of him who makes use of it, that is, in the sense agreeable to the subject. It would be a feeble objection to this, to allege that a man sometimes designedly employs equivocal expressions, with a view of holding out ideas quite different from his real thoughts, and that, in such case, the sense which agrees with the subject is not that which corresponds with the intention of the person speaking. We have already observed, that whenever a man can and ought to make known his intention, we assume for true against him what he has sufficiently declared (§266). And as good-faith ought to preside in conventions, they are always interpreted on the supposition that it actually did preside in them. Let us illustrate this rule by examples. The word *day* is understood of the *natural day,* or the time during which the sun affords us his light, and of the *civil day,* or the space of twenty-four hours. When it is used in a convention to point out a space of time, the subject itself manifestly shews that the parties mean the civil day, or the term of twenty-four hours. It was therefore a pitiful subterfuge, or rather a notorious perfidy, in Cleomenes,[74] when, having concluded a truce of some days with the people of Argos, and finding them asleep on the third night in reliance on the faith of the treaty, he killed a part of their number, and made the rest prisoners, alleging that the nights were not comprehended in the truce.* The word *steel* may be understood of the metal itself, or of certain instruments made of it:—in a convention which stipulates that *the enemy shall lay down their steel,* it evidently means *their weapons:* wherefore Pericles, in the example related above (§233), gave a fraudulent interpretation to those words, since it was contrary to what the nature of the subject manifestly pointed out. Q. Fabius Labeo, of whom we made mention in the same section, shewed equal dishonesty in the interpretation of his treaty with Antiochus; for a sovereign who stipulates that the half of his fleet or of his vessels shall be restored to him, undoubtedly means that the other party shall restore to him vessels which he can make use of, and not the half <252> of each vessel, when sawed into two. Pericles and Fabius are also condemned by the rule established above (§274), which forbids us to wrest the sense of the words contrary to the evident intention of the contracting parties.

If any one of those expressions which are susceptible of different significations occurs more than once in the same piece, we cannot make it a rule to take it every-where in the same signification. For we must, conformably to the preceding rule, take such expression, in each article, according as the subject requires,—*pro substrata materia,*[75] as the masters of the art say. The word *day,* for instance, has two significations, as we have just observed (§280). If therefore it be said in a convention, that there shall be a truce of fifty days, on condition that commissioners from both parties shall, during eight successive days, jointly endeavour to adjust the dispute,—the fifty days of the truce are civil days of twenty-four hours; but it would be absurd to understand them in the same sense in the

§281. Not necessary to give a term the same sense everywhere in the same deed.

---

* Puffendorf [[*Of the Law of Nature and Nations*]], lib. v. cap. xii. §7.
74. Cleomenes, king of Sparta, died ca. 490 B.C.
75. "According to the relevant subject."

second article, and to pretend that the commissioners should labour eight days and nights without intermission.

§282. We ought to reject every interpretation that leads to an absurdity; *Every interpretation that leads to an absurdity, ought to be rejected;* or, in other words, we should not give to any piece a meaning from which any absurd consequences would follow, but must interpret it in such a manner as to avoid absurdity. As it is not to be presumed that any one means what is absurd, it cannot be supposed that the person speaking intended that his words should be understood in a manner from which an absurdity would follow. Neither is it allowable to presume that he meant to indulge a sportive levity in a serious deed: for what is shameful and unlawful is not to be presumed. We call *absurd* not only what is *physically impossible,* but what is *morally* so,—that is to say, what is so contrary to reason, that it cannot be attributed to a man in his right senses. Those fanatic Jews, who scrupled to defend themselves when the enemy attacked them on the sabbath day, gave an absurd interpretation to the fourth commandment. Why did they not also abstain from dressing, walking, and eating? These also are *"works,"* if the term be strained to its utmost rigour. It is said that a man in England married three wives, in order that he might not be subject to the penalty of the law which forbids marrying two. This is doubtless a popular tale, invented with a view to ridicule the extreme circumspection of the English, who will not allow the smallest departure from the letter in the application of the law. That wise and free people have too often seen, by the experience of other nations, that the laws are no longer a firm barrier and secure defence, when once the executive power is allowed to interpret them at pleasure. But surely they do not mean that the letter of the law should on any occasion be strained to a sense that is manifestly absurd.

The rule we have just mentioned is absolutely necessary, and ought to be followed, even when the text of the law or treaty <253> does not, considered in itself, present either obscurity or ambiguity in the language. For it must be observed, that the uncertainty of the sense we are to give to a law or a treaty, does not solely proceed from the obscurity or other defect in the expression, but also from the limited nature of the human mind, which cannot foresee all cases and circumstances, nor take in at one view all the consequences of what is decreed or promised,—

and, finally, from the impossibility of entering into that immense detail. Laws and treaties can only be worded in a general manner; and it is the interpreter's province to apply them to particular cases, conformably to the intention of the legislature, or of the contracting powers. Now we are not in any case to presume that it was their intention to establish an absurdity: and therefore, when their expressions, taken in their proper and ordinary meaning, would lead to absurd consequences, it becomes necessary to deviate from that meaning, just so far as is sufficient to avoid absurdity. Let us suppose a captain has received orders to advance in a right line with his troops to a certain post: he finds a precipice in his way: surely his orders do not oblige him to leap headlong down: he must therefore deviate from the right line, so far as is necessary to avoid the precipice, but no farther.

The application of the rule is more easy, when the expressions of the law, or of the treaty, are susceptible of two different meanings. In this case we adopt without hesitation that meaning from which no absurdity follows. In the same manner, when the expression is such, that we may give it a figurative sense, we ought doubtless to do this, when it becomes necessary, in order to avoid falling into an absurdity.

It is not to be presumed that sensible persons, in treating together, or transacting any other serious business, meant that the result of their proceedings should prove a mere nullity. *The interpretation, therefore, which would render a treaty null and inefficient, cannot be admitted.* We may consider this rule as a branch of the preceding; for it is a kind of absurdity to suppose that the very terms of a deed should reduce it to mean nothing. *It ought to be interpreted in such a manner, as that it may have its effect, and not prove vain and nugatory:* and in this interpretation we proceed according to the mode pointed out in the foregoing section. In both cases, as in all interpretations, the question is, to give the words that sense which ought to be presumed most conformable to the intention of the parties speaking. If many different interpretations present themselves, by which we can conveniently avoid construing the deed into a nullity or an absurdity, we are to prefer that which appears the most agreeable to the intention of those who framed the deed: the particular circumstances of the case, aided by other rules of interpretation, will serve to

§283. and that which renders the act null and void of effect.

point it out. Thucydides relates,* that the Athe-<254>nians, after having promised to retire from the territories of the Boeotians, claimed a right to remain in the country under pretence that the lands actually occupied by their army did not belong to the Boeotians;—a ridiculous quibble, since, by giving that sense to the treaty, they reduced it to nothing, or rather to a puerile play. *The territories of the Boeotians* should evidently have been construed to mean all that was comprised within their former boundaries, without excepting what the enemy had seized during the war.

§284. Obscure expressions interpreted by others more clear in the same author.

If he who has expressed himself in an obscure or equivocal manner has spoken elsewhere more clearly on the same subject, he is the best interpreter of his own words. *We ought to interpret his obscure or equivocal expressions in such a manner, that they may agree with those clear and unequivocal terms which he has elsewhere used, either in the same deed, or on some other similar occasion.* In fact, while we have no proof that a man has changed his mind or manner of thinking, it is presumed that his thoughts have been the same on similar occasions; so that if he has anywhere clearly shewn his intention with respect to a certain thing, we ought to affix the same meaning to what he has elsewhere obscurely said on the same subject. Let us suppose, for instance, that two allies have reciprocally promised each other, in case of necessity, the assistance of ten thousand foot-soldiers who are to be supported at the expense of the party that sends them, and that, by a posterior treaty, they agree that the number of the auxiliary troops shall be fifteen thousand, without mentioning their support: the obscurity or uncertainty which remains in this article of the new treaty, is dissipated by the clear and express stipulation contained in the former one. As the allies do not give any indication that they have changed their minds with respect to the support of the auxiliary troops, we are not to presume any such change; and those fifteen thousand men are to be supported as the ten thousand promised in the first treaty. The same holds good, and with much stronger reason, when there is question of two articles of the same treaty,—when, for example, a prince promises to furnish ten thousand men, paid and maintained at

---

* [[*History of the Peloponnesian War,*]] Lib. iv. cap. xcviii.

his own expense, for the defence of the states of his ally,—and, in another article, only promises four thousand men, in case that ally be engaged in an offensive war.

It frequently happens, that, with a view to conciseness, people express imperfectly, and with some degree of obscurity, things which they suppose to be sufficiently elucidated by the preceding matter, or which they intend to explain in the sequel: and moreover, words and expressions have a different force, sometimes even a quite different signification, according to the occasion, their connection, and their relation to other words. The connection and train of the discourse is therefore another source of interpretation. *We must consider the whole discourse together, in order perfectly to conceive the sense of it, and to give to each expression, not so much the signification which it may individually ad-<255>mit of, as that which it ought to have from the context and spirit of the discourse.* Such is the maxim of the Roman law, *Incivile est, nisi totâ lege perspectâ, unâ aliquâ particulâ ejus propositâ, judicare, vel respondere.**[76]

§285. Interpretation founded on the connection of the discourse.

The very connection and relation of the things in question helps also to discover and establish the true sense of a treaty, or of any other piece. *The interpretation ought to be made in such a manner, that all the parts may appear consonant to each other,—that what follows may agree with what preceded,—unless it evidently appear, that, by the subsequent clauses, the parties intended to make some alteration in the preceding ones.* For it is to be presumed that the authors of a deed had an uniform and steady train of thinking,—that they did not aim at inconsistencies and contradictions,—but rather that they intended to explain one thing by another,—and, in a word, that one and the same spirit reigns throughout the same production or the same treaty. Let us render this more plain by an example. A treaty of alliance declares, that, in case one of the allies be attacked, each of the others shall assist him with a body of ten thousand foot, paid and supported; and in another article, it is said that the ally who is attacked shall be at liberty to demand the promised assistance

§286. Interpretation drawn from the connection and relation of the things themselves.

---

* Digest [[of Justinian]]. Lib. i. tit. iii. De Legibus, leg. 24.

76. "It is impertinent to give an opinion or make a response on any detail put forward without examining the whole law" (trans. Eds.).

in cavalry rather than in infantry. Here we see, that, in the first article, the allies have determined the quantum of the succour, and its value,— that of ten thousand foot; and, in the latter article, without appearing to intend any variation in the value or number, they leave the nature of the succours to the choice of the party who may stand in need of them. If therefore the ally who is attacked calls upon the others for cavalry, they will give him, according to the established proportion, an equivalent to ten thousand foot. But if it appears that the intention of the latter article was, that the promised succours should in certain cases be augmented,— if, for instance, it be said, that, in case one of the allies happen to be attacked by an enemy of considerably superior strength, and more powerful in cavalry, the succours shall be furnished in cavalry, and not in infantry,—it appears that, in this case, the promised assistance ought to be ten thousand horse.

As two articles in one and the same treaty may bear relation to each other, two different treaties may in like manner have a relative connection; and in this case, each serves to explain the other. For instance, one of the contracting parties has, in consideration of a certain object, promised to deliver to the other ten thousand sacks of wheat. By a subsequent agreement, it is determined, that, instead of wheat, he shall give him oats. The quantity of oats is not expressed; but it is determined by comparing the second convention with the first. If there be no circumstance to prove that it was the intention of the parties, in the second agreement, to diminish the value of what was to be delivered, we are to understand a quantity of oats proportioned to the price <256> of ten thousand sacks of wheat: but if it evidently appears, from the circumstances and motives of the second convention, that it was their intention to reduce the value of what was due under the former agreement,—in this case, ten thousand sacks of oats are to be substituted in lieu of the ten thousand sacks of wheat.

§287. Interpretation founded on the reason of the deed.   *The reason of the law,* or *of the treaty,*—that is to say, the motive which led to the making of it, and the object in contemplation at the time,— is the most certain clue to lead us to the discovery of its true meaning; and great attention should be paid to this circumstance, whenever there is question either of explaining an obscure, ambiguous, indeterminate passage in a law or treaty, or of applying it to a particular case. *When once we certainly know the reason which alone has determined the will of the person speaking, we ought to interpret and apply his words in a manner suitable to that reason alone.* Otherwise he will be made to speak and act contrary to his intention, and in opposition to his own views. Pursuant to this rule, a prince, who, on granting his daughter in marriage, has promised to assist his intended son-in-law in all his wars, is not bound to give him any assistance if the marriage does not take place.

But we ought to be very certain that we know the true and only reason of the law, the promise, or the treaty. In matters of this nature, it is not allowable to indulge in vague and uncertain conjectures, and to suppose reasons and views where there are none certainly known. If the piece in question is in itself obscure,—if, in order to discover its meaning, we have no other resource than the investigation of the author's views, or the motives of the deed,—we may then have recourse to conjecture, and, in default of absolute certainty, adopt, as the true meaning, that which has the greatest degree of probability on its side. But it is a dangerous abuse, to go, without necessity, in search of motives and uncertain views, in order to wrest, restrict, or extend the meaning of a deed which is of itself sufficiently clear, and carries no absurdity on the face of it. Such a procedure is a violation of that incontestable maxim,—that it is not allowable to interpret what has no need of interpretation (§263). Much less are we allowed,—when the author of a piece has in the piece itself declared his reasons and motives,—to attribute to him some secret reason, which may authorise us in giving an interpretation repugnant to the natural meaning of the expressions. Even though he should have entertained the views which we attribute to him,—yet, if he has concealed them, and announced different ones, it is upon the latter alone that we must build our interpretation, and not upon those which the author has not expressed:—we assume, as true, against him, what he has sufficiently declared (§266).

We ought to be the more circumspect in this kind of interpretation, as it frequently happens that several motives concur to determine the will of the party who speaks in a law or a promise. Perhaps the combined influence of all those motives was necessary <257> in order to determine

§288. Where many reasons have concurred to determine the will.

his will;—perhaps each one of them, taken individually, would have been sufficient to produce that effect. In the former case, *if we are perfectly certain that it was only in consideration of several concurrent reasons and motives that the legislature or the contracting parties consented to the law or the contract, the interpretation and application ought to be made in a manner agreeable to all those concurrent reasons,* and none of them must be overlooked. But in the latter case, *when it is evident that each of the reasons which have concurred in determining the will, was sufficient to produce that effect, so that the author of the piece in question would, by each of the reasons separately considered, have been induced to form the same determination which he has formed upon all the reasons taken in the aggregate, his words must be so interpreted and applied, as to make them accord with each of those reasons taken individually.* Suppose a prince has promised certain advantages to all foreign protestants and artisans who will come and settle in his states: if that prince is in no want of subjects, but of artisans only,—and if, on the other hand, it appears that he does not choose to have any other subjects than protestants,—his promise must be so interpreted, as to relate only to such foreigners as unite those two characters, of protestants and artisans. But if it is evident that this prince wants to people his country, and that, although he would prefer protestant subjects to others, he has in particular so great a want of artisans, that he would gladly receive them, of whatever religion they be,—his words should be taken in a disjunctive sense, so that it will be sufficient to be either a protestant or an artisan, in order to enjoy the promised advantages.

§289. What constitutes a sufficient reason for an act of the will.   To avoid tedious and complex circumlocution, we shall make use of the term, *"sufficient reason* for an act of the will," to express whatever has produced that act,—whatever has determined the will on a particular occasion; whether the will has been determined by a single reason, or by many concurrent reasons. That *sufficient reason,* then, will be sometimes found to consist in a combination of many different reasons, so that, where a single one of those reasons is wanting, the *sufficient reason* no longer exists: and in those cases where we say that many motives, many reasons, have concurred to determine the will, yet so as that each in particular would have been alone capable of producing the same effect,—

there will then be many *sufficient reasons* for producing one single act of the will. Of this we see daily instances. A prince, for example, declares war for three or four injuries received, each of which would have been sufficient to have produced the declaration of war.

The consideration of the reason of a law or promise not only serves to explain the obscure or ambiguous expressions which occur in the piece, but also to extend or restrict its several provisions independently of the expressions, and in conformity to the intention and views of the legislature or the contracting parties, rather than to their words. For, according to the remark of <258> Cicero,* the language, invented to explain the will, ought not to hinder its effect. *When the sufficient and only reason of a provision,* either in a law or a promise, *is perfectly certain, and well understood, we extend that provision to cases to which the same reason is applicable, although they be not comprised within the signification of the terms.* This is what is called *extensive interpretation.* It is commonly said, *that we ought to adhere rather to the spirit than to the letter.* Thus the Mahomedans justly extend the prohibition of wine, in the Koran, to all intoxicating liquors; that dangerous quality being the only reason that could induce their legislator to prohibit the use of wine. Thus also, if, at the time when there were no other fortifications than walls, it was agreed not to inclose a certain town with walls, it would not be allowable to fortify it with fossés and ramparts, since the only view of the treaty evidently was, to prevent its being converted into a fortified place.

§290. Extensive interpretation founded on the reason of the act.

But we should here observe the same caution above recommended (§287), and even still greater, since the question relates to an application in no wise authorised by the terms of the deed. We ought to be thoroughly convinced that we know the true and only reason of the law or

---

* Quid? verbis satis hoc cautum erat? Minime. Quae res igitur valuit? Voluntas: quae si, tacitis nobis, intelligi posset, verbis omnino non uteremur. Quia non potest, verba reperta sunt, non quae impedirent, sed quae indicarent voluntatem. [["Well, did the wording of the will provide adequately for this situation? Far from it. Then what was the deciding consideration? Intention; for if our intention could be made clear without speaking, we should not use words at all; but because it cannot, words have been invented, not to conceal but to reveal intention."]] Cicer. Orat. pro Caecina [[53]].

the promise, and that the author has taken it in the same latitude which must be given to it in order to make it reach the case to which we mean to extend the law or promise in question. As to the rest, I do not here forget what I have said above (§268), that the true sense of a promise is not only that which the person promising had in his mind, but also that which has been sufficiently declared,—that which both the contracting parties must reasonably have understood. In like manner, the true reason of a promise is that which the contract, the nature of the things in question, and other circumstances, sufficiently indicate: it would be useless and ridiculous to allege any by-views which the person might have secretly entertained in his own mind.

§291. Frauds tending to elude laws or promises. The rule just laid down serves also to defeat the pretexts and pitiful evasions of those who endeavour to elude laws or treaties. Good-faith adheres to the intention; fraud insists on the terms, when it thinks that they can furnish a cloak for its prevarications. The isle of Pharos near Alexandria was, with other islands, tributary to the Rhodians. The latter having sent collectors to levy the tribute, the queen of Egypt amused them for some time at her court, using in the mean while every possible exertion to join Pharos to the main land by means of moles: after which she laughed at the Rhodians, and sent them a message intimating that it was very unreasonable in them to pretend to levy on the main land a tribute which they had no title to demand except from the islands.* There existed a law <259> which forbade the Corinthians to *give* vessels to the Athenians:—they sold them a number at five drachmae each.† The following was an expedient worthy of Tiberius:[77] custom not permitting him to cause a virgin to be strangled, he ordered the executioner first to deflower the young daughter of Sejanus,[78] and then to strangle

---

* Puffendorf [[*Of the Law of Nature and Nations*]], lib. v. cap. xii. §18. He quotes Ammianus Marcellinus, lib. xxii. cap. xvi.

† Puffend. ibid.—Herodotus, lib. vi.—Five drachmae amounted to little more than three shillings sterling.

77. Tiberius, emperor of Rome, r. A.D. 14–37.

78. Lucius Aelius Sejanus (20 B.C.–A.D. 31), appointed praetorian prefect by Tiberius.

her.* To violate the spirit of the law while we pretend to respect the letter, is a fraud no less criminal than an open violation of it; it is equally repugnant to the intention of the law-maker, and only evinces a more artful and deliberate villany in the person who is guilty of it.

Restrictive interpretation, which is the reverse of *extensive interpretation,* is founded on the same principle. As we extend a clause to those cases, which, though not comprised within the meaning of the terms, are nevertheless comprised in the intention of that clause, and included in the reasons that produced it,—in like manner, we restrict a law or a promise, contrary to the literal signification of the terms,—our judgment being directed by the reason of that law or that promise: that is to say, *if a case occurs, to which the well-known reason of a law or promise is utterly inapplicable, that case ought to be excepted, although, if we were barely to consider the meaning of the terms, it should seem to fall within the purview of the law or promise.* It is impossible to think of every thing, to foresee every thing, and to express every thing; it is sufficient to enounce certain things in such a manner as to make known our thoughts concerning things of which we do not speak: and, as Seneca the rhetorician says,† there are exceptions so clear, that it is unnecessary to express them. The law condemns to suffer death whoever strikes his father: shall we punish him who has shaken and struck his father, to recover him from a lethargic stupor? shall we punish a young child, or a man in a delirium, who has lifted his hand against the author of his life? In the former case the reason of the law does not hold good; and to the two latter it is inapplicable. We are bound to restore what is intrusted to us: shall I restore what a robber has intrusted to me, at the time when the true proprietor makes himself known to me, and demands his property? A man has left his sword with me: shall I restore it to him, when, in a transport of fury, he demands it for the purpose of killing an innocent person?

§292. Restrictive interpretation.

---

* Tacit. Annal. lib. v. 9.
† [[Seneca, *De beneficiis*]] Lib. iv. Declam. xxvii.

§293. Its use, in order to avoid falling into absurdities, or into what is unlawful;

We have recourse to restrictive interpretation, in order to avoid falling into absurdities (see §282). A man bequeaths his house to one, and to another his garden, the only entrance into which is through the house. It would be absurd to suppose that he had bequeathed to the latter a garden into which he could not enter: we must therefore restrict the pure and simple donation of the house, and understand that it was given only upon condition of allowing a passage to the gar-<260>den. The same mode of interpretation is to be adopted whenever a case occurs, in which the law or the treaty, if interpreted according to the strict meaning of the terms, would lead to something unlawful. On such an occasion, the case in question is to be excepted, since nobody can ordain or promise what is unlawful. For this reason, though assistance has been promised to an ally in all his wars, no assistance ought to be given him when he undertakes one that is manifestly unjust.

§294. or what is too severe and burthensome.

When a case arises in which it would be too severe and too prejudicial to any one to interpret a law or a promise according to the rigour of the terms, a restrictive interpretation is then also used, and we except the case in question, agreeably to the intention of the legislature, or of him who made the promise: for the legislature intends only what is just and equitable; and, in contracts, no one can enter into such engagements in favour of another, as shall essentially supersede the duty he owes to himself. It is then presumed with reason, that neither the legislature nor the contracting parties have intended to extend their regulations to cases of this nature, and that they themselves, if personally present, would except them. A prince is no longer obliged to send succours to his allies, when he himself is attacked, and has need of all his forces for his own defence. He may also, without the slightest imputation of perfidy, abandon an alliance, when, through the ill success of the war, he sees his state threatened with impending ruin if he does not immediately treat with the enemy. Thus, towards the end of the last century, Victor Amadeus, duke of Savoy,[79] found himself under the necessity of separating from his allies, and of receiving law from France, to avoid losing his states. The

79. Victor Amadeus II, duke of Savoy, r. 1675–1720.

king his son[80] would have had good reasons to justify a separate peace in the year 1745: but upheld by his courage, and animated by just views of his true interest, he embraced the generous resolution to struggle against an extremity which might have dispensed with his persisting in his engagements.

We have said above (§280), that we should take the expressions in the sense that agrees with the subject or the matter. Restrictive interpretation is also directed by this rule. *If the subject or the matter treated of will not allow that the terms of a clause should be taken in their full extent, we should limit the sense according as the subject requires.* Let us suppose that the custom of a particular country confines the entail of fiefs to the male line properly so called: if an act of enfeoffment in that country declares that the fief is given to a person for himself and his male descendents, the sense of these last words must be restricted to the males descending from males; for the subject will not admit of our understanding them also of males who are the issue of females, though they are reckoned among the male descendents of the first possessor.

§295. How it ought to restrict the signification agreeably to the subject.

The following question has been proposed and debated,—"Whether promises include a tacit condition of the state of af-<261>fairs continuing the same,—or whether a change happening in the state of affairs can create an exception to the promise, and even render it void." The principle derived from the reason of the promise, must solve the question. *If it be certain and manifest, that the consideration of the present state of things was one of the reasons which occasioned the promise,—that the promise was made in consideration or in consequence of that state of things,—it depends on the preservation of things in the same state.* This is evident, since the promise was made only upon that supposition. When therefore that state of things, which was essential to the promise, and without which it certainly would not have been made, happens to be changed, the promise falls to the ground, when its foundation fails. And in particular cases where things cease for a time to be in the state that has produced or concurred to produce the promise, an exception is to

§296. How a change happening in the state of things may form an exception.

80. Charles Emmanuel III, son of Victor Amadeus II and king of Sardinia, r. 1730–73.

be made to it. An elective prince being without issue, has promised to an ally that he will procure his appointment to the succession. He has a son born: who can doubt that the promise is made void by this event? He who in a time of peace has promised succours to an ally, is not bound to give him any when he himself has need of all his forces for the defence of his own dominions. A prince, possessed of no very formidable power, has received from his allies a promise of faithful and constant assistance, in order to his aggrandisement,—in order to enable him to obtain a neighbouring state by election or by marriage: yet those allies will have just grounds for refusing him the smallest aid or support, and even form-ing an alliance against him, when they see him elevated to such a height of power, as to threaten the liberties of all Europe. If the great Gustavus had not been killed at Lutzen,[81] cardinal de Richelieu, who had con-cluded an alliance for his master with that prince, and who had invited him into Germany, and assisted him with money, would perhaps have found himself obliged to traverse the designs of that conqueror, when become formidable,—to set bounds to his astonishing progress, and to support his humbled enemies. The states-general of the United Prov-inces conducted themselves on these principles in 1668. In favour of Spain, which before had been their mortal enemy, they formed the triple alliance against Louis XIV. their former ally. It was necessary to raise a barrier to check the progress of a power which threatened to inundate and overwhelm all before it.

But we ought to be very cautious and moderate in the application of the present rule: it would be a shameful perversion of it, to take advan-tage of every change that happens in the state of affairs, in order to dis-engage ourselves from our promises: were such conduct adopted, there could be no dependence placed on any promise whatever. That state of things alone, in consideration of which the promise was made, is essen-tial to the promise: and it is only by a change in that state, that the effect of the promise can be lawfully prevented or suspended.—Such is the

81. Gustavus Adolphus, king of Sweden, was killed in the battle of Lützen in 1632.

<262> sense in which we are to understand that maxim of the civilians, *conventio omnis intelligitur rebus sic stantibus.*[82]

What we say of promises, must also be understood as extending to laws. A law which relates to a certain situation of affairs can only take place in that situation. We ought to reason in the same manner with respect to a commission. Thus, Titus[83] being sent by his father to pay his respects to the emperor, turned back on being informed of the death of Galba.[84]

In unforeseen cases, that is to say, when the state of things happens to be such as the author of a deed has not foreseen, and could not have thought of, *we should rather be guided by his intention than by his words, and interpret the instrument as he himself would interpret it if he were on the spot, or conformably to what he would have done if he had foreseen the circumstances which are at present known.* This rule is of great use to judges, and to all those in society who are appointed to carry into effect the testamentary regulations of the citizens. A father appoints by will a guardian for his children, who are under age. After his death the magistrate finds that the guardian he has nominated is an extravagant profligate, without property or conduct: he therefore dismisses him, and appoints another, according to the Roman laws,* adhering to the intention of the testator, and not to his words; for it is but reasonable to suppose,—and we are to presume it as a fact,—that the father never intended to give his children a guardian who should ruin them, and that he would have nominated another, had he known the vices of the person he appointed.

§297. Interpretation of a deed in unforeseen cases.

When the things which constitute the reason of a law or convention, are considered, not as actually existing, but simply as possible,—or, in other words, *when the fear of an event is the reason of a law or a promise, no other cases can be excepted from it, than those in which it can be proved to demonstration that the event is really impossible.* The bare possibility of

§298. Reasons arising from the possibility and not the existence of a thing.

---

* Digest [[of Justinian]]. lib. xxvi. tit. iii. De Confirm. Tutor. leg. 10.

82. "In every convention it must be understood that material conditions must remain the same" (trans. Eds.).

83. Titus Flavius Vespasianus (A.D. 39–81), son of Vespasian (r. A.D. 69–79), succeeded his father as Roman emperor, r. A.D. 79–81.

84. Servius Sulpicius Galba (3 B.C.–A.D. 69), Roman emperor, r. A.D. 68–69.

the event is sufficient to preclude all exceptions. If, for instance, a treaty declares that no army or fleet shall be conducted to a certain place, it will not be allowable to conduct thither an army or a fleet, under pretence that no harm is intended by such a step: for the object of a clause of this nature is not only to prevent a real evil, but also to keep all danger at a distance, and to avoid even the slightest subject of uneasiness. It is the same with the law which forbids walking the streets by night with a lighted torch or candle. It would be an unavailing plea for the transgressor of that law to allege that no mischief has ensued, and that he carried his torch with such circumspection, that no ill consequence was to be apprehended. The bare possibility of causing a conflagration was sufficient to have rendered it his duty to obey the law; and he has transgressed it by ex-<263>citing fears which it was the intention of the legislature to prevent.

§299. Expressions capable of an extensive and a limited sense.   At the beginning of this chapter, we observed that men's ideas and language are not always perfectly determinate. There is, doubtless, no language in which there do not occur expressions, words, or entire phrases, susceptible of a more or less extensive signification. Many a word is equally applicable to the genus or the species:—the word *fault* implies intentional *guilt* or simple *error:*—several species of animals have but one name common to both sexes, as *partridge, lark, sparrow,* &c.— when we speak of *horses* merely with a view to the services they render to mankind, *mares* also are comprehended under that name. In technical language a word has sometimes a more and sometimes a less extensive sense, than in vulgar use: the word *death,* among civilians, signifies not only natural death, but also civil death: *verbum,* in the Latin grammar, signifies only that part of speech called the *verb;* but, in common use, it signifies any *word* in general. Frequently also the same phrase implies more things on one occasion, and fewer on another, according to the nature of the subject or matter: thus, when we talk of *sending succours,* sometimes we understand a body of auxiliary troops maintained and paid by the party who sends them, at other times a body whose expenses are to be entirely defrayed by the party who receives them. It is therefore necessary to establish rules for the interpretation of those indeterminate expressions, in order to ascertain the cases in which they are to be understood in the more extensive sense, and those in which they are to be restricted to their more limited meaning. Many of the rules we have already given may serve for this purpose.

But it is to this head that the famous distinction, between things of a *favourable* and those of an *odious* nature, particularly belongs. Some writers have rejected the distinction,*—doubtless, for want of properly understanding it.[85] In fact, the definitions that have been given of what is *favourable* and what is *odious,* are not fully satisfactory, nor easily applied. After having maturely considered what the most judicious authors have written on the subject, I conceive the whole of the question to be reducible to the following positions, which convey a just idea of that famous distinction. When the provisions of a law or a convention are plain, clear, determinate, and attended with no doubt or difficulty in the application, there is no room for any interpretation or comment (§263). The precise point of the will of the legislature or the contracting parties, is what we must adhere to. But if their expressions are indeterminate, vague, or susceptible of a more or less extensive sense,—if that precise point of their intention cannot, in the particular case in question, be discovered and fixed by the other rules of interpretation,—we must presume it according to the laws of reason and <264> equity: and, for this purpose, it is necessary to pay attention to the nature of the things to which the question relates. There are certain things of which equity admits the extension rather than the restriction; that is to say, that, with respect to those things, the precise point of the will not being discovered in the expressions of the law or the contract, it is safer and more consistent with equity, to suppose and fix that point in the more extensive than in the more limited sense of the terms,—to give a latitude to the meaning of the expressions, than to restrict it. These are the things called *favourable. Odious* things, on the other hand, are those, of which the restriction tends more certainly to equity, than the extension. Let us fig-

§300. Of things favourable, and things odious.

---

* See Barbeyrac's remarks on Grotius and Puffendorf.

85. Jean Barbeyrac (1674–1744) commented on Grotius's *De jure belli* in his edition of 1720 (Amsterdam) and on Pufendorf's *Les devoirs de l'homme et du citoien* in his edition of 1707 (Amsterdam).

ure to ourselves the intention or the will of the legislature or the contracting parties, as a fixed point. At that point precisely should we stop, if it be clearly known;—if uncertain, we should at least endeavour to approach it. In things favourable, it is better to pass beyond that point, than not to reach it; in things odious, it is better not to reach it, than to pass beyond it.

§301. What tends to the common advantage, and to equality, is favourable; the contrary is odious.

It will not now be difficult to shew, in general, what things are *favourable,* and what are *odious.* In the first place, *every thing that tends to the common advantage in conventions, or that has a tendency to place the contracting parties on a footing of equality, is favourable.* The voice of equity, and the general rule of contracts, require that the conditions between the parties should be equal. We are not to presume, without very strong reasons, that one of the contracting parties intended to favour the other to his own prejudice; but there is no danger in extending what is for the common advantage. If, therefore, it happens that the contracting parties have not made known their will with sufficient clearness, and with all the necessary precision, it is certainly more conformable to equity to seek for that will in the sense most favourable to equality and the common advantage, than to suppose it in the contrary sense. For the same reason, *every thing that is not for the common advantage, every thing that tends to destroy the equality of a contract, every thing that onerates only one of the parties, or that onerates the one more than the other, is odious.* In a treaty of strict friendship, union, and alliance, every thing which, without being burthensome to any of the parties, tends to the common advantage of the confederacy, and to draw the bonds of union closer, is favourable. In unequal treaties, and especially in unequal alliances, all the clauses of inequality, and principally those that onerate the inferior ally, are odious. Upon this principle, that we ought, in case of doubt, to extend what leads to equality, and restrict what destroys it, is founded that well-known rule—*Incommoda vitantis melior quam commoda petentis est causa,**—*the party who endeavours to avoid a loss, has a better cause to support than he who aims at obtaining an advantage.* <265>

---

* Quintilian, Instit. Orat. lib. vii. cap. iv.

All those things which, without proving too burthensome to any one in particular, are useful and salutary to human society, are to be ranked in the class of favourable things: for a nation is already under a natural obligation with respect to things of this nature; so that if she has entered into any particular engagements of this kind, we run no risk in giving those engagements the most extensive meaning of which they are susceptible. Can we be afraid of violating the rules of equity by following the law of nature, and giving the utmost extent to obligations that tend to the common advantage of mankind? Besides, things which are useful to human society, are, from that very circumstance, conducive to the common advantage of the contracting parties, and are consequently favourable (see the preceding section). On the other hand, let us *consider as odious, every thing that is, in its own nature, rather injurious than useful to mankind.* Those things which have a tendency to promote peace are favourable; those that lead to war are odious.

§302. What is useful to human society, is favourable; the contrary is odious.

Every thing that contains a penalty, is odious. With respect to the laws, it is universally agreed, that, in case of doubt, the judge ought to incline to the merciful side, and that it is indisputably better to suffer a guilty person to escape, than to punish one who is innocent. Penal clauses in treaties lay a burthen upon one of the parties; they are therefore *odious* (§301).

§303. Whatever contains a penalty, is odious.

Whatever tends to render a deed void and ineffectual, either in the whole or in part, and consequently, *whatever introduces any change in things already agreed upon, is odious:* for men treat together with a view to their common benefit; and if I enjoy any particular advantage acquired by a lawful contract, I must not be deprived of it except by my own renunciation. When therefore I consent to new clauses that seem to derogate from it, I can lose my right only so far as I have clearly given it up; and consequently these new clauses are to be understood in the most limited sense they will admit of; as is the case in things of an odious nature (§300). If that which tends to render a deed void and ineffectual, is contained in the deed itself, it is evident that such passages ought to be construed in the most limited sense, in the sense best calculated to preserve the deed in force. We have already seen, that we should reject every interpretation which tends to render a deed void and ineffectual (§283).

§304. Whatever renders a deed void, is odious.

§305. What-
ever tends to
change the
present state
of things, is
odious; the
contrary is
favourable.

Whatever tends to change the present state of things, is also *to be ranked in the class of odious things:* for the proprietor cannot be deprived of his right except so far, precisely, as he relinquishes it on his part; and in case of doubt, the presumption is in favour of the possessor. It is less repugnant to equity to with-hold from the owner a possession which he has lost through his own neglect, than to strip the just possessor of what lawfully belongs to him. In the interpretation, therefore, we ought rather to hazard the former inconvenience than the latter. Here also may be applied, in many cases, the rule we have mentioned in §301, that the party who endeavours to avoid a loss, has a better cause to support than he who aims at obtaining an advantage. <266>

§306. Things
of a mixed
nature.

Finally, there are things which are at once of a *favourable* or an *odious* nature, according to the point of view in which they are considered. Whatever derogates from treaties, or changes the state of things, is odious; but if it is conducive to peace, it is, in that particular, favourable. A degree of odium always attaches to penalties: they may, however, be viewed in a favourable light on those occasions when they are particularly necessary for the safety of society. When there is question of interpreting things of this nature, we ought to consider whether what is favourable in them greatly exceeds what appears odious,—whether the advantage that arises from their being extended to the utmost latitude of which the terms are susceptible, will materially outweigh the severe and odious circumstances attending them; and if that is the case, they are to be ranked in the class of favourable things. Thus an inconsiderable change in the state of things or in conventions is reckoned as nothing, when it procures the inestimable blessings of peace. In the same manner, penal laws may be interpreted in their most extensive meaning, on critical occasions when such an instance of severity becomes necessary to the safety of the state. Cicero caused the accomplices of Catiline[86] to be executed by virtue of a decree of the senate,—the safety of the republic rendering it improper to wait till they should be condemned by the people. But where

---

86. Lucius Sergius Catilina, ca. 108–62 B.C., Roman politician and soldier notoriously denounced by Cicero for seeking to overthrow the republic.

there is not so great a disproportion in the case, and where things are in other respects equal, favour inclines to that side of the question which presents nothing odious;—that is to say, we ought to abstain from things of an odious nature, unless the attendant advantage so far exceed the odious part, as in a manner to conceal it from view. If there be any appearance, however small, of an equilibrium between the odious and the favourable in one of those things of a mixed nature, it is ranked in the class of odious things, by a natural consequence drawn from the principle on which we have founded the distinction between things of a favourable and things of an odious nature (§300), because, in case of doubt, we should in preference pursue that line of conduct by which we are least exposed to deviate from the principles of equity. In a doubtful case, we may reasonably refuse to give succours (though a thing favourable), when there is question of giving them against an ally,—which would be odious.

The following are the rules of interpretation, which flow from the principles we have just laid down.

§307. Interpretation of favourable things.

1. *When the question relates to things favourable, we ought to give the terms the utmost latitude of which they are susceptible according to the common usage of the language; and if a term has more than one signification, the most extensive meaning is to be preferred:* for equity ought to be the rule of conduct with all mankind wherever a perfect right is not exactly determined and known in its precise extent. When the legislature or the contracting parties have not expressed their will in terms that are precise and perfectly determinate, it is to be presumed that they <267> intended what is most equitable. Now, when there is question of favourable things, the more extensive signification of the terms accords better with equity than their more confined signification. Thus Cicero, in pleading the cause of Caecina, justly maintains that the interlocutory decree, ordaining, *"that the person expelled from his inheritance be reinstated in the possession,"* should be understood as extending to the man who has been forcibly prevented from entering upon it:* and the Digest decides it in

---

* Orat. pro Caecina, cap. xxiii.

the same manner.* It is true that this decision is also founded on the rule taken from parity of reasoning (§290). For it amounts to the same thing in effect, to drive a person from his inheritance, or forcibly to prevent him from entering upon it; and, in both cases, the same reason exists for putting him in possession.

2. *In questions relating to favourable things, all terms of art are to be interpreted in the fullest latitude of which they are susceptible, not only in common usage, but also as technical terms, if the person speaking understands the art to which those terms belong, or conducts himself by the advice of men who understand that art.*

3. *But we ought not, from the single reason that a thing is favourable, to take the terms in an improper signification: this is not allowable, except when necessary in order to avoid absurdity, injustice, or the nullity of the instrument,* as is practised on every subject (§§282, 283): for we ought to take the terms of a deed in their proper sense, conformably to custom, unless we have very strong reasons for deviating from it (§271).

4. *Though a thing appears favourable when viewed in one particular light,—yet, where the proper meaning of the terms would, if taken in its utmost latitude, lead to absurdity or injustice, their signification must be restricted according to the rules given above* (§§293, 294). For here, in this particular case, the thing becomes of a *mixed* nature, and even such as ought to be ranked in the class of odious things.

5. For the same reason, *although neither absurdity nor injustice results from the proper meaning of the terms,—if, nevertheless, manifest equity or a great common advantage requires their restriction, we ought to adhere to the most limited sense which the proper signification will admit, even in an affair that appears favourable in its own nature,*—because here also the thing is of a *mixed* kind, and ought, in this particular case, to be esteemed odious. As to the rest, it is to be carefully remembered that all these rules relate only to doubtful cases; since we are not allowed to go in quest of interpretations for what is already clear and determinate (§263). If any one has clearly and formally bound himself to burthen-

---

* Digest [[of Justinian]]. lib. xliii. tit. xvi. De Vi, et Vi Armata, legg. 1 et 3.

some conditions, he has knowingly and willingly done it, and cannot afterwards be admitted to appeal to equity.

Since odious things are those whose restriction tends more certainly to equity than their extension,—and since we ought to <268> pursue that line which is most conformable to equity, when the will of the legislature or of the contracting parties is not exactly determined and precisely known,—*we should, when there is question of odious things, interpret the terms in the most limited sense: we may even, to a certain degree, adopt a figurative meaning, in order to avert the oppressive consequences of the proper and literal sense, or any thing of an odious nature, which it would involve:* for we are to favour equity, and to do away every thing odious, as far as that can be accomplished without going in direct opposition to the tenor of the instrument, or visibly wresting the text. Now neither the limited nor even the figurative sense offers any violence to the text. If it is said in a treaty, that one of the allies shall assist the other with a certain number of troops at his own expense, and that the latter shall furnish the same number of auxiliary troops at the expense of the party to whom they are sent, there is something odious in the engagement of the former ally, since he is subject to a greater burthen than the other: but the terms being clear and express, there is no room for any restrictive interpretation. But if it were stipulated in this treaty, that one of the allies shall furnish a body of ten thousand men, and the other only of five thousand, without mentioning the expense, it ought to be understood that the auxiliary troops shall be supported at the expense of the ally to whose assistance they are sent; this interpretation being necessary, in order that the inequality between the contracting powers may not be carried too far. Thus the cession of a right or of a province, made to a conqueror in order to obtain peace, is interpreted in its most confined sense. If it be true that the boundaries of Acadia have always been uncertain, and that the French were the lawful possessors of it, that nation will be justified in maintaining that their cession of Acadia to the English by the treaty of Utrecht did not extend beyond the narrowest limits of that province.

In point of penalties, in particular when they are really odious, we ought not only to restrict the terms of the law, or of the contract, to

§308. Interpretation of odious things.

their most limited signification, and even adopt a figurative meaning, according as the case may require or authorise it,—but also to admit of reasonable excuses; which is a kind of restrictive interpretation, tending to exempt the party from the penalty.

The same conduct must be observed with respect to what may render an act void and without effect. Thus, when it is agreed that the treaty shall be dissolved whenever one of the contracting parties fails in the observance of any article of it, it would be at once both unreasonable and contrary to the end proposed in making treaties, to extend that clause to the slightest faults, and to cases in which the defaulter can allege well-grounded excuses.

§309.
Examples.

Grotius proposes the following question—"Whether, in a treaty which makes mention of allies, we are to understand those only who were in alliance at the time when the treaty was made, or <269> all the allies present and future?"* And he gives, as an instance, that article of the treaty concluded between the Romans and Carthaginians, after the war of Sicily,—that "neither of the two nations should do any injury to the allies of the other." In order to understand this part of the treaty, it is necessary to call to mind the barbarous law of nations observed by those ancient people. They thought themselves authorised to attack, and to treat as enemies, all with whom they were not united by any alliance. The article therefore signifies, that on both sides they should treat as friends the allies of their ally, and abstain from molesting or invading them: upon this footing it is in all respects so favourable, so conformable to humanity, and to the sentiments which ought to unite two allies, that it should, without hesitation, be extended to all the allies, present and future. The clause cannot be said to involve any thing of an odious nature, as cramping the freedom of a sovereign state, or tending to dissolve an alliance: for, by engaging not to injure the allies of another power, we do not deprive ourselves of the liberty to make war on them if they give us just cause for hostilities; and when a clause is just and reasonable, it does not become odious from the single circumstance that it *may* perhaps eventually occasion a rupture of the alliance. Were that to be the

* Lib. ii. cap. xvi. §13 [[*Law of War and Peace*]].

case, there could be no clause whatever, that might not be deemed odious. This reason, which we have touched upon in the preceding section and in §304, holds good only in doubtful cases: in the case before us, for instance, it ought to have prevented a too hasty decision that the Carthaginians had causelessly attacked an ally of the Romans. The Carthaginians, therefore, might, without any violation of the treaty, attack Saguntum, if they had lawful grounds for such an attack, or (in virtue of the voluntary law of nations) even apparent or specious grounds (Prelim. §21). But they might have attacked in the same manner the most ancient ally of the Romans; and the Romans might also, without breaking the treaty of peace, have confined themselves to the succouring of Saguntum. At present, treaties include the allies on both sides: but this does not imply that one of the contracting powers may not make war on the allies of the other if they give him cause for it,—but simply, that, in case of any quarrel arising between them, each of the contracting parties reserves to himself a power of assisting his more ancient ally: and, in this sense, the future allies are not included in the treaty.

Another example mentioned by Grotius is also taken from a treaty concluded between Rome and Carthage. When the latter city was reduced to extremities by Scipio Aemilianus, and obliged to capitulate,[87] the Romans promised "that Carthage should remain free, or in possession of the privilege of governing herself by her own laws."* In the sequel, however, those merciless conquerors pretended that the promised liberty regarded the <270> inhabitants, and not the city: they insisted that Carthage should be demolished, and that the wretched inhabitants should settle in a place at a greater distance from the sea. One cannot read the account of this perfidious and cruel treatment, without being concerned that the great, the amiable Scipio was obliged to be the instrument of it. To say nothing of the chicanery of the Romans respecting the meaning to be annexed to the word *"Carthage,"*—certainly, the *"liberty"* promised to the Carthaginians, though narrowly circumscribed by

---

* Αυτονομος. Appian. de Bello Punico.

87. Under the Roman general Scipio Aemilianus, the city of Carthage was destroyed in 146 B.C.

the existing state of affairs, should at least have extended to the privilege of remaining in their city. To find themselves obliged to abandon it and settle elsewhere,—to lose their houses, their port, and the advantages of their situation,—was a subjection incompatible with the smallest degree of liberty, and involved such considerable losses as they could not have bound themselves to submit to, unless by a positive engagement in the most express and formal terms.

§310. How we ought to interpret deeds of pure liberality.   Liberal promises, benefactions, and rewards, naturally come under the class of favourable things, and receive an extensive interpretation, unless they prove onerous or unreasonably chargeable to the benefactor, or that other circumstances evidently shew they are to be taken in a limited sense. For kindness, benevolence, beneficence, and generosity, are liberal virtues; they do not act in a penurious manner, and know no other bounds than those set by reason. But if the benefaction falls too heavy upon him who grants it, in this respect it partakes of the odious; and, in case of doubt, equity will not admit the presumption that it has been granted or promised in the utmost extent of the terms: we ought therefore, in such case, to confine ourselves to the most limited signification which the words are capable of receiving, and thus reduce the benefaction within the bounds of reason. The same mode should be adopted when other circumstances evidently point out the more limited signification as the more equitable.

Upon these principles, the bounties of a sovereign are usually taken in the fullest extent of the terms.* It is not presumed that he finds himself over-burthened by them: it is a respect due to majesty, to suppose that he had good reasons to induce him to confer them. They are therefore, in their own nature, altogether favourable; and, in order to restrict them, it must be proved that they are burthensome to the prince, or prejudicial to the state. On the whole, we ought to apply to deeds of

---

* Such is the decision of the Roman law.—Javolenus [[Javolenus Priscus, Roman jurist, praetor, and proconsul, A.D. 60–120]] says: "Beneficium imperatoris quam plenissime interpretari debemus"; and he gives this reason for it, "quod a divina ejus indulgentia proficiscatur." [["We should interpret the bounty of the emperor as generously as possible . . . because it proceeds from his divine permissiveness."]] Digest [[of Justinian]]. lib. i. tit. iv. de Constit. Princ. leg. 3.

pure liberality the general rule established above (§270); if those instruments are not precise and very determinate, they should be interpreted as meaning what the author probably had in his mind. <271>

Let us conclude this subject of interpretation with what relates to the collision or opposition of laws or treaties. We do not here speak of the collision of a treaty with the law of nature: the latter is unquestionably paramount, as we have proved elsewhere (§§160, 161, 170, and 293). There is a collision or opposition between two laws, two promises, or two treaties, when a case occurs in which it is impossible to fulfil both at the same time, though otherwise the laws or treaties in question are not contradictory, and may be both fulfilled under different circumstances. They are considered as contrary in this particular case; and it is required to shew which deserves the preference, or to which an exception ought to be made on the occasion. In order to guard against all mistake in the business, and to make the exception conformably to reason and justice, we should observe the following rules.

§311. Collision of laws or treaties.

1. *In all cases where what is barely permitted is found incompatible with what is positively prescribed, the latter claims a preference:* for the mere permission imposes no obligation to do or not to do: what is permitted is left to our own option: we are at liberty either to do it or forbear to do it. But we have not the same liberty with respect to what is prescribed: we are obliged to do that: nor can the bare permission in the former case interfere with the discharge of our obligation in the latter; but, on the contrary, that which was before permitted in general, ceases to be so in this particular instance, where we cannot take advantage of the permission without violating a positive duty.

§312. First rule in cases of collision.

2. In the same manner, *the law or treaty which permits, ought to give way to the law or treaty which forbids:* for the prohibition must be obeyed; and what was, in its own nature, or in general, permitted, must not be attempted when it cannot be done without contravening a prohibition: the permission, in that case, ceases to be available.

§313. 2d Rule.

3. All circumstances being otherwise equal, *the law or the treaty which ordains, gives way to the law or the treaty which forbids.* I say, "all circumstances being otherwise equal"; for many other reasons may occur, which will authorise the exception being made to the prohibitory law or treaty.

§314. 3d Rule.

The rules are general; each relates to an abstract idea, and shews what follows from that idea, without derogation to the other rules. Upon this footing, it is evident, that, in general, if we cannot obey an injunctive law without violating a prohibitory one, we should abstain from fulfilling the former: for the prohibition is absolute in itself, whereas every precept, every injunction, is in its own nature conditional, and supposes the power, or a favourable opportunity, of doing what is prescribed. Now when that cannot be accomplished without contravening a prohibition, the opportunity is wanting, and this collision of laws produces a moral impossibility of acting; for what is prescribed in general, is no longer so in the case where it cannot be done without committing an action <272> that is forbidden.* Upon this ground rests the generally received maxim that we are not justifiable in employing unlawful means to accomplish a laudable end,—as, for instance, in stealing with a view to give alms. But it is evident that the question here regards an absolute prohibition, or those cases to which the general prohibition is truly applicable, and therefore equivalent to an absolute one: there are, however, many prohibitions to which circumstances form an exception. Our meaning will be better explained by an example. It is expressly forbidden, for reasons to me unknown, to pass through a certain place under any pretence whatsoever. I am ordered to carry a message; I find every other avenue shut; I therefore turn back rather than take my passage over that ground which is so strictly forbidden. But if the prohibition to pass be only a general one with a view to prevent any injury being done to the productions of the soil, it is easy for me to judge that the orders with which I am charged ought to form an exception.

As to what relates to treaties, we are not obliged to accomplish what a treaty prescribes, any farther than we have the power. Now we have not a power to do what another treaty forbids: wherefore, in case of

---

* The prohibitory law creates, in that particular instance, an exception to the injunctive law. "Deinde utra lex jubeat, utra vetet. Nam saepe ea quae vetat, quasi exceptione quadam corrigere videtur illam quae jubet." [["Then, which law enjoins and which prohibits, for frequently the law that prohibits seems to have amended the law that enjoins by making an exception."]] Cicero, de Inventione, lib. ii. 145 [[146]].

collision, an exception is made to the injunctive treaty, and the prohibitory treaty has a superior claim to our observance,—provided, however, that all circumstances be in other respects equal; for it will presently appear, for instance, that a subsequent treaty cannot derogate from a prior one concluded with another state, nor hinder its effect directly or indirectly.

4. The dates of laws or treaties furnish new reasons for establishing the exception in cases of collision. *If the collision happen between two affirmative laws, or two affirmative treaties concluded between the same persons or the same states,* that which is of more recent date claims a preference over the older one: for it is evident, that, since both laws or both treaties have emanated from the same power, the subsequent act was capable of derogating from the former. But still this is on the supposition of circumstances being in other respects equal.—*If there be a collision between two treaties made with two different powers, the more ancient claims the preference:* for, no engagement of a contrary tenor could be contracted in the subsequent treaty; and if this latter be found, in any case, incompatible with that of more ancient date, its execution is considered as impossible, because the person promising had not the power of acting contrary to his antecedent engagements.

§315.
4th Rule.

5. *Of two laws or two conventions, we ought (all other circumstances being equal) to prefer the one which is less general, and which approaches nearer to the point in question:* because special matter <273> admits of fewer exceptions than that which is general; it is enjoined with greater precision, and appears to have been more pointedly intended. Let us make use of the following example from Puffendorf:*—One law forbids us to appear in public with arms on holidays: another law commands us to turn out under arms, and repair to our posts, as soon as we hear the sound of the alarm-bell. The alarm is rung on a holiday. In such case we must obey the latter of the two laws, which creates an exception to the former.

§316.
5th Rule.

6. *What will not admit of delay, is to be preferred to what may be done at another time.* For this is the mode to reconcile every thing, and fulfil

§317.
6th Rule.

* Jus Gent. [[*De jure naturae et gentium*]] lib. v. cap. xii. §23.

both obligations; whereas if we gave the preference to the one which might be fulfilled at another time, we would unnecessarily reduce ourselves to the alternative of failing in our observance of the other.

§318.
7th Rule.

7. *When two duties stand in competition, that one which is the more considerable, the more praiseworthy, and productive of the greater utility, is entitled to the preference.* This rule has no need of proof. But as it relates to duties that are equally in our power, and, as it were, at our option, we should carefully guard against the erroneous application of it to two duties which do not really stand in competition, but of which the one absolutely precludes the other,—our obligation to fulfil the former wholly depriving us of the liberty to perform the latter. For instance, it is a more praiseworthy deed to defend one nation against an unjust aggressor, than to assist another in an offensive war. But if the latter be the more ancient ally, we are not at liberty to refuse her our assistance and give it to the former; for we stand pre-engaged. There is not, strictly speaking, any competition between these two duties: they do not lie at our option: the prior engagement renders the second duty, for the present, impracticable. However, if there were question of preserving a new ally from certain ruin, and that the more ancient ally were not reduced to the same extremity, this would be the case to which the foregoing rule should be applied.

As to what relates to laws in particular, the preference is undoubtedly to be given to the more important and necessary ones. This is the grand rule to be observed whenever they are found to clash with each other; it is the rule which claims the greatest attention, and is therefore placed by Cicero at the head of all the rules he lays down on the subject.* It is

---

* "Primum igitur leges oportet contendere, considerando utra lex ad majores, hoc est, ad utiliores, ad honestiores, ac magis necessarias res pertineat. Ex quo conficitur ut, si leges duae, aut si plures, aut quotquot erunt, conservari non possint quia discrepent inter se, ea maxime conservanda putetur, quae ad maximas res pertinere videatur." [["In the first place then, one should compare the laws by considering which one deals with the most important matters, that is, the most expedient, honorable, or necessary. The conclusion from this is that if two laws (or whatever number there may be if more than two) cannot be kept because they are at variance, the one is thought to have the greatest claim to be upheld which has reference to the greatest matters." *De inventione* II.145.]] Cicero, ubi supra.

counteracting the general aim of the legislature, and the great end of the laws, to neglect one of great importance, under pretence of observing another which is less necessary, and of inferior consequence: in <274> fact, such conduct is criminal; for, a lesser good, if it exclude a greater, assumes the nature of an evil.

8. *If we cannot acquit ourselves at the same time of two things promised to the same person, it rests with him to choose which of the two we are to perform;* for he may dispense with the other on this particular occasion; in which case there will no longer be any collision of duties. But *if we cannot obtain a knowledge of his will, we are to presume that the more important one is his choice; and we should of course give that the preference.* And, *in case of doubt, we should perform the one to which we are the more strongly bound;*—it being presumable that he chose to bind us more strongly to that in which he is more deeply interested.

§319.
8th Rule.

9. Since the stronger obligation claims a preference over the weaker,— *if a treaty that has been confirmed by an oath happens to clash with another treaty that has not been sworn to,—all circumstances being in other respects equal, the preference is to be given to the former;* because the oath adds a new force to the obligation. But as it makes no change in the nature of treaties (§§225, &c.), it cannot, for instance, entitle a new ally to a preference over a more ancient ally whose treaty has not been confirmed by an oath.

§320.
9th Rule.

10. For the same reason, and, *all circumstances being in other respects equal, what is enjoined under a penalty claims a preference over that which is not enforced by one,—and what is enjoined under a greater penalty, over that which is enforced by a lesser;* for the penal sanction and convention give additional force to the obligation: they prove that the object in question was more earnestly desired,* and the more so in proportion as the penalty is more or less severe.

§321.
10th Rule.

---

* This is also the reason which Cicero gives: "Nam maxime conservanda est ea [*lex*] quae diligentissime sancta est." [["For that law is to be upheld, in which the penalties are most carefully prescribed." *De inventione* II.146.]] Cicero, ubi supra.

§322. General
remark on the
manner of
observing all
the preceding
rules.

All the rules contained in this chapter ought to be combined together, and the interpretation be made in such manner as to accord with them all, so far as they are applicable to the case. When these rules appear to clash, they reciprocally counterbalance and limit each other, according to their strength and importance, and according as they more particularly belong to the case in question.

CHAPTER XVIII

Of the Mode of terminating Disputes between Nations.

§323. General
direction on
this subject.

The disputes that arise between nations or their rulers, originate either from contested rights or from injuries received. A nation ought to preserve the rights which belong to her; and the care of her own safety and glory forbids her to submit to injuries. But in fulfilling the duty which she owes to her-<275>self, she must not forget her duties to others. These two views, combined together, will furnish the maxims of the law of nations respecting the mode of terminating disputes between different states.

§324. Every
nation is
bound to give
satisfaction
respecting the
just complaints
of another.

What we have said in Chap. I. IV. and V. of this book, dispenses with our proving here, that a nation ought to do justice to all others with respect to their pretensions, and to remove all their just subjects of complaint. She is therefore bound to render to each nation what is her due,— to leave her in the peaceable enjoyment of her rights,—to repair any damage that she herself may have caused, or any injury she may have done,—to give adequate satisfaction for such injuries as cannot be repaired, and reasonable security against any injury which she has given cause to apprehend. These are so many maxims evidently dictated by that justice which nations as well as individuals are, by the law of nature, bound to observe.

§325. How
nations may
abandon their
rights and just
complaints.

Every one is at liberty to recede from his right, to relinquish a just subject of complaint, and to forget an injury. But the ruler of a nation is not, in this respect, so free as a private individual. The latter may attend solely to the voice of generosity; and, in an affair which concerns none but himself alone, he may indulge in the pleasure which he derives from doing good, and gratify his love of peace and quiet. The representative of a nation, the sovereign, must not consult his own gratification, or suffer himself to be guided by his private inclinations. All his actions must be directed to the greatest advantage of the state, combined with the general interests of mankind, from which it is inseparable. It behoves the prince, on every occasion, wisely to consider, and firmly to execute, whatever is most salutary to the state, most conformable to the duties of the nation towards other states,—and, at the same time, to consult justice, equity, humanity, sound policy, and prudence. The rights of the nation are a property of which the sovereign is only the trustee; and he ought not to dispose of them in any other manner than he has reason to presume the nation herself would dispose of them. And as to injuries, it is often laudable in a citizen generously to pardon them: he lives under the protection of the laws; the magistrates are capable of defending or avenging him against those ungrateful or unprincipled wretches whom his indulgence might encourage to a repetition of the offence. A nation has not the same security: it is seldom safe for her to overlook or forgive an injury, unless she evidently possess sufficient power to crush the rash aggressor who has dared to offend her. In such a case, indeed, it will reflect glory on her, to pardon those who acknowledge their faults,—

Parcere subjectis, et debellare superbos;[88]

and she may do it with safety. But between powers that are nearly equal, the endurance of an injury without insisting on <276> complete satisfaction for it, is almost always imputed to weakness or cowardice, and seldom fails long to subject the injured party to further wrongs of a more atrocious nature. Why do we often see the very reverse of this conduct pursued by those who fancy themselves possessed of souls so highly exalted above the level of the rest of mankind? Scarcely can they receive concessions sufficiently humble from weaker states who have had the misfortune to offend them: but to those whom they would find it dangerous to punish, they behave with greater moderation.

88. "To spare the vanquished and subdue the arrogant." Virgil, *Aeneid* VI.853.

§326. Means
suggested by
the law of
nature, for
terminating
their disputes.

1. Amicable
accommo-
dation.

If neither of the nations who are engaged in a dispute thinks proper to abandon her right or her pretensions, the contending parties are, by the law of nature, which recommends peace, concord, and charity, bound to try the gentlest methods of terminating their differences. These are,—first, an amicable accommodation.—Let each party coolly and candidly examine the subject of the dispute, and do justice to the other; or let him whose right is too uncertain, voluntarily renounce it. There are even occasions when it may be proper for him who has the clearer right, to renounce it, for the sake of preserving peace,—occasions, which it is the part of prudence to discover. To renounce a right in this manner, is not abandoning or neglecting it. People are under no obligation to you for what you abandon: but you gain a friend in the party to whom you amicably yield up what was the subject of a dispute.

§327.
2. Compromise.

Compromise is a second method of bringing disputes to a peaceable termination. It is an agreement, by which, without precisely deciding on the justice of the jarring pretensions, the parties recede on both sides, and determine what share each shall have of the thing in dispute, or agree to give it entirely to one of the claimants on condition of certain indemnifications granted to the other.

§328.
3. Mediation.

Mediation, in which a common friend interposes his good offices, frequently proves efficacious in engaging the contending parties to meet each other half-way,—to come to a good understanding,—to enter into an agreement or compromise respecting their rights,—and, if the question relates to an injury, to offer and accept a reasonable satisfaction. The office of mediator requires as great a degree of integrity, as of prudence and address. He ought to observe a strict impartiality; he should soften the reproaches of the disputants, calm their resentments, and dispose their minds to a reconciliation. His duty is to favour well-founded claims, and to effect the restoration, to each party, of what belongs to him: but he ought not scrupulously to insist on rigid justice. He is a conciliator, and not a judge: his business is to procure peace; and he ought to induce him who has right on his side to relax something of his pretensions, if necessary, with a view to so great a blessing.

The mediator is not guarantee for the treaty which he has conducted, unless he has expressly undertaken to guarantee it. That is an engagement of too great consequence to be imposed <277> on any one, without his own consent clearly manifested. At present, when the affairs of the sovereigns of Europe are so connected, that each has an eye on what passes between those who are the most distant, mediation is a mode of conciliation much used. Does any dispute arise? The friendly powers, those who are afraid of seeing the flames of war kindled, offer their mediation, and make overtures of peace and accommodation.

When sovereigns cannot agree about their pretensions, and are nevertheless desirous of preserving or restoring peace, they sometimes submit the decision of their disputes to arbitrators chosen by common agreement. When once the contending parties have entered into articles of arbitration, they are bound to abide by the sentence of the arbitrators: they have engaged to do this; and the faith of treaties should be religiously observed. §329. 4. Arbitration.

If, however, the arbitrators, by pronouncing a sentence evidently unjust and unreasonable, should forfeit the character with which they were invested, their judgment would deserve no attention: the parties had appealed to it only with a view to the decision of doubtful questions. Suppose a board of arbitrators should, by way of reparation for some offence, condemn a sovereign state to become subject to the state she has offended, will any man of sense assert that she is bound to submit to such decision? If the injustice is of small consequence, it should be borne for the sake of peace; and if it is not absolutely evident, we ought to endure it, as an evil to which we have voluntarily exposed ourselves. For if it were necessary that we should be convinced of the justice of a sentence before we would submit to it, it would be of very little use to appoint arbitrators.

There is no reason to apprehend, that, by allowing the parties a liberty of refusing to submit to a manifestly unjust and unreasonable sentence, we should render arbitration useless: our decision is by no means repugnant to the nature of recognisances or arbitration articles. There can be no difficulty in the affair, except in case of the parties having signed vague and unlimited articles, in which they have not precisely specified the subject of the dispute, or marked the bounds of their opposite pretensions. It may then happen, as in the example just alleged, that the arbitrators will exceed their power, and pronounce on what has not been really submitted to their decision. Being called in to determine what satisfaction a state ought to make for an offence, they may condemn her to become subject to the state she has offended. But she certainly never gave them so extensive a power; and their absurd sentence is not binding. In order to obviate all difficulty, and cut off every pretext of which fraud might make a handle, it is necessary that the arbitration articles should precisely specify the subject in dispute, the respective and opposite pretensions of the parties, the demands of the one, and the objections of the other. These constitute the whole of what is submitted to the decision of the arbitrators; and it is upon <278> these points alone that the parties promise to abide by their judgment. If then their sentence be confined within these precise bounds, the disputants must acquiesce in it. They cannot say that it is manifestly unjust, since it is pronounced on a question which they have themselves rendered doubtful by the discordance of their claims, and which has been referred, as such, to the decision of the arbitrators. Before they can pretend to evade such a sentence, they should prove, by incontestable facts, that it was the offspring of corruption or flagrant partiality.

Arbitration is a very reasonable mode, and one that is perfectly conformable to the law of nature, for the decision of every dispute which does not directly interest the safety of the nation. Though the claim of justice may be mistaken by the arbitrators, it is still more to be feared that it will be overpowered in an appeal to the sword. The Swiss have had the precaution, in all their alliances among themselves, and even in those they have contracted with the neighbouring powers, to agree before-hand on the manner in which their disputes were to be submitted to arbitrators, in case they could not adjust them in an amicable manner. This wise precaution has not a little contributed to maintain the Helvetic republic in that flourishing state which secures her liberty, and renders her respectable throughout Europe.

§330. Conferences and congresses.   In order to put in practice any of these methods, it is necessary to speak with each other, and to confer together. Conferences and congresses are therefore a mode of conciliation, which the law of nature recommends to nations, as well calculated to bring their differences to an amicable termination. Congresses are assemblies of plenipotentiaries appointed to find out means of conciliation, and to discuss and adjust the reciprocal pretensions of the contending parties. To afford the prospect of a happy issue of their deliberations, such meetings should be formed and directed by a sincere desire of peace and concord. In the present century, Europe has witnessed two general congresses,—that of Cambray,* and that of Soissons,†—both tedious farces acted on the political theatre, in which the principal performers were less desirous of coming to an accommodation than of appearing to desire it.

In order at present to ascertain in what manner and how far a nation is bound to resort or accede to these various modes of accommodation, and which of them she ought to prefer, it becomes necessary, in the first place, to distinguish between cases that are evident, and those that are doubtful. Does the question relate to a right that is clear, certain, and incontestable? A sovereign, if he possesses sufficient strength, may peremptorily prosecute and defend that right, without exposing it to the doubtful issue of an arbitration. Shall he submit to negotiate and compound for a thing that evidently belongs to him, and which is disputed with-<279>out the least shadow of justice? Much less will he subject it to arbitration. But he ought not to neglect those methods of conciliation, which, without endangering his own right, may induce his opponent to listen to reason,—such as mediation and conferences. Nature gives us no right to have recourse to forcible means, except where gentle and pacific methods prove ineffectual. It is not permitted to be so inflexible in uncertain and doubtful questions. Who will dare to insist that another shall immediately, and without examination, relinquish to him a disputable right? This would be a means of rendering wars perpetual and inevitable. Both the contending parties may be equally convinced of the justice of their claims: why, therefore, should either yield to the other? In such a case, they can only demand an examination of the question, propose a conference or an arbitration, or offer to settle the point by articles of agreement.

§331. Distinction to be made between evident and doubtful cases.

* In 1724.
† In 1728.

§332. Of essential rights, and those of less importance.

In the disputes that arise between sovereigns, it is moreover necessary to make a proper distinction between essential rights and rights of inferior importance: for, according to the difference in the two cases, a different line of conduct is to be pursued. A nation is under many obligations of duty towards herself, towards other nations, and towards the great society of mankind. We know that the duties we owe to ourselves are, generally speaking, paramount to those we owe to others: but this is to be understood only of such duties as bear some proportion to each other. We cannot refuse, in some degree, to forget ourselves with respect to interests that are not essential, and to make some sacrifices, in order to assist other persons, and especially for the greater benefit of human society: and let us even remark, that we are invited by our own advantage, by our own safety, to make these generous sacrifices; for the private good of each is intimately connected with the general happiness. What idea should we entertain of a prince or a nation who would refuse to give up the smallest advantage for the sake of procuring to the world the inestimable blessings of peace? Every power therefore owes this respect to the happiness of human society, to shew himself open to every mode of conciliation, in questions relating to interests which are neither essential nor of great importance. If he exposes himself to the loss of something by an accommodation, by a compromise, or by an arbitration, he ought to be sensible what are the dangers, the evils, the calamities of war, and to consider that peace is well worth a small sacrifice.

But if any one would rob a nation of one of her essential rights, or a right without which she could not hope to support her national existence,—if an ambitious neighbour threatens the liberty of a republic,— if he attempts to subjugate and enslave her,—she will take counsel only from her own courage. She will not even attempt the mode of conferences on so odious a pretension: she will, in such a quarrel, exert her utmost efforts, exhaust every <280> resource, and gloriously lavish her blood to the last drop if necessary. To listen to the smallest proposition, is putting every thing to the risk. On such an occasion she may truly say—

Una salus ——— nullam sperare salutem:[89]

and if fortune prove unfavourable, a free people will prefer death to servitude. What would have become of Rome, had she listened to timid counsels, when Hannibal was encamped before her walls? The Swiss, ever so ready to embrace pacific measures or submit to legal decisions in disputes respecting less essential points, have uniformly spurned at all idea of compromise with those who harboured designs against their liberty. They even refused on such occasions to submit their disputes to arbitration, or to the judgment of the emperors.*

In doubtful causes which do not involve essential points, if one of the parties will not accede either to a conference, an accommodation, a compromise, or an arbitration, the other has only the last resource for the defence of himself and his rights,—an appeal to the sword; and he has justice on his side in taking up arms against so untractable an adversary. For, in a doubtful cause, we can only demand all the reasonable methods of elucidating the question, and of deciding or accommodating the dispute (§331).

§333. How we acquire a right of having recourse to force in a doubtful cause,

But let us never lose sight of what a nation owes to her own security, nor of that prudence by which she ought constantly to be directed. To authorise her to have recourse to arms, it is not always necessary that every conciliatory measure be first expressly rejected: it is sufficient that she have every reason to believe that the enemy would not enter into those measures with sincerity,—that they could not be brought to terminate in a happy result,—and that the intervening delay would only expose her to a greater danger of being overpowered. This maxim is incontestable; but its application in practice is very delicate. A sovereign

§334. and even without attempting other measures.

---

* When, in the year 1355, they submitted their differences with the dukes of Austria, in relation to the countries of Zug and Glaris, to the arbitration of Charles IV. it was not without this preliminary condition, that the emperor should not touch the liberty of those countries, nor their alliance with the other cantons. Tschudi, p. 429, &c.—Stettler, p. 77.—History of the Helvetic Confederacy, by De Watteville, book iv. at the beginning.

89. "There is only one hope of safety [for the vanquished]—not to hope for any well-being." Virgil, *Aeneid II,* 354.

who would not be considered as a disturber of the public peace, will not be induced abruptly to attack him who has not refused to accede to pacific measures, unless he be able to justify his conduct in the eyes of all mankind, by proving that he has reason to consider those peaceable appearances as an artifice employed for the purpose of amusing him, and taking him by surprise. To make his bare suspicions serve as sufficient authority for such a step, would be sapping every foundation on which rests the security of nations.

§335. Voluntary law of nations on this subject.   The faith of one nation has ever been suspected by another, <281> and sad experience but too plainly proves that this distrust is not illfounded. Independence and impunity are a touchstone that discovers the alloy of the human heart: the private individual assumes the character of candour and probity; and, in default of the reality, his dependence frequently obliges him to exhibit in his conduct at least the appearance of those virtues. The great man, who is independent, boasts still more of them in his discourse; but as soon as he finds himself possessed of superior strength, he scarcely endeavours to save appearances, unless his heart be moulded of materials which, unfortunately, are very rare indeed: and if powerful interests intervene, he will give himself a latitude in the pursuit of measures that would cover a private person with shame and infamy. When, therefore, a nation pretends that it would be dangerous for her to attempt pacific measures, she can find abundance of pretexts to give a colour of justice to her precipitation in having recourse to arms. And as, in virtue of the natural liberty of nations, each one is free to judge in her own conscience how she ought to act, and has a right to make her own judgment the sole guide of her conduct with respect to her duties in every thing that is not determined by the perfect rights of another (Prelim. §20), it belongs to each nation to judge whether her situation will admit of pacific measures, before she has recourse to arms. Now, as the voluntary law of nations ordains, that, for these reasons, we should esteem lawful whatever a nation thinks proper to do in virtue of her natural liberty (Prelim. §21), by that same voluntary law, nations are bound to consider as lawful the conduct of that power who suddenly takes up arms in a doubtful cause, and attempts to force his enemy to come to terms, without having previously tried pacific measures. Louis XIV. was in the heart of the Netherlands before it was known in Spain that he laid claim to the sovereignty of a part of those rich provinces in right of the queen his wife. The king of Prussia, in 1741, published his manifesto in Silesia, at the head of sixty thousand men. Those princes might have wise and just reasons for acting thus: and this is sufficient at the tribunal of the voluntary law of nations. But a thing which that law tolerates through necessity, may be found very unjust in itself: and a prince who puts it in practice, may render himself very guilty in the sight of his own conscience, and very unjust towards him whom he attacks, though he is not accountable for it to other nations, as he cannot be accused of violating the general rules which they are bound to observe towards each other. But if he abuses this liberty, he gives all nations cause to hate and suspect him; he authorises them to confederate against him; and thus, while he thinks he is promoting his interests, he sometimes irretrievably ruins them.

A sovereign ought, in all his quarrels, to entertain a sincere desire of rendering justice and preserving peace. He is bound, before he take up arms, and also after having taken them up, to offer equitable conditions: and then alone he is justifiable in ap-<282>pealing to the sword against an obstinate enemy who refuses to listen to the voice of justice or equity.

§336. Equitable conditions to be offered.

It is the business of the appellant to prove his right; for he ought to shew a good foundation for demanding a thing which he does not possess. He must have a title: and people are not obliged to respect that title any farther than he shews its validity. The possessor may therefore remain in possession till proof be adduced to convince him that his possession is unjust. As long as that remains undone, he has a right to maintain himself in it, and even to recover it by force, if he has been despoiled of it. Consequently it is not allowable to take up arms in order to obtain possession of a thing to which the claimant has but an uncertain or doubtful right. He is only justifiable in compelling the possessor, by force of arms if necessary, to come to a discussion of the question, to accede to some reasonable mode of decision or accommodation, or, finally, to settle the point by articles of agreement upon an equitable footing (§333).

§337. Possessor's right in doubtful cases.

§338. How
reparation of
an injury is to
be sought.

If the subject of the dispute be an injury received, the offended party ought to follow the rules we have just established. His own advantage, and that of human society, require, that, previous to taking up arms, he should try every pacific mode of obtaining either a reparation of the injury or a just satisfaction, unless there be substantial reasons to dispense with his recurrence to such measures (§334). This moderation, this circumspection, is the more becoming, and in general even indispensable, as the action which we look upon as an injury does not always proceed from a design to offend us, and is sometimes rather a mistake, than an act of malice. It even frequently happens that the injury is done by inferior persons, without their sovereign having any share in it: and on these occasions it is natural to presume that he will not refuse us a just satisfaction. When some petty officers, not long since, violated the territory of Savoy in order to carry off from thence a noted smuggling chief, the king of Sardinia[90] caused his complaints to be laid before the court of France; and Louis XV. thought it no derogation to his greatness to send an embassador extraordinary to Turin to give satisfaction for that violence. Thus an affair of so delicate a nature was terminated in a manner equally honourable to the two kings.

§339.
Retaliation.

When a nation cannot obtain justice, whether for a wrong or an injury, she has a right to do herself justice. But before she declare war (of which we shall treat in the following book), there are various methods practised among nations, which remain to be treated of here. Among those methods of obtaining satisfaction, has been reckoned what is called the law of retaliation, according to which we make another suffer precisely as much evil as he has done. Many have extolled that law, as being founded in the strictest justice:—and can we be surprised at their having proposed it to princes, since they have presumed to make it a rule even for the deity himself? The ancients called it the law of Rhadamanthus. The idea is wholly derived from the obscure <283> and false notion which represents evil as essentially and in its own nature worthy of punishment. We have shewn above (Book I. §169), what is the true origin

90. Charles Emmanuel III of Sardinia, r. 1730–73.

of the right of punishing;* whence we have deduced the true and just proportion of penalties (Book I. §171). Let us say then, that a nation may punish another which has done her an injury, as we have shewn above (see Chap. IV. and VI. of this Book), if the latter refuses to give her a just satisfaction: but she has not a right to extend the penalty beyond what her own safety requires. Retaliation, which is unjust between private persons, would be much more so between nations, because it would, in the latter case, be difficult to make the punishment fall on those who had done the injury. What right have you to cut off the nose and ears of the embassador of a barbarian who had treated your embassador in that manner? As to those reprisals in time of war which partake of the nature of retaliation, they are justified on other principles; and we shall speak of them in their proper place. The only truth in this idea of retaliation is, that, all circumstances being in other respects equal, the punishment ought to bear some proportion to the evil for which we mean to inflict it,—the very object and foundation of punishment requiring thus much.

It is not always necessary to have recourse to arms, in order to punish a nation. The offended party may, by way of punishment, deprive her of the privileges she enjoyed in his dominions,—seize on some of her property, if he has an opportunity,—and detain it till she has given him sufficient satisfaction.

§340. Various modes of punishing, without having recourse to arms.

When a sovereign is not satisfied with the manner in which his subjects are treated by the laws and customs of another nation, he is at liberty to declare that he will treat the subjects of that nation in the same manner as his are treated. This is what is called *retortion*. There is nothing in this, but what is conformable to justice and sound policy. No one can complain on receiving the same treatment which he gives to others. Thus the king of Poland, elector of Saxony, enforces the law of escheatage only against the subjects of those princes who make the Saxons liable to it. This retortion may also take place with respect to certain regulations, of

§341. Retortion.

* "Nam, ut Plato ait, nemo prudens punit quia peccatum est, sed, ne peccetur." [["For, as Plato says, no one (who is) prudent punishes because of sin but to stop sinning."]] Seneca, de Ira [[I.XIX.7]].

which we have no right to complain, and which we are even obliged to approve, though it is proper to guard against their effect, by imitating them. Such are the orders relating to the importation or exportation of certain commodities or merchandise. On the other hand, circumstances frequently forbid us to have recourse to retortion. In this respect, each nation may act according to the dictates of her own prudence.

§342. Reprisals. Reprisals are used between nation and nation, in order to do themselves justice when they cannot otherwise obtain it. If a nation has taken possession of what belongs to another,—if she refuses to pay a debt, to repair an injury, or to give adequate satisfaction < 284 > for it,—the latter may seize something belonging to the former, and apply it to her own advantage till she obtains payment of what is due to her, together with interest and damages,—or keep it as a pledge till she has received ample satisfaction. In the latter case, it is rather a stoppage or a seizure, than reprisals: but they are frequently confounded in common language. The effects thus seized on are preserved while there is any hope of obtaining satisfaction or justice. As soon as that hope disappears, they are confiscated, and then the reprisals are accomplished. If the two nations, upon this ground of quarrel, come to an open rupture, satisfaction is considered as refused from the moment that war is declared or hostilities commenced; and then also the effects seized may be confiscated.

§343. What is required to render them lawful. It is only upon evidently just grounds, or for a well-ascertained and undeniable debt, that the law of nations allows us to make reprisals. For he who advances a doubtful pretension, cannot in the first instance demand any thing more than an equitable examination of his right. In the next place, before he proceed to such extremities, he should be able to shew that he has ineffectually demanded justice, or at least that he has every reason to think it would be in vain for him to demand it. Then alone does it become lawful for him to take the matter into his own hands, and do himself justice. It would be too inconsistent with the peace, the repose, and the safety of nations, with their mutual commerce, and the duties which bind them to each other, that each one should be authorised to have immediate recourse to violent measures, without knowing whether there exist on the other side a disposition to do her justice, or to refuse it.

But in order perfectly to understand this article, it must be observed, that if, in a disputable case, our adversary either refuses to pursue or artfully evades the necessary steps for bringing the matter to the proof,—if he does not candidly and sincerely accede to some pacific mode of terminating the dispute,—especially if he is foremost in adopting violent measures,—he gives justice to our cause which before was problematical: we may then have recourse to reprisals, or the seizure of his effects, in order to compel him to embrace the methods of conciliation which the law of nature prescribes. This is the last remaining effort previous to a commencement of open hostilities.

We have observed above (§81), that the wealth of the citizens constitutes a part of the aggregate wealth of a nation,—that, between state and state, the private property of the members is considered as belonging to the body, and is answerable for the debts of that body (§82): whence it follows, that in reprisals we seize on the property of the subject just as we would on that of the state or sovereign. Every thing that belongs to the nation is subject to reprisals, whenever it can be seized, provided it be not a deposit intrusted to the public faith. As it is only in consequence of that confidence which the proprietor has placed in our good-faith, that we happen to have such deposit in our <285> hands, it ought to be respected, even in case of open war. Such is the conduct observed in France, England, and elsewhere, with respect to the money which foreigners have placed in the public funds.

§344. Upon what effects reprisals are made.

He who makes reprisals against a nation, on the property of its members indiscriminately, cannot be taxed with seizing the property of an innocent person for the debt of another: for in this case the sovereign is to compensate those of his subjects on whom the reprisals fall; it is a debt of the state or nation, of which each citizen ought only to pay his quota.*

§345. The state ought to compensate those who suffer by reprisals.

* On the subject of reprisals, it is necessary to observe, that when we adopt that expedient as being a gentler mode of proceeding than that of war, the reprisals ought not to be general. The grand pensionary De Witt [[Johan de Witt (1625–72), Dutch statesman]] very properly remarked—"I do not see any difference between general reprisals and open war." [[Note added in 1773/1797 editions.]]

§346. The
sovereign
alone can
order reprisals.

It is only between state and state that all the property of the individuals is considered as belonging to the nation. Sovereigns transact their affairs between themselves; they carry on business with each other directly, and can only consider a foreign nation as a society of men who have but one common interest. It belongs therefore to sovereigns alone to make and order reprisals on the footing we have just described. Besides, this violent measure approaches very near to an open rupture, and is frequently followed by one. It is therefore an affair of too serious a nature to be left to the discretion of private individuals. And accordingly we see, that, in every civilised state, a subject who thinks himself injured by a foreign nation, has recourse to his sovereign in order to obtain permission to make reprisals. This is what the French call applying for *letters of marque.*

§347. Reprisals against a nation for actions of its subjects, and in favour of the injured subjects.

We may make reprisals against a nation not only for the actions of the sovereign, but also for those of his subjects: and this may take place when the state or the sovereign participates in the act of his subject, and takes it upon himself; which he may do in several ways, as we have shewn in Chap. VI. of this Book.

In the same manner the sovereign demands justice, or makes reprisals, not only for his own concerns, but also for those of his subjects, whom he is bound to protect, and whose cause is that of the nation.

§348. But not in favour of foreigners.

But to grant reprisals against a nation in favour of foreigners, is to set himself up as judge between that nation and those foreigners; which no sovereign has a right to do. The cause of reprisals ought to be just: they ought even to be grounded on a denial of justice,—either an actual denial, or one which there is good reason to apprehend (§343). Now what right have we to judge whether the complaint of a stranger against an independent state is just, if he has really been denied justice? If it be objected, that we may espouse the quarrel of another state in a war that appears to us to be just,—to assist her, and even to unite with her,—the case is different. In granting succours against a nation, we do not detain her property or her people that happen to be within our territories under the public faith; and in declaring war against her, we suffer her to withdraw her subjects and her <286> effects, as will hereafter appear. In the case of reprisals granted to our own subjects, a nation cannot complain that we violate the public faith in seizing on her people or her property; because we are under no other obligation to grant security to that property and those people, than what arises from a reasonable supposition that their nation will not in the first instance violate, with respect to us or our subjects, the rules of justice which nations ought to observe towards each other. If she violate them, we have a right to obtain satisfaction; and the mode of reprisals is more easy, safe, and mild, than that of war. We cannot urge the same arguments in justification of reprisals ordered in favour of foreigners. For the security we owe to the subjects of a foreign power does not depend, as a condition, on the security which that power shall grant to all other nations, to people who do not belong to us, and are not under our protection. England having, in 1662, granted reprisals against the United Provinces, in favour of the knights of Malta,* the states of Holland asserted with good reason, that, according to the law of nations, reprisals can only be granted to maintain the rights of the state, and not for an affair in which the nation has no concern.†

* On that subject, the grand pensionary De Witt wrote as follows—"Nothing can be more absurd than that grant of reprisals: for—to say nothing of its proceeding from a board of admiralty who have no power to grant it without infringing on the sovereign authority of their prince—it is evident that no sovereign can grant or make reprisals, except for the defence or indemnification of his own subjects, whom he is, in the sight of God, bound to protect: but he can never grant reprisals in favour of any foreigner who is not under his protection, and with whose sovereign he has not any engagement to that effect, *ex pacto vel foedere*. Besides, it is certain that reprisals ought not to be granted except in case of an open denial of justice. Finally, it is also evident, that, even in case of a denial of justice, he cannot empower his subjects to make reprisals, until he has repeatedly demanded justice for them, and added, that, in the event of a refusal, he will be obliged to grant them letters of marque and reprisal."—From the answers of Mr. Boreel, it appears that this conduct of the British admiralty was strongly condemned by the court of France. The king of England testified his disapprobation of it, and gave orders for the release of the Dutch vessels whose seizure had been permitted by way of reprisal. [[Note added in 1773/1797 editions.]]

† See Bynckershock's Competent Judge of Embassadors, chap. xxii. §5.

§349. Those who have given cause for reprisals ought to indemnify those who suffer by them.   The individuals who by their actions have given cause for just reprisals, are bound to indemnify those on whom they fall; and the sovereign ought to compel them to do it. For we are under an obligation to repair the damage we have occasioned by our own fault. And although the sovereign, by refusing justice to the offended party, has brought on the reprisals against his subjects, those who were the first cause of them do not become the less guilty: the fault of the sovereign does not exempt them from repairing the consequences of theirs. However, if they were ready to give satisfaction to the party whom they had injured or offended, and their sovereign has prevented their doing it, they are not bound to do any thing more in that case, than they would before have been obliged to do in order to prevent the reprisals; and it is the sovereign's duty to repair the additional damage, which is the consequence of his own fault (§345). <287>

§350. What may be deemed a refusal to do justice.   We have said (§343) that we ought not to make reprisals, except when we are unable to obtain justice. Now justice is refused in several ways:— First, by a denial of justice, properly so called, or by a refusal to hear your complaints or those of your subjects, or to admit them to establish their right before the ordinary tribunals. Secondly, by studied delays, for which no good reasons can be given,—delays equivalent to a refusal, or still more ruinous. Thirdly, by an evidently unjust and partial decision. But it is necessary that this injustice should be manifest and palpable. In all cases susceptible of doubt, a sovereign ought not to listen to the complaints of his subjects against a foreign tribunal, nor to attempt to screen them from the effects of a sentence passed in due form: for that would be the means of exciting continual troubles. The law of nations directs that states should reciprocally pay that kind of deference to each other's jurisdiction, for the same reason as the civil law ordains within the state that every definitive sentence, passed in due form, shall be esteemed just. Between nation and nation, the obligation is neither so express nor so extensive: but it cannot be denied, that it is highly conducive to their peace, and conformable to their duties towards human society, to oblige their subjects, in all doubtful cases, and unless where there is a manifest wrong done to them, to submit to the sentences of the foreign tribunals before which their causes have been tried. (See above §84.)

As we may seize the things which belong to a nation, in order to compel her to do justice, we may equally, for the same reason, arrest some of her citizens, and not release them till we have received full satisfaction. This is what the Greeks called *Androlépsia.** At Athens the law permitted the relatives of him who had been assassinated in a foreign country, to seize three of the inhabitants of that country, and to detain them till the murderer was punished or delivered up.† But in the practice of modern Europe, this method is seldom resorted to, except with a view to obtain satisfaction for an injury of the same nature,—that is to say, to compel a sovereign to release a person whom he detains unjustly.

§351. Subjects arrested by way of reprisals.

The persons, however, who are thus arrested, being detained only as a security or pledge in order to oblige a nation to do justice,—if their sovereign obstinately persists in refusing it, we cannot take away their lives, or inflict any corporal punishment upon them, for a refusal, of which they are not guilty. Their property, their liberty itself, may be staked for the debts of the state; but not their lives, of which man has not the power of disposing. A sovereign has no right to put to death the subjects of a state which has done him an injury, except when they are engaged in war; and we shall see elsewhere, what it is that gives him that right. <288>

But the sovereign is authorised to employ forcible means against those who resist him in the exertion of his right, and to pursue such means as far as is necessary to overcome their unjust resistance. It is therefore lawful to repel those who undertake to oppose the making of just reprisals: and if, for that purpose, it be necessary to proceed even so far as to put them to death, the whole blame of that misfortune is imputable to their unjust and inconsiderate resistance. In such a case, Grotius would have us rather abstain from making reprisals.‡ Between private persons, and for things that are not of the highest importance, it is certainly worthy, not only of a christian, but, in general, of every man of principle, rather to abandon his right than to kill the person who unjustly resists him.

§352. Our right against those who oppose reprisals.

---

* Ἀνδροληψία, *seizure of men.*

† Demosthenes, Orat. adv. Aristocrat.

‡ De Jure Belli et Pacis, lib. iii. cap. ii. §6.

But, between sovereigns, the case is otherwise. To suffer themselves to be bullied, would be attended with consequences of too serious a nature. The true and just welfare of the state is the grand rule: moderation is ever laudable in itself; but the conductors of nations ought to practise that virtue so far only as it is consistent with the happiness and safety of their people.

§353. Just reprisals do not afford a just cause for war.

After having demonstrated the lawfulness of making reprisals when we can no otherwise obtain justice, we may thence readily conclude that a sovereign is not justifiable in making forcible opposition to, or waging war against, the party, who, by ordering or making reprisals in such a case, only exerts his just right.

§354. How we ought to confine ourselves to reprisals, or at length proceed to hostilities.

And as the law of humanity directs nations as well as individuals ever to prefer the gentlest measures when they are sufficient to obtain justice,—whenever a sovereign can, by the mode of reprisals, procure a just indemnification or a suitable satisfaction, he ought to confine himself to this method, which is less violent and less fatal than war. On this subject, I cannot avoid noticing an error which is too general to be wholly disregarded. If it happens that a prince, having reason to complain of some injustice or some acts of hostility, and not finding his adversary disposed to give him satisfaction, determines to make reprisals with the view of endeavouring to compel him to listen to the voice of justice before he proceeds to an open rupture,—if, without a declaration of war, he seizes on his effects, his shipping, and detains them as pledges,—you hear certain men cry out that this is robbery. If that prince had at once declared war, they would not have said a word; they would perhaps have praised his conduct. Strange forgetfulness of reason, and of every sound principle! Would we not, at this rate, be tempted to suppose that nations were bound to observe the laws of chivalry,—to challenge each other to the lists,—and decide their quarrels like a pair of doughty champions engaged in regular duel? It is the duty of sovereigns attentively to maintain the rights of their people, and to obtain justice by every lawful means,—still, however, prefer-<289>ring the gentlest methods: and we again repeat the assertion—it is evident that the mode of reprisals, of which we are speaking, is infinitely more gentle and less fatal than that of war. But since, between powers whose strength is nearly equal, reprisals often lead to war, they ought not to be attempted except in the last extremity. In such circumstances, the prince who has recourse to that expedient instead of proceeding to an open rupture, is undoubtedly entitled to praise for his moderation and prudence.

Those who run to arms without necessity, are the scourges of the human race, barbarians, enemies to society, and rebellious violators of the laws of nature, or rather the laws of the common father of mankind.

There are cases, however, in which reprisals would be justly condemnable, even when a declaration of war would not be so: and these are precisely those cases in which nations may with justice take up arms. When the question which constitutes the ground of a dispute, relates, not to an act of violence, or an injury received, but to a contested right,—after an ineffectual endeavour to obtain justice by conciliatory and pacific measures, it is a declaration of war that ought to follow, and not pretended reprisals, which, in such a case, would only be real acts of hostility without a declaration of war, and would be contrary to public faith as well as to the mutual duties of nations. This will more evidently appear, when we shall have explained the reasons which establish the obligation of declaring war previous to a commencement of hostilities.*

But if, from particular conjunctures, and from the obstinacy of an unjust adversary, neither reprisals, nor any of the methods of which we have been treating, should prove sufficient for our defence and for the protection of our rights, there remains only the wretched and melancholy alternative of war, which will be the subject of the following book.

<290> <291>

* See book iii. chap. iv.

THE
LAW
OF
NATIONS

ಖಿ BOOK III ಖಿ

Of War

CHAPTER I

Of War,—its different Kinds,—
and the Right of making War.

War is *that state in which we prosecute our right by force.* We also under- §1. Defini-
stand, by this term, the act itself, or the manner of prosecuting our right tion of war.
by force: but it is more conformable to general usage, and more proper
in a treatise on the law of war, to understand this term in the sense we
have annexed to it.

Public war is that which takes place between nations or sovereigns, §2. Public war.
and which is carried on in the name of the public power, and by its order.
This is the war we are here to consider:—*private war,* or that which is
carried on between private individuals, belongs to the law of nature
properly so called.

In treating of the right to security (Book II. Chap. IV.) we have shewn §3. Right of
that nature gives men a right to employ force, when it is necessary for making war.
their defence, and for the preservation of their rights. This principle is
generally acknowledged: reason demonstrates it; and nature herself has

engraved it on the heart of man. Some fanatics indeed, taking in a literal sense the moderation recommended in the gospel, have adopted the strange fancy of suffering themselves to be massacred or plundered, ra- <292>ther than oppose force to violence. But we need not fear that this error will make any great progress. The generality of mankind will, of themselves, guard against its contagion,—happy, if they as well knew how to keep within the just bounds which nature has set to a right that is granted only through necessity! To mark those just bounds,—and, by the rules of justice, equity, and humanity, to moderate the exercise of that harsh though too often necessary right,—is the intention of this third book.

§4. It belongs only to the sovereign power.

As nature has given men no right to employ force, unless when it becomes necessary for self-defence and the preservation of their rights (Book II. §49, &c.), the inference is manifest, that, since the establishment of political societies, a right, so dangerous in its exercise, no longer remains with private persons, except in those rencounters where society cannot protect or defend them. In the bosom of society, the public authority decides all the disputes of the citizens, represses violence, and checks every attempt to do ourselves justice with our own hands. If a private person intends to prosecute his right against the subject of a foreign power, he may apply to the sovereign of his adversary, or to the magistrates invested with the public authority: and if he is denied justice by them, he must have recourse to his own sovereign, who is obliged to protect him. It would be too dangerous to allow every citizen the liberty of doing himself justice against foreigners; as, in that case, there would not be a single member of the state who might not involve it in war. And how could peace be preserved between nations, if it were in the power of every private individual to disturb it? A right of so momentous a nature,—the right of judging whether the nation has real grounds of complaint,—whether she is authorised to employ force, and justifiable in taking up arms,—whether prudence will admit of such a step,—and whether the welfare of the state requires it,—that right, I say, can belong only to the body of the nation, or to the sovereign, her representative. It is doubtless one of those rights, without which there can be no salutary government, and which are therefore called rights of majesty (Book I. §45).

Thus the sovereign power alone is possessed of authority to make war. But as the different rights which constitute this power, originally resident in the body of the nation, may be separated or limited according to the will of the nation (Book I. §§31 and 45), it is from the particular constitution of each state, that we are to learn where the power resides, that is authorised to make war in the name of the society at large. The kings of England, whose power is in other respects so limited, have the right of making war and peace.* Those of Sweden have lost it. The brilliant but ruinous exploits of Charles XII.[1] suffici-<293>ently warranted the states of that kingdom to reserve to themselves a right of such importance to their safety.

War is either *defensive* or *offensive.* He who takes up arms to repel the attack of an enemy, carries on a defensive war. He who is foremost in taking up arms, and attacks a nation that lived in peace with him, wages offensive war. The object of a defensive war is very simple; it is no other than self-defence: in that of offensive war, there is as great a variety as in the multifarious concerns of nations: but, in general, it relates either to the prosecution of some rights, or to safety. We attack a nation with a view either to obtain something to which we lay claim, to punish her for an injury she has done us, or to prevent one which she is preparing to do, and thus avert a danger with which she seems to threaten us. I do not here speak of the justice of war: that shall make the subject of a particular chapter:—all I here propose is to indicate, in general, the various objects for which a nation takes up arms,—objects which may furnish lawful reasons, or unjust pretences, but which are at least susceptible of a colour of right. I do not therefore, among the objects of offensive war, set down conquest, or the desire of invading the property of others:—views of that nature, destitute even of any reasonable pretext to countenance them, do not constitute the object of regular warfare, but of robbery, which we shall consider in its proper place.

§5. Defensive and offensive war.

---

* I here speak of the right considered in itself. But as a king of England cannot, without the concurrence of parliament, either raise money or compel his subjects to take up arms, his right of making war is, in fact, but a slender prerogative, unless the parliament second him with supplies. [[Note added in 1773/1797 editions.]]

1. Charles XII of Sweden, r. 1697–1718.

CHAPTER II

Of the Instruments of War,—the raising of Troops, &c.—their Commanders, or the Subordinate Powers in War.

§6. Instruments of war.

The sovereign is the real author of war, which is carried on in his name, and by his order. The troops, officers, soldiers, and, in general, all those by whose agency the sovereign makes war, are only instruments in his hands. They execute his will and not their own. The arms, and all the apparatus of things used in war, are instruments of an inferior order. For the decision of questions that will occur in the sequel, it is of importance to determine precisely what are the things which belong to war. Without entering here into a minute detail, we shall only observe that whatever is peculiarly used in waging war, is to be classed among the instruments of war; and things which are equally used at all times, such as provisions, belong to peace, unless it be in certain particular junctures when those things appear to be specially destined for the support of war. Arms of all kinds, artillery, gun-powder, salt-petre and sulphur of which it is composed, ladders, gabions, tools, and all other implements for sieges, materials for building ships of war, tents, soldiers' clothes, &c. these always belong to war. <294>

§7. Right of levying troops.

As war cannot be carried on without soldiers, it is evident that whoever has the right of making war, has also naturally that of raising troops. The latter therefore belongs likewise to the sovereign (§4), and is one of the prerogatives of majesty (Book I. §45). The power of levying troops, or raising an army, is of too great consequence in a state, to be intrusted to any other than the sovereign. The subordinate authorities are not invested with it; they exercise it only by order or commission from the sovereign. But it is not always necessary that they should have an express order for the purpose. On those urgent exigencies which do not allow time to wait for the supreme order, the governor of a province, or the commandant of a town, may raise troops for the defence of the town or province committed to their care; and this they do by virtue of the power tacitly given them by their commission in cases of this nature.

I say that this important power is the appendage of sovereignty; it makes a part of the supreme authority. But we have already seen that those rights which together constitute the sovereign power, may be divided (Book I. §§31, 45), if such be the will of the nation. It may then happen that a nation does not intrust her chief with a right so dangerous to her liberty as that of raising and supporting troops, or at least that she limits the exercise of it, by making it depend on the consent of her representatives. The king of England, who has the right of making war, has also, indeed, that of granting commissions for raising troops; but he cannot compel any person to enlist, nor, without the concurrence of parliament, keep an army on foot.

§8. Obligation of the citizens or subjects.

Every citizen is bound to serve and defend the state as far as he is capable. Society cannot otherwise be maintained; and this concurrence for the common defence is one of the principal objects of every political association. Every man capable of carrying arms should take them up at the first order of him who has the power of making war.[2]

§9. Enlisting or raising of troops.

In former times, and especially in small states, immediately on a declaration of war, every man became a soldier; the whole community took up arms, and engaged in the war. Soon after, a choice was made, and armies were formed of picked men,—the remainder of the people pursuing their usual occupations. At present the use of regular troops is almost every-where adopted, especially in powerful states. The public authority raises soldiers, distributes them into different bodies under the command of generals and other officers, and keeps them on foot as long as it thinks necessary. As every citizen or subject is bound to serve the state, the sovereign has a right, in case of necessity, to enlist whom he pleases. But he ought to choose such only as are fit for the occupation of war; and it is highly proper that he should, as far as possible, confine his choice to volunteers, who enlist without compulsion.

2. This paragraph illustrates Vattel's belief that to some extent all successful monarchies needed to learn lessons from republics. Another example can be found in book 3, §50.

No person is naturally exempt from taking up arms in defence of the
state,—the obligation of every member of society being <295> the same.
Those alone are excepted, who are incapable of handling arms, or supporting the fatigues of war. This is the reason why old men, children,
and women, are exempted. Although there be some women who are
equal to men in strength and courage, yet such instances are not usual;
and rules must necessarily be general, and derived from the ordinary
course of things. Besides, women are necessary for other services in society; and, in short, the mixture of both sexes in armies would be attended with too many inconveniences.

A good government should, as far as possible, so employ all the citizens, and distribute posts and employments in such manner, that the
state may be the most effectually served in all its affairs. Therefore, when
not urged by necessity, it should exempt from military service all those
who are employed in stations useful or necessary to society. Upon this
ground, magistrates are usually exempted,—their whole time not being
too much for the administration of justice, and the maintenance of
order.

The clergy cannot naturally, and as matter of right, arrogate to themselves any peculiar exemption. To defend one's country, is an action not
unworthy of the most sacred hands. That article of the canon law which
forbids ecclesiastics to shed blood, is a convenient device to exempt from
personal danger those men who are often so zealous to fan the flame of
discord and excite bloody wars. Indeed, for the same reasons which we
have above alleged in favour of magistrates, an exemption from bearing
arms should be allowed to such of the clergy as are really useful,—to
those who are employed in teaching religion, governing the church, and
celebrating the public worship.*

---

* Formerly bishops went to war in virtue of their fiefs, and led with them their
vassals. The Danish bishops were not inattentive to a function which pleased them
better than the peaceful cares of episcopacy. The famous Absalom, bishop of Roschild, and afterwards archbishop of Lunden, was the principal general of king Waldemar I [[r. 1157–82]]. And since the use of regular troops has superseded that feudal
service, there have not been wanting some martial prelates, who eagerly courted the
command of armies. The cardinal De la Valette, and Sourdis archbishop of Bour-

But those immense multitudes of useless monks and friars,—those drones, who, under pretence of dedicating themselves to God, dedicate themselves in fact to sloth and effeminacy,—by what right do they pretend to a prerogative that is ruinous to the state? And if the prince exempts them from military service, is he not guilty of injustice to the other members, on whom he thus throws the whole burthen? I do not here mean to advise a sovereign to fill his armies with monks, but gradually to diminish a useless class of men, by depriving them of injurious and ill-<296>founded privileges. History mentions a martial bishop* whose weapon was a club, with which he knocked down the enemy, to avoid incurring the censure of the canon-law by shedding their blood. It would be much more reasonable, when monks are exempted from carrying arms, that they should be employed in the works as pioneers, and thus made to alleviate the toil of the soldiers. They have on many occasions zealously undertaken the task in cases of necessity. I could mention more than one famous siege, where monks have usefully served in defence of their country. When the Turks besieged Malta, the ecclesiastics, the women, the very children, all, according to their respective strength or capacity, contributed to that glorious defence which baffled the utmost efforts of the Ottoman empire.

There is another class of idle drones, whose exemption is a still more glaring abuse,—I mean those swarms of useless footmen who crowd the dwellings of the great and the wealthy,—and who, by the very nature of their employment, are themselves corrupted in displaying the luxury of their masters.

---

deaux, appeared in arms under the ministry of cardinal Richelieu, who also acted himself in a military capacity, at the attack of the pass of Susa. This is an abuse which the church very justly opposes. A bishop makes a better appearance in his proper station in his diocese, than in the army; and, at present, sovereigns are in no want of generals and officers, who will perform more useful services than can be expected from churchmen. In short, let every person keep to his vocation. All I dispute with the clergy is their exemption as matter of right, and in cases of necessity.

* A bishop of Beauvais, under Philip Augustus [[Philippe II of France, r. 1180–1223]]. He fought at the battle of Bouvines [[Bovines, 1214]].

§11. Soldiers' pay and quarters.   Among the Romans, while every citizen took his turn to serve in the army, their service was gratuitous. But when a choice is made, and standing armies are kept on foot, the state is bound to pay them, as no individual is under an obligation to perform more than his quota of the public service: and if the ordinary revenues are not sufficient for the purpose, the deficiency must be provided for by taxation. It is but reasonable that those who do not serve should pay their defenders.

When the soldier is not in the field, he must necessarily be provided with quarters. The burthen, in such case, naturally falls on housekeepers: but as that is attended with many inconveniences, and proves very distressing to the citizens, it becomes a good prince, or a wise and equitable government, to ease them of it as far as possible. In this particular, the king of France has made magnificent and ample provision in many towns, by the erection of barracks for the accommodation of the garrison.

§12. Hospitals for invalids.   The asylums prepared for indigent soldiers and officers who are grown grey in the service, and whom toil or the enemy's sword has rendered incapable of providing for their own subsistence, may be considered as part of the military pay. In France and England, magnificent establishments have been made in favour of invalids, which, while they discharge a debt of a sacred nature, do honour to the sovereign and the nation. The care of those unfortunate victims of war is the indispensable duty of every state, in proportion to its ability. It is repugnant, not only to humanity, but to the strictest justice, that generous citizens, heroes who have shed their blood for the safety of their country, should be left to perish with want, or unworthily forced to beg their bread. The honourable maintenance of such persons might <297> very properly be imposed upon rich convents, and large ecclesiastical benefices. Nothing can be more just than that those citizens who avoid all the dangers of war, should bestow part of their riches for the relief of their valiant defenders.

§13. Mercenary soldiers.   Mercenary soldiers are foreigners voluntarily engaging to serve the state for money, or a stipulated pay. As they owe no service to a sovereign whose subjects they are not, the advantages he offers them are their sole motive. By enlisting they incur the obligation to serve him; and the prince on his part promises them certain conditions which are settled in the articles of enlistment. Those articles, being the rule and measure of the respective obligations and rights of the contracting parties, are to be religiously observed. The complaints of some French historians against the Swiss troops, who on several occasions formerly refused to march against the enemy, and even withdrew from the service, because they were not paid,—those complaints, I say, are equally ridiculous and unjust. Why should the articles of enlistment be more strongly binding on one of the parties than on the other? Whenever the prince fails to perform what he has promised, the foreign soldiers are discharged from any further duty to him. I own it would be ungenerous to forsake a prince who, without any fault on his own part, is, by accident alone, rendered for a while unable to make good his payments. There may even be occasions when such an inflexibility on the part of the soldier would be, if not contrary to strict justice, at least very repugnant to equity. But this was never the case with the Switzers:—they never were known to quit the service on the first failure of payment; and when they perceived the good intentions of a sovereign labouring under a real inability to satisfy them, their patience and zeal always supported them under such difficulties. Henry the Fourth owed them immense sums: yet they did not, in his greatest necessities, abandon him; and that hero found the nation equally generous as brave. I here speak of the Switzers, because, in fact, those above alluded to were often mere mercenaries. But a distinction is to be made between troops of this kind and those Switzers who at present serve different powers, with the permission of their sovereign, and in virtue of alliances subsisting between those powers and the Helvetic body or some particular canton. The latter are real auxiliaries, though paid by the sovereigns whom they serve.

Much has been said on the question—Whether the profession of a mercenary soldier be lawful, or not,—whether individuals may, for money or any other reward, engage to serve a foreign prince in his wars? This question does not to me appear very difficult to be solved. Those who enter into such engagements without the express or tacit consent of their sovereign, offend against their duty as citizens. But if their sovereign leaves them at liberty to follow their inclination for a military life, they are perfectly free in that respect. Now, every free man may join whatever society he pleases, according as he finds it most to <298> his advantage. He may make its cause his own, and espouse its quarrels. He becomes in some measure, at least for a time, a member of the state in whose service he engages: and as an officer is commonly at liberty to quit the service when he thinks proper, and the private soldier at the expiration of his engagement,—if that state embark in a war which is evidently unjust, the foreigner may quit its service. And the mercenary soldier, having now learned the art of war, has rendered himself more capable of serving his country, if ever she require his assistance. This last consideration will furnish us with an answer to a question proposed on this head—Whether the sovereign can with propriety permit his subjects to serve foreign powers indiscriminately for money? He can, for this simple reason, that his subjects will thus learn an art, of which a thorough knowledge is both useful and necessary. The tranquillity, the profound peace, which Switzerland has so long enjoyed in the midst of all the commotions and wars which have agitated Europe,—that long repose would soon become fatal to her, did not her citizens, by serving foreign princes, qualify themselves for the operations of war, and keep alive their martial spirit.[3]

§14. What is to be observed in their enlistment.

Mercenary soldiers enlist voluntarily. The sovereign has no right to compel foreigners: he must not even employ stratagem or artifice in order to induce them to engage in a contract, which, like all others, should be founded on candor and good faith.

§15. Enlisting in foreign countries.

As the right of levying soldiers belongs solely to the nation or the sovereign (§7), no person must attempt to enlist soldiers in a foreign country, without the permission of the sovereign; and even with that permission, none but volunteers are to be enlisted: for the service of their country is out of the question here; and no sovereign has a right to give or sell his subjects to another.

The man who undertakes to enlist soldiers in a foreign country with-

---

3. Although Vattel's argument was common in Swiss circles, it is notable that the unintended consequence of mercenary employment of Swiss citizens was deemed to be the maintenance of republican valour, when this was transposed to the defense of Switzerland itself.

out the sovereign's permission,—and, in general, whoever entices away the subjects of another state,—violates one of the most sacred rights of the prince and the nation. This crime is distinguished by the name of kidnapping or man-stealing, and is punished with the utmost severity in every well-regulated state. Foreign recruiters are hanged without mercy, and with great justice. It is not presumed that their sovereign has ordered them to commit a crime: and supposing even that they had received such an order, they ought not to have obeyed it,—their sovereign having no right to command what is contrary to the law of nature. It is not, I say, presumed that these recruiters act by order of their sovereign: and with respect to such of them as have practised seduction only, it is generally thought sufficient to punish them when they can be detected and caught: if they have used violence, and made their escape, it is usual to demand a surrender of the delinquents, and to claim the persons they have carried off. But if it appears that they acted by order, such a proceeding in a foreign sovereign is justly considered as an injury, and <299> as a sufficient cause for declaring war against him, unless he make suitable reparation.

All soldiers, natives or foreigners, are to take an oath to serve faithfully, and not desert the service. This is no more than what they are already obliged to, the former as subjects, the latter by their engagement: but their fidelity is of so great importance to the state, that too many precautions cannot be taken for rendering it secure. Deserters merit severe and exemplary punishment; and the sovereign may, if he thinks it necessary, annex the penalty of death to desertion. The emissaries who solicit them to desert are far more guilty than the recruiters mentioned in the preceding section. §16. Obligation of soldiers.

Good order and subordination, so useful in all places, are nowhere so necessary as in the army. The sovereign should exactly specify and determine the functions, duties, and rights of military men,—of soldiers, officers, commanders of corps, and generals. He should regulate and fix the authority of commanders in all the gradations of rank,—the punishments to be inflicted on offenders,—the form of trials, &c. The laws and ordinances relative to these several particulars form the military code. §17. Military laws.

§18. Military discipline.

Those regulations, whose particular tendency is to maintain order among the troops, and to enable them to perform their military service with advantage to the state, constitute what is called military discipline. This is of the highest importance. The Switzers were the first among the modern nations that revived it in its ancient vigour. It was a good discipline, added to the valour of a free people, that produced, even in the infancy of their republic, those brilliant achievements which astonished all Europe. Machiavel says that the Switzers are the masters of all Europe in the art of war.* In our times, the Prussians have shewn what may be expected from good discipline and assiduous exercise: soldiers, collected from all quarters, have, by the force of habit and the influence of command, performed all that could be expected from the most zealous and loyal subjects.

§19. Subordinate powers in war.

Every military officer, from the ensign to the general, enjoys the rights and authority assigned him by the sovereign; and the will of the sovereign in this respect is known by his express declarations, contained either in the commissions he confers or in the military code,—or is, by fair deduction, inferred from the nature of the functions assigned to each officer: for every man who is intrusted with an employment, is presumed to be invested with all the powers necessary to enable him to fill his station with propriety, and successfully discharge the several functions of his office.

Thus the commission of a commander in chief, when it is simple and unlimited, gives him an absolute power over the army, a right to march it whither he thinks proper, to undertake such operations as he finds conducive to the service of the state, &c. <300> It is true, indeed, that the powers of a general are often limited; but the example of marshal Turenne sufficiently shews, that, when the sovereign is certain of having made a good choice, the best thing he can do in this respect is to give the general an unlimited power. Had the operations of the duke of Marlborough depended on the directions of the cabinet, there is little probability that all his campaigns would have been crowned with such distinguished success.

* Disc. on Livy.

When a governor is besieged in the place where he commands, and all communication with his sovereign is cut off, that very circumstance confers on him the whole authority of the state, so far as respects the defence of the town and the safety of the garrison.

These particulars merit the utmost attention, as they furnish a principle for determining what the several commanders, who are the subordinate or inferior powers in war, may execute with sufficient authority. Exclusive of the consequences which may be deduced from the very nature of their employments, we are likewise to consider the general practice and established usage in this respect. If it be a known fact, that, in the service of a particular nation, officers of a certain rank have been uniformly invested with such or such powers, it may reasonably be presumed that the person we are engaged with, is furnished with the same powers.

Every promise made by any of the subordinate powers, by any commander within his department, in conformity to the terms of his commission and to the authority which he naturally derives from his office and the functions intrusted to his care,—every such promise, I say, is, for the reasons above alleged, made in the name and by the authority of the sovereign, and equally obligatory on him, as if he had himself personally made it. Thus a governor capitulates for the town which he commands, and for the garrison; and what he has promised, the sovereign cannot invalidate. In the last war,[4] the general who commanded the French at Lintz[5] engaged to march back his troops on this side the Rhine. Governors of towns have often promised that, for a limited time, their garrisons should not carry arms against the enemy with whom they capitulated: and these capitulations have always been faithfully observed.

§20. How their promises bind the sovereign.

But if a subordinate power allows himself a greater latitude, and exceeds the authority annexed to his office, his promise becomes no more than a private engagement, or what is called *sponsio,* of which we have already treated (B. II. Ch. XIV.). This was the case of the Roman consuls at the Furcae Caudinae. They might indeed agree to deliver hostages, and

§21. In what cases their promises bind only themselves.

4. War of the Austrian Succession, 1741–48.
5. Philippe-Henri, Marquis de Ségur, 1724–1801.

that their army should pass under the yoke, &c. but they were not authorised to conclude a peace, as they took care to signify to the Samnites.

§22. Their
assumption of
an authority
which they do
not possess.

If a subordinate power assumes an authority which he does not possess, and thus deceives the party treating with him, though an enemy,—
he is naturally responsible for the damage caused by his deception, and
bound to make reparation. I say "though an ene-<301>my": for the faith
of treaties is to be observed between enemies, as all men of principle
agree, and as we shall prove in the sequel. The sovereign of that fraudulent officer ought to punish him, and oblige him to repair his fault:—
it is a duty which the prince owes to justice, and to his own character.

§23. How they
bind their
inferiors.

Promises, made by a subordinate power, are obligatory on those who
are subject to his control, and bind them in every particular in which he
is authorised and accustomed to command their obedience: for, with
respect to such particulars, he is vested with the sovereign authority,
which his inferiors are bound to respect in his person. Thus, in a capitulation, the governor of a town stipulates and promises for his garrison,
and even for the magistrates and citizens.

CHAPTER III

Of the just Causes of War.

§24. War
never to be
undertaken
without very
cogent reasons.

Whoever entertains a true idea of war,—whoever considers its terrible
effects, its destructive and unhappy consequences,—will readily agree
that it should never be undertaken without the most cogent reasons.
Humanity revolts against a sovereign, who, without necessity or without
very powerful reasons, lavishes the blood of his most faithful subjects,
and exposes his people to the calamities of war, when he has it in his
power to maintain them in the enjoyment of an honourable and salutary
peace. And if to this imprudence, this want of love for his people, he
moreover adds injustice towards those he attacks,—of how great a crime,
or rather, of what a frightful series of crimes, does he not become guilty!
Responsible for all the misfortunes which he draws down on his own
subjects, he is moreover loaded with the guilt of all those which he inflicts on an innocent nation. The slaughter of men, the pillage of cities,
the devastation of provinces,—such is the black catalogue of his enor-

mities. He is responsible to God, and accountable to human nature, for every individual that is killed, for every hut that is burned down. The violences, the crimes, the disorders of every kind, attendant on the tumult and licentiousness of war, pollute his conscience, and are set down to his account, as he is the original author of them all. Unquestionable truths! alarming ideas! which ought to affect the rulers of nations, and, in all their military enterprises, inspire them with a degree of circumspection proportionate to the importance of the subject!

Were men always reasonable, they would terminate their contests by the arms of reason only: natural justice and equity would be their rule, or their judge. Force is a wretched and melancholy expedient against those who spurn at justice, and re-<302>fuse to listen to the remonstrances of reason: but, in short, it becomes necessary to adopt that mode, when every other proves ineffectual. It is only in extremities that a just and wise nation or a good prince has recourse to it, as we have shewn in the concluding chapter of the second book. The reasons which may determine him to take such a step, are of two classes. Those of the one class shew that he has a right to make war,—that he has just grounds for undertaking it:—these are called *justificatory reasons.* The others, founded on fitness and utility, determine whether it be expedient for the sovereign to undertake a war:—these are called *motives.*

§25. Justificatory reasons, and motives for making war.

The right of employing force, or making war, belongs to nations no farther than is necessary for their own defence and for the maintenance of their rights (§3). Now if any one attacks a nation, or violates her perfect rights, he does her an injury. Then, and not till then, that nation has a right to repel the aggressor, and reduce him to reason. Further, she has a right to prevent the intended injury, when she sees herself threatened with it (Book II. §50). Let us then say in general, that the foundation or cause of every just war is injury, either already done, or threatened. The justificatory reasons for war shew that an injury has been received, or so far threatened as to authorise a prevention of it by arms. It is evident, however, that here the question regards the principal in the war, and not those who join in it as auxiliaries. When, therefore, we would judge whether a war be just, we must consider whether he who undertakes it has in fact received an injury, or whether he be really threatened with one. And in order to determine what is to be considered as

§26. What is in general a just cause of war.

an injury, we must be acquainted with a nation's *rights,* properly so called,—that is to say, her *perfect rights.* These are of various kinds, and very numerous, but may all be referred to the general heads of which we have already treated, and shall further treat in the course of this work. Whatever strikes at these rights is an injury, and a just cause of war.

§27. What war is unjust.

The immediate consequence of the premises is, that if a nation takes up arms when she has received no injury, nor is threatened with any, she undertakes an unjust war. Those alone, to whom an injury is done or intended, have a right to make war.

§28. The object of war.

From the same principle we shall likewise deduce the just and lawful object of every war, which is, to *avenge or prevent injury.* To *avenge* signifies here to prosecute the reparation of an injury, if it be of a nature to be repaired,—or, if the evil be irreparable, to obtain a just satisfaction,—and also to punish the offender, if requisite, with a view of providing for our future safety. The right to security authorises us to do all this (Book II. §§49–52). We may therefore distinctly point out, as objects of a lawful war, the three following—1. To recover what belongs or is due to us. 2. To provide for our future safety by punishing the aggressor or offender. 3. To defend ourselves, or to protect our-<303>selves from injury, by repelling unjust violence. The two first are the objects of an offensive, the third that of a defensive war. Camillus, when on the point of attacking the Gauls, concisely set forth to his soldiers all the subjects on which war can be grounded or justified—*omnia, quae defendi, repetique, et ulcisci fas sit.*[*][6]

§29. Both justificatory reasons and proper motives requisite in undertaking a war.

As the nation, or her ruler, ought, in every undertaking, not only to respect justice, but also to keep in view the advantage of the state,—it is necessary that proper and commendable motives should concur with the justificatory reasons, to induce a determination to embark in a war. These reasons shew that the sovereign has a right to take up arms, that

---

[*] Livy, lib. v. cap. 49.

6. "Everything, in a word, which it was their duty to defend, to recover, or to avenge" (trans. Eds.). The famous Roman soldier and statesman Marcus Furius Camillus (ca. B.C. 446–356) defended Rome against successive Gallic invasions when serving as dictator, as described by Plutarch and Livy.

he has just cause to do so. The proper motives shew that in the present case it is advisable and expedient to make use of his right. These latter relate to prudence, as the justificatory reasons come under the head of justice.

I call *proper and commendable motives* those derived from the good of the state, from the safety and common advantage of the citizens. They are inseparable from the justificatory reasons,—a breach of justice being never truly advantageous. Though an unjust war may for a time enrich a state, and extend her frontiers, it renders her odious to other nations, and exposes her to the danger of being crushed by them. Besides, do opulence and extent of dominion always constitute the happiness of states? Amidst the multitude of examples which might here be quoted, let us confine our view to that of the Romans. The Roman republic ruined herself by her triumphs, by the excess of her conquests and power. Rome, when mistress of the world, but enslaved by tyrants and oppressed by a military government, had reason to deplore the success of her arms, and to look back with regret on those happy times when her power did not extend beyond the bounds of Italy, or even when her dominion was almost confined within the circuit of her walls.

§30. Proper motives.

Vicious motives are those which have not for their object the good of the state, and which, instead of being drawn from that pure source, are suggested by the violence of the passions. Such are the arrogant desire of command, the ostentation of power, the thirst of riches, the avidity of conquest, hatred and revenge.

Vicious motives.

The whole right of the nation, and consequently of the sovereign, is derived from the welfare of the state; and by this rule it is to be measured. The obligation to promote and maintain the true welfare of the society or state gives the nation a right to take up arms against him who threatens or attacks that valuable enjoyment. But if a nation, on an injury done to her, is induced to take up arms, not by the necessity of procuring a just reparation, but by a vicious motive, she abuses her right. The viciousness of the motive tarnishes the lustre of her arms, which might otherwise have shone in the cause of justice:—the <304> war is not undertaken for the lawful cause which the nation had to engage in it: that cause is now no more than a pretext. As to the sovereign in particular,

§31. War undertaken upon just grounds, but from vicious motives.

the ruler of the nation,—what right has he to expose the safety of the state, with the lives and fortunes of the citizens, to gratify his passions? It is only for the good of the nation that the supreme power is intrusted to him; and it is with that view that he ought to exert it: that is the object prescribed to him even in his least important measures: and shall he undertake the most important and the most dangerous, from motives foreign or contrary to that great end? Yet nothing is more common than such a destructive inversion of views; and it is remarkable, that, on this account, the judicious Polybius gives the name of *causes** to the motives on which war is undertaken,—and of *pretexts*† to the justificatory reasons alleged in defence of it. Thus he informs us that the cause of the war which Greece undertook against the Persians was the experience she had had of their weakness, and that the pretext alleged by Philip, or by Alexander after him, was the desire of avenging the injuries which the Greeks had so often suffered, and of providing for their future safety.

§32. Pretexts.   Let us however entertain a better opinion of nations and their rulers. There are just causes of war, real justificatory reasons; and why should there not be sovereigns who sincerely consider them as their warrant, when they have besides reasonable motives for taking up arms? We shall therefore give the name of *pretexts* to those reasons alleged as justificatory, but which are so only in appearance, or which are even absolutely destitute of all foundation. The name of pretexts may likewise be applied to reasons which are, in themselves, true and well-founded, but, not being of sufficient importance for undertaking a war, are made use of only to cover ambitious views, or some other vicious motive. Such was the complaint of the czar Peter I. that sufficient honours had not been paid him on his passage through Riga. His other reasons for declaring war against Sweden I here omit.

Pretexts are at least a homage which unjust men pay to justice. He who screens himself with them shews that he still retains some sense of shame. He does not openly trample on what is most sacred in human

---

* Αιτιαι. Histor. lib. iii. cap. 6.
† Προφασεις.

society: he tacitly acknowledges that a flagrant injustice merits the indignation of all mankind.

Whoever, without justificatory reasons, undertakes a war merely from motives of advantage, acts without any right, and his war is unjust. And he, who, having in reality just grounds for taking up arms, is nevertheless solely actuated by interested views in resorting to hostilities, cannot indeed be charged with injustice, but he betrays a vicious disposition: his conduct is reprehensible, and sullied by the badness of his motives. War is so dreadful a scourge, that nothing less than manifest justice, joined to a kind of necessity, can authorise it, render it commendable, or at least exempt it from reproach. <305>

§33. War undertaken merely for advantage.

Nations that are always ready to take up arms on any prospect of advantage, are lawless robbers: but those who seem to delight in the ravages of war, who spread it on all sides, without reasons or pretexts, and even without any other motive than their own ferocity, are monsters, unworthy the name of men. They should be considered as enemies to the human race, in the same manner as, in civil society, professed assassins and incendiaries are guilty, not only towards the particular victims of their nefarious deeds, but also towards the state, which therefore proclaims them public enemies. All nations have a right to join in a confederacy for the purpose of punishing and even exterminating those savage nations. Such were several German tribes mentioned by Tacitus,—such those barbarians who destroyed the Roman empire: nor was it till long after their conversion to Christianity that this ferocity wore off. Such have been the Turks and other Tartars,—Genghis-khan, Timur-Bec or Tamerlane, who, like Attila, were scourges employed by the wrath of heaven, and who made war only for the pleasure of making it. Such are, in polished ages and among the most civilised nations, those supposed heroes, whose supreme delight is a battle, and who make war from inclination purely, and not from love to their country.

§34. Nations who make war without reason or apparent motives.

Defensive war is just when made against an unjust aggressor. This requires no proof. Self-defence against unjust violence is not only the right but the duty of a nation, and one of her most sacred duties. But if the enemy who wages offensive war has justice on his side, we have no right to make forcible opposition; and the defensive war then be-

§35. How defensive war is just or unjust.

comes unjust: for that enemy only exerts his lawful right:—he took up arms only to obtain justice which was refused to him; and it is an act of injustice to resist any one in the exertion of his right.

§36. How it may become just against an offensive war which at first was just.

All that remains to be done in such a case is to offer the invader a just satisfaction. If he will not be content with this, a nation gains one great advantage,—that of having turned the balance of justice on her own side; and his hostilities now becoming unjust, as having no longer any foundation, may very justly be opposed.

The Samnites, instigated by the ambition of their chiefs, had ravaged the lands of the allies of Rome. When they became sensible of their misconduct, they offered full reparation for the damages, with every reasonable satisfaction: but all their submissions could not appease the Romans; whereupon Caius Pontius, general of the Samnites, said to his men, "Since the Romans are absolutely determined on war, necessity justifies it on our side; an appeal to arms becomes lawful on the part of those who are deprived of every other resource"—*Justum est bellum, quibus necessarium; et pia arma, quibus nulla nisi in armis relinquitur spes.*[*][7]

§37. How an offensive war is just in an evident cause.

In order to estimate the justice of an offensive war, the nature of the subject for which a nation takes up arms must be first <306> considered. We should be thoroughly assured of our right before we proceed to assert it in so dreadful a manner. If, therefore, the question relate to a thing which is evidently just, as the recovery of our property, the assertion of a clear and incontestable right, or the attainment of just satisfaction for a manifest injury,—and if we cannot obtain justice otherwise than by force of arms,—offensive war becomes lawful. Two things are therefore necessary to render it just,—first, some right which is to be asserted,—that is to say, that we be authorised to demand something of another nation:—2. that we be unable to obtain it otherwise than by force of arms. Necessity alone warrants the use of force. It is a dangerous and terrible resource. Nature, the common parent of mankind, allows of it only in cases of the last extremity, and when all other means fail. It is

* Livy [[*Ab urbe condita*]], lib. ix. init.

7. "Just is the war that is necessary and the arms are righteous, where there is hope in nothing but arms" (trans. Eds.).

doing wrong to a nation, to make use of violence against her, before we know whether she be disposed to do us justice, or to refuse it.

Those who, without trying pacific measures, run to arms on every trifling occasion, sufficiently shew that justificatory reasons are, in their mouths, mere pretexts: they eagerly seize the opportunity of indulging their passions and gratifying their ambition under some colour of right.

In a doubtful cause, where the rights are uncertain, obscure, and disputable, all that can be reasonably required, is, that the question be discussed (Book II. §331), and that, if it be impossible fully to clear it up, the contest be terminated by an equitable compromise. If therefore one of the parties should refuse to accede to such conciliatory measures, the other is justifiable in taking up arms to compel him to an accommodation. And we must observe, that war does not decide the question; victory only compels the vanquished to subscribe to the treaty which terminates the difference. It is an error, no less absurd than pernicious, to say that war is to decide controversies between those who acknowledge no superior judge,—as is the case with nations. Victory usually favours the cause of strength and prudence rather than that of right and justice. It would be a bad rule of decision; but it is an effectual mode of compelling him who refuses to accede to such measures as are consonant to justice; and it becomes just in the hands of a prince who uses it seasonably and for a lawful cause. §38. In a doubtful cause.

War cannot be just on both sides. One party claims a right; the other disputes it:—the one complains of an injury; the other denies having done it. They may be considered as two individuals disputing on the truth of a proposition; and it is impossible that two contrary sentiments should be true at the same time. §39. War cannot be just on both sides.

It may however happen that both the contending parties are candid and sincere in their intentions; and, in a doubtful cause, it is still uncertain which side is in the right. Wherefore, since nations are equal and independent (Book II. §36, and Prelim. §§18, 19), and cannot claim a right of judgment over each other, it <307> follows, that, in every case susceptible of doubt, the arms of the two parties at war are to be accounted equally lawful, at least as to external effects, and until the decision of the cause. But neither does that circumstance deprive other §40. Sometimes reputed lawful.

nations of the liberty of forming their own judgment on the case, in order to determine how they are to act, and to assist that party who shall appear to have right on his side,—nor does that effect of the independence of nations operate in exculpation of the author of an unjust war, who certainly incurs a high degree of guilt. But if he acts in consequence of invincible ignorance or error, the injustice of his arms is not imputable to him.

§41. War undertaken to punish a nation. When offensive war has for its object the punishment of a nation, it ought, like every other war, to be founded on right and necessity. 1. On right:—an injury must have been actually received. Injury alone being a just cause of war (§26), the reparation of it may be lawfully prosecuted: or if in its nature it be irreparable (the only case in which we are allowed to punish), we are authorised to provide for our own safety, and even for that of all other nations, by inflicting on the offender a punishment capable of correcting him, and serving as an example to others. 2. A war of this kind must have necessity to justify it: that is to say, that, to be lawful, it must be the only remaining mode to obtain a just satisfaction; which implies a reasonable security for the time to come. If that complete satisfaction be offered, or if it may be obtained without a war, the injury is done away, and the right to security no longer authorises us to seek vengeance for it.—See Book II. §§49, 52.

The nation in fault is bound to submit to a punishment which she has deserved, and to suffer it by way of atonement: but she is not obliged to give herself up to the discretion of an incensed enemy. Therefore, when attacked, she ought to make a tender of satisfaction, and ask what penalty is required; and if no explicit answer be given, or the adversary attempts to impose a disproportionate penalty, she then acquires a right to resist, and her defence becomes lawful.

On the whole, however, it is evident that the offended party alone has a right to punish independent persons. We shall not here repeat what we have said elsewhere (Book II. §7) of the dangerous mistake or extravagant pretensions of those who assume a right of punishing an independent nation for faults which do not concern them,—who, madly setting themselves up as defenders of the cause of God, take upon them to punish the moral depravity or irreligion of a people not committed to their superintendency.

Here a very celebrated question, and of the highest importance, pre- §42. Whether
sents itself. It is asked, whether the aggrandisement of a neighbouring the aggran-
                                                                         disement of a
power, by whom a nation fears she may one day be crushed, be a suffi-   neighbouring
cient reason for making war against him,—whether she be justifiable in   power can
                                                                         authorise a war
taking up arms to oppose his aggrandisement, or to weaken him, with   against him.
the sole view of securing herself <308> from those dangers which the
weaker states have almost always reason to apprehend from an over-
grown power. To the majority of politicians this question is no problem:
it is more difficult of solution to those who wish to see justice and prudence ever inseparably united.

On the one hand, a state that increases her power by all the arts of
good government, does no more than what is commendable: she fulfils
her duties towards herself, without violating those which she owes to
other nations. The sovereign, who, by inheritance, by free election, or
by any other just and honourable means, enlarges his dominions by the
addition of new provinces or entire kingdoms, only makes use of his
right, without injuring any person. How then should it be lawful to attack a state which, for its aggrandisement, makes use only of lawful
means? We must either have actually suffered an injury or be visibly
threatened with one, before we are authorised to take up arms, or have
just grounds for making war (§§26, 27). On the other hand it is but too
well known from sad and uniform experience, that predominating powers seldom fail to molest their neighbours, to oppress them, and even
totally subjugate them, whenever an opportunity occurs, and they can
do it with impunity. Europe was on the point of falling into servitude
for want of a timely opposition to the growing fortune of Charles V. Is
the danger to be waited for? Is the storm, which might be dispersed at
its rising, to be permitted to increase? Are we to allow of the aggrandisement of a neighbour, and quietly wait till he makes his preparations to
enslave us? Will it be a time to defend ourselves when we are deprived
of the means?—Prudence is a duty incumbent on all men, and most
pointedly so on the heads of nations, as being commissioned to watch
over the safety of a whole people. Let us endeavour to solve this momentous question, agreeably to the sacred principles of the law of nature
and of nations. We shall find that they do not lead to weak scruples, and
that it is an invariable truth that justice is inseparable from sound policy.

§43. Alone
and of itself, it
cannot give a
right to attack
him.

And first, let us observe, that prudence, which is, no doubt, a virtue highly necessary in sovereigns, can never recommend the use of unlawful means for the attainment of a just and laudable end. Let not the safety of the people, that supreme law of the state, be alleged here in objection; for the very safety of the people itself, and the common safety of nations, prohibit the use of means which are repugnant to justice and probity. Why are certain means unlawful? If we closely consider the point, if we trace it to its first principles, we shall see that it is purely because the introduction of them would be pernicious to human society, and productive of fatal consequences to all nations. See particularly what we have said concerning the observance of justice (Book II. Ch. V.). For the interest, therefore, and even the safety of nations, we ought to hold it as a sacred maxim, that the end does not sanctify the means. And since war is not <309> justifiable on any other ground than that of avenging an injury received, or preserving ourselves from one with which we are threatened (§26), it is a sacred principle of the law of nations, that an increase of power cannot, alone and of itself, give any one a right to take up arms in order to oppose it.

§44. How the
appearances of
danger give
that right.

No injury has been received from that power (so the question supposes). We must therefore have good grounds to think ourselves threatened by him, before we can lawfully have recourse to arms. Now power alone does not threaten an injury:—it must be accompanied by the will. It is indeed very unfortunate for mankind, that the will and inclination to oppress may be almost always supposed, where there is a power of oppressing with impunity. But these two things are not necessarily inseparable: and the only right which we derive from the circumstance of their being generally or frequently united, is that of taking the first appearances for a sufficient indication. When once a state has given proofs of injustice, rapacity, pride, ambition, or an imperious thirst of rule, she becomes an object of suspicion to her neighbours, whose duty it is to stand on their guard against her. They may come upon her at the moment when she is on the point of acquiring a formidable accession of power,—may demand securities,—and, if she hesitates to give them, may prevent her designs by force of arms. The interests of nations are, in point of importance, widely different from those of individuals: the sovereign must not be remiss in his attention to them, nor suffer his generosity and greatness of soul to supercede his suspicions. A nation that has a neighbour at once powerful and ambitious, has her all at stake. As men are under a necessity of regulating their conduct in most cases by probabilities, those probabilities claim their attention in proportion to the importance of the subject: and (to make use of a geometrical expression) their right to obviate a danger is in a compound ratio of the degree of probability, and the greatness of the evil threatened. If the evil in question be of a supportable nature,—if it be only some slight loss,—matters are not to be precipitated: there is no great danger in delaying our opposition to it, till there be a certainty of our being threatened. But if the safety of the state lies at stake, our precaution and foresight cannot be extended too far. Must we delay to avert our ruin till it is become inevitable? If the appearances are so easily credited, it is the fault of that neighbour, who has betrayed his ambition by several indications. If Charles the Second, king of Spain,[8] instead of settling the succession on the duke of Anjou, had appointed for his heir Louis XIV. himself,—to have tamely suffered the union of the monarchy of Spain with that of France, would, according to all the rules of human foresight, have been nothing less than delivering up all Europe to servitude, or at least reducing it to the most critical and precarious situation. But then, if two independent nations think fit to unite, so as afterwards to form one joint empire, have they not a right to do it? And who is authorised to <310> oppose them? I answer, they have a right to form such a union, provided the views by which they are actuated be not prejudicial to other states. Now if each of the two nations in question be, separately and without assistance, able to govern and support herself, and to defend herself from insult and oppression, it may be reasonably presumed that the object of their coalition is to domineer over their neighbours. And on occasions where it is impossible or too dangerous to wait for an absolute certainty, we may justly act on a reasonable presumption. If a stranger levels a musket at me in the middle of a forest, I am not yet certain that he intends to kill me: but shall I, in order to be convinced of his design,

8. Charles II of Spain, r. 1665–1700.

allow him time to fire? What reasonable casuist will deny me the right to anticipate him? But presumption becomes nearly equivalent to certainty, if the prince who is on the point of rising to an enormous power, has already given proofs of imperious pride and insatiable ambition. In the preceding supposition, who could have advised the powers of Europe to suffer such a formidable accession to the power of Louis the Fourteenth? Too certain of the use he would have made of it, they would have joined in opposing it: and in this their safety warranted them.[9] To say that they should have allowed him time to establish his dominion over Spain, and consolidate the union of the two monarchies,—and that, for fear of doing him an injury, they should have quietly waited till he crushed them all,—would not this be, in fact, depriving mankind of the right to regulate their conduct by the dictates of prudence, and to act on the ground of probability? Would it not be robbing them of the liberty to provide for their own safety, as long as they have not mathematical demonstration of its being in danger? It would have been in vain to have preached such a doctrine. The principal sovereigns of Europe, habituated, by the administration of Louvois,[10] to dread the views and power of Louis XIV. carried their mistrust so far, that they would not even suffer a prince of the house of France to sit on the throne of Spain, though invited to it by the nation, whose approbation had sanctioned the will of her former sovereign. He ascended it, however, notwithstanding the efforts of those who so strongly dreaded his elevation; and it has since appeared that their policy was too suspicious.

§45. Another case more evident.   It is still easier to prove, that, should that formidable power betray an unjust and ambitious disposition by doing the least injustice to another, all nations may avail themselves of the occasion, and, by joining the injured party, thus form a coalition of strength, in order to humble that ambitious potentate, and disable him from so easily oppressing his

9. Vattel here argues that war was justified against Louis XIV in order to prevent universal monarchy in Europe.

10. François-Michel Le Tellier (1641–91), Marquis de Louvois, served as secretary of state for war under Louis XIV of France and was particularly concerned with the reform of the army.

neighbours, or keeping them in continual awe and fear. For an injury gives us a right to provide for our future safety, by depriving the unjust aggressor of the means of injuring us; and it is lawful and even praiseworthy to assist those who are oppressed, or unjustly attacked.

Enough has been said on this subject, to set the minds of politicians at ease, and to relieve them from all apprehension that a <311> strict and punctilious observance of justice in this particular would pave the way to slavery. It is perhaps wholly unprecedented that a state should receive any remarkable accession of power, without giving other states just causes of complaint. Let the other nations be watchful and alert in repressing that growing power, and they will have nothing to fear. The emperor Charles V. laid hold on the pretext of religion, in order to oppress the princes of the empire, and subject them to his absolute authority. If, by following up his victory over the elector of Saxony,[11] he had accomplished that vast design, the liberties of all Europe would have been endangered. It was therefore with good reason that France assisted the protestants of Germany:—the care of her own safety authorised and urged her to the measure. When the same prince seized on the duchy of Milan, the sovereigns of Europe ought to have assisted France in contending with him for the possession of it, and to have taken advantage of the circumstance, in order to reduce his power within just bounds. Had they prudently availed themselves of the just causes which he soon gave them to form a league against him, they would have saved themselves the subsequent anxieties for their tottering liberty.[12]

But, suppose that powerful state, by the justice and circumspection of her conduct, affords us no room to take exception to her proceedings, are we to view her progress with an eye of indifference? are we to remain quiet spectators of the rapid increase of her power, and imprudently expose ourselves to such designs as it may inspire her with?—No, beyond

§46. Other allowable means of defence against a formidable power.

11. The Holy Roman Emperor Charles V (r. 1530–56) defeated John Frederick, elector of Saxony, in 1547 at Mühlberg, outside Leipzig.

12. Once again Vattel underlines the danger of monarchs in Europe aspiring to expand their power and upset the existing balance between states. His strategy for ending the threat of universal monarchy is outlined in the following paragraphs.

all doubt. In a matter of so high importance, imprudent supineness would be unpardonable. The example of the Romans is a good lesson for all sovereigns. Had the potentates of those times concerted together to keep a watchful eye on the enterprises of Rome, and to check her encroachments, they would not have successively fallen into servitude. But force of arms is not the only expedient by which we may guard against a formidable power. There are other means, of a gentler nature, and which are at all times lawful. The most effectual is a confederacy of the less powerful sovereigns, who, by this coalition of strength, become able to hold the balance against that potentate whose power excites their alarms. Let them be firm and faithful in their alliance; and their union will prove the safety of each.

They may also mutually favour each other, to the exclusion of him whom they fear; and by reciprocally allowing various advantages to the subjects of the allies, especially in trade, and refusing them to those of that dangerous potentate, they will augment their own strength, and diminish his, without affording him any just cause of complaint, since every one is at liberty to grant favours and indulgences at his own pleasure.

§47. Political equilibrium.

Europe forms a political system, an integral body, closely connected by the relations and different interests of the nations inhabiting this part of the world. It is not, as formerly, a con-<312>fused heap of detached pieces, each of which thought herself very little concerned in the fate of the others, and seldom regarded things which did not immediately concern her. The continual attention of sovereigns to every occurrence, the constant residence of ministers, and the perpetual negotiations, make of modern Europe a kind of republic, of which the members— each independent, but all linked together by the ties of common interest—unite for the maintenance of order and liberty. Hence arose that famous scheme of the political balance, or the equilibrium of power; by which is understood such a disposition of things, as that no one potentate be able absolutely to predominate, and prescribe laws to the others.

§48. Ways of maintaining it.

The surest means of preserving that equilibrium would be, that no power should be much superior to the others,—that all, or at least the greater part, should be nearly equal in force. Such a project has been attributed to Henry the Fourth:* but it would have been impossible to carry it into execution without injustice and violence. Besides, suppose such equality once established, how could it always be maintained by lawful means? Commerce, industry, military pre-eminence, would soon put an end to it. The right of inheritance, vesting even in women and their descendents,—a rule, which it was so absurd to establish in the case of sovereignties, but which nevertheless is established,—would completely overturn the whole system.

It is a more simple, an easier, and a more equitable plan, to have recourse to the method just mentioned, of forming confederacies in order to oppose the more powerful potentate, and prevent him from giving law to his neighbours. Such is the mode at present pursued by the sovereigns of Europe. They consider the two principal powers, which on that very account are naturally rivals, as destined to be checks on each other; and they unite with the weaker, like so many weights thrown into the lighter scale, in order to keep it in equilibrium with the other. The house of Austria has long been the preponderating power: at present France is so in her turn. England, whose opulence and formidable fleets have a powerful influence, without alarming any state on the score of its liberty, because that nation seems cured of the rage of conquest,— England, I say, has the glory of holding the political balance. She is attentive to preserve it in equilibrium:—a system of policy, which is in itself highly just and wise, and will ever entitle her to praise, as long as she continues to pursue it only by means of alliances, confederacies, and other methods equally lawful.[13]

---

* Of France.

13. Vattel has attacked projects for perpetual peace associated with expanding French power as unworkable, and argues that only greater British involvement in European power politics can retain a political equilibrium which would maintain existing states—especially the smaller republics threatened by commercial monarchies. This argument becomes commonplace in republican reform politics in the decades up to the French Revolution.

§49. How he
who destroys
the equilib-
rium may
be restrained,
or even
weakened.

Confederacies would be a sure mode of preserving the equilibrium, and thus maintaining the liberty of nations, did all princes thoroughly understand their true interests, and make the welfare of the state serve as the rule in all their proceedings. Great potentates, however, are but too successful in gaining over par-<313>tisans and allies, who blindly adopt all their views. Dazzled by the glare of a present advantage, seduced by their avarice, deceived by faithless ministers,—how many princes become the tools of a power which will one day swallow up either themselves or their successors! The safest plan, therefore, is to seize the first favourable opportunity when we can, consistently with justice, weaken that potentate who destroys the equilibrium (§45)—or to employ every honourable means to prevent his acquiring too formidable a degree of power. For that purpose, all the other nations should be particularly attentive not to suffer him to aggrandise himself by arms: and this they may at all times do with justice. For if this prince makes an unjust war, every one has a right to succour the oppressed party. If he makes a just war, the neutral nations may interfere as mediators for an accommodation,—they may induce the weaker state to propose reasonable terms and offer a fair satisfaction,—and may save her from falling under the yoke of a conqueror. On the offer of equitable conditions to the prince who wages even the most justifiable war, he has all that he can demand. The justice of his cause, as we shall soon see, never gives him a right to subjugate his enemy, unless when that extremity becomes necessary to his own safety, or when he has no other mode of obtaining indemnification for the injury he has received. Now, that is not the case here, as the interposing nations can by other means procure him a just indemnification, and an assurance of safety.

In fine, there cannot exist a doubt, that, if that formidable potentate certainly entertain designs of oppression and conquest,—if he betray his views by his preparations and other proceedings,—the other states have a right to anticipate him: and if the fate of war declares in their favour, they are justifiable in taking advantage of this happy opportunity to weaken and reduce a power too contrary to the equilibrium, and dangerous to the common liberty.

This right of nations is still more evident against a sovereign, who, from an habitual propensity to take up arms without reasons or even so much as plausible pretexts, is continually disturbing the public tranquillity.

This leads us to a particular question nearly allied to the preceding. When a neighbour, in the midst of a profound peace, erects fortresses on our frontier, equips a fleet, augments his troops, assembles a powerful army, fills his magazines,—in a word, when he makes preparations for war,—are we allowed to attack him with a view to prevent the danger with which we think ourselves threatened? The answer greatly depends on the manners and character of that neighbour. We must inquire into the reasons of those preparations, and bring him to an explanation:— such is the mode of proceeding in Europe: and if his sincerity be justly suspected, securities may be required of him. His refusal in this case would furnish ample indication of sinister designs, and a sufficient reason to justify us in anticipating <314> them. But if that sovereign has never betrayed any symptoms of baseness and perfidy, and especially if at that time there is no dispute subsisting between him and us, why should we not quietly rest on his word, only taking such precautions as prudence renders indispensable? We ought not, without sufficient cause, to presume him capable of exposing himself to infamy by adding perfidy to violence. As long as he has not rendered his sincerity questionable, we have no right to require any other security from him.

§50. Behaviour allowable towards a neighbour preparing for war.

It is true, however, that if a sovereign continues to keep up a powerful army in profound peace, his neighbours must not suffer their vigilance to be entirely lulled to sleep by his bare word; and prudence requires that they should keep themselves on their guard. However certain they may be of the good-faith of that prince, unforeseen differences may intervene; and shall they leave him the advantage of being provided at that juncture with a numerous and well-disciplined army, while they themselves will have only new levies to oppose it? Unquestionably, no. This would be leaving themselves almost wholly at his discretion. They are therefore under the necessity of following his example, and keeping, as he does, a numerous army on foot:—and what a burden is this to a state! Formerly, and without going any farther back than the last century, it was pretty generally made an article in every treaty of peace, that the belligerent powers should disarm on both sides,—that they should disband their troops. If, in a time of profound peace, a prince was disposed to keep up any considerable number of forces, his neighbours took their measures accordingly, formed leagues against him, and obliged him to disarm. Why has not that salutary custom been preserved? The constant maintenance of numerous armies deprives the soil of its cultivators, checks the progress of population, and can only serve to destroy the liberties of the nation by whom they are maintained. Happy England! whose situation exempts it from any considerable charge in supporting the instruments of despotism. Happy Switzerland! if, continuing carefully to exercise her militia, she keeps herself in a condition to repel any foreign enemies, without feeding a host of idle soldiers who might one day crush the liberties of the people, and even bid defiance to the lawful authority of the sovereign. Of this the Roman legions furnish a signal instance. This happy method of a free republic,—the custom of training up all her citizens to the art of war,—renders the state respectable abroad, and saves it from a very pernicious defect at home. It would have been every-where imitated, had the public good been every-where the only object in view.

Sufficient has now been said on the general principles for estimating the justice of a war. Those who are thoroughly acquainted with the principles, and have just ideas of the various rights of nations, will easily apply the rules to particular cases. <315>

CHAPTER IV

Of the Declaration of War,— and of War in due form.

§51. Declaration of war.

The right of making war belongs to nations only as a remedy against injustice: it is the offspring of unhappy necessity. This remedy is so dreadful in its effects, so destructive to mankind, so grievous even to the party who has recourse to it, that unquestionably the law of nature allows of it only in the last extremity,—that is to say, when every other expedient proves ineffectual for the maintenance of justice. It is demonstrated in the foregoing chapter, that, in order to be justifiable in taking up arms, it is necessary—1. That we have a just cause of complaint. 2. That a reasonable satisfaction have been denied us. 3. The ruler of the nation, as we have observed, ought maturely to consider whether it be for the advantage of the state to prosecute his right by force of arms. But all this is not sufficient. As it is possible that the present fear of our arms may make an impression on the mind of our adversary, and induce him to do us justice,—we owe this farther regard to humanity, and especially to the lives and peace of the subjects, to declare to that unjust nation, or its chief, that we are at length going to have recourse to the last remedy, and make use of open force for the purpose of bringing him to reason. This is called *declaring war.* All this is included in the Roman manner of proceeding, regulated in their *fecial law.* They first sent the chief of the *feciales* or heralds, called *pater patratus,* to demand satisfaction of the nation who had offended them; and if within the space of thirty-three days that nation did not return a satisfactory answer, the herald called the gods to be witnesses of the injustice, and came away, saying that the Romans would consider what measures they should adopt. The king, and in after times the consul, hereupon asked the senate's opinion; and when war was resolved on, the herald was sent back to the frontier, where he declared it.* It is surprising to find among the Romans such justice, such moderation and prudence, at a time too when apparently nothing but courage and ferocity was to be expected from them. By such scrupulous delicacy in the conduct of her wars, Rome laid a most solid foundation for her subsequent greatness.

(marginal note) Necessity thereof.

A declaration of war being necessary as a further effort to terminate the difference without the effusion of blood, by making use of the principle of fear in order to bring the enemy to more equitable sentiments,— it ought, at the same time that it announces our settled resolution of making war, to set forth the <316> reasons which have induced us to take up arms. This is at present the constant practice among the powers of Europe.

(marginal note) §52. What it is to contain.

* Livy, lib. i. cap. 31.

§53. It is
simple or
conditional.

After a fruitless application for justice, a nation may proceed to a declaration of war, which is then *pure* and *simple*. But, to include the whole business in a single act instead of two separate ones, the demand of justice (called by the Romans *rerum repetitio*) may, if we think proper, be accompanied by a *conditional declaration* of war, notifying that we will commence hostilities unless we obtain immediate satisfaction on such or such subject. In this case there is no necessity for adding a *pure* and *simple* declaration of war,—the *conditional* one sufficing, if the enemy delays giving satisfaction.

§54. The right
to make war
ceases on
the offer of
equitable
conditions.

If the enemy, on either declaration of war, offers equitable conditions of peace, we are bound to refrain from hostilities; for as soon as justice is done to us, that immediately supercedes all right to employ force, which we are not allowed to use unless for the necessary maintenance of our rights. To these offers, however, are to be added securities; for we are under no obligation to suffer ourselves to be amused by empty proposals. The word of a sovereign is a sufficient security, as long as he has not disgraced his credit by any act of perfidy: and we should be contented with it. As to the conditions themselves,—besides the principal subject, we have a right to demand a reimbursement of the expenses incurred in our preparations for war.

§55. Formalities of a declaration of war.

It is necessary that the declaration of war be known to the state against whom it is made. This is all which the natural law of nations requires. Nevertheless, if custom has introduced certain formalities in the business, those nations, who, by adopting the custom, have given their tacit consent to such formalities, are under an obligation of observing them, as long as they have not set them aside by a public renunciation (Prelim. §26). Formerly the powers of Europe used to send heralds or embassadors to declare war; at present they content themselves with publishing the declaration in the capital, in the principal towns, or on the frontiers: manifestoes are issued; and through the easy and expeditious channels of communication which the establishment of posts now affords, the intelligence is soon spread on every side.

§56. Other
reasons for the
necessity of its
publication.

Besides the foregoing reasons, it is necessary for a nation to publish the declaration of war for the instruction and direction of her own subjects, in order to fix the date of the rights which belong to them from the moment of this declaration, and in relation to certain effects which the voluntary law of nations attributes to a war in form. Without such a public declaration of war, it would, in a treaty of peace, be too difficult to determine those acts which are to be considered as the effects of war, and those that each nation may set down as injuries of which she means to demand reparation. In the last treaty of Aix-la-Chapelle,[14] between France and Spain on the one side, and England on the other, it was agreed that all the prizes taken before the declaration of war should be restored. <317>

He who is attacked and only wages defensive war, needs not to make any hostile declaration,—the state of warfare being sufficiently ascertained by the enemy's declaration or open hostilities. In modern times, however, the sovereign who is attacked, seldom omits to declare war in his turn, whether from an idea of dignity, or for the direction of his subjects.

§57. Defensive war requires no declaration.

If the nation on whom we have determined to make war will not admit any minister or herald to declare it,—whatever the custom may otherwise be, we may content ourselves with publishing the declaration of hostilities within our own territories, or on the frontier; and if the declaration does not come to the knowledge of that nation before hostilities are commenced, she can only blame herself. The Turks imprison and maltreat even the embassadors of those powers with whom they are determined to come to a rupture: it would be a perilous undertaking for a herald to go and declare war against them in their own country. Their savage disposition, therefore, supercedes the necessity of sending one.

§58. When it may be omitted in an offensive war.

But no person being exempted from his duty for the sole reason that another has been wanting in *his,* we are not to omit declaring war against a nation previous to a commencement of hostilities, because that nation has on a former occasion attacked us without any declaration. That nation, in so doing, has violated the law of nature (§51); and her fault does not authorise us to commit a similar one.

§59. It is not to be omitted by way of retaliation.

The law of nations does not impose the obligation of declaring war, with a view to give the enemy time to prepare for an unjust defence. The

§60. Time of the declaration.

14. Treaty of Aix-la-Chapelle, 1748.

declaration, therefore, need not be made till the army has reached the frontiers; it is even lawful to delay it till we have entered the enemy's territories, and there possessed ourselves of an advantageous post: it must, however, necessarily precede the commission of any act of hostility. For thus we provide for our own safety, and equally attain the object of a declaration of war, which is, to give an unjust adversary the opportunity of seriously considering his past conduct, and avoiding the horrors of war, by doing justice. Such was the conduct of that generous prince, Henry the Fourth, towards Charles Emanuel duke of Savoy, who had wearied his patience by vain and fraudulent negotiations.*[15]

§61. Duty of the inhabitants on a foreign army's entering a country before a declaration of war.

If he who enters a country with an army kept under strict discipline, declares to the inhabitants that he does not come as an enemy, that he will commit no violence, and will acquaint the sovereign with the cause of his coming,—the inhabitants are not to attack him; and should they dare to attempt it, he has a right to chastise them. But they are not to admit him into any strong-holds, nor can he demand admission. It is not the business of subjects to commence hostilities without orders from their sovereign: but if they are brave and loyal, they will in the <318> mean time seize on all the advantageous posts, and defend themselves against any attempt made to dislodge them.

§62. Commencement of hostilities.

After a declaration of war on the part of the sovereign who has thus invaded the country, if equitable conditions are not offered him without delay, he may commence his operations: for, I repeat it, he is under no obligation to suffer himself to be amused. But, at the same time, we are never to lose sight of the principles before laid down (§§26 and 51) concerning the only legitimate causes of war. To march an army into a neighbouring country by which we are not threatened, and without having endeavoured to obtain, by reason and justice, an equitable reparation for the wrongs of which we complain, would be introducing a mode pregnant with evils to mankind, and sapping the foundations of the safety

* See Sully's Memoirs.

15. Between 1588 and 1593, Charles Emmanuel I took Saluzzo from France and after the murder of Henry III (1589) sent troops into France to assert his own claims to the throne against Henry IV (r. 1589–1610).

and tranquillity of states. If this mode of proceeding be not exploded and proscribed by the public indignation and the concurrence of every civilised people, it will become necessary to continue always in a military posture, and to keep ourselves constantly on our guard, no less in times of profound peace, than during the existence of declared and open war.

The sovereign declaring war can neither detain the persons nor the property of those subjects of the enemy who are within his dominions at the time of the declaration. They came into his country under the public faith. By permitting them to enter and reside in his territories, he tacitly promised them full liberty and security for their return. He is therefore bound to allow them a reasonable time for withdrawing with their effects; and if they stay beyond the term prescribed, he has a right to treat them as enemies,—as unarmed enemies, however. But if they are detained by an insurmountable impediment, as by sickness, he must necessarily, and for the same reasons, grant them a sufficient extension of the term. At present, so far from being wanting in this duty, sovereigns carry their attention to humanity still farther, so that foreigners, who are subjects of the state against which war is declared, are very frequently allowed full time for the settlement of their affairs. This is observed in a particular manner with regard to merchants; and the case is moreover carefully provided for, in commercial treaties. The king of England has done more than this. In his last declaration of war against France, he ordained that all French subjects who were in his dominions, should be at liberty to remain, and be perfectly secure in their persons and effects, "provided they demeaned themselves properly."

§63. Conduct to be observed towards the subjects of an enemy, who are in the country at the time of the declaration of war.

We have said (§56) that a sovereign is to make the declaration of war public within his dominions, for the information and direction of his subjects. He is also to make known his declaration of war to the neutral powers, in order to acquaint them with the justificatory reasons which authorise it,—the cause which obliges him to take up arms,—and to notify to them that such or such a nation is his enemy, that they may conduct themselves accordingly. We shall even see that this is necessary in <319> order to obviate all difficulty, when we come to treat of the right to seize certain things which neutral persons are carrying to the enemy, and of what is termed *contraband* in time of war. This *publi-*

§64. Publication of the war, and manifestoes.

cation of the war may be called *declaration,* and that which is notified directly to the enemy, *denunciation;* and indeed the Latin term is *denunciatio belli.*

War is at present published and declared by manifestoes. These pieces never fail to contain the justificatory reasons, good or bad, on which the party grounds his right to take up arms. The least scrupulous sovereign would wish to be thought just, equitable, and a lover of peace: he is sensible that a contrary reputation might be detrimental to him. The manifesto implying a declaration of war, or the declaration itself, printed, published, and circulated throughout the whole state, contains also the sovereign's general orders to his subjects relative to their conduct in the war.*

§65. Decorum and moderation to be observed in the manifestoes.

In so civilised an age, it may be unnecessary to observe, that, in those pieces which are published on the subject of war, it is proper to abstain from every opprobrious expression, indicative of hatred, animosity, and rage, and only calculated to excite similar sentiments in the bosom of the enemy. A prince ought to preserve the most dignified decorum, both in his words and in his writings. He ought to respect himself in the person of his equals: and though it is his misfortune to be at variance with a nation, shall he inflame the quarrel by offensive expressions, and thus deprive himself even of the hopes of a sincere reconciliation? Homer's heroes call each other *"dog"* and *"drunkard"*: but this was perfectly in character, since, in their enmity, they knew no bounds. Frederic Barbarossa, and other emperors, and the popes their enemies, treated each other with as little delicacy. Let us congratulate our age on the superior gentleness of its manners, and not give the name of unmeaning politeness to those attentions which are productive of real and substantial effects.

---

* It is remarked, as a very singular circumstance, that Charles the Second, king of Great Britain, in his declaration of war against France, dated February 9, 1668, promised security to French subjects who should *"demean themselves properly,"*—and moreover his protection and favour to such of them as might chuse to emigrate to his dominions. [[Note added in 1773/1797 editions.]]

Those formalities of which the necessity is deducible from the principles and the very nature of war, are the characteristics of a lawful war in due form (*justum bellum*). Grotius says,* that, according to the law of nations, two things are requisite to constitute a solemn or formal war—first, that it be, on both sides, made by the sovereign authority,—secondly, that it be accompanied by certain formalities. These formalities consist in the demand of a just satisfaction (*rerum repetitio*), and in the declaration of war, at least on the part of him who attacks;—for defensive war requires no declaration (§57), nor even, on urgent occasions, an express order from the sovereign. In effect, these <320> two conditions are necessarily required in every war which shall, according to the law of nations, be a legitimate one, that is to say, such a war as nations have a right to wage. The right of making war belongs only to the sovereign (§4); and it is only after satisfaction has been refused to him (§37), and even after he has made a declaration of war (§51), that he has a right to take up arms.

§66. What is a lawful war in due form.

A war in due form is also called a regular war, because certain rules, either prescribed by the law of nature, or adopted by custom, are observed in it.

Legitimate and formal warfare must be carefully distinguished from those illegitimate and informal wars, or rather predatory expeditions, undertaken, either without lawful authority, or without apparent cause, as likewise without the usual formalities, and solely with a view to plunder. Grotius relates several instances of the latter.† Such were the enterprises of the *grandes compagnies* which had assembled in France during the wars with the English,—armies of banditti, who ranged about Europe, purely for spoil and plunder: such were the cruises of the *buccaneers,* without commission, and in time of peace; and such in general are the depredations of pirates. To the same class belong almost all the expeditions of the Barbary corsairs: though authorised by a sovereign, they are undertaken without any apparent cause, and from no other motive than the lust of plunder. These two species of war, I say,—the lawful

§67. It is to be distinguished from informal and unlawful war.

* De Jure Belli et Pacis, lib. i. cap. iii. §4.
† Lib. iii. cap. iv [[*Law of War and Peace*]].

and the illegitimate,—are to be carefully distinguished, as the effects and the rights arising from each are very different.

§68. Grounds of this distinction. In order fully to conceive the grounds of this distinction, it is necessary to recollect the nature and object of lawful war. It is only as the last remedy against obstinate injustice that the law of nature allows of war. Hence arise the rights which it gives, as we shall explain in the sequel: hence likewise the rules to be observed in it. Since it is equally possible that either of the parties may have right on his side,—and since, in consequence of the independence of nations, that point is not to be decided by others (§40),—the condition of the two enemies is the same, while the war lasts. Thus, when a nation or a sovereign has declared war against another sovereign on account of a difference arisen between them, their war is what among nations is called a lawful and formal war; and its effects are, by the voluntary law of nations, the same on both sides, independently of the justice of the cause, as we shall more fully shew in the sequel.* Nothing of this kind is the case in an informal and illegitimate war, which is more properly called depredation. Undertaken without any right, without even an apparent cause, it can be productive of no lawful effect, nor give any right to the author of it. A nation attacked by such sort of enemies is not under any obligation to observe towards them the rules prescribed in formal war-<321>fare. She may treat them as robbers. The inhabitants of Geneva, after defeating the famous attempt to take their city by escalade,† caused all the prisoners whom they took from the Savoyards on that occasion, to be hanged up as robbers, who had come to attack them without cause and without a declaration of war. Nor were the Genevese censured for this proceeding, which would have been detested in a formal war.

---

* See chap. xii. of this book.
† In the year 1602.

CHAPTER V

Of the Enemy, and of Things belonging to the Enemy.

The enemy is he with whom a nation is at open war. The Latins had a particular term (*Hostis*) to denote a public enemy, and distinguished him from a private enemy (*Inimicus*). Our language affords but one word for these two classes of persons, who ought nevertheless to be carefully distinguished. A private enemy is one who seeks to hurt us, and takes pleasure in the evil that befalls us. A public enemy forms claims against us, or rejects ours, and maintains his real or pretended rights by force of arms. The former is never innocent; he fosters rancour and hatred in his heart. It is possible that the public enemy may be free from such odious sentiments, that he does not wish us ill, and only seeks to maintain his rights. This observation is necessary in order to regulate the dispositions of our heart towards a public enemy. §69. Who is an enemy.

When the sovereign or ruler of the state declares war against another sovereign, it is understood that the whole nation declares war against another nation: for the sovereign represents the nation, and acts in the name of the whole society (Book I. §§40, 41); and it is only in a body, and in her national character, that one nation has to do with another. Hence, these two nations are enemies, and all the subjects of the one are enemies to all the subjects of the other. In this particular, custom and principles are in accord. §70. All the subjects of the two states at war are enemies,

Enemies continue such, wherever they happen to be. The place of abode is of no consequence here. It is the political ties which determine the character. Whilst a man continues a citizen of his own country, he is the enemy of all those with whom his nation is at war. But we must not hence conclude that these enemies may treat each other as such, wherever they happen to meet. Every one being master in his respective country, a neutral prince will not allow them to use any violence in his territories. §71. and continue to be enemies in all places.

§72. Whether women and children are to be accounted enemies.

Since women and children are subjects of the state, and mem-<322>bers of the nation, they are to be ranked in the class of enemies. But it does not thence follow that we are justifiable in treating them like men who bear arms, or are capable of bearing them. It will appear in the sequel, that we have not the same rights against all classes of enemies.

§73. Things belonging to the enemy

When once we have precisely determined who our enemies are, it is easy to know what are the things belonging to the enemy (*res hostiles*). We have shewn that not only the sovereign with whom we are at war is an enemy, but also his whole nation, even the very women and children. Every thing, therefore, which belongs to that nation,—to the state, to the sovereign, to the subjects, of whatever age or sex,—every thing of that kind, I say, falls under the description of things belonging to the enemy.

§74. continue such every- where.

And, with respect to things, the case is the same as with respect to persons:—things belonging to the enemy continue such wherever they are. But we are not hence to conclude, any more than in the case of persons (§71), that we every-where possess a right to treat those things as things belonging to the enemy.

§75. Neutral things found with an enemy.

Since it is not the place where a thing is, which determines the nature of that thing, but the character of the person to whom it belongs,— things belonging to neutral persons, which happen to be in an enemy's country or on board an enemy's ships, are to be distinguished from those which belong to the enemy. But it is the owner's business to adduce evident proof that they are his property: for, in default of such proof, a thing is naturally presumed to belong to the nation in whose possession it is found.

§76. Lands possessed by foreigners in an enemy's country.

The preceding section relates to movable property: but the rule is different with respect to immovable possessions, such as landed estates. Since all these do in some measure belong to the nation, are part of its domain, of its territory, and under its government (Book I. §§204, 235, Book II. §114)—and since the owner is still a subject of the country as possessor of a landed estate,—property of this kind does not cease to be enemy's property (*res hostiles*), though possessed by a neutral foreigner. Nevertheless, war being now carried on with so much moderation and indulgence, protections are granted for houses and lands possessed by foreigners in an enemy's country. For the same reason, he who declares war does not confiscate the immovable property possessed in his country by his enemy's subjects. By permitting them to purchase and possess such property, he has in that respect admitted them into the number of his subjects. But the income may be sequestrated, in order to prevent its being remitted to the enemy's country.

Among the things belonging to the enemy, are likewise incorporeal things,—all his rights, claims, and debts, excepting however those kind of rights granted by a third party, and in which the grantor is so far concerned, that it is not a matter of indiffe-<323>rence to him, in what hands they are vested. Such, for instance, are the rights of commerce. But as debts are not of this number, war gives us the same rights over any sums of money due by neutral nations to our enemy, as it can give over his other property. §77. Things due to the enemy by a third party.

When Alexander, by conquest, became absolute master of Thebes, he remitted to the Thessalians a hundred talents which they owed to the Thebans.* The sovereign has naturally the same right over what his subjects may owe to enemies. He may therefore confiscate debts of this nature, if the term of payment happen in the time of war; or at least he may prohibit his subjects from paying while the war continues. But at present, a regard to the advantage and safety of commerce has induced all the sovereigns of Europe to act with less rigour in this point. And as the custom has been generally received, he who should act contrary to it, would violate the public faith; for strangers trusted his subjects only from a firm persuasion that the general custom would be observed. The state does not so much as touch the sums which it owes to the enemy: money lent to the public is every-where exempt from confiscation and seizure in case of war.

* Grotius, de Jure Belli & Pacis, lib. iii. cap. viii. §4.

CHAPTER VI

Of the Enemy's Allies—of warlike Associations— of Auxiliaries and Subsidies.

§78. Treaties
relative to war.
We have sufficiently spoken of treaties in general, and shall here touch on this subject only in its particular relations to war. Treaties relating to war are of several kinds, and vary in their objects and clauses, according to the will of those who make them. Besides applying to them all that we have said of treaties in general (Book II. Ch. XII. &c.), they may also be divided into treaties real and personal, equal and unequal, &c. But they have also their specific differences, viz. those which relate to their particular object, war.

§79. Defensive
and offensive
alliances.
Under this relation, alliances made for warlike purposes are divided in general into *defensive* and *offensive* alliances. In the former, the nation engages only to defend her ally in case he be attacked: in the latter, she unites with him for the purpose of making an attack,—of jointly waging war against another nation. Some alliances are both offensive and defensive; and there seldom is an offensive alliance which is not also a defensive one. But it is very usual for alliances to be purely defensive: and these are in general the most natural and lawful. It would be <324> a tedious and even a useless task to enumerate in detail all the varieties incident to such alliances. Some are made, without restriction, against all opponents: in others, certain states are excepted: others again are formed against such or such a nation expressly mentioned by name.

§80. Differ-
ence between
warlike associ-
ations and
auxiliary
treaties.
But a difference, of great importance to be observed, especially in defensive alliances, is that between an intimate and complete alliance, in which we agree to a union of interests,—and another, in which we only promise a stated succour. The alliance in which we agree to a union of interests, is a *warlike association:* each of the parties acts with his whole force; all the allies become principals in the war; they have the same friends and the same enemies. But an alliance of this nature is more particularly termed a *warlike association,* when it is offensive.

When a sovereign, without directly taking part in the war made by another sovereign, only sends him succours of troops or ships, these are called *auxiliaries.*

The auxiliary troops serve the prince to whom they are sent, according to their sovereign's orders. If they are purely and simply sent without restriction, they are to serve equally on the offensive and the defensive; and, for the particulars of their operations, they are to obey the directions of the prince to whose assistance they come. Yet this prince has not the free and entire disposal of them, as of his own subjects: they are granted to him only for his own wars; and he has no right to transfer them, as auxiliaries, to a third power.

Sometimes this succour from a potentate who does not directly take part in the war, consists in money; and then it is called a *subsidy.* This term is now often taken in another sense, and signifies a sum of money annually paid by one sovereign to another, in return for a body of troops, which the latter furnishes to the other to carry on his wars, or keeps in readiness for his service. The treaties for procuring such a resource are called *subsidiary treaties.* France and England have at present such treaties existing with several of the northern powers and princes in Germany, and continue them even in times of peace.

In order, now, to judge of the morality of these several treaties or alliances,—of their legitimacy according to the law of nations,—we must, in the first place, lay down this incontrovertible principle, that *It is lawful and commendable to succour and assist, by all possible means, a nation engaged in a just war; and it is even a duty incumbent on every nation, to give such assistance, when she can give it without injury to herself. But no assistance whatever is to be afforded to him who is engaged in an unjust war.* There is nothing in this which is not demonstrated by what we have said of the common duties of nations towards each other (Book II. Ch. I.). To support the cause of justice when we are able, is always commendable: but, in assisting the unjust, we partake of his crime, and become, like him, guilty of injustice.

If, to the principle we have now laid down, you add the consi-<325>deration of what a nation owes to her own safety, and of the care which it is so natural and so fit that she should take to put herself in a condition to resist her enemies, you will the more readily perceive how clear a right a nation has to make warlike alliances, and especially defensive alliances, whose sole tendency is to maintain all parties in the quiet and secure possession of their property.

But great circumspection is to be used in forming such alliances. Engagements by which a nation may be drawn into a war at a moment when she least expects it, ought not to be contracted without very important reasons, and a direct view to the welfare of the state. We here speak of alliances made in time of peace, and by way of precaution against future contingencies.

§85. Alliances made with a nation actually engaged in war.

If there be question of contracting an alliance with a nation already engaged in a war or on the point of engaging in one, two things are to be considered,—1. The justice of that nation's quarrel. 2. The welfare of the state. If the war which a prince wages or is preparing to wage, be unjust, it is not allowable to form an alliance with him; for injustice is not to be supported. If he is justifiable in taking up arms, it still remains to be considered whether the welfare of the state allows or requires us to embark in his quarrel: for it is only with a view to the welfare of the state that the sovereign ought to use his authority: to that all his measures should tend, and especially those of the most important nature. What other consideration can authorise him to expose his people to the calamities of war?

§86. Tacit clause in every warlike alliance.

As it is only for the support of a just war that we are allowed to give assistance or contract alliances,—every alliance, every warlike association, every auxiliary treaty, contracted by way of anticipation in time of peace, and with no view to any particular war, necessarily and of itself includes this tacit clause, that the treaty shall not be obligatory except in case of a just war. On any other footing, the alliance could not be validly contracted. (Book II. §§161, 168.)

But care must be taken that treaties of alliance be not thereby reduced to empty and delusive formalities. The tacit restriction is to be understood only of a war which is evidently unjust; for otherwise a pretence for eluding treaties would never be wanting. Is there question of contracting an alliance with a power actually at war?—It behoves you most religiously to weigh the justice of his cause: the judgment depends solely on you, since you owe him no assistance any farther than as his quarrel is just, and your own circumstances make it convenient for you to embark in it. But when once engaged, nothing less than the manifest injustice of his cause can excuse you from assisting him. In a doubtful case, you are to presume that your ally has justice on his side;—that being his concern.

But if you entertain strong doubts, you may very fairly and commendably interpose to effect an accommodation. Thus you may bring the justice of the cause to the test of evidence, by dis-<326>covering which of the contending parties refuses to accede to equitable conditions.

As every alliance implies the tacit clause above-mentioned, he who refuses to succour his ally in a war that is manifestly unjust, is not chargeable with a breach of alliance. §87. To refuse succours for an unjust war, is no breach of alliance.

When alliances have thus been contracted beforehand, the question is to determine, in the course of events, those cases in which our engagements come in force, and we are bound to act in consequence of the alliance. This is what is called *casus foederis*, or case of the alliance, and is to be discovered in the concurrence of the circumstances for which the treaty has been made, whether those circumstances have been expressly specified in it, or tacitly supposed. Whatever has been promised in the treaty of alliance, is due in the *casus foederis*, and not otherwise. §88. What the *casus foederis* is.

As the most solemn treaties cannot oblige any one to favour an unjust quarrel (§86), the *casus foederis* never takes place in a war that is manifestly unjust. §89. It never takes place in an unjust war.

In a defensive alliance, the *casus foederis* does not exist immediately on our ally being attacked. It is still our duty to examine whether he has not given his enemy just cause to make war against him: for we cannot have engaged to undertake his defence with the view of enabling him to insult others, or to refuse them justice. If he is in the wrong, we must induce him to offer a reasonable satisfaction; and if his enemy will not be contented with it,—then, and not till then, the obligation of defending him commences. §90. How it exists in a defensive war,

But if the defensive alliance contains a guarantee of all the territories at that time possessed by the ally, the *casus foederis* immediately takes place whenever those territories are invaded or threatened with an in- §91. and in a treaty of guarantee.

vasion. If they are attacked for a just cause, we must prevail on our ally to give satisfaction; but we may on good grounds oppose his being deprived of his possessions, as it is generally with a view to our own security that we undertake to guaranty them. On the whole, the rules of interpretation, which we have given in an express chapter,* are to be consulted, in order to determine, on particular occasions, the existence of the *casus foederis.*

§92. The succour is not due under an inability to furnish it, or when the public safety would be exposed.

If the state that has promised succours finds herself unable to furnish them, her inability alone is sufficient to dispense with the obligation: and if she cannot give her assistance without exposing herself to evident danger, this circumstance also dispenses with it. This would be one of those cases in which a treaty becomes pernicious to the state, and therefore not obligatory (Book II. §160). But we here speak of an imminent danger, threatening the very existence of the state. The case of such a danger is tacitly and necessarily reserved in every treaty. As to remote dangers, or those of no extraordinary magnitude,—since they < 327 > are inseparable from every military alliance, it would be absurd to pretend that they should create an exception: and the sovereign may expose the nation to them in consideration of the advantages which she reaps from the alliance.

In virtue of these principles, we are absolved from the obligation of sending assistance to an ally while we are ourselves engaged in a war which requires our whole strength. If we are able to oppose our own enemies, and to assist our ally at the same time, no reason can be pleaded for such dispensation. But, in such cases, it rests with ourselves to determine what our circumstances and strength will allow. It is the same with other things which may have been promised, as, for instance, provisions. There is no obligation to furnish an ally with them when we want them for our own use.

§93. Other cases.

We forbear to repeat in this place what we have said of various other cases in discoursing of treaties in general, as, for example, of the preference due to the more ancient ally (Book II. §167), and to a protector (ibid. §204), of the meaning to be annexed to the term *"allies,"* in a treaty

---

* Book ii. ch. xvii.

in which they are reserved (ibid. §309). Let us only add, on this last question, that, in a warlike alliance made against all opponents, *the allies excepted,* this exception is to be understood only of the present allies. Otherwise it would afterwards be easy to elude the former treaty by new alliances; and it would be impossible for us to know either what we are doing in concluding such a treaty, or what we gain by it.

A case which we have not spoken of is this:—Three powers have entered into a treaty of defensive alliance: two of them quarrel, and make war on each other:—how is the third to act? The treaty does not bind him to assist either the one or the other. For it would be absurd to say that he has promised his assistance to each against the other, or to one of the two in prejudice of the other. The only obligation, therefore, which the treaty imposes on him, is, to endeavour, by the interposition of his good offices, to effect a reconciliation between his allies: and if his mediation proves unsuccessful, he remains at liberty to assist the party who appears to have justice on his side.

Two of the parties in an alliance coming to a rupture.

To refuse an ally the succours due to him, without having any just cause to allege for such refusal, is doing him an injury, since it is a violation of the perfect right which we gave him by a formal engagement. I speak of evident cases, it being then only that the right is perfect; for, in those of a doubtful nature, it rests with each party to judge what he is able to do (§92): but he is to judge maturely and impartially, and to act with candor. And as it is an obligation naturally incumbent on us, to repair any damage caused by our fault, and especially by our injustice, we are bound to indemnify an ally for all the losses he may have sustained in consequence of our unjust refusal. How much circumspection therefore is to be used in forming engagements, which we cannot refuse to fulfil without material injury to our affairs or our <328> honour, and which, on the other hand, if complied with, may be productive of the most serious consequences!

§94. Refusal of the succours due in virtue of an alliance.

An engagement which may draw us into a war is of great moment: in it, the very existence of the state is at stake. He who in an alliance promises a subsidy or a body of auxiliaries, sometimes imagines that he only risks a sum of money or a certain number of soldiers; whereas he often exposes himself to war and all its calamities. The nation against

§95. The enemy's associates.

whom he furnishes assistance will look upon him as her enemy; and should her arms prove successful, she will carry the war into his country. But it remains to be determined whether she can do this with justice, and on what occasions. Some authors* decide in general, that whoever joins our enemy, or assists him against us with money, troops, or in any other manner whatever, becomes thereby our enemy, and gives us a right to make war against him:—a cruel decision, and highly inimical to the peace of nations! It cannot be supported by principles; and happily the practice of Europe stands in opposition to it.

It is true, indeed, that every associate of my enemy is himself my enemy. It is of little consequence whether any one makes war on me directly, and in his own name, or under the auspices of another. Whatever rights war gives me against my principal enemy, the like it gives me against all his associates: for I derive those rights from the right to security,—from the care of my own defence; and I am equally attacked by the one and the other party. But the question is, to know whom I may lawfully account my enemy's associates, united against me in war.

§96. Those who make a common cause with the enemy, are his associates; First, in that class I shall rank all those who are really united in a warlike association with my enemy, and who make a common cause with him, though it is only in the name of that principal enemy that the war is carried on. There is no need of proving this. In the ordinary and open warlike associations, the war is carried on in the name of all the allies, who are all equally enemies (§80).

§97. and those who assist him, without being obliged to it by treaties; In the second place, I account as associates of my enemy, those who assist him in his war without being obliged to it by any treaty. Since they freely and voluntarily declare against me, they, of their own accord, chuse to become my enemies. If they go no farther than furnishing a determined succour, allowing some troops to be raised, or advancing money,—and, in other respects, preserve towards me the accustomed relations of friendship or neutrality,—I may overlook that ground of complaint; but still I have a right to call them to account for it. This prudent caution, of not always coming to an open rupture with those who give such assistance to our enemy, that we may not force them to

* See Wolf, Jus Gentium, §§730 and 736.

join him with all their strength,—this forbearance, I say, has gradually introduced the custom of not looking on such assistance as an act of hostility, especially when it consists only in <329> the permission to enlist volunteers. How often have the Switzers granted levies to France, at the same time that they refused such an indulgence to the house of Austria, though both powers were in alliance with them! How often have they allowed one prince to levy troops in their country, and refused the same permission to his enemy, when they were not in alliance with either! They granted or denied that favour according as they judged it most expedient for themselves; and no power has ever dared to attack them on that account. But if prudence dissuades us from making use of all our right, it does not thereby destroy that right. A cautious nation chuses rather to overlook certain points than unnecessarily to increase the number of her enemies.

Thirdly, those who, being united with my enemy by an offensive alliance, actively assist him in the war which he declares against me,—those, I say, concur in the injury intended against me. They shew themselves my enemies, and I have a right to treat them as such. Accordingly the Switzers, whose example we have above quoted, seldom grant troops except for defensive war. To those in the service of France, it has ever been a standing order from their sovereigns, not to carry arms against the empire, or against the states of the house of Austria in Germany. In 1644, the captains of the Neufchatel regiment of Guy, on information that they were destined to serve under marshal Turenne in Germany, declared that they would rather die than disobey their sovereign, and violate the alliances of the Helvetic body. Since France has been mistress of Alsace, the Switzers who serve in her armies, never pass the Rhine to attack the empire. The gallant Daxelhoffer, captain of a Berne company in the French service, consisting of 200 men, and of which his four sons formed the first rank, seeing the general would oblige him to pass the Rhine, broke his espontoon, and marched back with his company to Berne.

§98. or who are in an offensive alliance with him.

Even a defensive alliance made expressly against me, or (which amounts to the same thing) concluded with my enemy during the war, or on the certain prospect of its speedy declaration, is an act of associ-

§99. How a defensive alliance associates with the enemy.

ation against me; and if followed by effects, I may look on the party who
has contracted it, as my enemy. The case is here precisely the same as
that of a nation assisting my enemy without being under any obligation
to do so, and chusing of her own accord to become my enemy. (See §97.)

§100.
Another case.

A defensive alliance, though of a general nature, and made before any
appearance of the present war, produces also the same effect, if it stipulates the assistance of the whole strength of the allies: for in this case
it is a real league or warlike association; and, besides, it were absurd that
I should be debarred from making war on a nation who opposes me with
all her might, and thus exhausting the source of those succours with
which she furnishes my enemy. In what light am I to consider an auxiliary who comes to make war on me at the head of all his forces? It
would be mockery on his part, to pretend that he is not my <330> enemy.
What more could he do, were he openly to declare himself such? He
shews no tenderness for me on the occasion: he only wishes that a tender
regard should be paid to himself. And shall I suffer him to preserve his
provinces in peace, and secure from all danger, whilst he is doing me all
the mischief in his power? No! the law of nature, the law of nations,
obliges us to be just, but does not condemn us to be dupes.

§101. In what
case it does not
produce the
same effect.

But if a defensive alliance has not been made against me in particular,
nor concluded at the time when I was openly preparing for war, or had
already begun it,—and if the allies have only stipulated in it, that each
of them shall furnish a stated succour to him who shall be attacked,—
I cannot require that they should neglect to fulfil a solemn treaty, which
they had an unquestionable right to conclude without any injury to me.
In furnishing my enemy with assistance, they only acquit themselves of
a debt: they do me no wrong in discharging it; and consequently they
afford me no just grounds for making war on them (§26). Neither can
I say that my safety obliges me to attack them; for I should thereby only
increase the number of my enemies, and, instead of a slender succour
which they furnish against me, should draw on myself the whole power
of those nations. It is, therefore, only the troops which they send as auxiliaries, that I am to consider as enemies. These are actually united with
my enemies, and fighting against me.

The contrary principles would tend to multiply wars, and spread them beyond all bounds, to the common ruin of nations. It is happy for Europe, that, in this instance, the established custom is in accord with the true principles. A prince seldom presumes to complain of a nation's contributing to the defence of her ally by furnishing him with succours which were promised in former treaties,—in treaties that were not made against that prince in particular. In the last war,[16] the United Provinces long continued to supply the queen of Hungary[17] with subsidies, and even with troops; and France never complained of these proceedings till those troops marched into Alsace to attack the French frontier. Switzerland, in virtue of her alliance with France, furnishes that crown with numerous bodies of troops, and, nevertheless, lives in peace with all Europe.

There is one case, however, which might form an exception to the general rule: it is that of a defensive war which is evidently unjust. For in such case there no longer exists any obligation to assist an ally (§§86, 87, 89). If you undertake to do it without necessity, and in violation of your duty, you do an injury to the enemy, and declare against him out of mere wantonness. But this is a case that very rarely occurs between nations. There are few defensive wars without at least some apparent reason to warrant their justice or necessity. Now, on any dubious occasion, each state is sole judge of the justice of her own cause; and the presumption is in favour of your ally (§86). Besides, it belongs to you alone to determine what conduct on your part will be <331> conformable to your duties and to your engagements; and consequently nothing less than the most palpable evidence can authorise the enemy of your ally to charge you with supporting an unjust war, contrary to the conviction of your own conscience. In fine, the voluntary law of nations ordains, that, in every case susceptible of doubt, the arms of both parties shall, with regard to external effects, be accounted equally lawful (§40).

16. War of the Austrian Succession, 1741–48.
17. Maria Theresa, r. 1740–80.

§102. Whether
it be necessary
to declare war
against the
enemy's
associates.

The real associates of my enemy being my enemies, I have against them the same rights as against the principal enemy (§95). And as their own conduct proclaims them my enemies, and they take up arms against me in the first instance, I may make war on them without any declaration; the war being sufficiently declared by their own act. This is especially the case of those who in any manner whatever concur to make an offensive war against me; and it is likewise the case of all those whom we have mentioned in §§96, 97, 98, 99, 100.

But it is not thus with those nations which assist my enemy in a defensive war: I cannot consider them as his associates (§101). If I am entitled to complain of their furnishing him with succours, this is a new ground of quarrel between me and them. I may expostulate with them, and, on not receiving satisfaction, prosecute my right, and make war on them. But in this case there must be a previous declaration (§51). The example of Manlius, who made war on the Galatians[18] for having supplied Antiochus with troops, is not a case in point. Grotius* censures the Roman general for having begun that war without a declaration. The Galatians, in furnishing troops for an offensive war against the Romans, had declared themselves enemies to Rome. It would appear, indeed, that, on peace being concluded with Antiochus, Manlius ought to have waited for orders from Rome before he attacked the Galatians; and then, if that expedition was considered as a fresh war, he should have not only issued a declaration, but also made a demand of satisfaction, previous to the commencement of hostilities (§51). But the treaty with the king of Syria had not yet received its consummation: and it concerned that monarch alone, without making any mention of his adherents. Therefore Manlius undertook the expedition against the Galatians, as a consequence or a remnant of the war with Antiochus. This is what he himself very well observed in his speech to the senate;† and he even added, that his first

* De Jure Belli et Pacis, lib. iii. cap. iii. §10.
† Livy, lib. xxxviii.
18. Gnaeus Manlius Vulso served as Roman consul in 189 B.C. and defeated the Galatian Gauls after accusing them of sending troops to support the Seleucids in the recent Roman-Syrian war.

measure was to try whether he could bring the Galatians to reasonable terms. Grotius more appositely quotes the example of Ulysses and his followers,—blaming them for having, without any declaration of war, attacked the Ciconians, who had sent succours to Priam during the siege of Troy.* <332>

CHAPTER VII

Of Neutrality—and the Passage of Troops through a Neutral Country.

Neutral nations are those who, in time of war, do not take any part in the contest, but remain common friends to both parties, without favouring the arms of the one to the prejudice of the other. Here we are to consider the obligations and rights flowing from neutrality.

§103. Neutral nations.

In order rightly to understand this question, we must avoid confounding what may lawfully be done by a nation that is free from all engagements, with what she may do if she expects to be treated as perfectly neutral in a war. As long as a neutral nation wishes securely to enjoy the advantages of her neutrality, she must in all things shew a strict impartiality towards the belligerent powers: for, should she favour one of the parties to the prejudice of the other, she cannot complain of being treated by him as an adherent and confederate of his enemy. Her neutrality would be a fraudulent neutrality, of which no nation will consent to be the dupe. It is sometimes suffered to pass unnoticed, merely for want of ability to resent it; we chuse to connive at it, rather than excite a more powerful opposition against us. But the present question is, to determine what may lawfully be done, not what prudence may dictate according to circumstances. Let us therefore examine, in what consists that impartiality which a neutral nation ought to observe.

§104. Conduct to be observed by a neutral nation.

It solely relates to war, and includes two articles,—1. To give no assistance when there is no obligation to give it,—nor voluntarily to fur-

* Grotius, ubi supra, not. 3.

nish troops, arms, ammunition, or any thing of direct use in war. I do not say "to give assistance equally," but "to give no assistance": for it would be absurd that a state should at one and the same time assist two nations at war with each other; and besides it would be impossible to do it with equality. The same things, the like number of troops, the like quantity of arms, of stores, &c. furnished in different circumstances, are no longer equivalent succours. 2. In whatever does not relate to war, a neutral and impartial nation must not refuse to one of the parties, on account of his present quarrel, what she grants to the other. This does not deprive her of the liberty to make the advantage of the state still serve as her rule of conduct in her negotiations, her friendly connections, and her commerce. When this reason induces her to give preferences in things which are ever at the free disposal of the possessor, she only makes use of her right, and is not chargeable with partiality. But to refuse any of those things to one of the parties purely <333> because he is at war with the other, and because she wishes to favour the latter, would be departing from the line of strict neutrality.

§105. An ally may furnish the succour due from him, and remain neuter.

I have said that a neutral state ought to give no assistance to either of the parties, when "under no obligation to give it." This restriction is necessary. We have already seen that when a sovereign furnishes the moderate succour due in virtue of a former defensive alliance, he does not become an associate in the war (§101). He may therefore fulfil his engagement, and yet observe a strict neutrality. Of this Europe affords frequent instances.

§106. Right of remaining neuter.

When a war breaks out between two nations, all other states that are not bound by treaties, are free to remain neuter; and if either of the belligerent powers attempted to force them to a junction with him, he would do them an injury, inasmuch as he would be guilty of an infringement on their independency in a very essential point. To themselves alone it belongs to determine whether any reason exists to induce them to join in the contest: and there are two points which claim their consideration,—1. The justice of the cause. If that be evident, injustice is not to be countenanced: on the contrary, it is generous and praiseworthy to succour oppressed innocence, when we possess the ability. If the case be dubious, the other nations may suspend their judgment, and not engage in a foreign quarrel. 2. When convinced which party has justice on his side, they have still to consider whether it be for the advantage of the state to concern themselves in this affair, and to embark in the war.

A nation making war, or preparing to make it, often proposes a treaty of neutrality to a state of which she entertains suspicions. It is prudent to learn betimes what she has to expect, and not run the risk of a neighbour's suddenly joining with the enemy in the heat of the war. In every case where neutrality is allowable, it is also lawful to bind ourselves to it by treaty. §107. Treaties of neutrality.

Sometimes even necessity renders this justifiable. Thus, although it be the duty of all nations to assist oppressed innocence (Book II. §4), yet, if an unjust conqueror, ready to invade his neighbour's possessions, makes me an offer of neutrality when he is able to crush me, what can I do better than to accept it? I yield to necessity; and my inability discharges me from a natural obligation. The same inability would even excuse me from a perfect obligation contracted by an alliance. The enemy of my ally threatens me with a vast superiority of force: my fate is in his hand: he requires me to renounce the liberty of furnishing any assistance against him. Necessity, and the care of my own safety, absolve me from my engagements. Thus it was that Louis the Fourteenth compelled Victor Amadeus duke of Savoy to quit the party of the allies.[19] But then the necessity must be very urgent. It is only the cowardly or the perfidious who avail themselves of the slightest grounds of alarm, to violate <334> their promises and desert their duty. In the late war, the king of Poland, elector of Saxony, and the king of Sardinia,[20] firmly held out against the unfortunate course of events, and, to their great honour, could not be brought to treat without the concurrence of their allies.

19. Victor Amadeus II, Duke of Savoy (r. 1675–1720), was forced to leave the Anglo-Dutch alliance against France during the War of the Spanish Succession (1701–13) after the siege of Turin in 1706.

20. During the War of the Austrian Succession (1741–48), Augustus III of Poland (r. 1734–63), who was also elector of Saxony as Frederick Augustus II, and Charles Emmanuel III of Savoy (r. 1730–73), opposed Empress Maria Theresa of Austria.

§108. Additional reason for making these treaties.

Another reason renders these treaties of neutrality useful, and even necessary. A nation that wishes to secure her own peace, when the flames of war are kindling in her neighbourhood, cannot more successfully attain that object than by concluding treaties with both parties, expressly agreeing what each may do or require in virtue of the neutrality. This is a sure mode to preserve herself in peace, and to obviate all disputes and cavils.

§109. Foundation of the rules of neutrality.

Without such treaties, it is to be feared that disputes will often arise respecting what neutrality does or does not allow. This subject presents many questions which authors have discussed with great heat, and which have given rise to the most dangerous quarrels between nations. Yet the law of nature and of nations has its invariable principles, and affords rules on this head, as well as on the others. Some things also have grown into custom among civilised nations, and are to be conformed to by those who would not incur the reproach of unjustly breaking the peace.* As to the rules of the natural law of nations, they result from a just combination of the laws of war, with the liberty, the safety, the advantages, the commerce, and the other rights of neutral nations. It is on this principle that we shall lay down the following rules.

§110. How levies may be allowed, money lent, and every kind of things sold, without a breach of neutrality.

First, No act on the part of a nation, which falls within the exercise of her rights, and is done solely with a view to her own good, without partiality, without a design of favouring one power to the prejudice of another,—no act of that kind, I say, can in general be considered as contrary to neutrality; nor does it become such, except on particular occasions when it cannot take place without injury to one of the parties, who has then a particular right to oppose it. Thus, the besieger has a right to prohibit access to the place besieged (see §117 in the sequel). Except in cases of this nature, shall the quarrels of others deprive me of the free exercise of my rights in the pursuit of measures which I judge advantageous to my people? Therefore, when it is the custom of a nation,

---

* The following is an instance.—It was determined by the Dutch, that, on a vessel's entering a neutral port after having taken any of the enemies of her nation prisoners on the high seas, she should be obliged to set those prisoners at liberty, because they were then fallen into the power of a nation that was in neutrality with the belligerent parties.—The same rule had been observed by England in the war between Spain and the United Provinces. [[Note added in 1773/1797 editions.]]

for the purpose of employing and training her subjects, to permit levies of troops in favour of a particular power to whom she thinks proper to intrust them,—the enemy of that power cannot look upon such permissions as acts of hostility, unless they are given with a view to the invasion of his territories, or the support of an odious and evidently <335> unjust cause. He cannot even demand, as matter of right, that the like favour be granted to him,—because that nation may have reasons for refusing him, which do not hold good with regard to his adversary; and it belongs to that nation alone to judge of what best suits her circumstances. The Switzers, as we have already observed, grant levies of troops to whom they please; and no power has hitherto thought fit to quarrel with them on that head. It must, however, be owned, that, if those levies were considerable, and constituted the principal strength of my enemy, while, without any substantial reason being alleged, I were absolutely refused all levies whatever,— I should have just cause to consider that nation as leagued with my enemy; and, in this case, the care of my own safety would authorise me to treat her as such.

The case is the same with respect to money which a nation may have been accustomed to lend out at interest. If the sovereign or his subjects lend money to my enemy on that footing, and refuse it to me because they have not the same confidence in me, this is no breach of neutrality. They lodge their property where they think it safest. If such preference be not founded on good reasons, I may impute it to ill-will against me, or to a predilection for my enemy. Yet if I should make it a pretence for declaring war, both the true principles of the law of nations, and the general custom happily established in Europe, would join in condemning me. While it appears that this nation lends out her money purely for the sake of gaining an interest upon it, she is at liberty to dispose of it according to her own discretion; and I have no right to complain.

But if the loan were evidently granted for the purpose of enabling an enemy to attack me, this would be concurring in the war against me.

If the troops, above alluded to, were furnished to my enemy by the state herself, and at her own expense, or the money in like manner lent by the state, without interest, it would no longer be a doubtful question whether such assistance were incompatible with neutrality.

Further, it may be affirmed on the same principles, that if a nation trades in arms, timber for ship-building, vessels, and warlike stores,—I cannot take it amiss that she sells such things to my enemy, provided she does not refuse to sell them to me also at a reasonable price. She carries on her trade without any design to injure me; and by continuing it in the same manner as if I were not engaged in war, she gives me no just cause of complaint.

§111. Trade of neutral nations with those which are at war. In what I have said above, it is supposed that my enemy goes himself to a neutral country to make his purchases. Let us now discuss another case,—that of neutral nations resorting to my enemy's country for commercial purposes. It is certain, that, as they have no part in my quarrel, they are under no obligation to renounce their commerce for the sake of avoiding to supply my <336> enemy with the means of carrying on the war against me. Should they affect to refuse selling me a single article, while at the same time they take pains to convey an abundant supply to my enemy, with an evident intention to favour him,—such partial conduct would exclude them from the neutrality they enjoyed. But if they only continue their customary trade, they do not thereby declare themselves against my interest; they only exercise a right which they are under no obligation of sacrificing to me.

On the other hand, whenever I am at war with a nation, both my safety and welfare prompt me to deprive her, as far as possible, of every thing which may enable her to resist or injure me. In this instance, the law of necessity exerts its full force. If that law warrants me, on occasion, to seize what belongs to other people, will it not likewise warrant me to intercept every thing belonging to war, which neutral nations are carrying to my enemy? Even if I should, by taking such measure, render all those neutral nations my enemies, I had better run that hazard than suffer him who is actually at war with me, thus freely to receive supplies, and collect additional strength to oppose me. It is therefore very proper, and perfectly conformable to the law of nations (which disapproves of multiplying the causes of war), not to consider those seizures of the goods of neutral nations as acts of hostility.

When I have notified to them my declaration of war against such or such a nation, if they will afterwards expose themselves to risk in supplying her with things which serve to carry on war, they will have no reason to complain if their goods fall into my possession; and I, on the other hand, do not declare war against them for having attempted to convey such goods. They suffer indeed by a war in which they have no concern; but they suffer accidentally. I do not oppose their right: I only exert my own; and if our rights clash with and reciprocally injure each other, that circumstance is the effect of inevitable necessity. Such collisions daily happen in war. When, in pursuance of my rights, I exhaust a country from which you derived your subsistence,—when I besiege a city with which you carried on a profitable trade,—I doubtless injure you; I subject you to losses and inconveniences; but it is without any design of hurting you. I only make use of my rights, and consequently do you no injustice.

But that limits may be set to these inconveniences, and that the commerce of neutral nations may subsist in as great a degree of freedom as is consistent with the laws of war, there are certain rules to be observed, on which Europe seems to be generally agreed.

The first is, carefully to distinguish ordinary goods which have no relation to war, from those that are peculiarly subservient to it. Neutral nations should enjoy perfect liberty to trade in the former: the belligerent powers cannot with any reason refuse <337> it, or prevent the importation of such goods into the enemy's country: the care of their own safety, the necessity of self-defence, does not authorise them to do it, since those things will not render the enemy more formidable. An attempt to interrupt or put a stop to this trade would be a violation of the rights of neutral nations, a flagrant injury to them;—necessity, as we have above observed, being the only reason which can authorise any restraint on their trade and navigation to the ports of the enemy. England and the United Provinces having agreed, in the treaty of Whitehall, signed on the 22d of August, 1689, to notify to all states not at war with France, that they would attack every ship bound to or coming from any port of that kingdom, and that they before-hand declared every such ship to be a lawful prize,—Sweden and Denmark, from whom some ships had been taken, entered into a counter-treaty on the 17th of March, 1693, for the purpose of maintaining their rights and procuring just satisfaction. And the two maritime powers, being con-

§112. Contraband goods.

vinced that the complaints of the two crowns were well founded, did them justice.*

Commodities particularly useful in war, and the importation of which to an enemy is prohibited, are called contraband goods. Such are arms, ammunition, timber for ship-building, every kind of naval stores, horses,—and even provisions, in certain junctures, when we have hopes of reducing the enemy by famine.†

§113. Whether such goods may be confiscated.

But in order to hinder the transportation of contraband goods to an enemy, are we only to stop and seize them, paying the value to the owner,—or have we a right to confiscate them? Barely to stop those goods would in general prove an ineffectual mode, especially at sea, where there is no possibility of entirely cutting off all access to the enemy's harbours. Recourse is therefore had to the expedient of confiscating all contraband <338> goods that we can seize on, in order that the fear of loss may operate as a check on the avidity of gain, and deter the merchants of neutral countries from supplying the enemy with such commodities. And indeed it is an object of such high importance to a

---

* See other instances in Grotius, de Jure Belli et Pacis, lib. iii. cap. i. §5, not. 6.

† The Pensionary De Witt, in a letter of January 14, 1654, acknowledges that it would be contrary to the law of nations to prevent neutrals from carrying corn to an enemy's country: but he says that we may lawfully prevent them from supplying the enemy with cordage and other materials for the rigging and equipment of ships of war.

In 1597, queen Elizabeth would not allow the Poles and Danes to furnish Spain with provisions, much less with arms,—alleging that "according to the rules of war, it is lawful to reduce an enemy even by famine, with the view of obliging him to sue for peace." The United Provinces, finding it necessary to observe a greater degree of circumspection, did not prevent neutral nations from carrying on every kind of commerce with Spain. It is true, indeed, that, while their own subjects sold both arms and provisions to the Spaniards, they could not with propriety have attempted to forbid neutral nations to carry on a similar trade. (Grotius, Hist. of the Disturbances in the Low Countries, book vi.) Nevertheless, in 1646, the United Provinces published an edict prohibiting their own subjects in general, and even neutral nations, to carry either provisions or any other merchandise to Spain, because the Spaniards, "after having, under the appearance of commerce, allured foreign vessels to their ports, detained them, and made use of them as ships of war." And for this reason the same edict declared that "the confederates, when blocking up their enemies' ports, would seize upon every vessel they saw steering towards those places." Ibid. book xv. p. 572. [[Note added in 1773/1797 editions.]]

nation at war to prevent, as far as possible, the enemy's being supplied with such articles as will add to his strength and render him more dangerous, that necessity and the care of her own welfare and safety authorise her to take effectual methods for that purpose, and to declare that all commodities of that nature, destined for the enemy, shall be considered as lawful prize. On this account she notifies to the neutral states her declaration of war (§63); whereupon, the latter usually give orders to their subjects to refrain from all contraband commerce with the nations at war, declaring that if they are captured in carrying on such trade, the sovereign will not protect them. This rule is the point where the general custom of Europe seems at present fixed, after a number of variations, as will appear from the note of Grotius which we have just quoted, and particularly from the ordinances of the kings of France, in the years 1543 and 1584, which only allow the French to seize contraband goods, and to keep them on paying the value. The modern usage is certainly the most agreeable to the mutual duties of nations, and the best calculated to reconcile their respective rights. The nation at war is highly interested in depriving the enemy of all foreign assistance; and this circumstance gives her a right to consider all those, if not absolutely as enemies, at least as people that feel very little scruple to injure her, who carry to her enemy the articles of which he stands in need for the support of the war: she therefore punishes them by the confiscation of their goods. Should their sovereign undertake to protect them, such conduct would be tantamount to his furnishing the enemy with those succours himself:—a measure which were undoubtedly inconsistent with neutrality. When a nation, without any other motive than the prospect of gain, is employed in strengthening my enemy, and regardless of the irreparable evil which she may thereby entail upon me,* she is certainly not my friend, and gives me a right to consider and treat her as an associate of my enemy. In order, therefore, to avoid perpetual subjects of complaint and rupture,

---

* In our time the king of Spain [[Philip V, r. 1700–1746]] prohibited all Hamburg ships from entering his harbours, because that city had engaged to furnish the Algerines with military stores; and thus he obliged the Hamburgers to cancel their treaty with the Barbarians.

it has, in perfect conformity to sound principles, been agreed that the belligerent powers may seize and confiscate all contraband goods which neutral persons shall attempt to carry to their enemy, without any complaint from the sovereign of those merchants; as, on the other hand, the power at war does not impute to the neutral sovereigns these practices of their subjects. Care is even taken to settle every particular of this kind in treaties of commerce and navigation. <339>

§114. Searching neutral ships.

We cannot prevent the conveyance of contraband goods, without searching neutral vessels that we meet at sea: we have therefore a right to search them. Some powerful nations have indeed, at different times, refused to submit to this search. "After the peace of Vervins,[21] queen Elizabeth, continuing the war against Spain, requested permission of the king of France to cause all French ships bound for Spain to be searched, in order to discover whether they secretly carried any military stores to that country: but this was refused, as an injury to trade, and a favourable occasion for pillage."* At present a neutral ship refusing to be searched, would from that proceeding alone be condemned as a lawful prize. But to avoid inconveniences, oppression, and every other abuse, the manner of the search is settled in the treaties of navigation and commerce. It is the established custom at present to give full credit to the certificates, bills of lading, &c. produced by the master of the ship, unless any fraud appear in them, or there be good reasons for suspecting it.

§115. Enemy's property on board a neutral ship.

If we find an enemy's effects on board a neutral ship, we seize them by the rights of war: but we are naturally bound to pay the freight to the master of the vessel, who is not to suffer by such seizure.†

---

* Grotius, ubi supra.

† "I have obtained" (said the ambassador Boreel, in a letter to the Grand Pensionary De Witt) "the abrogation of that pretended French law, that *enemies' property involves in confiscation the property of friends;* so that, if henceforward any effects belonging to the enemies of France be found in a free Dutch vessel, those effects alone shall be liable to confiscation; and the vessel shall be released, together with all the other property on board. But I find it impossible to obtain the object of the twenty-fourth article of my instructions, which says that *the immunity of the vessel shall extend to the cargo, even if enemies' property.*" De Witt's Letters and Negotiations, vol. i. p. 80.—Such a law as the latter would be more natural than the former. [[Note added in 1773/1797 editions.]]

21. In 1590.

The effects of neutrals, found in an enemy's ship, are to be restored to the owners, against whom there is no right of confiscation,—but without any allowance for detainder, decay, &c. The loss sustained by the neutrals on this occasion is an accident to which they exposed themselves by embarking their property in an enemy's ship; and the captor, in exercising the rights of war, is not responsible for the accidents which may thence result, any more than if his cannon kills a neutral passenger who happens unfortunately to be on board an enemy's vessel.

§116. Neutral property on board an enemy's ship.

Hitherto we have considered the commerce of neutral nations with the territories of the enemy in general. There is a particular case in which the rights of war extend still farther. All commerce with a besieged town is absolutely prohibited. If I lay siege to a place, or even simply blockade it, I have a right to hinder any one from entering, and to treat as an enemy whoever attempts to enter the place, or carry any thing to the besieged, without my leave; for he opposes my undertaking, and may contribute to the miscarriage of it, and thus involve me in all < 340 > the misfortunes of an unsuccessful war. King Demetrius[22] hanged up the master and pilot of a vessel carrying provisions to Athens at a time when he was on the point of reducing that city by famine.* In the long and bloody war carried on by the United Provinces against Spain for the recovery of their liberties, they would not suffer the English to carry goods to Dunkirk, before which the Dutch fleet lay.†

§117. Trade with a besieged town.

A neutral nation preserves, towards both the belligerent powers, the several relations which nature has instituted between nations. She ought to shew herself ready to render them every office of humanity reciprocally due from one nation to another: she ought, in every thing not directly relating to war, to give them all the assistance in her power, and of which they may stand in need. Such assistance, however, must be given with impartiality; that is to say, she must not refuse any thing to one of the parties on account of his being at war with the other (§104). But this is no reason why a neutral state, under particular connections

§118. Impartial offices of neutrals.

* Plutarch, in Demetrio.
† Grotius, ubi supra.
22. King Demetrius of Macedonia, r. 294–288 B.C.

of friendship and good-neighbourhood with one of the belligerent powers, may not, in every thing that is unconnected with war, grant him all
those preferences which are due to friends: much less does she afford any
grounds of exception to her conduct, if, in commerce, for instance, she
continues to allow him such indulgences as have been stipulated in her
treaties with him. She ought therefore, as far as the public welfare will
permit, equally to allow the subjects of both parties to visit her territories
on business, and there to purchase provisions, horses, and, in general,
every thing they stand in need of,—unless she has, by a treaty of neutrality, promised to refuse to both parties such articles as are used in war.
Amidst all the wars which disturb Europe, the Switzers preserve their
territories in a state of neutrality. Every nation indiscriminately is allowed free access, for the purchase of provisions if the country has a
surplus, and for that of horses, ammunition, and arms.

§119. Passage
of troops
through a neu-
tral country.
An innocent passage is due to all nations with whom a state is at peace
(Book II. §123); and this duty extends to troops as well as to individuals.
But it rests with the sovereign of the country to judge whether the passage be innocent; and it is very difficult for that of an army to be entirely
so. In the late wars of Italy,[23] the territories of the republic of Venice,
and those of the pope, sustained very great damages by the passage of
armies, and often became the theatre of the war.

§120. Passage
to be asked.
Since, therefore, the passage of troops, and especially that of a whole
army, is by no means a matter of indifference, he who desires to march
his troops through a neutral country, must apply for the sovereign's permission. To enter his territory without his consent, is a violation of his
rights of sovereignty and supreme dominion, by virtue of which, that
country is not to be disposed of for any use whatever, without his express
or tacit permission. <341> Now a tacit permission for the entrance of a
body of troops is not to be presumed, since their entrance may be productive of the most serious consequences.

23. Between 1745 and 1747 Italy became a major battleground in the War of the
Austrian Succession, with an alliance of Genoa, Naples, France, and Spain fighting
against the Austrian forces.

If the neutral sovereign has good reasons for refusing a passage, he is not obliged to grant it,—the passage in that case being no longer innocent.

§121. It may be refused for good reasons.

In all doubtful cases, we must submit to the judgment of the proprietor respecting the innocence of the use we desire to make of things belonging to another (Book II. §§128, 130), and must acquiesce in his refusal, even though we think it unjust. If the refusal be evidently unjust,—if the use, and, in the case now before us, the passage, be unquestionably innocent,—a nation may do herself justice, and take by force what is unjustly denied to her. But we have already observed that it is very difficult for the passage of an army to be absolutely innocent, and much more so for the innocence to be very evident. So various are the evils it may occasion, and the dangers that may attend it,—so complicated are they in their nature, and so numerous are the circumstances with which they are connected,—that to foresee and provide for every thing, is next to impossible. Besides, self-interest has so powerful an influence on the judgments of men, that if he who requires the passage is to be the judge of its innocence, he will admit none of the reasons brought against it; and thus a door is opened to continual quarrels and hostilities. The tranquillity, therefore, and the common safety of nations, require that each should be mistress of her own territory, and at liberty to refuse every foreign army an entrance, when she has not departed from her natural liberties in that respect, by treaties. From this rule, however, let us except those very uncommon cases which admit of the most evident demonstration that the passage required is wholly unattended with inconvenience or danger. If, on such an occasion, a passage be forced, he who forces it will not be so much blamed as the nation that has indiscreetly subjected herself to this violence. Another case, which carries its own exception on the very face of it, and admits not of the smallest doubt, is that of extreme necessity. Urgent and absolute necessity suspends all the rights of property (Book II. §§119, 123): and if the proprietor be not under the same pressure of necessity as you, it is allowable for you, even against his will, to make use of what belongs to him. When, therefore, an army find themselves exposed to imminent destruction or unable to return to their own country unless they pass

§122. In what case it may be forced.

through neutral territories, they have a right to pass in spite of the sovereign, and to force their way, sword in hand. But they ought first to request a passage, to offer securities, and pay for whatever damages they may occasion. Such was the mode pursued by the Greeks on their return from Asia, under the conduct of Agesilaüs.* <342>

Extreme necessity may even authorise the temporary seizure of a neutral town, and the putting a garrison therein, with a view to cover ourselves from the enemy, or to prevent the execution of his designs against that town, when the sovereign is not able to defend it. But when the danger is over, we must immediately restore the place, and pay all the charges, inconveniences, and damages, which we have occasioned by seizing it.

§123. The fear of danger authorises a refusal, When the passage is not of absolute necessity, the bare danger which attends the admission of a powerful army into our territory, may authorise us to refuse them permission to enter. We may have reason to apprehend that they will be tempted to take possession of the country, or at least to act as masters while they are in it, and to live at discretion. Let it not be said with Grotius,† that he who requires the passage is not to be deprived of his right on account of our unjust fears. A probable fear, founded on good reasons, gives us a right to avoid whatever may realise it; and the conduct of nations affords but too just grounds for the fear in question. Besides, the right of passage is not a perfect right, unless in a case of urgent necessity, or when we have the most perfect evidence that the passage is innocent.

§124. or a demand of every reasonable security. But, in the preceding section, I suppose it impracticable to obtain sufficient security which shall leave us no cause to apprehend any hostile attempts or violent proceedings on the part of those who ask permission to pass. If any such security can be obtained (and the safest one is, to allow them to pass only in small bodies, and upon delivering up their arms, as has been sometimes required),‡ the reason arising from fear no

---

* Plutarch's life of Agesilaüs.
† Book ii. chap. ii. §13. note 5 [[*Law of War and Peace*]].
‡ By the Eleans, and the ancient inhabitants of Cologne. See Grotius, ibid.

longer exists. But those who wish to pass should consent to give every reasonable security required of them, and consequently submit to pass by divisions and deliver up their arms, if the passage be denied them on any other terms. The choice of the security they are to give does not rest with them. Hostages or a bond would often prove very slender securities. Of what advantage will it be to me to hold hostages from one who will render himself master over me? And as to a bond, it is of very little avail against a prince of much superior power.

But, is it always incumbent on us to give every security a nation may require, when we wish to pass through her territories?—In the first place we are to make a distinction between the different reasons that may exist for our passing through the country; and we are next to consider the manners of the people whose permission we ask. If the passage be not essentially necessary, and can be obtained only on suspicious or disagreeable conditions, we must relinquish all idea of it, as in the case of a refusal (§122). But if necessity authorises me to pass, the conditions on which the passage will be granted may be accepted or rejected, according to the manners of the people I am treating with. Suppose I am to <343> cross the country of a barbarous, savage, and perfidious nation,—shall I leave myself at their discretion, by giving up my arms and causing my troops to march in divisions? No one, I presume, will condemn me to take so dangerous a step. Since necessity authorises me to pass, a kind of new necessity arises for my passing in such a posture as will secure me from any ambuscade or violence. I will offer every security that can be given without foolishly exposing myself; and if the offer is rejected, I must be guided by necessity and prudence,—and, let me add, by the most scrupulous moderation, in order to avoid exceeding the bounds of that right which I derive from necessity.

§125. Whether always necessary to give every kind of security required.

If the neutral state grants or refuses a passage to one of the parties at war, she ought in like manner to grant or refuse it to the other, unless a change of circumstances affords her substantial reasons for acting otherwise. Without such reasons, to grant to one party what she refuses to the other, would be a partial distinction, and a departure from the line of strict neutrality.

§126. Equality to be observed towards both parties as to the passage.

§127. No
complaint
lies against a
neutral state
for granting
a passage.

When I have no reason to refuse a passage, the party against whom it is granted has no right to complain of my conduct, much less to make it the ground of a hostile attack upon me, since I have done no more than what the law of nations enjoins (§119). Neither has he any right to require that I should deny the passage; for he must not pretend to hinder me from doing what I think agreeable to my duty. And even on those occasions when I might with justice refuse permission to pass, I am at liberty to abstain from the exertion of my right. But especially when I should be obliged to support my refusal by the sword, who will take upon him to complain of my having permitted the war to be carried into his country, rather than draw it on myself? No sovereign can require that I should take up arms in his favour, unless obliged to it by treaty. But nations, more attentive to their own interests than to the observance of strict justice, are often very loud on this pretended subject of complaint. In war especially, they stick at no measures; and if by their threats they can induce a neighbouring state to refuse a passage to their enemy, the generality of their rulers consider this conduct only as a stroke of good policy.

§128. This
state may
refuse it from
a fear of the
resentment of
the opposite
party;

A powerful state will despise these unjust menaces: firm and unshaken in what she thinks due to justice and to her own reputation, she will not suffer herself to be diverted by the fear of a groundless resentment: she will not even bear the menace. But a weak nation, unable to support her rights, will be under a necessity of consulting her own safety; and this important concern will authorise her to refuse a passage, which would expose her to dangers too powerful for her to repel.

§129. and lest
her country
should become
the theatre
of war.

Another fear may also warrant her in refusing a passage, namely, that of involving her country in the disorders and calamities of war. For, even if the party against whom a passage is requested, should observe such moderation as not to employ menaces for the purpose of intimidating the neutral nation into a <344> refusal, he will hardly fail to demand a passage for himself also: he will march to meet his enemy; and thus the neutral country will become the theatre of war. The infinite evils of such a situation are an unexceptionable reason for refusing the passage. In all these cases, he who attempts to force a passage, does an injury to the neutral nation, and gives her most just cause to unite her arms with those of his adversary. The Switzers, in their alliances with France, have promised not to grant a passage to her enemies. They ever refuse it to all sovereigns at war, in order to secure their frontiers from that calamity; and they take care that their territory shall be respected. But they grant a passage to recruits, who march in small bodies, and without arms.

The grant of permission to pass includes a grant of every thing which is naturally connected with the passage of troops, and without which the passage would be impracticable; such as the liberty of carrying with them whatever may be necessary for an army,—that of exercising military discipline on the soldiers and officers, and of purchasing at a fair price every thing the army may want, unless, through fear of scarcity, a particular exception has been made, to oblige them to carry with them their own provisions. §130. What is included in the grant of passage.

He who grants the passage is bound to render it safe, as far as depends on him. Good-faith requires this: and to act otherwise would be ensnaring those to whom the passage is granted. §131. Safety of the passage.

For this reason, and because foreigners can do nothing in a territory against the will of the sovereign, it is unlawful to attack an enemy in a neutral country, or to commit in it any other act of hostility. The Dutch East-India fleet having put into Bergen in Norway, in 1666, to avoid the English, the British admiral had the temerity to attack them there. But the governor of Bergen fired on the assailants; and the court of Denmark complained, though perhaps too faintly, of an attempt so injurious to her rights and dignity.* §132. No hostility to be committed in a neutral country.

To conduct prisoners, to convey spoil to a place of safety, are acts of war, consequently not to be done in a neutral country; and whoever should permit them would depart from the line of neutrality, by favouring one of the parties. But I here speak of prisoners and spoil not yet perfectly in the enemy's power, and whose capture is, as it were, not yet fully completed. A flying party, for instance, cannot make use of a neighbouring and neutral country as a place of deposit to secure their

* The author [[Robert Molesworth]] of the "Present State of Denmark," written in English, pretends that the Danes had engaged to deliver up the Dutch fleet, but that some seasonable presents made to the court of Copenhagen saved it. Chap. x.

prisoners and spoil. To permit this, would be giving countenance and support to their hostilities. When the capture is completed, and the booty absolutely in the enemy's power, no inquiry is made how he came by such effects, and he may dispose of them in a neutral country. A privateer carries his prize into a neutral port, <345> and there freely sells it; but he cannot land his prisoners there for the purpose of keeping them in confinement, because the detention and custody of prisoners of war is a continuation of hostilities.

§133. Neutral country not to afford a retreat to troops, that they may again attack their enemies.

On the other hand, it is certain, that, if my neighbour affords a retreat to my enemies when defeated and too much weakened to escape me, and allows them time to recover, and watch a favourable opportunity of making a second attack on my territories, this conduct, so prejudicial to my safety and interests, would be incompatible with neutrality. If therefore my enemies, on suffering a discomfiture, retreat into his country, although charity will not allow him to refuse them permission to pass in security, he is bound to make them continue their march beyond his frontiers as soon as possible, and not suffer them to remain in his territories on the watch for a convenient opportunity to attack me a-new; otherwise he gives me a right to enter his country in pursuit of them. Such treatment is often experienced by nations that are unable to command respect. Their territories soon become the theatre of war; armies march, encamp, and fight in it, as in a country open to all comers.

§134. Conduct to be observed by troops passing through a neutral country.

Troops to whom a passage is granted, are not to occasion the least damage in the country; they are to keep to the public roads, and not enter the possessions of private persons,—to observe the most exact discipline, and punctually pay for every thing with which the inhabitants supply them. And if the licentiousness of the soldiers, or the necessity of certain operations, as encamping or intrenching, has caused any damage, their commander or their sovereign is bound to make reparation. All this requires no proof. What right have an army to injure a country, when the most they could require was an innocent passage through it?

There can be no reason why the neutral state should not stipulate for a sum of money as an indemnification for certain damages which it would be difficult to estimate, and for the inconveniences naturally resulting from the passage of an army. But it would be scandalous to sell the very grant of passage,—nay even unjust, if the passage be attended with no damage, since, in that case, the permission is due. As to the rest, the sovereign of the country is to take care that the compensation be paid to the parties who have suffered the damage: for no right authorises him to reserve for his own use what is given for their indemnification. It is indeed too often the case that the weak sustain the loss, and the powerful receive the compensation.

Finally, as we are not bound to grant even an innocent passage except for just causes, we may refuse it to him who requires it for a war that is evidently unjust,—as, for instance, to invade a country without any reason, or even colourable pretext. Thus Julius Caesar denied a passage to the Helvetii, who were quitting their country in order to conquer a better. I conceive indeed that policy had a greater share in his refusal, than the love of justice; but, in short, justice authorised him on that occasion <346> to obey the dictates of prudence. A sovereign who is in a condition to refuse without fear, should doubtless refuse in the case we now speak of. But if it would be dangerous for him to give a refusal, he is not obliged to draw down the impending evil on his own head for the sake of averting it from that of his neighbour: nay, rashly to hazard the quiet and welfare of his people would be a very great breach of his duty.

§135. A passage may be refused for a war evidently unjust.

CHAPTER VIII

Of the Rights of Nations in War,—and first, of what we have a right to do, and what we are allowed to do, to the Enemy's Person in a just War.

What we have hitherto said concerns the right of making war:—let us now proceed to those rights which are to be respected during the war itself, and to the rules which nations should reciprocally observe, even when deciding their differences by arms. Let us begin by laying down the rights of a nation engaged in a just war: let us see what she is allowed to do to her enemy. The whole is to be deduced from one single principle,—from the object of a just war: for, when the end is lawful, he who

§136. General principle of the rights against an enemy in a just war.

has a right to pursue that end, has, of course, a right to employ all the means which are necessary for its attainment. The end of a just war is to *avenge or prevent injury* (§28)—that is to say, to obtain justice by force, when not obtainable by any other method,—to compel an unjust adversary to repair an injury already done, or give us securities against any wrong with which we are threatened by him. As soon, therefore, as we have declared war, we have a right to do against the enemy whatever we find necessary for the attainment of that end,—for the purpose of bringing him to reason, and obtaining justice and security from him.

§137. Difference between what we have a right to do and what is barely allowed to be done with impunity, between enemies.
The lawfulness of the end does not give us a real right to any thing further than barely the means necessary for the attainment of that end. Whatever we do beyond that, is reprobated by the law of nature, is faulty, and condemnable at the tribunal of conscience. Hence it is that the right to such or such acts of hostility varies according to circumstances. What is just and perfectly innocent in war in one particular situation, is not always so on other occasions. Right goes hand in hand with necessity and the exigency of the case, but never exceeds them.

But as it is very difficult, always to form a precise judgment of what the present case requires, and as, moreover it belongs to each nation to judge of what her own particular situation authorises her to do (Prelim. §16)—it becomes absolutely necessary that nations should reciprocally conform to general rules on this <347> subject. Accordingly, whenever it is certain and evident that such a measure, such an act of hostility, is necessary in general for overpowering the enemy's resistance, and attaining the end of a lawful war,—that measure, thus viewed in a general light, is, by the law of nations, deemed lawful in war, and consistent with propriety, although he who unnecessarily adopts it when he might attain his end by gentler methods, is not innocent before God and his own conscience. In this, lies the difference between what is just, equitable, irreprehensible in war, and what is only allowed between nations, and suffered to pass with impunity. The sovereign who would preserve a pure conscience, and punctually discharge the duties of humanity, ought never to lose sight of what we already have more than once observed,—that nature gives him no right to make war on his fellow-men, except in cases of necessity, and as a remedy, ever disagreeable, though often necessary, against obstinate injustice or violence. If his mind is duly impressed with this great truth, he will never extend the application of the remedy beyond its due limits, and will be very careful not to render it more harsh in its operation, and more fatal to mankind, than is requisite for his own security and the defence of his rights.

Since the object of a just war is to repress injustice and violence, and forcibly to compel him who is deaf to the voice of justice, we have a right to put in practice, against the enemy, every measure that is necessary in order to weaken him, and disable him from resisting us and supporting his injustice: and we may choose such methods as are the most efficacious and best calculated to attain the end in view, provided they be not of an odious kind, nor unjustifiable in themselves, and prohibited by the law of nature.

§138. The right to weaken an enemy by every justifiable method.

The enemy who attacks me unjustly, gives me an undoubted right to repel his violence; and he who takes up arms to oppose me when I demand only my right, becomes himself the real aggressor by his unjust resistance: he is the first author of the violence, and obliges me to employ forcible means in order to secure myself against the wrong which he intends to do me either in my person or my property. If the forcible means I employ produce such effect as even to take away his life, he alone must bear the whole blame of that misfortune: for if I were obliged to submit to the wrong rather than hurt him, good men would soon become the prey of the wicked. Such is the origin of the right to kill our enemies in a just war. When we find gentler methods insufficient to conquer their resistance and bring them to terms, we have a right to put them to death. Under the name of enemies, as we have already shewn, are to be comprehended, not only the first author of the war, but likewise all those who join him, and who fight in support of his cause.

§139. The right over the enemy's person.

But the very manner in which the right to kill our enemies is proved, points out the limits of that right. On an enemy's submitting and laying down his arms, we cannot with justice take <348> away his life. Thus, in a battle, quarter is to be given to those who lay down their arms; and, in a siege, a garrison offering to capitulate are never to be refused their lives. The humanity with which most nations in Europe carry on their wars at present, cannot be too much commended. If sometimes in the

§140. Limits of this right. An enemy not to be killed after ceasing to resist.

heat of action the soldier refuses to give quarter, it is always contrary to the inclination of the officers, who eagerly interpose to save the lives of such enemies as have laid down their arms.*

§141. A partic-
ular case, in
which quarter
may be refused.

There is, however, one case, in which we may refuse to spare the life of an enemy who surrenders, or to allow any capitulation to a town reduced to the last extremity. It is when that enemy has been guilty of some enormous breach of the law of nations, and particularly when he has violated the laws of war. This refusal of quarter is no natural consequence of the war, but a punishment for his crime,—a punishment which the injured party has a right to inflict. But in order that it be justly inflicted, it must fall on the guilty. When we are at war with a savage nation, who observe no rules, and never give quarter, we may punish them in the persons of any of their people whom we take (these belonging to the number of the guilty), and endeavour, by this rigorous proceeding, to force them to respect the laws of humanity. But wherever severity is not absolutely necessary, clemency becomes a duty. Corinth was utterly destroyed[24] for having violated the law of nations in the person of the Roman embassadors. That severity, however, was reprobated by Cicero and other great men. He who has even the most just cause to punish a sovereign with whom he is in enmity, will ever incur the reproach of cruelty, if he causes the punishment to fall on his innocent subjects. There are other methods of chastising the sovereign,—such as, depriving him of some of his rights, taking from him towns and provinces. The evil which thence results to the nation at large, is the consequence of that participation which cannot possibly be avoided by those who unite in political society.

* From several passages in Grotius's History of the Disturbances in the Low Countries, it appears that the war between the Dutch and Spaniards was carried on with unrelenting cruelty at sea, although the parties had agreed to observe the usual rules of moderation on land.—Intelligence being received by the confederate states, that the Spaniards had, by the advice of Spinola, embarked at Lisbon a body of troops destined for Flanders, they dispatched a squadron to wait for them in the strait of Calais, with orders to drown without mercy every soldier that was taken; and the order was punctually executed.—Book xiv. p. 550. [[Note added in 1773/1797 editions.]]

24. In 146 B.C.

This leads us to speak of a kind of retaliation sometimes practised in war, under the name of reprisals. If the hostile general has, without any just reason, caused some prisoners to be hanged, we hang an equal number of his people, and of the same rank,—notifying to him that we will continue thus to retaliate, for the purpose of obliging him to observe the laws of war. It is a dreadful extremity thus to condemn a prisoner to atone, by a miserable death, for his general's crime: and if we had previously <349> promised to spare the life of that prisoner, we cannot, without injustice, make him the subject of our reprisals.* Nevertheless, as a prince or his general has a right to sacrifice his enemies' lives to his own safety and that of his men,—it appears, that, if he has to do with an inhuman enemy who frequently commits such enormities, he is authorised to refuse quarter to some of the prisoners he takes, and to treat them as his people have been treated.† But Scipio's generosity is rather to be imitated:—that great man, having reduced some Spanish princes who had revolted against the Romans, declared to them that, on a breach of their faith, he would not call the innocent hostages to an account, but themselves; and that he would not avenge it on an unarmed enemy, but on those who should be found in arms.‡ Alexander the Great, having cause of complaint against Darius for some malpractices, sent him word, that if he continued to make war in such a manner, he would proceed to every extremity against him, and give him no quarter.§ It is thus an enemy who violates the laws of war is to be

§142.
Reprisals.

---

* In the French, we here find (apparently, very much out of place) a verbatim repetition of the long note which has already appeared in page 286. [[Note added in 1797 edition.]]

† Lysander [[commander of the Spartan fleet, d. 395 B.C.]], having captured the Athenian fleet, put the prisoners to death, on account of various cruelties practised by the Athenians during the course of the war, but principally on account of the barbarous resolution which they were known to have adopted, of cutting off the right hand of every prisoner, in case of victory declaring on their side. He spared Adeimantus alone, who had opposed that infamous resolution. Xenoph. Hist. Graec. lib. ii. cap. 1. [[Note added in 1773/1797 editions.]]

‡ Neque se in obsides innoxios, sed in ipsos, si defecerint, saeviturum; nec ab inermi, sed ab armato hoste, poenas expetiturum. Tit. Liv. [[*History of Rome*]] lib. xxviii.

§ Quint. Curt. lib. iv. cap. 1 & 11.

checked, and not by causing the penalty due to his crime to fall on innocent victims.

§143. Whether a governor of a town can be punished with death for an obstinate defence.

How could it be conceived in an enlightened age, that it is lawful to punish with death a governor who has defended his town to the last extremity, or who, in a weak place, has had the courage to hold out against a royal army? In the last century, this notion still prevailed; it was looked upon as one of the laws of war, and is not, even at present, totally exploded. What an idea! to punish a brave man for having performed his duty! Very different were the principles of Alexander the Great, when he gave orders for sparing some Milesians, *on account of their courage and fidelity.** "As Phyton was led to execution by order of Dionysius the tyrant for having obstinately defended the town of Rhegium of which he was governor, he cried out that he was unjustly condemned to die for having refused to betray the town, and that heaven would soon avenge his death." Diodorus Siculus terms this "an unjust punishment."† It is in vain to object, that an obstinate defence, especially in a weak place, against a royal army, only causes a fruitless effusion of blood. Such a defence may save the state, by delaying the enemy some days longer; and besides, courage supplies the de-<350>fects of the fortifications.‡ The

---

* Arrian. de Exped. Alexand. lib. i. cap. 20.

† Lib. xiv. cap. 113, quoted by Grotius, lib. iii. cap. 2, §16, n. 5 [[*Law of War and Peace*]].

‡ The false maxim which formerly prevailed on this subject, is noticed in the relation of the battle of Musselburgh [[1547]] (De Thou [[Jacques Auguste de Thou]], vol i. p. 287). "The general (the duke of Somerset), the regent of England, was on this occasion much admired for his clemency, which induced him to spare the lives of the besieged (the garrison of a castle in Scotland), notwithstanding that ancient maxim in war which declares that a weak garrison forfeit all claim to mercy on the part of the conqueror, when, with more courage than prudence, they obstinately persevere in defending an ill-fortified place against a royal army, and when, refusing to accept of reasonable conditions offered to them, they undertake to arrest the progress of a power which they are unable to resist."—Pursuant to that maxim, Caesar answered the Aduatici that he would spare their town, if they surrendered before the battering-ram touched their walls,—and the duke of Alva strongly blamed Prosper Colonna for having granted terms of capitulation to the garrison of a castle, who had refused to treat of a surrender until the cannon had been employed against them. [[Note added in 1773/1797 editions.]]

chevalier Bayard having thrown himself into Mezieres,[25] defended it with his usual intrepidity,* and proved that a brave man is sometimes capable of saving a place which another would not think tenable. The history of the famous siege of Malta[26] is another instance how far men of spirit may defend themselves, when thoroughly determined. How many places have surrendered, which might still have arrested the enemy's progress for a considerable time, obliged him to consume his strength and waste the remainder of the campaign, and even finally saved themselves, by a better-supported and more vigorous defence? In the last war, whilst the strongest places in the Netherlands opened their gates in a few days, the valiant general Leutrum was seen to defend Coni[27] against the utmost efforts of two powerful armies,—to hold out, in so indifferent a post, forty days from the opening of the trenches,—and finally to save the town, and, together with it, all Piémont. If it be urged, that, by threatening a commandant with death, you may shorten a bloody siege, spare your troops, and make a valuable saving of time,—my answer is, that a brave man will despise your menace, or, incensed by such ignominious treatment, will sell his life as dearly as he can,—will bury himself under the ruins of his fort, and make you pay for your injustice. But whatever advantage you might promise yourself from an unlawful proceeding, that will not warrant you in the use of it. The menace of an unjust punishment is unjust in itself: it is an insult and an injury. But, above all, it would be horrible and barbarous to put it in execution: and if you allow that the threatened consequences must not be realised, the threat is vain and ridiculous. Just and honourable means may be employed to dissuade a governor from ineffectually persevering to the last

---

* See his life. [[Champier, *Les Gestes, ensemble la vie du preulx chevalier Bayard* (Lyons, 1525).]]

25. The French soldier Pierre Terrail, seigneur de Bayard (1473–1524), defended Mézières with a tiny force against Charles V's imperial troops in 1521.

26. Between May and September 1565, the knights of Saint John of Jerusalem held Malta against the Ottoman Turks.

27. Karl Sigismond Friedrich Wilhelm Leutrum (1692–1755), commanding Piedmontese troops, defended the city of Coneo against Franco-Spanish forces in 1744 during the War of the Austrian Succession.

extremity: and such is the present practice of all prudent and humane generals. At a proper stage of the business, they summon a governor to surrender; they offer him honourable and advantageous terms of capitulation,—accompanied by a threat, that, if he delays too long, he will only be admitted to surrender as a prisoner of war, <351> and at discretion. If he persists, and is at length forced to surrender at discretion,—they may then treat both himself and his troops with all the severity of the law of war. But that law can never extend so far as to give a right to take away the life of an enemy who lays down his arms (§140), unless he has been guilty of some crime against the conqueror (§141).

Resistance carried to extremity does not become punishable in a subaltern, except on those occasions only when it is evidently fruitless. It is then obstinacy, and not firmness or valour:—true valour has always a reasonable object in view. Let us, for instance, suppose that a state has entirely submitted to the conqueror's arms, except one single fortress,—that no succour is to be expected from without,—no neighbour, no ally, concerns himself about saving the remainder of that conquered state:—on such an occasion, the governor is to be made acquainted with the situation of affairs, and summoned to surrender; and he may be threatened with death in case of his persisting in a defence which is absolutely fruitless, and which can only tend to the effusion of human blood.* Should this make no impression on him, he deserves to suffer the punishment with which he has been justly threatened. I suppose the justice of the war to be problematical, and that it is not an insupportable oppression which he opposes: for if this governor maintains a cause that is

---

* But it is not lawful to employ menaces of every kind in order to induce the governor or commandant of a town to surrender. There are some, against which nature revolts with horror.—Louis the Eleventh, being engaged in the siege of St. Omer, and incensed at the long resistance he experienced, informed the governor, Philip, son of Antony the Bastard of Burgundy, that, if he did not surrender the place, his father, (who was a prisoner in Louis's hands) should be put to death in his sight. Philip replied that he would feel the most poignant regret to lose his father, but that his honour was still dearer to him, and that he was too well acquainted with the king's disposition, to apprehend that he would disgrace himself by the perpetration of so barbarous a deed. [[Charles Pineau-Duclos,]] Hist. of Louis XI. book viii. [[Note added in 1773/1797 editions.]]

evidently just,—if he fights to save his country from slavery,—his misfortune will be pitied; and every man of spirit will applaud him for gallantly persevering to the last extremity, and determining to die free.

Fugitives and deserters, found by the victor among his enemies, are guilty of a crime against him; and he has undoubtedly a right to put them to death. But they are not properly considered as enemies: they are rather perfidious citizens, traitors to their country; and their enlistment with the enemy cannot obliterate that character, or exempt them from the punishment they have deserved. At present, however, desertion being unhappily too common, the number of the delinquents renders it in some measure necessary to shew clemency; and, in capitulations, it is usual to indulge the evacuating garrison with a certain number of covered waggons, in which they save the deserters. §144. Fugitives and deserters.

Women, children, feeble old men, and sick persons, come under the description of enemies (§§70, 72); and we have certain <352> rights over them, inasmuch as they belong to the nation with whom we are at war, and as, between nation and nation, all rights and pretensions affect the body of the society, together with all its members (Book II. §§81, 82, 344). But these are enemies who make no resistance; and consequently we have no right to maltreat their persons, or use any violence against them, much less to take away their lives (§140). This is so plain a maxim of justice and humanity, that at present every nation, in the least degree civilised, acquiesces in it. If sometimes the furious and ungovernable soldier carries his brutality so far as to violate female chastity, or to massacre women, children, and old men, the officers lament those excesses: they exert their utmost efforts to put a stop to them; and a prudent and humane general even punishes them whenever he can. But if the women wish to be spared altogether, they must confine themselves to the occupations peculiar to their own sex, and not meddle with those of men by taking up arms. Accordingly the military law of the Switzers, which forbids the soldier to maltreat women, formally excepts those females who have committed any acts of hostility.* §145. Women, children, the aged, and sick.

* See Simler, de Repub. Helvet.

§146. Clergy, men of letters, &c.

The like may be said of the public ministers of religion, of men of letters, and other persons whose mode of life is very remote from military affairs:—not that these people, nor even the ministers of the altar, are, necessarily and by virtue of their functions, invested with any character of inviolability, or that the civil law can confer it on them with respect to the enemy: but as they do not use force or violence to oppose him, they do not give him a right to use it against them. Among the ancient Romans the priests carried arms: Julius Caesar himself was sovereign pontiff:—and, among the christians, it has been no rare thing to see prelates, bishops, and cardinals, buckle on their armour, and take the command of armies. From the instant of their doing so, they subjected themselves to the common fate of military men. While dealing out their blows in the field of battle, they did not, it is to be presumed, lay claim to inviolability.

§147. Peasants, and, in general, all who do not carry arms.

Formerly, every one capable of carrying arms became a soldier when his nation was at war, and especially when it was attacked. Grotius however* produces instances of several nations and eminent commanders† who spared the peasantry in consideration of the immediate usefulness of their labours.‡ At present war is carried on by regular troops: the people, the peasants, the citizens, take no part in it, and generally have nothing to fear from the sword of the enemy. Provided the inhabitants submit to him who is master of the country, pay the contributions im-<353>posed, and refrain from all hostilities, they live in as perfect safety as if they were friends: they even continue in possession of what belongs to them: the country people come freely to the camp to sell their provisions, and are protected, as far as possible, from the calamities of war. A laudable custom, truly worthy of those nations who value themselves on their humanity, and advantageous even to the enemy who acts with such moderation. By protecting the unarmed inhabitants, keeping the soldiery under strict discipline, and preserving the country, a general

---

* Book iii. ch. ii. §11 [[*Law of War and Peace*]].

† Cyrus [[Cyrus the Great, founder of the Persian Empire, r. 576–529 B.C.]], Belisarius [[Flavius, Byzantine general serving under Justinian I, A.D. 505–65]], &c.

‡ Cyrus proposed to the king of Assyria, that both parties should reciprocally spare the cultivators of the soil, and make war only against those who appeared in arms:— and the proposal was agreed to. Xenoph. Cyrop. lib. v. cap. 4.

procures an easy subsistence for his army, and avoids many evils and dangers. If he has any reason to mistrust the peasantry and the inhabitants of the towns, he has a right to disarm them, and to require hostages from them: and those who wish to avoid the calamities of war, must submit to the laws which the enemy thinks proper to impose on them.

But all those enemies thus subdued or disarmed, whom the principles of humanity oblige him to spare,—all those persons belonging to the opposite party (even the women and children), he may lawfully secure and make prisoners, either with a view to prevent them from taking up arms again, or for the purpose of weakening the enemy (§138), or, finally, in hopes that, by getting into his power some woman or child for whom the sovereign has an affection, he may induce him to accede to equitable conditions of peace, for the sake of redeeming those valuable pledges. At present, indeed, this last-mentioned expedient is seldom put in practice by the polished nations of Europe: women and children are suffered to enjoy perfect security, and allowed permission to withdraw wherever they please. But this moderation, this politeness, though undoubtedly commendable, is not in itself absolutely obligatory; and if a general thinks fit to supersede it, he cannot be justly accused of violating the laws of war. He is at liberty to adopt such measures in this respect as he thinks most conducive to the success of his affairs. If, without reason, and from mere caprice, he refuses to indulge women with this liberty, he will be taxed with harshness and brutality,—he will be censured for not conforming to a custom established by humanity: but he may have good reasons for disregarding, in this particular, the rules of politeness, and even the suggestions of pity. If there are hopes of reducing by famine a strong place of which it is very important to gain possession, the useless mouths are not permitted to come out. And in this there is nothing which is not authorised by the laws of war. Some great men, however, have, on occasions of this nature, carried their compassion so far as to postpone their interests to the motions of humanity. We have already mentioned in another place how Henry the Great acted during the siege of Paris. To such a noble example let us add that of Titus at the siege of Jerusalem:[28] at first he was inclined to drive back into the city great

§148. The right of making prisoners of war.

28. Siege of Jerusalem, A.D. 70.

numbers of starving wretches, who came out of it: but he could not withstand the <354> compassion which such a sight raised in him; and he suffered the sentiments of humanity and generosity to prevail over the maxims of war.

§149. A prisoner of war not to be put to death. As soon as your enemy has laid down his arms and surrendered his person, you have no longer any right over his life (§140), unless he should give you such right by some new attempt, or had before committed against you a crime deserving death (§141). It was therefore a dreadful error of antiquity, a most unjust and savage claim, to assume a right of putting prisoners of war to death, and even by the hand of the executioner. More just and humane principles, however, have long since been adopted. Charles I. king of Naples,[29] having defeated and taken prisoner Conradin[30] his competitor, caused him to be publicly beheaded at Naples, together with Frederic of Austria, his fellow-prisoner. This barbarity raised a universal horror; and Peter the Third, king of Arragon,[31] reproached Charles with it as a detestable crime, and till then unheard of among christian princes.* The case, however, was that of a dangerous rival who contended with him for the throne. But supposing even the claims of that rival were unjust, Charles might have kept him in prison till he had renounced them, and given security for his future behaviour.

§150. How prisoners of war are to be treated. Prisoners may be secured; and, for this purpose, they may be put into confinement, and even fettered if there be reason to apprehend that they will rise on their captors, or make their escape. But they are not to be treated harshly, unless personally guilty of some crime against him who has them in his power. In this case he is at liberty to punish them: oth-

---

* Epist. Pet. Arrag apud Petr. de Vineis. [[Petrus de Vineis is Pierre de la Vigne (ca. 1190–1249), chancellor of Frederic II of Hohenstauffen. The letter from Peter III, king of Aragon, is in a collection that has not been identified.]]

29. Charles I of Naples, r. 1266–85.

30. Conradin, or Conrad V (1252–68), the last of the Hohenstaufen line, held the duchy of Swabia from 1262 and considered himself to be king of Jerusalem and of Sicily. Upon his defeat by Charles I of Naples, he was tried and beheaded.

31. Peter III of Aragon, r. 1276–85.

erwise he should remember that they are men, and unfortunate.* A man of exalted soul no longer feels any emotions but those of compassion towards a conquered enemy who has submitted to his arms. Let us in this particular bestow on the European nations the praise to which they are justly entitled. Prisoners of war are seldom ill treated among them. We extol the English and French, we feel our bosoms glow with love for them, when we hear the accounts of the treatment which prisoners of war, on both sides, have experienced from those generous nations. And what is more, by a custom which equally displays the honour and humanity of the Europeans, an officer, taken prisoner in war, is released on his <355> parole, and enjoys the comfort of passing the time of his captivity in his own country, in the midst of his family; and the party who have thus released him, rest as perfectly sure of him, as if they had him confined in irons.

Formerly a question of an embarrassing nature might have been proposed. When we have so great a number of prisoners that we find it impossible to feed them, or to keep them with safety, have we a right to put them to death? or shall we send them back to the enemy,—thus increasing his strength, and exposing ourselves to the hazard of being overpowered by him on a subsequent occasion? At present the case is attended with no difficulty. Such prisoners are dismissed on their parole,—bound by promise not to carry arms for a certain time or during the continuance of the war. And as every commander necessarily has a power of agreeing to the conditions on which the enemy admits his sur-

§151. Whether prisoners, who cannot be kept or fed, may be put to death.

---

* In 1593, the council of the Netherlands, at the persuasion of the count de Fuentes, resolved no longer to observe towards the United Provinces that moderation which humanity renders so necessary in war. They gave orders for putting to death every man who should be made prisoner, and, under the same penalty, prohibited the payment of any contributions to the enemy. But the complaints of the nobility and clergy, and, still more, the murmurs of the military, who saw themselves exposed to an infamous death in case of falling into the enemy's hands, obliged the Spaniards to re-establish those indispensable usages, which, in the words of Virgil [Aen. x. 532], are called *belli commercia*,—the ransom or exchange of prisoners, and the payment of contributions to avert pillage and devastation. The ransom of each prisoner was then settled at a month's pay. Grotius, Hist. of Netherlands, book iii. [[Note added in 1773/1797 editions.]]

render, the engagements entered into by him for saving his life or his liberty with that of his men, are valid, as being made within the limits of his powers (§§19, &c.); and his sovereign cannot annul them. Of this many instances occurred during the last war:[32]—several Dutch garrisons submitted to the condition of not serving against France or her allies, for one or two years: a body of French troops being invested in Lintz, were by capitulation sent back across the Rhine, under a restriction not to carry arms against the queen of Hungary for a stated time: and the sovereigns of those troops respected the engagements formed by them. But conventions of this kind have their limits, which consist in not infringing the rights of the sovereign over his subjects. Thus the enemy, in releasing prisoners, may impose on them the condition of not carrying arms against him till the conclusion of the war; since he might justly keep them in confinement till that period: but he cannot require that they shall for ever renounce the liberty of fighting for their country; because, on the termination of the war, he has no longer any reason for detaining them; and they, on their part, cannot enter into an engagement absolutely inconsistent with their character of citizens or subjects. If their country abandons them, they become free in that respect, and have in their turn a right to renounce their country.

But if we have to do with a nation that is at once savage, perfidious, and formidable, shall we send her back a number of soldiers who will perhaps enable her to destroy us?—When our own safety is incompatible with that of an enemy—even of an enemy who has submitted,—the question admits not of a doubt. But to justify us in coolly and deliberately putting to death a great number of prisoners, the following conditions are indispensably necessary:—1. that no promise have been made to spare their lives; and, 2. that we be perfectly assured that our own safety demands such a sacrifice. If it is at all consistent with prudence either to trust to their parole or to disregard their perfidy, a generous enemy will rather listen to the voice of huma-<356>nity than to that of a timid circumspection. Charles the Twelfth, being incumbered with his

32. War of the Austrian Succession.

prisoners after the battle of Narva,[33] only disarmed them and set them at liberty: but his enemy, still impressed with the apprehensions which his warlike and formidable opponents had excited in his mind, sent into Siberia all the prisoners he took at Pultowa. The Swedish hero confided too much in his own generosity: the sagacious monarch of Russia united perhaps too great a degree of severity with his prudence: but necessity furnishes an apology for severity, or rather throws a veil over it altogether. When admiral Anson took the rich Acapulco galleon near Manilla, he found that the prisoners outnumbered his whole ship's company: he was therefore under a necessity of confining them in the hold, where they suffered cruel distress.* But, had he exposed himself to the risk of being carried away a prisoner, with his prize and his own ship together, would the humanity of his conduct have justified the imprudence of it? Henry V. king of England, after his victory in the battle of Agincourt, was reduced, or thought himself reduced, to the cruel necessity of sacrificing the prisoners to his own safety. "In this universal route," says Father Daniel, "a fresh misfortune happened, which cost the lives of a great number of French. A remainder of their van was retreating in some order, and many of the stragglers rallied and joined it. The king of England, observing their motions from an eminence, supposed it was their intention to return to the charge. At the same moment he received information of an attack being made on his camp where the baggage was deposited. In fact, some noblemen of Picardy, having armed about six hundred peasants, had fallen upon the English camp. Thus circumstanced, that prince, apprehensive of some disastrous reverse, dispatched his aides-de-camp to the different divisions of the army, with orders for putting all the prisoners to the sword, lest, in case of a renewal of the battle, the care of guarding them should prove an impediment to his soldiers, or the prisoners should escape, and join their countrymen. The order was immediately carried into execution, and all the prisoners were

---

* See Anson's Voyage round the World.

33. Charles XII of Sweden (r. 1697–1718) defeated the forces of Czar Peter the Great at Narva in 1700 during the Great Northern War (1700–21).

put to the sword."* Nothing short of the greatest necessity can justify
so terrible an execution; and the general whose situation requires it, is
greatly to be pitied.

§152. Whether
prisoners of
war may be
made slaves.

Is it lawful to condemn prisoners of war to slavery? Yes, in cases which
give a right to kill them,—when they have rendered themselves personally guilty of some crime deserving of death. The ancients used to sell
their prisoners of war for slaves. They indeed thought they had a right
to put them to death. In every circumstance, when I cannot innocently
take away my prisoner's life, I have no right to make him a slave. If I
spare his life and condemn him to a state so contrary to the nature of
<357> man, I still continue with him the state of war. He lies under no
obligation to me: for, what is life without freedom? If any one counts
life a favour when the grant of it is attended with chains,—be it so: let
him accept the kindness, submit to the destiny which awaits him, and
fulfil the duties annexed to it. But he must apply to some other writer
to teach him those duties: there have been authors enough who have
amply treated of them. I shall dwell no longer on the subject: and indeed
that disgrace to humanity is happily banished from Europe.

§153.
Exchange and
ransom of
prisoners.

Prisoners of war, then, are detained, either to prevent their returning
to join the enemy again, or with a view to obtain from their sovereign a
just satisfaction, as the price of their liberty. There is no obligation to
release those who are detained with the latter view, till after satisfaction
is obtained. As to the former, whoever makes a just war, has a right, if
he thinks proper, to detain his prisoners till the end of the war: and
whenever he releases them, he may justly require a ransom, either as a
compensation at the conclusion of a peace, or, if during the continuance
of the war, for the purpose of at least weakening his enemy's finances at
the same time that he restores him a number of soldiers. The European
nations, who are ever to be commended for their care in alleviating the
evils of war, have, with regard to prisoners, introduced humane and salutary customs. They are exchanged or ransomed, even during the war;
and this point is generally settled beforehand by cartel. However, if a
nation finds a considerable advantage in leaving her soldiers prisoners

* [[Daniel]] Hist. of France, reign of Charles VI.

with the enemy during the war rather than exchanging them, she may certainly, unless bound by cartel, act in that respect as is most conducive to her interest. Such would be the case of a state abounding in men, and at war with a nation more formidable by the courage than the number of her soldiers. It would have ill suited the interests of the czar Peter the Great, to restore his prisoners to the Swedes for an equal number of Russians.

But the state is bound to procure, at her own expense, the release of her citizens and soldiers who are prisoners of war, as soon as she has the means of accomplishing it, and can do it without danger. It was only by acting in her service and supporting her cause, that they were involved in their present misfortune. For the same reason, it is her duty to provide for their support during the time of their captivity. Formerly prisoners of war were obliged to redeem themselves: but then the ransom of all those whom the officers or soldiers might take, was the perquisite of the individual captors. The modern custom is more agreeable to reason and justice. If prisoners cannot be delivered during the course of the war, at least their liberty must, if possible, make an article in the treaty of peace. This is a care which the state owes to those who have exposed themselves in her defence. It must, nevertheless, be allowed, that a nation may, after the example of the Romans, and for the purpose of stimulating her soldiers to the most vigorous resistance, enact a law to prohibit prisoners of war from <358> ever being ransomed. When this is agreed to by the whole society, nobody can complain. But such a law is very severe, and could scarce suit any but those ambitious heroes who were determined on sacrificing every thing in order to make themselves masters of the world.

§154. The state is bound to procure their release.

Since the present chapter treats of the rights which war gives us over the person of the enemy, this is the proper place to discuss a celebrated question on which authors have been much divided,—and that is, whether we may lawfully employ all sorts of means to take away an enemy's life? whether we be justifiable in procuring his death by assassination or poison? Some writers have asserted, that, where we have a right to take away life, the manner is indifferent. A strange maxim! but happily exploded by the bare ideas of honour, confused and indefinite as they

§155. Whether an enemy may lawfully be assassinated or poisoned.

are. In civil society, I have a right to punish a slanderer,—to cause my property to be restored by him who unjustly detains it: but shall the manner be indifferent? Nations may do themselves justice sword in hand, when otherwise refused to them: shall it be indifferent to human society that they employ odious means, capable of spreading desolation over the whole face of the earth, and against which, the most just and equitable of sovereigns, even though supported by the majority of other princes, cannot guard himself?

But in order to discuss this question on solid grounds, assassination is by all means to be distinguished from surprises, which are, doubtless, very allowable in war. Should a resolute soldier steal into the enemy's camp by night,—should he penetrate to the general's tent, and stab him,—in such conduct there is nothing contrary to the natural laws of war,— nothing even but what is perfectly commendable in a just and necessary war. Mutius Scaevola[34] has been praised by all the great men of antiquity; and Porsenna himself, whom he intended to kill, could not but commend his courage.* Pepin,[35] father of Charlemagne, having crossed the Rhine with one of his guards, went and killed his enemy in his chamber.† If any one has absolutely condemned such bold strokes, his censure only proceeded from a desire to flatter those among the great, who would wish to leave all the dangerous part of war to the soldiery and inferior officers. It is true indeed that the agents in such attempts are usually punished with some painful death. But that is because the prince or general who is thus attacked, exercises his own rights in turn,— has an eye to his own safety, and endeavours, by the dread of a cruel punishment, to deter his enemies from attacking him otherwise than by open force. He may proportion his severity towards an enemy according as his own safety requires. Indeed it would be more commendable on both sides to renounce every kind of hos-<359>tility which lays the en-

* See Livy, lib. ii. cap. 12.—Cicero, pro P. Sextio.—Valer. Max. lib. iii. cap. 3.— Plutarch, in Poplicol.

† Grotius, lib. iii. cap. 4, §18, n. 1 [[*Law of War and Peace*]].

34. Gaius Mucius Scaevola, ca. sixth century B.C., in Roman legend the hero who saved Rome from Porsenna's Etruscans.

35. Pepin the Younger, 714–68, king of the Franks 751–58.

emy under a necessity of employing cruel punishments in order to secure himself against it. This might be made an established custom,—a conventional law of war. The generous warriors of the present age dislike such attempts, and would never willingly undertake them, except on those extraordinary occasions when they become necessary to the very safety and being of their country. As to the six hundred Lacedaemonians, who, under the conduct of Leonidas,[36] broke into the enemy's camp, and made their way directly to the Persian monarch's[37] tent,* their expedition was justifiable by the common rules of war, and did not authorise the king to treat them more rigorously than any other enemies. In order to defeat all such attempts, it is sufficient to keep a strict watch; and it would be unjust to have recourse to cruel punishments for that purpose: accordingly such punishments are reserved for those only who gain admittance by stealth, alone or in very small number, and especially if under cover of a disguise.

I give, then, the name of *assassination* to a treacherous murder, whether the perpetrators of the deed be subjects of the party whom we cause to be assassinated, or of our own sovereign,—or that it be executed by the hand of any other emissary, introducing himself as a supplicant, a refugee, a deserter, or, in fine, as a stranger; and such an attempt, I say, is infamous and execrable, both in him who executes and in him who commands it. Why do we judge an act to be criminal, and contrary to the law of nature, but because such act is pernicious to human society, and that the practice of it would be destructive to mankind? Now what could be more terrible than the custom of hiring a traitor to assassinate our enemy? Besides, were such a liberty once introduced, the purest virtue, the friendship of the majority of the reigning sovereigns, would no longer be sufficient to ensure a prince's safety. Had Titus lived in the time of the *old man of the mountain*,[38]—though the happiness of man-

---

* Justin. [[Digest.]] lib. ii. cap. xi.

36. Leonidas, king of Sparta, ca. 489 B.C.

37. Xerxes I of Persia, r. 485–465 B.C.

38. The reference is to Hasan ibn al-Sabbah, founder of the Assassins, a secret order of the Ismaili sect of Islam. Folklore called him the Old Man of the Mountain.

kind centred in him,—though, punctual in the observance of peace and equity, he was respected and adored by all potentates,—yet, the very first time that the prince of the Assassins might have thought proper to quarrel with him, that universal affection would have proved insufficient to save him; and mankind would have lost their "darling." Let it not here be replied that it is only in favour of the cause of justice that such extraordinary measures are allowable: for all parties, in their wars, maintain that they have justice on their side. Whoever, by setting the example, contributes to the introduction of so destructive a practice, declares himself the enemy of mankind, and deserves the execration of all ages.* The assassination of William prince of Orange <360> was regarded with universal detestation, though the Spaniards had declared that prince a rebel. And the same nation denied, as an atrocious calumny, the charge of having had the least concern in that of Henry the Great, who was preparing for a war against them, which might have shaken their monarchy to its very foundations.

In treacherously administering poison there is something still more odious than in assassination: it would be more difficult to guard against the consequences of such an attempt; and the practice would be more dreadful; accordingly it has been more generally detested. Of this Grotius has accumulated many instances.† The consuls Caius Fabricius and

* See the dialogue between Julius Caesar and Cicero, in the Mélanges de Littérature et Poésies.—Farrudge, sultan of Egypt, sent to Timur-bec an embassador accompanied by two villains who were to assassinate that conqueror during the audience. This infamous plot being discovered—"It is not (said Timur) the maxim of kings to put embassadors to death: but as to this wretch, who, under the sacred garb of religion, is a monster of perfidy and corruption, it would be a crime to suffer him and his accomplices to live." Pursuant, therefore, to that passage of the Koran which says that "treachery falls on the traitor's own head," he ordered him to be dispatched with the same poignard with which he had intended to perpetrate the abominable deed. The body of the traitor was then committed to the flames, as an example to others. The two assassins were only condemned to suffer the amputation of their noses and ears,—Timur contenting himself with this punishment, and forbearing to put them to death, because he wished to send them back with a letter to the sultan. [[La Croix.]] Hist. of Timur-bec, book v. chap. 24. [[Note added in 1773/1797 editions.]]

† Book iii. chap. 4, §15 [[*Law of War and Peace*]].

Quintus Aemilius rejected with horror the proposal of Pyrrhus's[39] physician who made an offer of poisoning his master: they even cautioned that prince to be on his guard against the traitor,—haughtily adding, "It is not to ingratiate ourselves with you that we give this information, but to avoid the obloquy to which your death would expose us."* And they justly observe in the same letter, that it is for the common interest of all nations not to set such examples.† It was a maxim of the Roman senate, that war was to be carried on with arms, and not with poison.‡ Even under Tiberius,[40] the proposal of the prince of the Catti was rejected, who offered to destroy Arminius[41] if poison were sent him for that purpose: and he received for answer, that "it was the practice of the Romans to take vengeance on their enemies by open force, and not by treachery and secret machinations";§ Tiberius thus making it his glory to imitate the virtue of the ancient Roman commanders. This instance is the more remarkable, as Arminius had treacherously cut off Varus,[42] together with three Roman legions. The senate, and even Tiberius himself, thought it unlawful to adopt the use of poison, even against a perfidious enemy, and as a kind of retaliation or reprisals.

* Ουδε γαρ ταυτα ση χαριτι μηνυομεν, αλλ' όπως μη το σον παθος ήμιν διαβολην ενεγκη, Plut. in Pyrr.

† Sed communis exempli et fidei ergo visum est, uti te salvum velimus; ut esset, quem armis vincere possemus. [["But as a matter of general precedent and honor, it has seemed to us that we should desire your personal safety, in order that we may have the opportunity of vanquishing you in the field."]] Aul. Gell. Noct Attic. lib. iii. cap 8.

‡ Armis bella, non venenis, geri debere. [["War is to be fought with arms, not poison."]] Valer. Maxim. lib. vi. ch. 5, num. 1.

§ Non fraude, neque occultis, sed palam, et armatum, populum Romanum hostes suos ulcisci. Tacit. Annal. lib. ii. cap. 88.

39. Caius Luscinus Fabricius served as consul in 282 and 278 B.C. with Quintus Aemilius Papus. In 280 B.C. while serving as ambassadors from Rome, they rejected the approach of the physician employed by the Molossian king Pyrrhus of Epirus.

40. Emperor Tiberius, r. A.D. 14–37.

41. Arminius, chief of the Cherusci, defeated Varus and his Roman army at Teutoburg Forest in A.D. 9.

42. Publius Quinctilius Varus, 46 B.C.–A.D. 9, military governor appointed by Augustus, died at the battle of Teutoburg Forest.

Assassination and poisoning are therefore contrary to the laws of war, and equally condemned by the law of nature, and the <361> consent of all civilised nations. The sovereign who has recourse to such execrable means, should be regarded as the enemy of the human race; and the common safety of mankind calls on all nations to unite against him, and join their forces to punish him. His conduct particularly authorises the enemy whom he has attacked by such odious means, to refuse him any quarter. Alexander declared that "he was determined to proceed to the utmost extremities against Darius, and no longer to consider him as a fair enemy, but as a poisoner and an assassin."*

The interest and safety of men in high command require, that, so far from countenancing the introduction of such practices, they should use all possible care to prevent it. It was wisely said by Eumenes,[43] that "he did not think any general wished to obtain a victory in such manner as should set a pernicious example which might recoil on himself."† And it was on the same principle that Alexander formed his judgment of Bessus,[44] who had assassinated Darius.‡[45]

§156. Whether poisoned weapons may be used in war.

The use of poisoned weapons may be excused or defended with a little more plausibility. At least there is no treachery in the case, no clandestine machination. But the practice is nevertheless prohibited by the law of nature, which does not allow us to multiply the evils of war beyond all bounds. You must of course strike your enemy in order to get the better of his efforts: but if he is once disabled, is it necessary that he should

---

* Quint. Curt. lib. iv. cap. 11, num. 18.

† Nec Antigonum, nec quemquam ducum, sic velle vincere, ut ipse in se exemplum pessimum statuat. Justin. [[Digest]] lib. xiv. cap. 1, num. 12.

‡ Quem quidem [*Bessum*] cruci adfixum videre festino, omnibus regibus gentibusque fidei, quam violavit, meritas poenas solventem. [["I am assuredly in haste to see him (Bessus) nailed to a cross, paying the penalty he has deserved to all kings and nations for the loyalty which he has dishonoured."]] Q. Curt. lib. vi. ch. 3, num. 14.

43. Eumenes of Cardia, 362–316 B.C., Greek scholar and general, served under Alexander the Great.

44. Bessus, Persian nobleman who proclaimed himself king after murdering Darius III.

45. Darius III, king of Persia 336–330 B.C., deposed by Alexander prior to being assassinated by Bessus.

inevitably die of his wounds? Besides, if you poison your weapons, the enemy will follow your example; and thus, without gaining any advantage on your side for the decision of the contest, you have only added to the cruelty and calamities of war. It is necessity alone that can at all justify nations in making war: they ought universally to abstain from every thing that has a tendency to render it more destructive: it is even a duty incumbent on them, to oppose such practices. It is therefore with good reason, and in conformity to their duty, that civilised nations have classed among the laws of war the maxim which prohibits the poisoning of weapons;* and they are all warranted by their common safety to repress and punish the first who should offer to break through that law.

A still more general unanimity prevails in condemning the practice of poisoning waters, wells, and springs, because (say some authors) we may thereby destroy innocent persons,—we may destroy other people as well as our enemies. This is indeed an additional reason: but it is not the only nor even the true one; for we do not scruple to fire on an enemy's <362> ship, although there be neutral passengers on board. But though poison is not to be used, it is very allowable to divert the water,—to cut off the springs,—or by any other means to render them useless, that the enemy may be reduced to surrender.† This is a milder way than that of arms.

§157. Whether springs may be poisoned.

I cannot conclude this subject, of what we have a right to do against the person of the enemy, without speaking a few words concerning the dispositions we ought to preserve towards him. They may already be deduced from what I have hitherto said, and especially in the first chapter of the second book. Let us never forget that our enemies are men. Though reduced to the disagreeable necessity of prosecuting our right by force of arms, let us not divest ourselves of that charity which connects us with all mankind. Thus shall we courageously defend our country's rights without violating those of human nature.‡ Let our valour

§158. Dispositions to be preserved towards an enemy.

* Grotius, book iii. chap. 4, §16 [[*Law of War and Peace*]].
† Grotius, ibid. §17 [[*Law of War and Peace*]].
‡ The laws of justice and equity are not to be less respected even in time of war. The following I quote as a remarkable instance. Alcibiades, at the head of an Athenian

preserve itself from every stain of cruelty, and the lustre of victory will not be tarnished by inhuman and brutal actions. Marius[46] and Attila[47] are now detested; whereas we cannot forbear admiring and loving Caesar; his generosity and clemency almost tempt us to overlook the injustice of his undertaking. Moderation and generosity redound more to the glory of a victor, than his courage; they are more certain marks of an exalted soul. Besides the honour which infallibly accompanies those virtues, humanity towards an enemy has been often attended with immediate and real advantages. Leopold, duke of Austria, besieging Soleure in the year 1318, threw a bridge over the Aar, and posted on it a large body of troops. Soon after, the river having, by an extraordinary swell of its waters, carried away the bridge together with those who were stationed on it,—the besieged hastened to the relief of those unfortunate men, and saved the greatest part of them. Leopold, relenting at this act of generosity, raised the siege and made peace with the city.* The duke of Cumberland, after his victory at Dettingen,† appears to me still greater than in the heat of battle. As he was under the surgeon's hands, a French officer, much more dangerously <363> wounded than himself, being brought that way, the duke immediately ordered his surgeon to

---

army, was engaged in the siege of Byzantium, then occupied by a Lacedaemonian garrison; and finding that he could not reduce the city by force, he gained over some of the inhabitants, who put him in possession of it. One of the persons concerned in this transaction was Anaxilaüs, a citizen of Byzantium, who, being afterwards brought to trial for it at Lacedaemon, pleaded, in his defence, that, in surrendering the city, he had not acted through ill-will to the Lacedaemonians, or under the influence of a bribe, but with a view to save the women and children, whom he saw perishing with famine, for Clearchus, who commanded the garrison, had given to the soldiers all the corn that was found in the city. The Lacedaemonians, with a noble regard to justice, and such as seldom prevails on similar occasions, acquitted the culprit,—observing that he had not betrayed but saved the city,—and particularly attending to the circumstance of his being a Byzantine, not a Lacedaemonian. Xenoph Hist. Graec. lib. i. cap. 3. [[Note added in 1773/1797 editions.]]

* Watteville's Hist. of the Helvetic Confederacy, vol. i. p. 126.

† In the year 1743.

46. Gaius Marius, 157–86 B.C., Roman general and politician, famously cruel and rapacious.

47. Attila, 405–53, last and most powerful king of the Huns (r. 445–53), notorious for his barbarity.

quit him, and assist that wounded enemy. If men in exalted stations did but conceive how great a degree of affection and respect attends such actions, they would study to imitate them, even when not prompted to the practice by native elevation of sentiment. At present the European nations generally carry on their wars with great moderation and generosity. These dispositions have given rise to several customs which are highly commendable, and frequently carried to the extreme of politeness.* Sometimes refreshments are sent to the governor of a besieged town; and it is usual to avoid firing on the king's or the general's quarters. We are sure to gain by this moderation when we have to do with a generous enemy; but we are not bound to observe it any farther than can be done without injuring the cause we defend; and it is clear that a prudent general will, in this respect, regulate his conduct by the circumstances of the case, by an attention to the safety of the army and of the state, by the magnitude of the danger, and by the character and behaviour of the enemy. Should a weak nation or town be attacked by a furious conqueror who threatens to destroy it, are the defenders to forbear firing on his quarters? Far from it: that is the very place to which, if possible, every shot should be directed.

Formerly, he who killed the king or general of the enemy was commended, and greatly rewarded: the honours annexed to the *spolia opima* are well known. Nothing was more natural: in former times, the belligerent nations had, almost in every instance, their safety and very existence at stake; and the death of the leader often put an end to the war. In our days, a soldier would not dare to boast of having killed the en-

§159. Tenderness for the person of a king who is in arms against us.

---

* Timur-bec made war on Joseph Sofy, king of Carezem, and subdued his kingdom. During the course of the war, that great man proved himself to be possessed of all that moderation and politeness which is thought peculiar to our modern warriors. Some melons being brought to him whilst he was besieging Joseph in the city of Eskiskus, he resolved to send a part of them to his enemy, thinking it would be a breach of civility not to share those new fruits with that prince, when so near him; and accordingly he ordered them to be put into a gold bason, and carried to him. The king of Carezem received this instance of politeness in a brutal manner: he ordered the melons to be thrown into the fossé, and gave the bason to the city gatekeeper. La Croix, Hist. of Timur-bec, book v. ch. 27. [[Note added in 1773/1797 editions.]]

emy's king. Thus sovereigns tacitly agree to secure their own persons. It must be owned, that, in a war which is carried on with no great animosity, and where the safety and existence of the state are not involved in the issue, this regard for regal majesty is perfectly commendable, and even consonant to the reciprocal duties of nations. In such a war, to take away the life of the enemy's sovereign when it might be spared, is perhaps doing that nation a greater degree of harm than is necessary for bringing the contest to a happy issue. But it is not one of the laws of war that we should on every occasion spare the person of the hostile king: <364> we are not bound to observe that moderation except where we have a fair opportunity of making him prisoner.*

CHAPTER IX

Of the Right of War, with regard to Things belonging to the Enemy.

§160. Principles of the right over things belonging to the enemy.
A state taking up arms in a just cause has a double right against her enemy,—1. a right to obtain possession of her property with-held by the enemy; to which must be added the expenses incurred in the pursuit of that object, the charges of the war, and the reparation of damages: for, were she obliged to bear those expenses and losses, she would not fully recover her property, or obtain her due. 2. She has a right to weaken her enemy, in order to render him incapable of supporting his unjust vio-

---

* On this subject, let us notice a trait of Charles XII. of Sweden [[r. 1697–1718]], in which sound reason and the most exalted courage are equally conspicuous. That prince being engaged in the siege of Thorn in Poland [[1703]], and frequently walking round the city, was easily distinguished by the cannoneers, who regularly fired upon him as soon as they saw him make his appearance. The principal officers of his army, greatly alarmed at their sovereign's danger, wished to have information sent to the governor, that, if the practice was continued, no quarter should be granted either to him or to the garrison. But the Swedish monarch would never permit such a step to be taken,—telling his officers that the governor and the Saxon cannoneers were perfectly right in acting as they did,—that it was himself who made the attack upon them,—and that the war would be at an end if they could kill him; whereas they would reap very little advantage even from killing the principal officers of his army. [[Jacques Lacombe]] Histoire du Nord, p. 26. [[Note added in 1773/1797 editions.]]

lence (§138)—a right to deprive him of the means of resistance. Hence, as from their source, originate all the rights which war gives us over things belonging to the enemy. I speak of ordinary cases, and of what particularly relates to the enemy's property. On certain occasions, the right of punishing him produces new rights over the things which belong to him, as it also does over his person. These we shall presently consider.

We have a right to deprive our enemy of his possessions, of every thing which may augment his strength and enable him to make war. This every one endeavours to accomplish in the manner most suitable to him. Whenever we have an opportunity, we seize on the enemy's property, and convert it to our own use: and thus, besides diminishing the enemy's power, we augment our own, and obtain at least a partial indemnification or equivalent, either for what constitutes the subject of the war, or for the expenses and losses incurred in its prosecution:—in a word, we do ourselves justice.

§161. The right of seizing on them.

The right to security often authorises us to punish injustice or violence. It is an additional plea for depriving an enemy of <365> some part of his possessions. This manner of chastising a nation is more humane than making the penalty to fall on the persons of the citizens. With that view, things of value may be taken from her, such as rights, cities, provinces. But all wars do not afford just grounds for inflicting punishment. A nation that has with upright intentions supported a bad cause, and observed moderation in the prosecution of it, is entitled rather to compassion than resentment from a generous conqueror: and in a doubtful cause we are to suppose that the enemy sincerely thinks himself in the right (Prelim. §21; Book III. §40). The only circumstance, therefore, which gives an enemy the right to punish his adversaries, is their evident injustice unsupported even by any plausible pretext, or some heinous outrage in their proceedings: and, on every occasion, he ought to confine the punishment to what his own security and the safety of nations require. As far as consistent with prudence, it is glorious to obey the voice of clemency: that amiable virtue seldom fails of being more useful to the party who exerts it, than inflexible rigor. The clemency of Henry the Great[48] was of singular advantage in co-operating with his valour, when

§162. What is taken from the enemy by way of penalty.

48. Henry IV of France, r. 1589–1610.

that good prince found himself compelled to conquer his own kingdom. Those who would have continued his enemies if only subdued by arms, were won by his goodness, and became affectionate subjects.

§163. What is with-held from him, in order to oblige him to give just satisfaction. In fine, we seize on the enemy's property, his towns, his provinces, in order to bring him to reasonable conditions, and compel him to accept of an equitable and solid peace. Thus, much more is taken from him than he owes, more than is claimed of him: but this is done with a design of restoring the surplus by a treaty of peace. The king of France was, in the last war, known to declare that he aimed at nothing for himself: and by the treaty of Aix-la-Chapelle[49] he actually restored all his conquests.*

§164. Booty. As the towns and lands taken from the enemy are called *conquests,* all movable property taken from him comes under the denomination of *booty.* This *booty* naturally belongs to the sovereign making war, no less than the conquests; for he alone has such claims against the hostile nation, as warrant him to seize on her property and convert it to his own use. His soldiers, and even his auxiliaries, are only instruments which he employs in asserting his right. He maintains and pays them. Whatever they do is in his name, and for him. Thus there is no difficulty, even with regard to the auxiliaries. If they are not associates in the war, it is not carried on for their benefit; and they have no more right to the booty than to the conquests. But the sovereign may grant the troops what share of the booty he pleases. At present most nations allow them whatever they can make on certain occasions when the general allows of plundering,—such <366> as the spoil of enemies fallen in the field of battle, the pillage of a camp which has been forced, and sometimes that of a town taken by assault. In several services, the soldier has also the property of what he can take from the enemy's troops when he is out on a party or in a detachment, excepting artillery, military stores, magazines and convoys of provision and forage, which are applied to the wants and use

---

* The peace was become absolutely necessary to him; and he had, in return for his few conquests, Louisbourg, with all its dependencies, which were of more importance to him. [Note by the former translator.] [[The bracketed note by the 1797 editor refers to the note on p. 543 of the Dublin edition (1787) of *The Law of Nations.*]]

49. Treaty of Aix-la-Chapelle, 1748.

of the army. This custom being once admitted in an army, it would be injustice to exclude the auxiliaries from the right allowed to the national troops. Among the Romans, the soldier was obliged to bring in to the public stock all the booty he had taken. This the general caused to be sold; and after distributing a part of the produce among the soldiers, according to rank, he consigned the residue to the public treasury.

Instead of the custom of pillaging the open country and defenceless places, another mode has been substituted, which is at once more humane, and more advantageous to the belligerent sovereign—I mean that of *contributions*. Whoever carries on a just war has a right to make the enemy's country contribute to the support of his army, and towards defraying all the charges of the war. Thus he obtains a part of what is due to him; and the enemy's subjects, by consenting to pay the sum demanded, have their property secured from pillage, and the country is preserved. But a general who wishes to enjoy an unsullied reputation, must be moderate in his demand of contributions, and proportion them to the abilities of those on whom they are imposed. An excess in this point does not escape the reproach of cruelty and inhumanity: although there is not so great an appearance of ferocity in it as in ravage and destruction, it displays a greater degree of avarice or greediness. Instances of humanity and moderation cannot be too often quoted. A very commendable one occurred during those long wars which France carried on in the reign of Louis XIV. The sovereigns seeing it was their mutual interest as well as duty to prevent ravage, made it a practice, on the commencement of hostilities, to enter into treaties for regulating the contributions on a supportable footing: they determined the extent of hostile territory in which each might demand contributions, the amount of them, and the manner in which the parties sent to levy them were to behave. In these treaties it was expressed, that no body of men under a certain number should advance into the enemy's country beyond the limits agreed on, under the penalty of being treated as free-booters. By such steps they prevented a multitude of disorders and enormities, which entail ruin on the people, and generally without the least advantage to the belligerent sovereigns. Whence comes it that so noble an example is not universally imitated?

§165.
Contributions.

§166. Waste and destruc- tion.   If it is lawful to take away the property of an unjust enemy in order to weaken or punish him (§§161, 162), the same motives justify us in destroying what we cannot conveniently carry away. Thus, we waste a country, and destroy the provisions <367> and forage, that the enemy may not find a subsistence there: we sink his ships when we cannot take them or bring them off. All this tends to promote the main object of the war: but such measures are only to be pursued with moderation, and according to the exigency of the case. Those who tear up the vines and cut down the fruit-trees, are looked upon as savage barbarians, unless when they do it with a view to punish the enemy for some gross violation of the law of nations. They desolate a country for many years to come, and beyond what their own safety requires. Such a conduct is not dictated by prudence, but by hatred and fury.

§167. Ravaging and burning.   On certain occasions, however, matters are carried still farther: a country is totally ravaged, towns and villages are sacked, and delivered up a prey to fire and sword. Dreadful extremities, even when we are forced into them! Savage and monstrous excesses, when committed without necessity! There are two reasons, however, which may authorise them,—1. the necessity of chastising an unjust and barbarous nation, of checking her brutality, and preserving ourselves from her depredations. Who can doubt that the king of Spain and the powers of Italy have a very good right utterly to destroy those maritime towns of Africa, those nests of pirates, that are continually molesting their commerce and ruining their subjects? But what nation will proceed to such extremities, merely for the sake of punishing the hostile sovereign? It is but indirectly that he will feel the punishment: and how great the cruelty, to ruin an innocent people in order to reach him! The same prince whose firmness and just resentment was commended in the bombardment of Algiers, was, after that of Genoa, accused of pride and inhumanity.[50] 2. We ravage a country and render it un-inhabitable, in order to make it serve us as a barrier, and to cover our frontier against an enemy whose incursions

50. The prince in question is Louis XIV of France. The bombardment of Algiers, undertaken to effect deliverance of the Christian captives, occurred in 1682–83; the bombardment of Genoa in 1684.

we are unable to check by any other means. A cruel expedient, it is true: but why should we not be allowed to adopt it at the expense of the enemy, since, with the same view, we readily submit to lay waste our own provinces? The czar Peter the Great,[51] in his flight before the formidable Charles the Twelfth,[52] ravaged an extent of above fourscore leagues of his own empire, in order to check the impetuosity of a torrent which he was unable to withstand. Thus the Swedes were worn down with want and fatigue; and the Russian monarch reaped at Pultowa[53] the fruits of his circumspection and sacrifices. But violent remedies are to be sparingly applied: there must be reasons of suitable importance to justify the use of them. A prince who should without necessity imitate the czar's conduct, would be guilty of a crime against his people: and he who does the like in an enemy's country when impelled to it by no necessity or induced by feeble reasons, becomes the scourge of mankind. In the last century, the French ravaged and burnt the Palatinate.* <368> All Europe resounded with invectives against such a mode of waging war. It was in vain that the court attempted to palliate their conduct, by alleging that this was done only with a view to cover their own frontier:—that was an end to which the ravaging of the Palatinate contributed but little: and the whole proceeding exhibited nothing to the eyes of mankind but the revenge and cruelty of a haughty and unfeeling minister.

For whatever cause a country is ravaged, we ought to spare those edifices which do honour to human society, and do not contribute to increase the enemy's strength,—such as temples, tombs, public buildings, and all works of remarkable beauty. What advantage is obtained by destroying them? It is declaring one's self an enemy to mankind, thus wantonly to deprive them of these monuments of art and models of taste; and in that light Belisarius represented the matter to Tottila, king of the

§168. What things are to be spared.

---

* In 1674, and a second time, much more dreadfully, in 1689.

51. Peter the Great, czar of Russia, r. 1682–1725.

52. In 1697–1718, during the Great Northern War.

53. In 1709 Peter the Great decisively defeated the forces of King Charles XII of Sweden at Poltava. The Russian victory became a contributing factor in the destruction of Sweden's empire during the Great Northern War.

Goths.* We still detest those barbarians who destroyed so many wonders of art, when they over-ran the Roman empire. However just the resentment with which the great Gustavus was animated against Maximilian duke of Bavaria, he rejected with indignation the advice of those who wished him to demolish the stately palace of Munich,[54] and took particular care to preserve that admirable structure.

Nevertheless, if we find it necessary to destroy edifices of that nature in order to carry on the operations of war or to advance the works in a siege, we have an undoubted right to take such a step. The sovereign of the country, or his general, makes no scruple to destroy them, when necessity or the maxims of war require it. The governor of a besieged town sets fire to the suburbs, that they may not afford a lodgement to the besiegers. Nobody presumes to blame a general who lays waste gardens, vineyards, or orchards, for the purpose of encamping on the ground, and throwing up an intrenchment. If any beautiful production of art be thereby destroyed, it is an accident, an unhappy consequence of the war; and the general will not be blamed, except in those cases when he might have pitched his camp elsewhere without the smallest inconvenience to himself.

§169.
Bombarding towns.
In bombarding towns, it is difficult to spare the finest edifices. At present we generally content ourselves with battering the ramparts and defences of a place. To destroy a town with bombs and red-hot balls, is an extremity to which we do not proceed without cogent reasons. But it is nevertheless warranted by the laws of war, when we are unable by any other mode to reduce an important post, on which the success of the war may depend, or which enables the enemy to annoy us in a dangerous manner. It is also sometimes practised when we have no other means of forcing an enemy to make war with humanity, or punishing him for some instance of outrageous conduct. But it is only in cases of the last extremity, and with reluctance, that <369> good princes exert a

---

* See his letter in Procopius. It is quoted by Grotius, lib. iii. cap. 12, §2, not. 11 [[*Law of War and Peace*]].

54. Gustavus Adolphus had invaded Bavaria in 1632 and occupied Munich. He considered Maximilian I, elector of Bavaria, a Machiavellian supporter of his enemy Emperor Ferdinand II.

right of so rigorous a nature. In the year 1694, the English bombarded several maritime towns of France, on account of the great injury done to the British trade by their privateers. But the virtuous and noble-minded consort of William the Third did not receive the news of these exploits with real satisfaction. She expressed a sensible concern that war should render such acts of hostility necessary,—adding, that she hoped such operations would be viewed in so odious a light, as to induce both parties to desist from them in future.*

Fortresses, ramparts, and every kind of fortification, are solely appropriated to the purposes of war: and in a just war, nothing is more natural, nothing more justifiable, than to demolish those which we do not intend to retain in our own possession. We so far weaken the enemy, and do not involve an innocent multitude in the losses which we cause him. This was the grand advantage that France derived from her victories in a war in which she did not aim at making conquests.[55]

§170. Demolition of fortresses.

Safe-guards are granted to lands and houses intended to be spared, whether from pure favour, or with the proviso of a contribution. These consist of soldiers who protect them against parties, by producing the general's orders. The persons of these soldiers must be considered by the enemy as sacred: he cannot commit any hostilities against them, since they have taken their station there as benefactors, and for the safety of his subjects. They are to be respected in the same manner as an escort appointed to a garrison, or to prisoners of war, on their return to their own country.

§171. Safeguards.

What we have advanced is sufficient to give an idea of the moderation which we ought to observe, even in the most just war, in exerting our right to pillage and ravage the enemy's country. Except the single case in which there is question of punishing an enemy, the whole is reducible to this general rule—All damage done to the enemy unnecessarily, every act of hostility which does not tend to procure victory and bring the war to a conclusion, is a licentiousness condemned by the law of nature.

§172. General rule of moderation, respecting the evil which may be done to an enemy.

* [[Nicolas Chevalier,]] Histoire de Guillaume III. liv. vi. tom. 2. p. 66.
55. War of the Austrian Succession.

§173. Rule of
the voluntary
law of nations
on the same
subject.

But this licentiousness is unavoidably suffered to pass with impunity, and, to a certain degree, tolerated, between nation and nation. How then shall we, in particular cases, determine with precision, to what lengths it was necessary to carry hostilities in order to bring the war to a happy conclusion? And even if the point could be exactly ascertained, nations acknowledge no common judge: each forms her own judgment of the conduct she is to pursue in fulfilling her duties. If you once open a door for continual accusations of outrageous excess in hostilities, you will only augment the number of complaints, and inflame the minds of the contending parties with increasing animosity: fresh injuries will be perpetually springing up; and the sword will never be sheathed till one of the parties be utterly destroyed. The whole, therefore, <370> should, between nation and nation, be confined to general rules, independent of circumstances, and sure and easy in the application. Now the rules cannot answer this description, unless they teach us to view things in an absolute sense,—to consider them in themselves and in their own nature. As, therefore, with respect to hostilities against the enemy's person, the voluntary law of nations only prohibits those measures which are in themselves unlawful and odious, such as poisoning, assassination, treachery, the massacre of an enemy who has surrendered, and from whom we have nothing to fear,—so the same law, in the question now before us, condemns every act of hostility which, of its own nature, and independently of circumstances, contributes nothing to the success of our arms, and does not increase our strength, or weaken that of the enemy: and, on the other hand, it permits or tolerates every act which in itself is naturally adapted to promote the object of the war, without considering whether such act of hostility was unnecessary, useless, or superfluous, in that particular instance, unless there be the clearest evidence to prove that an exception ought to have been made in the case in question: for where there is positive evidence, the freedom of judgment no longer exists. Hence, the pillaging of a country, or ravaging it with fire, is not, in a general view of the matter, a violation of the laws of war: but if an enemy of much superior strength treats in this manner a town or province which he might easily keep in his possession as a means of obtaining an equitable and advantageous peace, he is universally accused of making war like a furious barbarian. Thus the wanton destruction of public monuments, temples, tombs, statues, paintings, &c. is absolutely condemned, even by the voluntary law of nations, as never being conducive to the lawful object of war. The pillage and destruction of towns, the devastation of the open country, ravaging, setting fire to houses, are measures no less odious and detestable on every occasion when they are evidently put in practice without absolute necessity or at least very cogent reasons. But as the perpetrators of such outrageous deeds might attempt to palliate them under pretext of deservedly punishing the enemy,—be it here observed, that the natural and voluntary law of nations does not allow us to inflict such punishments, except for enormous offences against the law of nations: and even then, it is glorious to listen to the voice of humanity and clemency, when rigour is not absolutely necessary. Cicero condemns the conduct of his countrymen in destroying Corinth to avenge the unworthy treatment offered to the Roman embassadors, because Rome was able to assert the dignity of her ministers, without proceeding to such extreme rigour. <371>

CHAPTER X

Of Faith between Enemies,—of Stratagems, Artifices in War, Spies, and some other Practices.

The faith of promises and treaties is the basis of the peace of nations, as we have shewn in an express chapter (Book II. Ch. XV.). It is sacred among men, and absolutely essential to their common safety. Are we then dispensed from it towards an enemy? To imagine that between two nations at war every duty ceases, every tie of humanity is broken, would be an error equally gross and destructive. Men, although reduced to the necessity of taking up arms for their own defence and in support of their rights, do not therefore cease to be men. They are still subject to the same laws of nature:—otherwise there would be no laws of war. Even he who wages an unjust war against us is still a man: we still owe him whatever that quality requires of us. But a conflict arises between our

§174. Faith to be sacred between enemies.

duties towards ourselves, and those which connect us with other men. The right to security authorises us to put in practice, against this unjust enemy, every thing necessary for repelling him, or bringing him to reason. But all those duties, the exercise of which is not necessarily suspended by this conflict, subsist in their full force: they are still obligatory on us, both with respect to the enemy and to all the rest of mankind. Now, the obligation of keeping faith is so far from ceasing in time of war by virtue of the preference which the duties towards ourselves are entitled to, that it then becomes more necessary than ever. There are a thousand occasions, even in the course of the war, when, in order to check its rage, and alleviate the calamities which follow in its train, the mutual interest and safety of both the contending parties requires that they should agree on certain points. What would become of prisoners of war, capitulating garrisons, and towns that surrender, if the word of an enemy were not to be relied on? War would degenerate into an unbridled and cruel licentiousness: its evils would be restrained by no bounds; and how could we ever bring it to a conclusion, and re-establish peace? If faith be banished from among enemies, a war can never be terminated with any degree of safety, otherwise than by the total destruction of one of the parties. The slightest difference, the least quarrel, would produce a war similar to that of Hannibal against the Romans, in which the parties fought, not for this or that province, not for sovereignty or for glory, but for the very existence of their respective nations.* Thus it is certain that the <372> faith of promises and treaties is to be held sacred in war as well as in peace, between enemies as well as between friends.

§175. What treaties are to be observed between enemies. The conventions, the treaties made with a nation, are broken or annulled by a war arising between the contracting parties, either because those compacts are grounded on a tacit supposition of the continuance of peace, or because each of the parties, being authorised to deprive his enemy of what belongs to him, takes from him those rights which he had conferred on him by treaty. Yet here we must except those treaties by which certain things are stipulated in case of a rupture,—as, for in-

* De salute certatum est. [["The fight was for survival."]]

stance, the length of time to be allowed on each side for the subjects of the other nation to quit the country,—the neutrality of a town or province, insured by mutual consent, &c. Since, by treaties of this nature, we mean to provide for what shall be observed in case of a rupture, we renounce the right of cancelling them by a declaration of war.

For the same reason, all promises made to an enemy in the course of a war are obligatory. For when once we treat with him whilst the sword is unsheathed, we tacitly but necessarily renounce all power of breaking the compact by way of compensation or on account of the war, as we cancel antecedent treaties: otherwise it would be doing nothing, and there would be an absurdity in treating with the enemy at all.

But conventions made during a war are like all other compacts and treaties, of which the reciprocal observance is a tacit condition (Book II. §202): we are no longer bound to observe them towards an enemy who has himself been the first to violate them. And even where there is question of two separate conventions which are wholly unconnected with each other,—although we are never justifiable in using perfidy on the plea of our having to do with an enemy who has broken his word on a former occasion, we may nevertheless suspend the effect of a promise in order to compel him to repair his breach of faith; and what we have promised him may be detained by way of security, till he has given satisfaction for his perfidy. Thus, at the taking of Namur in 1695, the king of England caused marshal Boufflers[56] to be put under arrest, and, notwithstanding the capitulation, detained him prisoner, for the purpose of obliging France to make reparation for the infractions of the capitulations of Dixmude and Deinse.* §176. On what occasions they may be broken.

Good-faith consists not only in the observance of our promises, but also in not deceiving on such occasions as lay us under any sort of obligation to speak the truth. From this subject arises a question which has been warmly debated in former days, and which appeared not a little intricate at a time when people did not entertain just or accurate ideas respecting the nature of a *lie*. Several writers, and especially divines, have §177. Of lies.

* [[Chevalier]] Histoire de Guillaume III. tom. ii. p. 148.
56. Louis François, Duc de Boufflers, 1644–1711, marshal of France, 1692.

made truth a kind of deity, to which, for its own sake, and independently
of its consequences, we <373> owe a certain inviolable respect. They
have absolutely condemned every speech that is contrary to the speaker's
thoughts: they have pronounced it to be our duty, on every occasion
when we cannot be silent, to speak the truth according to the best of
our knowledge, and to sacrifice to their divinity our dearest interests,
rather than be deficient in respect to her. But philosophers of more accurate ideas and more profound penetration have cleared up that notion,
so confused, and so false in its consequences. They have acknowledged
that truth in general is to be respected, as being the soul of human society, the basis of all confidence in the mutual intercourse of men,—
and, consequently, that a man ought not to speak an untruth, even in
matters of indifference, lest he weaken the respect due to truth in general,
and injure himself by rendering his veracity questionable even when he
speaks seriously. But in thus grounding the respect due to truth on its
effects, they took the right road, and soon found it easy to distinguish
between the occasions when we are obliged to speak the truth, or declare
our thoughts, and those when there exists no such obligation. The appellation of *lies* is given only to the words of a man who speaks contrary
to his thoughts, on occasions when he is under an obligation to speak
the truth. Another name (in Latin, *falsiloquium*)* is applied to any false
discourse to persons who have no right to insist on our telling them the
truth in the particular case in question.

These principles being laid down, it is not difficult to ascertain the
lawful use of truth or falsehood towards an enemy on particular occasions. Whenever we have expressly or tacitly engaged to speak truth, we
are indispensably obliged to it by that faith of which we have proved the
inviolability. Such is the case of conventions and treaties:—it is indispensably necessary that they should imply a tacit engagement to speak
the truth: for it would be absurd to allege that we do not enter into any
obligation of not deceiving the enemy under colour of treating with
him:—it would be downright mockery,—it would be doing nothing.
We are also bound to speak the truth to an enemy on all occasions when

---

* *Falsiloquy,* false-speaking, untruth, falsehood.

we are naturally obliged to it by the laws of humanity,—that is to say, whenever the success of our arms, and the duties we owe to ourselves, do not clash with the common duties of humanity, so as to suspend their force in the present case, and dispense with our performance of them. Thus, when we dismiss prisoners either on ransom or exchange, it would be infamous to point out the worst road for their march, or to put them in a dangerous one: and should the hostile prince or general inquire after a woman or child who is dear to him, it would be scandalous to deceive him.

But when, by leading the enemy into an error, either by words in which we are not obliged to speak truth, or by some feint, we <374> can gain an advantage in the war, which it would be lawful to seek by open force, it cannot be doubted that such a proceeding is perfectly justifiable. Nay, since humanity obliges us to prefer the gentlest methods in the prosecution of our rights,—if, by a stratagem, by a feint void of perfidy, we can make ourselves masters of a strong place, surprise the enemy, and overcome him, it is much better, it is really more commendable, to succeed in this manner, than by a bloody siege or the carnage of a battle.* But, the desire to spare the effusion of blood will by no means authorise us to employ perfidy, the introduction of which would be attended with consequences of too dreadful a nature, and would deprive sovereigns,

§178. Stratagems and artifices in war.

* There was a time when those who were taken in attempting to surprise a town were put to death. In 1597, prince Maurice [[of Nassau, Prince of Orange (1618–25), and capitain-general of the Dutch forces from 1587]] attempted to take Venloo by surprise: the attempt failed; and some of his men being made prisoners on the occasion, "were condemned to death,—the mutual consent of the parties having introduced that new rule, in order to obviate dangers of this kind." (Grotius Hist. of the Disturb. in the Netherlands.) Since that time, the rule has been changed: at present, military men who attempt to surprise a town in time of open war, are not, in case of being taken, treated in a different manner from other prisoners: and this custom is more consonant to reason and humanity. Nevertheless, if they were in disguise, or had employed treachery, they would be treated as spies: and this is perhaps what Grotius means: for I do not, in any other instance, find that such severity was used towards troops who were simply come to surprise a town in the silence of the night. It would be quite another affair, if such an attempt were made in a time of profound peace; and the Savoyards who were taken in the escalade of Geneva, deserved the punishment of death which was inflicted on them. [See page 508.] [[Note added in 1773/1797 editions.]]

once embarked in war, of all means of treating together, or restoring peace (§174).

Deceptions practised on an enemy either by words or actions, but without perfidy,—snares laid for him consistent with the rights of war,—are *stratagems,* the use of which has always been acknowledged as lawful, and had often a great share in the glory of celebrated commanders. The king of England, William III, having discovered that one of his secretaries regularly sent intelligence of every thing to the hostile general, caused the traitor to be secretly put under arrest, and made him write to the duke of Luxembourg, that the next day the allies would make a general forage, supported by a large body of infantry with cannon: and this artifice he employed for the purpose of surprising the French army at Steinkirk. But, through the activity of the French general, and the courage of his troops, though the measures were so artfully contrived, the success was not answerable.*

In the use of stratagems, we should respect not only the faith due to an enemy, but also the rights of humanity, and carefully avoid doing things the introduction of which would be pernicious to mankind. Since the commencement of hostilities between France and England,[57] an English frigate is said to have appeared off Calais, and made signals of distress, with a view of decoying out some vessel, and actually seized a boat and some sailors who generously came to her assistance. If the fact be true, that unworthy stratagem deserves a severe punishment. It tends < 375 > to damp a benevolent charity which should be held so sacred in the eyes of mankind, and which is so laudable even between enemies. Besides, making signals of distress is asking assistance, and, by that very action, promising perfect security to those who give the friendly succour. Therefore the action attributed to that frigate implies an odious perfidy.

Some nations, even the Romans, for a long time professed to despise every kind of artifice, surprise, or stratagem, in war; and others went so

---

* [[Antoine de Pas]] Memoires de Feuquieres, tom. iii. p. 87.
57. May 15, 1756.

far as to send notice of the time and place they had chosen for giving battle.* In this conduct there was more generosity than prudence. Such behaviour would indeed be very laudable, if, as in the frenzy of duels, the only business was to display personal courage. But in war the object is to defend our country, and by force to prosecute our rights which are unjustly with-held from us: and the surest means of obtaining our end are also the most commendable, provided they be not unlawful and odious in themselves.† The contempt of artifice, stratagem, and surprise, proceeds often, as in the case of Achilles, from a noble confidence in personal valour and strength: and it must be owned that when we can defeat an enemy by open force in a pitched battle, we may entertain a better-grounded belief that we have subdued him and compelled him to sue for peace, than if we had gained the advantage over him by surprise,—as Livy‡ makes those generous senators say, who did not approve of the insincere mode of proceeding which had been adopted towards Perseus.⁵⁸ Therefore, when plain and open courage can secure the vic-

---

* This was the practice of the ancient Gauls. See Livy.—It is said of Achilles, that he was for fighting openly, and not of a disposition to conceal himself in the famous wooden horse which proved fatal to the Trojans:—

> Ille non, inclusus equo Minervae
> Sacra mentito, male feriatos
> Troas, et laetam Priami choreis
>   Falleret aulam;
> Sed palam captis gravis. . . . Hor. lib. iv. od. 6.

> [["He would not have hidden within the horse that feigned sacrifice to Minerva, not striven to deceive the Trojans keeping ill-timed holiday, or Priam's court taking joy in dances but with open cruelty to his captives." Horace, *Odes* 4.6.13–17.]]

† Virg. Aen. ii. 390.
‡ Tit. Liv. lib. xlii. cap. 47.
58. Perseus, king of Macedonia (r. 179–168 B.C.). In books 39–44 of Livy's *History of Rome,* Livy argued that the leaders of the empire had always planned to subjugate Macedonia and were inconsistent and unfair to Perseus in justifying war against him. The result was the defeat of Perseus at Pydna in B.C. 168, along with his capture and imprisonment.

tory, there are occasions when it is preferable to artifice, because it procures to the state a greater and more permanent advantage.

§179. Spies.   The employment of spies is a kind of clandestine practice or deceit in war. These find means to insinuate themselves among the enemy, in order to discover the state of his affairs, to pry into his designs, and then give intelligence to their employer. Spies are generally condemned to capital punishment, and with great justice, since we have scarcely any other means of guarding against the mischief they may do us (§155). For this reason, a man of honour, who is unwilling to expose himself to an ignominious death from the hand of a common executioner, ever declines serving as a spy: and moreover he looks upon the office as unworthy of him, because it cannot be performed without some degree of treachery. The sovereign, therefore, has no right to require such a service of his subjects, unless perhaps <376> in some singular case, and that of the highest importance. It remains for him to hold out the temptation of a reward, as an inducement to mercenary souls to engage in the business. If those whom he employs make a voluntary tender of their services, or if they be neither subject to nor in any wise connected with the enemy, he may unquestionably take advantage of their exertions, without any violation of justice or honour. But is it lawful, is it honourable, to solicit the enemy's subjects to act as spies, and betray him? To this question the following section will furnish an answer.

§180. Clandestine seduction of the enemy's people.   It is asked in general whether it be lawful to seduce the enemy's men, for the purpose of engaging them to transgress their duty by an infamous treachery? Here a distinction must be made between what is due to the enemy notwithstanding the state of warfare, and what is required by the internal laws of conscience, and the rules of propriety. We may lawfully endeavour to weaken the enemy by all possible means (§138), provided they do not affect the common safety of human society, as do poison and assassination (§155). Now, in seducing a subject to turn spy, or the governor of a town to deliver it up to us, we do not strike at the foundation of the common safety and welfare of mankind. Subjects acting as spies to an enemy do not cause a fatal and unavoidable evil: it is possible to guard against them to a certain degree; and as to the security of fortresses, it is the sovereign's business to be careful in the choice of the governors to whom he intrusts them. Those measures, therefore, are not contrary to the external law of nations; nor can the enemy complain of them as odious proceedings. Accordingly they are practised in all wars. But are they honourable, and compatible with the laws of a pure conscience? Certainly no: and of this the generals themselves are sensible, as they are never heard to boast of having practised them. Seducing a subject to betray his country, engaging a traitor to set fire to a magazine, tampering with the fidelity of a governor, enticing him, persuading him to deliver up the town intrusted to his charge, is prompting such persons to commit detestable crimes. Is it honourable to corrupt our most inveterate enemy, and tempt him to the commission of a crime? If such practices are at all excusable, it can be only in a very just war, and when the immediate object is to save our country when threatened with ruin by a lawless conqueror. On such an occasion (as it should seem) the guilt of the subject or general who should betray his sovereign when engaged in an evidently unjust cause, would not be of so very odious a nature. He who himself tramples upon justice and probity, deserves in his turn to feel the effects of wickedness and perfidy.* And if ever it is excusable to depart from the strict <377> rules of honour, it is against such an enemy, and in such an extremity. The Romans, whose ideas concerning the rights of war were in general so pure and elevated, did not approve of such clandestine practices. They made no account of the consul Caepio's victory over Viriatus, because it had been obtained by means of bribery.[59] Valerius Maximus asserts that it was

---

* Xenophon very properly expresses the reasons which render treachery detestable, and which authorise us to repress it by other means than open force. "Treachery" (says he) "is more dreadful than open war, in proportion as it is more difficult to guard against clandestine plots than against an open attack: it is also more odious, because men engaged in overt hostilities may again treat together, and come to a sincere reconciliation, whereas nobody can venture to treat with or repose any confidence in a man whom he has once found guilty of treachery." Hist. Graec. lib. ii. cap. 3. [[Note added in 1773/1797 editions.]]

59. Viriatus (180–139 B.C.) sought to maintain Lusitanian independence and defeated the Roman general Quintus Fabius Maximus Servilianus in 140 B.C. The latter's successor, Servilius Caepio, contrived the murder of Viriatus in 139 B.C.

stained with a double perfidy;* and another historian says that the senate did not approve of it.†

§181. Whether the offers of a traitor may be accepted.

It is a different thing merely to accept of the offers of a traitor. We do not seduce him: and we may take advantage of his crime, while at the same time we detest it. Fugitives and deserters commit a crime against their sovereign; yet we receive and harbour them *by the rights of war,* as the civil law expresses it.‡ If a governor sells himself, and offers for a sum of money to deliver up his town, shall we scruple to take advantage of his crime, and to obtain without danger what we have a right to take by force? But when we feel ourselves able to succeed without the assistance of traitors, it is noble to reject their offers with detestation. The Romans, in their heroic ages, in those times when they used to display such illustrious examples of magnanimity and virtue, constantly rejected with indignation every advantage presented to them by the treachery of any of the enemy's subjects. They not only acquainted Pyrrhus with the atrocious design of his physician, but also refused to take advantage of a less heinous crime, and sent back to the Falisci, bound and fettered, a traitor who had offered to deliver up the king's children.§

* Viriati etiam caedes duplicem persidiae accusationem recepit; in amicis, quod eorum manibus interemptus est; in Q. Servilio Caepione consule, quia is sceleris hujus auctor, impunitate promissa, fuit, victoriamque non meruit, sed emit. lib. ix. cap. 6. [["Indeed the killing of Viriatus brought a double accusation of treachery, on the part of his friends, because he was done away with at their hands, and on the part of Q. Servilius Caepio the consul, because he was the instigator of this crime, promising immunity, and he did not earn but purchased his victory" (trans. Eds.).]] Although this instance seems to belong to another head (that of assassination), I nevertheless quote it here, because it does not appear from other authors that Caepio had induced Viriatus's soldiers to assassinate him. Among others, see Eutropius, lib. vi. cap. 8.

† Quae victoria, quia empta erat, a senatu non probata. [["Because this victory was purchased it was not commended by the senate."]] Auctor de Viris Illust. [[Sextus Aurelius Victor]] cap. 71.

‡ Transfugam jure belli recipimus. [["By the law of war we take back the deserter."]] Digest. [[Justinian]] l. xli. tit. 1, de adquir. Rer. Dom. leg. 51.

§ Eâdem fide indicatum Pyrrho regi medicum vitae ejus insidiantem; eâdem Faliscis vinctum traditum proditorem liberorum regis. [["This [Roman] sense of honor made them warn Pyrrhus against his physician who was plotting against his life; it made them hand over to the Faliscans as a prisoner the betrayer of their children."]] Tit. Liv. lib. xlii. cap. 47.

But when intestine divisions prevail among the enemy, we may without scruple hold a correspondence with one of the parties, and avail ourselves of the right which they think they have to injure the opposite party. Thus we promote our own interests, without seducing any person or being in anywise partakers of his guilt. If we take advantage of his error, this is doubtless allowable against an enemy.

Deceitful intelligence is that of a man who feigns to betray his own party, with a view of drawing the enemy into a snare. <378> If he does this deliberately, and has himself made the first overtures, it is treachery, and an infamous procedure: but an officer, or the governor of a town, when tampered with by the enemy, may, on certain occasions, lawfully feign acquiescence to the proposal with a view to deceive the seducer: an insult is offered to him in tempting his fidelity; and to draw the tempter into the snare, is no more than a just vengeance. By this conduct he neither violates the faith of promises, nor impairs the happiness of mankind: for criminal engagements are absolutely void, and ought never to be fulfilled; and it would be a fortunate circumstance if the promises of traitors could never be relied on, but were on all sides surrounded with uncertainties and dangers. Therefore a superior, on information that the enemy is tempting the fidelity of an officer or soldier, makes no scruple of ordering that subaltern to feign himself gained over, and to arrange his pretended treachery so as to draw the enemy into an ambuscade. The subaltern is obliged to obey. But when a direct attempt is made to seduce the commander in chief, a man of honour generally prefers, and ought to prefer, the alternative of explicitly and indignantly rejecting so disgraceful a proposal.*

§182.
Deceitful
intelligence.

* When the duke of Parma [[Alessandro Farnese, r. 1586–92]] was engaged in the siege of Bergen-op-zoom [[1588]], two Spanish prisoners, who were confined in a fort near the town, attempted to gain over a tavern-keeper, and an English soldier, to betray that fort to the duke. These men having acquainted the governor with the circumstance, received orders from him to feign acquiescence; and, accordingly, having made all their arrangements with the duke of Parma for the surprisal of the fort, they gave notice of every particular to the governor. He, in consequence, kept himself prepared to give a proper reception to the Spaniards, who fell into the snare, and lost near three thousand men on the occasion. Grotius, Hist. of the Disturb. in the Netherlands, book i. [[Note added in 1773/1797 editions.]]

CHAPTER XI

Of the Sovereign who wages an unjust War.

§183. An
unjust war
gives no right
whatever.

He who is engaged in war derives all his right from the justice of his cause. The unjust adversary who attacks or threatens him,—who withholds what belongs to him,—in a word, who does him an injury,—lays him under the necessity of defending himself, or of doing himself justice, by force of arms: he authorises him in all the acts of hostility necessary for obtaining complete satisfaction. Whoever therefore takes up arms without a lawful cause, can absolutely have no right whatever: every act of hostility that he commits is an act of injustice.

§184. Great
guilt of the
sovereign who
undertakes it.

He is chargeable with all the evils, all the horrors of the war: all the effusion of blood, the desolation of families, the rapine, the acts of violence, the ravages, the conflagrations, are his works and his crimes. He is guilty of a crime against the ene-<379>my, whom he attacks, oppresses, and massacres, without cause: he is guilty of a crime against his people, whom he forces into acts of injustice, and exposes to danger, without reason or necessity,—against those of his subjects who are ruined or distressed by the war,—who lose their lives, their property, or their health, in consequence of it: finally, he is guilty of a crime against mankind in general, whose peace he disturbs, and to whom he sets a pernicious example. Shocking catalogue of miseries and crimes! dreadful account to be given to the king of kings, to the common father of men! May this slight sketch strike the eyes of the rulers of nations,—of princes, and their ministers! Why may not we expect some benefit from it? Are we to suppose that the great are wholly lost to all sentiments of honour, of humanity, of duty, and of religion? And should our weak voice, throughout the whole succession of ages, prevent even one single war, how gloriously would our studies and our labour be rewarded!

§185. His
obligations.

He who does an injury is bound to repair the damage, or to make adequate satisfaction if the evil be irreparable, and even to submit to punishment, if the punishment be necessary, either as an example, or for the safety of the party offended, and for that of human society. In this predicament stands a prince who is the author of an unjust war. He is under an obligation to restore whatever he has taken,—to send back the prisoners at his own expense,—to make compensation to the enemy for the calamities and losses he has brought on him,—to reinstate ruined families,—to repair, if it were possible, the loss of a father, a son, a husband.

But how can he repair so many evils? Many are in their own nature irreparable. And as to those which may be compensated by an equivalent, where shall the unjust warrior find means to furnish an indemnification for all his acts of violence? The prince's private property will not be sufficient to answer the demands. Shall he give away that of his subjects?— It does not belong to him. Shall he sacrifice the national lands, a part of the state?—But the state is not his patrimony (Book I. §91): he cannot dispose of it at will. And although the nation be, to a certain degree, responsible for the acts of her ruler,—yet (exclusive of the injustice of punishing her directly for faults of which she is not guilty) if she is responsible for her sovereign's acts, that responsibility only regards other nations, who look to her for redress (Book I. §40, Book II. §§81, 82): but the sovereign cannot throw upon her the punishment due to his unjust deeds, nor despoil her in order to make reparation for them. And, were it even in his power, would this wash away his guilt, and leave him a clear conscience? Though acquitted in the eyes of the enemy, would he be so in the eyes of his people? It is a strange kind of justice which prompts a man to make reparation for his own misdeeds at the expense of a third person: this is no more than changing the object of his injustice. Weigh all these things, ye rulers of nations! and when clearly <380> convinced that an unjust war draws you into a multitude of iniquities which all your power cannot repair, perhaps you will be less hasty to engage in it.

§186. Difficulty of repairing the injury he has done.

The restitution of conquests, of prisoners, and of all property that still exists in a recoverable state, admits of no doubt when the injustice of the war is acknowledged. The nation in her aggregate capacity, and each individual particularly concerned, being convinced of the injustice of their possession, are bound to relinquish it, and to restore every thing which they have wrongfully acquired. But as to the reparation of any damage, are the military, the generals, officers, and soldiers, obliged in

§187. Whether the nation and the military are bound to any thing.

conscience to repair the injuries which they have done, not of their own will, but as instruments in the hands of their sovereign? I am surprised that the judicious Grotius should, without distinction, hold the affirmative.* It is a decision which cannot be supported except in the case of a war so palpably and indisputably unjust, as not to admit a presumption of any secret reason of state that is capable of justifying it,— a case in politics, which is nearly impossible. On all occasions susceptible of doubt, the whole nation, the individuals, and especially the military, are to submit their judgment to those who hold the reins of government,—to the sovereign: this they are bound to do, by the essential principles of political society and of government. What would be the consequence, if, at every step of the sovereign, the subjects were at liberty to weigh the justice of his reasons, and refuse to march to a war which might to them appear unjust? It often happens that prudence will not permit a sovereign to disclose all his reasons. It is the duty of subjects to suppose them just and wise, until clear and absolute evidence tells them the contrary. When, therefore, under the impression of such an idea, they have lent their assistance in a war which is afterwards found to be unjust, the sovereign alone is guilty: he alone is bound to repair the injuries. The subjects, and in particular the military, are innocent: they have acted only from a necessary obedience. They are bound, however, to deliver up what they have acquired in such a war, because they have no lawful title to possess it. This I believe to be the almost unanimous opinion of all honest men, and of those officers who are most distinguished for honour and probity. Their case, in the present instance, is the same as that of all those who are the executors of the sovereign's orders. Government would be impracticable if every one of its instruments was to weigh its commands, and thoroughly canvass their justice before he obeyed them. But if they are bound by a regard for the welfare of the state to suppose the sovereign's orders just, they are not responsible for them. <381>

* De Jure Belli et Pacis, lib. iii. cap. 10.

CHAPTER XII

Of the Voluntary Law of Nations, as it regards the Effects of Regular Warfare, independently of the Justice of the Cause.

All the doctrines we have laid down in the preceding chapter, are evidently deduced from sound principles,—from the eternal rules of justice: they are so many separate articles of that sacred law which nature, or the divine author of nature, has prescribed to nations. He alone whom justice and necessity have armed, has a right to make war; he alone is empowered to attack his enemy, to deprive him of life, and wrest from him his goods and possessions. Such is the decision of *the necessary law of nations,* or of the law of nature, which nations are strictly bound to observe (Prelim. §7): it is the inviolable rule that each ought conscientiously to follow. But in the contests of nations and sovereigns who live together in a state of nature, how can this rule be enforced? They acknowledge no superior. Who then shall be judge between them, to assign to each his rights and obligations,—to say to the one, "You have a right to take up arms, to attack your enemy, and subdue him by force,"—and to the other, "Every act of hostility that you commit will be an act of injustice; your victories will be so many murders, your conquests rapines and robberies?" Every free and sovereign state has a right to determine, according to the dictates of her own conscience, what her duties require of her, and what she can or cannot do with justice (Prelim. §16). If other nations take upon themselves to judge of her conduct, they invade her liberty, and infringe her most valuable rights (Prelim. §15): and, moreover, each party asserting that they have justice on their own side, will arrogate to themselves all the rights of war, and maintain that their enemy has none, that his hostilities are so many acts of robbery, so many infractions of the law of nations, in the punishment of which all states should unite. The decision of the controversy, and of the justice of the cause, is so far from being forwarded by it, that the quarrel will become more bloody, more

§188. Nations not rigidly to enforce the law of nature against each other.

calamitous in its effects, and also more difficult to terminate. Nor is this all: the neutral nations themselves will be drawn into the dispute, and involved in the quarrel. If an unjust war cannot, in its effect, confer any right, no certain possession can be obtained of any thing taken in war, until some acknowledged judge (and there is none such between nations) shall have definitively pronounced concerning the justice of the cause: and things so acquired will ever remain liable to be claimed, as property carried off by robbers.

§189. Why they ought to admit the voluntary law of nations.

Let us then leave the strictness of the necessary law of nature <382> to the conscience of sovereigns; undoubtedly they are never allowed to deviate from it. But as to the external effects of the law among men, we must necessarily have recourse to rules that shall be more certain and easy in the application, and this for the very safety and advantage of the great society of mankind. These are the rules of the voluntary law of nations (Prelim. §21). The law of nature, whose object it is to promote the welfare of human society, and to protect the liberties of all nations,— which requires that the affairs of sovereigns should be brought to an issue, and their quarrels determined and carried to a speedy conclusion,—that law, I say, recommends the observance of the voluntary law of nations, for the common advantage of states, in the same manner as it approves of the alterations which the civil law makes in the rules of the law of nature, with a view to render them more suitable to the state of political society, and more easy and certain in their application. Let us therefore apply to the particular subject of war the general observation made in our Preliminaries (§28)—a nation, a sovereign, when deliberating on the measures he is to pursue in order to fulfil his duty, ought never to lose sight of the *necessary* law, whose obligation on the conscience is inviolable: but in examining what he may require of other states, he ought to pay a deference to the voluntary law of nations, and restrict even his just claims by the rules of that law, whose maxims have for their object the happiness and advantage of the universal society of nations. Though the *necessary* law be the rule which he invariably observes in his own conduct, he should allow others to avail themselves of the *voluntary* law of nations.

The first rule of that law, respecting the subject under consideration, is, that *regular war, as to its effects, is to be accounted just on both sides.* This is absolutely necessary, as we have just shewn, if people wish to introduce any order, any regularity, into so violent an operation as that of arms, or to set any bounds to the calamities of which it is productive, and leave a door constantly open for the return of peace. It is even impossible to point out any other rule of conduct to be observed between nations, since they acknowledge no superior judge.

§190. Regular war, as to its effects, is to be accounted just on both sides.

Thus the rights founded on the state of war, the lawfulness of its effects, the validity of the acquisitions made by arms, do not, externally and between mankind, depend on the justice of the cause, but on the legality of the means in themselves,—that is, on every thing requisite to constitute a *regular war.* If the enemy observes all the rules of regular warfare (see Chap. III. of this Book), we are not entitled to complain of him as a violator of the law of nations. He has the same pretensions to justice as we ourselves have; and all our resource lies in victory or an accommodation.

Second rule. The justice of the cause being reputed equal between two enemies, *whatever is permitted to the one in virtue of the state of war, is also permitted to the other.* Accordingly, <383> no nation, under pretence of having justice on her side, ever complains of the hostilities of her enemy, while he confines them within the limits prescribed by the common laws of war. We have, in the preceding chapters, treated of what is allowable in a just war. It is precisely that, and no more, which the voluntary law equally authorises in both parties. That law puts things between both on a parity, but allows to neither what is in itself unlawful: it can never countenance unbridled licentiousness. If therefore nations transgress those bounds,—if they carry hostilities beyond what the internal and necessary law permits in general for the support of a just cause,—far be it from us to attribute these excesses to the voluntary law of nations: they are solely imputable to a depravation of manners, which produces an unjust and barbarous custom. Such are those horrid enormities sometimes committed by the soldiery in a town taken by storm.

§191. Whatever is permitted to one party, is so to the other.

§192. The
voluntary law
gives no more
than impunity
to him who
wages an
unjust war.

3. We must never forget that this voluntary law of nations, which is admitted only through necessity, and with a view to avoid greater evils (§§188, 189), *does not, to him who takes up arms in an unjust cause, give any real right that is capable of justifying his conduct and acquitting his conscience, but merely entitles him to the benefit of the external effect of the law, and to impunity among mankind.* This sufficiently appears from what we have said in establishing the voluntary law of nations. The sovereign, therefore, whose arms are not sanctioned by justice, is not the less unjust, or less guilty of violating the sacred law of nature, although that law itself (with a view to avoid aggravating the evils of human society by an attempt to prevent them) requires that he be allowed to enjoy the same external rights as justly belong to his enemy. In the same manner, the civil law authorises a debtor to refuse payment of his debts in a case of prescription: but he then violates his duty: he takes advantage of a law which was enacted with a view to prevent the endless increase of law-suits: but his conduct is not justifiable upon any grounds of genuine right.

From the unanimity that in fact prevails between states in observing the rules which we refer to the voluntary law of nations, Grotius assumes for their foundation an actual consent on the part of mankind, and refers them to the arbitrary law of nations. But, exclusive of the difficulty which would often occur in proving such agreement, it would be of no validity except against those who had formally entered into it. If such an engagement existed, it would belong to the conventional law of nations, which must be proved by history, not by argument, and is founded on facts, not on principles. In this work we lay down the natural principles of the law of nations. We deduce them from nature itself; and what we call the voluntary law of nations, consists in rules of conduct and of external right, to which nations are, by the law of nature, bound to consent; so that we are authorised to presume their consent, without seeking for a record of it in the annals of the world; because, <384> even if they had not given it, the law of nature supplies their omission, and gives it for them. In this particular, nations have not the option of giving or with-holding their consent at pleasure: the refusal to give it would be an infringement of the common rights of nations (Prelim. §21).

This voluntary law of nations, thus established, is of very extensive use, and is far from being a chimera, an arbitrary or groundless fiction. It flows from the same source, and is founded on the same principles, with the *natural and necessary law.* For what other reason does nature prescribe such and such rules of conduct to men, except because those rules are necessary to the safety and welfare of mankind? But the maxims of the necessary law of nations are founded immediately on the nature of things, and particularly on that of man, and of political society. The voluntary law of nations supposes an additional principle,—the nature of the great society of nations, and of their mutual intercourse. The necessary law enjoins to nations what is absolutely indispensable, and what naturally tends to their perfection and common happiness. The voluntary law tolerates what cannot be avoided without introducing greater evils.

CHAPTER XIII

Of Acquisitions by War, and particularly of Conquests.

If it be lawful to carry off things belonging to an enemy, with a view of weakening him (§160), and sometimes of punishing him (§162), it is no less lawful in a just war to appropriate them to our own use, by way of compensation, which the civilians term *expletio juris* (§161). They are retained as an equivalent for what is due by the enemy, for the expenses and damages which he has occasioned, and even (when there is cause to punish him) as a commutation for the punishment he has deserved. For when I cannot obtain the individual thing which belongs or is due to me, I have a right to an equivalent, which, by the rules of *expletive justice,* and in moral estimation, is considered as the thing itself. Thus, according to the law of nature, which constitutes the necessary law of nations, war founded on justice is a lawful mode of acquisition.

§193. How war is a method of acquisition.

But that sacred law does not authorise even the acquisitions made in a just war, any farther than as they are approved by justice,—that is to say, no farther than is requisite to obtain complete satisfaction in the

§194. Measure of the right it gives.

degree necessary for accomplishing the lawful ends we have just mentioned. An equitable conqueror, deaf to the suggestions of ambition and avarice, will make a just estimate of what is due to him,—that is to say, of the thing which has been the subject of the war (if the thing itself is no longer reco-<385>verable), and of the damages and expenses of the war,—and will retain no more of the enemy's property than what is precisely sufficient to furnish the equivalent. But if he has to do with a perfidious, restless, and dangerous enemy, he will, by way of punishment, deprive him of some of his towns or provinces, and keep them to serve as a barrier to his own dominions. Nothing is more allowable than to weaken an enemy who has rendered himself suspected and formidable. The lawful end of punishment is future security. The conditions necessary for rendering an acquisition, made by arms, just and irreproachable before God and our own conscience, are these—justice in the cause, and equity in the measure of the satisfaction.

§195. Rules of the voluntary law of nations.

But nations cannot, in their dealings with each other, insist on this rigid justice. By the rules of the voluntary law of nations, every regular war is on both sides accounted just, as to its effects (§190); and no one has a right to judge a nation, respecting the unreasonableness of her claims, or what she thinks necessary for her own safety (Prelim. §21). Every acquisition, therefore, which has been made in regular warfare, is valid according to the voluntary law of nations, independently of the justice of the cause, and the reasons which may have induced the conqueror to assume the property of what he has taken. Accordingly, nations have ever esteemed conquest a lawful title; and that title has seldom been disputed, unless where it was derived from a war not only unjust in itself, but even destitute of any plausible pretext.

§196. Acquisition of movable property.

The property of movable effects is vested in the enemy from the moment they come into his power; and if he sells them to neutral nations, the former proprietor is not entitled to claim them. But such things must be actually and truly in the enemy's power, and carried to a place of safety. Suppose a foreigner coming into our country buys a portion of the booty which a party of enemies have just taken from us: our men who are in pursuit of this party may very justly seize on the booty which that foreigner was over precipitate in buying. On this head Grotius quotes from De Thou the instance of the town of Lierre in Brabant, which having been captured and recaptured on the same day, the booty taken from the inhabitants was restored to them because it had not been twenty-four hours in the enemy's hands.* This space of twenty-four hours, together with the practice observed at sea,† is an institution of the law of nations established by agreement or custom, and is even a civil law in some states. The natural reason of the conduct adopted towards the inhabitants of Lierre is, that the enemy being taken as it were in the fact, and before they had carried off the booty, it was not looked upon as having absolutely become their property, or been lost to the inhabitants. Thus, at sea, a ship taken by <386> the enemy, may be retaken and delivered by other ships of her own party, as long as she has not been carried into some port, or into the midst of a fleet: her fate is not decided, nor is the owner's property irrecoverably lost, until the ship be in a place of safety with regard to the enemy who has taken her, and entirely in his power. But the ordinances of every state may make different regulations on this head between the citizens,‡ with a view either to prevent disputes or to encourage armed vessels to retake merchant ships that have fallen into the enemy's hands.

The justice or injustice of the cause does not here become an object of consideration. There would be no stability in the affairs of mankind, no safety in trading with nations engaged in war, if we were allowed to draw a distinction between a just and an unjust war, so as to attribute lawful effects to the one, which we denied to the other. It would be opening a door to endless discussions and quarrels. This reason is of such weight, that, on account of it, the effects of a public war, at least with regard to movables, have been allowed to expeditions which deserved no other name than that of predatory enterprises, though carried on by regular armies. When, after the wars of the English in France, the *grandes compagnies* ranged about Europe, sacking and pillaging wherever they came, none of the sufferers was ever known to claim the booty which

* Grotius, de Jure Belli et Pacis, lib. iii. cap. 6, §3, n. 7.
† See Grotius, ibid. and in the text.
‡ Grotius, ibid.

those plunderers had carried off and sold. At present it would be in vain
to claim a ship taken by the Barbary corsairs, and sold to a third party,
or retaken from the captors; though it is very improperly that the piracies
of those barbarians can be considered as acts of regular war. We here
speak of the external right: the internal right and the obligations of conscience undoubtedly require that we should restore to a third party the
property we recover from an enemy who had despoiled him of it in an
unjust war,—provided he can recognise that property, and will defray
the expenses we have incurred in recovering it. Grotius quotes many
instances of sovereigns and commanders who have generously restored
such booty, even without requiring any thing for their trouble or expense.* But such conduct is pursued only in cases where the booty has
been recently taken. It would be an impracticable task, scrupulously to
seek out the proprietors of what has been captured a long time back:
and moreover they have, no doubt, relinquished all their right to things
which they had no longer any hope of recovering. Such is the usual mode
of thinking with respect to captures in war, which are soon given up as
irrecoverably lost.

§197. Acqui-
sition of im-
moveables,—
or conquest.
Immovable possessions, lands, towns, provinces, &c. become the
property of the enemy who makes himself master of them: but it is only
by the treaty of peace, or the entire submission and extinction of the
state to which those towns and provinces belonged, that the acquisition
is completed, and the property becomes stable and perfect. <387>

§198. How to
transfer them
validly.
Thus a third party cannot safely purchase a conquered town or province, till the sovereign from whom it was taken has renounced it by a
treaty of peace, or has been irretrievably subdued, and has lost his sovereignty: for, while the war continues,—while the sovereign has still
hopes of recovering his possessions by arms,—is a neutral prince to come
and deprive him of the opportunity by purchasing that town or province
from the conqueror? The original proprietor cannot forfeit his rights by
the act of a third person; and if the purchaser be determined to maintain
his purchase, he will find himself involved in the war. Thus the king of
Prussia became a party with the enemies of Sweden, by receiving Stettin

---

* Grotius, lib. iii. cap. 16 [[*Law of War and Peace*]].

from the hands of the king of Poland and the czar, under the title of sequestration.* But when a sovereign has, by a definitive treaty of peace, ceded a country to the conqueror, he has relinquished all the right he had to it; and it were absurd that he should be allowed to demand the restitution of that country by a subsequent conqueror who wrests it from the former, or by any other prince, who has purchased it, or received it in exchange, or acquired it by any title whatever.

The conqueror who takes a town or province from his enemy, cannot justly acquire over it any other rights than such as belonged to the sovereign against whom he has taken up arms. War authorises him to possess himself of what belongs to his enemy: if he deprives him of the sovereignty of that town or province, he acquires it such as it is, with all its limitations and modifications. Accordingly, care is usually taken to stipulate, both in particular capitulations and in treaties of peace, that the towns and countries ceded shall retain all their liberties, privileges, and immunities. And why should they be deprived of them by the conqueror, on account of his quarrel with their sovereign? Nevertheless, if the inhabitants have been personally guilty of any crime against him, he may, by way of punishment, deprive them of their rights and privileges. This he may also do if the inhabitants have taken up arms against him, and have thus directly become his enemies. In that case, he owes them no more than what is due from a humane and equitable conqueror to his vanquished foes. Should he purely and simply incorporate them with his former states, they will have no cause of complaint.

§199. Conditions on which a conquered town is acquired.

Hitherto I evidently speak of a city or a country which is not simply an integrant part of a nation, or which does not fully belong to a sovereign, but over which that nation or that sovereign has certain rights. If the conquered town or province fully and perfectly constituted a part of the domain of a nation or sovereign, it passes on the same footing into the power of the conqueror. Thenceforward united with the new state to which it belongs,—if it be a loser by the change, that is a misfortune which it must wholly impute to the chance of war. Thus, if a town <388> which made part of a republic or a limited monarchy, and

* By the treaty of Schwedt, October 6, 1713.

enjoyed a right of sending deputies to the supreme council or the general assembly of the states, be justly conquered by an absolute monarch, she must never more think of such privileges: they are what the constitution of the new state to which she is annexed does not permit.

§200. Lands of private persons.

In the conquests of ancient times, even individuals lost their lands. Nor is it matter of surprise that in the first ages of Rome such a custom should have prevailed. The wars of that aera were carried on between popular republics and communities. The state possessed very little, and the quarrel was in reality the common cause of all the citizens. But at present war is less dreadful in its consequences to the subject: matters are conducted with more humanity: one sovereign makes war against another sovereign, and not against the unarmed citizens. The conqueror seizes on the possessions of the state, the public property, while private individuals are permitted to retain theirs. They suffer but indirectly by the war; and the conquest only subjects them to a new master.

§201. Conquest of the whole state.

But if the entire state be conquered, if the nation be subdued, in what manner can the victor treat it, without transgressing the bounds of justice? What are his rights over the conquered country? Some have dared to advance this monstrous principle, that the conqueror is absolute master of his conquest,—that he may dispose of it as his property,—that he may treat it as he pleases, according to the common expression of *treating a state as a conquered country;* and hence they derive one of the sources of despotic government. But, disregarding such writers, who reduce men to the state of transferable goods, or beasts of burthen,—who deliver them up as the property or patrimony of another man,—let us argue on principles countenanced by reason, and conformable to humanity.

The whole right of the conqueror is derived from justifiable self-defence (§§3, 26, 28), which comprehends the support and prosecution of his rights. When, therefore, he has totally subdued a hostile nation, he undoubtedly may, in the first place, do himself justice respecting the object which had given rise to the war, and indemnify himself for the expenses and damages he has sustained by it: he may, according to the exigency of the case, subject the nation to punishment, by way of example: he may even, if prudence so require, render her incapable of doing mischief with the same ease in future. But, for the attainment of these different objects, he is to prefer the gentlest methods,—still bearing in mind, that the doing of harm to an enemy is no farther authorised by the law of nature, than in the precise degree which is necessary for justifiable self-defence, and reasonable security for the time to come. Some princes have contented themselves with imposing a tribute on the conquered nation,—others, with depriving her of some of her rights, taking from her a province, or erecting fortresses to keep her in awe: others, <389> again, confining their quarrel to the sovereign alone, have left the nation in the full enjoyment of all her rights,—only setting over her a new sovereign, of their own appointment.

But if the conqueror thinks proper to retain the sovereignty of the conquered state, and has a right to retain it, the same principles must also determine the manner in which he is to treat that state. If it is against the sovereign alone that he has just cause of complaint, reason plainly evinces that he acquires no other rights by his conquest than such as belonged to the sovereign whom he has dispossessed: and, on the submission of the people, he is bound to govern them according to the laws of the state. If the people do not voluntarily submit, the state of war still subsists.

A conqueror who has taken up arms, not only against the sovereign, but against the nation herself, and whose intention it was to subdue a fierce and savage people, and once for all to reduce an obstinate enemy,— such a conqueror may with justice lay burthens on the conquered nation, both as a compensation for the expenses of the war, and as a punishment. He may, according to the degree of indocility apparent in their disposition, govern them with a tighter rein, so as to curb and subdue their impetuous spirit: he may even, if necessary, keep them for some time in a kind of slavery. But this forced condition ought to cease from the moment the danger is over,—the moment the conquered people are become citizens: for then the right of conquest is at an end, so far as relates to the pursuit of those rigorous measures, since the conqueror no longer finds it necessary to use extraordinary precautions for his own defence and safety. Then at length every thing is to be rendered conformable to the rules of a wise government, and the duties of a good prince.

When a sovereign, arrogating to himself the absolute disposal of a people whom he has conquered, attempts to reduce them to slavery, he perpetuates the state of warfare between that nation and himself. The Scythians said to Alexander the Great, "There is never any friendship between the master and slave: in the midst of peace the rights of war still subsist."* Should it be said, that in such a case there may be peace, and a kind of compact by which the conqueror consents to spare the lives of the vanquished, on condition that they acknowledge themselves his slaves,—he who makes such an assertion is ignorant that war gives no right to take away the life of an enemy who has laid down his arms, and submitted (§140). But let us not dispute the point: let the man who holds such principles of jurisprudence, keep them for his own use and benefit: he well deserves to be subject to such a law. But men of spirit, to whom life is nothing, less than nothing, unless sweetened with liberty, will always conceive themselves at war with that oppressor, though <390> actual hostilities are suspended on their part through want of ability. We may therefore safely venture to add, that if the conquered country is to be really subject to the conqueror as to its lawful sovereign, he must rule it according to the ends for which civil government has been established. It is generally the prince alone who occasions the war, and consequently the conquest. Surely it is enough that an innocent people suffer the calamities of war: must even peace itself become fatal to them? A generous conqueror will study to relieve his new subjects, and mitigate their condition: he will think it his indispensable duty. "Conquest (says an excellent man) ever leaves behind it an immense debt, the discharge of which is absolutely necessary to acquit the conqueror, in the eye of humanity."†

It fortunately happens that, in this particular as in every thing else, sound policy and humanity are in perfect accord. What fidelity, what assistance, can you expect from an oppressed people? Do you wish that your conquest may prove a real addition to your strength, and be well

---

* Inter dominum et servum, nulla amicitia est; etiam in pace, belli tamen jura servantur. Q. Curt. lib. vii. cap. 8.

† Montesquieu, in his Spirit of Laws. [[Book 10, chaps. 3–4.]]

affected to you?—treat it as a father, as a true sovereign. I am charmed
with the generous answer recorded of an embassador from Privernum.
Being introduced to the Roman senate, he was asked by the consul—
"If we shew you clemency, what dependence can we have on the peace
you are come to sue for?" "If" (replied the embassador) "you grant it on
reasonable conditions, it will be safe and permanent: otherwise, it will
not last long." Some took offence at the boldness of this speech; but the
more sensible part of the senate approved of the Privernian's answer,
deeming it the proper language of a man, and a freeman. "Can it be
imagined (said those wise senators) that any nation, or even any individual, will longer continue in an irksome and disagreeable condition,
than while compelled to submit to it? If those to whom you give peace
receive it voluntarily, it may be relied on: what fidelity can you expect
from those whom you wish to reduce to slavery?"*—"The most secure
dominion," said Camillus,[60] "is that which is acceptable to those over
whom it is exercised."†

Such are the rights which the law of nature gives to the conqueror,
and the duties which it imposes on him. The manner of exerting the
one, and fulfilling the other, varies according to circumstances. In general, he ought to consult the true interests <391> of his own state, and
by sound policy to reconcile them, as far as possible, with those of the
conquered country. He may, in imitation of the kings of France, unite
and incorporate it with his own dominions. Such was the practice of the
Romans: but they did this in different modes according to cases and

* Quid, si poenam (inquit consul) remittimus vobis, qualem nos pacem vobiscum
habituros speremus? Si bonam dederitis, inquit, et fidam et perpetuam; si malam,
haud diuturnam. Tum vero *minari, nec id ambigue Privernatem,* quidam, *et illis vo-
cibus ad rebellandum incitari pacatos populos.* Pars melior senatûs ad meliora responsa
trahere, et dicere viri et liberi vocem auditam: an credi posse ullum populum, aut
hominem denique, in eâ conditione cujus eum poeniteat, diutius quam necesse sit,
mansurum? ibi pacem esse fidam, ubi voluntarii pacati sint; neque eo loco, ubi ser-
vitutem esse velint, fidem sperandam esse. Tit. Liv. lib. viii. cap. 21.

† Certe id firmissimum longe imperium est, quo obedientes gaudent. Tit. Liv. lib.
viii. cap. 13.

60. Marius Furius Camillus, 446–364 B.C., Roman soldier and statesman. He
served as censor, and on five occasions as dictator.

conjunctures. At a time when Rome stood in need of an increase of population, she destroyed the town of Alba, which she feared to have as a rival: but she received all its inhabitants within her walls, and thereby gained so many new citizens. In after times the conquered cities were left standing, and the freedom of Rome was given to the vanquished inhabitants. Victory could not have proved so advantageous to those people as their defeat.

The conqueror may likewise simply put himself in the place of the sovereign whom he has dispossessed. Thus the Tartars have acted in China: the empire was suffered to subsist in its former condition, except that it fell under the dominion of a new race of sovereigns.

Lastly, the conqueror may rule his conquest as a separate state, and permit it to retain its own form of government. But this method is dangerous: it produces no real union of strength; it weakens the conquered country, without making any considerable addition to the power of the victorious state.

§202. To whom the conquest belongs. It is asked to whom the conquest belongs,—to the prince who has made it, or to the state? This question ought never to have been heard of. Can the prince, in his character of sovereign, act for any other end than the good of the state? Whose are the forces which he employs in his wars? Even if he made the conquest at his own expense, out of his own revenue, or his private and patrimonial estates, does he not make use of the personal exertions of his subjects in achieving it? does he not shed their blood in the contest? But supposing even that he were to employ foreign or mercenary troops, does he not expose his nation to the enemy's resentment? does he not involve her in the war? And shall he alone reap all the advantages of it? Is it not for the cause of the state, and of the nation, that he takes up arms? The nation therefore has a just claim to all the rights to which such war gives birth.

If the sovereign embarks in a war, of which his own personal interests are the sole ground,—as, for instance, to assert his right of succession to a foreign sovereignty,—the question then assumes a new face. In this affair the state is wholly unconcerned: but then the nation should be at liberty either to refuse engaging in it, or to assist her prince, at her own option. If he is empowered to employ the national force in support of his personal rights, he should, in such case, make no distinction between these rights and those of the state. The French law, which annexes to the crown all acquisitions made by the king, should be the law of all nations.

It has been observed (§196) that we may be obliged, if not externally, yet in conscience, and by the laws of equity, to re-<392>store to a third party the booty we have recovered out of the hands of an enemy who had taken it from him in an unjust war. The obligation is more certain and more extensive, with regard to a people whom our enemy had unjustly oppressed. For a people thus spoiled of their liberty never renounce the hope of recovering it. If they have not voluntarily incorporated themselves with the state by which they have been subdued,— if they have not freely aided her in the war against us,—we certainly ought so to use our victory, as not merely to give them a new master, but to break their chains. To deliver an oppressed people is a noble fruit of victory: it is a valuable advantage gained, thus to acquire a faithful friend. The canton of Schweitz having wrested the country of Glaris from the house of Austria, restored the inhabitants to their former liberties; and Glaris, admitted into the Helvetic confederacy, formed the sixth canton.*

§203. Whether we are to set at liberty a people whom the enemy had unjustly conquered.

CHAPTER XIV

Of the Right of Postliminium.

The right of postliminium is that, in virtue of which, persons and things taken by the enemy are restored to their former state, now coming again into the power of the nation to which they belonged.

§204. Definition of the right of postliminium.

The sovereign is bound to protect the persons and property of his subjects, and to defend them against the enemy. When, therefore, a subject, or any part of his property, has fallen into the enemy's possession, should any fortunate event bring them again into the sovereign's power,

§205. Foundation of this right.

---

* Histoire de la Confédération Helvétique, par M. De Watteville. liv. iii. under the year 1351.

it is undoubtedly his duty to restore them to their former condition,—to re-establish the persons in all their rights and obligations, to give back the effects to the owners,—in a word, to replace every thing on the same footing on which it stood previous to the enemy's capture.

The justice or injustice of the war makes no difference in this case,—not only, because, according to the voluntary law of nations, the war, as to its effects, is reputed just on both sides, but likewise because war, whether just or not, is a national concern; and if the subjects who fight or suffer in the national cause, should—after they have, either in their persons or their property, fallen into the enemy's power—be, by some fortunate incident, restored to the hands of their own people,—there is no reason why they should not be restored to their former condition. It is the same as if they had never been taken. If the war be just on the part of their nation, they were unjustly captured by the <393> enemy; and thus nothing is more natural than to restore them as soon as it becomes possible. If the war be unjust, they are under no greater obligation to suffer in atonement for its injustice, than the rest of the nation. Fortune brings down the evil on their heads, when they are taken: she delivers them from it, when they escape. Here again it is the same as if they never had been captured. Neither their own sovereign nor the enemy has any particular right over them. The enemy has lost by one accident what he had gained by another.

§206. How it takes effect.

Persons return, and things are recovered, by the right of postliminium, when, after having been taken by the enemy, they come again into the power of their own nation (§204). This right, therefore, takes effect as soon as such persons or things captured by the enemy fall into the hands of soldiers belonging to their own nation, or are brought back to the army, the camp, the territories of their sovereign, or the places under his command.

§207. Whether it takes effect among the allies.

Those who unite with us to carry on a war, are joint parties with us: we are engaged in a common cause; our right is one and the same; and they are considered as making but one body with us. Therefore when persons or things captured by the enemy are retaken by our allies or auxiliaries, or in any other manner fall into their hands, this, so far as relates to the effect of the right, is precisely the same thing as if they were come again into our own power; since, in the cause in which we are jointly embarked, our power and that of our allies is but one and the same. The right of postliminium therefore takes effect among those who carry on the war in conjunction with us; and the persons and things recovered by them from the enemy, are to be restored to their former condition.

But does this right take place in the territories of our allies? Here a distinction arises. If those allies make a common cause with us,—if they are associates in the war,—we are necessarily entitled to the right of post-liminium in their territories as well as in our own: for their state is united with ours, and, together with it, constitutes but one party in the war we carry on. But if, as in our times is frequently the practice, an ally only gives us a stated succour stipulated by treaty, and does not himself come to a rupture with our enemy, between whose state and his own, in their immediate relations, peace continues to be observed,—in this case, only the auxiliaries whom he sends to our assistance are partakers and associates in the war; and his dominions remain in a state of neutrality.

Now the right of postliminium does not take effect in neutral countries: for when a nation chooses to remain neuter in a war, she is bound to consider it as equally just on both sides, so far as relates to its effects,—and, consequently, to look upon every capture made by either party, as a lawful acquisition. To allow one of the parties, in prejudice to the other, to enjoy in her dominions the right of claiming things taken by the latter, or the <394> right of postliminium, would be declaring in favour of the former, and departing from the line of neutrality. §208. Of no validity in neutral nations.

Naturally, every kind of property might be recovered by the right of postliminium; and there is no intrinsic reason why moveables should be excepted in this case, provided they can be certainly recognised and identified. Accordingly, the ancients, on recovering such things from the enemy, frequently restored them to their former owners.* But the difficulty of recognising things of this nature, and the endless disputes which would arise from the prosecution of the owners' claims to them, have been deemed motives of sufficient weight for the general establishment §209. What things are recoverable by this right.

* See several instances in Grotius, book iii. chap. 16, §2 [[*Law of War and Peace*]].

of a contrary practice. To these considerations we may add, that, from the little hope entertained of recovering effects taken by the enemy and once carried to a place of safety, a reasonable presumption arises, that the former owners have relinquished their property. It is therefore with reason, that moveables or booty are excepted from the right of postliminium, unless retaken from the enemy immediately after his capture of them; in which case, the proprietor neither finds a difficulty in recognising his effects, nor is presumed to have relinquished them. And as the custom has once been admitted, and is now well established, there would be an injustice in violating it (Prelim. §26). Among the Romans, indeed, slaves were not treated like other movable property; they, by the right of postliminium, were restored to their masters, even when the rest of the booty was detained. The reason of this is evident: for, as it was at all times easy to recognise a slave, and ascertain to whom he belonged, the owner, still entertaining hopes of recovering him, was not supposed to have relinquished his right.

§210. Of those who cannot return by the right of postliminium.

Prisoners of war, who have given their parole,—territories and towns, which have submitted to the enemy, and have sworn or promised allegiance to him,—cannot of themselves return to their former condition by the right of postliminium: for faith is to be kept even with enemies (§174).

§211. They enjoy this right when retaken.

But if the sovereign retakes those towns, countries, or prisoners, who had surrendered to the enemy, he recovers all his former rights over them, and is bound to re-establish them in their pristine condition (§205). In this case they enjoy the right of postliminium without any breach of their word, any violation of their plighted faith. The enemy loses by the chance of war a right which the chance of war had before given him. But concerning prisoners of war, a distinction is to be made. If they were entirely free on their parole, the single circumstance of their coming again into the power of their own nation does not release them,—since, even if they had returned home, they would still have continued prisoners. The consent of the enemy who had captured them, or his total subjugation, can alone dis-<395>charge them. But if they have only promised not to effect their escape,—a promise which prisoners frequently make in order to avoid the inconveniences of a jail,—the only obligation incumbent on them, is, that they shall not, of themselves, quit the enemy's country, or the place assigned for their residence. And if the troops of their party should gain possession of the place where they reside, the consequence is, that, by the right of war, they recover their liberty, are restored to their own nation, and reinstated in their former condition.

When a town, reduced by the enemy's arms, is retaken by those of her own sovereign, she is, as we have above seen, restored to her former condition, and reinstated in the possession of all her rights. It is asked whether she thus recovers such part of her property as had been alienated by the enemy while he kept her in subjection. In the first place we are to make a distinction between movable property not recoverable by the right of postliminium (§202), and immovables. The former belongs to the enemy who gets it into his hands, and he may irrecoverably alienate it. As to immovables, let it be remembered that the acquisition of a town taken in war is not fully consummated, till confirmed by a treaty of peace, or by the entire submission or destruction of the state to which it belonged (§197). Till then, the sovereign of that town has hopes of retaking it, or of recovering it by a peace. And from the moment it returns into his power, he restores it to all its rights (§205), and consequently it recovers all its possessions, as far as in their nature they are recoverable. It therefore resumes its immovable possessions from the hands of those persons who have been so prematurely forward to purchase them. In buying them of one who had not an absolute right to dispose of them, the purchasers made a hazardous bargain; and if they prove losers by the transaction, it is a consequence to which they deliberately exposed themselves. But if that town had been ceded to the enemy by a treaty of peace, or was completely fallen into his power by the submission of the whole state, she has no longer any claim to the right of postliminium; and the alienation of any of her possessions by the conqueror is valid and irreversible; nor can she lay claim to them, if, in the sequel, some fortunate revolution should liberate her from the yoke of the conqueror. When Alexander made a present to the Thessalians of the sum due from them to the Thebans (see §77), he was so absolutely master of the republic of Thebes, that he destroyed the city, and sold the inhabitants.

The same decisions hold good with regard to the immovable property

§212. Whether this right extends to their property alienated by the enemy.

of individuals, prisoners or not, which has been alienated by the enemy
while he was master of the country. Grotius proposes the question with
respect to immovable property possessed in a neutral country by a prisoner of war.* But, according to the principles we have laid down, this
question is <396> groundless: for the sovereign who makes a prisoner
in war, has no other right over him than that of detaining his person
until the conclusion of the war, or until he be ransomed (§§148, &c.);
but he acquires no right to the prisoner's property, unless he can seize
on it. It is impossible to produce any natural reason why the captor
should have a right to dispose of his prisoner's property, unless the prisoner has it about him.

§213. Whether
a nation that
has been en-
tirely subdued
can enjoy the
right of post-
liminium.

When a nation, a people, a state, has been entirely subdued, it is asked
whether a revolution can entitle them to the right of postliminium. In
order justly to answer this question, there must again be a distinction of
cases. If that conquered state has not yet acquiesced in her new subjection, has not voluntarily submitted, and has only ceased to resist from
inability,—if her victor has not laid aside the sword of conquest and
taken up the sceptre of peace and equity,—such a people are not really
subdued: they are only defeated and oppressed; and, on being delivered
by the arms of an ally, they doubtless return to their former situation
(§207). Their ally cannot become their conqueror; he is their deliverer;
and all the obligation of the party delivered is to reward him. If the
subsequent conqueror, not being an ally to the state of which we speak,
intends to keep it under his own jurisdiction as the reward of his victory,
he puts himself in the place of the former conqueror, and becomes the
enemy of the state which the other had oppressed: that state may lawfully
resist him, and avail herself of a favourable opportunity to recover her
liberty. If she had been unjustly oppressed, he who rescues her from the
yoke of the oppressor ought generously to reinstate her in the possession
of all her rights (§203).

The question changes with regard to a state which has voluntarily
submitted to the conqueror. If the people, no longer treated as enemies
but as actual subjects, have submitted to a lawful government, they are

* Lib. iii. cap. 9, §6 [[*Law of War and Peace*]].

thenceforward dependent on a new sovereign; or, being incorporated with the victorious nation, they become a part of it, and share its fate. Their former state is absolutely destroyed; all its relations, all its alliances, are extinguished (Book II. §203). Whoever then the new conqueror may be, that afterwards subdues the state to which these people are united, they share the destiny of that state, as a part shares the fate of the whole. This has been the practice of nations in all ages,—I say, even of just and equitable nations,—especially with regard to an ancient conquest. The most moderate conqueror confines his generosity in this particular to the restoration of the liberties of a people who have been but recently subdued, and whom he does not consider as perfectly incorporated, or well cemented by inclination, with the state which he has conquered.

If the people in question shake off the yoke and recover their liberty by their own exertions, they regain all their rights; they return to their former situation; and foreign nations have no right to determine whether they have shaken off the yoke of lawful authority, or burst the chains of slavery. Thus, the <397> kingdom of Portugal,—which had been seized on by Philip II.[61] king of Spain, under pretence of an hereditary right, but in reality by force and the terror of his arms,—re-established the independency of her crown, and recovered her former rights, when she drove out the Spaniards, and placed the duke of Braganza[62] on the throne.

Provinces, towns, and lands, which the enemy restores by the treaty of peace, are certainly entitled to the right of postliminium: for the sovereign, in whatever manner he recovers them, is bound to restore them to their former condition, as soon as he regains possession of them (§205). The enemy, in giving back a town at the peace, renounces the right he had acquired by arms. It is just the same as if he had never taken it; and the transaction furnishes no reason which can justify the sovereign in refusing to reinstate such town in the possession of all her rights, and restore her to her former condition.

§214. Right of postliminium for what is restored at the peace;

61. In 1580.
62. John IV of Portugal, r. 1640–56.

§215. and for things ceded to the enemy.

But whatever is ceded to the enemy by a treaty of peace, is truly and completely alienated. It has no longer any claim to the right of post-liminium, unless the treaty of peace be broken and cancelled.

§216. The right of post-liminium does not exist after a peace.

And as things not mentioned in the treaty of peace remain in the condition in which they happen to be at the time when the treaty is concluded, and are, on both sides, tacitly ceded to the present possessor, it may be said in general, that the right of postliminium no longer exists after the conclusion of the peace. That right entirely relates to the state of war.

§217. Why always in force for prisoners.

Nevertheless, and for this very reason, there is an exception to be made here in favour of prisoners of war. Their sovereign is bound to release them at the peace (§154). But if he cannot accomplish this,—if the fate of war compels him to accept of hard and unjust conditions,—the enemy, who ought to set the prisoners at liberty when the war is terminated and he has no longer any thing to fear from them (§§150, 153), continues the state of war with respect to them, if he still detains them in captivity, and especially if he reduces them to slavery (§152). They have therefore a right to effect their escape from him if they have an opportunity, and to return to their own country, equally as in war time; since, with regard to them, the war still continues. And in that case, the sovereign, from his obligation to protect them, is bound to restore them to their former condition (§205).

§218. They are free even by escaping into a neutral country.

Further, those prisoners who are, without any lawful reason, detained after the conclusion of peace, become immediately free, when, once escaped from captivity, they have even reached a neutral country: for enemies are not to be pursued and seized on neutral ground (§132); and whoever detains an innocent prisoner after the peace, continues to be his enemy. This rule should and actually does obtain among nations who do not admit and authorise the practice of enslaving prisoners of war. <398>

§219. How the rights and obligations of prisoners subsist.

It is sufficiently evident from the premises, that prisoners are to be considered as citizens who may one day return to their country: and, when they do return, it is the duty of the sovereign to re-establish them in their former condition. Hence it clearly follows, that the rights of every one of those prisoners, together with his obligations (or the rights of others over him), still subsist undiminished,—only the exertion of them is, for the most part, suspended during the time of his captivity.

The prisoner of war therefore retains a right to dispose of his property, particularly in case of death: and as there is nothing in the state of captivity which can in this latter respect deprive him of the exercise of his right, the testament of a prisoner of war ought to be valid in his own country, unless rendered void by some inherent defect.

§220. Testament of a prisoner of war.

With nations which have established the indissolubility of the marriage ties, or have ordained that they should continue for life unless dissolved by the judgment of a court, those ties still subsist, notwithstanding the captivity of one of the parties, who, on his return home, is, by postliminium, again entitled to all his matrimonial rights.

§221. Marriage.

We do not here enter into a detail of what the civil laws of particular nations have ordained with respect to the right of postliminium: we content ourselves with observing that such local regulations are obligatory on the subjects of the state alone, and do not affect foreigners. Neither do we here examine what has been settled on that head by treaties: those particular compacts establish merely a conventional right, which relates only to the contracting parties. Customs confirmed by long and constant use are obligatory on those nations who have given a tacit consent to them; and they are to be respected, when not contrary to the law of nature: but those which involve an infringement of that sacred law are faulty and invalid; and, instead of conforming to such customs, every nation is bound to use her endeavours to effect their abolition. Among the Romans the right of postliminium was in force, even in times of profound peace, with respect to nations with which Rome had neither connections of friendship, rights of hospitality, nor alliance.* This was because those nations were, as we have already observed, considered in some measure as enemies. The prevalence of milder manners has almost every-where abolished that remnant of barbarism. <399>

§222. Regulations respecting postliminium, established by treaty or custom.

---

* [[Justinian's]] Digest. lib. xlix. de Capt. et Postlim. leg. v. §2.

CHAPTER XV

Of the Right of private Persons in War.

§223. Subjects cannot commit hostilities without the sovereign's order. The right of making war, as we have shewn in the first chapter of this book, solely belongs to the sovereign power, which not only decides whether it be proper to undertake the war, and to declare it, but likewise directs all its operations, as circumstances of the utmost importance to the safety of the state. Subjects, therefore, cannot, of themselves, take any steps in this affair; nor are they allowed to commit any act of hostility without orders from their sovereign. Be it understood, however, that, under the head of "hostilities," we do not here mean to include self-defence. A subject may repel the violence of a fellow-citizen when the magistrate's assistance is not at hand; and with much greater reason may he defend himself against the unexpected attacks of foreigners.

§224. That order may be general or particular. The sovereign's order, which commands acts of hostility and gives a right to commit them, is either general or particular. The declaration of war, which enjoins the subjects at large to attack the enemy's subjects, implies a general order. The generals, officers, soldiers, privateersmen, and partisans, being all commissioned by the sovereign, make war by virtue of a particular order.

§225. Source of the necessity of such an order. But, though an order from the sovereign be necessary to authorise the subjects to make war, that necessity wholly results from the laws essential to every political society, and not from any obligation relative to the enemy. For, when one nation takes up arms against another, she from that moment declares herself an enemy to all the individuals of the latter, and authorises them to treat her as such. What right could she have in that case to complain of any acts of hostility committed against her by private persons without orders from their superiors? The rule, therefore, of which we here speak, relates rather to public law in general, than to the law of nations properly so called, or to the principles of the reciprocal obligations of nations.

§226. Why the law of nations should have adopted this rule. If we confine our view to the law of nations, considered in itself,— when once two nations are engaged in war, all the subjects of the one may commit hostilities against those of the other, and do them all the mischief authorised by the state of war. But should two nations thus encounter each other with the collective weight of their whole force, the war would become much more bloody and destructive, and could hardly be terminated otherwise than by the utter extinction of one of the parties. The examples of ancient wars abundantly prove the truth of this assertion to any man who will for a moment recall to mind the first wars waged by Rome against the popular republics by which <400> she was surrounded. It is therefore with good reason that the contrary practice has grown into a custom with the nations of Europe,—at least with those that keep up regular standing armies or bodies of militia. The troops alone carry on the war, while the rest of the nation remain in peace. And the necessity of a special order to act is so thoroughly established, that, even after a declaration of war between two nations, if the peasants of themselves commit any hostilities, the enemy shews them no mercy, but hangs them up as he would so many robbers or banditti. The crews of private ships of war stand in the same predicament: a commission from their sovereign or admiral can alone, in case they are captured, insure them such treatment as is given to prisoners taken in regular warfare.

In declarations of war, however, the ancient form is still retained, by which the subjects in general are ordered, not only to break off all intercourse with the enemy, but also to *attack* him. Custom interprets this general order. It authorises, indeed, and even obliges every subject, of whatever rank, to secure the persons and things belonging to the enemy, when they fall into his hands; but it does not invite the subjects to undertake any offensive expedition without a commission or particular order. §227. Precise meaning of the order.

There are occasions, however, when the subjects may reasonably suppose the sovereign's will, and act in consequence of his tacit command. Thus, although the operations of war are by custom generally confined to the troops, if the inhabitants of a strong place, taken by the enemy, have not promised or sworn submission to him, and should find a favourable opportunity of surprising the garrison and recovering the place for their sovereign, they may confidently presume that the prince will approve of this spirited enterprise. And where is the man that shall dare to censure it? It is true, indeed, that, if the townsmen miscarry in the §228. What private persons may undertake, presuming on the sovereign's will.

attempt, they will experience very severe treatment from the enemy. But this does not prove the enterprise to be unjust, or contrary to the laws of war. The enemy makes use of his right, of the right of arms, which authorises him to call in the aid of terror to a certain degree, in order that the subjects of the sovereign with whom he is at war may not be willing to venture on such bold undertakings, the success of which might prove fatal to him. During the last war, the inhabitants of Genoa suddenly took up arms of their own accord, and drove the Austrians from the city:[63] and the republic celebrates an annual commemoration of that event by which she recovered her liberty.

§229.
Privateers.

Persons fitting out private ships to cruise against the enemy acquire the property of whatever captures they make, as a compensation for their disbursements, and for the risques they run: but they acquire it by grant from the sovereign, who issues out commissions to them. The sovereign allows them either the <401> whole or a part of the capture: this entirely depends on the nature of the contract he has made with them.

As the subjects are not under an obligation of scrupulously weighing the justice of the war, which indeed they have not always an opportunity of being thoroughly acquainted with, and respecting which, they are bound, in case of doubt, to rely on the sovereign's judgment (§187),— they unquestionably may with a safe conscience serve their country by fitting out privateers, unless the war be evidently unjust. But, on the other hand, it is an infamous proceeding on the part of foreigners, to take out commissions from a prince, in order to commit piratical depredations on a nation which is perfectly innocent with respect to them. The thirst of gold is their only inducement; nor can the commission they have received efface the infamy of their conduct, though it screens them from punishment. Those alone are excusable, who thus assist a nation whose cause is undoubtedly just, and that has taken up arms with no other view than that of defending herself from oppression. They would even deserve praise for their exertions in such a cause, if the hatred of oppression, and the love of justice, rather than the desire of riches,

63. December 5–11, 1767.

stimulated them to generous efforts, and induced them to expose their lives or fortunes to the hazards of war.

The noble view of gaining instruction in the art of war, and thus acquiring a greater degree of ability to render useful services to their country, has introduced the custom of serving as volunteers even in foreign armies; and the practice is undoubtedly justified by the sublimity of the motive. At present, volunteers, when taken by the enemy, are treated as if they belonged to the army in which they fight. Nothing can be more reasonable: they in fact join that army, and unite with it in supporting the same cause; and it makes little difference in the case, whether they do this in compliance with any obligation, or at the spontaneous impulse of their own free choice.

§230. Volunteers.

Soldiers can undertake nothing without the express or tacit command of their officers. To obey and execute, is their province,—not to act at their own discretion: they are only instruments in the hands of their commanders. Let it be remembered here, that, by a tacit order, I mean one which is necessarily included in an express order, or in the functions with which a person is intrusted by his superior. What is said of soldiers must also in a proper degree be understood of officers, and of all who have any subordinate command. Wherefore, with respect to things which are not intrusted to their charge, they may both be considered as private individuals, who are not to undertake any thing without orders. The obligation of the military is even more strict, as the martial law expressly forbids acting without orders; and this discipline is so necessary that it scarcely leaves any room for presumption. In war, an enterprise which wears a very advantageous appearance, and promises almost certain <402> success, may nevertheless be attended with fatal consequences. It would be dangerous, in such a case, to leave the decision to the judgment of men in subordinate stations, who are not acquainted with all the views of their general, and who do not possess an equal degree of knowledge and experience: it is therefore not to be presumed that he intends to let them act at their own discretion. Fighting without orders is almost always considered, in a military man, as fighting contrary to orders, or contrary to prohibition. There is, therefore, hardly any case except that of self-defence, in which the soldiers and inferior officers may

§231. What soldiers and subalterns may do.

act without orders. In that one case, the orders may safely be presumed; or rather, the right of self-defence naturally belongs to every one, and requires no permission. During the siege of Prague, in the last war,[64] a party of French grenadiers made a sally without orders and without officers,—possessed themselves of a battery, spiked a part of the cannon, and brought away the remainder into the city. The Roman severity would have punished those men with death. The famous example of the consul Manlius is well known, who, notwithstanding the victory gained by his son, caused capital punishment to be inflicted on him for having engaged the enemy without orders.* But the difference of times and manners obliges a general to moderate such severity. The mareschal Bel-lisle[65] publicly reprimanded those brave grenadiers, but secretly caused money to be distributed among them, as a reward of their courage and alacrity. At another famous siege in the same war, that of Coni,[66] the private men of some batallions that were stationed in the fossés, made, of their own accord, during the absence of their officers, a vigorous sortie which was attended with success. Baron Leutrum[67] was obliged to pardon their transgression, lest he should damp an ardour on which the safety of the place entirely depended. Such inordinate impetuosity should nevertheless be checked as far as possible; since it may eventually be productive of fatal consequences. Avidius Cassius inflicted capital punishment on some officers of his army, who had, without orders, marched forth at the head of a handful of men, to surprise a body of three thousand enemies, and had succeeded in cutting them to pieces. This rigour he justified by saying that there might have been an ambuscade,—*dicens evenire potuisse ut essent insidiae, &c.*†

* Tit. Liv. lib. viii. cap. 7.

† Volcatius Gallicanus, quoted by Grotius [[in *Law of War and Peace*]], book iii. chap. 18, §1, note 6. [["It might," he said, "have been an ambush, and the barbarians' awe for the Roman Empire might have been lost." Avidius Cassius, *Historia Augusta* IV.6.]]

64. Siege of Prague, 1741, during the War of the Austrian Succession.

65. Charles-Louis-Auguste Fouguet, Duc de Belle-Isle, 1684–1774, French soldier and diplomat.

66. Siege of Coni (Cuneo), 1744.

67. Karl Sigismond Friedrick Wilhelm Leutrum.

Is the state bound to indemnify individuals for the damages they have sustained in war? We may learn from Grotius that authors are divided on this question.* The damages under consideration are to be distinguished into two kinds,—those done by the state itself or the sovereign, and those done by the enemy. Of the first kind, some are done deliberately and by way of precaution, as when a field, a house, or a garden, belonging to a private person, is taken for the purpose of erecting on the spot a town rampart, <403> or any other piece of fortification,—or when his standing corn or his store-houses are destroyed, to prevent their being of use to the enemy. Such damages are to be made good to the individual, who should bear only his quota of the loss. But there are other damages, caused by inevitable necessity, as, for instance, the destruction caused by the artillery in retaking a town from the enemy. These are merely accidents,—they are misfortunes which chance deals out to the proprietors on whom they happen to fall. The sovereign, indeed, ought to shew an equitable regard for the sufferers, if the situation of his affairs will admit of it: but no action lies against the state for misfortunes of this nature,—for losses which she has occasioned, not wilfully, but through necessity and by mere accident, in the exertion of her rights. The same may be said of damages caused by the enemy. All the subjects are exposed to such damages: and woe to him on whom they fall! The members of a society may well encounter such risk of property, since they encounter a similar risk of life itself. Were the state strictly to indemnify all those whose property is injured in this manner, the public finances would soon be exhausted; and every individual in the state would be obliged to contribute his share in due proportion,—a thing utterly impracticable. Besides, these indemnifications would be liable to a thousand abuses, and there would be no end of the particulars. It is therefore to be presumed that no such thing was ever intended by those who united to form a society.

But it is perfectly consonant to the duties of the state and the sovereign, and, of course, perfectly equitable, and even strictly just, to relieve, as far as possible, those unhappy sufferers who have been ruined

§232. Whether the state is bound to indemnify the subjects for damages sustained in war.

* Lib. iii. cap. 20. §8 [[*Law of War and Peace*]].

by the ravages of war, as likewise to take care of a family whose head and support has lost his life in the service of the state. There are many debts which are considered as sacred by the man who knows his duty, although they do not afford any ground of action against him.* <404>

CHAPTER XVI

Of various Conventions made during the Course of the War.

§233. Truce and suspension of arms.

War would become too cruel and destructive, were all intercourse between enemies absolutely broken off. According to the observation of Grotius,† there still subsists a friendly intercourse in war, as Virgil‡ and Tacitus§ have expressed it. The occurrences and events of war lay enemies under the necessity of entering into various conventions. As we have already treated in general of the observance of faith between enemies, it is unnecessary for us in this place to prove the obligation of faithfully acting up to those conventions made in war: it therefore only remains

---

* It is in general the indispensable duty of every sovereign to adopt the most efficacious measures for the protection of his subjects engaged in war, in order that they may suffer by it as little as possible,—instead of voluntarily exposing them to greater evils. During the wars in the Netherlands, Philip the Second prohibited the release or exchange of prisoners of war. He forbade the peasants, under pain of death, to pay any contributions with a view to purchase an immunity from pillage and conflagration; and, under the same penalty, prohibited the use of safe-guards and protections. In opposition to this barbarous ordinance, the states-general adopted measures fraught with consummate wisdom. They published an edict, in which, after having described the destructive consequences of the Spanish barbarity, they exhorted the Flemings to attend to their own preservation, and threatened to retaliate on all who should obey the cruel ordinance of Philip. By such conduct they put an end to the dreadful proceedings to which it had given birth. [[Note added in 1773/1797 editions.]]

† Lib iii. cap. xxi. §1 [[*Law of War and Peace*]].

‡ —— Belli commercia Turnus
   Sustulit ista prior. Aen. x. 532.

[["Such trafficking in war Turnus first put away."]]

§ Ann. lib. xiv. cap. 33.

to explain the nature of them. Sometimes it is agreed to suspend hostilities for a certain time; and if this convention be made but for a very short period, or only regards some particular place, it is called a cessation or suspension of arms. Such are those conventions made for the purpose of burying the dead after an assault or a battle, and for a parley, or a conference between the generals of the hostile armies. If the agreement be for a more considerable length of time, and especially if general, it is more particularly distinguished by the appellation of a truce. Many people use both expressions indiscriminately.

The truce or suspension of arms does not terminate the war; it only suspends its operations.

§234. Does not terminate the war.

A truce is either partial or general. By the former, hostilities are suspended only in certain places, as between a town and the army besieging it. By the latter, they are to cease generally, and in all places, between the belligerent powers. Partial truces may also admit of a distinction with respect to acts of hostility, or to persons; that is to say, the parties may agree to abstain from certain acts of hostility during a limited time, or two armies may mutually conclude a truce or suspension of arms without regard to any particular place.

§235. A truce is either partial or general.

A general truce, made for many years, differs from a peace in little else than in leaving the question which was the original ground of the war, still undecided. When two nations are weary of hostilities, and yet cannot agree on the point which constitutes the subject of their dispute, they generally have recourse to this kind of agreement. Thus, instead of peace, long truces only have usually been made between the Christians and the Turks,—sometimes from a false spirit of religion, at other < 405 > times because neither party were willing to acknowledge the other as lawful owners of their respective possessions.

§236. General truce for many years.

It is necessary to the validity of an agreement, that it be made by one who possesses competent powers. Every thing done in war is done by the authority of the sovereign, who alone has the right both of undertaking the war, and directing its operations (§4). But from the impossibility of executing every thing by himself, he must necessarily communicate part of his power to his ministers and officers. The question, therefore, is, to determine what are the things of which the sovereign reserves the management in his own hands, and what those are which

§237. By whom these agreements may be concluded.

he is naturally presumed to intrust to the ministers of his will, to the generals and other officers employed in military operations. We have above (Book II. §207) laid down and explained the principle which is to serve as a general rule on this subject. If the sovereign has not given any special mandate, the person commanding in his name is held to be invested with all the powers necessary for the reasonable and salutary exercise of his functions,—for every thing which naturally follows from his commission. Every thing beyond that is reserved to the sovereign, who is not supposed to have delegated a greater portion of his power than is necessary for the good of his affairs. According to this rule, a general truce can only be concluded by the sovereign himself, or by some person on whom he has expressly conferred a power for that purpose. For it is by no means necessary to the success of the war, that a general should be invested with such an extensive authority: it would exceed the limits of his functions, which consist in directing the military operations in the place where he has the command, and not in regulating the general interests of the state. The conclusion of a general truce is a matter of so high importance, that the sovereign is always presumed to have reserved it in his own hands. So extensive a power suits only the viceroy or governor of a distant country, for the territories under him: and even in this case, if the truce be for a number of years, it is natural to suppose the sovereign's ratification necessary. The Roman consuls and other commanders had a power to grant general truces for the term of their commission; but if that term was considerable, or the truce made for a longer time, it required the ratification of the senate and people. Even a partial truce, when for a long time, seems also to exceed the ordinary powers of a general; and he can only conclude it under a reservation of its being ratified by the sovereign authority.

But, as to partial truces for a short period, it is often necessary, and almost always proper, that the general should have a power to conclude them:—it is necessary, when he cannot wait for the sovereign's consent: it is proper, on those occasions when the truce can only tend to spare the effusion of blood, and to promote the mutual advantage of the contracting parties. With such a power, therefore, the general or commander in <406> chief is naturally supposed to be invested. Thus, the governor of a town, and the general besieging it, may agree on a cessation of arms, for the purpose of burying the dead, or of coming to a parley: they may even settle a truce for some months, on condition that the town, if not relieved within that time, shall surrender, &c. Conventions of this kind only tend to mitigate the evils of war, and are not likely to prove detrimental to any one.

All these truces and suspensions of arms are concluded by the authority of the sovereign, who consents to some of them in his own person, and to others through the ministry of his generals and officers. His faith is pledged by such agreements, and he is bound to enforce their observance.

§238. The sovereign's faith engaged in them.

The truce binds the contracting parties from the moment of its being concluded, but cannot have the force of a law with regard to the subjects on both sides, till it has been solemnly proclaimed: and as an unknown law imposes no obligation, the truce does not become binding on the subjects, until duly notified to them. Hence, if, before they can have obtained certain information of its being concluded, they commit any act contrary to it,—any act of hostility,—they are not punishable. But as the sovereign is bound to fulfil his promises, it is incumbent on him to cause restitution to be made of all prizes taken subsequent to the period when the truce should have commenced. The subjects who through ignorance of its existence have failed to observe it, are not obliged to offer an indemnification, any more than their sovereign who was unable to notify it to them sooner: the non-observance of the truce in this case is merely an accident, not imputable to any fault on his part or on theirs. A ship being out at sea at the time when the truce is published, meets with a ship belonging to the enemy, and sinks her: as there is no guilt in this case, she is not liable to pay any damage. If she has made a capture of the vessel, all the obligation she lies under is to restore the prize, as she must not retain it in violation of the truce. But those who should, through their own fault, remain ignorant of the publication of the truce, would be bound to repair any damage they had caused contrary to its tenor. The simple commission of a fault, and especially of a slight one, may to a certain degree be suffered to pass with impunity; and it certainly does not deserve to be punished with equal severity as a premeditated

§239. When the truce begins to be obligatory.

transgression: but it furnishes no plea against the obligation to repair the damages accruing. In order, as far as possible, to obviate every difficulty, it is usual with sovereigns, in their truces as well as in their treaties of peace, to assign different periods for the cessation of hostilities, according to the situation and distance of places.

§240. Publication of the truce.

Since a truce cannot be obligatory on the subjects unless known to them, it must be solemnly published in all the places where it is intended that it should be observed.

§241. Subjects contravening the truce.

If any of the subjects, whether military men or private citizens, offend against the truce, this is no violation of the public <407> faith; nor is the truce thereby broken. But the delinquents should be compelled to make ample compensation for the damage, and severely punished. Should their sovereign refuse to do justice on the complaints of the party injured, he thereby becomes accessory to the trespass, and violates the truce.

§242. Violation of the truce.

Now, if one of the contracting parties, or any person by his order, or even with his simple consent, commits any act contrary to the truce, it is an injury to the other contracting party: the truce is dissolved; and the injured party is entitled immediately to take up arms, not only for the purpose of renewing the operations of the war, but also of avenging the recent injury offered to him.

§243. Stipulation of a penalty against the infractor.

Sometimes a penalty on the infractor of the truce is reciprocally stipulated: and then the truce is not immediately broken on the first infraction. If the party offending submits to the penalty, and repairs the damage, the truce still subsists, and the offended party has nothing farther to claim. But if an alternative has been agreed on, viz. that in case of an infraction the delinquent shall suffer a certain penalty, or the truce shall be broken, it is the injured party who has the choice of insisting on the penalty or taking advantage of his right to recommence hostilities: for if this were left at the option of the infractor, the stipulation of the alternative would be nugatory, since, by refusing to submit to the penalty simply stipulated, he would break the compact, and thereby give the injured party a right to take up arms again. Besides, in cautionary clauses of this kind, the alternative is not supposed to be introduced in favour of him who fails in his engagements; and it would be absurd to suppose that he reserves to himself the advantage of breaking them by his infraction rather than undergo the penalty. He might as well break them at once openly. The only object of the penal clause is to secure the truce from being so easily broken; and there can be no other reason for introducing it with an alternative, than that of leaving to the injured party a right, if he thinks fit, to dissolve a compact from which the behaviour of the enemy shews him he has little security to expect.

It is necessary that the time of the truce be accurately specified, in order to prevent all doubt or dispute respecting the period of its commencement, and that of its expiration. The French language, extremely clear and precise for those who know how to use it with propriety, furnishes expressions which bid defiance to the most subtle chicanery. The words *"inclusively"* and *"exclusively"* banish all ambiguity which may happen to be in the convention, with regard to the two terms of the truce, its beginning and end. For instance, if it be said that "the truce shall last from the first of March inclusively, until the fifteenth of April, also inclusively," there can remain no doubt; whereas, if the words had simply been, "from the first of March until the fifteenth of April," it might be disputed whether those two days, mentioned as the initial and final terms of the truce, were com-<408>prehended in the treaty, or not: and indeed authors are divided on this question. As to the former of those two days, it seems beyond all question to be comprised in the truce: for if it be agreed that there shall be a truce from the first of March, this naturally means that hostilities shall cease on the first of March. As to the latter day, there is something more of doubt,—the expression *"until"* seeming to separate it from the time of the armistice. However, as we often say *"until* such a day *inclusively,"* the word *"until"* is not necessarily exclusive, according to the genius of the language, And as a truce, which spares the effusion of human blood, is no doubt a thing of a favourable nature, perhaps the safest way is to include in it the very day of the term. Circumstances may also help to ascertain the meaning: but it is very wrong not to remove all ambiguity, when it may be done by the addition of a single word.

In national compacts, the word *"day"* is to be understood of a natural day, since it is in this meaning that a day is the common measure of time

§244. Time of the truce.

among nations. The computation by civil days owes its origin to the civil law of each nation, and varies in different countries. The natural day begins at sun-rise, and lasts twenty-four hours, or one diurnal revolution of the sun. If, therefore, a truce of a hundred days be agreed on, to begin on the first of March, the truce begins at sun-rise on the first of March, and is to continue a hundred days of twenty-four hours each. But as the sun does not rise at the same hour throughout the whole year, the parties, in order to avoid an overstrained nicety, and a degree of chicane unbecoming that candour which should prevail in conventions of this kind, ought certainly to understand that the truce expires, as it began, at the rising of the sun. The term of a day is meant from one sun to the other, without quibbling or disputing about the difference of a few minutes in the time of his rising. He who, having made a truce for a hundred days, beginning on the twenty-first of June, when the sun rises about four o'clock, should, on the day the truce is to end, take up arms at the same hour, and surprise his enemy before sun-rise, would certainly be considered as guilty of a mean and perfidious chicanery.

If no term has been specified for the commencement of the truce, the contracting parties, being bound by it immediately on its conclusion (§239), ought to have it published without delay, in order that it may be punctually observed: for it becomes binding on the subjects only from the time when it is duly published with respect to them (ibid.); and it begins to take effect only from the moment of the first publication, unless otherwise settled by the terms of the agreement.

§245. Effects of a truce; what is allowed, or not, during its continuance.

1st Rule. Each party may do at home what they have a right to do in time of peace.

The general effect of a truce is that every act of hostility shall absolutely cease. And in order to obviate all dispute respecting the acts which may be termed hostile, the general rule is, that, during the truce, each party may, within his own territories, and in the places where he is master, do whatever he would have <409> a right to do in time of profound peace. Thus a truce does not deprive a sovereign of the liberty of levying soldiers, assembling an army in his own dominions, marching troops within the country, and even calling in auxiliaries, or repairing the fortifications of a town which is not actually besieged. As he has a right to do all these things in time of peace, the truce does not tie up his hands. Can it be supposed that by such a compact he meant to debar himself from executing things which the continuation of hostilities could not prevent him from doing?

But to take advantage of the cessation of arms in order to execute without danger certain things which are prejudicial to the enemy, and which could not have been safely undertaken during the continuance of hostilities, is circumventing and deceiving the enemy with whom the compact has been made: it is a breach of the truce. By this second general rule we may solve several particular cases.

The truce concluded between the governor of a town and the general besieging it, deprives both of the liberty of continuing their works. With regard to the latter, this is manifest,—his works being acts of hostility. But neither can the governor, on his part, avail himself of the armistice, for the purpose of repairing the breaches or erecting new fortifications. The artillery of the besiegers does not allow him to carry on such works with impunity during the continuance of hostilities: it would therefore be detrimental to them that he should employ the truce in this manner; and they are under no obligation of submitting to be so far imposed upon: they will with good reason consider such an attempt as an infraction of the truce. But the suspension of arms does not hinder the governor from continuing within his town such works as were not liable to be impeded by the attacks or fire of the enemy. At the last siege of Tournay,[68] after the surrender of the town, an armistice was agreed on; during the continuance of which, the governor permitted the French to make all the necessary preparations for attacking the citadel, to carry on their works, and erect their batteries,—because the governor, on his part, was in the mean time busily employed within, in clearing away the rubbish with which the blowing up of a magazine had filled the citadel, and was erecting batteries on the ramparts. But all this he might have performed with little or no danger, even if the operations of the siege had commenced; whereas the French could not have carried on their works with such expedition, or made their approaches and erected their batteries, without losing a great number of men. There was therefore no equality in the case; and, on that footing, the truce was entirely in favour of the

§246. 2d. Rule. Not to take advantage of the truce in doing what hostilities would have prevented.

§247. For instance, continuing the works of a siege, or repairing breaches;

68. In 1745.

besiegers: and, in consequence of it, the capture of the citadel took place sooner, probably, by a fortnight, than it would otherwise have happened.

§248. or introducing succours.   If the truce be concluded either for the purpose of settling the terms of the capitulation or of waiting for the orders of the <410> respective sovereigns, the besieged governor cannot make use of it as a convenient opportunity to introduce succours or ammunition into the town: for this would be taking an undue advantage of the armistice for the purpose of deceiving the enemy;—a conduct which is inconsistent with candour and honesty. The spirit of such a compact evidently imports that all things shall remain as they were at the moment of its conclusion.

§249. Distinction of a particular case.   But this is not to be extended to a suspension of arms agreed on for some particular circumstance, as, for instance, burying the dead. In this case, the truce is to be interpreted with a view to its immediate object. Accordingly the firing ceases, either in all quarters, or only in a single point of attack, pursuant to agreement, that each party may freely carry off their dead: and during this intermission of the cannonade, it is not allowable to carry on any works which the firing would have impeded. This would be taking an undue advantage of the armistice, and consequently a violation of it. But it is perfectly justifiable in the governor, during such a cessation of hostilities, silently to introduce a reinforcement in some quarter remote from the point of attack. If the besieger, lulled by such an armistice, abates in his vigilance, he must abide the consequences. The armistice of itself does not facilitate the entrance of that reinforcement.

§250. Retreat of an army during a suspension of hostilities.   Likewise if an army in a bad position proposes and concludes an armistice for the purpose of burying the dead after a battle, it cannot pretend, during the suspension of arms, to extricate itself from its disadvantageous situation, and to march off unmolested, in sight of the enemy. This would be availing itself of the compact in order to effect a purpose which it could not otherwise have accomplished. This would be laying a snare: and conventions must not be converted into snares. The enemy, therefore, may justly obstruct the motions of that army the moment it attempts to quit its station: but if it silently files off in the rear, and thus reaches a safer position, it will not be guilty of a breach of faith; since nothing more is implied by a suspension of arms for the burial of the dead, than that neither party shall attack the other whilst this office of humanity is performing. The enemy, therefore, can only blame his own remissness:—he ought to have stipulated, that, during the cessation of hostilities, neither party should quit their post: or it was his business vigilantly to watch the motions of the hostile army: and on perceiving their design, he was at liberty to oppose it. It is a very justifiable stratagem to propose a cessation of arms for a particular object, with a view of lulling the enemy's vigilance, and covering a design of retreating.

But if the truce be not made for any particular object alone, we cannot honourably avail ourselves of it in order to gain an advantage, as, for instance, to secure an important post, or to advance into the enemy's country. The latter step would indeed be a violation of the truce; for every advance into the enemy's country is an act of hostility. <411>

Now, as a truce suspends hostilities without putting an end to the war, every thing must, during the continuance of the truce, be suffered to remain in its existing state, in all places of which the possession is contested: nor is it lawful, in such places, to attempt any thing to the prejudice of the enemy. This is a third general rule.

§251. 3d. Rule Nothing to be attempted in contested places, but every thing to be left as it was.

When the enemy withdraws his troops from a place, and absolutely quits it, his conduct sufficiently shews that he does not intend to occupy it any longer: and in this case we may lawfully take possession of it during the truce. But if by any indication it appears that a post, an open town, or a village, is not relinquished by the enemy, and that, though he neglects to keep it guarded, he still maintains his rights and claims to it, the truce forbids us to seize upon it. To take away from the enemy what he is disposed to retain, is an act of hostility.

§252. Places quitted or neglected by the enemy.

It is also an undoubted act of hostility to receive towns or provinces inclined to withdraw from the sovereignty of the enemy, and give themselves up to us. We therefore cannot receive them during the continuance of the truce, which wholly suspends all hostile proceedings.

§253. Subjects inclined to revolt against their prince not to be received during the truce;

Far more unlawful it is, during that period, to instigate the subjects of the enemy to revolt, or to tamper with the fidelity of his governors and garrisons. These are not only hostile proceedings, but odious acts of hostility (§180). As to deserters and fugitives, they may be received

§254. much less to be solicited to treason.

during the truce, since they are received even in time of peace, when there is no treaty to the contrary. And even if such a treaty did exist, its effect is annulled, or at least suspended, by the war which has since taken place.

§255. Persons or effects of enemies not to be seized during the truce.

To seize persons or things belonging to the enemy, when he has not, by any particular fault on his side, afforded us grounds for such seizure, is an act of hostility, and consequently not allowable during a truce.

§256. Right of postliminium during the truce.

Since the right of postliminium is founded only on the state of war (Chap. XIV. of this Book), it cannot take effect during the truce, which suspends all the acts of war, and leaves every thing in its existing state (§251). Even prisoners cannot during that season withdraw from the power of the enemy, in order to recover their former condition: for the enemy has a right to detain them while the war continues; and it is only on its conclusion that his right over their liberty expires (§148).

§257. Intercourse allowed during a truce.

During the truce, especially if made for a long period, it is naturally allowable for enemies to pass and repass to and from each other's country, in the same manner as it is allowed in time of peace; since all hostilities are now suspended. But each of the sovereigns is at liberty, as he would be in time of peace, to adopt every precaution which may be necessary to prevent this intercourse from becoming prejudicial to him. He has just grounds of suspicion against people with whom he is soon to recommence hostilities. He may even declare, at the <412> time of making the truce, that he will admit none of the enemy into any place under his jurisdiction.

§258. Persons detained by unsurmountable obstacles, after the expiration of the truce.

Those who, having entered the enemy's territories during the truce, are detained there by sickness or any other unsurmountable obstacle, and thus happen to remain in the country after the expiration of the armistice, may in strict justice be kept prisoners: it is an accident which they might have foreseen, and to which they have of their own accord exposed themselves; but humanity and generosity commonly require that they should be allowed a sufficient term for their departure.

§259. Particular conditions added to truces.

If the articles of truce contain any conditions either more extensive or more narrowly restrictive than what we have here laid down, the transaction becomes a particular convention. It is obligatory on the contracting parties, who are bound to observe what they have promised in due form: and the obligations thence resulting constitute a conventional right, the detail of which is foreign to the plan of this work.

As the truce only suspends the effects of war (§233), the moment it expires, hostilities may be renewed without any fresh declaration of war: for every one previously knows that from that instant the war will resume its course; and the reasons for the necessity of a declaration are not applicable to this case (§51).

§260. At the expiration of the truce, the war is renewed without any fresh declaration.

But a truce of many years very much resembles a peace, and only differs from it in leaving the subject of the war still undecided. Now as a considerable lapse of time may have effected a material alteration in the circumstances and dispositions of both the parties,—the love of peace, so becoming in sovereigns, the care they should take to spare their subjects' blood, and even that of their enemies,—these dispositions, I say, seem to require that princes should not take up arms again at the expiration of a truce in which all military preparatives had been totally laid aside and forgotten, without making some declaration which may invite the enemy to prevent the effusion of blood. The Romans have given us an example of this commendable moderation. They had only made a truce with the city of Veii;[69] and the enemy even renewed hostilities before the stipulated time was elapsed. Nevertheless, at the expiration of the term, the college of the feciales gave it as their opinion that the Romans should send to make a formal demand of satisfaction, previous to their taking up arms again.[*]

The capitulations on the surrender of towns are among the principal conventions made between enemies during the course of war. They are usually settled between the general of the besieging army and the governor of the besieged town, both acting in virtue of the authority annexed to their respective posts or commissions.

§261. Capitulations and by whom they may be concluded.

We have elsewhere (Book II. Chap. XIV.) laid down the principles of that authority which is vested in the subordinate < 413 > powers, together with general rules to aid in forming a decision respecting it. All this has recently been recapitulated in a few words, and particularly applied to

---

[*] Tit. Liv. lib. iv. cap. 30.
69. In 425 B.C.

generals and other military commanders in chief (§237). Since the general of an army, and the governor of a town, must naturally be invested with all the powers necessary for the exercise of their respective functions, we have a right to presume that they possess those powers: and that of concluding a capitulation is certainly one of the number, especially when they cannot wait for the sovereign's order. A treaty made by them on that subject is therefore valid, and binds the sovereigns, in whose name and by whose authority the respective commanders have acted.

§262. Clauses contained in them.
But let it be observed, that, if those officers do not mean to exceed their powers, they should scrupulously confine themselves within the limits of their functions, and forbear to meddle with things which have not been committed to their charge. In the attack and the defence, in the capture or the surrender of a town, the possession alone is the point in question, and not the property and right: the fate of the garrison is also involved in the transaction. Accordingly, the commanders may come to an agreement respecting the manner in which the capitulating town shall be possessed: the besieging general may promise that the inhabitants shall be spared, and permitted to enjoy their religion, franchises, and privileges: and as to the garrison, he may allow them to march out with their arms and baggage, with all the honours of war,—to be escorted and conducted to a place of safety, &c. The governor of the town may deliver it up at discretion, if reduced to that extremity by the situation of affairs: he may surrender himself and his garrison prisoners of war, or engage, that, for a stipulated time, or even to the end of the war, they shall not carry arms against the same enemy, or against his allies: and the governor's promise is valid and obligatory on all under his command, who are bound to obey him while he keeps within the limits of his functions (§23).

But should the besieging general take on him to promise that his sovereign shall never annex the conquered town to his own dominions, or shall, after a certain time, be obliged to restore it, he would exceed the bounds of his authority, in entering into a contract respecting matters which are not intrusted to his management. And the like may be said of a governor who in the capitulation should proceed to such lengths as for ever to alienate the town which he commands, and to deprive his sovereign of the right to retake it,—or who should promise that his garrison shall never carry arms, not even in another war. His functions do not give him so extensive a power. If, therefore, in the conferences for a capitulation, either of the hostile commanders should insist on conditions which the other does not think himself empowered to grant, they have still one expedient left, which is to agree to an armistice, during which every thing <414> shall continue in its present state, until they have received orders from higher authority.

At the beginning of this chapter we have given the reasons why we thought it unnecessary to prove in this place that all these conventions made during the course of the war, are to be inviolably adhered to. We shall therefore only observe, with respect to capitulations in particular, that, as it is unjust and scandalous to violate them, so the consequences of such an act of perfidy often prove detrimental to the party who has been guilty of it. What confidence can thenceforward be placed in him? The towns which he attacks will endure the most dreadful extremities, rather than place any dependence on his word. He strengthens his enemies by compelling them to make a desperate defence; and every siege that he is obliged to undertake, will become terrible. On the contrary, fidelity attracts confidence and affection; it facilitates enterprises, removes obstacles, and paves the way to glorious successes. Of this history furnishes us a fine example in the conduct of George Baste, general of the imperialists in 1602, against Battory and the Turks. The insurgents of Battory's party having gained possession of Bistrith, otherwise called Nissa, Baste recovered the town by a capitulation, which in his absence was violated by some German soldiers: but being informed of the transaction on his return, he immediately hanged up all the soldiers concerned, and out of his own purse paid the inhabitants all the damages they had sustained. This action had so powerful an influence on the minds of the rebels, that they all submitted to the emperor, without demanding any other surety than the word of general Baste.*

§263. Observance of capitulations, and its utility.

* Sully's Memoirs, by M. de l'Ecluse, vol. iv. p. 179.

§264. Prom-
ises made to
the enemy by
individuals.

Individuals, whether belonging to the army or not, who happen singly
to fall in with the enemy, are, by the urgent necessity of the circumstance,
left to their own discretion, and may, so far as concerns their own persons, do every thing which a commander might do with respect to himself and the troops under his command. If, therefore, in consequence of
the situation in which they are involved, they make any promise, such
promise (provided it do not extend to matters which can never lie within
the sphere of a private individual) is valid and obligatory, as being made
with competent powers. For when a subject can neither receive his sovereign's orders nor enjoy his protection, he resumes his natural rights,
and is to provide for his own safety by any just and honourable means
in his power. Hence, if that individual has promised a sum for his ransom, the sovereign, so far from having a power to discharge him from
his promise, should oblige him to fulfil it. The good of the state requires
that faith should be kept on such occasions, and that subjects should
have this mode of saving their lives or recovering their liberty. <415>

Thus a prisoner who is released on his parole, is bound to observe it
with scrupulous punctuality; nor has the sovereign a right to oppose such
observance of his engagement: for, had not the prisoner thus given his
parole, he would not have been released.

Thus also the country people, the inhabitants of villages or defenceless towns, are bound to pay the contributions which they have promised
in order to save themselves from pillage.

Nay more, a subject would even have a right to renounce his country,
if the enemy, being master of his person, refused to spare his life on any
other condition: for, when once the society to which he belongs is unable
to protect and defend him, he resumes his natural rights. And besides,
should he obstinately refuse compliance, what advantage would the state
derive from his death? Undoubtedly, while any hope remains, while we
have yet any means of serving our country, it is our duty to expose ourselves and to brave every danger for her sake. I here suppose that we have
no alternative but that of renouncing our country or perishing without
any advantage to her. If by our death we can serve her, it is noble to
imitate the heroic generosity of the Decii. But an engagement to serve
against our country, were it even the only means of saving our life, is

dishonourable; and a man of spirit would submit to a thousand deaths, rather than make so disgraceful a promise.

If a soldier, meeting an enemy in a by-place, makes him prisoner, but promises him his life or liberty on condition of his paying a certain ransom, this agreement is to be respected by the superiors: for it does not appear that the soldier, left entirely to himself on that occasion, has in any particular exceeded his powers. He might, on the other hand, have thought it imprudent to attack that enemy, and, under that idea, have suffered him to escape. Under the direction of his superiors, he is bound to obey: when alone, he is left to his own discretion. Procopius[70] relates the adventure of two soldiers, the one a Goth and the other a Roman, who, being fallen together into a pit, mutually promised each other that their lives should be spared: and this agreement was approved by the Goths.* <416>

CHAPTER XVII

Of Safe-conducts and Passports,—with Questions on the Ransom of Prisoners of War.

Safe-conducts and passports are a kind of privilege insuring safety to persons in passing and repassing, or to certain things during their conveyance from one place to another. From the usage and genius of the [*French*] language, it appears that the term *"passport"* is used, on ordinary occasions, when speaking of persons who lie under no particular exception as to passing and repassing in safety, and to whom it is only granted for greater security, and in order to prevent all debate, or to exempt them from some general prohibition. A *safe-conduct* is given to those who otherwise could not safely pass through the places where he who grants it is master,—as, for instance, to a person charged with some misdemeanor, or to an enemy. It is of the latter that we are here to treat.

§265. Nature of safe-conducts and passports.

---

* Hist. Goth. lib. ii. cap. 1, quoted by Puffendorf, book viii. chap. 7, §14.
70. Procopius of Caesarea, 500–565, Byzantine scholar and historian.

§266. From what authority they emanate.

All safe-conducts, like every other act of supreme command, emanate from the sovereign authority: but the prince may delegate to his officers the power of granting safe-conducts; and they are invested with that power, either by an express commission, or by a natural consequence of the nature of their functions. A general of an army, from the very nature of his post, can grant safe-conducts: and as they are derived, though mediately, from the sovereign authority, the other generals or officers of the same prince are bound to respect them.

§267. Not transferable from one person to another.

The person named in the safe-conduct cannot transfer his privilege to another: for he does not know whether it be a matter of indifference to the granter of the safe-conduct that another person should use it in his stead: and so far from presuming that to be the case, he is even bound to presume the contrary, on account of the abuses which might thence result; and he cannot assume to himself any farther privilege than was intended for him. If the safe-conduct is granted, not for persons, but for certain effects, those effects may be removed by others besides the owner. The choice of those who remove them is indifferent, provided there do not lie against them any personal exception sufficient to render them objects of just suspicion in the eye of him who grants the safe-conduct, or to exclude them from the privilege of entering his territories.

§268. Extent of the promised security.

He who promises security by a safe-conduct, promises to afford it wherever he has the command,—not only in his own territories, but likewise in every place where any of his troops may happen to be: and he is bound, not only to forbear violating <417> that security either by himself or his people, but also to protect and defend the person to whom he has promised it, to punish any of his subjects who have offered him violence, and oblige them to make good the damage.*

---

* At the famous interview at Peronne [[1468]], Charles duke of Burgundy [[r. 1467–77]], exasperated to find that Louis XI. [[r. 1461–83]] had engaged the people of Liege to take up arms against him, paid no respect to the safe-conduct which he had granted to that prince. If Louis had plotted and negotiated their defection while he was at Peronne, Charles would have been justifiable in disregarding a safe-conduct of which an improper use had been made. But the French monarch had dispatched agents to Ghent for that purpose, before there was any question of the meeting at Peronne; and Charles, in the transports of blind resentment excited by the disagree-

As the right arising from a safe-conduct proceeds entirely from the will of him who grants it, that will is the standard by which the extent of the right is to be measured; and the will is discoverable in the object for which the safe-conduct was granted. Consequently a person who has barely obtained permission to go away, does not thence derive a right to come back again; and a safe-conduct granted for the simple passage through a country does not entitle the bearer to repass through it on his return. When the safe-conduct is granted for a particular business, it must continue in force until that business is concluded, and the person has had time to depart: if it is specified to be granted for a journey, it will also serve for the person's return, since both passage and return are included in a journey. As this privilege consists in the liberty of going and coming in safety, it differs from a permission to settle in any particular place, and consequently cannot give a right to stop any-where for a length of time, unless on some special business, in consideration of which the safe-conduct was asked and granted.

§269. How to judge of the right derived from a safe-conduct.

A safe-conduct given to a traveller naturally includes his baggage, or his clothes and other things necessary for his journey, with even one or two domestics, or more, according to the rank of the person. But in all these respects, as well as in the others which we have just noticed above, the safest mode, especially when we have to do with enemies or other suspected persons, is to specify and distinctly enumerate the particulars, in order to obviate every difficulty. Accordingly, such is the practice which at present prevails; and, in granting safe-conducts, it is the custom expressly to include the baggage and domestics.

§270. Whether it includes baggage and domestics.

Though a permission to settle any-where, granted to the father of a family, naturally includes his wife and children, it is otherwise with a safe-conduct; because it seldom happens that a man settles in a place without having his family with him; whereas, on a journey, it is more usual to travel without them.

§271. Safe-conduct granted to the father does not include his family.

---

able and unexpected intelligence, committed a flagrant breach of the law of nations. [[Note added in 1773/1797 editions.]]

§272. Safe-conduct given in general to any one and his retinue.

A safe-conduct granted to a person for *himself and his retinue,* cannot give him a right of bringing with him persons justly suspected by the state, or who have been banished, or have fled from the country on account of any crime; nor can it serve as a protection to such men: for the sovereign who grants a safe-<418>conduct in those general terms, does not suppose that it will be presumptuously abused for the purpose of bringing persons into his territories who have been guilty of crimes or have particularly offended him.

§273. Term of the safe-conduct.

A safe-conduct given for a stated term, expires at the end of the term specified therein: and the bearer, if he does not retire before that time, may be arrested, and even punished, according to circumstances, especially if he has given room for suspicion by an affected delay.

§274. A person forcibly detained beyond the term.

But if forcibly detained, as by sickness, so as to be unable to depart in time, a proper respite should be allowed him: for a promise of security has been made to him; and though it was made only for a limited time, it is not by any fault of his own that he has been prevented from departing within the term. The case is different from that of an enemy coming into our country during a truce: to the latter we have made no particular promise: he at his own peril takes advantage of a general liberty allowed by the suspension of hostilities. All we have promised to the enemy is, to forbear hostilities for a certain time: and, at the expiration of that term, it is a matter of importance to us that we be at liberty to let the war freely take its course, without being impeded by a variety of excuses and pretexts.

§275. The safe-conduct does not expire at the death of him who gave it.

The safe-conduct does not expire at the decease or deposition of him who granted it; for it was given in virtue of the sovereign authority, which never dies, and whose efficacy exists independent of the person intrusted with the exercise of it. It is with this act as with other ordinances of the public power: their validity or duration does not depend on the life of him who enacted them, unless, by their very nature, or by express declaration, they are personally confined to him.

§276. How it may be revoked.

The successor, nevertheless, may revoke a safe-conduct, if he has good reasons for the revocation. Even he who has granted it, may in like case revoke it: nor is he always obliged to make known his reasons. Every privilege, when it becomes detrimental to the state, may be revoked,—

a gratuitous privilege, purely and simply,—a purchased privilege, on giving an indemnification to the parties concerned. Suppose a prince or his general is preparing for a secret expedition,—must he suffer any person, under cover of a safe-conduct antecedently obtained, to come and pry into his preparatives, and give the enemy intelligence of them? But a safe-conduct is not to be converted into a snare: if it be revoked, the bearer must be allowed time and liberty to depart in safety. If he, like any other traveller, be detained for some time in order to prevent his carrying intelligence to the enemy, no ill treatment is to be offered him; nor is he to be kept longer than while the reasons for his detainder subsist.

If a safe-conduct contains this clause, *"For such time as we shall think fit,"* it gives only a precarious right, and is revocable every moment: but, until it has been expressly revoked, it <419> remains valid. It expires on the death of him who gave it, who from that moment ceases to will the continuation of the privilege. But it must always be understood that when a safe-conduct expires in this manner, the bearer is to be allowed a proper time for his safe departure.

§277. Safe-conduct with the clause, *for such time as we shall think fit.*

After having discussed the right of making prisoners of war,—the obligation of the captor to release them at the peace by exchange or ransom,—and that of their sovereign to obtain their liberty,—it remains to consider the nature of those conventions whose object is the deliverance of these unfortunate sufferers. If the belligerent sovereigns have agreed on a cartel for the exchange or ransom of prisoners, they are bound to observe it with equal fidelity as any other convention. But if (as was frequently the practice in former times) the state leaves to each prisoner, at least during the continuance of the war, the care of redeeming himself,—such private conventions present a number of questions, of which we shall only touch on the principal ones.

§278. Conventions relating to the ransom of prisoners.

He who has acquired a lawful right to demand a ransom from his prisoner may transfer his right to a third person. This was practised in the last ages. It was frequent for military men to resign their prisoners, and transfer all the rights they had over them, into other hands. But, as the person who takes a prisoner is bound to treat him with justice and humanity (§150), he must not, if he wishes that his conduct should be free from censure, transfer his right, in an unlimited manner, to one who

§279. The right of demanding a ransom may be transferred.

might make an improper use of it: when he has agreed with his prisoner concerning the price of his ransom, he may transfer to whom he pleases the right to demand the stipulated sum.

§280. What may annul the convention made for the rate of the ransom.

When once the agreement is made with a prisoner for the price of his ransom, it becomes a perfect contract, and cannot be rescinded under pretence that the prisoner is discovered to be richer than was imagined: for it is by no means necessary that the rate should be proportioned to the wealth of the prisoner, since that is not the scale by which we measure the right to detain a prisoner of war (§§148, 153). But it is natural to proportion the price of the ransom to the prisoner's rank in the hostile army, because the liberty of an officer of distinction is of greater consequence than that of a private soldier or an inferior officer. If the prisoner has not only concealed but disguised his rank, it is a fraud on his part, which gives the captor a right to annul the compact.

§281. A prisoner dying before payment of ransom.

If a prisoner, having agreed on the price of his ransom, dies before payment, it is asked whether the stipulated sum be due, and whether the heirs are bound to pay it? They undoubtedly are, if the prisoner died in the possession of his liberty: for, from the moment of his release, in consideration of which he had promised a sum, that sum becomes due, and does not at all belong to his heirs. But if he had not yet obtained his liberty, the price which was to have been paid for it, is not a debt on him or <420> his heirs, unless he had made his agreement in a different manner: and he is not reputed to have received his liberty until the moment when he is perfectly free to depart at pleasure,—when neither the person who held him prisoner, nor that person's sovereign, opposes his release and departure.

If he has only been permitted to take a journey for the purpose of prevailing on his friends or his sovereign to furnish him with the means of ransoming himself, and dies before he is possessed of his full liberty, before he is finally discharged from his parole,—nothing is due for his ransom.

If, after having agreed on the price, he is detained in prison till the time of payment, and there dies in the interim, his heirs are not bound to pay the ransom,—such an agreement being, on the part of the person who held him prisoner, no more than a promise of giving him his liberty on the actual payment of a certain sum. A promise of buying and selling does not bind the supposed purchaser to pay the price of the article in question, if it happens to perish before the completion of the purchase. But if the contract of sale be perfect, the purchaser must pay the price of the thing sold, though it should happen to perish before delivery, provided there was no fault or delay on the part of the vender. For this reason, if the prisoner has absolutely concluded the agreement for his ransom, acknowledging himself, from that moment, debtor for the stipulated sum,—and is nevertheless still detained, no longer indeed as a prisoner, but as surety for the payment,—the price of the ransom is due, notwithstanding the circumstance of his dying in the interim.

If the agreement says that the ransom shall be paid on a certain day, and the prisoner happens to die before that day, the heirs are bound to pay the sum agreed on: for the ransom was due; and the appointed day was assigned merely as the term of payment.

From a rigid application of the same principles, it follows, that a prisoner, who has been released on condition of procuring the release of another, should return to prison, in case the latter happens to die before he has been able to procure him his liberty. But certainly such an unfortunate case is entitled to lenity; and equity seems to require that this prisoner should be allowed to continue in the enjoyment of that liberty which has been granted to him, provided he pays a fair equivalent for it, since he is now unable to purchase it precisely at the price agreed on.

§282. Prisoner released on condition of procuring the release of another.

If a prisoner, who has been fully set at liberty after having promised but not paid his ransom, happens to be taken a second time, it is evident, that, without being exempted from the payment of his former ransom, he will have to pay a second, if he wishes to recover his liberty.

§283. Prisoner retaken before he has paid his former ransom.

On the other hand, though the prisoner has agreed for the price of his ransom, if, before the execution of the compact,—before he is set at liberty in virtue of it,—he be retaken and delivered by his own party, he owes nothing. I here evidently <421> suppose that the contract for his ransom was not completed, and that the prisoner had not acknowledged himself debtor for the sum agreed on. The person who held him prisoner, had, as it were, only made him a promise of selling, and he had

§284. Prisoner rescued before he has received his liberty.

promised to purchase: but the purchase and sale had not actually passed into effect; the property was not actually transferred.

§285. Whether the things which a prisoner has found means to conceal, belong to him. The property of a prisoner's effects is not vested in the captor, except so far as he seizes on those effects at the time of his capture. Of this there is no doubt, in these modern times when prisoners of war are not reduced to slavery. And even by the law of nature, the property of a slave's goods does not, without some other reason, pass to the master of the slave. There is nothing in the nature of slavery, which can of itself produce that effect. Though a man obtains certain rights over the liberty of another, does it thence follow that he shall have a right over his property also? When, therefore, the enemy has not plundered his prisoner, or when the latter has found means to conceal something from the captor's search, whatever he has thus saved still continues to be his own property, and he may employ it towards the payment of his ransom. At present, even the plundering of prisoners is not always practised: the greedy soldier sometimes proceeds to such lengths; but an officer would think it an indelible stain on his character, to have deprived them of the smallest article. A party of private French troopers, who had captured a British general at the battle of Rocoux,[71] claimed no right to any thing belonging to their prisoner, except his arms alone.

§286. Hostage given for the release of a prisoner. The death of the prisoner extinguishes the captor's right. Wherefore, if any person is given as a hostage in order to procure a prisoner's enlargement, he ought to be released the moment the prisoner dies; and, on the other hand, if the hostage dies, his death does not reinstate the prisoner in the possession of his liberty. The reverse of this is true, if the one, instead of being simply a hostage for the other, had been substituted in his stead.

71. In 1746.

CHAPTER XVIII

Of Civil War.

It is a question very much debated, whether a sovereign is bound to observe the common laws of war towards rebellious subjects who have openly taken up arms against him? A flatterer, or a prince of a cruel and arbitrary disposition, will immediately pronounce that the laws of war were not made for rebels, for whom no punishment can be too severe. Let us proceed more soberly, and reason from the incontestable principles above laid down. In order clearly to discover what conduct the sove-<422>reign ought to pursue towards revolted subjects, we must, in the first place, recollect that all the sovereign's rights are derived from those of the state or of civil society, from the trust reposed in him, from the obligation he lies under of watching over the welfare of the nation, of procuring her greatest happiness, of maintaining order, justice, and peace within her boundaries (Book I. Chap. IV.). Secondly, we must distinguish the nature and degree of the different disorders which may disturb the state, and oblige the sovereign to take up arms, or substitute forcible measures instead of the milder influence of authority.

§287. Foundation of the sovereign's rights against the rebels.

The name of *rebels* is given to all subjects who unjustly take up arms against the ruler of the society, whether their view be to deprive him of the supreme authority, or to resist his commands in some particular instance, and to impose conditions on him.

§288. Who are rebels.

A popular commotion is a concourse of people who assemble in a tumultuous manner, and refuse to listen to the voice of their superiors, whether the design of the assembled multitude be levelled against the superiors themselves, or only against some private individuals. Violent commotions of this kind take place when the people think themselves aggrieved; and there is no order of men who so frequently give rise to them, as the tax-gatherers. If the rage of the malcontents be particularly levelled at the magistrates, or others vested with the public authority, and they proceed to a formal disobedience or acts of open violence, this is called a *sedition*. When the evil spreads,—when it infects the majority of the inhabitants of a city or province, and gains such strength that

§289. Popular commotion, insurrection, sedition.

even the sovereign himself is no longer obeyed,—it is usual more particularly to distinguish such a disorder by the name of *insurrection*.

§290. How the sovereign is to suppress them.   All these violences disturb the public order, and are state crimes, even when arising from just causes of complaint. For violent measures are forbidden in civil society: the injured individuals should apply to the magistrate for redress; and if they do not obtain justice from that quarter, they may lay their complaints at the foot of the throne. Every citizen should even patiently endure evils which are not insupportable, rather than disturb the public peace. A denial of justice on the part of the sovereign, or affected delays, can alone excuse the furious transports of a people whose patience has been exhausted,—and even justify them, if the evils be intolerable, and the oppression great and manifest. But what conduct shall the sovereign observe towards the insurgents? I answer, in general,—such conduct as shall at the same time be the most consonant to justice, and the most salutary to the state. Although it be his duty to repress those who unnecessarily disturb the public peace, he is bound to shew clemency towards unfortunate persons, to whom just causes of complaint have been given, and whose sole crime consists in the attempt to do themselves justice: they have been deficient in patience ra-
<423>ther than fidelity. Subjects who rise against their prince without cause, deserve severe punishment: yet, even in this case, on account of the number of the delinquents, clemency becomes a duty in the sovereign. Shall he depopulate a city, or desolate a province, in order to punish her rebellion? Any punishment, however just in itself, which embraces too great a number of persons, becomes an act of downright cruelty. Had the insurrection of the Netherlands against Spain been totally unwarrantable, universal detestation would still attend the memory of the duke of Alva,[72] who made it his boast that he had caused twenty thousand heads to be struck off by the hands of the common executioner. Let not his sanguinary imitators expect to justify their enormities by the plea of necessity. What prince ever suffered more outrageous in-

---

72. Don Fernando Álvarez de Toledo y Pimental, third duke of Alba, 1507–82, Spanish general and governor of the Spanish Netherlands (1567–73), named "the Iron Duke" by the Protestants for his cruelty.

dignities from his subjects than Henry the Great of France? Yet his victories were ever accompanied by an uniform clemency; and that excellent prince at length obtained the success he deserved: he gained a nation of faithful subjects; whereas the duke of Alva caused his master to lose the United Provinces. Crimes in which a number of persons are involved, are to be punished by penalties which shall equally fall on all the parties concerned: the sovereign may deprive a town of her privileges, at least till she has fully acknowledged her fault: as to corporal punishment, let that be reserved for the authors of the disturbances,—for those incendiaries who incite the people to revolt. But tyrants alone will treat, as seditious, those brave and resolute citizens who exhort the people to preserve themselves from oppression, and to vindicate their rights and privileges: a good prince will commend such virtuous patriots, provided their zeal be tempered with moderation and prudence. If he has justice and his duty at heart,—if he aspires to that immortal and unsullied glory of being the father of his people, let him mistrust the selfish suggestions of that minister who represents to him as rebels all those citizens who do not stretch out their necks to the yoke of slavery,—who refuse tamely to crouch under the rod of arbitrary power.

In many cases, the safest and at the same time the most just method of appeasing seditions is to give the people satisfaction. And if there existed no reasons to justify the insurrection (a circumstance which perhaps never happens), even in such case, it becomes necessary, as we have above observed, to grant an amnesty where the offenders are numerous. When the amnesty is once published and accepted, all the past must be buried in oblivion; nor must any one be called to account for what has been done during the disturbances: and in general, the sovereign, whose word ought ever to be sacred, is bound to the faithful observance of every promise he has made even to rebels,—I mean, to such of his subjects as have revolted without reason or necessity. If his promises are not inviolable, the rebels will have no security in treating with him: when they have once drawn <424> the sword, they must throw away the scabbard, as one of the ancients expresses it; and the prince, destitute of the more gentle and salutary means of appeasing the revolt, will have no other remaining expedient than that of utterly exterminating the insurgents.

§291. He is bound to perform the promises he has made to the rebels.

These will become formidable through despair; compassion will bestow succours on them; their party will increase, and the state will be in danger. What would have become of France, if the leaguers had thought it unsafe to rely on the promises of Henry the Great?[73] The same reasons which should render the faith of promises inviolable and sacred between individual and individual, between sovereign and sovereign, between enemy and enemy (Book II. §§163, 218, &c. and Book III. §174), subsist in all their force between the sovereign and his insurgent or rebellious subjects. However, if they have extorted from him odious conditions, which are inimical to the happiness of the nation or the welfare of the state,— as he has no right to do or grant any thing contrary to that grand rule of his conduct, which is at the same time the measure of his power, he may justly revoke any pernicious concessions which he has been obliged to make, provided the revocation be sanctioned by the consent of the nation, whose opinion he must take on the subject, in the manner and forms pointed out to him by the constitution of the state. But this remedy is to be used with great reserve, and only in matters of high importance, lest the faith of promises should be weakened and brought it into disrepute.*

§292. Civil war.   When a party is formed in a state, who no longer obey the sovereign, and are possessed of sufficient strength to oppose him,—or when, in a republic, the nation is divided into two opposite factions, and both sides take up arms,—this is called a *civil war.* Some writers confine this term to a just insurrection of the subjects against their sovereign, to distinguish that lawful resistance from *rebellion,* which is an open and unjust resistance. But what appellation will they give to a war which arises in a republic torn by two factions,—or in a monarchy, between two competitors for the crown? Custom appropriates the term of *"civil war"* to every war between the members of one and the same political society.

---

* An instance of this occurs in the transactions which took place after the insurrection at Madrid, in 1766. At the requisition of the cortes, the king [[Charles III, r. 1759–88]] revoked the concessions which he had been obliged to make to the insurgent populace: but he suffered the amnesty to remain in force. [[Note added in 1773/1797 editions.]]

73. Henry IV of France, r. 1589–1610.

If it be between part of the citizens on the one side, and the sovereign with those who continue in obedience to him on the other,—provided the malcontents have any reason for taking up arms, nothing further is required to entitle such disturbance to the name of *civil war,* and not that of *rebellion.* This latter term is applied only to such an insurrection against lawful authority, as is void of all appearance of justice. The sovereign indeed never fails to bestow the appellation of *rebels* on <425> all such of his subjects as openly resist him: but when the latter have acquired sufficient strength to give him effectual opposition, and to oblige him to carry on the war against them according to the established rules, he must necessarily submit to the use of the term "civil war."

It is foreign to our purpose in this place to weigh the reasons which may authorise and justify a civil war: we have elsewhere treated of the cases wherein subjects may resist the sovereign (Book I. Chap. IV.). Setting therefore, the justice of the cause wholly out of the question, it only remains for us to consider the maxims which ought to be observed in a civil war, and to examine whether the sovereign in particular is, on such an occasion, bound to conform to the established laws of war. §293. A civil war produces two independent parties.

A civil war breaks the bands of society and government, or at least suspends their force and effect: it produces in the nation two independent parties, who consider each other as enemies, and acknowledge no common judge. Those two parties, therefore, must necessarily be considered as thenceforward constituting, at least for a time, two separate bodies, two distinct societies. Though one of the parties may have been to blame in breaking the unity of the state and resisting the lawful authority, they are not the less divided in fact. Besides, who shall judge them? who shall pronounce on which side the right or the wrong lies? On earth they have no common superior. They stand therefore in precisely the same predicament as two nations, who engage in a contest, and, being unable to come to an agreement, have recourse to arms.

This being the case, it is very evident that the common laws of war,—those maxims of humanity, moderation, and honour, which we have already detailed in the course of this work,—ought to be observed by both parties in every civil war. For the same reasons which render the observance of those maxims a matter of obligation between state and §294. They are to observe the common laws of war.

state, it becomes equally and even more necessary in the unhappy circumstance of two incensed parties lacerating their common country. Should the sovereign conceive he has a right to hang up his prisoners as rebels, the opposite party will make reprisals:*—if he does not religiously observe the capitulations, and all other conventions made with his enemies, they will no longer rely on his word:—should he burn and ravage, they will follow his example; the war will become cruel, horrible, and every day more destructive <426> to the nation. The duke de Montpensier's[74] infamous and barbarous excesses against the reformed party in France are too well known: the men were delivered up to the executioner, and the women to the brutality of the soldiers. What was the consequence? the protestants became exasperated; they took vengeance of such inhuman practices; and the war, before sufficiently cruel as a civil and religious war, became more bloody and destructive. Who could without horror read of the savage cruelties committed by the baron Des Adrets?[75] By turns a catholic and a protestant, he distinguished himself by his barbarity on both sides. At length it became necessary to relinquish those pretensions to judicial authority over men who proved themselves capable of supporting their cause by force of arms, and to treat them, not as criminals, but as enemies. Even the troops have often refused to serve in a war wherein the prince exposed them to cruel reprisals. Officers who had the highest sense of honour, though ready to shed their blood in the field of battle for his service, have not thought it any part of their

---

* The prince of Condé [[Louis II de Bourbon, 1621–86]], commander of Louis XIII's forces against the reformed party, having hanged sixty-four officers whom he had made prisoners during the civil war, the protestants resolved upon retaliation; and the duke de Rohan, who commanded them, caused an equal number of catholic officers to be hanged. See Memoires de Rohan.

The duke of Alva made it a practice to condemn to death every prisoner he took from the confederates in the Netherlands. They, on their part, retaliated, and at length compelled him to respect the law of nations and the rules of war in his conduct towards them. Grotius, Ann. lib. ii. [[Note added in 1773/1797 editions.]]

74. François, Duc de Montpensier, 1542–92, fought for Henry IV of France in the 1580s and early 1590s.

75. François de Beaumont, Baron des Adrets, 1513–87, Huguenot leader during the Wars of Religion in France. He was notorious for his excessive violence, and for changing sides.

duty to run the hazard of an ignominious death. Whenever, therefore, a numerous body of men think they have a right to resist the sovereign, and feel themselves in a condition to appeal to the sword, the war ought to be carried on by the contending parties in the same manner as by two different nations; and they ought to leave open the same means for preventing its being carried to outrageous extremities, and for the restoration of peace.

When the sovereign has subdued the opposite party, and reduced them to submit and sue for peace, he may except from the amnesty the authors of the disturbances,—the heads of the party: he may bring them to a legal trial, and punish them, if they be found guilty. He may act in this manner particularly on occasion of those disturbances in which the interests of the people are not so much the object in view as the private aims of some powerful individuals, and which rather deserve the appellation of *revolt* than of *civil war*. Such was the case of the unfortunate duke of Montmorency:—he took up arms against the king,[76] in support of the duke of Orléans; and being defeated and taken prisoner at the battle of Castelnaudari,[77] he lost his life on a scaffold, by the sentence of the parliament of Toulouse. If he was generally pitied by all men of worth and sentiment, it was because they viewed him rather as an opponent to the exorbitant power of an imperious minister, than as a rebel against his sovereign,—and that his heroic virtues seemed to warrant the purity of his intentions.*

When subjects take up arms without ceasing to acknowledge the sovereign, and only for the purpose of obtaining a redress of their grievances, there are two reasons for observing the common laws of war towards them:—First, an apprehension lest the <427> civil war should become more cruel and destructive by the insurgents making retaliation, which, as we have already observed, they will not fail to do, in return for the severities exercised by the sovereign. 2. The danger of committing

§295. The effects of civil war distinguished according to cases.

* See the historians of the reign of Louis XIII. [[Le Vassor, Velly, Daniel, Mézeray.]]
76. King Louis XIII of France, r. 1610–43.
77. Louis XIII defeated the rebellion of his brother Gaston d'Orléans and Henri de Montmorency at Castelnaudary in September 1632.

great injustice by hastily punishing those who are accounted rebels. The flames of discord and civil war are not favourable to the proceedings of pure and sacred justice: more quiet times are to be waited for. It will be wise in the prince to keep his prisoners till, having restored tranquillity, he is able to bring them to a legal trial.

As to the other effects which the law of nations attributes to public war (See Chap. XII. of this Book), and particularly the acquisition of things taken in war,—subjects who take up arms against their sovereign without ceasing to acknowledge him, cannot lay claim to the benefit of those effects. The booty alone, the movable property carried off by the enemy, is considered as lost to the owners; but this is only on account of the difficulty of recognising it, and the numberless inconveniences which would arise from the attempt to recover it. All this is usually settled in the edict of pacification or the act of amnesty.

But when a nation becomes divided into two parties absolutely independent, and no longer acknowledging a common superior, the state is dissolved, and the war between the two parties stands on the same ground, in every respect, as a public war between two different nations. Whether a republic be split into two factions, each maintaining that it alone constitutes the body of the state,—or a kingdom be divided between two competitors for the crown,—the nation is severed into two parties who will mutually term each other rebels. Thus there exist in the state two separate bodies, who pretend to absolute independence, and between whom there is no judge (§293). They decide their quarrel by arms, as two different nations would do. The obligation to observe the common laws of war towards each other is therefore absolute,—indispensably binding on both parties, and the same which the law of nature imposes on all nations in transactions between state and state.

§296. Conduct to be observed by foreign nations.   Foreign nations are not to interfere in the internal government of an independent state (Book II. §54, &c.). It belongs not to them to judge between the citizens whom discord has roused to arms, nor between the prince and his subjects: both parties are equally foreigners to them, and equally independent of their authority. They may however interpose their good offices for the restoration of peace; and this the law of nature prescribes to them (Book II. Ch. I.). But if their mediation proves fruitless, such of them as are not bound by any treaty, may, with the view of regulating their own conduct, take the merits of the cause into consideration, and assist the party which they shall judge to have right on its side, in case that party requests their assistance or accepts the offer of it: they are equally at liberty, I say, to do <428> this, as to espouse the quarrel of one nation embarking in a war against another. As to the allies of the state thus distracted by civil war, they will find a rule for their conduct in the nature of their engagements, combined with the existing circumstances. Of this we have treated elsewhere. (See Book II. Chap. XII. and particularly §§196 and 197.) <429>

THE
LAW
OF
NATIONS

Of the Restoration of Peace;
and of Embassies

CHAPTER I

Of Peace, and the Obligation to cultivate it.

Peace is the reverse of war: it is that desirable state in which every one §1. What
quietly enjoys his rights, or, if controverted, amicably discusses them by peace is.
force of argument. Hobbs has had the boldness to assert that war is the
natural state of man. But if, by "the natural state of man," we understand
(as reason requires that we should) that state to which he is destined and
called by his nature, peace should rather be termed his natural state. For
it is the part of a rational being to terminate his differences by rational
methods; whereas it is the characteristic of the brute creation to decide
theirs by force.* Man, as we have already observed (Prelim. §10), alone

---

* Nam cum sint duo genera decertandi, unum per disceptationem, alterum per
vim,—cumque illud proprium sit hominis, hoc belluarum,—confugiendum est ad
posterius, si uti non licet superiore. [["For, since there are two ways of settling a
dispute: first, by discussion, second by physical force; and since the former is a char-

and destitute of succours, would necessarily be a very wretched creature. He stands in need of the intercourse and assistance of his species, in order to enjoy the sweets of life, to develop his faculties, and live in a manner suitable to his nature. Now, it is in peace alone that all these advantages are to be found: it is in peace that men respect, <430> assist, and love each other: nor would they ever depart from that happy state, if they were not hurried on by the impetuosity of their passions, and blinded by the gross deceptions of self-love. What little we have said of the effects of war will be sufficient to give some idea of its various calamities; and it is an unfortunate circumstance for the human race, that the injustice of unprincipled men should so often render it inevitable.

§2. Obligation of cultivating it.   Nations who are really impressed with sentiments of humanity,—who seriously attend to their duty, and are acquainted with their true and substantial interests,—will never seek to promote their own advantage at the expense and detriment of other nations: however intent they may be on their own happiness, they will ever be careful to combine it with that of others, and with justice and equity. Thus disposed, they will necessarily cultivate peace. If they do not live together in peace, how can they perform those mutual and sacred duties which nature enjoins them? And this state is found to be no less necessary to their happiness than to the discharge of their duties. Thus the law of nature every way obliges them to seek and cultivate peace. That divine law has no other end in view than the welfare of mankind: to that object all its rules and all its precepts tend: they are all deducible from this principle, that men should seek their own felicity; and morality is no more than the art of acquiring happiness. As this is true of individuals, it is equally so of nations, as must appear evident to any one who will but take the trouble of reflecting on what we have said of their common and reciprocal duties in the first chapter of the second book.

§3. The sovereign's obligation to it.   This obligation of cultivating peace binds the sovereign by a double tie. He owes this attention to his people, on whom war would pour a torrent of evils; and he owes it in the most strict and indispensable man-

---

acteristic of man, and the latter of the brute, we must resort to force only in case we may not avail ourselves of discussion."]] Cicero, de Offic. lib. i. cap. 2.

ner, since it is solely for the advantage and welfare of the nation that he is intrusted with the government (Book I. §39). He owes the same attention to foreign nations, whose happiness likewise is disturbed by war. The nation's duty in this respect has been shewn in the preceding chapter; and the sovereign, being invested with the public authority, is at the same time charged with all the duties of the society, or body of the nation (Book I. §41).

The nation or the sovereign ought not only to refrain, on their own part, from disturbing that peace which is so salutary to mankind: they are moreover bound to promote it as far as lies in their power,—to prevent others from breaking it without necessity, and to inspire them with the love of justice, equity, and public tranquillity,—in a word, with the love of peace. It is one of the best offices a sovereign can render to nations, and to the whole universe. What a glorious and amiable character is that of peace-maker! Were a powerful prince thoroughly acquainted with the advantages attending it,—were he to conceive what pure and effulgent glory he may derive from that endearing character, together with the gratitude, the love, the venera-<431>tion, and the confidence of nations,—did he know what it is to reign over the hearts of men,— he would wish thus to become the benefactor, the friend, the father of mankind; and in being so, he would find infinitely more delight than in the most splendid conquests. Augustus,[1] shutting the temple of Janus, giving peace to the universe, and adjusting the disputes of kings and nations,—Augustus, at that moment, appears the greatest of mortals, and, as it were, a god upon earth. §4. Extent of this duty.

But those disturbers of the public peace,—those scourges of the earth, who, fired by a lawless thirst of power, or impelled by the pride and ferocity of their disposition, snatch up arms without justice or reason, and sport with the quiet of mankind and the blood of their subjects,—those monstrous heroes, though almost deified by the foolish admiration of the vulgar, are in effect the most cruel enemies of the human race, and ought to be treated as such. Experience shews what a train of calamities war entails even upon nations that are not immedi- §5. Of the disturbers of the public peace.

1. Gaius Octavian, Emperor Augustus, r. 27 B.C.–A.D. 14.

ately engaged in it. War disturbs commerce, destroys the subsistence of mankind, raises the price of all the most necessary articles, spreads just alarms, and obliges all nations to be upon their guard, and to keep up an armed force. He, therefore, who without just cause breaks the general peace, unavoidably does an injury even to those nations which are not the objects of his arms; and by his pernicious example he essentially attacks the happiness and safety of every nation upon earth. He gives them a right to join in a general confederacy for the purpose of repressing and chastising him, and depriving him of a power which he so enormously abuses. What evils does he not bring on his own nation, lavishing her blood to gratify his inordinate passions, and exposing her to the resentment of a host of enemies! A famous minister of the last century[2] has justly merited the indignation of his country, by involving her in unjust or unnecessary wars. If by his abilities and indefatigable application he procured her distinguished successes in the field of battle, he drew on her, at least for a time, the execration of all Europe.

§6. How far war may be continued.

The love of peace should equally prevent us from embarking in a war without necessity, and from persevering in it after the necessity has ceased to exist. When a sovereign has been compelled to take up arms for just and important reasons, he may carry on the operations of war till he has attained its lawful end, which is, to procure justice and safety (Book III. §28).

If the cause be dubious, the just end of war can only be to bring the enemy to an equitable compromise (Book III. §38); and consequently the war must not be continued beyond that point. The moment our enemy proposes or consents to such compromise, it is our duty to desist from hostilities.

But if we have to do with a perfidious enemy, it would be imprudent to trust either his words or his oaths. In such case, justice allows and prudence requires that we should avail ourselves of a successful war, and follow up our advantages, till we < 432 > have humbled a dangerous and excessive power, or compelled the enemy to give us sufficient security for the time to come.

2. Cardinal Richelieu, chief minister (1624–42) to King Louis XIII of France.

Finally, if the enemy obstinately rejects equitable conditions, he himself forces us to continue our progress till we have obtained a complete and decisive victory, by which he is absolutely reduced and subjected. The use to be made of victory has been shewn above (Book III. Chap. VIII. IX. XIII.).

When one of the parties is reduced to sue for peace, or both are weary of the war, then thoughts of an accommodation are entertained, and the conditions are agreed on. Thus peace steps in, and puts a period to the war.

§7. Peace the end of war.

The general and necessary effects of peace are the reconciliation of enemies, and the cessation of hostilities on both sides. It restores the two nations to their natural state.

§8. General effects of peace.

CHAPTER II

Treaties of Peace.

When the belligerent powers have agreed to lay down their arms, the agreement or contract in which they stipulate the conditions of peace, and regulate the manner in which it is to be restored and supported, is called the *treaty of peace.*

§9. Definition of a treaty of peace.

The same power who has the right of making war, of determining on it, of declaring it, and of directing its operations, has naturally that likewise of making and concluding the treaty of peace. These two powers are connected together, and the latter naturally follows from the former. If the ruler of the state is empowered to judge of the causes and reasons for which war is to be undertaken,—of the time and circumstances proper for commencing it,—of the manner in which it is to be supported and carried on,—it is therefore his province also to set bounds to its progress, to point out the time when it shall be discontinued, and to conclude a peace. But this power does not necessarily include that of granting or accepting whatever conditions he pleases, with a view to peace. Though the state has intrusted to the prudence of her ruler the general care of determining on war and peace, yet she may have limited

§10. By whom it may be concluded.

his power in many particulars by the fundamental laws. Thus Francis the First, king of France, had the absolute disposal of war and peace: and yet the assembly of Cognac declared that he had no authority to alienate any part of the kingdom by a treaty of peace. (See Book I. §265.)

A nation that has the free disposal of her domestic affairs, and of the form of her government, may intrust a single person or an assembly with the power of making peace, although she has not given them that of making war. Of this we have an instance < 433 > in Sweden, where, since the death of Charles XII.[3] the king cannot declare war without the consent of the states assembled in diet; but he may make peace in conjunction with the senate. It is less dangerous for a nation to intrust her rulers with this latter power, than with the former. She may reasonably expect that they will not make peace till it suits with the interest of the state. But their passions, their own interest, their private views, too often influence their resolutions when there is question of undertaking a war. Besides, it must be a very disadvantageous peace indeed, that is not preferable to war; whereas, on the other hand, to exchange peace for war, is always very hazardous.

When a prince who is possessed only of limited authority has a power to make peace, as he cannot of himself grant whatever conditions he pleases, it is incumbent on those who wish to treat with him on sure grounds, to require that the treaty of peace be ratified by the nation, or by those who are empowered to perform the stipulations contained in it. If, for instance, any potentate, in negotiating a treaty of peace with Sweden, requires a defensive alliance or guaranty as the condition, this stipulation will not be valid, unless approved and accepted by the diet, who alone have the power of carrying it into effect. The kings of England are authorised to conclude treaties of peace and alliance; but they cannot, by those treaties, alienate any of the possessions of the crown without the consent of parliament. Neither can they, without the concurrence of that body, raise any money in the kingdom: wherefore, whenever they conclude any subsidiary treaty, it is their constant rule to

3. In 1718.

lay it before the parliament, in order that they may be certain of the concurrence of that assembly to enable them to make good their engagements. When the emperor Charles V. required of Francis the First, his prisoner, such conditions as that king could not grant without the consent of the nation, he should have detained him till the states-general of France had ratified the treaty of Madrid,[4] and Burgundy had acquiesced in it: thus he would not have lost the fruits of his victory by an oversight which appears very surprising in a prince of his abilities.

We shall not here repeat what we have said on a former occasion concerning the alienation of a part of the state (Book I. §§263, &c.), or of the whole state (ibid. §§68, &c.). We shall therefore content ourselves with observing, that, in case of a pressing necessity, such as is produced by the events of an unfortunate war, the alienations made by the prince in order to save the remainder of the state, are considered as approved and ratified by the mere silence of the nation, when she has not, in the form of her government, retained some easy and ordinary method of giving her express consent, and has lodged an absolute power in the prince's hands. The states-general are abolished in France by disuse and by the tacit consent of the nation. Whenever, therefore, that kingdom is reduced to any calamitous exigency, it belongs to the king alone to determine by <434> what sacrifices he may purchase peace: and his enemies will treat with him on a sure footing. It would be a vain plea on the part of the people, to say that it was only through fear they acquiesced in the abolition of the states-general. The fact is that they did acquiesce, and thereby suffered the king to acquire all the powers necessary for contracting with foreign states in the name of the nation. In every state there must necessarily be some power with which other nations may treat on secure grounds. A certain historian* says, that, "by the fundamental laws, the kings of France cannot, to the prejudice of their successors, renounce any of their rights, by any treaty, whether voluntary or compulsory." The fundamental laws may indeed with-hold from the king the power of

§11. Alienations made by a treaty of peace.

---

* The abbé de Choisy, Hist. de Charles V. p. 492.
4. King Francis I of France (r. 1515–47) signed the Treaty of Madrid in 1526.

alienating, without the nation's consent, what belongs to the state; but they cannot invalidate an alienation or renunciation made with that consent.* And if the nation has permitted matters to proceed to such lengths that she now has no longer any means of expressly declaring her consent, her silence alone, on such occasions, is in reality a tacit consent. Otherwise there would be no possibility of treating on sure grounds with such a state: and her pretending thus beforehand to invalidate all future treaties, would be an infringement of the law of nations, which ordains that all states should retain the means of treating with each other (Book I. §262), and should observe their treaties (Book II. §§163, 269, &c.).

It is to be observed, however, that, in our examination whether the consent of the nation be requisite for alienating any part of the state, we mean such parts as are still in the nation's possession, and not those which have fallen into the enemy's hands during the course of the war: for, as these latter are no longer possessed by the nation, it is the sovereign alone, if invested with the full and absolute administration of the government, and with the power of making war and peace,—it is he alone, I say, who is to judge whether it be expedient to relinquish those parts of the state, or to continue the war for the recovery of them. And even though it should be pretended that he cannot by his own single authority make any valid alienation of them,—he has, nevertheless, according to our supposition, that is, if invested with full and absolute power,—he has, I say, a right to promise that the nation shall never again take up arms for the recovery of those lands, towns, or provinces, which he relinquishes: and this suffices for securing the quiet possession of them to the enemy into whose hands they are fallen. <435>

---

* The renunciation made by Anne of Austria, consort of Louis the Thirteenth, was good and valid, because it was confirmed by the general assembly of the cortes, and registered in all the offices. The case was otherwise with that made by Maria Theresa, which was not sanctioned by those formalities,—consequently, not stamped with the national approbation, and the character of a law of the state. The cardinals who examined this affair by order of the pope, whom Charles II. had consulted, paid no regard to Maria Theresa's renunciation, as not deeming it of sufficient force to invalidate the laws of the country, and to supersede the established custom. Memoirs of M. de St. Philippe [[San Felipe]], vol. i. p. 29. [[Note added in 1773/1797 editions.]]

The necessity of making peace authorises the sovereign to dispose of the property of individuals; and the eminent *domain* gives him a right to do it (Book I. §244). He may even, to a certain degree, dispose of their persons, by virtue of the power which he has over all his subjects. But as it is for the public advantage that he thus disposes of them, the state is bound to indemnify the citizens who are sufferers by the transaction (ibid.).

§12. How the sovereign may in a treaty dispose of what concerns individuals.

Every impediment by which the prince is disabled from administering the affairs of government, undoubtedly deprives him of the power of making peace. Thus a king cannot make a treaty of peace during his minority, or while in a state of mental derangement: this assertion does not stand in need of any proof: but the question is, whether a king can conclude a peace while he is a prisoner of war, and whether the treaty thus made be valid? Some celebrated authors* here draw a distinction between a monarch whose kingdom is patrimonial, and another who has only the *usufructus* of his dominions. We think we have over-thrown that false and dangerous idea of a patrimonial kingdom (Book I. §§68, &c.), and evidently shewn that the notion ought not to be extended beyond the bare power with which a sovereign is sometimes intrusted, of nominating his successor, of appointing a new prince to rule over the state, and dismembering some parts of it, if he thinks it expedient;— the whole, however, to be uniformly done for the good of the nation, and with a view to her greater advantage. Every legitimate government, whatever it be, is established solely for the good and welfare of the state. This incontestable principle being once laid down, the making of peace is no longer the peculiar province of the king; it belongs to the nation. Now it is certain that a captive prince cannot administer the government, or attend to the management of public affairs. How shall he who is not free command a nation? How can he govern it in such manner as best to promote the advantage of the people, and the public welfare? He does not indeed forfeit his rights; but his captivity deprives him of the power of exercising them, as he is not in a condition to direct the use of them to its proper and legitimate end. He stands in the same predic-

§13. Whether a king, being a prisoner of war, can make peace.

* See Wolf, Jus Gent. §982.

ament as a king in his minority, or labouring under a derangement of his mental faculties. In such circumstances, it is necessary that the person or persons whom the laws of the state designate for the regency, should assume the reins of government. To them it belongs to treat of peace, to settle the terms on which it shall be made, and to bring it to a conclusion, in conformity to the laws.

The captive sovereign may himself negotiate the peace, and promise what personally depends on him: but the treaty does not become obligatory on the nation till ratified by herself, or by those who are invested with the public authority during the <436> prince's captivity, or, finally, by the sovereign himself after his release.

But, if it is a duty incumbent on the state to use her best efforts for procuring the release of the most inconsiderable of her citizens who has lost his liberty in the public cause, the obligation is much stronger in the case of her sovereign, whose cares, attention, and labours, are devoted to the common safety and welfare. It was in fighting for his people, that the prince who has been made prisoner, fell into that situation, which, to a person of his exalted rank, must be wretched in the extreme: and shall that very people hesitate to deliver him at the expense of the greatest sacrifices? On so melancholy an occasion, they should not demur at any thing short of the very existence of the state. But, in every exigency, the safety of the people is the supreme law; and, in so severe an extremity, a generous prince will imitate the example of Regulus. That heroic citizen, being sent back to Rome on his parole, dissuaded the Romans from purchasing his release by an inglorious treaty, though he was not ignorant of the tortures prepared for him by the cruelty of the Carthaginians.*

§14. Whether peace can be made with a usurper. When an unjust conqueror, or any other usurper, has invaded the kingdom, he becomes possessed of all the powers of government when once the people have submitted to him, and, by a voluntary homage, acknowledged him as their sovereign. Other states, as having no right to intermeddle with the domestic concerns of that nation, or to interfere in her government, are bound to abide by her decision, and to look no

---

* See Tit. Liv. epitom. lib. xviii and other historians.

farther than the circumstance of actual possession. They may therefore broach and conclude a treaty of peace with the usurper. They do not thereby infringe the right of the lawful sovereign:—it is not their business to examine and judge of that right: they leave it as it is, and only look to the possession, in all the affairs they have to transact with that kingdom, pursuant to their own rights and those of the nation whose sovereignty is contested. But this rule does not preclude them from espousing the quarrel of the dethroned monarch, and assisting him, if he appears to have justice on his side: they then declare themselves enemies of the nation which has acknowledged his rival, as, when two different states are at war, they are at liberty to assist either party whose pretensions appear to be best founded.

The principal in the war, the sovereign in whose name it has been carried on, cannot justly make a peace without including his allies,—I mean those who have given him assistance without directly taking part in the war. This precaution is necessary in order to secure them from the resentment of the enemy: for though the latter has no right to take offence against his adversary's allies, whose engagements were purely of a defensive nature, and who have done nothing more than faithfully execute their <437> treaties (Book III. §101)—yet it too frequently happens that the conduct of men is influenced by their passions rather than by justice and reason. If the alliance was not of prior date to the commencement of the war, and was formed with a view to that very war,—although these new allies do not engage in the contest with all their force, nor directly as principals, they nevertheless give to the prince against whom they have joined, just cause to treat them as enemies. The sovereign, therefore, whom they have assisted, must not omit including them in the peace.

§15. Allies included in the treaty of peace.

But the treaty concluded by the principal is no farther obligatory on his allies than as they are willing to accede to it, unless they have given him full power to treat for them. By including them in his treaty, he only acquires a right, with respect to his reconciled enemy, of insisting that he shall not attack those allies on account of the succours they have furnished against him,—that he shall not molest them, but shall live in peace with them as if nothing had happened.

§16. Associates to treat, each for himself.

Sovereigns who have associated in a war,—all those who have directly taken part in it,—are respectively to make their treaties of peace, each for himself. Such was the mode adopted at Nimeguen, at Ryswick, and at Utrecht.[5] But the alliance obliges them to treat in concert. To determine in what cases an associate may detach himself from the alliance, and make a separate peace, is a question which we have examined in treating of associations in war (Book III. Chap. VI.), and of alliances in general (Book II. Chap. XII. and XV.).

§17. Mediation.

It frequently happens that two nations, though equally tired of the war, do nevertheless continue it merely from a fear of making the first advances to an accommodation, as these might be imputed to weakness; or they persist in it from animosity, and contrary to their real interests. On such occasions, some common friends of the parties effectually interpose by offering themselves as mediators. There cannot be a more beneficent office, and more becoming a great prince, than that of reconciling two nations at war, and thus putting a stop to the effusion of human blood: it is the indispensable duty of those who have the means of performing it with success. This is the only reflection we shall here make on a subject we have already discussed (Book II. §328).

§18. On what footing peace may be concluded.

A treaty of peace can be no more than a compromise. Were the rules of strict and rigid justice to be observed in it, so that each party should precisely receive every thing to which he has a just title, it would be impossible ever to make a peace. First, with regard to the very subject which occasioned the war, one of the parties would be under a necessity of acknowledging himself in the wrong, and condemning his own unjust pretensions; which he will hardly do, unless reduced to the last extremity. But if he owns the injustice of his cause, he must at the same time condemn every measure he has pursued in support of it: he must restore what he has unjustly taken, must reimburse the expenses of the war, and repair the damages. And how can a just <438> estimate of all the damages be formed? What price can be set on all the blood that has been shed, the loss of such a number of citizens, and the ruin of families? Nor is this all. Strict justice would further demand, that the author of

5. Nimeguen, 1678–79; Ryswick, 1697; Utrecht, 1713.

an unjust war should suffer a penalty proportioned to the injuries for which he owes satisfaction, and such as might ensure the future safety of him whom he has attacked. How shall the nature of that penalty be determined, and the degree of it be precisely regulated? In fine, even he who had justice on his side, may have transgressed the bounds of justifiable self-defence, and been guilty of improper excesses in the prosecution of a war whose object was originally lawful: here then are so many wrongs, of which strict justice would demand reparation. He may have made conquests and taken booty beyond the value of his claim. Who shall make an exact calculation, a just estimate of this? Since, therefore, it would be dreadful to perpetuate the war, or to pursue it to the utter ruin of one of the parties,—and since, however just the cause in which we are engaged, we must at length turn our thoughts towards the restoration of peace, and ought to direct all our measures to the attainment of that salutary object,—no other expedient remains than that of coming to a compromise respecting all claims and grievances on both sides, and putting an end to all disputes, by a convention as fair and equitable as circumstances will admit of. In such convention no decision is pronounced on the original cause of the war, or on those controversies to which the various acts of hostility might give rise; nor is either of the parties condemned as unjust,—a condemnation to which few princes would submit;—but, a simple agreement is formed, which determines what equivalent each party shall receive in extinction of all his pretensions.

The effect of the treaty of peace is to put an end to the war, and to abolish the subject of it. It leaves the contracting parties no right to commit any acts of hostility on account either of the subject itself which had given rise to the war, or of any thing that was done during its continuance: wherefore they cannot lawfully take up arms again for the same subject. Accordingly, in such treaties, the contracting parties reciprocally engage to preserve *perpetual peace:* which is not to be understood as if they promised never to make war on each other for any cause whatever. The peace in question relates to the war which it terminates: and it is in reality perpetual, inasmuch as it does not allow them to revive the same war by taking up arms again for the same subject which had originally given birth to it.

§19. General effect of the treaty of peace.

A special compromise, however, only extinguishes the particular means to which it relates, and does not preclude any subsequent pretensions to the object itself, on other grounds. Care is therefore usually taken to require a general compromise, which shall embrace not only the existing controversy, but the very thing itself which is the subject of that controversy: stipulation is made for a general renunciation of all pretensions what-< 439 >ever to the thing in question: and thus, although the party renouncing might in the sequel be able to demonstrate by new reasons that the thing did really belong to him, his claim would not be admitted.

§20. Amnesty.   An amnesty is a perfect oblivion of the past; and the end of peace being to extinguish all subjects of discord, this should be the leading article of the treaty: and accordingly, such is at present the constant practice. But though the treaty should be wholly silent on this head, the amnesty, by the very nature of peace, is necessarily implied in it.

§21. Things not mentioned in the treaty.   As each of the belligerent powers maintains that he has justice on his side,—and as their pretensions are not liable to be judged by others (Book III. §188)—whatever state things happen to be in at the time of the treaty, is to be considered as their legitimate state; and if the parties intend to make any change in it, they must expressly specify it in the treaty. Consequently all things not mentioned in the treaty are to remain on the same footing on which they stand at the period when it is concluded. This is also a consequence of the promised amnesty. All damages caused during the war are likewise buried in oblivion; and no action can be brought for those of which the treaty does not stipulate the reparation: they are considered as having never happened.

§22. Things not included in the compromise or amnesty.   But the effect of the compromise or amnesty cannot be extended to things which have no relation to the war that is terminated by the treaty. Thus, claims founded on a debt, or on an injury which had been done prior to the war, but which made no part of the reasons for undertaking it, still stand on their former footing, and are not abolished by the treaty, unless it be expressly extended to the extinction of every claim whatever. The case is the same with debts contracted during the war, but for causes which have no relation to it,—or with injuries done during its continuance, but which have no connection with the state of warfare.

Debts contracted with individuals, or injuries which they may have received from any other quarter, without relation to the war, are likewise not abolished by the compromise and amnesty, as these solely relate to their own particular object,—that is to say, to the war, its causes, and its effects. Thus, if two subjects of the belligerent powers make a contract together in a neutral country,—or if the one there receives an injury from the other,—the performance of the contract, or the reparation of the injury and damage, may be prosecuted after the conclusion of the treaty of peace.

Finally, if the treaty expresses that all things shall be restored to the state in which they were before the war, this clause is understood to relate only to immovable possessions, and cannot be extended to movables, or booty, which immediately becomes the property of the captors, and is looked on as relinquished by the former owners on account of the difficulty of recognising it, and the little hope they entertain of ever recovering it. <440>

When the last-made treaty mentions and confirms other treaties of prior date, these constitute a part of the new one, no less than if they were literally transcribed and included in it: and any new articles relating to former conventions are to be interpreted according to the rules which we have laid down in a preceding part of this work (Book II. Chap. XVII. and particularly §286). §23. Former treaties, mentioned and confirmed in the new, are a part of it.

CHAPTER III

Of the Execution of the Treaty of Peace.

A treaty of peace becomes obligatory on the contracting parties from the moment of its conclusion,—the moment it has passed through all the necessary forms; and they are bound to have it carried into execution without delay.* From that instant all hostilities must cease, unless a par- §24. When the obligation of the treaty commences.

---

* It is an essential point, to neglect none of the formalities which can ensure the execution of the treaty, and prevent new disputes. Accordingly, care must be taken to have it duly recorded in all the proper offices and courts. M. Van Beuningen,

ticular day has been specified for the commencement of the peace. But this treaty does not bind the subjects until it is duly notified to them. The case is the same in this instance, as in that of a truce (Book II. §239). If it should happen that military men, acting within the extent of their functions and pursuant to the rules of their duty, commit any acts of hostility before they have authentic information of the treaty of peace, it is a misfortune, for which they are not punishable: but the sovereign, on whom the treaty of peace is already obligatory, is bound to order and enforce the restitution of all captures made subsequent to its conclusion: he has no right whatever to retain them.

§25. Publica-
tion of the
peace.

And in order to prevent those unhappy accidents, by which many innocent persons may lose their lives, public notice of the peace is to be given without delay, at least to the troops. But at present, as the body of the people cannot of themselves undertake any act of hostility, and do not personally engage in the war, the solemn proclamation of the peace may be deferred, provided that care be taken to put a stop to all hostilities; which is easily done by means of the generals who direct the operations, or by proclaiming an armistice at the head of the armies. The peace of 1735, between the emperor and France,[6] was not <441> proclaimed till long after. The proclamation was postponed till the treaty was digested at leisure,—the most important points having been already adjusted in the preliminaries. The publication of the peace replaces the two nations in the state they were in before the war. It again opens a free

---

writing to the Grand Pensionary De Witt in 1662, thus observes—"The articles and conditions of this alliance contain various matters of different natures, the majority of which fall under the cognisance of the privy council,—several, under that of the admiralty,—others, under that of the civil tribunals, the parliaments, &c.—escheatage, for instance, which comes under the cognisance of the chambre des comptes [*exchequer*]. Thus the treaty must be recorded in all those different places." This advice was followed; and the states general required that the treaty concluded the same year should be recorded in all the parliaments of the kingdom. See the king's reply on this subject, in his letter to the count D'Estrades, page 399. [[Note added in 1773/1797 editions.]]

6. Louis XV of France supported Stanislaw Leszczyński's compaign to return to the Polish throne, inaugurating the War of the Polish Succession (1733–38) against Emperor Charles VI and Russia.

intercourse between them, and reinstates the subjects on both sides in the enjoyment of those mutual privileges which the state of war had suspended. On the publication, the treaty becomes a law to the subjects; and they are thenceforward bound to conform to the regulations stipulated therein. If, for instance, the treaty imports that one of the two nations shall abstain from a particular branch of commerce, every subject of that nation, from the time of the treaty's being made public, is obliged to renounce that commerce.

When no particular time has been assigned for the execution of the treaty, and the performance of the several articles, common sense dictates that every point should be carried into effect as soon as possible: and it was, no doubt, in this light that the contracting parties understood the matter. The faith of treaties equally forbids all neglect, tardiness, and studied delays, in the execution of them. §26. Time of the execution.

But in this affair, as in every other, a legitimate excuse, founded on a real and insurmountable obstacle, is to be admitted; for nobody is bound to perform impossibilities. The obstacle, when it does not arise from any fault on the side of the promising party, vacates a promise which cannot be made good by an equivalent, and of which the performance cannot be deferred to another time. If the promise can be fulfilled on another occasion, a suitable prolongation of the term must be allowed. Suppose one of the contracting nations has, by the treaty of peace, promised the other a body of auxiliary troops: she will not be bound to furnish them, if she happen to stand in urgent need of them for her own defence. Suppose she has promised a certain yearly quantity of corn: it cannot be demanded at a time when she herself labours under a scarcity of provisions: but, on the return of plenty, she is bound to make good the quantity in arrear, if required. §27. A lawful excuse to be admitted.

It is further held as a maxim, that the promiser is absolved from his promise, when, after he has made his preparations for performing it according to the tenor of his engagement, he is prevented from fulfilling it, by the party himself to whom it was made. The promisee is deemed to dispense with the fulfilment of a promise, of which he himself obstructs the execution. Let us therefore add, that if he who had promised a thing by a treaty of peace, was ready to perform it at the time agreed §28. The promise is void when the party to whom it was made, has himself hindered the performance of it.

on, or immediately and at a proper time if there was no fixed term,—
and the other party would not admit of it, the promiser is discharged
from his promise: for the promisee, not having reserved to himself a right
to regulate the performance of it at his own pleasure, is accounted to
renounce it by not accepting of it <442> in proper season and at the
time for which the promise was made. Should he desire that the performance be deferred till another time, the promiser is in honour bound
to consent to the prolongation, unless he can shew, by very good reasons,
that the promise would then become more inconvenient to him.

§29. Cessation of contributions.

To levy contributions is an act of hostility which ought to cease as
soon as peace is concluded (§24). Those which are already promised, but
not yet paid, are a debt actually due; and, as such, the payment may be
insisted on. But, in order to obviate all difficulty, it is proper that the
contracting parties should clearly and minutely explain their intentions
respecting matters of this nature: and they are generally careful to do so.

§30. Products of the thing restored or ceded.

The fruits and profits of those things which are restored by a treaty
of peace are due from the instant appointed for carrying it into execution: and if no particular period has been assigned, they are due from
the moment when the restitution of the things themselves was agreed
to: but those which were already received or become payable before the
conclusion of the peace, are not comprised in the restitution; for the
fruits and profits belong to the owner of the soil; and, in the case in
question, possession is accounted a lawful title. For the same reason, in
making a cession of the soil, we do not include in that cession the rents
and profits antecedently due. This Augustus justly maintained against
Sextus Pompey,[7] who, on receiving a grant of the Peloponnesus, claimed
the imposts of the preceding years.*

§31. In what condition things are to be restored.

Those things, of which the restitution is, without further explanation,
simply stipulated in the treaty of peace, are to be restored in the same
state in which they were when taken: for the word "restitution" naturally

* Appian. de Bell. Civ. lib. v. quoted by Grotius, lib. ii. cap. 20, §22 [[*Law of War
and Peace*]].

7. Sextus Pompey, also known as Magnus Pius, the youngest son of Pompey the
Great, led the opposition to the Second Triumvirate of Octavian, Marc Antony, and
Lepidus, before being executed without trial in 35 B.C.

implies that every thing should be replaced in its former condition. Thus, the restitution of a thing is to be accompanied with that of all the rights which were annexed to it when taken. But this rule must not be extended to comprise those changes which may have been the natural consequences and effects of the war itself, and of its operations. A town is to be restored in the condition it was in when taken, as far as it still remains in that condition, at the conclusion of the peace. But if the town has been rased or dismantled during the war, that damage was done by the right of arms, and is buried in oblivion by the act of amnesty. We are under no obligation to repair the ravages that have been committed in a country which we restore at the peace: we restore it in its existing state. But, as it would be a flagrant perfidy to ravage that country after the conclusion of the peace, the case is the same with respect to a town whose fortifications have escaped the devastation of war: to dismantle it previous to the restoration, would be a violation of good-faith and honour. If the captor has repaired the breaches, and put the place in the same state it was in before the siege, he is bound to restore it in <443> that state. If he has added any new works, he may indeed demolish these: but if he has razed the ancient fortifications, and constructed others on a new plan, it will be necessary to come to a particular agreement respecting this improvement, or accurately to define in what condition the place shall be restored. Indeed this last precaution should in every case be adopted, in order to obviate all dispute and difficulty. In drawing up an instrument solely intended for the restoration of peace, it should be the object of the parties to leave, if possible, no ambiguity whatever,— nothing which may have a tendency to rekindle the flames of war. I am well aware, however, that this is not the practice of those who value themselves now-a-days on their superior abilities in negotiation: on the contrary, they study to introduce obscure or ambiguous clauses into a treaty of peace, in order to furnish their sovereign with a pretext for broaching a new quarrel, and taking up arms again on the first favourable opportunity. How contrary such pitiful finesse is to the faith of treaties, we have already observed (Book II. §231): it is a disparagement of that candour and magnanimity which should beam forth in all the actions of a great prince.

§32. The interpretation of a treaty of peace is to be against the superior party.

But, as it is extremely difficult wholly to avoid ambiguity in a treaty, though worded with the greatest care and the most honourable intentions,—and to obviate every doubt which may arise in the application of its several clauses to particular cases,—recourse must often be had to the rules of interpretation. We have already devoted an entire chapter to the exposition of those important rules:* wherefore, instead of entering at present into tedious repetitions, we shall confine ourselves to a few rules more particularly adapted to the special case before us,—the interpretation of treaties of peace. 1. In case of doubt, the interpretation goes against him who prescribed the terms of the treaty: for as it was in some measure dictated by him, it was his own fault if he neglected to express himself more clearly: and by extending or restricting the signification of the expressions to that meaning which is least favourable to him, we either do him no injury, or we only do him that to which he has wilfully exposed himself; whereas, by adopting a contrary mode of interpretation, we would incur the risk of converting vague or ambiguous terms into so many snares to entrap the weaker party in the contract, who has been obliged to subscribe to what the stronger had dictated.

§33. Names of ceded countries.

2. The names of countries ceded by treaty are to be understood according to the usage prevailing at the time among skilful and intelligent men: for it is not to be presumed that weak or ignorant persons should be intrusted with so important a concern as that of concluding a treaty of peace; and the articles of a contract are to be understood of what the contracting parties most probably had in contemplation, since the object in contemplation is the motive and ground of every contract. <444>

§34. Restoration not to be understood of those who have voluntarily given themselves up.

3. The treaty of peace naturally and of itself relates only to the war which it terminates. It is, therefore, in such relation only, that its vague clauses are to be understood. Thus the simple stipulation of restoring things to their former condition does not relate to changes which have not been occasioned by the war itself: consequently this general clause cannot oblige either of the parties to set at liberty a free people who have voluntarily given themselves up to him during the war. And as a people,

* Book II. Chap. XVII.

when abandoned by their sovereign, become free, and may provide for their own safety in whatever manner they think most advisable (Book I. §202)—if such people, during the course of the war, have voluntarily, and without military compulsion, submitted and given themselves up to the enemy of their former sovereign, the general promise of restoring conquests shall not extend to them. It were an unavailing plea, to allege that the party who requires all things to be replaced on their former footing, may have an interest in the independence of the former of those people, and that he evidently has a very great one in the restoration of the latter. If he wished to obtain things which the general clause does not of itself comprise, he should have clearly and specifically expressed his intentions relative to them. Stipulations of every kind may be inserted in a treaty of peace: but if they bear no relation to the war which it is the view of the contracting parties to bring to a conclusion, they must be very expressly specified; for the treaty is naturally understood to relate only to its own particular object.

CHAPTER IV

Of the Observance and Breach of the Treaty of Peace.

The treaty of peace concluded by a lawful power is undoubtedly a public treaty, and obligatory on the whole nation (Book II. §154). It is likewise, by its nature, a real treaty; for if its duration had been limited to the life of the sovereign, it would be only a truce, and not a treaty of peace. Besides, every treaty which, like this, is made with a view to the public good, is a real treaty (Book II. §198). It is therefore as strongly binding on the successors as on the prince himself who signed it, since it binds the state itself, and the successors can never have, in this respect, any other rights than those of the state.

§35. The treaty of peace binds the nation and successors.

After all we have said on the faith of treaties and the indispensable obligation which they impose, it would be superfluous to use many words in shewing how religiously treaties of peace in particular should be observed both by sovereigns and people. These treaties concern and

§36. It is to be faithfully observed.

bind whole nations; they are of the highest importance; the breach of them infallibly rekindles the <445> flames of war;—all which considerations give additional force to the obligation of keeping our faith, and punctually fulfilling our promises.

§37. The plea of fear or force does not dispense with the observance.

We cannot claim a dispensation from the observance of a treaty of peace, by alleging that it was extorted from us by fear, or wrested from us by force. In the first place, were this plea admitted, it would destroy, from the very foundations, all the security of treaties of peace; for there are few treaties of that kind, which might not be made to afford such a pretext, as a cloak for the faithless violation of them. To authorise such an evasion, would be a direct attack on the common safety and welfare of nations:—the maxim would be detestable, for the same reasons which have universally established the sacredness of treaties (Book II. §220). Besides it would generally be disgraceful and ridiculous to advance such a plea. At the present day, it seldom happens that either of the belligerent parties perseveres to the last extremity before he will consent to a peace. Though a nation may have lost several battles, she can still defend herself: as long as she has men and arms remaining, she is not destitute of all resource. If she thinks fit, by a disadvantageous treaty, to procure a necessary peace,—if by great sacrifices she delivers herself from imminent danger or total ruin,—the residue which remains in her possession is still an advantage for which she is indebted to the peace: it was her own free choice to prefer a certain and immediate loss, but of limited extent, to an evil of a more dreadful nature, which, though yet at some distance, she had but too great reason to apprehend.

If ever the plea of constraint may be alleged, it is against an act which does not deserve the name of a treaty of peace,—against a forced submission to conditions which are equally offensive to justice and to all the duties of humanity. If an unjust and rapacious conqueror subdues a nation, and forces her to accept of hard, ignominious, and insupportable conditions, necessity obliges her to submit: but this apparent tranquillity is not a peace; it is an oppression which she endures only so long as she wants the means of shaking it off, and against which men of spirit rise on the first favourable opportunity. When Ferdinand Cortes[8] attacked

8. Hernando Cortés, 1485–1547, conqueror of the Aztec empire from 1519.

the empire of Mexico without any shadow of reason, without even a plausible pretext,—if the unfortunate Montezuma[9] could have recovered his liberty by submitting to the iniquitous and cruel conditions of receiving Spanish garrisons into his towns and his capital, of paying an immense tribute, and obeying the commands of the king of Spain,— will any man pretend to assert that he would not have been justifiable in seizing a convenient opportunity to recover his rights, to emancipate his people, and to expel or exterminate the Spanish horde of greedy, insolent, and cruel usurpers? No! such a monstrous absurdity can never be seriously maintained. Although the law of nature aims at protecting the safety and peace of nations by enjoining the faithful observance of promises, it does not <446> favour oppressors. All its maxims tend to promote the advantage of mankind: that is the great end of all laws and rights. Shall he, who with his own hand tears asunder all the bonds of human society, be afterwards allowed to claim the benefit of them? Even though it were to happen that this maxim should be abused, and that a nation should, on the strength of it, unjustly rise in arms and recommence hostilities,—still it is better to risk that inconvenience than to furnish usurpers with an easy mode of perpetuating their injustice, and establishing their usurpation on a permanent basis. Besides, were you to preach up the contrary doctrine which is so repugnant to all the feelings and suggestions of nature, where could you expect to make proselytes?

Equitable agreements, therefore, or at least such as are supportable, are alone entitled to the appellation of treaties of peace: these are the treaties which bind the public faith, and which are punctually to be observed, though in some respects harsh and burthensome. Since the nation consented to them, she must have considered them as in some measure advantageous under the then existing circumstances; and she is bound to respect her promise. Were men allowed to rescind at a subsequent period those agreements to which they were glad to subscribe on a former occasion, there would be an end to all stability in human affairs.

§38. How many ways a treaty of peace may be broken.

9. Montezuma, 1466–1520, Aztec emperor defeated by Cortés in the battle of Tenochtitlán in 1520.

The breach of a treaty of peace consists in violating the engagements annexed to it, either by doing what it prohibits, or by not doing what it prescribes. Now the engagements contracted by treaty may be violated in three different ways,—either by a conduct that is repugnant to the nature and essence of every treaty of peace in general,—by proceedings which are incompatible with the particular nature of the treaty in question,—or, finally, by the violation of any article expressly contained in it.

§39. By a conduct contrary to the nature of every treaty of peace.

First, a nation acts in a manner that is repugnant to the nature and essence of every treaty of peace, and to peace itself, when she disturbs it without cause, either by taking up arms and recommencing hostilities without so much as a plausible pretext, or by deliberately and wantonly offending the party with whom she has concluded a peace, and offering such treatment to him or his subjects, as is incompatible with the state of peace, and such as he cannot submit to, without being deficient in the duty which he owes to himself. It is likewise acting contrary to the nature of all treaties of peace to take up arms a second time for the same subject that had given rise to the war which has been brought to a conclusion, or through resentment of any transaction that had taken place during the continuance of hostilities. If she cannot allege at least some plausible pretext borrowed from a fresh cause, which may serve to palliate her conduct, she evidently revives the old war that was extinct, and breaks the treaty of peace.

§40. To take up arms for a fresh cause is no breach of the treaty of peace.

But to take up arms for a fresh cause is no breach of the treaty of peace: for, though a nation has promised to live in peace, she has not therefore promised to submit to injuries and wrongs <447> of every kind, rather than procure justice by force of arms. The rupture proceeds from him who, by his obstinate injustice, renders this method necessary.

But here it is proper to recall to mind what we have more than once observed,—namely, that nations acknowledge no common judge on earth,—that they cannot mutually condemn each other without appeal,—and, finally, that they are bound to act in their quarrels as if each was equally in the right. On this footing, whether the new cause which gives birth to hostilities be just or not, neither he who makes it a handle for taking up arms, nor he who refuses satisfaction, is reputed to break the treaty of peace, provided the cause of complaint on the one hand,

and the refusal of satisfaction on the other, have at least some colour of reason, so as to render the question doubtful. When nations cannot come to any agreement on questions of this kind, their only remaining resource is an appeal to the sword. In such case the war is absolutely a new one, and does not involve any infraction of the existing treaty.

And as a nation, in making a peace, does not thereby give up her right of contracting alliances and assisting her friends, it is likewise no breach of the treaty of peace, to form a subsequent alliance with the enemies of the party with whom she has concluded such treaty,—to join them, to espouse their quarrel, and unite her arms with theirs,—unless the treaty expressly prohibits such connections. At most she can only be said to embark in a fresh war in defence of another people's cause.

§41. A subsequent alliance with an enemy is likewise no breach of the treaty.

But I here suppose these new allies to have some plausible grounds for taking up arms, and that the nation in question has just and substantial reasons for supporting them in the contest. Otherwise, to unite with them just as they are entering on the war or when they have already commenced hostilities, would be evidently seeking a pretext to elude the treaty of peace, and no better, in fact, than an artful and perfidious violation of it.

It is of great importance to draw a proper distinction between a new war and the breach of an existing treaty of peace, because the rights acquired by such treaty still subsist notwithstanding the new war; whereas they are annulled by the rupture of the treaty on which they were founded. It is true, indeed, that the party who had granted those rights, does not fail to obstruct the exercise of them during the course of the war, as far as lies in his power,—and even may, by the right of arms, wholly deprive his enemy of them, as well as he may wrest from him his other possessions. But in that case he with-holds those rights as things taken from the enemy, who, on a new treaty of peace, may urge the restitution of them. In negotiations of that kind, there is a material difference between demanding the restitution of what we were possessed of before the war, and requiring new concessions: a little equality in our successes entitles us to insist on the former, whereas nothing less than a decided superiority can give us a claim to the latter. It often happens, when nearly equal success <448> has attended the arms of both parties,

§42. Why a distinction is to be made between a new war and a breach of the treaty.

that the belligerent powers agree mutually to restore their conquests, and to replace every thing in its former state. When this is the case, if the war in which they were engaged was a new one, the former treaties still subsist: but if those treaties were broken by taking up arms a second time for the same subject, and an old war was revived, they remain void; so that, if the parties wish they should again take effect, they must expressly specify and confirm them in their new treaty.

The question before us is highly important in another view also,— that is, in its relation to other nations who may be interested in the treaty, inasmuch as their own affairs require them to maintain and enforce the observance of it. It is of the utmost consequence to the guarantees of the treaty, if there are any,—and also to the allies, who have to discover and ascertain the cases in which they are bound to furnish assistance. Finally, he who breaks a solemn treaty is much more odious than the other who, after making an ill-grounded demand, supports it by arms. The former adds perfidy to injustice: he strikes at the foundation of public tranquillity; and as he thereby injures all nations, he affords them just grounds for entering into a confederacy in order to curb and repress him. Wherefore, as we ought to be cautious of imputing the more odious charge, Grotius justly observes, that, in a case of doubt, and where the recurrence to arms may be vindicated by some specious pretext resting on a new ground, "it is better that we should, in the conduct of him who takes up arms anew, presume simple injustice, unaccompanied by perfidy, than account him at once guilty both of perfidy and injustice."*

§43. Justifiable self-defence is no breach of the treaty. Justifiable self-defence is no breach of the treaty of peace. It is a natural right which we cannot renounce: and in promising to live in peace, we only promise not to attack without cause, and to abstain from injuries and violence. But there are two modes of defending our persons or our property: sometimes the violence offered to us will admit of no other remedy than the exertion of open force; and under such circumstances we may lawfully have recourse to it. On other occasions we may obtain redress for the damage and injury by gentler methods; and to these we ought of course to give the preference. Such is the rule of conduct which

* Lib. iii. cap. 20, §28 [[*Law of War and Peace*]].

ought to be observed by two nations that are desirous of maintaining peace, whenever the subjects of either have happened to break out into any act of violence. Present force is checked and repelled by force. But if there is question of obtaining reparation of the damage done, together with adequate satisfaction for the offence, we must apply to the sovereign of the delinquents; we must not pursue them into his dominions, or have recourse to arms, unless he has refused to do us justice. If we have reason to fear that the offenders will escape,—as, for instance, if a band of unknown per-<449>sons from a neighbouring country have made an irruption into our territory,—we are authorised to pursue them with an armed force into their own country, until they be seized: and their sovereign cannot consider our conduct in any other light than that of just and lawful self-defence, provided we commit no hostilities against innocent persons.

When the principal contracting party has included his allies in the treaty, their cause becomes, in this respect, inseparable from his; and they are entitled, equally with him, to enjoy all the conditions essential to a treaty of peace; so that any act, which, if committed against himself, would be a breach of the treaty, is no less a breach of it, if committed against the allies whom he has caused to be included in his treaty. If the injury be done to a new ally, or to one who is not included in the treaty, it may indeed furnish a new ground for war, but is no infringement of the treaty of peace. §44. Causes of rupture on account of allies.

The second way of breaking a treaty of peace is by doing any thing contrary to what the particular nature of the treaty requires. Thus every procedure that is inconsistent with the rules of friendship, is a violation of a treaty of peace which has been concluded under the express condition of thenceforward living in amity and good understanding. To favour a nation's enemies,—to give harsh treatment to her subjects,—to lay unnecessary restrictions on her commerce, or give another nation a preference over her without reason,—to refuse assisting her with provisions, which she is willing to pay for, and we ourselves can well spare,—to protect her factious or rebellious subjects,—to afford them an asylum,—all such proceedings are evidently inconsistent with the laws of friendship. To this list, may, according to circumstances, be also added— §45. 2. The treaty is broken by what is contrary to its particular nature.

the building of fortresses on the frontiers of a state,—expressing distrust against her,—levying troops, and refusing to acquaint her with the motives for such step, &c. But, in affording a retreat to exiles,—in harbouring subjects who chuse to quit their country, without any intention of injuring it by their departure, and solely for the advantage of their private affairs,—in charitably receiving emigrants who depart from their country with a view to enjoy liberty of conscience elsewhere,—there is nothing inconsistent with the character of a friend. The private laws of friendship do not, according to the caprice of our friends, dispense with our observance of the common duties of humanity which we owe to the rest of our species.

§46.
3. By the violation of any article.

Lastly, the peace is broken by the violation of any of the express articles of the treaty. This third way of breaking it is the most decisive, the least susceptible of quibble or evasion. Whoever fails in his engagements annuls the contract, as far as depends on him:—this cannot admit of a doubt.

§47. The violation of a single article breaks the whole treaty.

But it is asked, whether the violation of a single article of the treaty can operate a total rupture of it? Some writers,* here <450> drawing a distinction between the articles that are connected together (*connexi*), and those that stand detached and separate (*diversi*), maintain, that, although the treaty be violated in the detached articles, the peace nevertheless still subsists with respect to the others. But, to me, the opinion of Grotius appears evidently founded on the nature and spirit of treaties of peace. That great man says that all the articles of one and the same treaty are conditionally included in each other, as if each of the contracting parties had formally said, "I will do such or such thing, provided that, on your part, you do so and so":† and he justly adds, that, when it is designed that the engagement shall not be thereby rendered ineffectual, this express clause is inserted,—that, "though any one of the articles of the treaty may happen to be violated, the others shall nevertheless subsist in full force." Such an agreement may unquestionably be made. It may likewise be agreed that the violation of one article shall only annul

---

* See Wolf, Jus Gent. §§1022, 1023.
† Lib. iii. cap. xix. §14 [[*Law of War and Peace*]].

those corresponding to it, and which, as it were, constitute the equivalent to it. But if this clause be not expressly inserted in the treaty of peace, the violation of a single article overthrows the whole treaty, as we have proved above, in speaking of treaties in general (Book II. §202).

It is equally nugatory to attempt making a distinction in this instance between the articles of greater and those of lesser importance. According to strict justice, the violation of the most trifling article dispenses the injured party from the observance of the others, since they are all, as we have seen above, connected with each other, as so many conditions. Besides, what a source of disputes will such a distinction lay open!—Who shall determine the importance of the article violated?—We may, however, assert with truth, that, to be ever ready to annul a treaty on the slightest cause of complaint, is by no means consonant to the reciprocal duties of nations, to that mutual charity, that love of peace, which should always influence their conduct.

§48. Whether a distinction may here be made between the more and the less important articles.

In order to prevent so serious an inconvenience, it is prudent to agree on a penalty to be suffered by the party who violates any of the less important articles: and then, on his submitting to the penalty, the treaty still subsists in full force. In like manner, there may, to the violation of each individual article, be annexed a penalty proportionate to its importance. We have treated of this subject in our remarks on truces (Book III. §243), to which we refer the reader.

§49. Penalty annexed to the violation of an article.

Studied delays are equivalent to an express denial, and differ from it only by the artifice with which he who practises them seeks to palliate his want of faith: he adds fraud to perfidy, and actually violates the article which he should fulfil.

§50. Studied delays.

But if a real impediment stand in the way, time must be allowed; for no one is bound to perform impossibilities. And for the same reason, if any unsurmountable obstacle should render the <451> execution of an article not only impracticable for the present, but forever impossible, no blame is imputable to him who had engaged for the performance of it; nor can his inability furnish the other party with a handle for annulling the treaty: but the latter should accept of an indemnification, if the case will admit of it, and the indemnification be practicable. However, if the thing which was to have been performed in pursuance of the article in

§51. Unsur-mountable impediments.

question be of such a nature, that the treaty evidently appears to have been concluded with a sole view to that particular thing, and not to any equivalent,—the intervening impossibility undoubtedly cancels the treaty. Thus, a treaty of protection becomes void when the protector is unable to afford the promised protection, although his inability does not arise from any fault on his part. In the same manner also, whatever promises a sovereign may have made on condition that the other party should procure him the restoration of an important town, he is released from the performance of every thing which he had promised as the purchase of the recovery, if he cannot be put in possession. Such is the invariable rule of justice. But rigid justice is not always to be insisted on:—peace is so essential to the welfare of mankind, and nations are so strictly bound to cultivate it, to procure it, and to re-establish it when interrupted,— that, whenever any such obstacles impede the execution of a treaty of peace, we ought ingenuously to accede to every reasonable expedient, and accept of equivalents or indemnifications, rather than cancel a treaty of peace already concluded, and again have recourse to arms.

§52. Infractions of the treaty of peace by the subjects; We have already in an express chapter (Book II. Chap. VI.) examined how and on what occasions the actions of subjects may be imputed to the sovereign and the nation. It is by that circumstance we must be guided in determining how far the proceedings of the subjects may be capable of annulling a treaty of peace. They cannot produce such effect unless so far as they are imputable to the sovereign. He who is injured by the subjects of another nation, takes satisfaction for the offence, himself, when he meets with the delinquents in his own territories, or in a free place, as, for instance, on the open sea; or, if more agreeable to him, he demands justice of their sovereign. If the offenders are refractory subjects, no demand can be made on their sovereign; but whoever can seize them, even in a free place, executes summary justice on them himself. Such is the mode observed towards pirates: and, in order to obviate all misunderstandings, it is generally agreed that the same treatment be given to all private individuals who commit acts of hostility without being able to produce a commission from their sovereign.

§53. or by allies. The actions of our allies are still less imputable to us than those of our subjects. The infractions of a treaty of peace by allies, even by those who have been included in it, or who joined in it as principals, can there-fore produce no rupture of it except with regard to themselves, and do not affect it in what concerns their <452> ally, who, on his part, reli-giously observes his engagements. With respect to him, the treaty sub-sists in full force, provided he do not undertake to support the cause of those perfidious allies. If he furnishes them with such assistance as he cannot be bound to give them on an occasion of this nature, he espouses their quarrel, and becomes an accomplice in their breach of faith. But if he has an interest in preventing their ruin, he may interpose, and, by obliging them to make every suitable reparation, save them from an op-pression of which he would himself collaterally feel the effects. It even becomes an act of justice to undertake their defence against an impla-cable enemy who will not be contented with an adequate satisfaction.

When the treaty of peace is violated by one of the contracting parties, the other has the option of either declaring the treaty null and void, or allowing it still to subsist: for a contract which contains reciprocal en-gagements, cannot be binding on him with respect to the party who on his side pays no regard to the same contract. But if he chuses not to come to a rupture, the treaty remains valid and obligatory. It would be absurd that he who had been guilty of the violation should pretend that the agreement was annulled by his own breach of faith: this would indeed be an easy way of shaking off engagements, and would reduce all treaties to empty formalities. If the injured party be willing to let the treaty sub-sist, he may either pardon the infringement,—insist on an indemnifi-cation or adequate satisfaction,—or discharge himself, on his part, from those engagements corresponding with the violated article,—those promises he had made in consideration of a thing which has not been performed. But if he determines on demanding a just indemnification, and the party in fault refuses it, then the treaty is necessarily broken, and the injured party has a very just cause for taking up arms again. And indeed this is generally the case; for it seldom happens that the infractor will submit to make reparation, and thereby acknowledge himself in fault.

§54. Right of the offended party against him who has violated the treaty.

CHAPTER V

Of the Right of Embassy, or the Right of sending and receiving public Ministers.

§55. It is necessary that nations be enabled to treat and communicate together.

It is necessary that nations should treat and hold intercourse together, in order to promote their interests,—to avoid injuring each other,—and to adjust and terminate their disputes. And as they all lie under the indispensable obligation of giving their consent and concurrence to whatever conduces to the general advantage and welfare (Prelim. §13)—of procuring the means of accommodating and terminating their differences <453> (Book II. §323, &c.)—and as each has a right to every thing which her preservation requires (Book I. §§18)—to every thing which can promote her perfection without injuring others (ibid. §23), as also to the necessary means of fulfilling her duties,—it results from the premisses, that each nation is at once possessed of the right to treat and communicate with others, and bound by reciprocal obligation to consent to such communication as far as the situation of her affairs will permit her.

§56. They do this by the agency of public ministers.

But nations or sovereign states do not treat together immediately; and their rulers or sovereigns cannot well come to a personal conference in order to treat of their affairs. Such interviews would often be impracticable: and, exclusive of delays, trouble, expense, and so many other inconveniences, it is rarely, according to the observation of Philip de Commines,[10] that any good effect could be expected from them. The only expedient, therefore, which remains for nations and sovereigns, is to communicate and treat with each other by the agency of procurators or mandatories,—of delegates charged with their commands, and vested with their powers,—that is to say, *public ministers.* This term, in its more extensive and general sense, denotes any person intrusted with the management of public affairs, but is more particularly understood to designate one who acts in such capacity at a foreign court.

At present there are several orders of public ministers, and in the se-

10. Philippe de Commines, French diplomat and chronicler, ca. 1447–1511.

quel we shall speak of them; but whatever difference custom has introduced between them, the essential character is common to them all; I mean that of *minister,* and, in some sort, *representative* of a foreign power,—a person charged with the commands of that power, and delegated to manage his affairs: and that quality is sufficient for our present purpose.

Every sovereign state then has a right to send and to receive public ministers; for they are necessary instruments in the management of those affairs which sovereigns have to transact with each other, and the channels of that correspondence which they have a right to carry on. In the first chapter of this work may be seen who are those sovereigns, and what those independent states, that are entitled to rank in the great society of nations. They are the powers to whom belongs the right of embassy.

§57. Every sovereign state has a right to send and receive public ministers.

An unequal alliance, or even a treaty of protection, not being incompatible with sovereignty (Book I. §§5, 6)—such treaties do not of themselves deprive a state of the right of sending and receiving public ministers. If the inferior ally or the party protected has not expressly renounced the right of entertaining connections and treating with other powers, he necessarily retains that of sending ministers to them, and of receiving their ministers in turn. The same rule applies to such vassals and tributaries as are not subjects (Book I. §§7, 8).

§58. An unequal alliance, or a treaty of protection, does not take away this right.

Nay more, this right may even belong to princes or communities not possessed of sovereign power: for, the rights whose assemblage constitutes the plenitude of sovereignty, are not indivi-<454>sible: and if, by the constitution of the state, by the concession of the sovereign, or by reservations which the subjects have made with him, a prince or community remains possessed of any one of those rights which usually belong to the sovereign alone, such prince or community may exercise it, and avail themselves of it in all its effects and all its natural or necessary consequences, unless they have been formally excepted. Though the princes and states of the empire are dependent on the emperor and the empire, yet they are sovereign in many respects: and as the constitutions of the empire secure to them the right of treating with foreign powers and contracting alliances with them, they incontestably have also that

§59. Right of the princes and states of the empire in this respect.

of sending and receiving public ministers. The emperors, indeed, when they felt themselves able to carry their pretensions very high, have sometimes disputed that right, or at least attempted to render the exercise of it subject to the controul of their supreme authority,—insisting that their permission was necessary to give it a sanction. But since the peace of Westphalia,[11] and by means of the imperial capitulations, the princes and states of Germany have been able to maintain themselves in the possession of that right; and they have secured to themselves so many other rights, that the empire is now considered as a republic of sovereigns.

§60. Cities that have the right of banner.   There are even cities which are and which acknowledge themselves to be in a state of subjection, that have nevertheless a right to receive the ministers of foreign powers, and to send them deputies, since they have a right to treat with them. This latter circumstance is the main point upon which the whole question turns: for whosoever has a right to the end, has a right to the means. It would be absurd to acknowledge the right of negotiating and treating, and to contest the necessary means of doing it. Those cities of Switzerland, such as Neufchatel and Bienne, which have the right of banner, have, by natural consequence, a right to treat with foreign powers, although the cities in question be subject to the dominion of a prince: for the right of *banner*, or of arms, comprehends that of granting succours of troops,* provided such grants be not inconsistent with the service of the prince. Now, if those cities are entitled to grant troops, they must necessarily be at liberty to listen to the applications made to them on the subject by a foreign power, and to treat respecting the conditions. Hence it follows that they may also depute an agent to him for that purpose, or receive his ministers. And as they are at the same time vested with the administration of their own internal police, they have it in their power to insure respect to such foreign ministers as come to them. What is here said of the rights of those cities is confirmed by ancient and constant practice. However exalted and extraordinary such rights may appear, they will not be thought

* See the History of the Helvetic Confederacy, by M. de Watteville.
II. 1648.

strange, if it be considered that those very cities were already possessed of extensive privileges at <455> the time when their princes were themselves dependent on the emperors, or on other liege lords who were immediate vassals of the empire. When the princes shook off the yoke of vassalage, and established themselves in a state of perfect independence, the considerable cities in their territories made their own conditions; and, instead of rendering their situation worse, it was very natural that they should take advantage of the existing circumstances, in order to secure to themselves a greater portion of freedom and happiness. Their sovereigns cannot now advance any plea in objection to the terms on which those cities consented to follow their fortunes, and to acknowledge them as their only superiors.

Viceroys and chief governors of a sovereignty or remote province have frequently the right of sending and receiving public ministers; but, in that particular, they act in the name and by the authority of the sovereign whom they represent, and whose rights they exercise. That entirely depends on the will of the master by whom they are delegated. The viceroys of Naples, the governors of Milan, and the governors-general of the Netherlands for Spain, were invested with such power.

§61. Ministers of viceroys.

The right of embassy, like all the other rights of sovereignty, originally resides in the nation as its principal and primitive subject. During an interregnum, the exercise of that right reverts to the nation, or devolves on those whom the laws have invested with the regency of the state. They may send ministers in the same manner as the sovereign used to do; and these ministers possess the same rights as were enjoyed by those of the sovereign. The republic of Poland sends embassadors while her throne is vacant; nor would she suffer that they should be treated with less respect and consideration than those who are sent while she has a king. Cromwell effectually maintained the embassadors of England in the same rank and respectability which they possessed under the regal authority.

§62. Ministers of the nation or of the regents during an interregnum.

Such being the rights of nations, a sovereign who attempts to hinder another from sending and receiving public ministers, does him an injury, and offends against the law of nations. It is attacking a nation in one of her most valuable rights, and disputing her title to that which nature herself gives to every independent society: it is offering an insult to nations in general, and tearing asunder the ties by which they are united.

§63. Of him who molests another in the exercise of the right of embassy.

§64. What is allowable in this respect in time of war.

But this is to be understood only of a time of peace: war introduces other rights. It allows us to cut off from an enemy all his resources, and to hinder him from sending ministers to solicit assistance. There are even occasions when we may refuse a passage to the ministers of neutral nations, who are going to our enemy. We are under no obligation to allow them an opportunity of perhaps conveying him intelligence of a momentous nature, and concerting with him the means of giving him assistance, &c. This admits of no doubt, for instance, in the case of a besieged town. No right can authorise the minister of a neutral power, or any other person whatsoever, to enter the place without the <456> besieger's consent. But, in order to avoid giving offence to sovereigns, good reasons must be alleged for refusing to let their ministers pass: and with such reasons they must rest satisfied, if they are disposed to remain neuter. Sometimes even a passage is refused to suspected ministers in critical and dubious junctures, although there do not exist any open war. But this is a delicate proceeding, which, if not justified by reasons that are perfectly satisfactory, produces an acrimony that easily degenerates into an open rupture.

§65. The minister of a friendly power is to be received.

As nations are obliged to correspond together, to attend to the proposals and demands made to them, to keep open a free and safe channel of communication for the purpose of mutually understanding each other's views and bringing their disputes to an accommodation,—a sovereign cannot, without very particular reasons, refuse admitting and hearing the minister of a friendly power, or of one with whom he is at peace. But in case there be reasons for not admitting him into the heart of the country, he may notify to him that he will send proper persons to meet him at an appointed place on the frontier, there to hear his proposals. It then becomes the foreign minister's duty to stop at the place assigned: it is sufficient that he obtains a hearing; that being the utmost that he has a right to expect.

§66. Of resident ministers.

The obligation, however, does not extend so far as to include that of suffering at all times the residence of perpetual ministers, who are desirous of remaining at the sovereign's court, although they have no business to transact with him. It is natural, indeed, and perfectly conformable to the sentiments which nations ought mutually to entertain for each other, that a friendly reception should be given to those resident ministers, when there is no inconvenience to be apprehended from their stay. But if there exist any substantial reason to the contrary, the advantage of the state undoubtedly claims a preference; and the foreign sovereign cannot take it amiss if his minister be requested to withdraw, when he has fulfilled the object of his commission, or when he has not any business to transact. The custom of keeping every-where ministers constantly resident is now so firmly established, that whoever should refuse to conform to it, must allege very good reasons for his conduct, if he wishes to avoid giving offence. These reasons may arise from particular conjunctures; but there are also ordinary reasons ever subsisting, and such as relate to the constitution of a government and the state of a nation. Republics would often have very good reasons of the latter kind, to excuse themselves from continually suffering the residence of foreign ministers, who corrupt the citizens,—gain them over to their masters, to the great detriment of the republic,—and excite and foment parties in the state, &c. And even though no other evil should arise from their presence than that of inspiring a nation, originally plain, frugal, and virtuous, with a taste for luxury, the thirst of gain, and the manners of courts,—that alone would be more than sufficient to justify the conduct of wise and provident rulers in dis-<457>missing them. The Polish government is not fond of resident ministers; and indeed their intrigues with the members of the diet have furnished but too many reasons for keeping them at a distance. In the war of 1666, a nuncio publicly complained in the open diet, of the French embassador's unnecessarily prolonging his stay in Poland, and declared that he ought to be considered as a spy. In 1668, other members of that body moved for a law to regulate the length of time that an embassador should be allowed to remain in the kingdom.*

The greater the calamities of war are, the more it is incumbent on nations to preserve means for putting an end to it. Hence it becomes necessary, that, even in the midst of hostilities, they be at liberty to send ministers to each other, for the purpose of making overtures of peace,

§67. How the ministers of an enemy are to be admitted.

* Wicquefort's Embassador, book i. §1.

or proposals tending to moderate the transports of hostile rage. It is true, indeed, that the minister of an enemy cannot come without permission; accordingly a passport or safe-conduct is asked for him, either through the intervention of some common friend, or by one of those messengers who are protected by the laws of war, and of whom we shall speak in the sequel,—I mean a trumpeter, or drummer. It is true also, that, for substantial reasons, the safe-conduct may be refused, and admission denied to the minister. But this liberty, which is authorised by the care that every nation is bound to bestow on her own safety, is no bar to our laying it down as a general maxim, that we are not to refuse admitting and hearing an enemy's minister; that is to say, that war alone, and of itself, is not a sufficient reason for refusing to hear any proposal coming from an enemy; but that, to warrant such refusal, there must exist some reason of a particular nature, and which rests upon very good grounds,—as, for instance, when an artful and designing enemy has by his own conduct given us just cause to apprehend that his only intention, in sending his ministers and making proposals, is to disunite the members of a confederacy, to lull them into security by holding out false appearances of peace, and then to overpower them by surprise.

§68. Whether ministers may be received from or sent to a usurper. Before we conclude this chapter, it will be proper to discuss a celebrated question, which has been often debated. It is asked whether foreign nations may receive the embassadors and other ministers of a usurper, and send their ministers to him. In this particular, foreign powers take for their rule the circumstance of actual possession, if the interest of their affairs so require: and indeed there cannot be a more certain rule, or one that is more agreeable to the law of nations and the independency of states. As foreigners have no right to interfere in the domestic concerns of a nation, they are not obliged to canvas and scrutinise her conduct in the management of them, in order to determine how far it is either just or unjust. They may, if they think proper, suppose the right to be annexed to the posses-<458>sion. When a nation has expelled her sovereign, other powers, who do not chuse to declare against her and to risk the consequences of her enmity or open hostility, consider her thenceforward as a free and sovereign state, without taking on themselves to determine whether she has acted justly in withdrawing from her allegiance to the prince by whom she was governed. Cardinal Mazarin[12] received Lockhart,[13] whom Cromwell had sent as embassador from the republic of England, and refused to see either king Charles the Second, or his ministers. If a people, after having expelled their prince, submit to another,—if they change the order of succession, and acknowledge a sovereign to the prejudice of the natural and appointed heir,—foreign powers may, in this instance also, consider what has been done as lawful: it is no quarrel or business of theirs. At the beginning of the last century, Charles duke of Sudermania, having obtained the crown of Sweden to the prejudice of his nephew Sigismund king of Poland, was soon acknowledged by most sovereigns. Villeroy, minister of the French monarch Henry the Fourth, in his dispatches of the 8th of April 1608, plainly said to the president Jeannin, "All these reasons and considerations shall not prevent the king from treating with Charles, if he finds it to be his interest, and that of his kingdom." This remark was sensible and judicious. The king of France was neither the judge nor the guardian of the Swedish nation, that he should, contrary to the interest of his own kingdom, refuse to acknowledge the king whom Sweden had chosen, under pretence that a competitor termed Charles a usurper. Had the charge been even founded in justice, it was an affair which did not fall under the cognisance of foreigners.

Therefore, when foreign powers have received the ministers of a usurper, and sent theirs to him, the lawful prince, on recovering the throne, cannot complain of these measures as an injury, nor justly make them the ground of a war, provided those powers have not proceeded to greater lengths, nor furnished any assistance against him. But to acknowledge the dethroned prince or his heir after the state has solemnly acknowledged the person to whom the sceptre has been transferred, is an injury done to the latter, and a profession of enmity to the nation that has chosen him. Such a step, hazarded in favour of James the Second's son, was, by William the Third and the British nation, alleged as one of the principal reasons of the war which England soon after de-

12. Cardinal Mazarin, a chief minister of France, 1642–61.
13. Sir William Lockhart, 1621–76.

clared against France. Notwithstanding all the caution and all the protestations of Louis the Fourteenth, his acknowledgement of young Stuart as king of England, Scotland, and Ireland, under the title of James the Third, was considered by the English as an injury done both to the king and to the nation. <459>

CHAPTER VI

Of the several Orders of public Ministers,—
of the representative Character,—and of
the Honours due to Ministers.

§69. Origin of the several orders of public ministers.   In former days, people were scarcely acquainted with more than one order of public ministers, in Latin termed *legati,* which appellation has been rendered by that of *"embassadors."* But when courts were become more proud, and at the same time more punctilious in the article of ceremony, and especially when they had introduced the idea of extending the minister's representation even to that of his master's dignity, it was thought expedient to employ commissioners of less exalted rank on certain occasions, in order to avoid trouble, expense, and disputes. Louis the Eleventh of France[14] was perhaps the first who set the example. Thus several orders of ministers being established, more or less dignity was annexed to their character, and proportionate honours were required for them.

§70. Representative character.   Every minister in some measure represents his master, as every agent or delegate represents his constituent. But this representation relates to the affairs of his office: the minister represents the subject in whom reside the rights which he is to exercise, preserve, and assert,—the rights respecting which he is to treat in his master's stead. Although such representation is admitted in a general view, and so far as respects the essence of affairs, it is with an abstraction of the dignity of the constituent. In process of time, however, princes would have ministers to represent

14. Louis XI of France, r. 1461–83.

them, not only in their rights and in the transaction of their affairs, but also in their dignity, their greatness, and their pre-eminence. It was, no doubt, to those signal occasions of state, those ceremonies for which embassadors are sent, as, for instance, marriages, that this custom owes its origin. But so exalted a degree of dignity in the minister is attended with considerable inconvenience in conducting business, and, besides occasioning trouble and embarrassment, is often productive of difficulties and disputes. This circumstance has given birth to different orders of public ministers, and various degrees of representation. Custom has established three principal degrees. What is, by way of pre-eminence, called the *representative character,* is the faculty possessed by the minister, of representing his master even in his very person and dignity.

The representative character, so termed by way of pre-eminence, or in contradistinction to other kinds of representation, constitutes the minister of the first rank, the embassador. It places him above all other ministers who are not invested with the same character, and precludes their entering into competition with the embassador. At present there are embassadors <460> ordinary and extraordinary: but this is no more than an accidental distinction, merely relative to the subject of their mission. Yet almost every-where some difference is made in the treatment of these different embassadors. That, however, is purely matter of custom. §71. Embassadors.

Envoys are not invested with the representative character, properly so called, or in the first degree. They are ministers of the second rank, on whom their master was willing to confer a degree of dignity and respectability, which, without being on a level with the character of an embassador, immediately follows it, and yields the pre-eminence to it alone. There are also *envoys ordinary* and *extraordinary;* and it appears to be the intention of princes that the latter should be held in greater consideration. This likewise depends on custom. §72. Envoys.

The word *Resident* formerly related only to the continuance of the minister's stay; and it is frequent in history for embassadors in ordinary to be designated by the simple title of residents. But since the practice of employing different orders of ministers has been generally established, the name of resident has been confined to ministers of a third order, to whose character general custom has annexed a lesser degree of §73. Residents.

respectability. The resident does not represent the prince's person in his dignity, but only in his affairs. His representation is in reality of the same nature as that of the envoy: wherefore we often term him, as well as the envoy, a minister of the second order,—thus distinguishing only two classes of public ministers, the former consisting of embassadors who are invested with the representative character in pre-eminence, the latter comprising all other ministers who do not possess that exalted character. This is the most necessary distinction, and indeed the only essential one.

§74. Ministers.   Lastly, a custom of still more recent origin has introduced a new kind of ministers without any particular determination of character. These are called simply *ministers,* to indicate that they are invested with the general quality of a sovereign's mandatories, without any particular assignment of rank and character. It was likewise the punctilio of ceremony which gave rise to this innovation. Use had established particular modes of treatment for the embassador, the envoy, and the resident. Disputes between ministers of the several princes often arose on this head, and especially about rank. In order to avoid all contest on certain occasions when there might be room to apprehend it, the expedient was adopted of sending ministers not invested with any one of the three known characters. Hence they are not subjected to any settled ceremonial, and can pretend to no particular treatment. The minister represents his master in a vague and indeterminate manner, which cannot be equal to the first degree; consequently he makes no demur in yielding pre-eminence to the embassador. He is entitled to the general regard due to a confidential person intrusted by a sovereign with the management of his affairs; and he possesses all the rights <461> essential to the character of a public minister. This indeterminate quality is such that the sovereign may confer it on one of his servants whom he would not choose to invest with the character of embassador: and, on the other hand, it may be accepted by a man of rank, who would be unwilling to undertake the office of resident, and to acquiesce in the treatment at present allotted to men in that station. There are also *ministers plenipotentiary,* and of much greater distinction than simple ministers. These also are without any particular attribution of rank and character, but by custom are now placed immediately after the embassador, or on a level with the envoy extraordinary.

We have spoken of *consuls* in treating of commerce (Book II. §34). Formerly *agents* were a kind of public ministers; but in the present increase and profusion of titles, this is given to persons simply appointed by princes to transact their private affairs, and who not unfrequently are subjects of the country where they reside. They are not public ministers, and consequently not under the protection of the law of nations. But a more particular protection is due to them than to other foreigners or citizens, and likewise some attentions in consideration of the prince whom they serve. If that prince sends an agent with credentials and on public business, the agent thenceforward becomes a public minister; his title making no difference in the case. The same remark is also applicable to deputies, commissioners, and others intrusted with the management of public affairs. *[margin: §75. Consuls, agents, deputies, commissioners, &c.]*

Among the several characters established by custom, it rests with the sovereign to determine with what particular one he chooses to invest his minister; and he makes known the minister's character in the *credentials* which he gives him for the sovereign to whom he sends him. Credentials are the instrument which authorises and establishes the minister in his character with the prince to whom they are addressed. If that prince receives the minister, he can receive him only in the quality attributed to him in his credentials. They are, as it were, his general letter of attorney, his *mandate patent, mandatum manifestum.* *[margin: §76. Credentials.]*

The *instructions* given to the minister contain his master's *secret mandate,* the orders to which the minister must carefully conform, and which limit his powers. Here we might apply all the rules of the law of nature respecting procurations and mandates, whether open or secret. But exclusive of their being more particularly applicable to the subject of treaties, we may with the less impropriety dispense with such details in this work, as the custom has wisely been established, that no engagements into which a minister may enter, shall have any validity between sovereigns, unless ratified by his principal. *[margin: §77. Instructions.]*

We have seen above that every sovereign, every community, and even every individual, who has a right to treat with foreign powers, has also that of sending embassadors. (See the preceding chapter.) The question admits of no difficulty, so far as respects simple ministers or mandatories, considered in general as persons <462> intrusted with the affairs, and *[margin: §78. Right of sending embassadors.]*

vested with the powers, of those who have a right to treat. Further, the ministers of every sovereign are, without hesitation, allowed to enjoy all the rights and prerogatives belonging to ministers of the second order. Powerful monarchs indeed deny to some petty states the right of sending embassadors: but let us see with what reason. According to the generally established custom, the embassador is a public minister representing the person and dignity of a sovereign; and, as this representative character procures him particular honours, great princes are therefore unwilling to admit the embassador of an inconsiderable state, from a repugnance to paying him honours of so distinguished a kind. But it is manifest that every sovereign has an equal right of causing himself to be represented in the first as well as in the second or the third degree: and the sovereign dignity is entitled to distinguished respect in the great society of nations. We have shewn (Book II. Ch. III.) that the dignity of independent nations is essentially the same; that a sovereign prince, however low he may rank in the scale of power, is as completely sovereign and independent as the greatest monarch, in the same manner as a dwarf is a man equally with a giant; although indeed the political giant makes a more conspicuous figure in the general society than the dwarf, and has, on that account, a greater portion of respect and more signal honours paid to him. It is evident then that every prince, every state, truly possessed of sovereignty, has a right to send embassadors, and that to contest their right in this instance is doing them a very great injury; it is, in fact, contesting their sovereign dignity. And if they have that right, their embassadors cannot be refused those regards and honours which custom particularly assigns to the representative of a sovereign. The king of France admits no embassadors from the princes of Germany, as refusing to their ministers the honours annexed to the first degree of representation; yet he receives embassadors from the princes of Italy. The reason alleged for this conduct is that he considers the latter to be more perfectly sovereign princes than the former, because, though equally vassals of the emperor and the empire, they are not equally dependent on the imperial authority. The emperors, nevertheless, claim the same rights over the princes of Italy, as over those of Germany. But France, seeing that the former do not actually constitute a part of the Germanic body, nor assist at the diets, countenances their absolute independence, in order as much as possible to detach them from the empire.

I shall not here enter into a detail of the honours due and actually paid to embassadors: these are matters which altogether depend on institution and custom: I shall only observe, in general, that they are entitled to those civilities and distinctions which usage and the prevailing manners of the time have pointed out as proper expressions of the respect due to the representative of a sovereign. And it must be observed here, with regard to things <463> of institution and custom, that, when a practice is so established, as to impart, according to the usages and manners of the age, a real value and a settled signification to things which are in their own nature indifferent, the natural and necessary law of nations requires that we should pay deference to such institution, and act, with respect to such things, in the same manner as if they really possessed all that value which the opinion of mankind has annexed to them. For instance, according to the general usage of all Europe it is the peculiar prerogative of an embassador to wear his hat in presence of the prince to whom he is sent. This right expresses that he is acknowledged as the representative of a sovereign: to refuse it therefore to the embassador of a state which is truly independent, would be doing an injury to that state, and, in some measure, degrading it. The Switzers, who formerly were much deeper adepts in the art of war than in the etiquette of courts, and far from being punctilious on the score of mere ceremony, have, on some occasions, submitted to be treated in a manner unbecoming the dignity of their nation. In 1663, their embassadors suffered the king of France, and the nobles of his court, to refuse them those honours which custom has rendered essential to the embassadors of sovereigns, and particularly that of being covered before the king at their audience.* Some of their number, who knew better what they owed to the glory of their republic, strongly insisted on that essential and distinctive honour: but the opin-

§79. Honours due to embassadors.

---

* In Wicquefort, may be seen a particular account of the whole transaction. That writer is justifiable in expressing a degree of indignation against the Swiss embassadors: but he ought not to have insulted the whole nation by coarsely asserting that "they prefer money to honour." Embassad. book i. §19. See also §18.

ion of the majority prevailed, and at length they all yielded, on being assured that the embassadors of their nation had not worn their hats in presence of Henry the Fourth. Allowing the fact to have been true, the argument was not unanswerable. The Switzers might have replied, that in Henry's time their nation was not yet solemnly acknowledged free and independent of the empire, as it had lately been by the treaty of Westphalia in 1648. They might have said, that, although their predecessors had not been duly attentive to support the dignity of their sovereigns, that gross error could not impose on their successors any obligation to commit a similar one. At present, as the nation is more enlightened, and more attentive to points of that nature, she will not fail to support her dignity in a more becoming manner. Whatever extraordinary honours may in other respects be paid to her embassadors, she will not in future suffer herself to be so far blinded by those empty marks of distinction, as to overlook that peculiar prerogative which custom has rendered essential. When Louis the Fifteenth visited Alsace in 1744, the Helvetic body declined sending embassadors to compliment him according to custom, until informed whether they would be allowed to wear their hats: and on the refusal of <464> that just demand, none were sent. Switzerland may reasonably hope that his most christian majesty will no longer insist on a claim which does not enhance the lustre of his crown, and can only serve to degrade an ancient and faithful ally.

CHAPTER VII

Of the Rights, Privileges, and Immunities of Embassadors and other Public Ministers.

§80. Respect due to public ministers.

The respect which is due to sovereigns should redound to their representatives, and especially their embassadors, as representing their master's person in the first degree. Whoever offends and insults a public minister, commits a crime the more deserving of severe punishment, as he might thereby involve his country and his sovereign in very serious difficulties and trouble. It is just that he should be punished for his fault, and that the state should, at the expense of the delinquent, give full satisfaction to the sovereign who has been offended in the person of his minister. If the foreign minister is himself the aggressor, and offends a citizen, the latter may oppose him without departing from the respect due to the character which the offender bears, and give him a lesson which shall both efface the stain of the outrage, and make the author of it blush for his misconduct. The person offended may further prefer a complaint to his own sovereign, who will demand for him an adequate satisfaction from the minister's master. The great concerns of the state forbid a citizen, on such occasions, to entertain those thoughts of revenge which the point of honour might suggest, although they should in other respects be deemed allowable. Even according to the maxims of the world, a gentleman is not disgraced by an affront for which it is not in his own power to procure satisfaction.

The necessity and right of embassies being established (see Chap. V. of this Book), the perfect security and inviolability of embassadors and other ministers is a certain consequence of it: for if their persons be not protected from violence of every kind, the right of embassy becomes precarious, and the success very uncertain. A right to the end inseparably involves a right to the necessary means. Embassies then being of such great importance in the universal society of nations, and so necessary to their common well-being, the persons of ministers charged with those embassies are to be held *sacred* and *inviolable* among all nations (see Book II. §218). Whoever offers violence to an embassador, or to any other public minister, not only injures the sovereign whom that minister represents, but also attacks the common <465> safety and well-being of nations: he becomes guilty of an atrocious crime against mankind in general.*

§81. Their persons sacred and inviolable.

---

* An enormous infraction of the law of nations caused the ruin of the powerful empire of Khovarezm or Kakesm, and opened a door to the Tartars for the subjugation of almost all Asia. The famous Gengis-khan, wishing to establish a commercial intercourse between his states and those of Persia and the other provinces subject to Mohammed Cotheddin, sultan of Khovarezm, sent to that prince an embassador accompanied by a caravan of merchants. On the arrival of that caravan at Otraw, the governor caused them to be arrested, together with the embassador, and wrote word

§82. Particular
protection due
to them.

This safety is particularly due to the minister, from the sovereign to whom he is sent. To admit a minister, to acknowledge him in such character, is engaging to grant him the most particular protection, and that he shall enjoy all possible safety. It is true, indeed, that the sovereign is bound to protect every person within his dominions, whether native or foreigner, and to shelter him from violence: but this attention is in a higher degree due to a foreign minister. An act of violence done to a private person is an ordinary transgression, which, according to circumstances, the prince may pardon: but if done to a public minister, it is a crime of state, an offence against the law of nations; and the power of pardoning, in such case, does not rest with the prince in whose dominions the crime has been committed, but with him who has been offended in the person of his representative. However, if the minister has been insulted by persons who were ignorant of his character, the offence is wholly unconnected with the law of nations, and falls within the class of ordinary transgressions. A company of young rakes, in a town of Switzerland, having, in the night-time, insulted the British minister's house without knowing who lived in it, the magistracy sent a message to the minister, to know what satisfaction he required. He prudently answered, that it was the magistrates' concern to provide for the public safety by such means as they thought best; but that, as to his own part, he required nothing, not thinking himself affronted by persons who could have had no design against him, as not knowing his house. Another particular circumstance in the protection due to foreign ministers,

---

to the sultan that they were a company of spies. Mohammed thereupon ordered him to have the prisoners put to death. Gengis-khan demanded satisfaction of the sultan for this barbarous massacre; and, finding him backward to give it, he took up arms. The conquest of the whole empire of Khovarezm soon followed; and Mohammed himself, reduced to the condition of a wretched fugitive, died of a broken heart in a desert island of the Caspian sea.

Canson, the last sultan of the Mammelucs, having put to death the embassadors of the Turkish emperor Selim the First, the injured monarch took a signal vengeance for the atrocious deed. He conquered all the dominions of Canson, and having defeated and captured that prince near Cairo, he caused him to be hanged at one of the gates of the city. Marigny [[François Augier de Marigny]], Hist. of the Arabs, vol. ii. pp. 105, 427. [[Note added in 1773/1797 editions.]]

is this:—according to the destructive maxims introduced by a false point of honour, a sovereign is under a necessity of shewing indulgence to a person wearing a sword, who instantly revenges an affront done to him by a private individual: but violent proceedings against a public minister can never be allowed or ex-<466>cused, unless where the latter has himself been the aggressor, and, by using violence in the first instance, has reduced his opponent to the necessity of self-defence.

Though the minister's character is not displayed in its full extent, and does not thus ensure him the enjoyment of all his rights, till he is acknowledged and admitted by the sovereign, to whom he delivers his credentials,—yet, on his entering the country to which he is sent, and making himself known, he is under the protection of the law of nations; otherwise it would not be safe for him to come. Until he has had his audience of the prince, he is, on his own word, to be considered as a minister; and besides, exclusive of the notice of his mission usually given by letter, the minister has, in case of doubt, his passports to produce, which will sufficiently certify his character.

§83. When it commences.

These passports sometimes become necessary to him in the countries through which he passes on his way to the place of his destination; and, in case of need, he shews them, in order to obtain the privileges to which he is entitled. It is true, indeed, that the prince alone to whom the minister is sent, is under any obligation or particular engagement to ensure him the enjoyment of all the rights annexed to his character. Yet the others through whose dominions he passes, are not to deny him those regards to which the minister of a sovereign is entitled, and which nations reciprocally owe to each other. In particular they are bound to afford him perfect security. To insult him, would be injuring his master, and the whole nation to which he belongs: to arrest him and offer him violence, would be infringing the right of embassy, which belongs to all sovereigns (§§57, 63). The French monarch, Francis the First, had therefore very good reason to complain of the murder of his embassadors Rincon and Fregose, as an atrocious violation of public faith and of the law of nations. Those two ministers, the one destined for Constantinople, the other for Venice, having embarked on the Po, were stopped and murdered; and, according to all appearances, the deed had been per-

§84. What is due to them in countries through which they pass.

petrated by order of the governor of Milan.* The emperor Charles the
Fifth having taken no pains to discover the persons concerned in the
murder, authorised a belief that he had himself ordered it, or at least
that he tacitly approved of the act after its commission. And as he did
not give any suitable satisfaction for it, Francis had a very just cause for
declaring war against him, and even calling for the assistance of all other
nations: for an affair of this nature is not a private dispute, a doubtful
question in which each party pretends to have justice on his side: it is a
quarrel which involves the concern of all nations, since they are all
equally interested in maintaining the sacred inviolability of that right
and of those means which enable them to hold communication with
each other, and to treat of their affairs. If an in-<467>nocent passage,
and even perfect security, are due to a private individual, much more are
they due to the minister of a sovereign, who is going to execute his master's orders, and who travels on the affairs of a nation. I say, "an innocent
passage": for the minister's journey is justly suspected, if a sovereign has
reason to apprehend that he will make an improper use of the liberty
granted him of entering his territories, by plotting against his interests
while in the country, or that he is going to convey intelligence to his
enemies, or to stir up others against him. We have already said (§64) that
he may in such case refuse him a passage: but he is not to maltreat him,
nor suffer any violence to be offered to his person. If he has not reason
sufficient for denying him a passage, he may take precautions against the
abuse which the minister might make of it. These maxims the Spaniards
found established in Mexico, and the neighbouring provinces. In those
countries, embassadors were respected throughout their whole journey;
but they could not deviate from the high road without forfeiting their
rights:†—a prudent and judicious reservation, introduced as a guard
against the admission of spies under the name of embassadors. Thus,
while the negotiations for peace were carried on at the famous congress
of Westphalia amidst the dangers of war and the din of arms, the several
couriers sent or received by the plenipotentiaries had each his particular

* Memoires de Martin du Bellay, liv. ix.
† Solis's history of the Conquest of Mexico.

route designated; and out of the prescribed tract, his passport could afford him no protection.*

What we have here observed, relates to nations that are at peace with each other. On the breaking out of a war, we cease to be under any obligation of leaving the enemy in the free enjoyment of his rights: on the contrary, we are justifiable in depriving him of them, for the purpose of weakening him, and reducing him to accept of equitable conditions. His people may also be attacked and seized wherever we have a right to commit acts of hostility. Not only, therefore, may we justly refuse a passage to the ministers whom our enemy sends to other sovereigns; we may even arrest them if they attempt to pass privately, and without permission, through places belonging to our jurisdiction. Of such proceeding the last war furnishes a signal instance. A French embassador, on his route to Berlin, touched, through the imprudence of his guides, at a village within the electorate of Hanover, whose sovereign, the king of England, was at war with France. The minister was there arrested, and afterwards sent over to England. As his Britannic majesty had in that instance only exerted the rights of war, neither the court of France nor that of Prussia complained of his conduct.

§85. Embassadors going to an enemy's country.

The reasons which render embassies necessary, and embassadors sacred and inviolable, are not less cogent in time of war than <468> in profound peace. On the contrary, the necessity and indispensable duty of preserving some resource by which the minds of the belligerent parties may be brought to a mutual understanding, and peace be restored, is a fresh reason why the persons of ministers, as instruments in the preliminary conferences and final reconciliation, should be still more sacred and inviolable. *Nomen legati*, says Cicero, *ejusmodi esse debet, quod, non modo inter sociorum jura, sed etiam inter hostium tela, incolume versetur.†* Accordingly, one of the most sacred laws of war is that which ensures perfect security to persons who bring messages or proposals from the

§86. Embassies between enemies.

---

* Wicquefort's Embassador, b. i. §17.

† In Verrem, orat. i. [[Orat. II, 1.85: "The very name *legatus* should inspire such respect that its bearer should be able to move unharmed not only among allies who acknowledge our rights but among enemies whose swords are drawn against us!"]]

enemy. It is true, indeed, that the embassador of an enemy must not approach without permission: and as there does not always exist a convenient opportunity of obtaining such permission through the medium of neutral persons, the defect has been supplied by the establishment of certain privileged messengers for carrying proposals from enemy to enemy, in perfect safety.

§87. Heralds, trumpeters, and drummers.
The privileged messengers I allude to are heralds, trumpeters, and drummers, who, from the moment they make themselves known, and as long as they confine themselves within the terms of their commission, are, by the laws of war and those of nations, considered as sacred and inviolable. This regulation is absolutely necessary: for, exclusive of the duty incumbent on us to reserve the means of restoring peace (as above mentioned), there occur, even during the course of the war, a thousand occasions, when the common safety and advantage of both parties require that they should be able to send messages and proposals to each other. The institution of heralds succeeded that of the Roman *feciales:* at present, however, they are seldom employed: drummers or trumpeters are sent, and, after them, according to the exigence of the occasion, ministers, or officers furnished with powers. Those drummers and trumpeters are held sacred and inviolable; but they are to make themselves known by the marks peculiar to them. Maurice, prince of Orange,[15] highly resented the conduct of the garrison of Ysendick, who had fired at his trumpeter:* on which occasion the prince observed that no punishment can be too severe for those who violate the law of nations. Other instances may be seen in Wicquefort, and particularly the reparation which the duke of Savoy, as general of Charles the Fifth's army, caused to be made to a French trumpeter, who had been dismounted and despoiled by some German soldiers.†

* Wicquefort, book i. §3.
† Ibid.
15. Maurice, prince of Orange, r. 1618–25.

In the wars of the Netherlands the duke of Alva hanged up a trumpeter belonging to the prince of Orange, saying that he was not obliged to allow safety to a trumpeter sent him by the chief of the rebels.* On this as on many other occasions, that sanguinary general was undoubtedly guilty of a flagrant violation of the laws of war, which, as we have proved above (Book III. <469> Chap. XVIII.), ought to be observed even in civil wars: for, unless both parties can with perfect safety interchange messages and reciprocally send confidential persons to each other, how can they, on those unfortunate occasions, ever come to talk of peace? what channel remains open for negotiating a salutary accommodation? The same duke of Alva, in the war which the Spaniards afterwards made on the Portuguese[16] whom they also termed rebels, caused the governor of Cascais to be hanged for having given orders to fire on a trumpeter sent to demand a surrender of the town.† In a civil war, or when a prince takes up arms for the purpose of subduing a body of people who think themselves absolved from their allegiance to him, an attempt to compel the enemies to respect the laws of war while he himself does not observe them on his own part, is in fact equal to a determined resolution of carrying those wars to the extreme of cruelty, and converting them into a scene of inordinate and endless murder, by the long series of mutual retaliations which will naturally ensue.

§88. Ministers, trumpeters, &c. to be respected even in a civil war.

But, as a prince, when influenced by substantial reasons, may refuse to admit and listen to embassadors, in like manner the general of an army, or any other commander, is not always obliged to permit the approach of a trumpeter or drummer, and to give him a hearing. If, for instance, the governor of a besieged town is apprehensive that a summons to surrender may intimidate the garrison, and excite premature ideas of capitulation, he undoubtedly may, on seeing the trumpeter advance, send him orders to retire, informing him that if he comes a second time on the same errand and without permission, he shall be fired upon. This conduct is no violation of the laws of war: but such a mode of

§89. Sometimes they may be refused admittance.

* Ibid.
† Wicquefort, book i.
16. In 1580–81.

proceeding ought not to be adopted without very cogent reasons, because, by irritating the besiegers, it exposes the garrison to be treated by them with the extreme of rigour, untempered with mercy or moderation. To refuse to hear a trumpeter's message without alleging a substantial reason for the refusal, is equivalent to a declaration that the party is determined to persevere in irreconcilable hostility.

§90. Every thing which has the appearance of insult to them, must be avoided.

Whether we admit or refuse to hear a herald or a trumpeter, we ought carefully to avoid every thing which might wear the appearance of an insult offered to him. Not only does the law of nations claim that respect, but prudence moreover recommends such caution and delicacy. In 1744, the Bailly de Givry sent a trumpeter with an officer to summon the redoubt of Pierre-longe in Piémont. The Savoyard officer who commanded in the redoubt, a brave man, but of a blunt and fiery disposition, feeling his indignation roused by a summons to surrender a post which he deemed tenable and secure, returned an insulting answer to the French general. The officer to whom the answer was given, judiciously took advantage of the circumstance, and delivered it to the Bailly de Givry in the hearing of the French <470> troops. It set them in a flame; and their native valour being stimulated by the eager desire of avenging an affront, their impetuosity was irresistible: though the attack was attended with considerable carnage, the losses they sustained only added fresh fuel to their courage, till at length they carried the redoubt: and thus the imprudent commandant was accessary to his own death, the slaughter of his men, and the loss of his post.

§91. By and to whom they may be sent.

The prince, the general of the army, and every commander in chief within his department, have alone the right of sending a trumpeter or drummer; and, on the other hand, it is only to the commander in chief that they can send such messengers. Should a general, besieging a town, attempt to send a trumpeter to any subaltern, to the magistracy, or the townsmen, the governor might justly treat that trumpeter as a spy. The French monarch, Francis the First, while engaged in war with Charles the Fifth, sent a trumpeter to the diet of the empire, then assembled at Spires. The trumpeter was seized by order of the emperor, who threatened to hang him because he was not sent to him.* But he did not dare

* Wicquefort, ubi supra.

to put his threat in execution; for, loudly as he complained on the subject, he was nevertheless convinced in his own mind that the diet had a right, even without his consent, to listen to the proposals brought by a trumpeter. On the other hand, a drummer or trumpeter from a subaltern is seldom received, unless for some particular object depending on the present authority of that subaltern acting in his function. At the siege of Rhynberg in 1598, a colonel of a Spanish regiment having taken upon him to summon the town, the governor sent the drummer orders to withdraw, informing him at the same time, that, if any other drummer or trumpeter had the audacity to come on the same errand from a subaltern, he would cause the messenger to be hanged.*

The inviolability of a public minister,—or the protection to which he has a more sacred and particular claim than any other person, whether native or foreigner,—is not the only privilege he enjoys: the universal practice of nations allows him moreover an entire independence on the jurisdiction and authority of the state in which he resides. Some authors† maintain that this independence is merely a matter of institution between different states, and will have it referred to the arbitrary law of nations, which owes its origin to manners, customs, or particular conventions: in a word, they deny it to be grounded on the natural law of nations. It is true, indeed, that the law of nature gives men a right to punish those who injure them: consequently it empowers sovereigns to punish any foreigner who disturbs the public tranquillity, who offends them, or maltreats their subjects: it authorises them to compel such foreigner to <471> conform to the laws, and to behave properly towards the citizens. But it is no less true, that the natural law at the same time imposes on all sovereigns the obligation of consenting to those things without which it would be impossible for nations to cultivate the society that nature has established among them,—to keep up a mutual correspondence,—to treat of their affairs, or to adjust their differences. Now, embassadors and other public ministers are necessary instruments for the maintenance of that general society, of that mutual correspondence between nations. But their ministry cannot effect the intended purpose,

§92. Independence of foreign ministers.

---

* Idem, ibid.
† See Wolf, Jus Gent. §1059.

unless it be invested with all the prerogatives which are capable of ensuring its legitimate success, and of enabling the minister freely and
faithfully to discharge his duty in perfect security. The law of nations,
therefore, while it obliges us to grant admission to foreign ministers, does
also evidently oblige us to receive those ministers in full possession of
all the rights which necessarily attach to their character,—all the privileges requisite for the due performance of their functions. It is easy to
conceive that independence must be one of those privileges; since, without it, that security which is so necessary to a public minister, would be
enjoyed on a very precarious footing. He might be molested, persecuted,
maltreated, under a thousand pretences. A minister is often charged with
commissions that are disagreeable to the prince to whom he is sent. If
that prince has any power over him, and especially a sovereign authority,
how is it to be expected that the minister can execute his master's orders
with due fidelity, firmness, and freedom of mind? It is a matter of no
small importance that he have no snares to apprehend,—that he be not
liable to be diverted from his functions by any chicanery,—that he have
nothing to hope, nothing to fear, from the sovereign to whom he is sent.
In order, therefore, to the success of his ministry, he must be independent of the sovereign authority and of the jurisdiction of the country,
both in civil and criminal matters. To this it may be added, that the
nobility and other persons of eminence would be averse to undertaking
an embassy, if such commission were to subject them to a foreign authority,—not unfrequently in countries where they have little friendship
to expect for their own nation, and where they must support disagreeable
claims, and enter into discussions naturally productive of acrimony. In
a word, if an ambassador may be indicted for ordinary offences, be crim-
inally prosecuted, taken into custody, punished,—if he may be sued in
civil cases,—the consequence will often be, that he will neither possess
the power, the leisure, nor the freedom of mind, which his master's affairs require. And how shall he be able to support the dignity of representation in such a state of subjection?—On the whole, therefore, it is
impossible to conceive that the prince who sends an embassador or any
other minister, can have any intention of subjecting him to the authority
of a foreign power: and this consideration furnishes an additional ar-

gument which completely establishes the < 472 > independency of a public minister. If it cannot be reasonably presumed that his sovereign means to subject him to the authority of the prince to whom he is sent, the latter, in receiving the minister, consents to admit him on the footing of independency: and thus there exists between the two princes a tacit convention which gives a new force to the natural obligation.

The established practice is perfectly conformable to the principles here laid down. All sovereigns claim a perfect independency for their embassadors and ministers. If it be true that there was a king of Spain, who, from a desire of arrogating to himself a jurisdiction over the foreign ministers resident at his court, wrote to all the christian princes, informing them that if his embassadors should commit any crime in the places of their respective residence, it was his pleasure that they should forfeit all their privileges, and be tried according to the laws of the country,*— one solitary instance is of no weight in an affair of this nature; nor have his successors on the Spanish throne adopted a similar mode of thinking.

This independency of the foreign minister is not to be converted into licentiousness: it does not excuse him from conforming to the customs and laws of the country in all his external actions, so far as they are unconnected with the object of his mission and character:—he is independent; but he has not a right to do whatever he pleases. Thus, for instance, if there exist a general prohibition against passing in a carriage near a powder magazine, or over a bridge,—against walking round and examining the fortifications of a town, &c.—the embassador is bound to respect such prohibitions.† Should he forget his duty,—should he

§93. How the foreign minister is to behave.

---

* The fact is advanced by Antony de Vera, in his "Idea of a Perfect Embassador": but Wicquefort suspects the authenticity of the anecdote,—not having, as he says, met with it in any other writer. Embassad. book i. §29.

† The king of England having received information that the French and Spanish embassadors had severally collected considerable numbers of armed men for the purpose of supporting on a solemn occasion their respective claims to precedency, made a general request to all the foreign ministers not to send their carriages to attend the public entry of the Venetian embassador. The count D'Estrades, at that time minister from the court of France, having complied with his majesty's desire,—Louis XIV. testified his dissatisfaction at the deference paid by the count to the British monarch's message, "which was no more than a simple request not to send carriages;—whereas,

grow insolent and be guilty of irregularities and crimes,—there are, according to the nature and importance of his offences, various modes of repressing him: and these we shall speak of, after we have said a few words concerning the line of conduct to be pursued by a public minister in the place of his residence. He must not avail himself of his independency for <473> the purpose of violating the laws and customs; he should rather punctually conform to them as far as they may concern him, although the magistrate has no compulsive power over him; and he is especially bound to a religious observance of the rules of justice towards all who have any dealings with him. As to what concerns the prince to whom he is sent, the embassador should remember that his ministry is a ministry of peace, and that it is on that footing only he is received. This reason forbids his engaging in any evil machinations:—let him serve his master without injuring the prince who receives him. It is a base treachery to take advantage of the inviolability of the embassadorial character, for the purpose of plotting in security the ruin of those who respect that character,—of laying snares for them,—of clandestinely injuring them,—of embroiling and ruining their affairs. What would be infamous and abominable in a private guest, shall that be allowable and becoming in the representative of a sovereign?

Here arises an interesting question.—It is but too common for embassadors to tamper with the fidelity of the ministers of the court to which they are sent, and of the secretaries and other persons employed in the public offices. What ideas are we to entertain of this practice? To corrupt a person,—to seduce him,—to engage him by the powerful allurement of gold to betray his prince and violate his duty,—is, according to all the established principles of morality, undoubtedly a wicked ac-

---

even if he had issued an express order (as being at liberty to give what orders he pleases in his own kingdom), you should have replied that you receive no commands but from me: and if, after that, he had attempted to use violence, the part which remained for you to act, was that of withdrawing from his court."—I think the French monarch entertained erroneous ideas on the subject; since every sovereign must surely have a right to prohibit all foreign ministers doing any thing in his dominions which may tend to produce disorder, and which, moreover, is not necessary to the exercise of their ministerial functions. [[Note added in 1773/1797 editions.]]

tion. How comes it then that so little scruple is made of it in public affairs? A wise and virtuous politician* sufficiently gives us to understand that he absolutely condemns that scandalous resource: but, fearful of provoking the whole tribe of politicians to assail him at once like a nest of hornets, he proceeds no farther than barely advising them not to practise such manoeuvres except when every other resource fails. As to me, whose pen is employed in developing the sacred and immutable principles of justice, I must, in duty to the moral world, openly aver that the mode of corruption is directly repugnant to all the rules of virtue and probity, and a flagrant violation of the law of nature. It is impossible to conceive an act of a more flagitious nature, or more glaringly militant against the reciprocal duties of men, than that of inducing any one to do evil. The corruptor is undoubtedly guilty of a crime against the wretch whom he seduces: and as to the sovereign whose secrets are thus treacherously explored, is it not both an offence and an injury committed against him, to abuse the friendly reception given at his court, and to take advantage of it for the purpose of corrupting the fidelity of his servants? He has a right to banish the corruptor from his dominions, and to demand justice of his employer.

If ever bribery be excusable, it is when it happens to be the only possible mode by which we can completely discover and <474> defeat a heinous plot, capable of ruining or materially endangering the state in whose service we are employed. In the conduct of him who betrays such a secret, there may, according to circumstances, be no criminality. The great and lawful advantage accruing from the action which we induce him to perform, together with the urgent necessity of having recourse to it, may dispense with our paying too scrupulous an attention to the questionable complexion of the deed on his part. To gain him over, is no more than an act of simple and justifiable self-defence. It every day happens, that, in order to foil the machinations of wicked men, we find ourselves under a necessity of turning to our account the vicious dispositions of men of similar stamp. On this footing it was, that Henry the Fourth said to the Spanish minister that "it is justifiable conduct in

---

* Mons. Pequet, Discours sur l'Art de negocier, p. 91.

an embassador to have recourse to bribery for the purpose of detecting the intrigues that are carried on against his sovereign's interests";* adding that the affair of Marseilles,[17] that of Metz,[18] and several others, sufficiently shewed that he had good reason for endeavouring to penetrate the schemes which his enemies were plotting at Brussels against the tranquillity of his kingdom. That great prince, it is to be presumed, did not consider bribery and seduction as on all occasions excusable in a foreign minister, since he himself gave orders for the arrest of Bruneau, the Spanish embassador's secretary, who had tampered with Mairargues for the clandestine surrender of Marseilles to the Spaniards.

In barely taking advantage of the offers made to us by a traitor whom we have not seduced, our conduct is less inconsistent with justice and honour. But the examples of the Romans, which we have already quoted (Book III. §§155, 181), and in which there was question of declared enemies,—those examples, I say, sufficiently shew that true greatness of soul disdains even that resource, lest the adoption of it should hold out an encouragement to infamous treachery. A prince or a minister, whose ideas of honour are not inferior to those of the ancient Romans above noticed, will never stoop to embrace the proposals of a traitor, except when compelled by some dire uncontroulable necessity: and even then he will regret the degrading circumstance of owing his preservation to so unworthy an expedient.

But I do not here mean to condemn an embassador for employing civilities and polite attentions, and even presents and promises, with a view to gain friends for his sovereign. To conciliate men's affection and good will, is not seducing them, or impelling them to the perpetration of criminal deeds: and as to those new friends, it is their business to keep a strict watch over their own hearts, lest their attachment to a foreign prince should ever warp them from the fidelity which they owe to their lawful sovereign. <475>

---

* See Sully's Memoirs, and the French historians.
17. In 1601.
18. In 1601.

Should an embassador forget the duties of his station,—should he render himself disagreeable and dangerous,—should he form cabals and schemes prejudicial to the peace of the citizens, or to the state or prince to whom he is sent,—there are various modes of punishing him, proportionate to the nature and degree of his offence. If he maltreats the subjects of the state,—if he commits any acts of injustice or violence against them,—the injured subjects are not to seek redress from the ordinary magistrates, since the embassador is wholly independent of their jurisdiction: and for the same reason, those magistrates cannot proceed directly against him. On such occasions, therefore, the plaintiffs are to make application to their sovereign, who demands justice from the embassador's master, and, in case of a refusal, may order the insolent minister to quit his dominions.

§94. How he may be punished,

1. for ordinary transgressions;

Should a foreign minister offend the prince himself,—should he fail in the respect which he owes him, or, by his intrigues, embroil the state and the court,—the offended prince, from a wish to keep measures with the offender's sovereign, sometimes contents himself with simply requiring that the minister be recalled; or if the transgression be of a more serious nature, he forbids his appearance at court in the interval while his master's answer is expected; and in cases of a heinous complexion, he even proceeds so far as to expel him from his territories.

§95.
2. for faults committed against the prince.

Every sovereign has an unquestionable right to proceed in this manner; for, being master in his own dominions, no foreigner can stay at his court or in his territories, without his permission. And though sovereigns are generally obliged to listen to the overtures of foreign powers, and to admit their ministers, this obligation entirely ceases with regard to a minister, who, being himself deficient in the duties attached to his station, becomes dangerous to or justly suspected by the sovereign, to whom he can come in no other character than that of a minister of peace. Can a prince be obliged to suffer that a secret enemy, who is raising disturbances in the state and plotting its ruin, shall remain in his dominions, and appear at his court? Ridiculous was the answer of Philip the Second to queen Elizabeth, on her request that he would recall his embassador who was carrying on dangerous plots against her. The Spanish monarch refused to recall him, saying, that "the condition of princes would be

§96. Right of ordering away an embassador who is guilty, or justly suspected.

very wretched indeed, if they were obliged to recall a minister whenever his conduct did not suit the humour or the interest of those with whom he was negotiating."* Much more wretched would be the condition of princes, if they were bound to suffer in their states, and at their court, a minister who was disagreeable or justly suspected, an incendiary, an enemy disguised under the character of an embassador, who should avail himself of his inviolability, for the purpose of boldly plotting schemes of a per-<476>nicious tendency. The queen, justly offended at Philip's refusal, put a guard on the embassador.†

§97. Right of repressing him by force if he behaves as an enemy.

But is a prince on every occasion bound to confine his resentment to the simple expulsion of an embassador, however great the enormities of which the latter may have been guilty?—Such is the doctrine maintained by some authors, who ground their opinion on the absolute independency of a public minister. I own he is independent of the jurisdiction of the country: and I have already said, that, on this account, the common magistrate cannot proceed against him. I further admit, that, in all cases of ordinary transgression, all instances of offensive or disorderly behaviour, which, though injurious to individuals or to society, do not endanger the safety of the state or of the sovereign, there is that degree of respect due to the embassadorial character which is so necessary for the correspondence of nations, and to the dignity of the prince represented, that a complaint be first made to him of the conduct of his minister, together with a demand of reparation; and that, if no satisfaction is obtained, the offended sovereign be then content with simply ordering the embassador to quit his dominions, in case the serious nature of the offences absolutely require that a stop be put to them. But shall an embassador be suffered with impunity to cabal against the state where he resides, to plot its ruin, to stir up the subjects to revolt, and boldly to foment the most dangerous conspiracies, under the assurance of being supported by his master? If he behaves as an enemy, shall it not be allowable to treat him as such? The question admits not of a doubt with regard to an embassador who proceeds to overt acts, who takes up arms,

* Wicquefort, book i. §29.
† Idem, ibid.

and uses violence. In such case, those whom he attacks may repel him; self-defence being authorised by the law of nature. Those Roman embassadors, who, being sent to the Gauls, fought against them with the people of Clusium, divested themselves of the embassadorial character.* Can any one therefore imagine that the Gauls were bound to spare them in the hour of battle?

The question is more difficult with respect to an embassador who, without proceeding to overt acts, broaches plots of a dangerous tendency,—who, by his occult machinations, excites the subjects to revolt, and who forms and encourages conspiracies against the sovereign or the state. Shall it be deemed unlawful to repress and inflict exemplary punishment on a traitor who abuses the sacred character with which he is invested, and who is himself the first to set the example of violating the law of nations? that sacred law provides no less for the safety of the prince who receives an embassador, than for that of the embassador himself. But, on the other hand, if we allow the offended prince a right to punish a foreign minister in such cases, the subjects of contest <477> and rupture between sovereigns will become very frequent; and it is much to be feared that the embassadorial character will cease to enjoy that protection and inviolability which are so essential to it. There are certain practices connived at in foreign ministers, though not always strictly consistent with the rules of rectitude: there are others, again, which are not to be corrected by actual punishment, but simply by ordering the minister to depart. How shall we, in every case, be able to ascertain the precise boundaries of those different degrees of transgression? When there exists a premeditated design of persecuting a minister, an odious colouring will be given to his intrigues; his intentions and proceedings will be calumniated by sinister constructions; even false accusations will be raised against him. Finally, such plots as we here allude to are generally conducted with caution: they are carried on so secretly, that to obtain full proof of them is a matter of extreme difficulty, and indeed hardly pos-

§98. Embassador forming dangerous plots and conspiracies.

---

* Livy, book v. chap. 26 [[chap. 36]], where the historian peremptorily decides that those embassadors violated the law of nations: "Legati, contra jus gentium, arma capiunt." [["The legates took up arms in defiance of the law of nations."]]

sible without the formalities of justice,—formalities to which we cannot subject a minister who is independent of the jurisdiction of the country.

In laying down the grounds of the voluntary law of nations (Prelim. §21), we have seen, that, in particular conjunctures, nations must, with a view to the general advantage, necessarily recede from certain rights, which, taken in themselves and abstracted from every other consideration, should naturally belong to them. Thus, although the sovereign who has justice on his side, be alone really entitled to all the rights of war (Book III. §188), he is nevertheless obliged to look upon his enemy as enjoying equal rights with himself, and to treat him accordingly (ibid. §§190, 191). The same principles must be our rule in the present case. We may therefore venture to affirm, that, in consideration of the extensive utility, nay the absolute necessity of embassies, sovereigns are bound to respect the inviolability of an embassador as long as it is not incompatible with their own safety and the welfare of their state. Consequently, when the intrigues of the embassador have transpired, and his plots are discovered,—when the danger is past, so that there no longer exists a necessity of laying hands on him in order to guard against it,—the offended sovereign ought, in consideration of the embassadorial character, to renounce his general right of punishing a traitor and a secret enemy who conspires against the safety of the state,—and to content himself with dismissing the guilty minister, and requiring that punishment be inflicted on him by the sovereign to whose authority he is subject.

Such in fact is the mode of proceeding established by common consent among the generality of nations, especially those of Europe. Wicquefort* gives us several instances of some of the principal European sovereigns, who, on discovering embassadors to be guilty of odious machinations, have limited their resentment to the expulsion of the offenders, without even making <478> application to have them punished by their masters, of whom they did not expect to obtain a compliance with such a demand. To these instances let us add that of the duke of Orléans, regent of France.[19] That prince having detected a dangerous

---

* Embassad. book i. §§27, 28, 29.
19. Duke of Orléans, r. 1715–23.

conspiracy[20] which had been formed against him by the prince de Cellamare, embassador from Spain, behaved with great moderation on the occasion,—not adopting any severer measures than those of setting a guard over the guilty minister, seizing his papers, and causing him to be conducted out of the kingdom. Another remarkable instance, of very ancient date, stands recorded by the Roman historians,—that in which Tarquin's[21] embassadors were concerned. Having repaired to Rome under pretence of claiming the private property belonging to their master who had been expelled from his kingdom, they tampered with the profligate young nobility, and engaged them in a black and infamous conspiracy against the liberties of their country. Although such conduct would have authorised the rulers of the Roman state to treat them as enemies, the consuls and senate nevertheless respected the law of nations in the persons of those embassadors.* The offenders were sent back to their employer, without having received any personal injury: but, from Livy's account of the transaction, it appears that the letters which they had from the conspirators to Tarquin, were taken from them.

This example leads us to the true rule of the law of nations, in the cases now in question. An embassador cannot be punished, because he is independent: and for the reasons we have alleged, it is not proper to treat him as an enemy, till he himself proceeds to overt acts of violence: but we are justifiable in adopting against him every measure which the circumstances of the case may reasonably require for the purpose of defeating his machinations, and averting the evil which he has plotted. If, in order to disconcert and prevent a conspiracy, it were necessary to arrest or even put to death an embassador who animates and conducts it, I do not see why we should for a moment hesitate to take either of those steps,—not only because the safety of the state is the supreme law, but also because, independent of that maxim, the embassador's own deeds

§99. What may be done to him according to the exigency of the case.

---

* Et quamquam visi sunt (*legati*) commisisse ut hostium loco essent, jus tamen gentium valuit. [["But, notwithstanding they appeared to have deserved nothing less than being treated as enemies, the law of nations prevailed."]] Tit. Liv. [[*Ab urbe condita*]] lib. ii. cap. 4.

20. In 1718.

21. Lucius Tarquinius Superbus was the last king of Rome, reigning between B.C. 535 and 510. His expulsion marked the beginning of the Roman republic.

give us a perfect and particular right to proceed to such extremities. A
public minister, I grant, is independent; and his person is sacred: but it
is unquestionably lawful to repel his attacks, whether of a secret or of
an open nature, and to defend ourselves against him, whenever he acts
either as an enemy or a traitor. And if we cannot accomplish our own
preservation without harm thence resulting to him, it is he himself who
has laid us under a necessity of not sparing him. On such an occasion,
it may with great truth be asserted that the minister has by his own act
excluded himself from the protection of the law of nations. Suppose
the Venetian senate,—though apprised of the marquis of Bedamar's
conspiracy,[22] and <479> impressed with a thorough conviction of that
minister's being the prime mover and director of the whole business,—
had nevertheless been, in other particulars, destitute of sufficient information to enable them to crush the detestable plot,—suppose they had
been uncertain with respect to the number and rank of the conspirators,
the designs they had in agitation, and the particular quarter where the
meditated mischief was to burst forth,—whether an intention was entertained of exciting a revolt among the marine or the land forces, or
effecting the clandestine capture of some important fortress,—would
they, under such circumstances, have been bound to suffer the embassador to depart unmolested, and thus afford him an opportunity of joining and heading his accomplices, and of bringing his designs to a successful issue?—No man will seriously answer in the affirmative:—the
senate therefore would have had a right to arrest the marquis and all his
household, and even to extort from them their detestable secret. But
those prudent republicans, seeing the danger was removed and the conspiracy totally suppressed, chose to keep measures with Spain: wherefore
they prohibited all accusation of the Spaniards as concerned in the plot,
and contented themselves with simply requesting the embassador to
withdraw, in order to screen himself from the rage of the populace.

§100. Embas-
sador attempt-
ing against the
sovereign's life.
In this case the same rule is to be followed, which we have already laid
down (Book III. §136) in treating of what may lawfully be done to an
enemy. Whenever an embassador acts as an enemy, we are justifiable in

22. In 1618.

adopting against him every measure that is necessary for the purpose of defeating his evil designs, and ensuring our own safety. It is on the same principle, and under the idea which represents the embassador as a public enemy when he behaves as such, that we proceed to determine the treatment he ought to receive in case he pursues his criminal career to the last stage of enormity. If an embassador commit any of those atrocious crimes which sap the very foundations of the general safety of mankind,—if he attempt to assassinate or poison the prince who has received him at his court,—he unquestionably deserves to be punished as a treacherous enemy guilty of poisoning or assassination (see Book III. §155). The embassadorial character, which he has so basely prostituted, cannot shield him from the sword of justice. Is the law of nations to protect such a criminal, when the personal security of all sovereigns, and the general safety of mankind, loudly demand that his crime should be expiated by the sacrifice of his forfeit life? It is true indeed that we have little room to apprehend that a public minister will proceed to such dreadful enormities: for it is generally men of honour who are invested with the character of embassadors; and even if there should, among the number, be some whose consciences are callous to every scruple, the difficulties, nevertheless, and the magnitude of the danger, are sufficient to deter them from the attempt. Yet such crimes are not wholly <480> unexampled in history. Monsieur Barbeyrac* instances the assassination of the lord of Sirmium by an embassador of Constantinus Diogenes, governor of the neighbouring province for Basilius II. emperor of Constantinople; and for his authority he quotes the historian Cedrenus. The following fact is likewise to the purpose. In the year 1382, Charles III. king of Naples, having sent to his competitor, Louis duke of Anjou, a knight named Matthew Sauvage, in the character of a herald, to challenge him to single combat,—the herald was suspected of carrying a demi-lance whose point was tinged with a poison of so subtle a nature, that whoever should look stedfastly on it, or even suffer it to touch his clothes, would instantly drop down dead. The duke, being apprised of

* In his notes on Bynkershoek's treatise on the Competent Judge of Embassadors, ch. xxiv. §5, note 2.

the danger, refused to admit the herald into his presence, and ordered him to be taken into custody. The culprit was interrogated, and, upon his own confession, suffered the punishment of decapitation. Charles complained of the execution of his herald, as an infraction of the laws and usages of war: but Louis, in his reply, maintained that he had not violated those laws in his treatment of Sauvage, who had been convicted by his own confession.* Had the crime imputed to the herald been clearly substantiated, he was an assassin, whom no law could protect. But the very nature of the accusation sufficiently proves that it was a false and groundless charge.

§101. Two remarkable instances respecting the immunities of public ministers.

The question of which we have been treating has been debated in England and France, on two famous occasions. In the former of those countries, the question arose in the case of John Leslie, bishop of Ross, embassador from Mary queen of Scots.[23] That minister was continually intriguing against queen Elizabeth, plotting against the tranquillity of the state, forming conspiracies, and exciting the subjects to rebellion. Five of the most able civilians, being consulted by the privy council, gave it as their opinion, that "an embassador raising a rebellion against the prince at whose court he resides, forfeits the privileges annexed to his character, and is subject to the punishment of the law." They should rather have said, that he may be treated as an enemy. But the council contented themselves with causing the bishop to be arrested, and after having detained him a prisoner in the Tower for two years, set him at liberty when there was no longer any danger to be apprehended from his intrigues, and obliged him to depart from the kingdom.† This instance may serve to confirm the principles which we have laid down; and the like may be said of the following. Bruneau, secretary to the Spanish embassador in France, was detected in the very act of treating with Mairargues, in a time of profound peace, for the surrender of Marseilles to the Spaniards. The <481> secretary was thereupon committed to prison,

---

* History of the Kings of the Two Sicilies, by Monsieur D'Egly [[Monthenault D'Egly]].

† [[William Camden]] Cambden's Annal. Angl. ad ann. 1571, 1573.

23. Mary, Queen of Scots, r. 1542–67.

and was subjected to a judicial examination by the parliament before whom Mairargues was tried. That body, however, did not pronounce sentence of condemnation on Bruneau, but referred his case to the king, who restored him to his master, on condition that the latter should order him to depart immediately from the kingdom. The embassador warmly complained of the imprisonment of his secretary: but Henry IV. very judiciously answered, that "the law of nations does not forbid putting a public minister under an arrest, in order to hinder him from doing mischief." The king might have added, that a nation has even a right to adopt, against a public minister, every measure which may be necessary for the purpose of warding off the mischief he meditates against her,— of defeating his projects, and preventing their evil consequences. It was on this principle that the parliament were authorised to interrogate Bruneau, for the purpose of discovering all the parties concerned in so dangerous a conspiracy. The question, whether foreign ministers who violate the law of nations do thereby forfeit their privileges, was warmly debated at Paris: but, without waiting to have the point decided, the king restored Bruneau to his master.*

It is not lawful to maltreat an embassador by way of retaliation: for the prince who uses violence against a public minister, is guilty of a crime; and we are not to take vengeance for his misconduct, by copying §102. Whether reprisals may be made on an embassador.

---

* See the discussion of the question, and the discourse which Henry IV. held on this subject, to the Spanish embassador, in the Memoires de Nevers, vol. ii. p. 858, et seq. in Matthieu, vol. ii. book 3, and other historians.

Joseph Sofi, king of Carezem, having imprisoned an embassador of Timur-Bec, Timur's secretary of state wrote him a letter couched in strong terms of expostulation on the subject of that infraction of the law of nations,—informing him that "it is a maxim with kings to consider the person of an embassador as sacred: for which reason he is always held exempt from the punishment of death or imprisonment, if the sovereign to whom he is sent has even the slightest knowledge of the law of nations, or the embassador himself does but possess sufficient prudence to refrain from the commission of any heinous offence, and to behave with common decency." La Croix, Hist. of Timur-Bec, book ii. chap. 26.—The same historian, in his account of Barcouc, sultan of Egypt, who put Timur's embassador to death, observes,—"that it was an infamous action;—that to insult an embassador, is a violation of the law of nations, and a deed at which nature herself shudders." Ibid. book v. chap. 17. [[This paragraph added in 1773/1797 editions.]]

his example. We never can, under pretence of retaliation, be authorised to commit actions which are in their own nature unjustifiable: and such undoubtedly would be any instance of ill-treatment inflicted on an un-offending minister as a punishment for his master's faults. If it be an indispensable duty to pay a general regard to this rule in cases of retal-iation, it is more particularly obligatory with regard to an embassador, on account of the respect due to his character. The Carthaginians having violated the law of nations in the persons of the Roman embassadors, the embassadors of that perfidious nation were brought to Scipio, who, being asked how he would have them to be treated, replied, "Not in the manner that the Carthaginians have treated ours." Ac-<482>cordingly he dismissed them in safety:* but at the same time he made preparations for chastising by force of arms the state which had violated the law of nations.† There cannot be a better pattern for sovereigns to follow on such an occasion. If the injury for which we would make retaliation does not concern a public minister, there exists a still stronger certainty that we must not retaliate on the embassador of the sovereign against whom our complaint lies. The safety of public ministers would be very pre-carious, if it were liable to be affected by every casual difference that might arise. But there is one particular case in which it appears perfectly justifiable to arrest an embassador, provided no ill treatment be given to him in other respects. When, for instance, a prince has, in open violation of the law of nations, caused our embassador to be arrested, we may arrest and detain his, as a pledge for the life and liberty of ours. But, should this expedient prove unsuccessful, it would become our duty to liberate the unoffending minister, and to seek redress by more efficacious measures. Charles the Fifth caused the French embassador, who had made

---

* Appian, quoted by Grotius, lib. ii. cap. 28, §7 [[*Law of War and Peace*]].—According to Diodorus Siculus, Scipio said to the Romans, "Do not imitate that conduct with which you reproach the Carthaginians." Εκιπιων ουκ εφη δειν πραττειν ὁ τοις Καρχηδονιοις εγκαλουσι. Diod. Sic. Excerpt. Peiresc. p. 290.

† Livy, book xxx. chap. 28, §7. That historian makes Scipio say "Though the Car-thaginians have violated the faith of the truce, and the law of nations, in the person of our embassadors, I will do nothing against theirs that is unworthy of the maxims of the Roman people, and of my own principles."

him a declaration of war, to be put under an arrest; whereupon Francis the First caused Granvelle, the emperor's embassador, to be arrested in like manner. At length, however, it was agreed that both those ministers should be conducted to the frontier, and released at the same time.*

We have derived the independence and inviolability of the embassadorial character from the natural and necessary principles of the law of nations. These prerogatives are farther confirmed by the uniform practice and general consent of mankind. We have seen above (§84) that the Spaniards found the right of embassies established and respected in Mexico. The same principle also prevails even among the savage tribes of North America: and if we thence turn our eye to the other extremity of the globe, we find that embassadors are highly respected in China. In India also the same rule is observed, though with less scrupulous punctuality:†—the king of Ceylon, for instance, has sometimes imprisoned the embassadors of the Dutch East-India company. Being master of the places which produce cinnamon, he knows that the Dutch, in consideration of a profitable commerce, will over-look many irregularities in his conduct: and, with the true disposition of a barbarian, he takes an undue advantage of that circumstance. The Koran enjoins the moslems to respect public ministers: and if the Turks have not in all in-<483>stances uniformly observed that precept, their violations of it are rather imputable to the ferocity of particular princes than to the principles of the nation at large. The rights of embassadors were formerly very well known among the Arabs. A writer of that nation‡ relates the following incident. Khaled, an Arabian chief, having come, in the character of embassador, to the army of the emperor Heraclius, used insolent language to the general: whereupon the latter observed to him, that "embassadors were protected from all kind of violence by the law which universally prevailed among nations: and it was probably that consid-

§103. Agreement of nations concerning the privileges of embassadors.

---

* Mezeray's Hist. of France, vol. ii. p. 470.

† General Hist. of Voyages, artic. China, and Indies. [[Prévost, *Histoire générale des voyages* (Paris, 1746–1801).]]

‡ Alvakedi's History of the Conquest of Syria. [[Alvakedi was translated by Ockley, and incorporated into the latter's *History of the Saracens.*]]

eration which had emboldened the Arab to speak to him in so indecent a manner."* It would be quite unnecessary, in this place, to accumulate the various examples with which the history of the European nations presents us: the enumeration would be endless; and the established customs of Europe on this subject are sufficiently known. Saint Louis, when at Acra in Palestine, gave a remarkable instance of the protection due to public ministers:—an embassador from the Old Man of the Mountain, or prince of the Assassins, speaking insolently to the French monarch, the grand masters of the orders of the Temple and the Hospital informed that minister, that, "were it not for the respect paid to the character with which he was invested, they would cause him to be thrown into the sea."† The king however dismissed him without suffering the slightest injury to be done him. Nevertheless, as the prince of the Assassins was on his own part guilty of grossly violating the most sacred rights of nations, it would have been reasonable to suppose that his embassador had no claim to protection, except indeed on this single consideration, that, as the privilege of inviolability is founded on the necessity of keeping open a safe channel of communication, through which sovereigns may reciprocally make proposals to each other, and carry on negotiations both in peace and in war, the protection should therefore extend even to the envoys of those princes, who, guilty themselves of violating the law of nations, would otherwise have no title to our respect.

§104. Free exercise of religion.   There are rights of another nature, which, though not necessarily annexed to the character of a public minister, are nevertheless allowed to him by established custom in almost every country. One of the principal of these is the free exercise of his religion. It is indeed highly proper that a minister, and especially a resident minister, should enjoy the free exercise of his religion within his own house, for himself and his retinue. But it cannot be said, that this right, like those of independence and inviolability, is absolutely necessary to the success of his commission, particularly in the case of a non-resident minister, the only one whom nations are bound to admit (§66). The mi-<484>nister may, in this re-

---

* Ockley's History of the Saracens, vol. i.
† Choisy's History of St. Louis.

spect, do what he pleases in his own house, into which no body has a right to pry, or to enter. But if the sovereign of the country where he resides, should, for substantial reasons, refuse him permission to practise his religion in any manner which might render it an object of public notice, we must not presume to condemn the conduct of that sovereign, much less to accuse him of violating the law of nations. At present embassadors are not debarred the free exercise of their religion in any civilised country: for a privilege which is founded on reason, cannot be refused when it is attended with no ill consequence.

Among those rights that are not necessary to the success of embassies, there are, on the other hand, some which are not founded on a general consent of nations, but which are nevertheless, by the custom of several countries, annexed to the embassadorial character. Of this number is the exemption of things brought into or sent out of the country by a foreign minister, from the customary duties on importation and exportation. There is no necessity that he should be favoured with any distinction in that respect, since his payment of those duties will not render him the less capable of discharging his functions. If the sovereign is pleased to exempt him from them, it is an instance of civility which the minister could not claim as matter of right, any more than that his baggage, or any chests or packages which he imports from abroad, shall not be searched at the custom-house. Thomas Chaloner, the English embassador in Spain, sent home a bitter complaint to queen Elizabeth his mistress, that the custom-house officers had opened his trunks in order to search them. But the queen returned him for answer, that it was "the duty of an embassador to wink at every thing which did not directly offend the dignity of his sovereign."* §105. Whether an embassador be exempted from all imposts.

The independency of the embassador exempts him indeed from every personal imposition, capitation, or other duty of that nature, and in general from every tax relating to the character of a subject of the state. But as for duties laid on any kind of goods or provisions, the most absolute independency does not exempt him from the payment of them: even sovereigns themselves are subject to them. In Holland, the follow-

* Wicquefort's Embass. book i. §28. towards the end.

ing rule is observed:—embassadors are exempt from the taxes on consumption,—doubtless, because those taxes are more directly of a personal nature: but they pay the duties on importation and exportation.

However extensive their exemption may be, it is manifest that it solely relates to things intended for their own use. Should they abuse and make a shameful traffic of it by lending their name to merchants, the sovereign has unquestionably a right to put a stop to the fraud, even by suppressing the privilege. Such things have been known in several places; and the sordid avarice of some ministers, who made a trade of their exemption, has oblig-<485>ed the sovereign to deprive them of it. At present the foreign ministers at Petersburgh are subject to the duties on importation: but the empress has the generosity to indemnify them for the loss of a privilege which they had no right to claim, and which, from the frequency of its abuse, she had been obliged to abolish.

§106. Obligation founded on use and custom.

But here it is asked, whether a nation may abolish what general custom has established with respect to foreign ministers? Let us then consider what obligation custom and received usage can impose on nations, not only in what concerns ministers, but also in any other instance, in general. The usages and customs of other nations are no farther obligatory on an independent state, than as she has expressly or tacitly given her consent to them. But when once a custom, indifferent in itself, has been generally established and received, it carries the force of an obligation on the states which have tacitly or expressly adopted it. Nevertheless, if, in process of time, any nation perceives that such custom is attended with inconveniences, she is at liberty to declare that she no longer chuses to conform to it: and when once she has made this explicit declaration, no cause of complaint lies against her for refusing thenceforward to observe the custom in question. But such a declaration should be made beforehand, and at a time when it does not affect any particular nation: it is too late to make it when the case actually exists: for it is a maxim universally received, that a law must never be changed at the moment of the actual existence of the particular case to which we would apply it. Thus, on the subject before us, a sovereign who has previously notified his intentions, and received an embassador only on that footing, is not obliged to allow him the enjoyment of all the privileges, or to pay

him all the honours, which custom had before annexed to the embassadorial character,—provided that the privileges and honours which are
with-held be not essential to the nature of the embassy, and necessary
to ensure its legitimate success. To refuse privileges of this latter kind,
would be the same thing in effect as refusing the embassy itself, a conduct
which a state is not at liberty to pursue generally and on every occasion
(§65), but in those instances only where the refusal is founded on some
very substantial reason. To with-hold honours which are consecrated by
custom and become in a manner essential, is an expression of contempt,
and an actual injury.

Here it must be further observed, that, when a sovereign intends to
break through an established custom, the rule should be general. To refuse certain customary honours or privileges to the embassador of one
nation, and to continue the enjoyment of them to others, is an affront
to that nation, a mark of contempt, or at least of ill-will.

Sometimes princes send to each other secret ministers, whose char- §107. A min-
acter is not public. If a minister of this kind be insulted by a person ister whose
character is
unacquainted with his character, such insult is no violation of the law not public.
of nations: but the prince who receives this embassador, and knows him
to be a public minister, is bound by the <486> same ties of duty towards
him as towards a publicly acknowledged embassador, and under equal
obligation to protect him, and, as far as in his power, to ensure him the
full enjoyment of that inviolability and independence which the law of
nations annexes to the embassadorial character. No excuse, therefore, can
be offered for the conduct of Francis Sforza, duke of Milan,[24] in putting
to death Maraviglia, secret minister of Francis the First. Sforza had often
treated with that secret agent, and had acknowledged him as the French
monarch's minister.*

We cannot introduce in any more proper place an important question §108. A
of the law of nations, which is nearly allied to the right of embassies. It sovereign
in a foreign
is asked, what are the rights of a sovereign who happens to be in a foreign country.

---

* See the Memoirs of Martin Du Bellay, book iv. and Father Daniel's History of
France, vol. v. p. 300, &c.
24. Francis Sforza, Duke of Milan, r. 1450–66.

country, and how the master of the country is to treat him? If that prince be come to negotiate, or to treat about some public affair, he is doubtless entitled in a more eminent degree to enjoy all the rights of embassadors. If he be come as a traveller, his dignity alone, and the regard due to the nation which he represents and governs, shelters him from all insult, gives him a claim to respect and attention of every kind, and exempts him from all jurisdiction. On his making himself known, he cannot be treated as subject to the common laws; for it is not to be presumed that he has consented to such a subjection: and if a prince will not suffer him in his dominions on that footing, he should give him notice of his intentions. But if the foreign prince forms any plot against the safety and welfare of the state,—in a word, if he acts as an enemy,—he may very justly be treated as such. In every other case he is entitled to full security, since even a private individual of a foreign nation has a right to expect it.

A ridiculous notion has possessed the minds even of persons who deem themselves superior in understanding to the common herd of mankind. They think that a sovereign who enters a foreign country without permission, may be arrested there.* But on what reason can such an act of violence be grounded? The absurdity of the doctrine carries its own refutation on the face of it. A foreign sovereign, it is true, ought to give notice of his coming, if he wishes to receive such treatment as he is entitled to expect. It would moreover be prudent in him to make application for passports, in order that designing malevolence may not have any pretext, any hope of finding specious reasons to pal-<487>liate an act of injustice and violence. I further allow, that,—as the presence of a foreign sovereign may on certain occasions be productive of serious

---

* It is surprising to see a grave historian give into this opinion. See Gramond's Hist. Gall. lib. xii. The cardinal De Richelieu also alleged this trifling reason, when he gave orders for arresting Charles Lewis, the elector Palatine, who had attempted to pass through France incognito: he said, that "No foreign prince was permitted to pass through the kingdom without a passport." But he added better reasons, drawn from the prince Palatine's designs against Brissac and the other places left by Bernard duke of Saxe-Weymar, and to which France pretended to have a greater right than any other power, because those conquests had been made with the money furnished by that kingdom. See the History of the Treaty of Westphalia, by Father Bougant [[Bougeant]], vol. ii. in 12mo. pag. 88.

consequences,—if the times are in any-wise critical, and the motives of his journey liable to suspicion, he ought not to undertake it without the consent and approbation of the prince whose territories he means to enter. When Peter the Great determined personally to visit foreign countries in quest of the arts and sciences to enrich his empire, he travelled in the retinue of his own embassadors.

A foreign prince unquestionably retains all his rights over his own state and subjects, and may exercise them in every instance that does not affect the sovereignty of the country in which he is a sojourner. The king of France, therefore, appears to have been too punctilious in refusing to permit the emperor Sigismund, when at Lyons, to confer the dignity of duke on the count of Savoy, who was a vassal of the empire (see Book II. §40). Less difficulty would have been made with any other prince: but the court was scrupulously careful to guard against the old claims of the emperors. On the other hand, it was with very good reason that the same court expressed considerable displeasure at the conduct of queen Christina,[25] who, whilst residing in France, caused one of her domestics to be executed in her own house: for an execution of that kind is an act of territorial jurisdiction: and besides, Christina had abdicated the crown.[26] Her reservations, her birth, her dignity, might indeed entitle her to great honours, or, at most, to an entire independence,—but not to all the rights of an actual sovereign. The famous instance of Mary queen of Scots, so often quoted in questions on this subject, is not a very apposite example: for that princess was no longer in possession of the crown at the time when she came to England, and was arrested, tried, and condemned to death.

The deputies sent to the assembly of the states of a kingdom or a republic, are not public ministers like those of whom we have spoken above, as they are not sent to foreign powers: but they are public persons, and in that character are possessed of privileges which it is our duty to establish before we take leave of this subject. The states which have a right to meet by deputies for the purpose of deliberating on public af-

§109. Deputies to the states.

25. Queen Christina of Sweden, r. 1632–54.
26. In 1654.

fairs, are, from that very circumstance, entitled to demand perfect security for their representatives, together with every exemption and immunity that is necessary to the free discharge of their functions. If the persons of the deputies be not inviolable, their constituents cannot be assured of their fidelity in asserting the rights of the nation, and courageously defending the public interests. And how could those representatives duly acquit themselves of their functions, if people were allowed to molest them by arrests, either for debt or for ordinary offences? Between the nation and the sovereign, in this case, the same reasons hold good, on which, between state and state, the immunities of embassadors are founded. We may therefore safely venture to assert that the rights of the nation, and the public faith, secure those deputies from violence of every kind, and even from <488> any judicial prosecution, during the term of their ministry. Such indeed is the rule observed in all countries, and particularly at the diets of the empire, the parliaments of England, and the cortes of Spain. Henry the Third of France[27] caused the duke and the cardinal de Guise to be killed at the meeting of the states at Blois.[28] Unquestionably the security of the assembly was violated by that action: but those two princes were factious rebels, whose audacious views aimed at nothing less than depriving their sovereign of his crown. And if it was equally certain that Henry was no longer possessed of sufficient power to bring them to a formal trial, and punish them according to the laws, the necessity of justifiable self-defence gave the king a right to adopt the mode which he pursued, and furnishes a sufficient apology for his conduct. It is the misfortune of weak and unskilful princes, that they suffer themselves to be reduced to extremities, from which they cannot extricate themselves without a violation of every established rule. It is said that Pope Sixtus the Fifth, on hearing of the catastrophe of the duke de Guise, commended that resolute act, as a necessary stroke of policy: but when he was told that the cardinal had likewise been killed, he burst into a violent paroxysm of rage.* This, indeed, was carrying his haughty

---

* See the French historians [[Daniel, Mézeray, Velly]].
27. Henry III, r. 1574–89.
28. In 1588 the French Estates General met at Blois.

pretensions to an excessive height. The pontiff readily allowed that urgent necessity had authorised Henry to violate the security of the states, and to break through all the forms of justice: and could he pretend that this prince, rather than be deficient in respect for the Roman purple, should risk both his crown and his life?

CHAPTER VIII

Of the Judge of Embassadors in Civil Cases.

Some authors will have an embassador to be subject, in civil cases, to the jurisdiction of the country where he resides,—at least in such cases as have arisen during the time of his embassy; and, in support of their opinion, they allege that this subjection is by no means derogatory to the embassadorial character: "for," say they, "however sacred a person may be, his inviolability is not affected by suing him in a civil action." But it is not on account of the sacredness of their person that embassadors cannot be sued: it is because they are independent of the jurisdiction of the country to which they are sent; and the substantial reasons on which that independency is grounded, may be seen in a preceding part of this work (§92). Let us here add that it is in every respect highly proper, and even necessary, that an embassador should be exempt from judicial prosecution even in civil causes, in order that he may be free from molestation in the exercise of his functions. For a similar reason, it was not allowed among the Romans to summon a priest whilst he <489> was employed in his sacred offices:* but at other times he was open to the law. The reason which we have here alleged for the exemption, is also assigned in the Roman law: *"Ideo enim non datur actio* (adversus legatum) *ne ab officio suscepto legationis avocetur,*† *ne impediatur*

§110. The embassador is exempt from the civil jurisdiction of the country where he resides.

---

* Nec pontificem (in jus vocari oportet) dum sacra facit. [["One should not bring a priest before the law while he is performing religious rites" (trans. Eds.).]] [[Justinian's]] Digest. lib. ii. tit. 4, De in Jus vocando, leg. 2.

† [[Justinian's]] Digest. lib. v. tit. 1, De Judiciis, &c. leg. 24, §2.

legatio.*[29] But there was an exception as to those transactions which had taken place during the embassy. This was reasonable with regard to those *legati* or ministers of whom the Roman law here speaks, who, being sent only by nations subject to the empire, could not lay claim to the independency enjoyed by a foreign minister. As they were subjects of the state, the legislature was at liberty to establish whatever regulations it thought most proper respecting them: but a sovereign has not the like power of obliging the minister of another sovereign to submit to his jurisdiction: and even if such power was vested in him by convention or otherwise, the exercise of it would be highly improper: because, under that pretext, the embassador might be often molested in his ministry, and the state involved in very disagreeable quarrels, for the trifling concerns of some private individuals, who might and ought to have taken better precautions for their own security. It is, therefore, only in conformity to the mutual duties which states owe to each other, and in accord with the grand principles of the law of nations, that an embassador or public minister is at present, by the universal custom and consent of nations, independent of all jurisdiction in the country where he resides, either in civil or criminal cases. I know there have occurred some instances to the contrary: but a few facts do not establish a custom: on the contrary, those to which I allude, only contribute, by the censure passed on them, to prove the custom such as I have asserted it to be. In the year 1668, the Portuguese resident at the Hague was, by an order of the court of justice, arrested and imprisoned for debt. But an illustrious member of that same court† very justly thinks that the procedure was unjustifiable, and contrary to the law of nations. In the year 1657, a resident of the elector of Brandenburg was also arrested for debt in England. But he was set at liberty, as having been illegally arrested; and

---

* Ibid. leg. xxvi.

† M. de Bynkershoek's Competent Judge of Embassadors, chap. xiii. §1.

29. "Now for that reason a lawsuit is not granted (against an ambassador) in case he is called away from the diplomatic post he has taken up, and lest diplomacy be hampered."

even the creditors and officers of justice who had offered him that insult were punished.*

But if an embassador chooses to renounce a part of his independency, and to subject himself in civil affairs to the jurisdiction of the country, he is undoubtedly at liberty to do so, provided it be done with his master's consent. Without such consent, the embassador has no right to renounce privileges in which the dig-<490>nity and service of his sovereign are concerned,—which are founded on the master's rights, and instituted for his advantage, not for that of the minister. It is true, indeed, that the embassador, without waiting for his sovereign's permission, acknowledges the jurisdiction of the country when he commences a suit as plaintiff in a court of justice. But the consequence, in that case, is inevitable; and besides, in a civil cause, on a point of private interest, no inconvenience attends it; since the embassador has it at all times in his power to avoid commencing a suit, or may, if such a step be necessary, intrust the prosecution of his cause to an attorney or lawyer.

§111. How he may voluntarily subject himself to it.

Let us here add, by the way, that an embassador ought never to institute a prosecution on a criminal charge. If he has been insulted, he should make his complaint to the sovereign; and the delinquent is to be prosecuted by the public.

It may happen that the minister of a foreign power is at the same time a subject of the state where he is employed; and in this case, as a subject, he is unquestionably under the jurisdiction of the country in every thing which does not directly relate to his ministry. But the question is, to determine in what cases those two characters, of subject and foreign minister, are united in the same person. To produce such union, it is not sufficient that the minister was born a subject of the state to which he is sent; for, unless the laws expressly prohibit every citizen to leave his country, he may legally have renounced his country, and placed himself

§112. A minister who is a subject of the state where he is employed.

* Ibid.—It is not long since the world witnessed the circumstance of a foreign minister in France being pursued by his creditors, and refused a passport by the French court. See Journal Politique de Bouillon, Feb. 1, 1771, page 54, and Jan. 15, p. 57. [[*Journal politique* (March 1766–95), later called *Gazette des Gazettes,* published at Bouillon. Note added in 1773/1797 editions.]]

in subjection to a new master. He may likewise, without renouncing his country for ever, become independent of it during the whole time that he spends in the service of a foreign prince; and the presumption is certainly in favour of such independency: for the state and functions of a public minister naturally require that he should depend only on his master (§92), on the prince who has intrusted him with the management of his affairs. Whenever, therefore, there does not exist any circumstance which furnishes a proof or indication to the contrary, a foreign minister, though antecedently a subject of the state, is reputed to be absolutely independent of it during the whole time of his commission. If his former sovereign does not choose to allow him such independency in his dominions, he may refuse to admit him in the character of a foreign minister, as is the practice in France, where, according to monsieur De Callieres, "the king no longer receives any of his own subjects as ministers of foreign princes."*

But a subject of the state may still continue its subject, notwithstanding his acceptance of a commission from a foreign prince. His subjection is expressly established when the sovereign acknowledges him as minister only with a reserve that he shall remain a subject of the state. The states-general of the United Provinces, in a decree of the 19th of June 1681, declare, "That no subject <491> of the state shall be received as embassador or minister of another power, but on condition that he shall not divest himself of his character of subject, even with regard to jurisdiction both in civil and criminal affairs,—and that whoever, in making himself known as embassador or minister, has not mentioned his quality of subject of the state, shall not enjoy those rights or privileges which peculiarly belong to the ministers of foreign powers."†

Such a minister may likewise retain his former subjection *tacitly;* and then, by a natural consequence drawn from his actions, state, and whole behaviour, it is known that he continues a subject. Thus, independent of the declaration abovementioned, those Dutch merchants who obtain the title of residents of certain foreign princes, and nevertheless continue

* [[Callières]] Manner of negotiating with Sovereigns, chap. vi.
† Bynkershock, ubi supra, chap. xi.

to carry on their commerce, thereby sufficiently denote that they remain subjects. Whatever inconveniences may attend the subjection of a minister to the sovereign with whom he resides, if the foreign prince chooses to acquiesce in such a state of things, and is content to have a minister on that footing, it is his own concern; and should his minister on any ignominious occasion be treated as a subject, he has no cause of complaint.

It may likewise happen that a foreign minister shall become a subject of the sovereign to whom he is sent, by accepting of a post under him: and in this case he cannot lay claim to independence except in such things alone as directly relate to his ministry. The prince by whom he is delegated, in allowing of this voluntary subjection, agrees to risk the inconveniences that attend it. Thus, in the last century, the baron De Charnacé[30] and the count D'Estrades[31] were embassadors from France to the states-general, and at the same times officers in their high mightinesses' army.

The independency of a public minister is the true reason of his exemption from the jurisdiction of the country in which he resides. No legal process can be directly issued against him, because he is not subject to the authority of the prince or the magistrates. But it is asked whether that exemption of his person extends indiscriminately to all his property? In order to solve this question, we must consider by what circumstances property may be subjected to, and by what others it may be exempted from, the jurisdiction of a country. In general, whatever lies within the extent of a country, is subject to the authority and jurisdiction of the sovereign (Book I. §205, and Book II. §§83, 84). If any dispute arises concerning effects or goods within or passing through the country, it is to be decided by the judge of the place. In virtue of this dependence, the mode of stoppage or seizure has been established in many countries, for the purpose of compelling a foreigner to repair to the spot where the seizure has been made, and there to answer questions that are to be put to him, though not directly relating to the effects seized. But a foreign

§113. Immunity of the minister extends to his property.

30. Baron De Charnacé, r. 1639–40.
31. Count D'Estrades, r. 1640–48.

minister, <492> as we have already shewn, is independent of the jurisdiction of the country: and his personal independence in civil cases
would be of little avail, unless it extended to every thing which he finds
necessary in order to enable him to live with dignity, and quietly to attend to the discharge of his functions. Besides, whatever he has brought
with him or purchased for his own use as minister, is so connected with
his person as to partake of the same fate with it. Since the minister entered the territory on the footing of independence, he could not have it
in contemplation to subject his retinue, his baggage, or his necessaries,
to the jurisdiction of the country. Every thing, therefore, which directly
belongs to his person in the character of a public minister,—every thing
which is intended for his use, or which serves for his own maintenance
and that of his household,—every thing of that kind, I say, partakes of
the minister's independency, and is absolutely exempt from all jurisdiction in the country. Those things, together with the person to whom
they belong, are considered as being out of the country.

§114. The
exemption
cannot extend
to effects
belonging to
any trade the
minister may
carry on;

But this exemption cannot extend to such property as evidently belongs to the embassador under any other relation than that of minister.
What has no affinity with his functions and character, cannot partake
of the privileges which are solely derived from his functions and character. Should a minister, therefore, (as it has often been the case) embark
in any branch of commerce, all the effects, goods, money, and debts,
active and passive, which are connected with his mercantile concerns,—
and likewise all contests and law-suits to which they may give rise,—fall
under the jurisdiction of the country. And although, in consequence of
the minister's independency, no legal process can, in those law-suits, be
directly issued against his person, he is nevertheless, by the seizure of the
effects belonging to his commerce, indirectly compelled to plead in his
own defence. The abuses which would arise from a contrary practice,
are evident. What could be expected from a merchant vested with a privilege to commit every kind of injustice in a foreign country? There exists
not a shadow of reason for extending the ministerial immunity to things
of that nature. If the sovereign who sends a minister is apprehensive of
any inconvenience from the indirect dependency in which his servant
thus becomes involved, he has only to lay on him his injunctions against

engaging in commerce,—an occupation, indeed, which ill accords with the dignity of the ministerial character.

To what we have said, let us add two illustrations: 1. In doubtful cases, the respect due to the ministerial character requires that things should always be explained to the advantage of that character. I mean that when there is room for doubt whether a thing be really intended for the use of the minister and his household, or whether it belongs to his commerce, the decision must be given in favour of the minister; otherwise there would be a risk of violating his privileges. 2. When I say that we may <493> seize such of the minister's effects as have no relation to his public character, particularly those that belong to his commercial concerns, this is to be understood only on the supposition that the seizure be not made for any cause arising from his transactions in quality of minister, as for instance, articles supplied for the use of his family, house-rent, &c. because any claims which may lie against him in that relation, cannot be decided in the country, and consequently cannot be subjected to its jurisdiction by the indirect mode of seizure.

All landed estates, all immovable property, by whomsoever possessed, are subject to the jurisdiction of the country (Book I. §205, and Book II. §§83, 84). Are they to be exempted from it on the single ground that their owner has been appointed embassador by a foreign power? There can exist no reason for the exemption in such case. It is not in his public character that the embassador possesses that property; nor is it attached to his person, so as, like himself, to be reputed out of the territory. If the foreign prince apprehends any ill consequences from that state of dependency in which his minister may stand on account of some of his possessions, he may make choice of another person to fill the office. Let us conclude, therefore, that immovable property possessed by a foreign minister does not change its nature in consequence of the character conferred on the owner, but continues subject to the jurisdiction of the state in which it lies. All contests and law-suits concerning that property are to be carried before the tribunals of the country; and those same tribunals may decree its seizure in order to satisfy any legal claim. It is, however, easily conceived, that, if the embassador lives in a house of his own, that house is excepted from the rule, as actually serving for his

§115. nor to immovable property which he possesses in the country.

immediate use;—it is excepted, I mean, in whatever may affect the present use which the embassador makes of it.

It may be seen, in monsieur de Bynkershoek's treatise,* that custom coincides with the principles laid down in this and the preceding sections. In suing an embassador in either of the two cases just mentioned,—that is to say, on the subject of any immovable property lying in the country, or of movable effects which have no connection with the embassy,—the embassador is to be summoned in the same manner as an absent person, since he is reputed to be out of the country, and his independency does not permit any immediate address to his person in an authoritative manner, such as sending an officer of a court of justice to him.

§116. How justice may be obtained against an embassador.

By what mode, then, may satisfaction be obtained of an embassador who refuses to do justice to those who have dealings with him? It is asserted by many that he must be sued before the tribunal to whose jurisdiction he was subject antecedently to his appointment as embassador. In this there appears to me an impropriety. If the necessity and importance of his functions set him above all prosecution in the foreign country where he resides, shall any man be allowed to molest him in the performance of his ministerial duties by summoning him to appear be-<494>fore the tribunals of his own country? The interest of the public service forbids such a procedure. It is absolutely necessary that the minister should solely depend on his sovereign, to whom he belongs in a peculiar manner. He is an instrument in the hand of the conductor of the nation; and no circumstance whatever ought to be permitted to divert or obstruct his services. Neither would it be just that the absence of a person who is intrusted with the interests of the sovereign and the nation, should prove detrimental to him in his private concerns. In all countries, those who are absent on the service of the state enjoy privileges which secure them from the inconveniences attendant on the state of absentees. But these privileges of the ministers of the state should, as far as possible, be so modelled and tempered, as not to be unreasonably burthensome or injurious to private persons who have dealings with

---

* On the Competent Judge of Embassadors, chap. xvi. §6.

them. How then are those different interests—the service of the state and the administration of justice—to be reconciled? All private persons, whether citizens or foreigners, who have any demands against a minister—if they cannot obtain satisfaction from himself—should apply to his master, who is obliged to do them justice in such manner as may be most consistent with the public service. It rests with the prince to determine whether it be most proper to recall his minister, to appoint a tribunal before which he may be sued, or to order an adjournment of the cause, &c. In a word, the good of the state does not allow that any person whatever should have it in his power to disturb the minister in his functions, or to divert his attention from them, without the sovereign's permission; and the sovereign, whose duty it is to distribute impartial and universal justice, ought not to countenance his minister in refusing it, or wearying out his adversaries by unjust delays.

CHAPTER IX

Of the Embassador's House and Domestics.

The independency of the embassador would be very imperfect, and his security very precarious, if the house in which he lives were not to enjoy a perfect immunity, and to be inaccessible to the ordinary officers of justice. The embassador might be molested under a thousand pretexts; his secrets might be discovered by searching his papers, and his person exposed to insults. Thus all the reasons which establish his independence and inviolability, concur likewise in securing the freedom of his house. In all civilised nations, this right is acknowledged as annexed to the embassadorial character: and an embassador's house, at least in all the ordinary affairs of life, is, equally with his person, considered as being out of the country. Of this, a remarkable instance occurred, not many years ago, at Petersburg. On the third of April, 1752, thirty soldiers, with an officer at <495> their head, entered the house of baron Greiffenheim the Swedish minister, and carried off two of his domestics, whom they conducted to prison, under a pretence that those two men had clandes-

§117. The embassador's house.

tinely sold liquors which the imperial farm alone has the privilege of selling. The court, incensed at such a proceeding, caused the authors of this act of violence to be immediately taken into custody, and the empress ordered satisfaction to be made to the offended minister; she likewise sent to him and to all the other foreign ministers, a declaration, in which she expressed her concern and resentment at what had happened, and communicated the orders which she had given to the senate to institute a prosecution against the commissioner of the office established for the prevention of the clandestine sale of liquors,—he being the chief delinquent.

The house of an embassador ought to be safe from all outrage, being under the particular protection of the law of nations, and that of the country: to insult it, is a crime both against the state and against all other nations.

§118. Right of asylum. But the immunity and freedom of the embassador's house is established only in favour of the minister and his household; as is evident from the very reasons upon which it is grounded. Can he take advantage of the privilege, in order to convert his house into an asylum, to afford shelter and protection to the enemies of the prince, and to malefactors of every kind, and thus screen them from the punishments which they have deserved? Such proceedings would be contrary to all the duties of an embassador, to the spirit by which he ought to be animated, and to the lawful purposes for which he has been admitted into the country. This is what nobody will presume to deny. But I proceed farther, and lay it down as a certain truth, that a sovereign is not obliged to tolerate an abuse so pernicious to his state, and so detrimental to society. I grant, indeed, that when there is question only of certain ordinary transgressions, and these committed by persons who often prove to be rather unfortunate than criminal, or whose punishment is of no great importance to the peace of society, the house of an embassador may well serve as an asylum for such offenders; and it is better that the sovereign should suffer them to escape, than expose the embassador to frequent molestation under pretence of a search after them, and thus involve the state in any difficulties which might arise from such proceedings. And as the house of an embassador is independent of the ordinary jurisdiction, no magistrate, justice of the peace, or other subordinate officer, is in any case entitled to enter it by his own authority, or to send any of his people to enter it, unless on occasions of urgent necessity, when the public welfare is threatened with imminent danger which admits of no delay. Whatever concerns a point of such weight and delicacy,—whatever affects the rights and the dignity of a foreign power,—whatever may embroil the state with that power,—is to be laid immediately before the sovereign, and to be determined either by himself in person, or, under his direction, by the privy council. <496> Thus, it belongs to the sovereign to decide, on occasion, how far the right of asylum, which an embassador claims as belonging to his house, is to be respected: and if the question relates to an offender whose arrest or punishment is of great importance to the state, the prince is not to be with-held by the consideration of a privilege which was never granted for the detriment and ruin of states. In the year 1726, the famous duke de Ripperda having sheltered himself in the house of lord Harrington, embassador from England, the council of Castille decided "that he might be taken out of it, even by force; since, otherwise, those regulations which had been made for the purpose of maintaining a more regular and intimate correspondence between sovereigns, would on the contrary operate to the subversion and utter ruin of their authority;—and that, if persons who had been intrusted with the finances, the power, and the secrets of the state, were, when guilty of violating the duties of their office, allowed to take shelter under a privilege which had been granted to the houses of embassadors in favour only of ordinary offenders,—such an extension of the right of asylum would be productive of consequences the most pernicious and detrimental to all the powers on earth, who, if the practice once became established, would be reduced to the necessity, not only of enduring the presence of every man who was plotting their destruction, but even of seeing him supported in their own court."*— Nothing could be said on this head with greater truth and judgment.

The abuse of the privilege has no-where been carried to a greater extent than at Rome, where the embassadors of crowned heads claim it

* Memoirs of the abbé Du Montgon, vol. i.

for the whole ward in which their house is situated. The popes, once so formidable to sovereigns, have for above two centuries been in their turn under a necessity of observing the most delicate and cautious circumspection in their conduct towards them. It is in vain that they have endeavoured to suppress, or at least to reduce within proper bounds, an abusive privilege, for which, prescription, however great its antiquity, ought not to be allowed as a sufficient plea in opposition to justice and reason.

§119. Exemption of an embassador's carriages;   An embassador's carriages and equipages are equally privileged with his house, and for the same reasons: to insult them, is an attack on the embassador himself, and on the sovereign whom he represents. They are independent of all subordinate authority—of guards, custom-house officers, magistrates and their agents,—and must not be stopped or searched without a superior order. But in this instance, as in that of the embassador's house, the abuse is not to be confounded with the right. It would be absurd that a foreign minister should have the power of conveying off in his coach a criminal of consequence,—a man, in the seizure of whose person the state were highly interested; and that he should do this under the very eyes of the sovereign, who thus would see himself defied in his own kingdom and court. Where < 497 > is the sovereign who would suffer this? The marquis De Fontenay, the French embassador at Rome, sheltered the Neapolitan exiles and rebels, and at last undertook to convey them out of Rome in his own carriages: but the carriages were stopped at the city gates by some Corsicans of the pope's guard, and the Neapolitans committed to prison. The embassador warmly complained of the procedure: but the pope answered "that his motive had only been that of arresting men whom the embassador had assisted in escaping from confinement; and that, since the embassador took the liberty of harbouring villains, and affording protection to every criminal in the papal territory,—at least *he,* who was sovereign of the state, ought to be allowed to have them retaken wherever they could be found; as the rights and privileges of embassadors were not to be carried to such lengths." The embassador replied, "that it would not appear, on examination, that he had granted an asylum to any subjects of the pope, but solely to some Neapolitans, whom he might very lawfully shelter from the persecutions of the Spaniards."* By this answer, the minister tacitly conceded that he would not have been authorised to complain of the stoppage of his carriages, if he had employed them for the purpose of favouring the escape of any of the pope's subjects, and aiding criminals to elude the pursuit of justice.

The persons in an embassador's retinue partake of his inviolability; his independency extends to every individual of his household: so intimate a connection exists between him and all those persons, that they share the same fate with him; they immediately depend on him alone, and are exempt from the jurisdiction of the country, into which they would not have come without such reservation in their favour. The embassador is bound to protect them; and no insult can be offered to them, which is not at the same time an insult to himself. If the domestics and household of a foreign minister were not solely dependent on him, it is evident at first sight, how easily he might be harassed, molested, and disturbed in the exercise of his functions. These maxims are at present every-where adopted and confirmed by custom. *§120. of his retinue;*

The embassador's wife is intimately united with him, and more particularly belongs to him than any other person of his household. Accordingly she participates in his independence and inviolability: she even receives distinguished honours, which, in a certain degree, cannot be refused to her without affronting the embassador; and for which there exists, in the generality of courts, an established ceremonial. The respect due to the embassador extends likewise to his children, who also partake of his immunities. *§121. of his wife and family;*

The embassador's secretary is one of his domestics: but the secretary of the embassy holds his commission from the sovereign himself; which makes him a kind of public minister, enjoying in his own right the protection of the law of nations, and the <498> immunities annexed to his office, independently of the embassador, to whose orders he is indeed but imperfectly subjected,—sometimes not at all, and always in such degree only, as their common master has been pleased to ordain. *§122. of the secretary of the embassy;*

---

* Wicquefort's Embassad. book i. §28, towards the end.

§123. of the embassador's couriers and dispatches.

Couriers sent or received by an embassador, his papers, letters, and dispatches, all essentially belong to the embassy, and are consequently to be held sacred; since, if they were not respected, the legitimate objects of the embassy could not be attained, nor would the embassador be able to discharge his functions with the necessary degree of security. The states-general of the United Provinces decided, whilst the president Jeannin resided with them as embassador from France, that to open the letters of a public minister is a breach of the law of nations.* Other instances may be seen in Wicquefort. That privilege, however, does not—on certain momentous occasions when the embassador himself has violated the law of nations by forming or countenancing plots or conspiracies against the state—deprive us of the liberty to seize his papers for the purpose of discovering the whole secret, and detecting his accomplices; since, in such an emergency, the embassador himself may lawfully be arrested and interrogated (§99). An example is furnished us in the conduct of the Roman government, who seized the letters which a treasonable junto had committed to the hands of Tarquin's embassadors (§98).

§124. The embassador's authority over his retinue.

The persons in a foreign minister's retinue being independent of the jurisdiction of the country, cannot be taken into custody or punished without his consent. It would nevertheless be highly improper that they should enjoy an absolute independence, and be at liberty to indulge in every kind of licentious disorder, without control or apprehension. The embassador must necessarily be supposed to possess whatever degree of authority is requisite for keeping them in order:† and some writers will

* Wicquefort, book i. §27.

† It is his duty to watch over their conduct, and to exert his authority in order to prevent them from transgressing the bounds of their station, and committing actions which may give just offence to the sovereign at whose court he resides,—an event which may sometimes be productive of very serious and disagreeable consequences. The French court having sent the count De Harcourt to England to mediate an accommodation between Charles I. and his parliament, several gentlemen of that minister's suite repaired to the royal army, and fought against the parliamentarians: on which account the parliament immediately declined all further negotiation with the count De Harcourt. Du Port's Hist. of Conspir. vol. iv. p. 261. [[Note added in 1773/1797 editions.]]

have that authority to include even a power over life and death. When the marquis De Rôny, afterwards duke De Sully, was in England as embassador extraordinary from France, a gentleman of his retinue committed a murder, which caused a great noise among the people of London. The embassador assembled some French noblemen who had accompanied him on his mission, tried the murderer, and sentenced him to lose his head. He then acquainted the lord mayor of London that he had pronounced sentence on the criminal, desiring that magistrate to furnish him with an executioner and proper attendants to have <499> the punishment inflicted. But he afterwards consented to deliver up the criminal to the English, in order that they might execute justice on him as they thought proper: and Monsieur De Beaumont, the French embassador in ordinary, prevailed on the British monarch to pardon the young man, who was related to that minister by the ties of consanguinity.* It rests entirely at the option of the sovereign to invest his embassador with such an extensive power over the persons of his suite: and the marquis De Rôny was confidently certain of having his conduct approved by his master, who did, in fact, express his approbation of the whole transaction. In general, however, it is to be presumed that the embassador is possessed only of a coercive power sufficient to restrain his dependents by other punishments which are not of a capital or infamous nature. He may punish the faults committed against himself and against his master's service, or send the delinquents to their sovereign, in order to their being punished. But should any of his people commit crimes against society which deserve a severe punishment, the embassador ought to make a distinction between such of his domestics as belong to his own nation, and others who are subjects of the country where he resides. The shortest and most natural way with the latter is to dismiss them from his service, and deliver them up to justice. As to those of his own nation, if they have offended the sovereign of the country, or committed any of those atrocious crimes in whose punishment all nations are interested, and whose perpetrators are, for that reason, usually surrendered by one state when demanded by another,—why should he not

* Sully's Memoirs, vol. vi. chap. i.

give them up to the nation which calls for their punishment? If the transgression be of a different kind, he is to send them to his sovereign. Finally, if the case be of a doubtful nature, it is the embassador's duty to keep the offender in irons till he receives orders from his court. But if he passes a capital sentence on the criminal, I do not think he can have it executed in his own house; an execution of that nature being an act of territorial superiority which belongs only to the sovereign of the country. And although the embassador, together with his house and household, be reputed out of the country, that is nothing more than a figurative mode of speech intended to express his independency, and all the rights necessary to the lawful success of the embassy: nor can that fiction involve privileges which are reserved to the sovereign alone,—which are of too delicate and important a nature to be communicated to a foreigner, and, moreover, not necessary to the embassador for the due discharge of his functions. If the offence has been committed against the embassador or against the service of his master, the embassador may send the delinquent to his sovereign. If the crime concerns the state where the minister resides, he may try the criminal, and, if he finds him worthy of death, deliver him up to the justice of the country, as did the marquis De Rôny. <500>

§125. When the rights of an embassador expire.

When the commission of an embassador is at an end,—when he has concluded the business for which he came into the country,—when he is recalled or dismissed,—in a word, when he is obliged to depart on any account whatever, his functions cease: but his privileges and rights do not immediately expire: he retains them till his return to his sovereign, to whom he is to make a report of his embassy.* His safety, his independence, and his inviolability, are not less necessary to the success of the embassy in his return, than at his coming. Accordingly, when an embassador departs on account of a war arising between his master and the sovereign at whose court he was employed, he is allowed a sufficient

* "It was, at that time," says Joinville, "an established custom, as well in pagan as in christian countries, that, when two princes were at war, if one of them happened to die, the embassadors whom they had mutually sent to each other, remained prisoners and slaves." p. 72. [[Note added in 1773/1797 editions.]]

time to quit the country in perfect security: and moreover, if he was returning home by sea, and happened to be taken on his passage, he would be released without a moment's hesitation, as not being subject to lawful capture.

For the same reasons the embassador's privileges still exist at those times when the activity of his ministry happens to be suspended, and he stands in need of fresh powers. Such a case occurs in consequence of the death of the prince whom the minister represents, or of the sovereign at whose court he resides. On either occasion it becomes necessary that the minister should be furnished with new credentials. The necessity, however, is less cogent in the latter than in the former case, especially if the successor of the deceased prince be the natural and necessary successor; because, while the authority whence the minister's power emanated, still subsists, it is fairly presumable that he retains his former character at the court of the new sovereign. But if his own master is no more, the minister's powers are at an end; and he must necessarily receive fresh credentials from the new prince, before he can be authorised to speak and act in his name. In the interim, however, he still continues to be the minister of his nation, and, as such, is entitled to enjoy all the rights and honours annexed to that character.

§126. Cases when new credentials are necessary.

At length I have reached the end of my proposed career. I do not flatter myself with the idea of having given a perfect, full, and complete treatise of the law of nations; nor was that, indeed, my design; for it would have been too great a degree of confidence in my own abilities to have made such an attempt on a subject so extensive and so copious. I shall think I have done a great deal, if my principles are approved as solid, luminous, and sufficient to enable intelligent persons to give a proper solution of any minute questions that may arise in particular cases; and shall be happy if the result of my labours proves in any wise serviceable to those men in power who love mankind and respect justice,—and furnishes them with weapons for the purpose of defending the cause of right, and compelling the unjust to observe at least some measures, and to keep within the bounds of decency.

§127. Conclusion.

E N D.

Essay on the Foundation of Natural Law and on the First Principle of the Obligation Men Find Themselves Under to Observe Laws[1]

Translated by T. J. Hochstrasser

> What is the goal of those who teach natural law and ethics? Is it not to bring men to the observance of justice and the practice of virtue?
> — *The Author*

I. Natural laws, natural jurisprudence, and moral science are three things that are often confused in ordinary language because they all three have the same object: to know how to order the customs and conduct of men. But in handling a topic clearly and securely it is necessary to separate out carefully those issues that are in reality distinct.

II. A *law* is in general a rule by which we are obliged to determine our actions; and *natural laws,* in particular, are those that we derive from nature, or whose rationale is found in the essence and nature of man, and of things in general.

III. *Natural jurisprudence* is a general theory of the duties of man, considered simply as man, or a science, which teaches us what is *naturally good* or *bad* in man, what he must and must not do.

IV. Moral science or *ethics* is a practical science, which teaches us how we should direct our faculties to practice what is *good,* and avoid what

---

1. [[For persons and books referred to in these essays, see the biographical sketches and the bibliography of works cited by Vattel. *Droit* has been translated as "right" or "law," according to context. *Utile/utilité* has been translated as "self-interest," "expediency," or "interest," according to context. *Honnêteté* and its cognates have been translated as "integrity."]]

is *bad*. Often the term *moral science* is employed to designate the study of behavior in general, and in this sense it includes *natural law* and *ethics*. Sometimes *moral science* seems to mean the theory of our *duties,* insofar as we are obliged to employ them, for ourselves, as rational creatures; and *natural law* includes the theory of these same duties insofar as we are *bound* to them in respect of other men, as members of human society, or as others have the *right* to require that we observe them. But our distinction (§III) is more tidy and convenient, and it contains everything, for *natural law* comprises also our *duties* toward ourselves.

V. With that established, we look for the *foundation* of natural law, and the *principle* which compels us to practice what it prescribes for us, and avoid what it forbids us. On these two points there have been major disputes among the learned.

VI. If by the *foundation* of natural law we understand the source from which can be derived the rules and precepts; the principle in which is found what can provide an explanation for why these rules and precepts are as they are, then we would not wish to look further than in *the essence and nature of man and things in general.* For, since natural law is the science which tells us what is *naturally good* or *bad* in man (§III), how shall we determine what is *naturally* good or bad for him, if not through his essence and nature, and by the nature and essence of things, through considering the degree of suitability between actions and this essence and this nature? This truth is confirmed *a posteriori* or by experience. To determine whether someone has given an accurate idea of the laws of nature, examine what there is in man and in other things that is in accordance with their essence and nature, and you will see how you will understand clearly from that why our free actions must be regulated and determined in the manner that natural law prescribes.[2] It would be easy to give examples of this. But each person can put this to the test for himself.

2. See Wolff, *Phil. Pract. Univ.,* part I, §cxxxvii.

VII. All the authors of different systems are obliged to agree with what we have just established, whatever their sense may be of the principle of obligation, which we shall speak of presently. Those who delude themselves that natural law was invented for the benefit of human society, must agree that the source of this view can only be the nature and essence of things and of man in particular. For, I ask you, where could these would-be inventors have learned with such certainty that some actions are useful to the human race and that others are harmful, if not by considering the harmony or disharmony of these actions with the nature of man and the nature of things? Therefore it is on this nature that they have had to base their whole theory of rules and the laws of natural jurisprudence.

VIII. The same must be said of those who assign the instituting of natural law to the arbitrary will of God. For, at the same time as they recognize God as a wise being, who ordains nothing without wisdom, they must agree that God could only give laws suitable to the nature of things, and particularly to the essence and nature of man, whom he instructs to observe them; laws whose rationale is found in this essence and nature. We can go further: how do these authors know that God has laid down such-and-such laws rather than others quite contrary to them? Doubtless it is because knowing that God is a wise being, they consider, rightly, that he could only give laws that are the most appropriate to man, the most advantageous to the good of society in general, and to that of each individual in particular. But how will they know these most advantageous of laws? They will consider the nature of man and things, and they will see which laws are most appropriate to them. They are required to draw on the same source as us. This is sufficient to show that natural law is founded on the essence and nature of things and of men in particular. Cicero recognized this when he said that law is established by nature: *natura ipsa constitutum est jus.*

IX. We attain knowledge of these laws through *reason.* This faculty of the soul teaches us what is the essence and nature of man and of things in general, and makes us see the aptness or inappropriateness of actions in relation to this essence and nature: from this we derive general rules or laws which constitute the body of natural jurisprudence.

X. But it is not enough that these laws exist and that they are known: for men to be obliged to obey them they must also be effective. Everyone agrees that they are so bound, but authors disagree on the principle of this *obligation*. Some derive it from the *authority of a superior,* which can only be God, the author of nature; others base it on the very *beauty* of *virtue,* which, by its nature, is *preferable to vice.* Finally, others say that man, being a rational and sociable creature, must act in conformity with this character. Let us try to determine the true and first principle of this *obligation* and reveal where all these authors agree and are right, and where their views err. To succeed in this it is absolutely necessary to develop a clear and distinct idea of things, and to provide good definitions. We shall see that it is as a result of having neglected this rule that clever authors have caused themselves so much embarrassment in this matter, and have seemed to fall into views that are so mutually opposed.

XI. To determine what *obligation* is requires first an examination of what is commonly understood when this term is employed. Ask any man who says, "We are *obliged* to do something," and you will see that he means that we are under a kind of necessity to do this very thing; that we are compelled, bound, tied—as if forced—although not *forced* or *constrained* physically by an external cause that acts violently upon us, but *morally,* and in a way that free beings can be engaged to do something even against the urging of their passions. Now, what are the reasons which bring free beings to act even against their inclination, without physical compulsion or external causes? They can only be *motives,* which being immediate to the soul, perceived and evaluated by reason, make us feel the necessity of acting in such a fashion and resolve the will, often against the heart's inclination and despite the resistance of the passions. How therefore are we compelled to take a certain action? It is through the linkage of a powerful motive with this action. Thus, there are two issues to consider in respect of *obligation:* 1. The principle which gives birth to or which constitutes it, which creates the obligation; 2. The condition in which we find ourselves when we are so obligated.

XII. Hence it follows that obligation is characterized as *active* and *passive*. *Active obligation* is the connection of the motive with the action. *Passive obligation* is a moral necessity[3] to act or not to act.[4] The former is the principle which sways the intelligent being, and the latter is the condition in which this being finds himself.

XIII. Passive obligation produces active obligation just as cause gives birth to effect. For, if it is morally necessary to act, it is necessary to wish to act. Now, there is no will in the soul without motivation; therefore to bring about the moral necessity to undertake a particular action, some motivation must be linked to this action, which you cannot separate from it.[5]

XIV. There is good reason why we pause to demonstrate this origin for passive obligation. It proves the reality of our definition and shows that we are in agreement with the most famous writers, though sometimes with this difference—that these authors have restricted themselves to showing the effect of obligation, without explaining clearly its content. Some have defined *passive obligation* and not *active obligation:* "Obligation," says Pufendorf, "is a moral quality by virtue of which we are compelled, by a moral necessity, to accept or endure something."[6] But he does not say in what this *moral quality* consists. Grotius also uses this expression, that an action is *morally necessary,* to say that we are obliged to do it; but he does not in any way define *obligation.*[7]

XV. Those who only have extremely confused ideas of all this will perhaps object that it is *duty* which creates *obligation,* and that we are obliged to undertake certain actions because they are in line with our *duty,* and abstain from others because they conflict with it. Nothing is

---

3. A thing is *morally necessary* when it cannot fail to happen, given the nature of the intelligent being which produces it; just as it is said that a thing is *physically necessary* when it cannot fail to happen, given the nature of the physical agent that creates it.

4. See Wolff, *Phil. Pract. Univ.,* part I, §cxviii.

5. *Idem,* §cxix.

6. *Droit de la nature et des gens,* book 1, ch. i, §xxi.

7. *De Jure Belli ac Pacis,* l. I, c. 1, §x.

more common than this way of speaking; it is why it matters to throw light on the problem, although, as we shall see, it consists only of pure gibberish. Let us see therefore what is this *duty* on which *obligation* is based.

XVI. Our *duty* is no more than the way in which we must determine or direct our actions so that they are good and right.[8]

XVII. Now, a free action is *good* or *right* when it has its justification in the essence and attributes of the being that produces it,[9] that is to say, when a reason or explanation can be given through the essence and attributes of this being as to why his action has had to be so and not otherwise.[10] This recalls what we have said (§VI) about the match or mismatch of actions with the essence of the nature of man and of things, which creates the foundation of natural law and the source of the laws that compose it. It still remains to find out the nature of the *obligation* we are under to live according to our *duty*, and, in consequence, the objection we have just witnessed is only empty verbiage. The same outcome will hold good if the term *duty* is considered in another sense, according to which particular *duty* is an action decided on in accordance with law, in such a way that we are *compelled* to resolve on it in this way. For in this sense, it is *obligation*, which constitutes *duty*, and so, it does not stem from duty.

XVIII. Mr. Barbeyrac in his notes on Grotius and Pufendorf provides no definition of *obligation* at all; except that, while saying that there is no obligation without a superior, he makes it appear that we are subject to the will of a superior, which compels us to bring our conduct into conformity with this superior's laws. But it is plainly a confusion to interpret *obligation* as *dependency* or *submission*. We still have to explain why this dependence binds us; why we must preserve this submission.

---

8. In Latin *rectae.* The correctness of an action, *rectitudo,* means what is understood by the words right, just, good, praiseworthy, etc.

9. The difference which exists between free actions, in respect to this correctness, is what is called the *morality* of actions.

10. Wolff, *Theol. nat.,* part I, §dcccl.

If we ask this learned man, "Why must we obey a superior?" he will not reply, "Because we are obliged to." This would be to say nothing and to explain *like with like*. Will he say that it is because this obedience is just, in conformity with the rules of order, or because this superior can punish us if we rebel against him? But in that case he is citing to us the *motives* which are linked to this action of obedience, and he falls back on our definition, according to which *obligation* is the *connection or link of motive with action.*

XIX. Now this definition is adequately established if the first principle of *obligation* can be found which binds us to the observance of natural law, to a principle which is truly primary, which does not stem from any other. Then it is clear that we can only find it in a general motive which moves us, without drawing its effectiveness from any other, and which, in contrast, all the others relate to as branches or subsidiary motives, which draw all their strength from this common source.

XX. Given that motives act on us in accordance with our desires, to discover what we are looking for, we must see if there is in our soul an affection or essential and basic desire, which does not derive from another, and on which all the others rely. We do not need a long period of reflection to convince us that there is no inclination, desire, or affection more essential to us, or more basic and general, than *self-love,* which causes us to desire and seek for our happiness or the perfection of our condition, whether internal or external, i.e., the perfection of our soul, the well-being of our body, and the prosperity of our fortune.

XXI. That being so, the most *general* motive that influences us, this *basic* motive which stems from no other, can only be what relies on this general and basic inclination. Now, what is this motive, which stems from self-love or our desire for happiness? It is, for sure, our *well-being,* our *expediency,* our *advantage.* Experience reveals this truth clearly to the eyes of whoever wishes to pay some attention to what takes place inside his own mind. Let us investigate carefully, let us examine attentively the way in which our wishes are formed, and we shall see that we never determine on an action through the perception of some *benefit* that we think we perceive in it, whether for perfection or peace and the pleasure of our soul, or for the well-being of our body, or for the profit of our fortune. Every motive returns, ultimately, to real or perceived *expediency*. But we must observe in passing that if our greatest good comprises the perfection of our soul, then the motives that relate to it—for example, those which derive from obedience owed to a being such as God, independent of all fear, beauty, and virtue—these motives, I say, may be considered as the noblest with good reason. After them, those that are concerned with the good of the body are the most rational; finally, the motives that provide us with the condition of our fortune take the third place.

XXII. If our expediency and our well-being are therefore the predominant motivation, the most basic motive that drives us, we must conclude that this *good,* this *expediency,* is the first principle of all *obligation,* and in particular of the obligation to keep to natural law. There is no doubt that our expediency is linked to this observance, for natural law is a science that teaches us what is naturally *good* or *bad* in man (§III); and the natural laws that comprise this law only prescribe some actions and forbid others as a result of the harmony or disharmony of these actions with our nature and the nature of things (§VI).

XXIII. Man is a social animal; society is natural to him; indeed, it is even essential to him if he is to pass his life happily. From this observation the judicious Grotius adopted the sociability of man as the foundation of natural law; and that is very reasonable provided that we do not take it as the first principle of *obligation,* but only as the next principle from which the duty derives for all men to follow the laws which must govern the natural society which exists among them, and without which they cannot survive.

XXIV. Each individual has as a general and overriding motive his own self-interest, and this motive creates the obligation to which he is liable: it is the unvarying principle of his decisions, against which it would be absurd to claim that he could be made to act. But if society is useful and even necessary to him, and this society is unable to subsist without laws or general rules observed by all its members, he is obliged, by virtue of his own expediency, to follow them. He ought not even consider sacrificing them to an immediate advantage, because they are what guarantee him peaceful enjoyment of all his other goods.

XXV. That is the foundation of civil laws and the principle of the submission that we owe to them. Men, who are required by their needs to form individual societies, will definitely not give up their own self-interest and expediency on entering them. On the contrary, it was doubtless on account of this very benefit that they each decided to make these commitments. But readily perceiving that such a host of evils and disadvantages might arise among people so often blinded by or taken up with their passions (if every individual had the freedom to decide, in particular instances, what was the best course of action for him), they understood that they had to establish laws that were sufficient to guarantee the happiness of society. They adjusted them, so far as was possible for a majority, to the interest of each member. Everyone felt that these laws, if they were to achieve the desired effect, must be observed religiously; that exceptions could not be made from them without weakening or destroying them, and that therefore on this occasion they had to sacrifice an immediate advantage to a greater good, since laws are the basis of our peace and security. That is the true principle of the obligation we have to observe them, a principle to which all men subject themselves without difficulty.

XXVI. The view that I established (§XXI) on the principle of obligation is not new, and I find in a note of Mr. Barbeyrac, on the great work of Pufendorf,[11] a passage in which I see with a particular pleasure, that a learned Englishman shared exactly the same views: "According to him, *duty* or *obligation,* in respect of man, can only be a reason or motive put forward in an appropriate manner, which makes him decide to choose or to prefer one way of acting over another; and this reason or motive can only be the avoidance or acquisition of a very high degree of unhappiness or happiness, which cannot be avoided or gained by acting in another manner. He does not acknowledge any other obligation—or if

---

11. Book I, ch. vi, §v, note 4.

there be some other type, he believes that by examining it carefully it will be seen to resolve itself into the same kind." Thus Mr. Bernard expresses the thoughts of Mr. Gastrell:[12] which are precisely in line with what I have tried to establish.

XXVII. But let us see what Mr. Barbeyrac puts forward in the same note: "The motive for *obligation,* or what brings about most effective compliance with it, should not be confused with the *foundation* of *obligation* or the reason why we are absolutely required to do one thing or another. This reason is nothing other than the will of a superior, whose power, in relation to our own good or evil, then stimulates our will to determine our present duty." The whole problem between this learned commentator and ourselves derives from the fact that he does not define *obligation* as we have done (§XVIII). *Expediency,* he says, is the *motive* for *obligation,* it is not the *foundation:* we are *required* to obey a superior. But we may ask him: what, therefore, is the *foundation* of obligation, and for what reason am I to obey a superior? You will tell me that it is my duty to obey him because I am dependent on him. That still does not enlighten me.

XXVIII. I continue: why must I respect this dependency? Why must I fulfill my duty? And if I violate it, what will happen? You will punish me, you will say. And there we have the motive that creates my *obligation* to this *duty:* by breaking with it, I bring harm to myself. But if I could avoid the punishment, would this transgression still be an offense? Yes, you say—and why? Because I must obey a superior who has a legitimate authority over me: my disobedience would be a bad act. But why should I not commit an evil act when it will draw down no punishment upon me? You cannot respond with anything more rational than this: "In committing an evil act, an act contrary to order and reason, you depart from the perfection of your being." And that brings us back to my view, which bases *obligation* on expediency, for it is without doubt advantageous to

12. *Nouvelles de la République des Lettres,* April 1700, p. 408. [[In 1699 the French Reformed theologian Jacques Bernard began a continuation of Pierre Bayle's *Nouvelles de la République des Lettres* (1684–87), which appeared until 1710.]]

me to be perfect. Let us not pursue any further a matter we have already touched upon (§XVIII).

XXIX. I flatter myself that by developing ideas carefully and defining the meaning of terms precisely, as I have tried to do, the reader will see a way of reconciling Mr. Barbeyrac with us, and that this scholar will himself come to agree.[13] The will of a superior, as we have just seen, is not the first principle or the *foundation of obligation.* But it is, doubtless, a proximate principle of real substance: firstly, because disregarding the integrity inherent in the action that is prescribed for us, it is fine and praiseworthy to obey a legitimate superior; and secondly, because this superior can recompense or punish us, independently of the good or evil that our action naturally entails. And when this superior is recognized as very wise, and all-powerful, his will alone imposes on us a true obligation, even if we might not perceive the integrity of the action that he prescribes to us, or the relation that it can have in itself with our happiness. I would go further: even if we believed we saw something harmful to us in the situation—in a word, when we do not know the *reasons* for the law that he gives us. For we can relate to him; we rely on his wisdom for the integrity of the action and on his goodness for the usefulness of this very action; and it is by virtue of this legitimate trust that we can say when he prescribes a law that his will takes the place of reasons.[14] Moreover, while this act might be unimportant in itself, whether in terms of its integrity or our self-interest, or even contrary to it, the act becomes good and praiseworthy as soon as he prescribes it, and he is the master through his omnipotence who can attach such a reward as he considers appropriate, and compensate us a hundredfold for the harm that it will have caused us. To God alone, as a wise and all-powerful superior, is this unlimited trust due. But as a result the occasion for action can only exist when this sovereign legislator gives us revealed laws. For natural laws, we only know them to be the laws of God, by the *reasons*

13. At the time of writing Mr. Barbeyrac was still alive.
14. "Thus will may stand in the place of reason." Wolff, *Phil. Prac. Univ.,* part I, §cxxxii, in note.

for these laws—by the reasons which show their justice and expediency; so, if we do not see wise reasons for undertaking a particular action or abstaining from it, we cannot know if it is the will of God that we should do it or avoid it. Let us recall here a passage of Mr. Barbeyrac, even if it is a little long; the reader, on comparing it with what we have just said, will see clearly the heart of the problem, how our principles cause it to vanish, and how they may serve to reconcile opinions which at first sight seem so opposed:[15] "The author [*Grotius*] here imagines that there might be an *obligation* to do or not do certain things, even if he did not have to answer to anybody for his conduct. And there is no need to be astonished that his ideas on this point are not quite in order, since we still see today, not only that the majority of philosophers and scholastic theologians, but also some authors who elsewhere are very judicious and in no way slaves to scholastic prejudice, are all obstinate in maintaining that the rules of natural law and ethics, impose in themselves an absolute obligation, independent of the will of God. Nevertheless, some argue in a way that suggests that there is only a dispute over the meaning of words between the latter and others who are not of the same opinion. I am going to try, albeit in a few words, to update thoroughly the state of the debate, and the basis of the disagreement I have with the author. It is not a matter here of arguing whether by disregarding the will of an intelligent being or even the will of God our minds can discover the ideas and relations from which the rules of natural law and ethics can be deduced. We must agree in good faith with the supporters of the view that I am combating, that the rules are effectively based on the very nature of things; that they are in conformity with the order that we conceive as necessary to the beauty of the universe; that there is a certain proportion or lack of proportion, aptitude or unsuitability between the majority of actions and their objects, which makes sure that we find beauty in some and ugliness in others. But from that alone it does not follow that anyone is properly *obliged* to do or not do one thing or an-

15. Translation of *On the Law of War and Peace,* of Grotius, book I, ch. I, §x, no. 2, note 4.

other. The fitness or unsuitability, which we can call the *natural morality* of actions, is indeed a reason which can cause action or its refusal, but it is not a reason which imposes an absolute requirement, such as the idea of *obligation* implies. This necessity can only come from a *superior,* i.e., from an intelligent being outside ourselves, who has the power to restrict our freedom and to prescribe rules of conduct for us. For proof, here is my reasoning. If there were some obligation, independent of the will of a superior, either the nature of things would have to impose it or our own reason. The very nature of things could not impose any obligation on us, in any real sense. That there may be a harmonious or disharmonious relationship between our ideas, this alone does not require a recognition of this relationship—something further is required to compel us to make our acts and life conform. Nor can reason by itself place us under an indispensable necessity to follow the ideas of harmony or disharmony that it sets before our eyes as based on the nature of things." (I do not copy the proof that the author gives of it, which is found word for word in his reply to the *Judgment* of Mr. Leibniz, which I shall look at shortly.[16] Let us move on to his conclusion.) "From all these points I conclude that the maxims of reason, however congruent they may be with the nature of things, and with the makeup of our

16. [[The great German natural jurist Samuel Pufendorf published an abridgment of his *De jure naturae et gentium* (*On the Law of Nature and Nations,* 1672) as *De officio hominis et civis juxta legem naturalem* (*On the Duty of Man and Citizen According to Natural Law*) in 1673. The latter work was translated into French as *Les devoirs de l'homme et du citoien* in 1707 by the Swiss Huguenot Jean Barbeyrac and became famous throughout Europe. Barbeyrac's successive editions were increasingly heavily annotated, and his fourth edition of 1718 included a French translation, with Barbeyrac's response, of Gottfried Wilhelm Leibniz's critique of Pufendorf's *De Officio* in a Latin letter composed in 1701. Barbeyrac gave Leibniz's letter the title "Jugement d'un anonyme sur l'original de cet abrégé." The letter had been printed in 1709 as the *Epistola Viri Excellentissimi ad Amicum, quâ monita quaedam ad principia Pufendorfiani operis, De Officio hominis et civis, continentur,* but had circulated in manuscript since its composition. Barbeyrac's response has been published for the first time in English from the Latin original in Samuel Pufendorf, *The Whole Duty of Man, According to the Law of Nature,* ed. I. Hunter and D. Saunders (Indianapolis: Liberty Fund, 2003). Vattel is here concerned, as he notes, with Barbeyrac's fourth edition of *Les devoirs* of 1718.]]

being, are in no way binding, until this very same reason has revealed to us the Author of existence and of the nature of things, who gives the force of law to these maxims by his will, and imposes on us an indispensable necessity of conforming to them by virtue of the right he has to limit our liberty as he considers appropriate, and to set such boundaries for the faculties he has given us as seem good to him. It is true that God can ordain nothing contrary to the ideas of harmony or disharmony with which reason furnishes us in certain acts; but that does not alter the fact that the obligation to regulate ourselves according to those ideas stems uniquely from his will. It matters not whether this will is arbitrary or not; it is always the will alone which imposes the necessity. Finally, a proof that the will of God is the source of every duty and obligation, lies in that fact that when those who have a religion, adopt the rules of virtue and the maxims of natural law, they must do so, not chiefly because they recognize that these rules are in conformity with the natural and unvarying ideas of order, harmony, and justice, but rather because God, their sovereign master, wishes them to follow the rules in their conduct." A charming proof, which precisely defines what is at issue. But perhaps there is a path of reconciliation between us. We reply to all this reasoning that men would be obliged to follow natural laws even by setting aside the will of God, because they are praiseworthy and useful. But this will undoubtedly adds a great weight to this obligation: it is a very legitimate and solid foundation although this foundation is not a basic principle since it derives itself from another from whom it draws its strength—I mean, our self-interest. Will not the learned commentator on Grotius be obliged to agree, and will he not admit that his note is useless against a similar system? He adds, "that ultimately it would otherwise be fairly purposeless that God prescribed anything (*to men*), since they would already be held to it: the will and authority of God would only in this case be a kind of accessory, which would not contribute anything further than to make the obligation stronger." That issue, I do not consider as a difficulty. In no way does it detract from the authority of God to say that everything he ordains for us in natural laws is so *fine* and *useful* in itself that we would be *obliged* to adopt it, even if God had not ordered it.

XXX. Another few words about self-interest. There is something ambiguous about this term: some define it unreasonably narrowly, and seem to mean by it a crude expediency restricted to property. It is what gives rise to this note by Mr. Barbeyrac: "There are here two extremes to avoid: one is the work of those who by confusing *integrity* and *expediency,* and measuring this expediency according to their own particular interest, destroy thereby every idea of virtue and vice, all natural law and morality; the other, on the part of those who believing (with reason) that the practice of all the virtues, and of all the rules of natural law, is truly and infallibly to the advantage of all men in every respect, confuse this *expediency* with the natural *integrity* of actions. The first is only an ineluctable consequence of the other, and a feature from which we can discern what is truly honorable from what is only so in the erroneous opinion of men. When I say, *we should repay evil with good, but not good with evil; and men must obey the will of their creator, God,* there is in these statements a congruence so clear and evident that, however little attention we pay to them, we cannot refrain from acquiescing, and judging the views they contain both fine and honorable, without needing to think at all about the advantage which flows from following them. We are convinced from that point on that any action contrary to these maxims is a sin against reason, and we are forced to blame ourselves. The concept of duty derives from that recognition alone, as does the rational end to follow duty. It is true that to give full force to all these like maxims where we reveal a natural beauty and harmony, we must have been convinced of the truth of the second example I gave. But even when everything is properly reduced to this basic rule, there is no need at all to consider the unlimited expediency which flows from it as a way of perceiving the obligation we are under to conform to it. More to the point: it is precisely not on account of this self-interest that we must currently perform what is in line with the will of God: it is solely because we admit we are his dependents and that it is fine and honorable to obey him; and this would still be so even if (which would be impossible) he demanded something absolutely without purpose. Whatever view we take of self-interest, we must not view it simply in itself, but in terms of the product of the natural and wonderful union that the Creator has established between the duty and happiness of his creatures. In a word, to set up expediency itself as the most real and universal foundation of moral integrity and of obligation as such, is to muddle concepts and to make what is secondary into the principal. Let us also recognize that those who have not known about or have imperfectly understood this expediency have insufficiently acknowledged the intrinsic integrity of the majority of actions that conform with natural law."[17] It is surely sufficient to respond that when we say that *self-interest* provides the foundation or the principle of obligation, we are speaking of a noble and agreed expediency, which is located mainly in the observance and practice of virtue—because this observance and practice bring us closer to perfection. I would argue that that point alone is enough to bring this reasoning tumbling down, and to lighten the difficulties in which the author entangles himself, from which he cannot extract himself with the help of his principles. When we have a correct understanding of *self-interest;* when we have constituted it mainly in the perfection of the soul, a perfection that already defines our happiness in itself, and which reconciles us with the good will of the Creator, what danger is there in confusing the meaning of *integrity* with *expediency*? Furthermore—the doctrine of those who by distinguishing between *integrity* and *expediency* maintain that there are honest things that are not useful and useful ones that are not honest—is it not, as the ancients have observed, as pernicious as it is insecure? On this point let us consider the fine words of Cicero: *The usage of this word has been corrupted and perverted and has gradually come to the point where, separating moral rectitude from expediency, it is accepted that a thing may be morally right without being expedient, and expedient without being morally right. No more pernicious doctrine than this could be introduced into human life.*[18] *And so, we have heard, Socrates used to pronounce a curse upon those who first drew a conceptual distinction between things naturally*

---

17. Translation of *On the Law of Nature and Nations* of Pufendorf, book II, ch. III, §x, note 6.

18. *De officiis,* book II, ch. iii.

inseparable. [19] Now that we know what we must understand by the word *expediency,* let us conclude with Horace: *Self-interest itself is almost the mother of justice and fairness.* [20]

XXXI. Since we have begun to examine the reasoning that Mr. Barbeyrac develops to support his hypothesis, let us add some reflections on what the same scholar, at the end of his translation of the treatise *On the Duties of Man and Citizen,* sets up against the judgment that Mr. Leibniz had delivered on this work of Pufendorf. This discussion will conclude by highlighting the use that we can make of our principles. We conclude this dissertation with these remarks not with the goal of criticizing an able man, but so as to demonstrate the advantage of a precise method, and to show how by defining ideas, by making them clear and defining terms, we can unravel almost painlessly the debates in which many scholars have obstructed us.

XXXII. "The anonymous author,"[21] says Mr. Barbeyrac,[22] "manifestly confuses *duty* with the *effects* or the *motives for its observance;* the strength that *duty* has in its own right with the force it exercises over the minds of men in the way that most of them are constituted." He should say *all* men here rather than *most.* For Mr. Leibniz's statement that duties have no force without motives is true of all men without exception; we have established this earlier by showing how *obligation* is nothing other than the *link between motive and action* (§XI and XII); and this philosopher, without any reference to another life, had grounded his view in the same fashion: "If we are born with such dispositions, and if we have not been brought up in such a way that we find a great pleasure in virtue and a great distaste for vices (it is fortunate that everyone has not!), there will be nothing that can deter us from a major crime, when we will be able, through committing it, to acquire great rewards with impunity."[23]

---

19. *Ibid.,* book III, ch. iii. [[Translations taken from Loeb edition edited by Walter Miller (Cambridge, Mass.: Harvard University Press, 1913).]]

20. *Satires* 3, book 1.

21. Mr. Leibniz.

22. P. 444. I use the 4th edition published in Amsterdam in 1718. [[See note 16.]]

23. P. 442.

And above all there will be nothing that can induce us to sacrifice our goods and our lives for the sake of our country, or for the support of law and justice.[24] For in the imaginary instance a man would have no motive to make this sacrifice, not even those people who can argue for the *beauty* of virtue. However, Mr. Barbeyrac opposes a doctrine which seems to us so self-evident: "We are *obliged,*" he says,[25] "not only not to do harm to anyone in the course of obtaining some advantage for ourselves, but also to give up on occasion our goods, honors, and even our lives, quite independent of any consideration of the life to come; and for this sole reason, that these are the *duties* which the wise Author of natural law and sovereign leader of the universe has imposed upon us." What does the term *obliged* mean here? If Mr. Barbeyrac has the same concept of obligation that we have (§XI and XII), then for sure what he proposes is unsustainable: for there is no motive remaining to be linked to the action in the case in question. If this scholar means that it is a rule of *law,* a maxim of the *virtue* of sometimes sacrificing our property, etc., we would agree with him. But how does this relate to a man who, as we imagine him here, has no taste for virtue and in no way prefers it to vice? It is not a matter of determining the maxims of *right* or *virtue,* but of knowing the outcomes to which men will be brought or obligated in one case or another. How will we be able to impose on them a requirement for action, without recourse to the constraints of physical force? They are bound to these actions, says our author, by this single reason—that they are the *duties* which the wise Author of natural law and sovereign Leader of the universe has imposed on them. But what purchase has this reason on a man who has no expectation of this sovereign Legislator, and who has no love for virtue, and supports as well the hypothesis against which we are reasoning?

XXXIII. "Which of these two moral outlooks, I ask you," adds Mr. Barbeyrac, "is the most pure, noble, and conformable to the ideas of the wise pagan authors who have distinguished so clearly between *integrity*

24. P. 441.
25. P. 445.

and *expediency?*" Without getting into an argument about the epithets *pure* and *noble,* let us ask in turn what is the goal of those who teach natural law and ethics? Is it not to bring men to an observance of justice and to the practice of virtue? Which moral system is therefore the most reasonable and useful? The one that, based on the nature of man, bears him toward virtue through considering his best interests? Or the one that is so *pure* and *noble* that it is outside our reach and entirely useless as an influence on our will? As for the ideas of the *wise pagan authors,* we have seen that the *wisest* had sharply turned away from *a clear separation of integrity and expediency. Socrates,* says Cicero, *execrated those who were the first in their opinions to have separated things that nature had closely united.*

XXXIV. Mr. Barbeyrac continues: "But how does the reasoning of our anonymous author match up with what he says here, that *there is a level of natural law which can exist even in the case of an atheist?* And also with what he argues later (§XV) *that there would be some natural obligation, even if someone argued that there is no Divinity?"* The anonymous author, or Mr. Leibniz, has not contradicted himself. He argues (p. 445)[26] *that to neglect consideration of a life to come, which has an inseparable link with divine Providence, is to destroy several duties of life.* He does not say that it would destroy all of them: on the contrary, he concedes that there would still be a large number of duties for an atheist, because there are, in fact, several where the *reasons* or *motives* which bind us, reside in their *expediency,* even in respect of this life; and an atheist can also in several instances readily find sufficient motives in the *beauty* of virtue alone. Mr. Barbeyrac, at the same time as he accuses his adversary of a contradiction, cannot prevent himself stating in the two following pages (446 & 447), what destroys this alleged contradiction. We can read these pages, and I pass on to another passage.

---

26. From the cited [[1718 fourth French]] edition of *On the Duties of Man and the Citizen,* in which the "Judgment of an Anonymous Author" (Mr. Leibniz) has been interpolated with the reflections of the editor.

XXXV. "There is no middle course: either the *obligation* of the rules of justice among men is absolutely independent of the Divinity, and based uniquely on the very nature of things, as is the case with *the principles of arithmetic and geometry,* or it is not based on the nature of things in any respect."[27] And why might there be no *middle ground*? There is one to be sure, and here it is: *obligation* derives from the very nature of things, but the Divinity is among the number of these things, whose nature determines the rules of *justice* and *injustice,* and provides the *motives* which constitute *obligation.* Moreover, we have noted earlier (§XXIX) that the will of God is also an immediate and very powerful principle of *obligation.* It is not difficult to prove what Mr. Leibniz advances— that the opinion of those who derive every right from the will of a superior is devoid of foundation, and that we need always to come back to the nature of things. When a man who has no other lights but those of reason identifies that one action is *good* and that another is *bad,* what proof does he have that it is the will of God that creates the former and is absent from the latter? His reason, you will say, teaches him that God wishes for all that is *good.* Very well. But this response itself demonstrates that the intrinsic quality of the action is already a reason to prefer it, disregarding the will of God; and that the very will of God orders itself according to this reason. This will is therefore not the *first principle,* the *foundation* of the preference that places the *good* above the *bad:* it adds only a great weight to reason derived from the nature of things; and when it is clearly known, it must take the place of everything, and provide us with a sufficient reason to determine our action without further investigation, on the particular merits of the prescribed end (§XXIX).

XXXVI. "The nature of things in itself," adds Mr. Barbeyrac,[28] "could not impose on us an *obligation,* as such. Whether there is this or that relation of equality and proportion, harmony or disharmony in the nature of things, that alone does not require us to recognize this relation: something further is required to limit our freedom and subject our ac-

27. P. 470.
28. P. 470.

tions to regulation in a particular manner." It is true that the relations of harmony or disharmony, which exist between things, do not in themselves require recognition of these relations; but the influence that these very things can have on our happiness by virtue of these connections is a powerful motive which compels us to act or not since *obligation* is the link between motive and action (§XI). There is the *extra factor* that Mr. Barbeyrac requests *to limit our freedom and subject our actions to regulation in a particular manner.*

XXXVII. "Nor can reason," he continues,[29] "considered in itself, and independent of the Creator who has given it to us, place us under an absolute necessity of following these ideas, although it approves them as based on the nature of things. For, first, the passions set against these abstract and speculative ideas, ideas based on emotion and sensibility etc." If reason shows us clearly that by following *these ideas based on the nature of things* we are working toward our greater *good,* to our true happiness, then it sets us under a necessity of following it; since this *necessity* is nothing other than *passive obligation* (§XII), which derives from *active obligation* (§XII), which consists of the link between motive and action (§XI & XII). Given that self-love and a desire for happiness are the strongest and most all-encompassing of our passions (§XX), will that passion be able to overcome the counsels of reason successfully, when reason will show us clearly the link between our happiness and a certain action? Rather it will enlighten us as to the truly appropriate route to our happiness, and our passions themselves will bring us to perform our duty.

XXXVIII. "Why," says our author on the same page, "should we follow the lights of our own minds, rather than the inclination of our hearts, if there is no external principle—no being beyond us—to whom we are subject?" It is because we understand that the lights of our minds will lead us more securely to happiness than the inclination of our hearts. And setting aside this thought, what might be this principle external to our will? And how might this being beyond ourselves compel us to follow

29. P. 471.

his orders freely, rather than our inclination? For sure, he can only make us his subjects by *motives* capable of influencing our wills. He might force us through physical action, but this would no longer be a matter of a required obligation, for we would no longer be acting freely. For sure, it is true that regard for a sovereign Master, our Creator, is highly efficacious in placing an *obligation* on us to practice the duties of morality. It is why Mr. Leibniz said earlier that *to neglect consideration of the life to come, which has an inseparable link with divine Providence, is to deprive natural law of the finest of its parts, and to destroy at the same time several duties of life.* Indeed, although every *good action* is *useful* in itself, and every *bad action harmful,* there are a thousand instances in which we do not see clearly enough the influence that actions have in themselves on our happiness, however much this reflection bears down on the strength of our inclinations. But the concept of a wise God, a good and just disposer of *good* and *evil*—this concept, I say, is always at the forefront of our minds—and directs us to an action that we know to conform to his will, even though we do not perceive at that moment the reasons bound up in the very nature of this action which should bring us to give it our preference. Besides, we should note that this concept of a divinity only acts on us as a motive. Why therefore is it so powerful in making up our minds and placing us under such a strong obligation? It is because we are convinced that nothing is more important for our happiness than a perfect obedience toward an omnipotent Being, who holds our fate in his hands and whose orders are always wise and just.

XXXIX. Mr. Barbeyrac has foreseen this reply. Let us look at his response.[30] "Reason, you say, shows us clearly that by following the rules of harmony, based on the nature of things, we will act in a fashion more in line with our interests, than if we allow ourselves to be led by our passions. But is not every man free to give up his interest, insofar as there is nothing besides to prevent him, and there is no other person who is concerned that he does not act against his interests, and has the right to require that he pursue them?" It is not a matter here of some petty in-

---

30. P. 471 & 472.

terests, or some advantages of fortune which we recognize each man is free to renounce; it is a question of our greatest interest, since the author himself says that *all things considered, our interest requires that we follow what reason dictates.* And he has to be understood in this sense, for otherwise all his reasoning would be meaningless against ours. But, good God, what a moral system! And for what kind of beings will it be created? If every man were free to give up his greatest interest, what would become of obligation? Where would duties be? What obligation, I ask you, or what duties would there be for a man who gave up his temporal and eternal happiness? If he is capable by himself of renouncing it, what could there be *besides to prevent him*? And why should the *rights* of *another person concerned* about his conduct matter to him? I agree that this *other person* will have the right to restrain him as a madman is restrained with a tourniquet; but this person will never be able to *oblige* him to act *voluntarily.* Our author would never have advanced such unsustainable paradoxes if he had worked out clear notions of these matters, and if he had begun by providing good definitions of terms. We have shown (§XI & XII) that *obligation* can only be understood as the connection between motive and action, from which it follows that there is no *obligation* at all for a man who renounces all his interests. And as for *duty,* however we may define this term, we shall never be able to show that a man capable of giving up happiness has duties. If we say that our *duty* is the manner in which we must determine our actions, whether they are good or bad (§XVI), or that a *duty* is an action resolved in conformity with law, insofar as we are *obliged* to resolve it in this way; we have shown (§XVII) that all the strength of *duty* in this sense, comes from *obligation,* as we have defined it (§XII). If *duties,* as they are often defined in theology, are things that we must practice if we wish to please God and to be happy, it is all the more clear that there is no duty for the man who has given up all interest. What does it matter to such a man that God approves, *wishes,* or *commands* an action? Why would he obey him if he does not care at all about doing what is *fine* and *praiseworthy,* or working to be happy? Now, he will not care one bit if he can renounce all interest. Finally, in a particular sense our *duties* in respect of others are things that they have the *right* to require from us, that we *owe* them, so that they could *with justice* do us *harm* if we refuse to fulfill our obligation. But in this sense also, what would these *duties* become for anyone who gave us his own interests? And how could he be brought to recognize them other than by force? Will he do for anyone else what he will not do for himself?

XL. Here is another objection: "But what we must reflect carefully on above all is that our reason, considered outside all dependence on the Creator from whom we possess it, is ultimately nothing other than ourselves. Now, no one can impose on himself an absolute necessity to act or not in one way or another."[31] This is a pure begging of the question. The objection is based on the view that we have already refuted, that all *obligation* comes from an external principle, the will of a superior. Besides, we should note that it is not our *reason* that imposes *obligation* on us: reason only makes apparent the link between motive and action that constitutes *obligation.* This link comes from the nature of things, and it is the Creator who established it when he made the world as it is. There is also a response which anticipates what Mr. Barbeyrac adds: "For necessity to truly exist, it cannot cease at the will of the person subject to it—otherwise it is reduced to nothing." This necessity or *obligation* for sure cannot cease at our behest, for we cannot separate a motive from an action to which it is joined by the nature of things.

XLI. I believed that these few reflections on what the learned translator of Pufendorf objects to in *Judgment of an Anonymous Author* could serve to shed more light on the subject, and it is in the same light that I shall conclude by recalling the fine words of the anonymous author, or Mr. Leibniz:[32] "What we have just argued is very useful in relation to the practice of true piety; for it is not enough to be subject to God as if we were in obedience to a tyrant; for we must not only fear him on account of his greatness but also love him because of his goodness. These are the maxims of right reason, as well as the precepts of Scripture, and they are where the good principles of jurisprudence lead, which are in accord

31. P. 472.
32. §xvi, p. 476.

with sound theology and which lead to a true virtue. Those who perform good actions not through a motive of hope or fear in respect of a superior but following the inclination of their hearts, do not act with justice. On the contrary, those who act most justly are those who imitate in some way the justice of God. For when we have done good through love of God or our neighbor, we take pleasure in our action itself (such is the nature of love), and we need no further spur or command of a superior. It is of such a person that it is said *'the law is not made for the just.'*[33] It is indeed against reason to argue that law or constraint alone creates the just man. However, we must concede that those who have not reached this point of perfection are only made subject to obligation through hope and fear. It is above all in the expectation of divine punishment that we find a full and complete necessity, which has power to compel all men to follow the rules of justice and equity."

33. Timothy I, 9.

Dissertation on This Question: "Can Natural Law Bring Society to Perfection Without the Assistance of Political Laws?"

Translated by T. J. Hochstrasser

I. This question, proposed in 1742 by the Academy of Dijon, struck me as chosen with real wisdom; for any reliable and principled handling of this topic requires reflection on the foundation of the nature and goal of politics. Men are not often given the chance to undertake such researches.

II. So as to advance this interesting subject in a clear and precise manner, and to determine the issue unambiguously, it is necessary above all to define the meaning of terms precisely, and to make clear and distinct the concepts that match them. That is the key point in matters of moral theory, and once it is resolved, the solution follows naturally and presents itself. Let us see therefore what are the *perfection* of society, *natural law,* and *political laws.*

III. The perfection of a thing consists generally in the harmony or agreement of everything within it in the direction of a common goal; so we need to see what is the goal of society if we want to get to know exactly what constitutes its perfection.

IV. Man naturally desires perfection and happiness, and he enjoys gifts of intelligence and free will to attain them. But he cannot work toward that goal without a peaceful life, and the resources to provide for his security and all his needs. There is no one who can obtain these advantages without the help of others. This is what induced men to create a society in which they promised such reciprocity. The perfection of this society therefore consists in the provision of arrangements such that not only do all members enjoy personal security, but also their labor yields the necessities and even the comforts of life; as a result there are no obstacles to each pursuing his own perfection, in accordance with the views of God.

V. So that a society can be well founded, so that everything is in order, and each individual can pursue his own business in peace, there must be rules of conduct based on wise reasoning and to which all the members submit. These rules are *laws*. We recognize two forms of them: *natural* and *civil law*.

VI. *Natural law* comprises rules of conduct based on the nature of things, and in particular on the nature of man. We get to know it through reason. This faculty of the soul reveals to us the agreement or disagreement which exists between free actions and the nature of things and man in particular. Moreover, it demonstrates that if we want to act as rational beings, we must scrutinize carefully these different relationships that actions have with the nature of things, and above all with the nature of man—relations between *good* and *evil*, and the *good* and the *bad*. Reason teaches us that we are under obligation to practice the former and avoid the latter. Finally, we cannot doubt that in so acting we are fulfilling the will of the Creator, who has imposed the rule of law on us by the same means that he has established the world as it is.

VII. The ancient philosophers had the same idea of the law of nature as we do. Here is the definition that they gave of it: *Law is the height of reason innate in nature, which commands those actions which must be undertaken and forbids the contrary.*[1] Cicero adds in the same place: *The same reason, when it finds confirmation and completion in the mind of man, is law.* And the same philosopher, in the company of the wisest men of the ancient world, relates the whole of natural law to this general rule that man must live in a way that conforms to his nature, *living in harmony with nature.* Indeed, from the nature of man can be deduced all the duties and commands of natural law, in the same way that mathema-

---

1. Cicero, *de Legib.* I. I.

ticians deduce all the laws of movement from this single proposition based on the nature of bodies: "Every body remains in its state of rest or movement so long as no external force compels it to leave that condition."

VIII. From there it follows that *natural law is universal.* Since it requires us to do all that is most suited to our nature, there is no situation in which it can let us down; for in every situation in which there is a *better* option to take, we are ordered to take it; and if it were possible to find a case of perfect indifference, no law would be of any use in resolving the matter.

IX. Lastly, let us also note that if natural law is essential to man, based on his nature and the nature of things, it is eternal, immutable, and prescribed by God. This was the view of the Roman jurists. *Indeed,* said the emperor Justinian, *natural laws, which are observed for the most part the world over, remain established and unchanging, established by a divine Providence.* [2] From which it follows self-evidently that no law can be contrary to the law of nature.

X. This is a very important feature to note of political or civil laws, which are rules of conduct, established by a public authority for the good of society, and furnished with a positive *obligation,* by virtue of the penalties linked to their neglect. As they cannot be contrary to natural law in any way (para. IX), and have universal application (para. VIII), political laws correspond at bottom with natural laws. What separates them is, first, that they are written or pronounced formally and that they reduce natural law to general rules to cover every instance of the same kind; and, secondly, that they are provided with civil power, and accompanied with the positive obligation that the threat of punishment adds to natural obligation.

XI. It is not possible to deduce natural law in the form of general rules directed to the good of society and adapted to circumstances, without causing it to undergo some slight alterations, or some deviation in par-

---

2. *Instit.* Book I, title II, para. II, *De jure nat. gent. et civ.*

ticular instances, and this has given rise to this definition of civil law which is found in law six of the Digest: *On justice and law: civil law neither departs wholly from the law of nature or nations, nor is it a slave to it in every particular. Therefore when we add or subtract something from common law, we create particular or civil law.*

XII. According to the idea that we have furnished of the law of nature, it is clear that this law is sufficient in itself to bring society to perfection; and if that were all that were required, I reckon that the issue would be settled. A law founded on the nature of things, especially on the nature of man, and which is, in consequence, wisdom and justice itself; a law, which applies in all instances; a law, in a word, which provides *wisely for everything,* is, without doubt, appropriate to regulate society perfectly. It would invariably produce this outcome if men were as they should be; if they tried to *live in conformity with their nature,* while never abusing their freedom. Given the parallel between the laws of nature and the laws of motion according to the axiom or proposition cited earlier (para. VII), if men took care to follow all the precepts that flow from it, just as bodies follow the laws given to them, then the moral world in human society would bear witness to the same order and harmony that we look on with wonder in the material world.

XIII. When I say, "If men were as they ought to be," I do not at all ask that they exceed their humanity, but only that they make full use of their faculties. Let us imagine one thousand people of both sexes, chosen from the most rational and virtuous in Europe, and that together they form a kind of small republic. Who can doubt that this society would not be better regulated by natural law alone, than has been any other state with the support of political laws? These one thousand people will be enlightened enough to get to know natural law, and to be convinced that their best interest requires that they conform to it exactly. As a result, their society will be as perfect a human society as any such can. They will have a body of law, just, wise, and complete, which is known to all the members and accompanied by sufficient incentives to shape their will. Without the need for subordination to the authority of a government, they will acknowledge themselves under the *obligation* of this law that they derive from nature to provide for the common good. They will focus their talents and labor on this goal; everyone will compete to preserve order and peace. If differences arise, they will choose arbitrators to resolve them. And if it should happen that one individual, possessed by the force of a violent passion, departs from his duty, then the others, whose reason would not be obscured by the same clouds, would they not readily and with one will restrain him without provoking the least social dislocation? Some might vainly object that regulations would be required for trade, for example, or for crucial periods of war and epidemic disease, and a sovereign authority to ensure that they are observed. But reason will promote wise measures in these instances to the people as we have imagined them, and natural law will oblige them to preserve those rules devotedly, as they will tend to social benefit.

XIV. But men are very different both from what they ought to be and from these one thousand people of whom we have just spoken. Two considerations make natural law useless in respect of them: first, the majority do not know in all instances what it determines, either because they lack the necessary insight or because their passions and prejudices throw up an illusion and cast them into error, by representing to them as legitimate or neutral conduct that is in fact criminal. There are even subtle circumstances in which the slightest prejudice can prevent an honest man from seeing the truth that otherwise he would discern. Secondly, men are not always sufficiently enlightened as to their true interests to be aware of the incentives with which natural law is accompanied, and often in the midst of passion these motivations do not present themselves to their minds, or do not strike them with sufficient force. Two considerations bring the man of reason to adherence to this law: first, the obedience which he owes to his Creator; and secondly, the advantages which flow naturally from this adherence. Virtue adorns the soul and ennobles it through its beauty, and in its results and consequences it is always more reliably useful than vice: *The good hate to sin through love of virtue.* But experience shows only too well how few of these motives hold sway over the generality of men. Most scarcely think of God in the fever of their passions, or if they think of him in more collected moments, his goodness conveys to them an illusion, and they imagine that after having satisfied their desires, they will easily win pardon. Are they truly so blind as to underestimate their Creator? As for the second motivation, how small is the number of those who know and are aware of it! It would be a pleasant means of preventing a criminal by making him aware that through his crimes he dishonors the dignity of his being, and that poverty, accompanied by virtue, is of more lasting worth than a criminal wealth. A reason which is fine and persuasive in the mind of a wise man would become absurd in the eyes of a wretch degraded by vice.

XV. It has therefore been necessary, for the good of society, to repair these defects and to supply what is missing in natural law—not in itself—but with regard to the corruption of men. So that this law, perfect in itself, may become sufficient to regulate a society of men, such as they are, these steps need to be taken: *first,* that it may be known to everyone and have a determinate meaning, which is the same for everyone. This is the way to head off disputes and the swarm of other difficulties that might emerge from the ignorance, passions, and prejudices which produce such a bewildering diversity of human opinions. It would be too dangerous, in a myriad of examples, to assign to each person the task of determining in their own fashion what the natural law decides in one case or another. For example, this law states that a man whose reason is not yet mature, and who does not have the good sense required to handle business, is not in a condition to make contracts, and that if someone had abused his lack of knowledge to make him take on burdensome obligations, then the contract would be void. There is nothing more just than this rule, but also nothing better calculated to produce a multitude of quarrels and injustices among men who are ignorant, prejudiced, and self-interested. Individuals would be perpetually at odds, so as to know whether or not a youth is really in a fit state to handle his affairs, and the judges would frequently be perplexed in deciding the issue. The honorable magistrate could easily fall into error, and the wicked one would have his hands free to practice his iniquity. Civil laws have prevented this abuse, by setting an age below which a man is a *juvenile;* i.e., that he is judged incapable of forming a contract; and the laws have fixed the period of his *majority* at the time when experience has shown that subjects of the State commonly have the degree of reason sufficient to regulate their own affairs. So it is for the benefit and peace of society that general laws have had to be derived from natural law, which can be acknowledged by everyone, where the meaning is fixed and the application clear. *Secondly,* a source of authority is needed to compel a respect for the laws on the part of those who are not amenable to the voices of reason, and which adds to natural obligation, which is too weak for the majority of men, a new positive obligation through the means of penalties attached to disobedience. It is the only motive that can influence the will of the wicked. *The evil hate to sin through fear of punishment.*

XVI. But if by setting up a public authority natural law experiences the two changes or additions that we have just touched on, then it becomes public law. For the political or civil laws, to be precise, differ from natural law only in these two respects (para. X).

XVII. Thus, given the depravity of mankind, the good regulation of society has been seen to depend on two steps: *first,* extending the knowledge of natural law by making its application easy, and as a result reducing it to clearly publicized general rules; *secondly,* establishing a public authority, and adding a positive obligation to natural obligation, through the means of punishments (para. XV). To do that is nothing other than to establish civil or political laws (para. XVI); and thus it is demonstrated that *in the current condition of the human race, natural law cannot bring society to perfection without the assistance of political laws.*

XVIII. We have already remarked that those laws must never be contrary to the law of nature. It is only in examples where there is a necessary deviation that they can be separated; for it would be impossible to do otherwise without giving up all the benefits that these laws produce for society: natural law itself states that one must always choose the lesser of two evils. For example, Louis XIV [of France] wisely established under his ordinance of April 1667 that every transaction that exceeds the sum or value of one hundred *livres,* even a voluntary trust, must be signed off in front of lawyers or under formal signature; and that witnesses will not be recognized outside the content of those documents. It is certain that, according to natural law, a man who has acknowledged a debt, whether major or minor, or who has received money on trust, and who has promised verbally to pay back or return it, is no less obligated than if he had made undertakings in writing. However, French law wisely determines that he cannot be compelled because it is more useful to head off a host of lawsuits than harmful for one man to be deprived of the sum of money he is owed. Besides, it is up to the creditor to know the law and take precautions, and if he neglects them then he has no right to complain.

XIX. If the help of state laws is necessary to provide natural law with its full force, we must not imagine that that is sufficient and that we can neglect the study of the latter. On the contrary, the two categories of law must always be kept together, and lend each other mutual support. The legislator who wishes to provide a State with good laws, must know natural law to perfection, and be governed by its always infallible rulings. It is indeed the true source of law, as the ancients rightly remarked: *may I reach back to the source of law through nature,* says Cicero.[3] When political or civil laws are established, those to whom their execution is entrusted must exercise fairness in interpretation, and apply the study of natural law. Knowledge of it is even necessary for members of the public. Cases repeatedly present themselves which the legislator has not foreseen, and in which we have no other guide than nature.

XX. A good philosophy is the only means of reaching to a precise and reliable knowledge of the law of nature—a knowledge that is essential to anyone who wishes to be well trained in the law. This is why Cicero said that jurisprudence must not be drawn from anything in the Praetorian Edict or the Twelve Tables, but from the heart of the deepest philosophy: *the science of law is to be derived not from the praetorian edict, as several writers now suggest, nor from the Twelve Tables, as earlier au-*

---

3. Cicero, as above. [[*De legibus.*]]

thorities argued, but deep from within the resources of philosophy.[4] Also, the wisest of the ancient philosophers, convinced that there is no more useful social science than morality, devoted their chief reflections to this part of philosophy. Is there, indeed, a science worthier of human attention than the one that teaches them the ways of being wise and happy? *This is,* says Pliny, *the most beautiful part of philosophy—to discover and practice jurisprudence.*[5] He speaks of a jurisprudence founded on morality or on natural law. However, this very part of philosophy is today the most neglected. Most modern philosophers only study physics or mathematics. And among the awards that the famous Academies offer to the learned to stimulate their researches, there is not one devoted to moral theory. Is there none of these Royal Societies that wishes to merit the eulogy Cicero offered of Socrates? *Socrates was the first, however, who summoned philosophy from heaven, relocated it in cities and introduced it into homes, and compelled consideration of the meaning of life, customs, good, and evil.*[6]

---

4. *De Leg.* I. 5 [[The Praetorian Edict was a guide to Roman legal procedure which each praetor (magistrate) issued before it was standardized under Emperor Hadrian (A.D. 117–38). The Twelve Tables were the earliest code of Roman law, established by ten consuls between 455 and 450 B.C.]]

5. *Ep. L.* I. 10. [[Pliny the Younger, *Epistulae* (*Letters*).]]

6. *Tuscul.* I. V [[Cicero, *Tusculan Disputations*]].

DIALOGUE Between the Prince of ****
and His Confidant, on Certain Essential
Elements of Public Administration

TRANSLATED BY KENNETH GOODWIN

*It was the day of the crowning of the Prince of ****, who had been named as Successor to the Throne. The Count of ****, the Prince's Confidant, entered the bedroom early in the morning. He found that the Prince had risen, and seeing that he appeared to be very busy, remained a little distance away. When the Prince looked up, the Count began to address him thus:*

THE COUNT. This is the loveliest day of my life and a very happy one for the **** [people of this country]. You, my Prince, are going to reign over them.

THE PRINCE. Ah! My dear Count, thank Heaven that today will be really happy for the ****! It will nevertheless be dreadful for me.

THE COUNT. How so? You seem to fear something that most men regard as the greatest good fortune, being in a position almost above humanity [*la Condition humaine*].

THE PRINCE. The crown is scarcely a benefit destined for the particular advantage of its possessor. I consider it a burden, as difficult an office as it is important.

THE COUNT. Ah, my dear Prince! (Allow me to use this expression; nothing is more fitting.) Since you have such an idea of Royalty, I am certain that you will fulfill its functions perfectly.

THE PRINCE. If the task was less daunting, I would risk promising myself that. But who could cope in dealing with so many important matters that are so varied and so complicated? I believe, however, that I can categorize them under two general headings, the Glory of the Supreme Being and the Happiness of the Nation. There you have the twin objects of my actions and my cares. They are the great ends for every just government.

THE COUNT. You could make this fine aim a great deal simpler since both goals are intertwined and are dependent upon each other. In all your steps in the short term, choose the one that pleases you more. Be constant to it and, being an enlightened Prince, you will achieve your other goal.

THE PRINCE. What you've just said, my dear Count, is all very well, and at first sight seems very reasonable. However, I still have something of a problem. I have been told so often that we must sacrifice everything to the Glory of God, that the goods of this world are not those recommended to us by our Religion.

THE COUNT. The desire to please God must without any doubt be the great motivation which animates every intelligent Being, and this motivation should be reflected in our deeds. This is what I call "glorifying God." But this Supreme Being has no need of men. He demands nothing from us for himself, and if he gives us our Laws, it is as an infinitely good and wise Father and for our own good. It would be very easy to demonstrate that for every thinking Being without exception, the paths of sound Religion [*saine Religion*] and those of real happiness are one and the same. Practicing Virtue is the art of making oneself happy. But now, let us speak about the State, of the Nation as a whole. You understand that Religion can flourish, spread, and be fully effective among men only in the kindly shade of peace, safety, and good order, which in turn can be derived only from the establishment of a well-governed Civil Society.

THE PRINCE. All this is certain. If men used to live without Laws, or without any form of Government, each living in his own small world, reason and experience show us equally that Religion was not able to make itself heard, be studied, enjoyed, or practiced, in the midst of such awful confusion.

THE COUNT. You see then that Religion is very much interested in the prosperity of the State and that you will serve it extremely well by working to encourage this prosperity. Can you conceive of anything more agreeable to the Common Father of all men than to procure the happiness of an infinite number of His Creatures, by maintaining and securing an Establishment under whose shade men can cultivate their Souls, improve their Morals, enlighten themselves, understand their Maker, and serve him by helping their brothers. Allow me in this regard to quote the words of a Pagan Philosopher: *Nihil est enim illi principi Deo, qui omnem hunc mundum regit, quod quidem in terris fiat, acceptus, quim concilia catusque hominum jure sociati, qui Civitates appellantur.*[1] CICERO spoke thus in this fine piece called *Scipio's Dream*.

THE PRINCE. What an admirable Pagan! It is quite shameful that several of our Doctors, with so much help that CICERO did not enjoy, should appear so inferior to him in their reasoning about Morality.

THE COUNT. These wise Romans had an excellent maxim. One never saw them separate the interests of Religion from the true welfare of the State. On the contrary, they used to apply themselves constantly to maintain these two great designs in perfect harmony.

THE PRINCE. Their Religion was false, however. And we, who have happily discovered the true faith, will struggle to reconcile it with the welfare of the State. We shall see it often put into direct opposition to the happiness of the Nation!

THE COUNT. In the Roman Republic, the same men presided over Religious Ceremonies and the Affairs of State. They did not recognize the distinction between the Clergy and the Laity. Senators were High Priests, Augurs, performed Altar Rituals, ensured Justice, and commanded

---

1. "For to the Supreme God who governs this whole universe nothing is more pleasing than those companies and unions of men that are called cities." [[Cicero's *Somnium Scipionis* (*Scipio's Dream*) formed a digression within the sixth book of his *De republica* (*On the Republic*), in which the consul who commanded at the destruction of Carthage in 146 B.C., Publius Cornelius Scipio Aemilianus (185–129 B.C.), meets the adopted grandfather who had defeated Hannibal in the Second Punic War, Publius Cornelius Scipio Africanus (236–184 B.C.).]]

Armies. As these were only different Ministries of the Republic, they were often carried out by the same persons.

THE PRINCE. Should not all citizens, however, irrespective of their social rank, work toward the same goal? Do they not have a common interest, the prosperity of the State?

THE COUNT. You should appreciate, Prince, that men carry their passions and their individual interests even into the most sacred matters.

THE PRINCE. Alas! I know this only too well nowadays. I know too that such men are more false, more difficult to unmask, when they are members of a state which makes them wear a brave face in everyday affairs. How can I identify those who merit my confidence?

THE COUNT. In my view, here are the means. When you find a wise Pastor—moderate, charitable, motivated by a true zeal for the good of the Kingdom—listen to him, my Prince, and follow his advice in all matters pertaining to Religion.

THE PRINCE. But there are others who only speak to me about the sacrifices that are owed to God. They say that everything should give way before the greater interest of the Faith.

THE COUNT. Do not listen to such imposing talk. It is all too often used by the fanatic or the hypocrite. True Piety, enlightened Piety, will not hold you to vague and obscure ramblings. It will constantly reveal its Doctrine to you, in happy harmony with the practice of reasonable Morality and sound Politics. Have you not agreed just now that true Religion can never be opposed to the welfare of the State? It is, on the contrary, its most firm support. The God who approves of and protects Civil Societies, would he allow into the Religion he has imparted to mankind, any Dogma, any Practice or any Maxim contrary to the well-being of such necessary institutions? When you see a dogmatic Doctor holding forth in an incomprehensible manner, or who crosses the threshold into vulgarity, and is quite useless in his profession, always refusing to compromise, and pursuing anyone who does not think like him, can you doubt that pride and a domineering nature are his motivating impulses, rather than zeal for a Religion which teaches only sweetness and charity? You will be doing him a kindness if you accuse him of fanaticism. Reject zeal of this kind and guard against such counsels when these people call upon you to use your power to persecute their adversaries.

THE PRINCE. But ought I not protect our Religion and fight its enemies?

THE COUNT. Of course you must, my Prince. The means, however, must be well chosen. It is an error and bad faith to support Religion by violence and force. Content to force everyone to bend their heads beneath the yoke, false Religion is never impeded by the fear of making hypocrites. But true Religion desires only the happiness of mankind. It scorns enforced submission and lays claim to reign only in our hearts. The Truth alone persuades, it does not enter into souls by violence. And by the same token, when a Pastor does not act in good faith, if he is wise and prudent he would refrain from advising or ever soliciting persecution. The blood of Martyrs from every Sect, every Religion, whether true or false, pours oil upon the flames, a sprinkling which produces in its turn thousands of followers of these Sects. Add to this consideration the frightful evils arising in a State which result from persecution, and I am certain that you will reject all advice from Persecutors with revulsion and deal with them severely.

THE PRINCE. Praise be to God for helping me to understand so clearly that true Religion does not ever demand anything which is detrimental to the public good. In working for His Creatures, I will no longer be afraid of failing the Supreme Being. The happiness of my People will be my guiding rule. I believe it better for Religion to be in the hands of a Prince, and far safer than leaving it to the wiles of Theologians. If Religion, however, does not entail anything contrary to the well-being of the State, would it be equally true to say that nothing can be of value to the Kingdom unless at the same time it is given the approbation of Religion, or at least tolerated by it? Some would raise many questions with me over this.

THE COUNT. I would be very happy if I could alleviate any doubts for you. Whereas in ordinary Morals, SOCRATES and CICERO roundly condemned those who distinguished between the useful and the honest,[2] I would want in any ordered State [*Etat police*] for everyone to indignantly reject this idea, along with those who wish to set Religion against the good of the State, and he who dares boast that what damages Religion is beneficial to Society. The first among these people is the wrongheaded, ignorant, and fanatic Theologian; the second is the false and superficial Politician.

THE PRINCE. I relish your maxims, my dear Count, and it appears to me that this is how things should be. Help me, though, to resolve some difficulties that occur to me. Take Luxury, for example. People vaunt its utility in a large Kingdom, but without giving in to too much austerity, it would seem that Religion does not approve of it.

THE COUNT. Yet, Prince, Luxury is as unsuitable to the good of the State as it is to the purity of Religion.

THE PRINCE. One reads about it in pompous eulogies and one hears these matters being discussed in daily conversation. They say that in a large State, Luxury is the lifeblood of commerce, industry, and labor. It is a source of riches, through the high regard that foreigners have for elegance and arts of every kind, of which Luxury is the source. You cannot deny that there is something of the truth in all of this.

THE COUNT. Before proceeding further, we must first agree on what we define as Luxury. I understand by this term, excessive expenditure that goes beyond normal amounts. I am not talking about the necessary and the useful alone, or yet the convenient or even the agreeable and what decency demands from its depiction according to rank and station. I say also that in the usual course of affairs, this spending exceeds the capacities of anyone who indulges in it and it always carries with it some element of frivolity.

THE PRINCE. Well! Luxury, as you have just defined it, provides employment for a huge number of workers, enables them to gain their live-

2. Cicero, *de Offic.* lib. II. cap. 3. & lib. III. cap. 3.

lihood, makes them richer, and through the prestige that it gives to our tastes and Manufactures, every year brings considerable revenue into the Country.

THE COUNT. I can tell you another singular fact. We do not have close at hand, the wherewithal required by Luxury. We lack gold and silver mines and those for precious stones. The delicious wines of our Kingdom are hardly the only things needed for our delicate and sumptuous tables. Hungary, Spain, and the Islands furnish them at great expense, and our much-vaunted fabrics do not stop us from seeking out foreign alternatives. While I would agree that Luxury brings more money into the Country than goes out, more money goes out than is useful.

THE PRINCE. Nevertheless, riches are very necessary for the defense of the Realm. They supply a large part of our armed forces.

THE COUNT. I scarcely know anyone today who doubts it. The Duc de SULLY[3] will teach you to put this precept into a proper perspective. When the Kingdom provides you, at much less cost, with larger, more dependable, braver, and more frugal Armed Forces, would you be any less powerful with reduced revenue? But I don't want to give up easily. Let us consider the Luxury that increases the wealth of the Kingdom and thus furnishes the means to extend its power. The case for that has not yet been made.

THE PRINCE. I think I understand your line of argument, but do continue.

THE COUNT. Firstly, here's a fine and delicate question to consider: to know if our well-kept and well-cultivated agricultural lands would not provide us with exports as large and with a surer return than all the Manufactures sustained by Luxury. Furthermore, it is clear that Luxury has caused the neglect of the purely useful or necessary arts like the cultivation of the Land and the work of artisans. It depopulates the Country-

---

3. See his Memoires. [[Vattel was most likely using the *Mémoires de Maximilien de Béthune Duc de Sully, principal ministre de Henry le Grand* (London [Paris], 1752).]]

side, everybody heads for the Towns, where the means are to be found of getting rich quickly and with less of a struggle. The Laboring class, that unique pool of good Soldiers, is thereby diminished. Yet, after all of these facts, I am told that Luxury increases the force of the State!

THE PRINCE. Oh, my dear Count! You are beginning to alarm me, and I see that those who praise this public menace are shallow Politicians. They have put before me only their most positive contentions.

THE COUNT. That is not the half of it. Let us now see this menace in its other guises. Can it be denied that Luxury sustains and strengthens the spirit of softness and frivolity which characterizes this Century? And what damage has it not caused to your Army? How would they under similar circumstances sustain the glory of our forefathers who were hardened to toil, indefatigable on the field of honor, and when peace obliged them to lay down their arms, sought their amusement only in games and exercises where they recaptured the memory of their battles?

THE PRINCE. Honor, so natural to my Nobility, will sustain our courage. My Nobles will fly from their ablutions straight to the battlefield, and one could hardly accuse them of being driven mad by Luxury.

THE COUNT. I do know that, Prince, and have seen it myself. And please Heaven that this bright flame will always burn despite the universal depravity of morals! Though by unique fortune effeminate leanings ought never diminish the courage of our young Warriors, Valor is not the only quality necessary for Soldiers. Wise heads are required to direct all those arms. Certainly too, I do not see how a young Lord can do this, while occupied with his pleasures, his appearance, his accoutrements, jewelry, and baubles. Neither do I see, I can say, how he would be able to acquire the prudence and wisdom so necessary in a General; nor by what happy chance resolve and greatness of spirit would find a place within him in the midst of so many trifles.

THE PRINCE. History confirms only too well the truth you have uttered. After the Romans had given in to the excesses of Luxury, they fell into soft ways and their warrior virtues did not hold out for long. CAESAR understood only too well the effect of these effeminate morals. At the battle of Pharsala,[4] he ordered his Soldiers to strike the enemy in the face. What was in his mind regarding the youth of the city, who were fighting under POMPEY's orders? Soft living had not yet been able to extinguish the courage of these young Romans. It had sufficient influence on them, though, to make them fear being disfigured even more than death itself.

THE COUNT. I too have often seen in our Armies that discomfort, tiredness, and inclement weather spread an almost general despondency and discouragement among the men that the sight of the greater dangers had not been able to undermine. Our Warriors scorn death in battle and on the march, but cannot bear the loss of their equipment.

THE PRINCE. Ah! I see the reason for that. Honor places upon them the obligation to face danger bravely, and unfortunately it cannot shame them for any effeminate posturing as unworthy of a Warrior, worse even than cowardice. Oh, Count! How impatient I am to eradicate the harmful causes of such a shameful weakness! If I could only bring back the times of manly and virtuous simplicity!

THE COUNT. You would certainly make the Nation more powerful, more respectable to its neighbors, more redoubtable to its enemies. What is more, you would even make our citizens happier. All these refinements of Luxury become essential for someone immersed in his own pleasure. Their loss would torment him, but their enjoyment does not make him happy. Consider these things, the air of laziness, of boredom and disgust, that nearly always can be discerned in the so-called fortunates of the century.

THE PRINCE. What am I waiting for to take action? I want to begin my Reign with such a salutary reform.

4. [[Julius Caesar defeated General Gnaeus Pompey, his fellow member of the Triumvirate and the Roman consul, in 48 B.C. at Pharsala, the ancient city of Thessaly in northeastern Greece.]]

THE COUNT. This enthusiasm is all to the good and is worthy of admiration and of praise! I have no fear of a little vivacity even when engaged in an undertaking where one has to proceed with measured tread. I understand your prudence.

THE PRINCE. Quite right, Count. I sense that this work will take time, prudence, and appropriate and well-managed measures. Help me to carry it through. You have excited me against luxury. I am asking for your advice in the war that I am going to declare upon it.

THE COUNT. You have convinced me, my Prince, that you want to attack this enemy with all the application humanity demands. You intend to put down its tyranny without upsetting its unfortunate victims, without reducing to penury those who perpetuate its existence. When Luxury has put down so many deep roots in a Kingdom, it becomes a deep-seated illness that must be given proper treatment. Too strong a medicine will send the ailing body into dangerous convulsions. We are talking about an illness that has several causes and several symptoms, each one of which has to be treated with the appropriate remedy.

THE PRINCE. I can, for example, forbid a particular product, anything that Luxury draws from abroad. Nothing prevents me from disallowing its use.

THE COUNT. I see no objections to such a wise move. In that way, you could save for the Kingdom all the money that those foreign goods lose us. There is another area of Luxury that you could remove without difficulty, and by a single authoritative act that would be remarkably easy to enforce. I am speaking about the inordinate number of useless servants whom people employ merely for show. Nothing prevents your delivering us from this vain and ruinous extravagance. Fix the number of lackeys or other domestic servants people are allowed to employ, in accordance with their rank, and you will stop them from drawing on ploughboys or men from the army. Those of your subjects who are the most healthy and robust will no longer be enticed into lives of idleness and corruption through service in the houses of the rich and powerful.

THE PRINCE. Would it not be easy to destroy luxury in all its manifestations! But I would be somewhat uneasy about laying down a limit on everybody's expenditure for the table, furniture, or clothes.

THE COUNT. Nothing could be truer, Prince, and you would have to determine how far to go in this regard. I can hardly advise you how to proceed with such Orders in Council. Sumptuary Laws are convenient, essential in a small State and especially in a Republic. In a large Kingdom, however, or in the situation where we find ourselves, you will cause a sort of revolution by fiercely attacking all these trifles to which men are so attached. There are more subtle, indirect ways more suited to circumstances and that I believe are more effective in their results. I place your own example at the top of the list. If a populace has, over a long period of time, been accustomed to follow the example of their Masters, to flatter them and imitate them, should you not wait until the Nation's eyes and hearts are turned toward you? *"Our Kings,"* Montaigne wrote, *"can do what they please in such external reformations; their own inclination stands in this case for a law. Quidquid Principes faciunt, praecipere videntur.*[5] *Whatever is done at court, passes for a rule throughout the rest of France."*[6] If your Courtiers see for themselves that the excesses of Luxury and frivolity displease you, one will no longer see them ruin themselves through trivialities. Unconsciously, they will bring themselves back within the bounds of reason and decency. They will set the tone for the Nobility, and the leading citizens and all the nation will soon follow their lead.

THE PRINCE. It was excellent in the olden days when the Nobility and the most eminent in the kingdom alone held positions where people took notice of them. Today, the country is full of these new men who, while

---

5. [["What princes themselves do, they seem to prescribe." Quintilian, *Declamationes*, 3.]]

6. *Essays*, Book I, Chap. XLIII. [[Vattel was using *Les essais de Michel de Montaigne, nouvelle edition*, London, 1724, 3 vols. Montaigne's essay "Des lois somptuaires" ("Of Sumptuary Laws") contained a critique of the dangerous influence of the frivolous manners of the French court (*Montaigne's Essays in Three Books*, trans. Charles Cotton, London, 1743, 325–28).]]

not being admitted to Court, spread a contagious luxury in the cities, mainly in the capital.

THE COUNT. It is a good thing that you know about such abuses and that you are aware of their consequences.

THE PRINCE. Of course I know about them, Count, and I know the remedy. I will cut off the source of these quick-made fortunes, and I will deliver my people from these men who together become their tyrants and corruptors.

THE COUNT. Oh, Prince, how you have filled one faithful Subject with joy. In one single stroke, through such a necessary reform in the administration of your finances, you will be giving a new face to this fine Kingdom. We shall no longer see useless limbs bloated with blood and foulness whilst the rest of the body perishes from exhaustion. Wealth will circulate afar in a wider and more sustained manner. Honest abundance will be come from the fruits of our labors, and it will circulate with an equality that conforms to the good of the State, just as it does to justice and common humanity.

THE PRINCE. I can appreciate what the followers concerned with the favorites of PLUTUS[7] tell me, that opulent financiers are an ever-present resource to meet the pressing needs of the State. A vain attraction, capable of dazzling only the poorest eyesight! Is not money distributed more equally always in the hands of the citizens themselves? I would no longer need large amounts. It will flow into my Coffers in abundance when the needs of State demand it. I am confident of being able to provide all I need even during the most trying times when I govern a rich and happy People with wisdom.

THE COUNT. I do not doubt it, Prince. You will win the confidence and the hearts of your Subjects. They will happily give you all you demand of them for their defense, and you are going to put them into a position where they can satisfy your needs.

---

7. [[God of wealth and money in Greek mythology.]]

THE PRINCE. Of course, I want to provide them with all the necessities of life. I sense that in order to secure a comfortable state for them they must refrain from delivering themselves up to ruinous fantasies and from seeking out trivialities that nowise bring them happiness. Here is a very important point for the success of my undertaking. We must mark out the real limits of Luxury and clearly indicate the expenditure that is to be permitted and what we will agree not to forbid. I would not want to reduce my Subjects to petty meanness, force the rich to live as if they were poor, and snuff out the arts and industry.

THE COUNT. I had not counted on pushing the reform that far. A great and rich Kingdom should not present itself as a poor State. Such austerity would perhaps not be entirely fitting and might prove to be a dangerous introduction into a state. Praiseworthy magnificence is acceptable when it does not exceed the means of those who indulge in it. The tastes of rich people for truly beautiful things, for the best of the arts, can only be beneficial to the Kingdom. They galvanize industry, and excite genius and talent. Far from your opposing these tastes, expand them yourself, by protecting the Fine Arts so that they serve to heighten the luster of your grandeur. Ensure that they convey a lofty impression of us to the whole world. The magnificence of our public buildings, for example, sits well upon a powerful Nation. They will imbue the State with esteem, gain the respect of foreigners, and contribute to the majesty of the State. The Great will imitate you according to their means, and all the Citizens will follow suit in proportion to their rank. Take care that when men's inclinations turn them toward praiseworthy undertakings, they are not acting out of fear. The form and effects of their tastes will continue to be characterized by wisdom and solidity.

THE PRINCE. It has to be done if I am to achieve fully and without opposition my goal of drawing men away from frivolity, and inspiring them to seek wise and wholesome pursuits.

THE COUNT. You have reached the second matter I wanted to put to you, Prince, and which together should serve as a means of destroying Luxury and set a limit on the kinds of magnificence that can be admitted. Regulate the tastes of your subjects and everything will follow. To regulate their tastes, give them a fine education. This is the soundest basis of all good order in a State, the fecund source of its advantages, which lead in turn to its success. Just as a poor education is the polluted source from which all public misfortunes flow. I tremble when thinking about the effect that the present system has upon young people of quality to-day. What can you expect from a young man who has been fed on and molded by frivolity, who has sought after pleasures, is taken with elegant dress, and concerned with how he looks and with cultivating effeminate manners. Far from becoming embarrassed, he derives all his glory from these miserable things. He calls it *"good manners,"* and he looks down on anyone who is not able to be, or who does not want to be, as frivolous as he is. It gives me no joy to say this, and I do not make any exaggeration in stating that these *"good manners"* will lead a powerful state to its ruin. "These are superficial errors," said MONTAIGNE,[8] and warned us "but they are of ill augury, and enough to inform us that the whole fabric is crazy and tottering, when we see the roughcast of our walls to cleave and split."

THE PRINCE. I promise you, my dear Count, that I will begin by banning these so-called *"good manners"* at my Court. The breath of contempt will soon make these puerilities vanish into thin air. And as a result, the ambition of the Fathers will answer me through the education that they provide for their children. I will let it be known far and wide that throughout the course of my reign, no one will be able to aspire to any position unless he has made himself capable of filling it.

THE COUNT. May you enjoy a long reign over a nation that you will make glorious! You will make it happy, and you will not fail to be happy yourself.

THE PRINCE. You are my lucky augur, my dear Count. The first words I have heard since ascending the Throne are those from a faithful Servant. May Heaven grant that I never listen to any others.

8. *Ibid.* See at the end. [[Montaigne's "Des lois somptuaires" ("Of Sumptuary Laws"), *Montaigne's Essays,* trans. Charles Cotton (London, 1743), 327.]]

Biographical Sketches of Authors Referred to by Vattel

AMMIANUS MARCELLINUS (A.D. 330–95): A Greek from Antioch, Ammianus served as a soldier in the Roman army. He later wrote a history of Rome and on "civilitas," the moral and institutional restraints that an emperor ought to observe. His work *Res gestae libri* was published in thirty-one volumes, of which only the last eighteen survive.

ANSON, GEORGE (1697–1762): First Baron Anson, admiral and naval reformer, appointed First Lord of the Admiralty in 1757. He is notable for his work *A Voyage Round the World* (1748), in which he recounted his experiences circumnavigating the globe.

APPIAN (or Appianus) (A.D. ca. 95–ca. 165): Known as Appian of Alexandria, he earned recognition for his rhetorical skills in pleading cases in Rome and was appointed Procurator Augusti of Egypt in 147. He wrote *Roman History* in twenty-four books, of which thirteen survive. His work gives accounts of various peoples and countries up to their incorporation into the Roman Empire.

ARISTOTLE (384–322 B.C.): Greek philosopher, polymath, and student of Plato, he wrote on everything from anatomy to rhetoric. His major works— *Physics, Metaphysics, On the Soul, Politics, Nicomachean Ethics, Rhetoric,* and *On the Heavens*—have had a long-lasting influence on the development of every aspect of Western philosophical thought.

ARRIAN (L. Flavius Arrianus) (A.D. ca. 92–ca. 175): Of Greek origin, born in Nicomedia (now Izmit, west Turkey), he was important in the Roman administration and became proconsul of Baetica. He is best known for his work as a historian; of his many books, his *Anabasis Alexandri* is the oldest-surviving complete account of the campaigns of Alexander the Great.

AUGIER DE MARIGNY, FRANÇOIS (1690–1762): French writer known for the *Histoire des Arabes* (1750), which covers 636 years of the Islamic world, from the first successors of Mohammed in the seventh century to 1258 when the last caliph was toppled from power by the Tartars. His work was based on the writings of the Coptic bishop Severus.

AULUS GELLIUS (A.D. ca. 125–ca. 180): Studied grammar and rhetoric in Rome and philosophy in Athens, eventually holding judicial office in Rome. His work *Noctes Atticae,* comprising twenty books, was in the form of a "commonplace" book, in which he noted things of interest, including notes on grammar, geometry, philosophy, and conversations.

BACALLAR Y SANNA, VICENTE (Marquis de San Felipe) (1669–1728): Spanish nobleman and author. His works included *Mémoires pour servir à l'histoire d'Espagne sous le règne de Philippe V* (1756) and *Monarchia Hebrea* (1745).

BELLAY, MARTIN DU (1495–1559): Born in Langey, France. Bellay's work *Les mémoires de Mess. M. Du Bellay* was originally started by his older brother Guillaume, who was a successful general and diplomat for Francis I. After Guillaume's death, Bellay incorporated his brother's writing into his own to form a single work.

BERNARD, JACQUES (1658–1718): Born in Nions, Dauphiné, Bernard was a French theologian trained at Geneva. After preaching reformed doctrines in France, he left for Gouda in the 1680s, where he became pensionary minister. His *Abrégé de l'histoire de l'Europe* appeared monthly between 1686 and 1688; it was followed by *Lettres historiques* (1692–98) and his continuation of Bayle's *Nouvelles de la république des lettres* (1699–1710, 1716–18). From 1705 he was minister of the Walloon Church at Leiden.

BILAIN, ANTOINE (d. 1672): French jurist who wrote on French foreign policy. His books presented legal arguments in support of Louis XIV's claims against neighboring powers.

BODIN, JEAN (1530–96): Born in Angers, France. Bodin was a jurist, natural law philosopher, and advocate of free trade. Part of the circle of the Duc d'Alençon, he also served as a delegate in the Third Estate of the Estates-General, working with D'Hôpital advocating religious tolerance between extremist Protestants and Catholics. He wrote *La démonomanie des sorciers* (1580), but it is his book of political theory, *Six livres de la République* (1576), on the nature of sovereignty, that established his reputation.

BOIZARD, JEAN: Early eighteenth-century writer about whom little is known, except that he was the royal treasurer for a time in France. His book *Traité des monnoyes* (1714) explains monetary systems, financial terms, the variety of forms of money, and how money is made.

BONTEKOE, WILLEM (1587–1657): Born in Hoorn, Holland, Bontekoe was a boat captain in the Dutch East India Company who compiled a journal of his eventful journey to Sumatra. His story, *Voyages of the Dutch to the East-Indies* (1646), recounted shipwrecks and adventure on the high seas and became a best-seller, going through many editions in the seventeenth and eighteenth centuries.

BOUGEANT, GUILLAUME HYACINTHE (1690–1743): Born in Quimper, Brittany, he became a Jesuit priest and taught classics at the Colleges of Caen and Nevers. His work *Amusement philosophique sur le langage des bêtes* (1737) caused his exile from Paris. However, his historical works on the Thirty Years' War and on the Treaty of Westphalia reestablished his reputation. His three comedies in which he satirized Jansenists were widely translated.

BOURBON CONDÉ, ANNE GENEVIÈVE DE (1619–79): The only daughter of Henry II, prince of Condé, she moved in court circles and was involved in the factional religious politics of the day. She instigated the first and second Frondes and was a lifelong enemy of Mazarin. An avowed Jansenist, she gave up court life in 1653 and retired to a convent in Port Royal. She wrote *Abrégé du memoire de Madame la Duchesse de Longueville*.

BUDDEUS [Budaeus], JOHANN FRANZ (1667–1729): Born in Anklam, Pomerania. German Lutheran theologian, professor of Greek and Latin at Coburg (1692), professor of moral philosophy at Halle (1693), and professor of theology at Jena (1705). His writings most commented-upon across Europe were *Historia juris naturae et synopsis juris naturae et gentium iuxta disciplinam Hebraeorum* (1695) and *Elementa philosophiae practicae* (1697).

BULLINGER, HEINRICH (1504–75): One of the key figures of the Reformation in Zurich and a close ally of Zwingli, whom he succeeded in 1531 as head of the Zurich congregation. Bullinger published widely, including histories of the Reform (1564), the Swiss Confederation (1568), and Zurich (1573–74).

BYNKERSHOEK, CORNELIUS VAN (1673–1743): Born in Holland. Writer on international maritime law, publishing *De dominio maris* in 1702. He also wrote on and specialized in diplomatic rights and public law and proposed the "three-mile limit rule," which stated that a nation may claim sovereignty over a territorial distance of three miles from shore, roughly the distance a cannon could then shoot.

CAESAR (Gaius Julius Caesar) (100–44 B.C.): Roman political and military leader who played a key role in changing the Roman Republic into an empire, an act which famously precipitated his murder. He wrote several memoirs of his different successful military campaigns, including *De bello Africo, De bello Alexandrino,* and *De bello Gallico.*

CALLIÈRES, FRANÇOIS DE (1645–1717): Born in Thorigny, France, Callières was sieur de Rochelay et de Gigny and private secretary to Louis XIV, as well as a diplomat and man of letters. A member of the Académie Française, he published eight books, including *De la manière de négocier avec les souverains* (1716), which was considered a preeminent guide to diplomacy.

CAMDEN, WILLIAM (1551–1623): English antiquarian, archaeologist, and headmaster of Westminster School. He wrote *Britannia,* the first comprehensive, county-by-county topographical survey of Great Britain, and *Annales rerum gestarum Anglicarum et Hibernicarum regnante Elizabetha* (1615), a detailed historical account of the reign of Elizabeth I.

CAMPANELLA, TOMMASO (1568–1639): Born in Calabria in southern Italy, Campanella became a Dominican monk in 1583. He was well known for his heterodox theological beliefs and radical political views. His opposition to Spanish rule in Italy led to a life of intermittent imprisonment. His most famous work, *La città del sole,* written during imprisonment, was published in Italian in 1602 and in Latin as *Civitas solis* in 1623.

CHAMPIER, SYMPHORIEN (1471–1538): Born in Lyons, France. Doctor of medicine and cofounder of the College of the Doctors of Lyon with François Rabelais. *Categorie medicinales,* on the logic of medical analysis and argumentation, is the best known of his many works.

CHARLEVOIX, PIERRE FRANÇOIS XAVIER (1682–1761): Born in St. Quentin, France, Charlevoix was a Jesuit teacher and explorer who wrote chronicles of his traveling adventures. His work *Histoire et description générale de la Nouvelle France* was among the earliest written descriptions of North America.

CHAUVELIN, HENRI-PHILIPPE (Abbé) (1716–70): Little is known of Chauvelin except that he was canon of Our Lady of Paris and adviser to the Parlement of Paris. The lengthy title of his work translates as "Tradition of the facts which express the system of independence that the Bishops opposed, in the various centuries, with the invariable principles of the sovereign justice of the king on all his subjects indistinctly; and need for letting act the secular judges against their companies, to maintain the observation of the law, and the public tranquillity."

CHEVALIER, NICOLAS (1650–1720): Little is known about him other than that he wrote *Histoire de Guillaume III, roi de la Grande Bretagne,* a biography of King William III of England.

CHOISY, FRANÇOIS TIMOLÉON DE (1644–1724): Born in Paris. An extravagant cross-dresser and flamboyant character in Louis XIV's court who later underwent a religious conversion, he was ordained and became the abbé of Choisy. He was author of six historical and religious works, but it was his *Mémoires* (1737), a salacious account of his years at court, that proved his most popular publication.

CICERO (Marcus Tullius Cicero) (106–43 B.C.): Born in Arpinium, Italy. An orator, statesman, political theorist, and philosopher of ancient Rome. He was famous for his skillful prosecutions in court, for his views on the rhetorical arts, and for defining philosophy as an education in citizenship.

COMMINES, PHILIPPE DE (1447–1511): Flemish diplomat and writer who served in the courts of Burgundy and France. In his *Mémoires de Messire Philippe Commines* (1552), he analyzed the contemporary political scene with the aim of instructing the reader in statecraft. He was an advocate of political machination over military action.

CREVIER, JEAN BAPTISTE LOUIS (1693–1765): Born in Paris. Professor of rhetoric at the College of Beauvais for twenty years. He produced major works on Roman history, two editions of Livy, and *Rhétorique français* (1767).

CURTIUS RUFUS, QUINTUS: First-century A.D. historian and the author of *Historiae Alexandri Magni,* a biography of Alexander the Great in ten books that focused on character rather than events.

DANIEL, GABRIEL (1649–1728): Born in Rouen, France. A Jesuit, Daniel was appointed historiographer of France by Louis XIV. Among philosophical, theological, and historical treatises, he wrote the epic *Histoire de France* (1713) in seventeen volumes, which was quickly translated into four languages.

DE LA VEGA, GARCILASO (1539–1616): Born in Cuzco, Peru. Although he left Peru for Spain and was conscripted into military service at a young age, his writings on Inca life, history, and subsequent Spanish conquest earned him the sobriquet "El Inca." He was the first Spanish writer to sympathize with the Inca plight.

DEMOSTHENES (384–322 B.C.): Athenian orator and statesman. He was instrumental in his city's uprising against Alexander the Great. Defeat forced him into exile, where he took his own life. The corpus of his work that survives amounts to sixty-three texts, including many of his political and judicial orations.

DIODORUS SICULUS (ca. 80–20 B.C.): Greek historian from Agyrium in Sicily (hence "Siculus") whose forty books, of which only fifteen survive, provide a history of the world from mythical times to 60 B.C.

DUPORT DU TERTRE, FRANÇOIS-JOACHIM (1716–59): Born in St. Malo, France, he was a Jesuit priest and historical writer. He left the priesthood to become an independent author and wrote the *Abrégé de l'histoire d'Angleterre* (1751) and *Project utile pour le progrès de la littérature* (1756).

ETTERLIN, PETERMAN (d. 1509): Swiss chronicler and historian of Lucerne. Served as a captain in the wars against Charles of Burgundy (1474–77).

EUTROPIUS (A.D. ca. 320–ca. 390): A Roman, Eutropius held the office of secretary in Constantinople at the height of the Byzantine era, working under both Emperors Julian and Valens. His book *Eurtopii breviarium ab urbe condita* is a ten-book compendium of the history of Rome.

FREDERICK II OF PRUSSIA (Frederick the Great) (1712–86): An "enlightened despot" from the Hohenzollern dynasty, he was responsible for transforming Prussia from a small kingdom into a European power through a series of military conquests. He wrote several works, including *Anti-Machiavel* (1739) and *Instructions militaires du roi de Prusse pour ses généraux* (1762).

GRAMOND, GABRIEL-BARTHÉLEMY DE (1590–1654): Born in Toulouse, France. Little is known of this author except that he was a nobleman and adviser to the president of the Parlement of Toulouse.

GROTIUS, HUGO (1583–1645): Born in Delft. A jurist in the Dutch republic, a great and prolific humanist scholar, an European diplomat, and an ecumenical theologian. His works include *De iure praedae* (1605) and *De jure belli ac pacis* (1625), by which he was seen to have laid the foundations of international law, and *De veritate religionis Christianae* (1627).

GUICCIARDINI, FRANCESCO (1483–1540): Born in Florence, Italy. A statesman and a political and historical writer, he worked for the Medici popes and was appointed governor of Modena, Reggio, and Parma. Among his many histories and political discourses, the *History of Italy* (*Storia d'Italia*) (1537–40) established his reputation.

HEISS VON KOGENHEIM, JOHANN: Of German origin. Although precise details of his life are unknown, in the late seventeenth century he was the resident historian at the court of Louis XIV.

HERODOTUS (fifth century B.C.): Born in Halicarnassus, in Asia Minor. Called the "Father of History" for his detailed account of the Greco-Persian wars from 500 to 479 B.C.

HOBBES, THOMAS (1588–1679): English philosopher and author of many works concerning ethics, politics, history, and human nature, such as *De cive* (1642), *De corpore* (1655), *De homine* (1658) and *Questions Concerning Liberty, Necessity, and Chance* (1656). *Leviathan* (1651), his major work, cemented his reputation, which has endured.

HORACE (Quintus Horatius Flaccus) (65–8 B.C.): Born in Venusia, Italy. Leading Roman lyric poet and satirist in the time of Augustus. The themes of his odes and epistles were love, friendship, and the pleasures of life. His works included *Satires* (35–30 B.C.) *Epodes* (30 B.C.) and three books of *Odes* (23 B.C.).

JOINVILLE, JEAN DE (ca. 1224/5–1317): French nobleman from Champagne, medieval historian, crusader, friend and servant of Louis IX, the French king canonized in 1297. Joinville's history of this king was completed in 1309 at the request of the then queen, Jean of Navarre.

JUSTINIAN I (Flavius Petrus Sabbatius Justinianus) (A.D. 483–565): Known as the last Roman Emperor, he was ruler of the Eastern Empire and is notable for his conquests and for re-taking Rome and the Western Empire from the Ostrogoths. His lasting legacy was the great codification of Roman law.

LACOMBE, JACQUES (1724–1811): French lawyer and author. His writings included histories of northern Europe and of Queen Christina.

LANCELOTTI, GIOVANNI PAOLO (1522–90): Italian jurist and historian.

LA PIMPIE SOLIGNAC, PIERRE JOSEPH DE (1687–1773): Little is known of this French author except that he served on the staff of King Stanislas of Poland. He wrote *Les amours d'Horace* (1728), which was an attempt to re-create the life and times of Horace, and *L'histoire générale de Pologne* (1752).

LEIBNIZ, GOTTFRIED WILHELM (1646–1716): German philosopher and polymath who served the house of Hanover as court counselor, diplomat, librarian, and much else. Of his prodigious writings on virtually all areas of philosophy, science, mathematics, technology, law, and history, only a few were published in his lifetime, most importantly *Essais de théodicée* (1710).

LE VASSOR, MICHEL (1646–1718): French Protestant, historian, and critic of Louis XIV. Through his various writings and membership in the circle of Pierre Jurieu, he underscored the instability in the European state system caused by aspirations to universal monarchy.

LIVY (Titus Livius) 59 B.C.–A.D. 17): Born in Patavium, Italy. Historian and historical interpreter on a grand scale, rejecting the contemporary method of yearly chronological history. He focused instead on themes, such as public morality, and on periods of thought, exemplified by his epic work of Roman history, comprising one hundred forty-three books.

LUCRETIUS (Titus Lucretius Carus) (ca. 94–ca. 49 B.C.): Roman poet, philosopher, and Epicurean. His poem *De rerum natura* was accredited with influencing Virgil and naturalizing Greek philosophical ideas and discourse in the Latin language.

MACHIAVELLI, NICOLÒ (1469–1527): Florentine political philosopher, musician, poet, and playwright. Famous for such works as *The Prince* (1505) and *Discourses on Livy* (1519). Accused of justifying reason-of-state in politics, he sought to show how republics could maintain themselves in early modern Europe.

MARIANA, JUAN DE (1536–1624): Born in Talavera, Spain. A Jesuit and a Spanish historian whose work was noted for its accuracy and style. His major work, *Historiae de rebus Hispaniae* (1592–1605), consisted of thirty books; his other important work, *De rege et regis institutione* (1598), debated whether it was lawful to overthrow a tyrant. He concluded that it was, which led to his imprisonment by the Inquisition.

MATTHIEU, PIERRE (1563–1621): French historian and poet, popularizer of Charron and Montaigne and chronicler of the history of the French court and kingly life.

MÉZERAY, FRANÇOIS EUDES DE (1610–83): Official historiographer of France and in 1649 admitted to the Académie Française. He wrote summaries of French and Latin chronicles in his three-volume *Abrégé chronologique* (1667).

MOLESWORTH, ROBERT (First Viscount Molesworth) (1656–1725): Supporter of William of Orange and a prominent member of the Irish Privy Council, he was very much involved in the European political scene, which he commented upon in his various writings.

MONTAIGNE, MICHEL DE (1533–92): Born near Bordeaux. French Renaissance scholar and statesman during the Wars of Religion. The first edition of his famous *Essays* was published in 1580 and a later edition in 1588.

MONTESQUIEU, CHARLES-LOUIS DE SECONDAT, BARON DE LA BRÈDE ET DE (1689–1755): Born near Bordeaux. French nobleman, magistrate, and prolific author. His *Lettres persanes* (1721) brought him to prominence in European literary circles. His magisterial reflection on the nature of law and the likely future of France, *De l'esprit des lois* (*The Spirit of the Laws*) (1748), became one of the most influential works of the century.

MONTGON, CHARLES ALEXANDER DE (1690–1770): The Abbé de Montgon was a French diplomat and the secret agent of King Philippe V of Spain. His *Mémoires de M. l'Abbé de Montgon* (1748–49) in ten volumes reveal his machinations regarding the succession to the thrones of Spain and France and his negotiations with Portugal. His duplicity was discovered and he was condemned to exile. His memoirs proved a significant source in European diplomatic history.

MONTHENAULT D'EGLY, CHARLES PHILIPPE DE (1696–1749): Wrote *Histoire des rois des deux Siciles* (1741).

NEVERS, LOUIS DE GONZAGE, DUC DE (1539–95): Leading French Catholic soldier in the Wars of Religion, whose memoirs related his experiences in battle.

NOEL, ALEXANDRE (also Natalis Alexander) (1630–1724): Born in Rouen, France. Dominican priest and professor of theology, he lectured on theology, philosophy, and ecclesiastical law at the Sorbonne before becoming archbishop of Rouen. He was a Thomist and his writings, *Selecta historiae ecclesiasticae capita* (1676–86) in twenty-six volumes and *Selecta historiae veteris testamenti* (1689), comprised a pioneering study of comparative religion.

OCKLEY, SIMON (1678–1720): Born in Exeter, England. Ockley was a British Orientalist and fellow of Jesus College Cambridge, where he lectured on Arabic history. He translated many Arabic texts into English. His central work was the two-volume *Conquest of Syria, Persia, and Egypt by the Saracens* (1708–18).

OSSAT, ARNAULD D' (1536–1604): Born in Gascony, France. Bishop of Bayeux and a French diplomat, he played a major role in negotiating the reconciliation of Henry IV in 1595 with the Holy See. He was named Conseiller d'Etat in 1587 and served Henry IV in Italy.

OVID (Publius Ovidius Naso) (43 B.C.–A.D. 17): Born in Sulmonia, Italy. Roman poet who wrote about love and mythology. His themes and style were influential in art and literature throughout the Renaissance. Much of his work has survived, such as *Amores* (10 B.C.) in five volumes and *Heroides* (5 B.C.), consisting of twenty-one letters. *Metamorphoses* (A.D. 8), describing the creation and history of the world, remains his most famous work.

PAPON, JEAN (1507–90): Lieutenant general of Ballifs de Forez.

PAS, ANTOINE DE (Marquis de Feuquieres) (1648–1711): An important figure in the French military. His *Mémoires sur la guerre* (1730) recounted his battle experiences serving Louis XIV.

PECQUET, ANTOINE (1704–62): Held the position "premier commis" in the French ministry of Foreign Affairs during the reign of King Louis XV. He wrote *Discours sur l'art de négocier* (1737), later published as *De l'art de négocier avec les souverains, par M. Pecquet* (1738).

PINEAU-DUCLOS, CHARLES (1704–72): French biographer and novelist. He was secretary of the Académie Français and succeeded Voltaire as the official historiographer of France.

PLINY THE YOUNGER (Gaius Plinius Caecilius Secundus) (A.D. ca. 63–ca. 113): Born in Comum, Italy. Roman magistrate serving as senator, quaestor, tribune, praetor, consul, augur, and ambassador between A.D. 81 and A.D. 110. His numerous letters (*Epistulae*) described Roman life in the first century.

PLUMARD DE DANGUEL, LOUIS-JOSEPH (John Nickolls, pseud.) (1722–77): Born in Mans, France, de Danguel was a political economist whose essay *Remarques sur les avantages et les désavantages de la France et de la Gr. Bretagne* (1754) was a comparative study of the condition of workers, agriculture, taxation, and the fishing industry.

PLUTARCH (Mestrius Plutarchus) (A.D. 40–ca. 120): Born in Chaeronea, Greece. Biographer and essay writer as well as an ambassador for Chaeronea at Rome. In total he wrote forty-four biographies and seventy-eight works on moral, political, philosophical, and scientific topics in essay or dialogue form.

POLYBIUS (ca. 200–118 B.C.): Born in Megalopolis. An officer of the Achaean League, he is considered reliable as a historian because of his presence at the destruction of both Carthage and Corinth. In Rome at the end of the Punic Wars, he wrote the *Histories,* comprising forty books, in which he attempted to trace the causes of the rise of Rome and the Mediterranean world from 220 to 146 B.C.

PRÉVOST, ANTOINE FRANÇOIS (Abbe Prévost) (1697–1763): Born in Hesdin, Artois. Prévost served as Jesuit priest for many years before leaving the church and fleeing to London and Utrecht. These experiences formed the basis of his *Mémoires et aventures d'un homme de qualité* (1728) and *Le philosophe Anglais* (1731), the seventh volume of which became the novel *Manon Lescault* (1731), which was forbidden in France as a scandalous work.

PUFENDORF, SAMUEL (1632–94): Born in Chemnitz, Saxony. A German jurist and historian, he was seen, along with Grotius, as one of the major voices in defining natural law and jurisprudence in the late seventeenth and eighteenth centuries. While a professor at Heidelberg, he introduced natural and civil law into the curriculum. He also served Charles XI of Sweden and the elector of Brandenburg.

QUINTILIAN (Marcus Fabius Quintilianus) (A.D. ca. 40–ca. 96): Born in Calahorra, Spain. The first professor of any subject to hold an official appointment in Rome. In his *Institutio oratoria* he described how to train men for leadership and what qualities they should possess, advocating the importance of rhetoric and education.

REBMANN, HANS (or JOHANN) RUDOLF (1566–1605): Born in Bern, Switzerland. Rebmann was a poet noted for writing in the German vernacular.

ROHAN, HENRI, DUC DE (1579–1638): Born in Blain, Brittany. A favorite of Henry IV, he made his name as a soldier and leader of the Huguenot forces and died after being wounded in battle. He wrote *Le parfait capitaine* (1631) and *Traité du gouvernement des treize cantons* (1630s) in which he applied the lessons of Caesar's military tactics to contemporary warfare.

SCHODELER, WERNHER (1490–1541): Born in Bremgarten (Bern), Switzerland. Little is known about him except that he was a town clerk who spent much of his time writing the *Eidgennössische Chronik,* an illuminated chronicle of Switzerland. It was published ca. 1535, six years before he died of the plague.

SELDEN, JOHN (1584–1654): Born in West Tarring, Sussex. Scholar, jurist, and legal antiquary who studied law and became keeper of records at the Inner Temple and a member of Parliament. His various works included *Titles of Honour* (1614), *De diis Syris* (1617), *History of Tithes* (1618), *Mare clausum* (1618)—a rejection of Grotius's *Mare Liberum* concerning sovereignty of the sea—and *De jure naturali et gentium juxta disciplinam Ebraerorum* (1640).

SENECA (Lucius Annaeus Seneca) (ca. 4 B.C.–A.D. 65): Born in Cordova, Spain. Undogmatic Stoic and polymath, politician and courtier, eventually tutor of Nero. He was forced to commit suicide at the age of seventy after falling from Nero's favor. His extensive oeuvre comprises essays on ethics and natural phenomena, as well as nine tragedies.

SEXTUS AURELIUS VICTOR (A.D. ca. 320–90): Little is known about his life except that he was prefect of the Roman province of Pannonia Secunda, present-day Serbia, Bosnia, and Croatia. Four works that have been published together as *Historia Romana* have been ascribed to him, although his authorship remains contested.

SHARAF AD-DIN ʿALI YAZDI (d. 1454): A Persian historian from Yazd, in Samarkand. He was well known to Shāh Rokh Mirza, who was the fourth son of Tamerlane and the ruler of Central Asia. His main work was *The History of Timur-Bec, Known by the Name of Tamerlain the Great* (London, 1723).

SIMLER, JOSIAS (1530–76): Born in Kappel, Switzerland. A Swiss theologian and classicist, Simler was professor of theology in Zürich and penned the first known study of the Alps in *De Alpibus commentarius* (ca. 1574). His *De Helvetorium republica* (1576) focused on Swiss constitutional issues.

SOCRATES (ca. 470–399 B.C.): Athenian philosopher and teacher. Socrates served as a soldier in the Peloponnesian War and was later appointed to the Athenian Assembly. His life and writings are known through the works of Plato, Aristotle, and Xenophon, among others.

SOLÍS Y RIVADENEIRA, ANTONIO DE (1610–86): Born in Alcala de Henares, Spain. Dramatist, poet, and historian of the conquest of Mexico. His *Historia de la conquista de México* (1686) covered the initial journey of Juan de Grijalva in 1518 to Cortes's defeat of Montezuma in 1520. His work celebrated the achievements of the conquistadors.

STETTLER, MICHAEL (1580–1642): Citizen of Bern and one of the most influential historians in seventeenth-century Switzerland. His works included the famous *Chronikon oder Grundliche Beschreibung der fürnembsten Geschichte und Thaten.*

STUMPF, JOHANNES (1500–78): Originally from Bruchsal, in Germany, he studied at Heidelberg. Stumpf converted to Protestantism during the early 1520s and became an ally and close friend of Zwingli.

SULLY, MAXIMILIEN DE BÉTHUNE, DUC DE (1560–1641): Born in Rosny. French Protestant and nobleman who fought in the Wars of Religion before serving Henry IV in numerous offices, becoming well known for fostering agriculture and commerce. His famous *Mémoires* were published in 1638, with additional volumes appearing posthumously in 1662.

TACITUS (Publius Cornelius Tacitus) (ca. A.D. 55–117): Roman orator and historian of imperial Rome, he became prefect consul under Nerva in 97. His *Annals* and *Histories* examined the reigns of Tiberius, Claudius, and Nero.

TERTULLIAN (Florens Quintus Septimius Tertullianus) (A.D. ca. 155–230): Born in Carthage. He was the first notable Latin theological thinker of early Christianity and a church leader, whose work later influenced St. Thomas Aquinas. Known as the "Father of the Latin Church," he introduced the term "Trinity" into Christian eschatology. His many works included *De testimonio animae, De monogamia, De patientia,* and *De spectaculis,* which were polemical, moral, and ascetic treatises.

THOU, JACQUES AUGUSTE DE (1553–1617): French historian who moved in the court circles of Henry III. He was appointed "président à mortier" in

1596 and was instrumental in negotiating the Edict of Nantes with the Protestants. He later replaced Sully in the Conseil des Finances. His *Historia sui temporis* (1620), in eighteen books, focused on the history of his own time, especially the Wars of Religion.

THUCYDIDES (ca. 454–399 B.C.): Born in Athens. His unfinished *History of the Peloponnesian War,* comprising eight books, became famous as the earliest surviving work of contemporary history that was factual and avowedly devoid of mythical and religious inspiration.

TRIBBECHOV, ADAM (1641–87): Born in Lübeck, Germany. German theologian. Professor of moral philosophy, then of history, at the new University of Kiel, later church administrator in Gotha. His writings included *De philosophia morum inter barbaros praecipue orientales* (1666) and *De doctoribus scholasticis et corrupta per eos divinarum humanarumque rerum scientia* (1665).

TSCHUDI, AEGIDIUS (also Giles) (1505–72): Born in Glarus, Switzerland. He devoted himself to the Counter-Reformation, using his authority as chief magistrate. He is better known as a historian of the Swiss Confederation, although his work was published posthumously. *Beschreibung Galliae Comatae* (1758) was a topographical, historical, and antiquarian description of ancient Helvetia; his major work, *Chronicon helveticorum* (1734–36), related Swiss history from 1001 to 1470.

TURRETINI [Turretin] [Turretinus], FRANÇOIS (1623–87): Born in Geneva of Italian descent. Pastor of the Italian church at Geneva, where he used his position to redefine Calvinist orthodoxy. He was appointed professor of theology in 1653, and his polemic *Institutio theologiae elencticae* in three parts (1679–85) was used as a standard text in Reformed circles.

VALERIUS MAXIMUS: Early-first-century Roman author. Little is known about him except that he was a professional rhetorician. His book *Factorum et dictorum memorabilium,* dedicated to Tiberius, was a collection of anecdotes and miscellany about Roman history for the use of orators.

VARRO, MARCUS TERENTIUS (116–27 B.C.): Born in Rieti, Italy. A Roman scholar, writer, and supporter of Pompey in the civil wars of the Triumvirate, reaching the offices of tribune and then praetor. After Pompey's defeat he was granted a pardon by Caesar and in 47 B.C. was appointed to run the public library planned by Caesar. He wrote hundreds of works, of which only two survive, *De Lingua Latina* in twenty-five books and *Rerum rusticarum libri III,* on agricultural topics.

VELLY, PAUL FRANÇOIS (Abbé) (1709–59): Prolific French historian and theological author.

VERTOT, RENÉ-AUBERT DE (1655–1735): Born in Benetot, Normandy. A Capuchin abbé and prolific historian with histories of, among other matters, the Knights of Malta and the revolutions in Sweden and Portugal.

VIRGIL (Publius Vergilius Maro) (70–19 B.C.): Born in Mantua, Italy. The most famous of his works is the *Aeneid,* an epic poem on the history of Rome comprising six books. Other works included the *Eclogues* and *Georgics.*

VOGEL, FRANZ ADAM (d. 1749): Born in Colmar. Lawyer and *grand-juge* of the Swiss Guard stationed in France. Author of *Code criminal de l'empereur Charles V* (1735).

VOPISCUS, FLAVIUS: In 59 B.C. he was tribune to the plebs and involved with the factions against Cataline, becoming praetor in 54 B.C.

WATTENWYL (French spelling is Watteville), ALEXANDER LUDWIG VON (1714–81): Born in Berne, Switzerland, of a patrician family, Wattenwyl became a magistrate and historian and was one of the first to attempt a modern history of the Swiss Confederation based on original source material. Between 1763 and 1766 Wattenwyl participated in the reform-oriented Helvetic Society, where he defended anti-Rousseauian positions. Wattenwyl's views on Bernese constitutional history were summarized in his posthumously published *Über die Staatsverfassung der Stadt und Republik Bern* (Schweizerisches Museum, 1783). He was also the author of *Histoire de la Confédération helvétique* (1754).

WICQUEFORT, ABRAHAM DE (1598–1682): Born in Amsterdam. A Dutch diplomat to France, in 1675 Wicquefort was accused of high treason after selling secret dispatches to the English ambassador. He escaped the death penalty; however, all his goods were confiscated, and he was imprisoned in Lowenstein, where he wrote *The Embassador and His Functions* (1716) about his experiences.

WITT, JOHAN DE (1625–72): Born in Dordrecht. In 1650 he became leader of the deputation of Dordrecht to the States of Holland. He later ruled the Republic of United Provinces and was assassinated by his enemies in the

Orange party, whom he had opposed throughout his political career. He wrote a book on mathematics, *Elementa curvarum linearum* (1659) and *Waardije van lyf-renten naer proportie van los-renten* (1671), on political economy.

WOLFF, CHRISTIAN (1679–1754): Born in Breslau, Silesia. A German philosopher and polymath, he composed a vast philosophical system comprehending all sciences, first in German, then in Latin, and dominated philosophy in Germany and beyond for decades in the middle of the eighteenth century.

XENOPHON (ca. 428–353 B.C.): Born in Ephesus. Soldier, mercenary, and historian. His history *Hellenica* focused on events of 411 to 362 B.C. *Anabasis* (*The Inland Expedition* [of Cyrus]) is a record of his travels in the expedition against the Persians and was used as a field guide by Alexander the Great.

BIBLIOGRAPHY

Works Referred to by Vattel

COLLECTIONS

Canon in nona actione [*Can. in nona actione*], *Corpus Iuris Canonici.* In *The 1917 or Pio-Benedictine Code of Canon Law in English Translation,* edited by Edward N. Peters. San Francisco: Ignatius Press, 2001.

Extravagantes communes [*Extravag. Commun.*]. In *Corpus Iuris Canonici,* edited by Emilius Ludwid Richter. Reprint of the 1879–81 edition. Graz, 1959.

Hardouin, Jean. *Conciliorum collectio regia maxima.* 12 vols. Paris, 1715.

OTHER SOURCES

Ammianus Marcellinus. *Res gestae XXXI.* In Ammianus Marcellinus, *Roman History III. Books 27–31. Excerpta Valesiana,* translated by J. C. Rolfe. Loeb Classical Library no. 331. Cambridge, Mass.: Harvard University Press, 1939.

Anonymous. *Mémoires pour server à l'histoire du differend entre le Pape et le Canton de Lucerne. à L***.* Lucerne, 1727.

Anson, George. *A Voyage Round the World* [*Anson's Voyage Round the World*]. London, 1748. Modern edition, London: Oxford University Press, 1974.

Appian. *De bello punico.* In Appian, *Roman History.* Translated by Horace White. 2 vols. Loeb Classical Library, nos. 2, 3. Cambridge, Mass.: Harvard University Press, 1912.

Aristotle. *Politics.* Translated by H. Rackham. Loeb Classical Library, no. 264. Cambridge, Mass.: Harvard University Press, 1932.

Arrian. *Anabasis Alexandri I* [*de Exped. Alexand.*]. In Arrian, *The Anabasis of Alexander 1–4,* translated by P. A. Brunt and E. Iliff Robson. Loeb

Classical Library, no. 236. Cambridge, Mass.: Harvard University Press, 1929.

Augier de Marigny, François. *Histoire des Arabes sous le gouvernement des califes* [*Hist. of the Arabs*]. Paris, 1750. Published in English as *The History of the Arabians, Under the Government of the Caliphs*. London, 1758.

Aulus Gellius. *Noctes Atticae III* [*Aul. Gell. Noct. Attic. lib. iii*]. In Aulus Gellius, *Attic Nights, Books 1–5,* translated by J. C. Rolfe. Loeb Classical Library, no. 195. Cambridge, Mass.: Harvard University Press, 1927.

Bacallar y Sanna, Vicente (Marquis de San Felipe). *Mémoires pour servir à l'histoire d'Espagne sous le règne de Philippe V* [*Memoirs of M. de St. Phillippe*] [*Memoirs of Mons. de St. Phillipe*] [*Memoirs of M. St. Phillip; Memorial of the marquis de St. Philip*]. Translated by Maudave. Paris, 1756. Published in English as *Memoirs of Elizabeth Farnese*. London, 1746.

Bellay, Martin Du. *Les mémoires de Mess. M. Du Bellay* [Memoirs of Martin Du Bellay]. Paris, 1569. Modern edition, *Mémoires de Martin et Guillaume Du Bellay,* edited by V. L. Bourrilly and F. Vindry. Paris: Renouard, H. Laurens, succ., 1908–19.

Bernard, Jacques, ed. *Nouvelles de la République des Lettres*. Amsterdam, 1698–1710.

Bilain, Antoine. *Traité des droits de la reyne tres-chrestienne sur divers estats de la Monarchie d'Espagne* [*A treatise on the right of the queen to several states of the Spanish monarchy*]. Paris, 1667.

Bodin [Bodinus], Jean. *Six livres de la République* [*Republic*]. Paris, 1576. Published in English in Jean Bodin, *On Sovereignty*. Edited and translated by Julian H. Franklin. Cambridge Texts in the History of Political Thought. Cambridge: Cambridge University Press, 1992.

Boizard, Jean. *Traité des monnoyes, de leurs circonstances & dépendances* [*Treatise on Coin*]. Paris, 1714.

Bontekoe, Willem. *Journael ofte gedenckwaerdige beschrijvinge van de Oost-Indische reyse van Willem Ysbrantsz Bontekoe* [*Voyages of the Dutch to the East-Indies*]. Hoorn, 1646. Published in English as *Memorable Description of the East-Indian Voyage, 1618–25*. Translated and edited by C. B. Bodde-Hodgkinson and Pieter Geyl. London: Routledge, 1929.

Bougeant, Guillaume Hyacinthe. *Histoire des guerres et des négociations qui précédèrent le traité de Westphalie sous le règne de Louis XIII* [*History of the Treaty of Westphalia*]. Paris, 1751.

Bourbon Condé, Anne Geneviève de. *Abrégé du Mémoire de Madame la Du-*

chesse de Longueville, contre Madame la Duchesse de Nemours, touchant la compétence des trois Estats de Neuf-chastel. N.p., 1670–80.

Buddeus [Budaeus], Johann Franz. *Elementa philosophiae practicae, instrumentalis et theoreticae [Elementa Philos. Pract.]*. Magdeburg, 1697. Published in English as *Elements of Instrumental Philosophy.* 1717.

Burke, William. *An Account of the European Settlements in the Americas.* London, 1757.

Bynkershoek, Cornelius van. *De foro legatorum liber singularis [Competent Judge of Embassadors]*. Leiden, 1721. Published in English as *De foro legatorum liber singularis—a monograph on the jurisdiction over ambassadors in both civil and criminal cases.* Translated by Gordon J. Laing. Oxford: Clarendon Press, 1946.

Caesar. *De bello Gallico.* In Caesar, *The Gallic Wars,* translated by H. J. Edwards. Loeb Classical Library, no. 72. Cambridge, Mass.: Harvard University Press, 1917.

Callières, François de. *De la manière de négocier avec les souverains [Manner of negotiating with Sovereigns]*. Brussels, 1716. Published in English as *The Art of Negotiating with Sovereign Princes.* London, 1716; *On the Manner of Negotiating with Princes.* Translated by A. F. Whyte. Washington, D.C.: University Press of America, 1983.

Camden, William. *Annales rerum Anglicarum et Hibernicarum, regnante Elizabetha [Annal. Angl.]*. London, 1615. Published in English as *Annales, or, the True and Royall History of the Famous Empresse Elizabeth Queene of England, France, and Ireland [History of Queen Elizabeth]*. London, 1625. Excerpts published in William Camden, *The History of the Most Renowned and Victorious Princess Elizabeth, Late Queen of England.* Chicago/London: University of Chicago Press, 1970.

Campanella, Tommaso. *Civitas solis (La città del sole).* Frankfurt, 1623.

Champier, Symphorien. *Les gestes, ensemble la vie du preulx chevalier Bayard [Life]*. Lyons, 1525. Modern edition edited by Denis Crouzet. Paris: Impr. nationale, 1992.

Charlevoix, Pierre François Xavier. *Histoire et description générale de la Nouvelle France, avec le journal historique d'un voyage fait par ordre du roi dans l'Amérique septentrionnale [History of New France]*. Paris, 1744.

Chauvelin, Henri-Philippe (Abbé). *Tradition des faits, qui manifestent le système d'indépendance que les évêques ont opposé dans les différens siècles aux principes invariables de la justice souveraine du roi sur tous ses sujets indistinctement; et la nécessité de laisser agir les juges séculiers contre leurs entre-*

prises, pour maintenir l'observation des loix, et la tranquillité publique. N.p., [1753].

Chevalier, Nicolas. *Histoire de Guillaume III, roi de la Grande Bretagne.* Amsterdam, 1692.

Choisy, François Timoléon de. *Histoire de Charles Cinquième roi de France* [*Choisy's History of Charles V*] [*abbé de Choisy, Hist. de Charles V*]. Paris, 1689.

———. *Histoire de France sous les règnes de S. Louis, de Philippe de Valois, du roi Jean, de Charles V., et de Charles VI* [*Choisy's History of St. Louis*]. Paris, 1688–95.

Cicero. *De divinatione* [*de Divinat.*]. In Cicero, *On Old Age. On Friendship. On Divination,* translated by W. A. Falconer. Loeb Classical Library, no. 154. Cambridge, Mass.: Harvard University Press, 1923.

———. *De inventione.* In Cicero, *On Invention. The Best Kind of Orator. Topics,* translated by H. M. Hubbell. Loeb Classical Library, no. 386. Cambridge, Mass.: Harvard University Press, 1949.

———. *De legibus* [*de Legib.*]. In Cicero, *On the Republic. On the Laws,* translated by Clinton W. Keynes. Loeb Classical Library, no. 213. Cambridge, Mass.: Harvard University Press, 1928.

———. *De natura Deorum* [*De Natura Deorum*]. In Cicero, *On the Nature of Gods. Academics,* translated by H. Rackham. Loeb Classical Library, no. 268. Cambridge, Mass.: Harvard University Press, 1933.

———. *Fragment. Ex lib. ii De Republica.* In Cicero, *On the Republic. On the Laws,* translated by Clinton W. Keynes. Loeb Classical Library, no. 213. Cambridge, Mass.: Harvard University Press, 1928.

———. *De officiis III* [*De Offic.*]. In Cicero, *On Duties,* translated by Walter Miller. Loeb Classical Library, no. 30. Cambridge, Mass.: Harvard University Press, 1913.

———. *In Verrem I* [*Orat. i*]. In Cicero, *The Verrine Orations I: Against Caecilius. Against Verres,* translated by L. H. G. Greenwood. Loeb Classical Library, no. 221. Cambridge, Mass.: Harvard University Press, 1928.

———. *In Verrem I* [*Orat. ii,* i.85]. In Cicero, *The Verrine Orations II: Against Verres,* part 2, books 3–5, translated by L. H. G. Greenwood. Loeb Classical Library, no. 293. Cambridge, Mass.: Harvard University Press, 1935.

———. *Pro Caecina* [*Orat. pro Caecina*]. In Cicero, *Pro Lege Manilia. Pro Caecina. Pro Cluentio. Pro Rabirio Perduellionis Reo,* translated by H. Grose Hodge. Loeb Classical Library, no. 198. Cambridge, Mass.: Harvard University Press, 1927.

———. *Pro Roscio Comoedo* [*Orat. pro Q. Roscio, comoedo*]. In Cicero, *Pro Quinctio. Pro Roscio Amerino. Pro Roscio Comoedo. The Three Speeches on the Agrarian Law Against Rullus.* Translated by J. H. Freese. Loeb Classical Library, no. 240. Cambridge, Mass.: Harvard University Press, 1930.

———. *Pro Sestio* [*Pro P. Sextio*]. In Cicero, *Pro Sestio. In Vatinium,* translated by R. Gardner. Loeb Classical Library, no. 309. Cambridge, Mass.: Harvard University Press, 1958.

———. *Somnium Scipionis* [*Som. Scip.; De republica VI.xiii*]. In Cicero, *On the Republic. On the Laws,* translated by Clinton W. Keynes. Loeb Classical Library, no. 213. Cambridge, Mass.: Harvard University Press, 1928.

———. *Tusculan Disputations* [*Tuscul.*]. Translated by J. E. King. Loeb Classical Library, no. 141. Cambridge, Mass.: Harvard University Press, 1927.

Commines, Philippe de. *Mémoires de Messire Philippe Commines* [*Memoires of Commines*]. Paris, 1552. Published in English as *Memoirs of Philip de Commines, Lord of Argenton.* Praeger Series in War Studies. London, 1991.

Crevier, Jean Baptiste Louis. *Histoire des empereurs romains* [*History of the Emperors*]. Paris, 1750–56. Published in English as *The History of the Roman Emperors.* Translated by John Mill. London, 1814.

Curtius Rufus, Quintus [Q. Curt.]. *History of Alexander.* [*Quint. Curt.*]. In Quintus Curtius, *History of Alexander,* translated by J. C. Rolfe. 2 vols. Loeb Classical Library, nos. 368, 369. Cambridge, Mass.: Harvard University Press, 1946.

Daniel, Gabriel. *Histoire de France* [*Father Daniel's History of France*] [*Hist. of France*]. Paris, 1713. Published in English as *The History of France.* London, 1726.

D'Egly, Charles Philippe de Monthenault. *Histoire des rois des deux Siciles* [*History of the Kings of the Two Sicilies*] [*History of the Two Sicilies*]. Paris, 1741.

Demosthenes. *Against Aristocrates* [*Orat. Adv. Aristocrat.*]. In Demosthenes, *Against Meidias. Against Androtion. Against Aristocrates. Against Timocrates. Against Aristogeiton 1 and 2 (21–26),* translated by J. H. Vince. Loeb Classical Library, no. 299. Cambridge, Mass.: Harvard University Press, 1935.

Diodorus Siculus. *Library of History.* Vol. IX, books 18–19.65. Translated by R. M. Geer. Loeb Classical Library, no. 377. Cambridge, Mass.: Harvard University Press, 1947.

Duport du Tertre, François-Joachim. *Histoire des conjurations, conspirations et révolutions célèbres* [Conspiracies] [*Du Port's Hist. of Conspir.*]. Paris, 1754.

Etterlin, Peterman. *Kronica von der loblichen Eydtgnoschaft* [Etterlin]. Basel, 1507. Reprint, Winterthur, 1978.

Eutropius. *Eutropii breviarium ab urbe condita* [*Eutropius*]. Published in English as *The Breviarium ab urbe condita of Eutropius.* Translated by H. W. Bird. Liverpool: Liverpool University Press, 1993.

Frederick II of Prussia. *Memoirs of the House of Brandenburg.* Translated by M. Darget. London, 1748.

Gramond, Gabriel-Barthélemy de. *Historiarum Galliae ab excessu Henrici IV libri XVIII, quibus rerum per Gallos tota Europa gestarum accurata narratio continetur, autore Gabr. Bartholomaeo Gramondo, . . .* [*Hist. Gall.*]. Tolosae: apud A. Colomerium, 1643.

Grotius, Hugo. *Annales et historiae de rebus Belgicis* [*Ann.*] [*Annals of the Netherlands*] [*Hist. of the Disturb. in the Netherlands*] [*Hist. of the Disturbances in the Low Countries*] [*Hist. of the Disturbances in the Netherlands*] [*Hist. of Netherlands*] [*Hist. of the Troubles in the Low Countries*] [*History of the Disturbances in the Low Countries*] Amsterdam, 1657. Published in English as *De rebus belgicis, or, The Annals and History of the Low-Countrey-Warrs.* London, 1665.

———. *The Free Sea* [*Mare Liberum*]. Edited by D. Armitage. Indianapolis: Liberty Fund, 2004.

———. *The Rights of War and Peace, in Three Books: Wherein Are Explained, the Law of Nature and Nations, and the Principal Points Relating to Government* [*De Jure Belli et Pacis*] [*Law of War and Peace*]. Edited and translated by Jean Barbeyrac. London, 1738. Modern edition edited by R. Tuck. Indianapolis: Liberty Fund, 2005.

Guicciardini, Francesco. *The History of Italy, from the Year 1490, to 1532 . . . In twenty books. Translated into English by the Chevalier Austin Parke Goddard.* London, 1753–56.

Heiss von Kogenheim, Johann. *Histoire de l'Empire* [*History of the Empire*]. Paris, 1684. Published in English as *History of the Empire.* Translated by Bourgeois de Chastenet. London, 1727–29.

Herodotus. *The History of Herodotus.* Translated by G. Rawlinson. 4 vols. London: J. Murray, 1862.

Hobbes, Thomas. *De Cive, or the Citizen* [*De Cive*]. Published in English as Thomas Hobbes, *De Cive, or the Citizen—English Version.* Edited by Howard Warrender. Clarendon Edition of the Works of Thomas Hobbes.

Oxford, 1984. Published in Latin as Thomas Hobbes, *De Cive—Latin Version*. Edited by Howard Warrender. Clarendon Edition of the Works of Thomas Hobbes. Oxford, 1984.

Horace. *Carmina IV* [Hor. lib. iv. od. 6]. In Horace, *Odes and Epodes*, translated by Niall Rudd. Loeb Classical Library, no. 33. Cambridge, Mass.: Harvard University Press, 2004.

———. *Satires, Epistles. The Art of Poetry* [*Ars poetica*]. Translated by H. Rushton Fairclough. Loeb Classical Library, no. 33. New York: G. P. Putnam, 1926.

Joinville, John de. *Histoire de saint Louis, Credo et lettre à Louis X.* Accompagné d'une traduction par M. Natalis de Wailly. Paris: Firmin-Didot, 1874.

Justinian I [Justin.]. *Digests (Pandects)* [*Digest.*]. In *The Digest of Justinian*, translated by Alan Watson. Philadelphia: University of Philadelphia Press, 1997.

———. *Institutes I* [*Instit. lib. i*]. In *The Institutes of Justinian: Text, Translation, and Commentary*, edited and translated by J. A. C. Thomas. New York: American Elsevier, 1975.

Lacombe, Jacques. *Abrégé chronologique de l'histoire du Nord* [*Histoire du Nord*]. Paris, 1762.

Lancelotti, Giovanni Paolo (Johannis Pauli). *Institutiones juris canonici: Cum notis variorum, praecipue arcana dominationis papalis, episcopalis, et clericalis in Ecclesia Romana detegentibus; In usum auditorii Thomasiani* [*Thomas. Nat. ad Lancell.*]. Halle, 1715–17.

La Pimpie Solignac, Pierre Joseph de. *L'histoire générale de Pologne de Mr. de Solignac* [*History of Poland*]. Paris, 1750.

Leibniz, Gottfried Wilhelm. *Codex juris gentium diplomaticus.* [*Codex Juris Gent. Diplomat.*] [*diplomatic code of the law of nations*] [Leibnitii Codex *Juris Gent. Diplomat.*] [*diplomatic Code of the Law of Nations*] [Leibnitii Codex *Juris Gent. Diplomat.*] [Leibnitz, *Cod. Jur. Gent. Diplomat.*]. Hanover, 1693.

Le Vassor, Michel. *The History of King Lewis XIII* [*Hist. of Louis XIII*]. London, 1700–1702.

Livy [Tit. Liv]. *Ab urbe condita I.* In Livy, *History of Rome, Books 1–2*, translated by B. O. Foster. Loeb Classical Library, no. 114. Cambridge, Mass.: Harvard University Press, 1919.

———. *Ab urbe condita II.* In Livy, *History of Rome, Books 1–2*, translated by B. O. Foster. Loeb Classical Library, no. 114. Cambridge, Mass.: Harvard University Press, 1919.

————. *Ab urbe condita IV.* In Livy, *History of Rome, Books 3–4,* translated by B. O. Foster. Loeb Classical Library, no. 133. Cambridge, Mass.: Harvard University Press, 1922.

————. *Ab urbe condita V.* In Livy, *History of Rome, Books 5–7,* translated by B. O. Foster. Loeb Classical Library, no. 172. Cambridge, Mass.: Harvard University Press, 1924.

————. *Ab urbe condita VI.* In Livy, *History of Rome, Books 5–7,* translated by B. O. Foster. Loeb Classical Library, no. 172. Cambridge, Mass.: Harvard University Press, 1924.

————. *Ab urbe condita VII.* In Livy, *History of Rome, Books 5–7,* translated by B. O. Foster. Loeb Classical Library, no. 172. Cambridge, Mass.: Harvard University Press, 1924.

————. *Ab urbe condita VIII.* In Livy, *History of Rome, Books 8–10,* translated by B. O. Foster. Loeb Classical Library, no. 191. Cambridge, Mass.: Harvard University Press, 1926.

————. *Ab urbe condita IX.* In Livy, *History of Rome, Books 8–10,* translated by B. O. Foster. Loeb Classical Library, no. 191. Cambridge, Mass.: Harvard University Press, 1926.

————. *Ab urbe condita XXVIII.* In Livy, *History of Rome, Books 28–30,* translated by F. G. Moore. Loeb Classical Library, no. 381. Cambridge, Mass.: Harvard University Press, 1949.

————. *Ab urbe condita XXX.* In Livy, *History of Rome, Books 28–30,* translated by F. G. Moore. Loeb Classical Library, no. 381. Cambridge, Mass.: Harvard University Press, 1949.

————. *Ab urbe condita XXXVIII.* In Livy, *History of Rome, Books 38–39,* translated by E. T. Sage. Loeb Classical Library, no. 313. Cambridge, Mass.: Harvard University Press, 1936.

————. *Ab urbe condita XLII.* In Livy, *History of Rome, Books 40–42,* translated by E. T. Sage and A. C. Schlesinger. Loeb Classical Library, no. 332. Cambridge, Mass.: Harvard University Press, 1938.

————. *Epitom. lib. XVIII.* In Livy, *Summaries, Fragments, and Obsequens,* translated by A. C. Schlesinger. Loeb Classical Library, no. 404. London: Heinemann, 1959.

Lucretius. *De rerum natura* [unreferenced]. In Lucretius, *On the Nature of Things,* translated by W. H. D. Rouse, revised by Martin F. Smith. Loeb Classical Library, no. 181, rev. ed. Cambridge, Mass.: Harvard University Press, 1992.

Machiavelli, Nicolò. *Discorsi sopra la prima deca di Tito Livio* [*Disc. on Livy*].

1531. Published in English as *Discourses on Livy.* Translated by Harvey C. Mansfield and Nathan Tarcov. Chicago: University of Chicago Press, 1996.

Mariana, Juan de. *De rege et regis institutione [de Rege et Regis Institut.].* Toledo, 1599.

Matthieu, Pierre. *Histoire de France sous les regnes de François I, Henri II, François II, Charles IX, Henri III, Henri IV, and Louis XIII* [Matthieu vol. ii book 3]. 2 vols. Paris, 1631.

Mézeray, François Eudes de. *A General Chronological History of France [Hist. of France] [History of France].* London, 1683.

Molesworth, Robert. *Etat présent du Danemark, par M. Molesworth, envoyé d'Angleterre à la Cour de Danemark* [Present State of Denmark]. Amsterdam: Jansons à Waesberge, 1732.

Montaigne, Michel de. *Les essais de Michel de Montaigne, nouvelle edition.* 3 vols. London, 1724.

Montesquieu, Charles de Secondat, Baron de. *The Spirit of the Laws [Spirit of Laws].* Edited by A. M. Cohler et al. Cambridge: Cambridge University Press, 1989.

Montgon, Charles Alexander de. *Mémoires de M. l'Abbé de Montgon [Memoirs of the abbé De Montgon].* Lausanne, 1748–49.

Nevers, Louis de Gonzage, Duc de. *Les Mémoires de Monsieur le Duc de Nevers [Memoires de Nevers].* Paris, 1665.

Noell [Natalis], Alexandre. *Historia ecclesiastica [Dissert. Hist. Eccl.]* [Natal. Alex. *Dissert. Hist. Eccles.*]. Paris, 1676.

Ockley, Simon. *The Conquest of Syria, Persia, and Egypt by the Saracens [Alvakedi's History of the Conquest of Syria].* London, 1708–18.

———. *The History of the Saracens [History of the Saracens].* London, 1718. Reprint, Whitefish, Mont.: Kessinger, 2003.

Ossat, Arnauld d'. *Lettres de illustrissime et reverendissime Cardinale d'Ossat [Letters of Cardinal d'Ossat].* Paris, 1624.

Ovid. *Tristia* I. In Ovid, *Tristia. Ex Porto,* translated by A. L. Wheeler, revised by G. P. Gould. Loeb Classical Library, no. 151. Cambridge, Mass.: Harvard University Press, 1988.

Papon, Jean. *Recueil d'arrests notables des cours souveraines de France [Arrêts Notables].* Paris, 1565.

Pas, Antoine de, Marquis de Feuquières. *Mémoires sur la guerre [Memoires de Feuquieres].* [Paris?], 1730. Published in English as *Memoirs Historical and Military.* London, 1736.

Pecquet, Antoine. *Discours sur l'art de négocier.* Paris, 1737.

Pineau-Duclos, Charles. *The History of King Louis XI, King of France.* London, 1746.

Pliny the Younger [Gaius Plinius Caecilius Secundus]. *Epistulae [Ep. L].* In *Letters, I Books 1–7,* translated by Betty Radice. Loeb Classical Library. New York: Heinemann, 1969.

Plumard de Danguel, Louis-Joseph [John Nickolls, pseud.]. *Remarques sur les avantages et les désavantages de la France et de la Gr. Bretagne, par rapport au commerce.* Leiden [Paris], 1754. Published in English as *Remarks on the Advantages and Disadvantages of France and Great-Britain with Respect to Commerce.* London, 1754.

Plutarch. *Agesilaus [Life of Agesilaüs].* In Plutarch, *Agesilaus and Pompey. Pelopidas and Marcellus,* translated by Bernadotte Perrin. Loeb Classical Library, no. 87. Cambridge, Mass.: Harvard University Press, 1917.

———. *Demetrios [in Demetrio.].* In Plutarch, *Demetrius and Antony. Pyrrhus and Gaius Marius [Plut. in Pyrr.],* translated by Bernadotte Perrin. Loeb Classical Library, no. 101. Cambridge, Mass.: Harvard University Press, 1920.

———. *Fabius [life of Fabius Maximus].* In Plutarch, *Pericles and Fabius Maximus. Nicias and Crassus,* translated by Bernadotte Perrin. Loeb Classical Library, no. 65. Cambridge, Mass.: Harvard University Press, 1916.

———. *Publicola [in Poplicol.].* In Plutarch, *Theseus and Romulus. Lycurgus and Numa. Solon and Publicola,* translated by Bernadotte Perrin. Loeb Classical Library, no. 46. Cambridge, Mass.: Harvard University Press, 1914.

Polybius. *Historiae III [Histor. lib. iii].* In Polybius, *Histories Books 3–4,* translated by W. R. Paton. Loeb Classical Library, no. 137. Cambridge, Mass.: Harvard University Press, 1922.

Prévost, Antoine François. *Histoire générale des voyages, ou Nouvelle collection de toutes les relations de voyages par mer et par terre qui ont été publiées jusqu'à présent dans les différentes langues.* 20 vols. Paris, 1746–1801.

Pufendorf, Samuel. *Les devoirs de l'homme et du citoien.* 4th ed. Amsterdam, 1718. Modern English edition, *The Whole Duty of Man, According to the Law of Nature.* Edited by I. Hunter and D. Saunders. Indianapolis: Liberty Fund, 2003.

———. *Of the Law of Nature and Nations [Law of Nature and Nations; De jure naturae et gentium].* Edited by Jean Barbeyrac. Translated by Basil Kennet. 4th ed. London, 1729. Reprint, Clark, N.J.: Lawbook Exchange, 2005.

Quintilian. *Institutio Oratoria VII [Inst. Orat.] [Instit. Orat.].* In Quintilian,

The Orator's Education, Books 6–8, translated by Donald A. Russell. Loeb Classical Library, no. 126. Cambridge, Mass.: Harvard University Press, 2002.

———. *The Major Declamations Attributed to Quintilian* [*Declamations*]. Translated by L. A. Sussman. Frankfurt am Main; New York: Verlag P. Lang, 1987.

Rebmann, Hans Rudolf. *Ein neuw, lustig, ernsthafft, poetisch Gastmal, vnd Gespräch zweyer Bergen, in der löblichen Eydgnossschafft, vnd im Berner Gebiet gelegen . . .* Bern, 1606.

Ricci, Pietro Andrea. *Synopsis, decreta et resolutiones sac. congr. Immunitatis super controversijs iurisdictionalibus complectens.* [*Synops. Decret. et Resol. S. Congreg. Immunit.*]. Praeneste: Typis Barberinis apud Antonium Ruzzolum, 1708.

Rohan, Henri, Duc de. *Mémoires du Duc de Rohan sur les choses qui se sont passées en France depuis la mort de Henri le Grand jusqu'à la Paix faite avec les Réformés* [*Memoires de Rohan*]. [Paris?], 1644. Published in English as *The Memoires of the Duke of Rohan.* Translated by George Bridges. London, 1660.

Schodeler [Schodoler], Wernher. *Eidgenössische Chronik* [*Schodeler*]. Bremgarten an der Reuss, [ca. 1510–35]. Reprint, Luzern: Faksimile-Verlag, 1980.

Selden, John. *Mare clausum, of the Dominion, or, Ownership of the Sea* [*Mare Clausum*]. London, 1635. Reprint, Clark, N.J.: Lawbook Exchange, 2002.

Seneca. *De beneficiis.* In Seneca, *Moral Essays,* vol. 3. Translated by John W. Basore. Loeb Classical Library, no. 310. Cambridge, Mass.: Harvard University Press, 1935.

———. *De ira I.* In Seneca, *Moral Essays. De providentia. De constantia. De ira. De clementia,* translated by John W. Basore. Loeb Classical Library, no. 214. Cambridge, Mass.: Harvard University Press, 1928.

Sextus Aurelius Victor. *De Viris Illustribus [Auctor de Viris Illust.].* In *Sexti Aurelii Victoris Liber de Caesaribus. Praecedunt Origo gentis Romanae et Liber de viris illustribus urbis Romae. Subsequitur Epitome de Caesaribus,* edited by Franz Pichlmayr and Roland Gründel. Leipzig: B. G. Teubneri, 1966.

Sharaf ad-Din ʿAli Yazdi. *The History of Timur-Bec, Known by the Name of Tamerlain the Great* [Hist. of Timur-Bec]. From the Persian by Cherefeddin Ali. Translated into French by Petis de la Croix and into English by John Darby. 2 vols. London, 1723.

Simler, Josias. *De Helvetiorum republica* [*de Repub. Helvet.*]. Zürich, 1576.

Socrates of Constantinople [Scholasticus]. *Ecclesiastical History* [*Hist. Eccles.*]. Whitefish, Mont.: Kessinger, 2003.

Solís y Rivadeneira, Antonio de. *Historia de la conquista de México*. Spain, 1686. Modern edition, Prologue and appendices by Edmundo O'Gorman. Notes by José Valero Silva. Mexico City, 1973. Published in English as *History of the Conquest of Mexico by the Spaniards*. Translated by Thomas Townsend. London, 1742.

Stettler, Michael. *Chronikon oder Grundliche Beschreibung der fürnembsten Geschichte und Thaten, welche sich in gantzer Helvetia, den jüngsten Jahren nach, von ihrem Anfang her gerechnet, . . . bis auff das 1627. Jahr/participirt, verlauffen*. Bern, 1627.

Stumpf, Johannes. *Gemeiner loblicher Eydgnoschafft Stetten/Landen vnd Völckeren Chronick wirdiger thaaten beschreybung*. Zürich, 1554.

Sully, Maximilien de Béthune, Duc de. *Mémoires de Maximilien de Béthune Duc de Sully, principal ministre de Henry le Grand, mis en ordre: Avec des rémarques* [*Memoirs digested by M. de l'Ecluse*] [*Sully's Memoirs*] [*Sully's Memoirs*, by M. de l'Ecluse]. Edited by Pierre Mathurin de L'Écluse des Loges. London [Paris], 1752.

Tacitus, *Annales I*. In Tacitus, *Histories 4–5. Annals 1–3*, translated by Clifford H. Moore and John Jackson. Loeb Classical Library, no. 249. Cambridge, Mass.: Harvard University Press, 1931.

———. *Annales II* [Tacit. *Annal.* lib. ii]. In Tacitus, *Histories 4–5. Annals 1–3*, translated by Clifford H. Moore and John Jackson. Loeb Classical Library, no. 249. Cambridge, Mass.: Harvard University Press, 1931.

———. *Annales III*. In Tacitus, *Histories 4–5. Annals 1–3*, translated by Clifford H. Moore and John Jackson. Loeb Classical Library, no. 249. Cambridge, Mass.: Harvard University Press, 1931.

———. *Annales XII*. In Tacitus, *Annals 4–6, 11–12*, translated by John Jackson. Loeb Classical Library, no. 312. Cambridge, Mass.: Harvard University Press, 1937.

———. *Annales XIII*. In Tacitus, *Annals 13–16*, translated by John Jackson. Loeb Classical Library, no. 322. Cambridge, Mass.: Harvard University Press, 1937.

———. *Annales XIV*. In Tacitus, *Annals 13–16*, translated by John Jackson. Loeb Classical Library, no. 322. Cambridge, Mass.: Harvard University Press, 1937.

Tertullian. *Tertullian De exhortatione castitatis* [*Exhort. Castit.*]: Ermahnung zur Keuscheit. In *Tertullian,* edited by Hans-Veit Friedrich. Stuttgart: Teubner, 1990.

Thou [De Thou], Jacques Auguste de. *A. Thuani historiarum sui temporis.* Geneva, 1620. Published in English as *Monsieur de Thou's History of His Own Times.* Translated by Bernhard Wilson. London, 1729–30.

Thucydides. *The History of the Peloponnesian War, Books 3–4.* Translated by C. F. Smith. Loeb Classical Library, no. 109, rev. ed. Cambridge, Mass.: Harvard University Press, 1930.

Tribbechov, Adam. *Exercitationes ad baronii annales ubi desiit Isaacus Casaubonus: In Acad. Kiloniensi ad disputandum propositae Kilonium [ad Baron. Annal.].* Kiel: Reumann, 1667; later edition Leipzig: Reumann, 1708.

Tschudi, Aegidius. *Chronicon Helveticorum.* Basle, 1734–36. Reprint, Bern: Allgemeine Geschichtsforschende Gesellschaft der Schweiz, 1968–2000.

Turretini [Turretin] [Turretinus], François. *Compendium theologicae didactoelencticae [Turretin, Hist. Ecclesiast. Compendium].* Published in English as *Institutes of Elenctic Theology.* Edited by James T. Dennison. Translated by George Musgrave Giger. Phillipsburg, N.J.: P & R Publications, 1992.

Valerius Maximus [*Valer. Maxim.*]. *Factorum et dictorum memorabilium* [*Valer. Max.*]. In Valerius Maximus, *Memorable Doings and Sayings,* translated by D. R. Shackleton Bailey. 2 vols. Loeb Classical Library, nos. 492, 493. Cambridge, Mass.: Harvard University Press, 2000.

Varro. *De lingua Latina V [de Ling. Lat. lib. iv].* In Varro, *On the Latin Language,* translated by Roland G. Kent. Loeb Classical Library, no. 333. Cambridge, Mass.: Harvard University Press, 1951.

Vattel, Emer de. *Le loisir philosophique ou pièces diverses de philosophie, de morale, et d'amusement.* Geneva, 1747.

———. *Mélanges de littérature, de morale, et de politique.* Neuchâtel: Edit. du Journal Helvétique, 1760.

Vega, Garcilaso de la. *Royal Commentaries of the Incas and General History of Peru [Garcillasso de la Vega].* Edited and translated by Harold V. Livermore. Lisbon, 1609. Austin: University of Texas Press, 1966.

Velly, (Abbé) Paul François. *Histoire de France, depuis l'établissement de la monarchie jusqu'au règne de Louis XIV—Nouvelle édition* [Abbé Velly, *History of France*] [*Hist. of France*]. Vols. 1–7 by Velly. Vols. 8–17 by C. Villaret. Vols. 18–30 by J. J. Garnier. Paris, 1755–86.

———. *Poliergie, ou Mélange de littérature et de poësies.* Amsterdam: Arkstée et Merkus, 1757.

Vertot, René-Aubert de. *History of the Revolutions in Sweden, Occasioned by the Change in Religion* [*History of the Revolutions in Sweden*]. London, 1696.

————. *Revolutions of Portugal.* Translated by G. Roussillon. London, 1721.

Virgil. *Aeneid II.* In Virgil, *Eclogues, Georgics, Aeneid Books 1–6,* translated by H. Rushton Fairclough, revised by G. P. Goold. Loeb Classical Library, no. 63. Cambridge, Mass.: Harvard University Press, 1916.

————. *Aeneid VI.* In Virgil, *Eclogues, Georgics, Aeneid Books 1–6,* translated by H. Rushton Fairclough, revised by G. P. Goold. Loeb Classical Library, no. 63. Cambridge, Mass.: Harvard University Press, 1916.

————. *Aeneid X* [Aen.]. In Virgil, *Aeneid 7–12, Appendix Vergiliana,* translated by H. Rushton Fairclough, revised by G. P. Goold. Loeb Classical Library, no. 64. Cambridge, Mass.: Harvard University Press, 1918.

————. *Eclogues.* In Virgil, *Eclogues, Georgics, Aeneid Books 1–6,* translated by H. Rushton Fairclough, revised by G. P. Goold. Loeb Classical Library, no. 63. Cambridge, Mass.: Harvard University Press, 1916.

Vogel, Franz Adam. *Traité historique et politique des alliances entre la France et les XIII. Cantons: Depuis Charles VII jusqu'à présent par Mr. Vogel G[rand] J[uge] D[es] G[ardes] S[uisses]. Suivant la copie imprimée-Paris* [*Vogel's Historical and Political Treatise*]. 1733.

Vopiscus, Flavius. *Probus* [*Prob.*]. In *Historia Augusta III,* translated by David Magie. Loeb Classical Library, no. 263. Cambridge, Mass.: Harvard University Press, 1932.

Wattenwyl (French spelling is Watteville), Alexander Ludwig von. *Histoire de la Confédération helvétique* [*History of the Helvetic Confederacy*] [*Hist. of the Helvetic Confederacy*]. Bern: Gottschall, 1754.

Wicquefort, Abraham de. *The Embassador and His Functions* [*The Ambassador*] [*Embassador*] [*Embassad.*] [*Embass.*]. Translated by John Digby. London, 1716. Reprint, Leicester: Leicester University, 1997.

Witt, Johan de. *Brieven geschreven ende gewisselt tusschen den Heer Johan de Witt.* [*De Witt's Letters and Negotiations*] Gravenhage, 1723–25. Modern edition, *Brieven van Johan de Witt.* Edited by Robert Fruin. Amsterdam: J. Müller, 1919.

Wolf[f], Christian. *Ius naturae et ius gentium* [*Jus Gent.*] [*Law of Nations*] [*Law of Nature*] [Wolf, *Jus Gent.*] [Wolf, *Jus Gentium*] [Wolf, *Jus Nat.*] [Wolfii, *Jus Gent.*] [Wolfius, *Jus Gent.*] [Wolfius, *Jus Nat.*]. Halle, 1740–46. Reprinted in J. Ecole et al., eds., *Christian Wolff: Gesammelte Werke,* series 2 (Latin), vol. 61. Hildesheim [Zurich] New York, 1960.

————. *Ius gentium methodo scientifica pertractatum.* Translated by Joseph H. Drake. Oxford: Clarendon Press, 1934.

————. *Philosophia practica universalis methodo scientifica pertractata* [*Phil. Pract. Univ.*]. Frankfurt, 1738–39. Reprinted in *Gesammelte Schriften.* Abtl. 2, *Lateinische Schriften.* Band 10–11. Hildesheim: Olms, 1971–78.

————. *Theologia naturalis scientifica pertractata* [*Theol. nat.*]. 2 vols. Frankfurt, 1736–37.

Xenophon [Xenoph.]. *Constitution of Lacedaemon* [*Lacedaemon. Respublica.*]. In Xenophon, *Hiero. Agesilaus. Constitution of the Lacedaemonians. Ways and Means. Cavalry Commander. Art of Horsemanship. On Hunting. Constitution of the Athenians,* translated by E. C. Marchant and G. W. Bowersock. Loeb Classical Library, no. 183. Cambridge, Mass.: Harvard University Press, 1925.

————. *Cyropaedia V* [*Cyrop.*]. In Xenophon, *Cyropaedia 5–8,* translated by Walter Miller. Loeb Classical Library, no. 52. Cambridge, Mass.: Harvard University Press, 1914.

————. *Hellenica.* [*Hist. Graec.*] In Xenophon, *Hellenica Books 1–4,* translated by Carleton L. Brownson. Loeb Classical Library, no. 88. Cambridge, Mass.: Harvard University Press, 1918.

Writings on Vattel

Bandelier, André. "De Berlin à Neuchâtel: La genèse du Droit des gens d'Emer de Vattel." In *Schweizer im Berlin des 18. Jahrhunderts,* 45–56, edited by Martin Fontius and Helmut Holzhey, Berlin: Akademie Verlag, 1996.

Baudenet D'Annoux, Henry. *Le développement de la neutralité de Grotius à Vattel.* Orléans: A. Gout, 1910.

Beaulac, Stéphane. "Emer de Vattel and the Externalization of Sovereignty." *Journal of the History of International Law* 5 (2003): 237–92.

————. "The Westphalian Legal Orthodoxy—Myth or Reality?" *Journal of the History of International Law* 2 (2000): 148–77.

Béguelin, Eduard. "En souvenir de Vattel." In *Recueil de travaux,* 35–176. Neuchâtel: Attinger, 1929.

Brierly, J. L. *The Law of Nations.* 6th ed. Oxford: Clarendon, 1963.

Bull, Hedley. *The Anarchical Society: A Study of Order in World Politics.* London: Macmillan, 1977.

Butler, Peter F. "Legitimacy in a States-System: Vattel's Law of Nations." In *The Reason of States,* edited by Michael Donelan, 45–63. London: Allen and Unwin, 1978.

Cavallar, Georg. *The Rights of Strangers: Theories of International Hospitality, the Global Community, and Political Justice Since Vitoria,* 306–17. Aldershot: Ashgate, 2002.

Dufour, Alfred. "Religion, église, état dans la pensée d'Emer de Vattel." *Musée Neuchâtelois* 2002: 169–92.

Fenwick, Charles G. "The Authority of Vattel." *American Political Science Review* 7 (1913): 395–410.

Guggenheim, Paul. *Emer de Vattel et l'étude des relations internationales en Suisse.* Genève: Georg et Cie, 1956.

———. "La souveraineté dans l'histoire du droit des gens de Vitoria à Vattel." In *Mélanges offerts à Juray Andrassy,* edited by Vladimir Ibler, 111–21. La Haye: Martin Nijhoff, 1968.

Haggenmacher, Peter. "L'Etat souverain comme sujet du droit international, de Vitoria à Vattel." *Droits: Revue française de théorie juridique* 16 (1992): 11–20. Paris: PUF.

Hochstrasser, Timothy J. *Natural Law Theories in the Early Enlightenment,* 177–83. Cambridge: Cambridge University Press, 2000.

Hurell, Andrew. "Vattel: Pluralism and Its Limits." In *Classical Theories of International Relations,* edited by Ian Clark and Iver B. Neumann, 233–55. New York: St. Martin's Press, 1996.

Jouannet, Emmanuelle. "La critique de la pensée classique durant l'entre-deux guerres: Vattel et Van Vollenhoven (Quelques réflexions sur le modèle classique du droit international)." *Miskolc Journal of International Law* 1 (2004): 45–63.

———. *Emer de Vattel et l'émergence doctrinale du droit international classique.* Paris: A. Pedrone, 1998.

———. "Vattel et la sujétion directe de l'Etat au droit international." In *L'Etat Moderne: Regards sur la pensée politique de l'Europe Occidentale entre 1715 et 1848,* edited by Simone Goyard-Fabre, 153–79. Paris: J. Vrin, 2000.

Kant, Immanuel. "Perpetual Peace." In *Kant: Political Writings,* edited by H. S. Reiss. Cambridge: Cambridge University Press, 1991.

Kapossy, Béla. *Iselin contra Rousseau: Sociable Patriotism and the History of Mankind.* Basel: Schwabe, 2006.

Kelsen, Hans. "Quincy Wright's *A Study of War* and the Bellum Justum Theory." *Ethics* 3, no. 3 (1943): 208–11.

Koskenniemi, Martti. *From Apology to Utopia: The Structure of International Legal Argument,* 89–97. Helsinki: Finnish Lawyers' Publishing Co., 1989.

Lapradelle, Albert de. Introduction to *The Law of Nations or the Principles of Natural Law,* by Emer de Vattel, iii–lix. Carnegie ed. Washington, D.C., 1916. Reprint, New York: Oceana, 1964.

Linklater, Andrew. *Men and Citizens in the Theory of International Relations.* London: Macmillan, 1982.

Manz, Johannes. *Emer de Vattel: Versuch einer Würdigung; Unter besonderer Berücksichtigung seiner Auffassung von der individuellen Freiheit und der souveränen Gleichheit.* Diss. Zürich, 1971.

Midgley, E. B. F. *The Natural Law Tradition and the Theory of International Relations,* 184–95. London: Elek, 1975.

Montmorency, J. E. G. de. "Emerich de Vattel." *Journal of the Society of Comparative Legislation,* n.s., 10 (1909): 17–39. Reprinted in *Great Jurists of the World,* edited by John Macdonell and Edward Manson, 477–504. Boston: Little, Brown, 1914.

Nussbaum, A. *A Concise History of the Law of Nations.* New York: Macmillan, 1954.

Onuf, Nicholas Greenwood. "Civitas Maxima: Wolff, Vattel, and the Fate of Republicanism." *American Journal of International Law* 88 (1994): 280–303.

Rabkin, Jeremy. "Grotius, Vattel, and Locke: An Older View of Liberalism and Nationality." *Review of Politics* 59 (1997): 292–322.

Remec, Peter Pavel. *The Position of the Individual in International Law According to Grotius and Vattel.* The Hague: M. Nijhoff, 1960.

Ruddy, Francis Stephen. "The Acceptance of Vattel." *Grotian Society Papers* 1972: 177–96. The Hague: M. Nijhoff.

———. *International Law in the Enlightenment: The Background of Emmerich de Vattel's Le Droit des Gens.* Dobbs Ferry, N.Y.: Oceana, 1975.

Schmitt, Carl. *Der Nomos der Erde im Völkerrecht des Jus Publicum Europaeum.* 4th ed. Berlin: Duncker and Humblot, 1997.

Senellart, Michel. "La qualification de l'ennemi chez Emer de Vattel." *Astérion,* no. 2 (juillet 2004) 31–51.

Staub, Hans. *Die Völkerrechtlichen Lehren Vattels im Lichte der naturrechtlichen Doktrin: Ein Beitrag zur Gründungsgeschichte des Völkerrechts.* Berlin: Vahlen, 1922.

Thévenaz, Henri. "Vattel ou La destinée d'un livre." *Schweizerisches Jahrbuch für Internationales Recht* 14 (1957): 9–16.

Tuck, Richard. *The Rights of War and Peace: Political Thought and the International Order from Grotius to Kant,* 191–96. Oxford: Oxford University Press, 1999.

Van Vollenhoven, Cornelius. *Du droit de paix. De iure pacis.* La Haye: M. Nijhoff, 1932.

———. *Les trois phases du* Droit des gens. La Haye: M. Nijhoff, 1919.

Whelan, Frederick G. "Vattel's Doctrine of the State." *History of Political Thought* 9 (1988): 59–90. Reprinted in *Grotius, Pufendorf, and Modern Natural Law,* edited by K. Haakonssen, 403–34. Brookfield, Vt.: Dartmouth Publishing, 1998.

Wright, Quincy. Preface to *The Position of the Individual in International Law According to Grotius and Vattel,* by Peter Pavel Remec. The Hague: M. Nijhoff, 1960.

———. *A Study of War.* 2 vols. Chicago: University of Chicago Press, 1942.

Zurbuchen, Simone. "Die schweizerische Debatte über die Leibniz-Wolffsche Philosophie und ihre Bedeutung für Emer von Vattels philosophischen Werdegang." In *Reconceptualizing Nature, Science, and Aesthetics: Contribution à une nouvelle approche des Lumières helvetiques,* edited by Patrick Coleman, Anne Hofmann, and Simone Zurbuchen, 91–113. Genève: Slatkine, 1998.

INDEX

This index uses modern American spelling, with original usage enclosed in parentheses or cross-referenced when necessary. Declarations, councils, treaties, and the like will be found under their main element; thus the treaty of Madrid is located under *M*. For names including the French prefix *de* or *d'*, please check under the main element (François de Callières, for instance, will be under *C*).

abandonment: of sovereignty, 212; usucaption and prescription, 331–38

Absalum, bishop of Roschild, 474n

absurdities, interpretation of treaties leading to, 418–19, 428

academicians, as enemies, 550

accommodation, amicable, 450

Achilles, 581

active and passive obligation, 751–52; basis for, 766

Adeimantus, 545n

Adrets, François de Beaumont, baron des, 646

Adrian (Hadrian; Roman emperor), 125

Adriatic Sea, Venetian control of, 254–55

Aduatici, 546n

aged people, as enemies, 549

agents, ambassadorial, 693

Agesilaüs, 536

aggrandizement of neighboring power as just cause for war, 491–99

Agincourt, battle of, 555–56

agriculture: government support for, 128–31; peasants, as enemies, 550–51

Aix-la-Chapelle, treaty of, 400, 503, 568

Alba (Alva), Don Fernando Álvarez de Toledo y Pimental, 3rd duke of, 546n, 642–43, 646n, 703

Albert II the Wise (king of Austria), 402

Albigenses (Cathars), 183n

Alcibiades, 563–64n

Alexander VI (pope), 173, 215n

Alexander the Great, 486, 511, 545, 546, 562, 600, 607

Algerian corsairs. *See* piracy

alienation of property, 237–42; by corporations, 232–33; nation, alienation of part of, 240–42; in peace treaties, 657–59; public property, 237–40

alliances, 512–23; aggrandizing powers, controlling, 496; *casus foederis* in, 515–16; civil wars of other nations, involvement in, 648–49; declarations of war against enemies' allies, 522–23; defensive, 512, 519–21; embassy and, 686; enemies' associates and allies, 517–23; equal alliances vs. equal treaties, 348; just

alliances (*continued*)
    cause for, 513–14; in just war only,
    514–16; with nations already at war,
    514; offensive, 512, 519; peace trea-
    ties and, 661–62, 675, 677, 680–
    81; personal, 355, 362–64; post-
    liminium, 604–5; precedence of
    more ancient allies regarding trea-
    ties, 344; real, 355–59, 364–65; re-
    fusal of help as injury in, 517;
    ruptures between former allies, 517;
    troops or funds provided by, 513;
    unequal, 349–55, 683–85; warlike
    associations vs., 512
alluvion, right of, 244–45, 247–49
Alphonso VIII (king of Castile), 231n
Alphonso V (king of Portugal), 121,
    216n
Alva (Alba), Don Fernando Álvarez
    de Toledo y Pimental, 3rd duke of,
    546n, 642–43, 646n, 703
Alvakedi, 721n
ambassadors. *See* embassy
ambiguous or equivocal expressions,
    416–18, 420–21, 432–33
Ambrose of Milan, 176
America: Canada (*see* Canada); Euro-
    pean colonization of (*see* coloniza-
    tion); Indians (*see* Native
    Americans); Spanish attacks on, 275
American Revolution, ix
amicable accommodation, 450
Ammianus Marcellinus, 329n, 426n,
    797
amnesties, 664
Amurath (Murad) II (sultan), 388
Anaxilaüs, 564n
Ancona, 280
androlepsia, 465
Anne (queen of England), 573
Anne of Austria (regent of France),
    657–58n
Anson, George, 555, 797
Antaeus, 291

antichresis, 398
anticipation, right of, 234
Antiochus IV Epiphanes (Seleucid
    ruler), 394, 417, 522
Antoninus (Roman emperor), 125
Antony the Bastard of Burgundy,
    548n
Appian[us], 668n, 797
Arabs, 310, 721–22. *See also* Islam
Aragon. *See* Spain, and individual
    rulers
arbitrary law of nations, 17, 705
arbitration: between nations, 451–52;
    between subjects and sovereigns,
    109
Arbroath, declaration of, 106–7nn
Aristotle, 83, 797
armies. *See* entries at military
Arminius, 561
arrest of subject by way of reprisal,
    465
Arrian (Lucius Flavius Arrianus),
    546n, 797
artifices and stratagems in war, 579–81
arts, national encouragement of, 146–
    47
assassination: of enemies, 557–63; of
    sovereigns, 103, 156, 170, 178–79,
    716–19
the Assassins, 559–60, 722
asseverations used in treaties, 392
associations, warlike, vs. alliances, 512
asylum in ambassador's house, 738–40
asylums for invalid soldiers, 476
Atahualpa (Incan emperor), 290
atheism, 765–66
Athenians. *See* Greeks
Attila the Hun, 487, 564
Augier de Marigny, François, 698n,
    798
August[us] III (king of Poland), x,
    525n
Augustus Caesar (Roman emperor),
    653n, 668

Aulus Gellius, 561n, 798
Austria: commercial trading rights, 251; Swiss protectorates of dukes of, 209, 212; Vienna, Turkish siege of, 263; War of the Austrian Succession, 425, 481n, 521n, 534n, 554, 573n, 614, 616
authority: of body politic over its members, 81–82; Catholic independence from, 174–79; embassy, authority to send, 683, 704–5; of judges, 189; over clergy, 164–70; over peace treaties, 655–57, 659–60; over public ministers, 112; over public property, 229–30; over religious matters, 168–69; over reprisals, 462; over treaties and conventions, 338–39, 372–73; over truces, 619–21; of sovereign, 100
auxiliary treaties, 512
auxiliary troops, 513
Avidius Cassius, 616

Bacallar y Sanna, Vicente, marquis de San Felipe (marquis de St. Philippe), 284n, 387n, 658n, 798
Bacon, Sir Francis, 205
balance of powers, 496–99
balance of trade, 139
banishment, 225–28, 307–8, 323
banks and banking, 144
banner, right of. See embassy
barbarians: migration of peoples, 328–29; Roman empire, admission to, 328–29; Tacitus on, 108, 161n, 306n, 394, 427n, 487, 809; Teutoburg Forest, battle of, 561n; war made without reason or motive by, 487
Barbary corsairs. See piracy
Barbeyrac, Jean: on embassy, 717; on law of nature and law of nations, 9–10; on national responsibility for actions of citizens, 301n; on natural law, 755–58, 759n, 761, 763–67, 768–69, 770; on obligation, 752–53; on sovereigns, 111; translations and commentaries, xvi; on treaties, 433n
Barkuk or Barquq (Barcouc; sultan of Egypt), 719n
Bartolus, 283n
Basilius II (Byzantine emperor), 717
Baste, George, 631
Battory, 631
Baune, Renauld de, 174n
Bayard, chevalier de, 547
Bayle, Pierre, 756n
bays, sovereignty over, 255–56
Beaumont, François de, baron des Adrets, 646
Beaumont, Monsieur De (French ambassador to Britain), 743
Bedamar, marquis of, 716
Belisarius, 550n, 571–72
Bellay, Martin Du, 700n, 725n, 798
Belle-Isle, Charles-Louis-Auguste Fouget, duc de, 616
Benedict XIV (pope), 199–200, 268, 286n
Bernard, duke of Saxe-Weymar, 726n
Bernard, Jacques, 756, 798
Bernouilli, Jacob, 205
Bessus, 562
Béthune, Maximilien de, duc de Sully, xi, 161, 238, 504n, 631, 710, 743, 789, 809
Beuningen, Coenraad van, 296n, 665n
biblical citations: 1 Samuel 19–20, 112n; Timothy 1:9, 771
Bilaine, Antoine, 102n, 798
Bodinus (Jean Bodin), 144, 254, 283n, 293n, 315, 318, 798
Boeotians, 420
Boizard, Jean, 142n, 799
bombardment of towns, 570, 572–73
Boniface VIII (pope), 170–71
Bontekoe, Willem, 321, 799

booty, 568–69, 593–603
Boreel (ambassador), 463n, 532n
Borgia, Cesare, 289
Boufflers, Louis François, duc de, 577
Bougeant, Guillaume Hyacinthe, 390n, 726n, 799
Bouillon, French ambassador to Britain, 291n
boundaries: rivers and streams as, 242–47; settlement of, 308
Bourbon Condé, Anne Geneviève de, 305n, 799
Brandenburg, French refugees in, 329
breaches of peace treaties, 673–81
Breda, treaty of, 254
Breslau, Treaty of, 370
bribery by ambassadors, 709–10
bridges and highways, maintenance of, 139–41
Brienne, Jean, count de, 286n
Britain: Aix-la-Chapelle, treaty of, 400, 503, 568; arts and sciences, national encouragement of, 147; balance of powers, maintaining, 497; Civil War and Commonwealth, 106–8, 282, 685, 689; commerce of, 131, 132, 137n; contraband goods, 529; Glorious Revolution, 290, 364–65; Lisbon earthquake, public collections following, 264; maritime law of, 251, 252–54; neutrality and use of ports, 526n; obligations and rights between nations, former nonrecognition of, 273n; peace, right to make, 656; prisoners of war, treatment of, 553; Prussian vessels, seizure of, 304; religion, sovereign's authority in matters of, 168–69; reprisals against Netherlands in favor of Knights of Malta, 463; self-preservation and perfection as aim of, 89–91; sovereign succession in, 116, 122; standing army, lack of

need for, 500; taxation in, 230; treaty keeping of, 343; valor, national reputation for, 200; Vattel's admiration of, xviii–xix; war, right of sovereign to make, 471
Brühl, count, x–xi, xix, 19n2
Bruneau (secretary to Spanish ambassador in France), 710, 718–19
Brutus (Marcus Junius Brutus Caepio), 154
Budaeus or Buddeus, Johann Franz, 10, 799
Bullinger, Heinrich, 212n, 799
Burgundy, Antony the Bastard of, 548n
Burgundy, Charles, duke of, 634n
Burgundy, Philip, duke of, 389
Burgundy, Philip, son of Antony the Bastard of, 548n
burial of dead during time of truce, 626–27
Burlamaqui, Jean-Jacques, x
burning of enemy property, 570–73
Busiris (king of Egypt), 291
buying, right of, 133, 134
Bynkershoek, Cornelius van, 463n, 717n, 730n, 732n, 736, 799–800

Caecina, 437
Caepio (Servilius Caepio), 583
Caesar, Gaius Julius. See Julius Caesar
Caius Luscinus Fabricius, 560–61
Caius Pontius, 488
Callières, François de, 732, 800
Cambray, congress of, 453
Camden, William, 413, 718n, 800
Camillus (Marius Furius Camillus), 484n, 601
Campanella, Tommaso, 302, 800
Canada: Hudson's Bay, 255; missionaries to Hurons, 166
canals, bridges, and highways, maintenance of, 139–41

Can Natural Law Bring Society to Perfection Without the Assistance of Political Laws? (Vattel): editions and translations, xxiii; text, 773–81; Vattel's writing of, xi

Canson (Mameluke sultan), 698n

capital punishment. *See* killing

capitulation of towns and cities, 629–32

Caraffa (papal legate), 389

carriages of ambassadors, 707–8n, 740–41

Carthage: commerce of, 131; treaties with Rome, 351–52, 354–55, 440–42, 660; wars with Rome, 354–55, 455, 576, 660

Castile. *See* Spain, and individual rulers

casus foederis in alliances, 515–16

Cathars (Albigenses), 183n

Catholicism, 169–85; asylum, embassies in Rome as places of, 739–40; British rejection of Catholic kings, 116; celibacy of clergy, 174–76, 199–200; convents/monasteries, 175, 199–200, 475; division of New World between Spain and Portugal by papacy, 215; Dutch ships, protection offered to, 268; excommunication, 180–82; as foreign power, 173–74; French Canada, missionaries to Hurons of, 166; immunity of clergy, 177–79; independence from civil authority, 174–79; laws and customs pernicious to state, 184–85; power of papacy, 170–73; property of church, 179–80, 184; titles and honors conferred by pope, 286–87; treaties violated by pope, 388–90; Vattel's anti-Catholic sentiments, xviii–xix

Catiline (Lucius Sergius Catilina), 436

Caudine Forks, battle of, 374–82, 481–82

Cedrenus, 717

celibacy of clergy, 174–76, 199–200

Cellamare, prince de, 715

Cesarini (papal legate), 388

Ceylon, 278, 721

Chaloner, Thomas, 723

Champier, Symphorien, 547n, 800

Charlemagne, 282–83, 293

Charles, duke of Burgundy, 634n

Charles, duke of Sudermania, 689

Charles I (king of England), 107–8, 282n

Charles II (king of England), 506n, 689

Charles IV the Fair (king of France), 119–20

Charles V (king of France), 390

Charles VI (king of France), 112

Charles VIII (king of France), 173

Charles IX (king of France), 110

Charles IV (Holy Roman Emperor), 212, 283, 455n

Charles V (Holy Roman Emperor), 241–42, 283, 495, 656–57, 700, 702n, 704–5

Charles VI (Holy Roman Emperor), 347n, 365, 397, 666n

Charles I (king of Naples), 552

Charles III (king of Naples), 717–18

Charles II (king of Spain), 365, 493, 658n

Charles III (king of Spain), 644n

Charles XII (king of Sweden), 222n, 471, 554–55, 566n, 571, 656

Charles Emmanuel I, duke of Savoy, 504

Charles Emmanuel III of Savoy (king of Sardinia), 429n, 458n, 525n

Charles Louis, elector Palatine, 726n

Charlevoix, Pierre François Xavier, 166, 800

Charnacé, baron De, 733

Chauvelin, Henri-Philippe, 178n, 800–801

Chêne, Marie de, xii

Chevalier, Nicolas, 573n, 577n, 801

children: of ambassadors, 741; citizenship of, 219; as enemies, 510, 549; inheritance rights, 237; as prisoners of war, 551; safe-conducts for individuals not covering, 635; of vagrants, 220

China, 174, 309, 312, 721

Chitty, Joseph, xxi–xxii, 90n6, 137n

Choisy, François Timoléon de, 341n, 390n, 657n, 722n, 801

Christiern II (king of Denmark), 172, 401

Christina (queen of Sweden), 727

Churchill, John, 1st Duke of Marlborough, 205, 415, 480

Cicero: on absurdity in philosophy, 118n; on assassination, 560n; biographical information, 801; on common interests, 269n; on embassy, 701; enemy property, treatment of, 575; on great and elevated souls, 271; on infractions of natural law by other nations, 76n; on interpretation of treaties, 414, 425, 436, 437, 444n, 446, 447n; on justice, 19; on killing of enemies, 558n; on lying and perjury, 390–91; on natural law, 749, 762, 763, 765, 774, 780; on obligations and rights between nations, 259–61, 273n; on peace, 651–52n; quarter, giving or refusing to give, 544; on religion, 148–49, 161, 162n; on religion and good governance, 785; on Socrates, 781; on superstition, 148–49; on the useful vs. the honest, 787–88

cinnamon trade, 278

cities. See towns and cities

citizens and subjects: ambassadors subjects of state where employed, 731–33; children of citizens born out of country, 219; defined, 217–18; enemies, promises made by individuals to, 632–33; enemies, whole nation as, 509–10, 612–18; foreigners as, 314–15; glory of nation and, 204–5; indemnification against losses in war, 617–18; marriage to aliens, 319; martial duty of, 473, 615; national obligations regarding actions by and against, 298–301; naturalization as, 218; peace treaties violated by, 680; quitting country, possibility of, 220–25; reprisal, arrest by way of, 465; soldiers, garrisoning of, 476; valor and military virtues of, 200–201; voluntary submission of nation to foreign power, rights in cases of, 208; war, rights and obligations of private persons in, 612–18

civil laws, 92–93

civil war, 641–49; British Civil War and Commonwealth, 106–8, 282, 685, 689; common laws of war to be observed in, 645–47; defined, 644–45; effects of, 647–48; embassy, respect for, 703; foreign nations and allies, involvement of, 648–49; interference in quarrel between sovereign and subjects, 290–91; obedience owed by subjects to sovereigns, 109; obligations and rights of sovereign in, 641, 642–44; popular commotions, sedition, and insurrections, 641–42; rebels, defined, 641; resistance, right of, 101n, 103–12, 288–89; truces, revolts during, 627; two independent parties produced by, 645; tyrants, right to overthrow, 101n, 103–12

civitas maxima, concept of, xv

clandestine seduction of enemies, 582–84

Clearchus, 564n

Clement, James, 156

Cleomenes (king of Sparta), 417
clergy: Catholic, 174–79; celibacy of,
    174–76; as enemies, 550; indepen-
    dence of, 174–79; sovereign au-
    thority over, 164–68; in war, 474–75
Cloelia, 404
coastal seas, 252–58
Codrus (king of Athens), 153
coinage and coining, 141–44
colonization, 214–17; division of New
    World between Spain and Portugal
    by papacy, 215; domain over desert
    and uninhabited places, 306–7, 311;
    exile of people from their land,
    307–8; India, European commerce
    and colonization of, 131, 138; Na-
    tive Americans, lands of, 216–17,
    310; New England, Puritans in,
    216–17; of Pennsylvania, 217;
    Vattel's views on, xv
Colonna, Prosper, 546n
commanders of armies, 480–82, 615
commerce: ambassadors, carried on
    by, 734–35; besieged towns, trading
    with, 533; consuls, 279–80, 693;
    contraband goods, 505, 529–32;
    free trade, 274; laws of, 132–36,
    144; luxury and, 792; merchandise,
    innocent right of passage for, 327–
    28; monopolies, 138, 278–79; mu-
    tual commerce between nations,
    273–80; of nations considered in
    themselves, 131–39; neutral ships,
    searching of, 532–33; neutral states
    trading with states at war, 528–34;
    treaties, commercial, 136–37, 275–
    78, 360
Commines, Philippe de, 205, 682, 801
commissioners, ambassadorial, 693
common property, 229, 232, 233–36
Commonwealth, British, 106–8, 282,
    685, 689
companies, 138, 232–33. See also East
    Indies companies

compromise, 450, 662–64
Condé, Henri II, prince of, 305n, 801
Condé, Louis II de Bourbon, prince
    of, 305n, 646n
Coneo (Coni), siege of, 547, 616
confederacies, 84, 498
conferences and congresses to settle
    disputes between nations, 452–53
confiscation of contraband goods,
    530–32
conflict of laws or treaties, 443–47
conquest, 308, 568, 593, 596–603,
    606–9
Conradin or Conrad V, duke of
    Swabia, 552
Consalvi, Cardinal, ix, xviii–xix
conspiracies, ambassadorial, 713–19
Constance, council of, 327
Constantine I the Great (Roman em-
    peror), 163, 169
Constantius Diogenes, 717
constitutional obligations and rights,
    91–96
consuls, 279–80, 693
context and interpretation of treaties,
    421–26
Conti, Armand de Bourbon, prince
    of, 305
continental shelf, 252–58
contraband goods, 505, 529–32
contracts, private, made by sovereign,
    382–86
contributions from enemies, 569, 668
conventional law of nations. See trea-
    ties and conventions
convents, 175, 199–200, 475
Corea, 315
corporations, 138, 232–33. See also
    East Indies companies
corsairs. See piracy
Cortés, Hernando (Ferdinand
    Cortes), 672–73
counterfeiters, 143
counterintelligence, 580, 585

countries, 217–28; children of citizens born out of, 219; citizens, natives, and inhabitants distinguished, 217–18; defined, 153–54; establishment of nation in, 213–17 (*see also* domain); exile and banishment from, 225–28; independent families in, 310–11; love of country, encouraging, 152–55; migration from, 127, 198–200, 220–25; multiple nations, possessed by, 309; private persons possessing, 309–10; refugees, 225; settlement, natural or acquired, 220; vagrants, 220. *See also* nations

couriers, ambassadorial, 742

courts, 188–89

credentials of ambassadors, 693, 745

Crevier, Jean Baptiste Louis, 395n, 801

criminal laws, 191–92

Croix, Petis de la, 98n, 414n, 560n, 565n, 719n

Cromwell, Oliver, 282, 285n, 685

Crousaz, Jean-Pierre de, x

Cueva, Bertrand de la, 121

Cujas, Jacques, 415n

Cumberland, duke of, 564–65

currency, 141–44

Curtius (Marcus Curtius), 154

Curtius Rufus (Quintus Curtius Rufus), 562n, 600n, 801

customary law of nations, 77–78; embassy and, 705, 724–25; hostages, treatment of, 406; on postliminium, 611; usucaption and prescription, 338

customs, 139, 723

Cyrus the Great, 550n

Damien[s], Robert François, 103n

Danguel, Louis-Joseph Plumard de (John Nickolls), 132n, 806

Daniel, Gabriel, 341n, 555–56, 725n, 728n, 801

Darius III (king of Persia), 545, 562

David (biblical king), 111–12

Daxelhoffer, Captain, 519

death: burial of dead during time of truce, 626–27; ransom of prisoners and, 638–39, 640; safe-conducts not expiring at, 636. *See also* killing

debts: of ambassadors, 731; enemies, owed to, 511; pledges given for fulfillment of, 398–400; of sovereign and state, contracts regarding, 384–85

deceitful intelligence, 580, 585

deception of the enemy, 576–81

the Decii, 154

declarations of war, 500–506, 522–23

defense, right of, 297

defensive alliances, 512, 519–21

defensive war, 471, 487–88, 503, 515

Demetrius (Greco-Bactrian king), 300–301

Demetrius (king of Macedonia), 533

Demosthenes, 465n, 802

Denmark: arbitration between subjects and sovereigns in, 109; contraband goods, 529, 530n; Great Northern War, 288n; papacy, power of, 172; safe passage, granting of, 539

deputies, ambassadorial, 693

deputies sent to legislative assemblies, 727–29

Descartes, René, 205

desert, domain over, 306–7

deserters, 549

destruction of enemy property, 570–73

Dialogue Between the Prince of **** and His Confidant (Vattel): publication history, xxiii–xxiv; significance of, xxiii–xxiv; text of, 783–96; Vattel's economic reform theory and, xviin21, xxiv

dialogues of Vattel, xi

Digest of Justinian. *See* Justinian I

dignity and equality of nations, 75, 281

Diodorus Siculus, 546, 802

Diogenes, xi

Diomede (king of Thrace), 291

Dionysius the Tyrant, 546

diplomacy. *See* embassy

discipline, military, 480, 615–16

dismemberment of state, 240–42

dispatches, ambassadorial, 742

disputes between nations, settling, 448–67; amicable accommodation, 450; arbitration, 451–52; compromise, 450, 662–64; conferences and congresses for purposes of, 452–53; equitable conditions, offering, 457; essential rights vs. rights of less importance, 453–54; evident vs. doubtful cases, 453, 455, 457; just complaints, abandonment of, 448–49; just complaints, duty to resolve, 448; justice, refusal of, 464; mediation, 450–51, 648–49, 662; natural law, means suggested by, 450–52; possession as 9/10ths of law, 457; reparations, 458; reprisals, 460–67; retaliation, 458–59, 503; retortion, 459–60. *See also* war

distributive justice, 189–90

Dlugoss, Jan, 388n

domain, 301–11; desert and uncultivated land, 306–7; establishment of, 213–17; extent of, 302–3; independent families in, 310–11; innocent use, right of, 326–31; jurisdiction and, 303–5; prohibitions on entering, 309; sovereignty and, 303; treaties, settlement by, 308; usucaption and prescription, 331–38; violations of, 308–9

domestic servants: of ambassadors, 737–44; conscription of footmen, 475; luxury and surplus of, 792–93;

Queen Christina of Sweden's execution of, 727; safe-conducts and, 635–36

donations of sovereign, 385–86

D'Orléans, Abbé, 305

d'Orléans, Gaston, 647

drafting troops, 473–75, 500

Dreux, battle of, 201

Le droit des gens (Vattel). *See Law of Nations*

drummers, ambassadorial, 702–5

Du Bellay, Martin, 700n, 725n, 798

dueling or single combat, 194–97

Duport du Tertre, François-Joachim, 121n, 742n, 802

Dutch. *See* Netherlands

duty, 751–52. *See also* obligations and rights

East Indies companies, 138, 251, 539, 721

l'Ecluse, abbé de, 631n

economics: balance of trade, 139; government, end or purpose of, 126–28; luxury, civic dangers of, 150–51, 788–96. *See also* commerce

education: happiness, obtaining, 145–46; of youth, 146

Edward I (king of England), 254

Edward III (king of England), 120

Egeria, 160

D'Egly, Charles Philippe de Monthenault, 718n, 805

Egypt, 290, 426, 560n, 698n, 719n

elderly people, as enemies, 549

Eleans, 536n

elective sovereigns, 113

Elizabeth (empress of Russia), 116

Elizabeth I (queen of England), 122, 530n, 532, 711, 718, 723

embassy, 682–745; agents, deputies, and commissioners, 693; between allies, 686; ambassadors proper, 691; asylum in ambassador's house,

embassy (*continued*)
738–40; attempts to hinder, 685–
86; authority to send, 683, 704–5;
carriages of ambassadors, 707–8n,
740–41; in civil wars, 703; commencement of ambassadorial
status, 699; commerce carried on
by ambassadors, 734–35; consuls,
279–80, 693; credentials of ministers, 693, 745; of enemies, 687–88;
enemies, to or through country of,
701–2; expiration of rights of,
744–45; heralds, trumpeters,
drummers, and other messengers,
702–5, 717–18; house and servants
of ambassador, 737–44; immunity
and independence of (*see* immunity of ambassadors); indeterminate character, ministers of, 692;
instructions for ministers, 693; legislative assemblies, deputies sent
to, 727–29; orders of public ministers for, 690–96; passage, right of,
699–701; plenipotentiary ministers, 692; proxies or plenipotentiaries, treaties made by, 339–40;
refusal of, 703–4; religion, ministers' right to free exercise of, 722–
23; representative character of,
690–91; resident ministers, 686–
87, 691–92; respect and honors due
to, 695–97; right of, 682–90, 693–
95; secretary of, 741; secret or non-
public ministers, 725; security of
ministers' persons, 697–704; sovereigns in foreign countries, 725–27;
treaties made by subordinate powers with proper permission, 372–
73; with usurpers, 688–90; of
viceroys and regents, 685; in war,
686–88
emigration. *See* migration
eminent domain, 232–33, 659
empire, 308

enemies, 509–11; ambassadors and,
701–2; associates and allies of, 517–
23; clandestine seduction of, 582–
84; counterintelligence against,
580, 585; debts owed to, 511; defined, 509; disposition toward,
563–66; embassy from, 687–88;
faith between, 575–85; killing of,
543–49, 557–63; lying to, 577–81;
neutral ships, property found on,
532; neutral's property found on
ships of, 533; poisoning or assassination of, 557–63; as prisoners of
war, 551–57, 606–7; promises made
by individuals to, 632–33; property
of, 510–11, 566–75; rights in just
war regarding (*see* obligations and
rights in just wars); terror, right to
use, 614; traitors, accepting offers
of, 584–85, 627–28; treaties between, 576–77 (*see also* peace treaties); truces between (*see* truces);
whole nation as, 509–10, 612–18
England. *See* Britain
English Channel, French terms for,
254
enlisting troops, 473–75, 500
equality: in alliances, 348; as favorable
thing in interpretation of treaties,
434; of nations, 75, 281; in treaties,
346–48
equilibrium of powers, 496–99
equitable conditions: in disputes between nations, offering, 457; of
peace offered after declarations of
war, 502
equivocal or ambiguous expressions,
416–18, 420–21, 432–33
escheatage, 317–18
*Essay on the Foundation of Natural
Law* (Vattel): editions and translations, xxiii; text, 747–71; Vattel's
theory of obligation in, xvi;
Vattel's writing of, xi

D'Estrades, count, 665n, 707–8n, 733
ethics or moral science, defined, 747–48
Ethiopia, 315
Etrurians, 371
Etterlin, Peterman, 155n, 212n, 802
Eugenius IV (pope), 388
Eumenes of Cardia, 562
Europe: balance or equilibrium of powers in, 496–99; conferences and congresses, 452–53; universal monarchy, Vattel's fear of, 491–99. *See also* specific nations
Eutropius, 584n
exchange of goods, 141–44
exchanges of prisoners, 556–57
excommunication, Catholic practice of, 180–82
executive power: laws, execution of, 192–93; of sovereign, 187, 192–93
exile, 225–28, 307–8, 323
expletive justice, 593
external attacks, government's duty to protect nation against, 198–203
external obligations and rights, 74–75
external vs. internal religion, 157, 161–62

Fabius Labeo (Quintus Fabius Labeo), 394n, 408n
Fabius Maximus (Quintus Fabius Maximus Servilianus), 583n
Fabius Maximus (Quintus Fabius Maximus Verrucosus), 379
faith between enemies, 575–85
faith of treaties, 386–95, 411
falsiloquy, 578
families: of ambassadors, 741; independent, 310–11; safe-conducts for individuals not covering, 635–36
farming: government support for, 128–31; peasants, as enemies, 550–51
Farnese, Alessandro, duke of Parma, 585n

Farouq (Farrudge; sultan of Egypt), 560n
favorable vs. odious things in interpretation of treaties, 433–42
fecial law of Romans, 7, 377n
federal republics, 84
Ferdinand I (king of Aragon and Sicily), 120
Ferdinand II (king of Aragon and Naples) and IV (king of Castile and Sicily), 120, 121, 215n
Ferdinand II (Holy Roman Emperor), 572
Ferdinand II (king of Spain), 393
feudatory states, 84
Feuquieres, Antoine de Pas, marquis de, 580n, 806
figurative expressions in interpretation of treaties, 415–16
fishing rights, 246–47, 251, 252–58
footmen, conscription of, 475. *See also* domestic servants
foreign armies entering a country before declaration of war, 504
foreign countries: civil wars of other nations, involvement in, 648–49; embassies to (*see* embassy); enlistment of soldiers in, 478–79, 519, 521, 527; right to dwell in, 323, 328–31; sovereigns in, 725–27; voluntary submission of another nation to (*see* voluntary submission to foreign power)
foreigners: enemy country, property in, 510–11; reprisals, arrested as means of, 465; reprisals in favor of, 462–63; in time of war, 505, 506n; treatment of, 311–19, 327–31, 459–60
foreign trade. *See* commerce
forgers of money, 143
formal and lawful wars, 507–8
fortresses and fortifications of enemy, destruction of, 573

Fouget, Charles-Louis-Auguste, duc de Belle-Isle, 616

France: Aix-la-Chapelle, treaty of, 400, 503, 568; arts and sciences, national encouragement of, 147; contraband goods, 529, 531, 532; embassies to, 694–96; James II of England, support for, 364–65; pleasant reception of foreigners in, 331; prisoners of war, treatment of, 553; ravages of Catholicism in, 170, 177–78; regicide in, 103; religion, sovereign's authority in matters of, 168; sovereign succession in, 113, 119–20; sponsio of La Trimouille with Switzerland, 381–82, 403; taxation in, 231; Treaty of Madrid, 241–42; unequal alliances with Sweden and Switzerland, 349–50; valor, national reputation for, 200; Vattel on rivalry between Britain and, xviii–xix, 90; War of the Austrian Succession, 425, 481n, 521n, 534n, 554, 573n, 614, 616; War of the Polish Succession, 666; War of the Spanish Succession, 365, 493–94, 525; wines, British duties on, 139

Francis I (king of France), 241, 403, 405, 656–57, 699–700, 704–5, 721, 725

fraud's adherence to terms in interpretation of treaties, 426–27

Frederick I, elector of Brandenburg, 285

Frederick I (Holy Roman Emperor), 169

Frederick II (Holy Roman Emperor), 169, 181, 182, 318

Frederick III (Holy Roman Emperor), 255

Frederick II the Great (king of Prussia), x, xix, 284n, 370, 802

Frederick Augustus II (elector of Saxony), x, 525n

Frederick of Austria (king of the Romans), 389, 552

Frederick William, elector of Brandenburg, 329

Frederick William I (king of Prussia), ix, 225

freedom. See liberty and independence

Fregose (ambassador of Francis I), 699–700

French Canada, missionaries to Hurons of, 166

Friedrich. See entries at Frederick

friendship: between nations, 267; Vattel's theory of obligation and, xvi

fugitives, 225, 549

Fulstin, Herburt de, 388n

fundamental laws, 92, 101

Galatian Gauls, 522–23

Galba (Servius Sulpicius Galba, Roman emperor), 431n

garrisoning of soldiers, 476

Gaston d'Orléans, 647

Gastrell, Francis, 756

Gauls, 522–23, 581n, 713

Genghis Khan, 487, 697–98n

Genoa, 614

George II (king of England), 347n

Gepidae, 329

Germanic tribes. See barbarians, and specific tribes

Germany: Cologne, ancient inhabitants of, 536n; embassy, right of, 683–85; France's denial of embassy from, 694; treaties, power of states and cities to make, 339

Givry, Bailly de, 704

Glorious Revolution, 290, 364–65

glory of a nation, 203–6, 267–68

good faith: adherence to intention in interpretation of treaties, 426–27; with enemies, 577

Goths, 329, 572, 633

government: agriculture, encouraging, 128–31; authority of body politic over its members, 81–82; coinage, rights and duties with respect to, 142–44; commerce and, 131–39; constitution and, 91–96; dignity and majesty of state not affected by form of, 282; economic security as end or purpose of, 126–28; external attacks, end or purpose as protection against, 198–203; happiness for nation, procurement of, 145–55; interference in government of another nation, no right to, 289–93; ministers of state, 112; people's knowledge of intentions of, 150–51; of public property, 233; reform of, 94; sovereign (*see* sovereigns and sovereignty); toll roads, duties regarding, 140; types of, 82–85

governors defending enemy towns, killing of, 546–49

Gramond, Gabriel-Barthélemy de, 726n, 802

granaries, public, 130–31

Gray, John de, archbishop of Canterbury, 181n

Great Northern War, 288n, 486, 571

Greeks: enemies, debts to, 511; enemies, killing of, 546; passage of troops through neutral countries, 536; postliminium, 607; reprisals, 465; treaties of, 392–94, 417, 420, 426; wars, motives for, 486

Gregory VII (pope), 171n

Gregory IX (pope), 171n

Greiffenheim, baron, 737–38

Grotius, Hugo: on alliances, 523; Barbeyrac's translation of, 9; biographical information, 802–3; on church and laws pernicious to state, 184; on civil war, 646n; on contraband goods, 530n, 531, 532n, 533n; on counterintelligence, 585n; on debts of sovereign and state, 384n; on Dutch revolt, 107n, 209n, 553n; on enemies, 511n, 550; examples used by, 20; foreigners, treatment of, 314n, 317n; on hostages, 401n, 406n; on killing of enemies, 544n, 546n; on law of nature and law of nations, 7–8; on maritime law, 250n, 251; on national responsibility for actions of citizens, 301n; on natural law, 752, 753, 754, 758, 761; on obligations and rights between nations, 273n; on passage of troops through neutral countries, 536; on peace treaties, 668n, 676, 678; on poisoning weapons and wells, 563n; on postliminium, 605n, 608; on property acquired by war, 594–96; on reprisals, 465; on soldiers acting without orders, 616n; on sovereigns and sovereignty, 101n, 107n, 115n, 119; on surprise attacks, 579n; on treaties, 342, 345, 359, 369, 375, 379, 393, 395, 415, 433n, 440–42; on usucaption and prescription, 332n; on war, 507; on war against those guilty of gross transgressions of law of nature, 265

guaranties given for observance of treaties, 395–98, 515–16

Guicciardini, Francesco, 120, 381n, 803

Gustavus Adolphus (king of Sweden), 350, 430, 572

Hadrian (Adrian; Roman emperor), 125

Hannibal of Carthage, 355, 455, 576

happiness: government's duty to procure for nation, 145–55; religion and good of state, 784–88; self-interest and mutuality, tension between, xvi–xvii

Harcourt, count De, 742n
Harrington, Lord, 739
Hasan ibn al-Sabbah (the Old Man of the Mountain), 559–60, 722
Heiss von Kogenheim, Johann, 182n, 803
Helvetii, 307–8, 541
Henry (infante of Portugal), 216n
Henry, landgrave of Thuringia, 182
Henry IV (king of Castile), 121
Henry V (king of England), 555–56
Henry VIII (king of England), 170n
Henry II (king of France), 389
Henry III (king of France), 156n, 170n, 504n, 728–29
Henry IV the Great (king of France): alienation of public property reversed by, 238; assassination of, 156n, 170n; balance of powers, maintaining, 497; Charles Emmanuel I (duke of Savoy) and, 504; in civil war, 642–43, 644, 646n; embassy and, 689, 696, 709–10, 719; enemies, treatment of, 560, 567–68; independence of clergy and, 174n; mercenary soldiers of, 477; Philip II of Spain and, 289; siege of Paris and, 263; Vattel's admiration for, xi, 204
Henry IV (Holy Roman Emperor), 169
Heraclius (Byzantine emperor), 721
heralds, 702–5, 717–18
Herburt, Jean, 388n
Hercules, 260, 291
hereditary or successive sovereignties, 113–22
Herodotus, 803
herring fisheries off British coast, 252
highways, maintenance of, 139–41, 328
Hobbes, Thomas, 8–9, 651, 803
Holland. See Netherlands
Holy Roman Empire. See Germany, and specific emperors

honors: of ambassadors, 695–96; of nations or sovereigns, 281–88
Horace, 399n, 581n, 763, 803
hospitality, 313–14
hospitals for invalid soldiers, 476
hostages: for passage of troops through neutral country, 537; for prisoners of war, 640; treaties, as securities for observance of, 400–406
hostis vs. inimicus, 509
house of ambassador, 737–44
Hudson's Bay, 255
human nature: foundation of natural law in, 748–50; made for society, 754
Hungary, 255
Hurons, 166

immemorial prescription, 334–35, 337
immigration. See migration
immunity of ambassadors, 705–22; asylum in ambassador's house, 738–40; bribery, 709–10; carriages and equipages, 740–41; civil jurisdiction, submission to, 729–37; couriers and dispatches, 742; customary law of nations regarding, 705, 724–25; debt, 731; dismissal or recall of errant ministers, 711–12; families of ambassadors, 741; house and servants, 737–44; plots and conspiracies, 713–19; property, 733–36; punishment of ambassadors, 711–18; reprisals, 719–21; secretary of embassy, 741; sovereigns in foreign countries, 725–27; subjects of state where employed as ambassadors, 731–33; treason, ministers soliciting, 707–10. See also embassy
immunity of clergy, 177–79
imperfect obligations and rights, 74–75

import duties, 139

impossibility/possibility affecting interpretation of treaties, 431–32

imposts, ambassadorial exemption from, 723–24

inalienability of sovereignty, 115–16, 123–25

inalienable rights, 319–26

Incas, 290

indemnification: of citizens against losses in war, 617–18; reprisals, 464

independence. *See* liberty and independence

India, 131, 138, 251, 721

Indians. *See* Native Americans

indulgences, 184

inexhaustible things, right to use, 323–24

informal and unlawful wars, 507–8

inhabitants, natives, and citizens distinguished, 217–18

inheritance: of foreigners, 315–19; laws of, 237; of safe-conducts, 636–37

inimicus vs. *hostis,* 509

injustice. *See* justice

Innocent III (pope), 181, 183

Innocent IV (pope), 182

Innocent X (pope), 389n

innocent use, right of, 324–31

instruments of war (armies, troops, and commanders), 413, 472–82, 500

insurrections, 641–42. *See also* civil war

intention and interpretation of treaties, 421–26

internal obligations and rights, 74–75

internal police, 193–94

internal vs. external religion, 157, 161–62

interpretation of treaties, 407–48; absurdities, interpretations leading to, 418–19, 428; ancient treaties, 413; change in state of things affecting, 429–31, 436; conflicts with laws or other treaties, 443–47; context and intention, importance of ("reason of the act"), 421–26; degrees, terms admitting of, 415, 432–33; equivocal or ambiguous expressions, 416–18, 420–21, 432–33; evidently false or fanciful interpretations, 408–9; favorable vs. odious things, 433–42; figurative expressions, 415–16; fraud's adherence to terms, 426–27; general principles of, 407–9; good faith's adherence to intention, 426–27; intentions of contracting parties, 409–10, 411–12, 414; liberality, acts of, 442–43; mental reservations nonadmissable, 414; nullification, grounds for, 419–20, 435, 440; nullification, interpretations leading to, 419–20; peace treaties, 670; penalties, 435, 439–40; plain meaning rule, 408–9, 412–14; possibility/impossibility affecting, 431–32; real vs. personal treaties, distinguishing, 358–59; restrictive or strict, 427–29; rules for, importance of, 410–11, 448; subterfuges, 393, 408–9; "sufficient reason for an act of the will," 424–25; technical terms, 414–15; unforeseen cases, 431; wording of treaties, caution in constructing, 393

invalid soldiers, asylums for, 476

Isabella (queen of Castile), 120, 121, 215n

Isabella Clara Eugenia (regent of Netherlands), 115n

Islam: ambassadors, respect for, 721; Arabs, 310, 721–22; Asian conquests of, 265, 293; the Assassins, 559–60; ban on wine in Koran, 425; nomadic Arabs, 310; treaties, keeping, 342, 343n. *See also* Turkish empire

Italy, 534n, 570, 694
Ives (Ivo) de Chartres, 181

James I (king of England), 253, 291n
James II (king of England), 290, 364–65, 689
"James III" (Prince James Francis Edward Stuart, the Young Pretender), 364–65, 689–90
Jan III Sobieski (king of Poland), 263
Jane (infanta of Castile), 121
Japan, 312
Javolenus Priscus, 442n
Jean de Joinville, 744n, 803
Jeannin, president (French ambassador to Netherlands), 689, 742
Jerusalem, kingdom of, 120
Jerusalem, siege of (A.D. 10), 551–52
Jews, 273
Joan (queen of France and Navarre), 143n
Joan of Hochberg, 163n
John (prince of Bohemia), 122n
John (king of England), 181–82
John II (king of France), 143n
John II (king of Portugal), 101n
John IV de Braganza (king of Portugal), 178–79, 609
John XXII (pope), 107n, 389
John de Gray, archbishop of Canterbury, 181n
John-Frederick, elector of Saxony, 495n
joint property, 229
Joinville, Jean de, 744n, 803
José of Braganza, archbishop of Braga, 179
Joseph Sofy/Sofi (king of Carazem), 565n, 719n
judiciary, 185–97; appointment of judges, 187–88; authority of judges, sovereign support for, 189; courts, 188–89; internal police, 193–94; punishment of transgres-

sors, 190–92; supreme courts, 188–89. See also laws
Julian the Apostate (Roman emperor), 163, 406
Julius Caesar, 308, 329n, 541, 546n, 550, 560n, 564, 790–91, 800
jurisdiction: civil jurisdiction, ambassadorial submission to, 729–37; domain and, 303–5; maritime, 257; over ambassadors, 705–7; over lakes and rivers, 249
jus detractus, 318
justice, 185–97; distributive, 189–90; dueling or single combat, 194–97; establishment and enforcement through laws, 185–86; expletive, 593; between nations, 296–98; pardons, 193; refusal of justice in disputes between nations, 464; sovereign's duties with regard to, 186–89; treaty violation as act of injustice, 343
Justinian I the Great (Byzantine emperor), biographical information, 803
Justinian I the Great, Digest and Institutes: civil actions against ambassadors, 729n; foreigners, treatment of, 318n; on justice, 186; on law of nature and law of nations, 6, 775n, 776; on postliminium, 611n; on treaties, 356n, 408n, 421n, 431n, 437–38, 438n, 442n
just war: aggrandizement of neighboring power, 491–99; alliances, just cause for, 513–14; alliances only in, 514–16; both sides, accounted as just on, 591; both sides, war not just on, 489–90; defensive, 487–88; just causes of, 482–86; justificatory reasons and motives, 483, 484–87; just reprisals not affording cause for, 466; lawful wars in due form, 507–8; natural law of nations on,

589–90; object of, 484; obligations and rights in (*see* obligations and rights in just wars); postliminium, 604; preparation for war, responding to, 499–500; punishment as object of, 490

Kakesm (Khovarezm), 697n
Kandy (Ceylon), 278, 721
Kant, Immanuel, xvi
Khaled, 721
Khovarezm (Kakesm), 697n
killing: of ambassadors, 697–701; of enemy soldiers, 543–46; of governors defending enemy towns, 546–49; poisoning or assassination of enemies, 557–63; of prisoners of war, 552–56, 646; of soldiers acting without orders, 616; of sovereign, 103, 156, 170, 178–79, 565–66, 716–19; of spies, 582
kings. *See* sovereigns and sovereignty
Knights of Malta (Knights of St. John of Jerusalem), 463, 547n
knowledge of natural law obtained through reason, 749–50
knowledge of self, national importance of, 91
Koran: ambassadors, respect for, 721; ban on wine in, 425

Labbe, P., 120n
Lacedaemonians. *See* Sparta and Spartans
Lacombe, Jacques, 566n, 803
la Croix, Petis de, 98n, 414n, 560n, 565n, 719n
Ladislaus or Uladislaus (king of Naples), 255
lakes, 242, 247–49
Lancellotti, Giovanni Paolo, 176n, 804
La Pimpie Solignac, Pierre-Joseph de, 388n, 804

Lars Porsenna, 404, 558
La Trimouille (La Trémoille), Louis I de, viscount of Thouars, 381–82, 403
Laupen, battle of, 201
la Valette, Cardinal De, 474–75n
la Vega, Garcillaso de, 290n, 801
lawful wars in due form, 507–8
law of nations: basic principles of, 17–19, 67–79; conventional (*see* treaties and conventions); customary (*see* customary law of nations); defined, 67–69; necessary (*see* necessary law of nations); positive, 78; on private persons in just war, 612–13; small states, defense of sovereignty of, xix; treaty violation as violation of, 387–91; Vattel's application of theory of natural law to, xiii–xix, 5 (*see also* natural law of nations); Vattel's study of, x; Vattel's writings on, importance of, ix, xix–xx; voluntary (*see* voluntary law of nations)
The Law of Nations (Vattel): economic reform theory in, xvii–xviii; editions and translations of, xi*n*10, xxi–xxii, 2; examples, use of, 19–20; mutual aid and self-interest, tension between, xvi–xvii (*see also* mutuality, self-interest vs.); significance of, ix, xix–xx; Vattel's application of theory of natural law to law of nations in, xiii–xix; Vattel's writing of, xi
law of nature. *See* natural law; natural law of nations
laws: Catholicism productive of laws and customs pernicious to state, 184–85; civil, 92–93; of commerce, 132–36, 144; conflict of laws or treaties, 443–47; constitution and, 92–93; criminal, 191–92; defined, 747; enforcement of, 186; execu-

laws (*continued*)
tion of, 192–93; fecial law of
Romans, 7, 377n; foreigners subject
to, 312–13; fundamental, 92, 101;
inheritance, 237; justice established
through, 185–86; on migration,
222–23, 224; military, 479–80; obedience to, 93; political, 92, 773–81;
on property, 232; Roman marriage
laws, 175; of the seas (*see* maritime
law); sovereign and, 101–9. *See also*
judiciary; justice
l'Ecluse, abbé de, 631n
Lee, Sir George, 304n
legislative assemblies, deputies sent
to, 727–29
legislative power and right to change
constitution, 94–95
Leibniz, Gottfried Wilhelm, x, 122,
183n, 205, 239n, 759, 763–71, 804
Leo X (pope), 172
Leonidas (Spartan leader), 559
Leopold, duke of Austria, 564
Leslie, John, bishop of Ross, 718
Leszcyński, Stanislaw, 666n
Le Tellier, François-Michel, marquis
de Louvois, 494
letters, men of, as enemies, 550
letters of marque, 462
Letters Rogatory, 300
Leutrum, Karl Sigismond Friedrick
Wilhelm, 547, 616
Le Vassor, Michel, 291n, 804
levying troops, 473–75, 500
Lewis. *See* entries at Louis
liberality, interpretation of treaties involving acts of, 442–43
liberty and independence, 74; ambassadorial immunity (*see* immunity
of ambassadors); ambassadorial
right to free exercise of religion,
722–23; definition of nation as free
persons living together in state of
nature, 68; as favorable thing in in-

terpretation of treaties, 434; infractions, right to suppress, 77;
philosophical discussion, freedom
of, 147–49; religion and liberty of
conscience, 157, 161; trade, freedom
of, 274; unjustly conquered people, freeing of, 603; Vattel's belief
in importance of, xvii–xviii
lies, 390–91, 577–81
Lisbon earthquake, 264
Livy (Titus Livius): biographical information, 804; on conquest,
601n; on declarations of war, 501;
on embassy, 713n, 715; on killing of
enemies, 545n, 558n; necessity,
right of, 321n; on peace treaties,
660n; stratagems and artifices in
war, 581; on treaties, 371, 374, 376,
394, 404n, 406n; on truces, 629n;
on voluntary submission to foreign
power, 208n; on war, 484n
Lockhart, Sir William, 689
Loisir Philosophique (Vattel), 186n
Longueville, Madame de, 117n, 120n,
305
Louis, duke of Anjou, 717–18
Louis VI the Fat (king of France),
97n
Louis VII (king of France), 97n
Louis VIII (king of France), 182–83n
Louis IX (St. Louis; king of France),
722
Louis XI (king of France), 205, 548n,
634n, 690
Louis XII (king of France), 99, 153,
341, 381–82
Louis XIII (king of France), 291n,
348n, 646n, 647, 657n
Louis XIV (king of France): Algiers,
bombardment of, 570n; Breda,
treaty of, terms for English Chan-
nel used in, 254; Charles II of
Spain and, 493–94; contributions
from enemies, 569; Cromwell's

form of address to, 285n; dueling outlawed by, 194; on embassy, 707–8n; Netherlands and, 263, 272, 430, 457; on sovereignty, 102; War of the Spanish Succession and, 364–66, 493–94, 524; written requirements for debts under, 779–80

Louis XV (king of France), 103n, 147, 458, 666n, 696

Louis IV of Bavaria (Holy Roman Emperor), 122, 169–70, 389

Louvois, François-Michel Le Tellier, marquis de, 494

love: of country, encouraging, 152–55; between nations, mutuality of, 267

Low Countries. *See* Netherlands

Lucretius (Titus Lucretius Carus), 169n, 804

Ludwig, marquis of Brandenburg, 122n

Ludwig IV (Holy Roman Emperor), 122n

Lupfen, count of, 327

Luxembourg, duke of, 580

luxury: of Catholic clergy, 180; civic dangers of, 150–51, 788–96; defined, 788; social mobility and, 793–94

Lycurgus, 146

lying, 390–91, 577–81

Lyons, council of, 182

Lysunder, 545n

Machiavelli, Nicolò, 289, 480, 804

Madrid, treaty of, 241–42, 403, 657

Magellan, Straits of, 255

Magnus Pius (Sextus Pompey), 668

Mahomet. *See* entries at Muhammad, Muhammed

Maine, Henry Summer, 304n

Mairargues (French officer), 710, 719

"Majesty," as title, 285–86

Malta, siege of, 547

Maltese Knights (Knights of St. John of Jerusalem), 463, 547n

manifestos declaring war, 500–506

Manlius (Gnaeus Manlius Vulso), 394, 522–23, 616

Mansfield, Lord (Mr. Murray), 304n

Maraviglia (secret minister of Francis I), 725

Marcus Aurelius (Roman emperor), xi, 125

Margaret, duchess of Karinthia, 122n

Mariana, Juan de, 103–4n, 106n, 114n, 231n, 804

Maria Theresa (queen of Hungary and empress of Austria), 521, 525n, 554, 658n

Marie de Medicis (regent of France), 291n

Marigny, François Augier de, 698n, 798

maritime law, 249–58; children born at sea, citizenship of, 219; coastal seas, 252–58; jurisdiction, 257; neutral ships, searching of, 532–33; possession of or dominion over open seas, 249–52; privateers, 614–15. *See also* piracy

Marius (Gaius Marius), 564

marriage: of aliens, 319; of prisoners of war, 611; women, right to carry off, 321–22

Martin I (king of Aragon) and II (king of Sicily), 120

Martin IV (pope), 183n

Mary (queen of Scots), 718, 727

Matthieu, Pierre, 719n, 805

Maurice, prince of Orange, 579n, 702n

Maximilian I (elector of Bavaria), 572

Maximilian I (Holy Roman Emperor), 341, 381n

Mazarin, Cardinal, 689

mediation, 450–51, 648–49, 662

Medicis, Marie de (regent of France), 291n
Mediterranean Sea, 257
mental reservations nonadmissable in interpretation of treaties, 414
mercenary soldiers, 476–79
merchants. See commerce
messengers, ambassadorial, 702–5
Methuen, treaty of, 137n
Mexico, 672–73, 700, 721
Mézeray, François Eudes de, 110n, 201, 241n, 242n, 283, 341n, 721n, 728n, 805
migration: allowing or disallowing citizens to quit country, 220–25; exile or banishment, 225–28, 307–8, 323; of individuals, 127, 198–200, 220–25, 328–29; nomadic peoples, 220, 310–11; of peoples, 220, 307–8, 328–29; tax on, 221n. See also colonization
military actions during truces, 624–28
military discipline, 480, 615–16
military prowess, national cultivation of, 201
military troops, 472–82; acting without orders, 615–16; allies, provided to, 513; booty, 568–69; foreign countries, levying of troops in, 478–79, 519, 521, 527; fugitives and deserters, 549; luxury, dangers of, 790–91; mercenaries, 476–79; neutral states, passage through, 534–41; officers, 480–82, 615; retreat during truce, 626–27; standing armies, 476, 500; volunteers, 615
militia of Switzerland, 500
ministers of religion. See clergy
ministers of state. See public ministers
Mirabeau, Victor Riqueti de, xviii
missionaries: China, missionaries driven from, 174; French Canada,

missionaries to Hurons of, 166; persuasion, right of, 294
Mithridates (king of Armenia), 394
Modestinus, 331
Mohammed. See entries at Muhammad, Muhammed
Molesworth, Robert, viscount, 539n, 805
monarchs. See sovereigns and sovereignty
monasteries, 175, 199–200, 475
money, 141–44
monopolies, 138, 278–79
Montaigne, Michel de, 793, 796, 805
Montesquieu, Charles-Louis de Secondat, baron de la Brède et de, xviii, 116n, 175n, 185n, 304n, 600n, 805
Montezuma (Aztec emperor), 673
Montgon, Charles Alexandre de, 739n, 805
Monthenault D'Egly, Charles Philippe de, 718n, 805
Montmollin, Marie de, ix
Montpensier, François, duc de, 646
moral persons, nations as, 67, 85
moral science or ethics, defined, 747–48
Morat, battle of, 201
mortgages given for observance of treaties, 398
Mortgarten, battle of, 201
motives for war, 483, 484–87
Mucius Scaevola (Gaius Mucius Scaevola), 558
Muffelburgh, battle of, 546n
Muhammad II (sultan), 413
Muhammed Cotheddin (sultan of Khovarezm), 697–98n
Muhammed the Prophet, 343n
Murad (Amurath) II (sultan), 388
Murray, Mr. (later Lord Mansfield), 304n
Muslims. See Islam

mutuality: of love and friendship between nations, 267; self-interest vs., xvi–xvii, 73–74; treaties dissolved by mutual consent, 371–72

Natalis, Alexander (Alexandre Noel), 171n, 805
nations, 81–85; alienation of part of, 240–42; citizens, actions by and against, 298–301; conquest, ownership of, 602–3; conquest of entire state, 608–9; constitutions of, 91–96; countries vs., 153–54 (see also countries); defined, 67, 68, 81; equality and dignity of, 75, 281; establishment of a nation in a country, 213–17 (see also domain); exiled or banished persons, duties toward, 227–28; external attacks, preventing, 198–203; as free persons living together in state of nature, 68; glory of, 203–6, 267–68; government of (see government); independence from another state of which it is a member, obtaining, 210–12; indivisibility of sovereignty of, 117–18; law of (see law of nations; natural law of nations); liberty and independence of (see liberty and independence); as moral persons, 67, 85; obligations and rights between (see obligations and rights between nations); obligations and rights toward themselves, 85–91 (see also obligations and rights); power relative to other nations, 202–3; religion, public establishment of, 157–59; self-determination of actions not affecting rights of other nations, 75; self-knowledge, importance of, 91; self-love, encouraging, 152–55; self-preservation and perfection as duties of, 86–91; small states, de-

fense of sovereignty of, xix; sovereigns, national obligations and rights invested in, 99; sovereignty or dependence of, 83–85; strength of, 198–200; submission to foreign power, voluntary (see voluntary submission to foreign power); titles, honors, rank, and precedence, 281–88; wealth of, 201–2, 228–29, 788–96
Native Americans: ambassadors, respect for, 700, 721; Aztecs, Spanish conquest of, 672–73; colonization of lands of, 216–17, 310; French Canada, missionaries to Hurons of, 166; Incan empire, Spanish interference in, 290
natives, citizens, and inhabitants distinguished, 217–18
naturalization, 218
natural law, 747–71; defined, 69–70n, 747; human nature, foundation in, 748–50; Leibniz's critique of Pufendorf and Barbeyrac's response to, 763–71; obligation of, 750–61; perfection via, 773–81; reason, knowledge of natural law obtained through, 749–50; self-interest as basis for obligation of, 753–63; society between persons and nations formed by, 71–73, 261–62; treaties regarding things already due by, 345–46; universality of, 775; usucaption and prescription established by, 332–36; Vattel's application to law of nations, xiii–xix, 5 (see also natural law of nations); Vattel's study of, x; Vattel's writings on, importance of, ix; will of God and foundations of, 749, 758–61, 763–71
natural law of nations, 68–69; defined, 69–70n; disputes, means of settling, 450–52; embassy, immu-

natural law of nations (*continued*)
nity and independence of, 705–7,
721–22; as foundation of obligations and rights between nations,
259–62; on neutrality and neutral
states, 526; obligation of nation to
act according to its nature, 85–86;
society formed by, 72–73; unequal
treaties conformable with, 354–55;
usucaption and prescription, 336;
Vattel's theory of, xiii–xix, 5; on
war, 589–90

natural resources, right to use, 323–24

navigation, rights of, 246–47, 251

necessary law of nations, 16–17, 70–
71; defined, 70; immutability of,
70; lawful vs. unlawful treaties or
conventions and, 70–71; positive
law distinguished, 78; voluntary
law distinguished, 78–79; on war,
589

necessity, right of, 320–22

Negropont, 413

Nemours, Madame de, 117n, 120n, 305

Nepesinians, 371

Nerva (Roman emperor), 125

Netherlands: ambassadorial exemption from imposts in, 723–24; arbitration between subjects and
sovereigns in, 109; commerce of,
131, 138, 278, 280; contraband
goods, 529, 530n; Louis XIV and,
263, 272, 430, 457; maritime treaty
with Austria, 251; neutrality and
use of ports, 526n; papal protection of Dutch ships, 268; police
in, 194; ranking and precedence of
nations, effect of form of government on, 282; regency of Isabella
Clara Eugenia, 115n; religious toleration in, 162; reprisals by Britain in
favor of Knights of Malta, 463;
Spain, revolt against, 104, 107n,
209n, 533, 544n, 553n, 585n, 618n,

642–43, 703; subjects of state
where employed as ambassadors,
732–33; War of the Austrian Succession, 521

Neufchâtel (modern-day Neuchâtel):
arbitration between subjects and
sovereigns in, 109; embassy, right
of, 684; guardianship of Madame
de Longueville, 305; reformed religion embraced in, 163n; subject to
Prussian prince but not part of
Prussia, 84; succession to sovereignty in, 117n, 120; Vattel and, xi–
xiii, xix

Neugebauer (Polish historian), 388n

neutrality and neutral states, 523–41;
acts done with view to self-interest
and without partiality, 526–28;
commerce with states at war, 528–
34; conduct regarded as neutral,
523–24; declarations of war, 505–6;
defined, 523; hostilities against,
539–40; impartiality, duty of, 533–
34; natural law of nations on, 526;
obligation to give succor and, 524;
passage of troops through, 534–41;
postliminium in, 605; prisoners of
war escaping into, 610; property
found with enemies, 510; right of,
524–25; searching of neutral ships,
532–33; treaties of, 525–26

Nevers, Louis de Gonzage, duc de,
719n, 805

New England, Puritans in, 216–17

Newton, Isaac, 147, 205

Nicholas V (pope), 216n

Nickolls, John (Louis-Joseph Plumard
de Danguel), 132n, 806

Nimeguen, peace of, 662

Noel, Alexandre (Alexander Natalis),
171n, 805–6

nomads, 310–11

noncombatants as enemies, treatment
of, 510, 549–51

Norway, 288n, 539
Novara, battle of, 84n4
Numa, 160
Nuremberg, burgrave of, 327

oaths: of soldiers, 479; treaties, use
  in, 390–92
obedience to sovereigns, 109
obligations and rights, 73–74; active
  and passive obligation, 751–52; basis for, 766; civil war, sovereign in,
  641, 642–44; constitutional, 91–96;
  definition of obligation, 750–53;
  duty and, 751–52; external vs. internal, 74–75; inalienable rights,
  319–26; in just wars (see obligations
  and rights in just wars); law of nations and, 67–68; Leibniz's critique
  of Pufendorf and Barbeyrac's response to, 763–71; between nations
  (see obligations and rights between
  nations); of nation toward itself,
  85–91; natural law, obligation of,
  750–61; of neutrality, 524–25; perfect vs. imperfect, 74–75, 297; of
  prisoners of war, 610–11; self-
  determination of national actions
  not affecting rights of other nations, 75; self-interest as basis for,
  753–63; silence, loss of rights by,
  210; of soldiers, 479–80; of sovereigns, 96–112; Vattel's theory of,
  xvi; war, right of making, 469–71;
  will of God and foundations of
  natural law, 749, 758–61, 763–71
obligations and rights between nations: ancients' ignorance of, 273;
  citizens, actions by and against,
  298–301; commerce, right of, 274–
  75; compelling assistance from another nation, 266; difference of
  religion, effects of, 268; disputes,
  settlement of (see disputes between
  nations, settling); domain, effect

of, 301–11; embassy, right of, 682–
  90, 693–95; foreigners, treatment
  of, 311–19, 327–31; foundations of,
  259–61; inalienable rights, 319–26;
  injury or offense to other nations,
  avoiding, 271–72; innocent use,
  right of, 324–31; interference in
  government of another nation, no
  right to, 289–93; justice, 296–98;
  in just wars (see obligations and
  rights in just wars); limitations due
  to present state of humanity, 268–
  71; love between nations, mutuality of, 267; passage (see passage,
  right of); peace treaties, observation of, 671–73; perfection of others, contributing to, 264–65;
  preservation of others, assisting,
  262–64; requiring assistance from
  another nation, 266; security, right
  of, 288–95; titles, honors, rank,
  and precedence, 281–88; treaties,
  obligation to observe terms of,
  342–43 (see also treaties and conventions); unequal treaties, 352–53;
  usucaption and prescription, 331–
  38
obligations and rights in just wars,
  541–75; disposition toward enemies, 563–66; faith between enemies, 575–85; killing of enemy,
  543–49, 557–63; noncombatants as
  enemies, treatment of, 510, 549–51;
  person of the enemy, 541–66; postliminium, 603–11; prisoners of
  war, 551–57, 606–7, 610–11; private
  persons, 612–18; property of the
  enemy, 566–75; reprisals, 543–44;
  right of making war, 469–71; safe-
  conducts, 635
Ockley, Simon, 343n, 721n, 722n, 806
odious vs. favorable things in interpretation of treaties, 433–42
offensive alliances, 512, 519

offensive war, 471, 488–89, 503
officers, military, 480–82, 615
older people, as enemies, 549
the Old Man of the Mountain
    (Hasan ibn al-Sabbah), 559–60,
    722
open seas. *See* maritime law
D'Orléans, Abbé, 305
d'Orléans, Gaston, 647
Orléans, Philippe II, duc d', 714–15
Orte, governor of Bayonne, 110
Ossat, Arnauld d', 174n, 806
Otho IV (Holy Roman Emperor), 181
Ovid (Publius Ovidius Naso), 3n,
    806
Oxenstierna, Axel, 205

papacy. *See* Catholicism, and individ-
    ual popes
Papon, Jean, 177n, 806
pardon, 193
Paris, Matthew, 182n
Paris, siege of, 263
Pas, Antoine de, marquis de
    Feuquières, 580n, 806
passage, right of, 322–23, 327–28; am-
    bassadors, 699–701; military troops
    passing through neutral states,
    534–41; property/merchandise,
    327–28; safe-conducts in war, 633–
    37
passive and active obligation, 751–52,
    766
passports, 633–34, 699–701
Patkul, General, 222n
patrimonial sovereignty, 123–26
patriotism: importance of encourag-
    ing, 152–55; Vattel's concept of, xix
Paul, Dr., 304n
Paul III (pope), 177
Paul V (pope), 172
peace, 651–55; defined, 651–52; effects
    of, 655; end of war as, 655; obliga-
    tion to cultivate, 652–54; post-

liminium, 609–10; treaties of (*see*
    peace treaties)
peace treaties, 655–81; alienation of
    property in, 657–59; alliances and,
    675, 677, 680–81; allies and associ-
    ates, 661–62; amnesties as part of,
    664; authority to make, 655–57,
    659–60; binding nature of, 671;
    breaches of, 673–81; citizens or
    subjects violating, 680; commence-
    ment of obligations under, 665–
    67; compromise as, 662–64;
    contributions, cessation of, 668;
    defined, 655; effects of, 663–64; ex-
    ecution of, 665–71; former treaties,
    incorporation of, 665; interpreta-
    tion of, 670; invalidity of, 667,
    681; mediation of, 662; new cause
    for war and, 674, 675–76; obliga-
    tion to observe, 672–73; obstacles
    to implementing, 667, 679–80;
    penalties for violating, 679; prop-
    erty restored in, 668–69; publica-
    tion of, 666–67; self-defense no
    breach of, 676–77; single article
    violated as violation of whole
    treaty, 678–79; studied delays, 679;
    terms of, 663–65; with usurpers,
    660–61
peasants, as enemies, 550–51
Pecquet, Antoine, 709, 806
Pedius (Quintus Pedius), 356
penalties: enemy property taken by
    way of, 567–68; peace treaties, vio-
    lation of, 679; in treaties, interpre-
    tation of, 435, 439–40; truces,
    violation of, 622–23. *See also*
    punishment
Penn, William, 217
Pentherrieder, 284n
Pepin the Younger (king of the
    Franks), 558
perfection: constitution as means of,
    92; contribution of other nations

to, 264–65, 267; happiness of nation, encouraging, 151–52; nation, as aim of, 86, 88–89; natural law and political laws, 773–81; obligations and rights, perfect, 74–75, 297; society, as aim of, 73; sovereign's duty to perfect nation, 99–100; of treaties, 360; war, not an argument for, 265

Pericles, 394, 417

perjury, 390–91

Peronne, interview at, 634–35n

Perseus (king of Macedonia), 581

personal treaties and alliances, 355, 362–64

Peter III (king of Aragon), 183n, 552

Peter II (king of Portugal), 179n

Peter I the Great (emperor of Russia), 147, 285, 288, 315, 486, 555, 571

Pharos, 426

Philip (archduke of Austria), 341

Philip, duke of Burgundy, 389

Philip, son of Antony the Bastard of Burgundy, 548n

Philip I (king of Castile), 393n

Philip II Augustus (king of France), 475n

Philip III the Bold (king of France), 183n

Philip IV the Fair (king of France), 143n, 171

Philip II (king of Spain), 104, 107n, 115n, 289, 384n, 609, 618n, 711–12

Philip V of Anjou (king of Spain), 365, 531n

Philip de Valois, 119, 142n, 183

Philip of Macedon, 486

Philippe II, duc d'Orléans, 714–15

Philippe de Commines, 205, 682, 801

Philippe-Henri, marquis de Séqur, 481n

philosophical discussion, freedom of, 147–49

Phyton, 546

piety, 155–56. *See also* religion

pillaging, 568–69

Pineau-Duclos, Charles, 341n, 548n, 806

piracy: citizens, national responsibility for actions of, 301; contraband goods and, 531n; as informal and unlawful war, 507; papal protection of Dutch ships, 268; privateers, 614–15; property acquired by, 596; ravaging of North African hideouts by Spain and Italy, 570

Pius II (pope), 121

Pius V (pope), 172, 177

plain meaning rule for interpretation of treaties, 408–9, 412–13

pledges given for observance of treaties, 398–400

plenipotentiaries: ambassadorial ministers, 692; treaties made by, 339–40

Pliny the Younger (Gaius Plinius Caecilius Secundus), 781, 806

plots, ambassadorial, 713–19

Plumard de Danguel, Louis-Joseph (John Nickolls), 132n, 807

Plutarch (Mestrius Plutarchus), 379n, 533n, 536n, 558n, 807

poisoning of enemies, 557–63

Poland, 263, 530n, 596–97, 666

police, internal, 193–94

political law, 92, 773–81

Polybius, 301n, 486, 807

Pompey, 668n, 791

Pomponius (Titus Pomponius Atticus), 317–18

pontifex maximus, choice of, 168

popular commotions, 641. *See also* civil war

population of country, encouraging, 127, 198–200

Porsenna (Lars Porsenna), 404, 558

ports, 255

Portugal: attempted assassination of John de Braganza, 178–79; com-

Portugal (*continued*)
merce of, 137n, 138, 274; division of New World between Spain and Portugal by papacy, 215; Lisbon earthquake, 264; open seas, appropriation of, 250; rules of sovereign succession in, 116; Spanish conquest and reversal, 609, 703
port wine trade between Britain and Portugal, 137n
positive law of nations, 78
possession as 9/10ths of law, 457
possibility/impossibility affecting interpretation of treaties, 431–32
postliminium, 603–11, 628
power of the purse, 230
Praetorian Edict, 780, 781n
Pragmatic Sanction, 397
Prague, siege of, 616
precedence of nations or sovereigns, 281–88
preparation for war, responding to, 499–500
prescription, 331–38
pretexts for war, 486–87
Prévost, Antoine François, 721n, 807
princes. *See* sovereigns and sovereignty
prisoners of war, 551–57; in civil wars, 646; concealed property of, 640; death before ransom, 638–39, 640; exchanges, 556–57; hostages for, 640; killing of, 552–56, 646; marriage of, 611; neutral states, escaping into, 610; peace treaties, authority to make, 659–60; postliminium, 606–7, 610–11; promises made to enemies by, 633n; ransom of, 556–57, 637–40; as slaves, 556–57; wills of, 611; women and children as, 551
private contracts made by sovereign, 382–86

private enemies, 509
privateers, 614–15. *See also* piracy
private persons' obligations and rights in war, 612–18
private property, 229, 236–37; domain, as part of, 302–3; of foreigners, 315–19; reprisals involving, 461; war, acquisition by, 598
private war, 469
Privernians, 601
Probus (Marcus Aurelius Probus, Roman emperor), 328
Procopius of Caesarea, 633
property, 228–37; alienation (*see* alienation of property); ambassadorial, 733–36; common property, 229, 232, 233–36; contraband goods, 505, 529–32; disposal of by sovereign, 659; eminent domain, 232–33; of enemies, 510–11, 566–75; joint property, 229; laws governing, 232; national wealth, 201–2, 228–29, 788–96; necessity, right of, 320–22; of neutral parties, 529–32; passage, right of, 327–28; peace treaty, restoration by, 668–69; pledges given for observance of treaties, 398–400; possession as 9/10ths of law, 457; postliminium, 603–11; private (*see* private property); public (*see* public property); right to use everything in primitive state, 320; safe-conducts covering, 635; of unjustly conquered people, 603; unowned things, national right to appropriate, 307; usucaption and prescription, 331–38; war, acquisitions by, 568–69, 593–603. *See also* domain
prostitution, as metaphor for bad government, 151
protection of a foreign power, nations submitting to. *See* voluntary submission to foreign power

proxies, treaties made by, 339–40

Prussia, 162, 304, 480, 596–97

publications: declarations of war, 500–506, 522–23; of peace treaties, 666–67; of truces, 621–22

public enemies, 509

public ministers: ambassadorial (*see* embassy); defined, 682–83; sovereign authority over, 112

public property: acquisition of, 229; alienation of, 237–40; defined, 228–29; eminent domain, 232–33; government of, 233; laws governing, 232; preservation and repair of, 235–36; sovereign's authority over, 229–30; use of, 233–36

public war, 469

public ways, 139–41, 328

Pufendorf, Samuel: biographical information, 807; examples used by, 20; on law of nature and law of nations, 9; on natural law, 752, 753, 755, 759n, 762n, 763, 771; on promises made by individuals to enemies, 633n; on sovereigns and sovereignty, 119; on treaties, 360, 361, 381, 414n, 417n, 426n, 433n, 445; Vattel's study of, x

punishment: of ambassadors, 711–18; injustice, right of punishing, 297; just war, as object of, 490; retaliation by one nation against another, 458–59, 503; security rights of nations and right of, 289; of transgressors, 190–92; unequal treaties as means of, 354–55. *See also* penalties

Puritans in New England, 216–17

purse, power of, 230

Pyrrhus (king of Epirus and Macedon), 561

quarter, giving or refusing to give, 543–44

Quintilian (Marcus Fabius Quintilianus), 434n, 807

Quintus Aemilius Papus, 561

Quintus Curtius Rufus, 562n, 600n, 801

rank of nations or sovereigns, 281–88

ransom of prisoners, 556–57, 637–40

rape of the Sabine women, 321

ravaging of enemy property, 570–73

Ravaillac (assassin of Henry IV of France), 156

Raymond, count of Toulouse, 182–83n

real treaties and alliances, 355–59, 364–65

reason, knowledge of natural law obtained through, 749–50

"reason of the act" in interpretation of treaties, 421–26

Rebmann, Hans Rudolf, 155n, 807

refugees, 225

regents, 117

regicide, 103, 156, 170, 178–79, 716–19

Regulus, 660

religion, 155–85; abuse of, 166; ambassadorial right to free exercise of, 722–23; atheism, 765–66; Catholic (*see* Catholicism); changing publicly established religion, 163–64; defined, 157; difference of religion and relationship between nations, 268; general truces between Turks and Christians, 619; happiness and good of state, 784–88; interference with government of another nation on grounds of, 291, 292–95; internal vs. external, 157, 161–62; liberty of conscience, 157, 161; ministers of (*see* clergy); missionizing (*see* missionaries); nations, rights and obligations of, 157–59; piety, 155–56; public establishment of, 157–59, 160–61, 163–64; sovereigns, rights and duties of, 159–70,

religion (*continued*)
787; superstition vs., 148–49; toleration of, 162; treaties between parties not professing the same faith, 342, 392; will of God and foundations of natural law, 749–50, 758–61, 763–71
renunciation of sovereignty: national allegiance to sovereign, renouncing, 210–12; by sovereign, 115–16
reparations, 289, 458
reprisals, 460–67, 545–46, 719–21
republics: ranking and precedence of nations, effect of form of government on, 282; as type of government, 82–85; Vattel's views on, 473n
res communes, 228. *See also* public property
resistance, right of, 101n, 103–12, 288–89
restrictive or strict interpretation of treaties, 427–29
retaliation, 458–59, 503
retinue. *See* domestic servants
retortion, 459–60
Rhadamanthus, law of, 458
Rhadamistus (king of Iberia and Armenia), 394
Rhodians, 426
Ricci, Pierro Andrea, 177n
Richelieu, Cardinal, 348n, 349–50, 430, 475, 654n, 726n
rights. *See* obligations and rights
Rincon (ambassador of Francis I), 699–700
Ripperda, duke de, 739
rivers and streams, 242–47, 249, 323–24
roads, maintenance of, 139–41, 328
robbers, treatment of enemies waging unlawful war as, 508
Robert II (king of Scotland), 390
Rohan, Henri, duc de, 646n, 808

Romans: aggrandizing powers, failure to address, 496; arts and sciences, national encouragement of, 147; on assassination, 561; barbarians admitted to empire, 328–29; booty, 569; Carthage, foreign commerce with, 131; Carthage, treaties with, 351–52, 354–55, 440–42, 660; Carthage, wars with, 354–55, 455, 576, 660; conquests of, 598, 601–2; education of youth, 146; embassy, 710, 713, 715, 729–30, 742; fecial law, 7, 377n; foreigners, treatment of, 317–18; on law of nature and law of nations, 5–7; marriage, laws encouraging, 175; military discipline of, 616; peace treaties of, 660; pontifex maximus, choice of, 168; postliminium among, 606, 611; promises made by individuals to enemies, 633; ranking and precedence of nations, effect of form of government on, 282; *sponsio*, 374–82; standing army, dangers of, 500; stratagems and artifices in war, 580–81; treaties of, 394; truces, 629; voluntary submission of nation to foreign power of, 208; wars of, 485, 488, 613; women, right to carry off, 321–22
Rôny, marquis De, 743–44
Roques, Pierre, x
Rousseau, Jean-Jacques, xii–xiii, xviii
Royal Academy of Sciences, 147
royalty. *See* sovereigns and sovereignty
Russia: arts and sciences, national encouragement of, 147; embassy in, 724, 737–38; foreigners, treatment of, 315; Great Northern War, 288n, 486, 571; rules of sovereign succession in, 116; Schwedt, treaty of, 596–97
Ruyter, Michiel de, 205

Ryder, Sir Dudley, 304n
Ryswick, treaty of, 662

Sabine women, rape of, 321
sacredness or faith of treaties, 386–95, 411
safe-conducts, 633–37
safeguards granted to enemy property, 573
St. Bartholomew's Day Massacre, 110
St. Jacques, battle of, 205–6
St. John of Jerusalem, Knights of (Knights of Malta), 463, 547n
St. Philippe, marquis de (Vicente Bacallar y Sanna, marquis de San Felipe), 284n, 387n, 658n, 798
Saint-Pierre, Abbé de, xviii
Salic law (succession through male line only), 113
Samnites, 374–82, 482, 488
1 Samuel 19–20, 112n
San Felipe, Vicente Bacallar y Sanna, marquis de (marquis de St. Philippe), 284n, 387n, 658n, 798
Sapor I (king of Persia), 394–95
Sarnicki, S., 388n
Saul (biblical king), 111–12
Sauvage, Matthew, 717–18
Saxony in Great Northern War, 288n
Schodeler, Wernher, 155n, 808
scholars, as enemies, 550
Schwedt, treaty of, 596–97
sciences, national encouragement of, 146–47
Scipio Aemilianus (Publius Cornelius Scipio Aemilianus), 441, 545, 785
Scipio Africanus (Publius Cornelius Scipio Africanus Major), 354–55, 406
Scotland, 106–7n, 390, 546n, 718, 727
Scythians, 314, 600
searching of neutral ships, 532–33
seas, law of. See maritime law
secretary of embassy, 741

secret or non-public ambassadors, 725
security: of ambassadors, 697–704; for passage of troops, 536–37; passports, 633–34; right of, 288–95; safe-conducts, 633–37
security given for observance of treaties, 395–406; antichresis, 398; guaranties, 395–98, 515–16; hostages, 400–406; mortgages, 398; pledges, 398–400
sedition, 641
seduction of enemies, clandestine, 582–84
Sejanus (Lucius Aelius Sejanus), 426–27
Selden, John, 250n, 253n, 254, 808
self-interest: love of country (self-love), promoting, 152–55; mutuality vs., xvi–xvii, 73–74; nation's obligation to preserve itself and its members, 86–88; neutral states acting with view to self-interest and without partiality, 526–28; obligation of natural law, as basis for, 753–63; peace treaty not breached by acts of self-defense, 676–77; sovereign's duty to promote self-preservation of nation, 99–100; treaties conflicting with, 345–46
self-knowledge, 91, 100
Selim I (Turkish sultan), 698n
selling, right of, 133
Sempach, battle of, 155, 201
Seneca (Lucius Annaeus Seneca), 427n, 808
Séqur, Philippe-Henri, marquis de, 481n
servants. See domestic servants
settlement, natural or acquired, 220
settling disputes between nations. See disputes between nations, settling
Sextus Aurelius Victor, 379n, 808
Sextus Pompey (Magnus Pius), 668

Seymour, Edward, duke of Somerset, 546n

Sforza, Francis, duke of Milan, 725

Sharaf Ad-Din 'Ali Yazdi, 97–98n, 808

shipwrecks, right to, 256

shores of seas, 255

sick persons: as enemies, 549; invalid soldiers, asylums for, 476

Sigismund (Holy Roman Emperor), 283, 327, 727

Sigismund Augustus (king of Poland), 144, 689

silence, loss of rights by, 210

Simler, Josias, 212n, 549n, 808

single combat or dueling, 194–97

Sixtus V (pope), 170

slaves: postliminium and, 606; prisoners of war as, 556–57

small states, defense of sovereignty of, xix

Smith, Adam, 137n

social mobility and luxury, 793–94

society: end or purpose of, 86; foundations of natural law and, 749; between nations, 72–73, 261–62; perfection as aim of, 73; perfection via natural law/political laws, 773–81; between persons, 71–72, 261–62; persons made for, 754

Socrates, 763, 765, 781, 787–88, 809

Sofy/Sofi, Joseph (king of Carazem), 565n, 719n

Soissons, congress of, 453

soldiers, 472–82

Solignac, Pierre-Joseph de La Pimpie, 388n, 803

Solís y Rivadeneira, Antonio de, 700n, 809

Somerset, Edward Seymour, duke of, 546n

Sourdis, archbishop of Bourdeaux, 474–75n

sovereigns and sovereignty, 96–112, 783–96; abandonment of, 212; ambassadors, authority to send, 683; arbitration between subjects and, 109; assassination of, 103, 156, 170, 178–79, 716–19; civil revolts against (see civil war); clergy, authority over, 164–70; conquest, ownership of, 602–3; debts of sovereign and state, 384–85; deposed sovereigns, treaties made by, 363–65; derivation and extent of authority of, 100; dismemberment of state, 241–42; domain and, 303; donations of, 385–86; elective, 113; excommunication, Catholic practice of, 181–82; executive power belonging to, 187, 192–93; in foreign countries, 725–27; glory of nation as duty of, 203–4; inalienability, 115–16, 123–25; indivisibility of sovereignty, 117–18; interference in conduct of another sovereign, no right to, 290; justice, duties with regard to, 186–89; killing of sovereign, 103, 156, 170, 178–79, 565–66, 716–19; laws of nation and, 101–9; levying troops, right of, 473–74; limitations on obligations and rights between nations, 271; love of subjects by, 153; luxury, civic dangers of, 150–51, 788–96; national obligations and rights invested in, 99; obedience owed by subjects to, 109; obligations and rights, 96–112; pardoning power, 193; patrimonial, 123–26; peace, obligation to cultivate, 652–53; peace treaties, authority to make, 655–57, 659–60; person, inviolability of, 103; prerogatives of, 100; private contracts made by sovereign, 382–86; private property and, 236–37; public ministers, authority over, 112; public

property, alienation of, 238–39; public property, authority over, 229–30; public property, preservation and repair of, 236; purpose of, 96–99; regents, 117; religion, rights and duties regarding, 159–70, 787; renunciation of allegiance to, 210–12; renunciation of sovereignty by, 115–16; representative character of, 99; reprisals, authority to order, 462; resistance, right of, 101n, 103–12, 288–89; *sponsio* and, 379–82, 481–82; successive or hereditary, 113–22; taxing powers, 230–32; titles, honors, rank, and precedence, 281–88; treaties concluded by sovereigns, 338–39, 356–57, 372, 382–86; truces, authority to conclude, 619–21; tyrants, right to overthrow, 101n, 103–12; unequal treaties and alliances impinging on, 351–52; universal monarchy in Europe, Vattel's fear of, 491–99; violations of treaties by, 390–91; war, right of making, 470–71
sovereignty of states, 83–85
Spain: Aix-la-Chapelle, treaty of, 400, 503, 568; America attacked by, 275; commerce of, 275, 280; contraband goods, 530n, 531n, 532; division of New World between Spain and Portugal by papacy, 215; Dutch revolt, 104, 107n, 209n, 533, 544n, 553n, 585n, 618n, 642–43, 703; Incan empire, interference in, 290; Portuguese conquest and reversal, 609, 703; ravaging of North African pirate hideouts by, 570; sovereigns deposed in, 106n; sovereign succession in, 120, 121; War of the Spanish Succession, 365, 493–94, 525
Sparta and Spartans: arts and sciences, national encouragement of, 147; assassination of enemies, 559; disposition toward enemies, 564n; education of youth in, 146; government of, 82n; killing of enemies by, 545n; Rousseau's followers and, xiii; treaties of, 417
spies, use of, 581–82
sponsio, 379–82, 481–82
springs, poisoned, 563
Spurius Postumius, 374, 376, 378
St. *See* entries at Saint
standing armies, 476, 500
state assemblies, deputies sent to, 727–29
states. *See* nations
Steno (Sten Sture the Younger), 172, 401
Stettler, Michael, 212n, 327n, 455n, 809
straits, 255–56
stratagems and artifices in war, 579–81
strict or restrictive interpretation of treaties, 427–29
Stuart, James (the Young Pretender), 364–65, 689–90
Stumpf, Johannes, 212n, 809
subjects. *See* citizens and subjects
submission of nation to foreign power, voluntary. *See* voluntary submission to foreign power
subordinate powers: military officers as, 480–82, 615; treaties made without proper permission by (*sponsio*), 379–82, 481–82; treaties made with proper permission by, 372–73; truces, authority to conclude, 620–21
subsidies for war, allies providing, 513
subterfuges in treaties, 393, 408–9
successive or hereditary sovereignties, 113–22
"sufficient reason for an act of the will," 424–25

Sully, Maximilien de Béthune, duc de, xi, 161, 238, 504n, 631, 710, 743, 789, 809

sumptuary laws, 793–96

superstition, 148–49

supplicants, 225

supreme courts, 188–89

surprise attacks, 579–81

surrender or capitulation of towns and cities, 629–32

suspension of hostilities, 618–19. *See also* truces

Sweden: arbitration between subjects and sovereigns in, 109; Charles, duke of Sudermania, usurpation by, 689; contraband goods, 529; Great Northern War, 288n, 486, 571; papacy, power of, 172; peace, right to make, 656; Schwedt, treaty of, 596–97; unequal alliance with France, 350; war, right to make, 471

Switzerland: abandonment by sovereign, 212; alliances of, 519, 521; assistance provided between states of, 263–64; Catholic church, importunities of, 173, 178n, 184; dispute settlement by, 455; embassies to France, 695–96; embassy, cities with right of, 684; foreign levying of troops in, 519, 521, 527; glory of nation, as exemplar of, 205–6; heroic patriotism in, 154–55; Letters Rogatory, 300; mercenary soldiers from, 477, 478n; migration laws, 224; military discipline in, 480; military prowess of, 201; militia of, 500; neutrality of, 527, 534, 538; passage of troops through, refusal of, 538; religion, different establishments of, 158; religion, sovereign's authority in matters of, 169; robbers, treatment of enemies waging unlawful war as, 508; *sponsio* of La

Trimouille with, 381–82, 403; treaties, power of cities to make, 339; treaty keeping of, 343; unequal alliance with France, 350; unjustly conquered people, freeing of, 603; valor, national reputation for, 200; Vattel's Swiss heritage, importance of, xii–xiii, xix; Vaud, possession of, 399–400; voluntary submission of Lucerne to Austria, 209; women as enemies, military treatment of, 549. *See also* Neufchâtel

tacit agreements: maritime rights, regarding, 252; treaties, faith of, 394–95

Tacitus (Publius Cornelius Tacitus), 108, 161n, 306n, 394, 427n, 487, 809

Tamerlane (Timur-Bec), 97–98n, 413–14, 487, 560n, 565n, 719n

Tarquin (Roman king), 715, 742

Tartars, 487, 697–98n

Taurians, 314n

taxes and taxation, 230; ambassadorial exemption from imposts, 723–24; contributions from enemies, 569, 668; imposition of, 230–31; migration tax, 221n; national wealth and, 202; sovereigns and, 230–32; toll roads, 139–41

Tellier, François-Michel Le, marquis de Louvois, 494

Tenchtheri, 329n

terminating disputes between nations. *See* disputes between nations, settling

territory of nation. *See* domain

terror, right of warring enemies to use, 614

Tertullian (Florens Quintus Septimius Tertullianus), 199n, 809

Teutoburg Forest, battle of, 561n

Thebes, 511, 607

Theodosian Code, 169n, 175n

Theodosius I (Roman emperor), 176

Thessalians, 511, 607

Thomasius, Christian, 176n

Thou, Jacques Auguste de, 389n, 546n, 595, 809–10

Thouars, Louis I de La Trimouille (La Trémoille), viscount of, 381–82, 403

Thucydides, 420, 810

Tiberius (Roman emperor), 426–27, 561

Timothy 1:9, 771

Timur-Bec (Tamerlane), 97–98n, 413–14, 487, 560n, 565n, 719n

titles of nations or sovereigns, 281–88

Titus (Roman emperor), 431, 551–52, 559–60

Titus Livius. See Livy

Titus Veturius Calvinus, 374

toleration of religion, 162

tolls and toll roads, 139–41, 328

Tottila (king of the Goths), 571–72

Toulouse, Raymond, count of, 182–83n

Tournay, siege of, 625

towns and cities: bombardment of, 570, 572–73; capitulation of, 629–32; conquest of, 596–98, 606–8; embassy, right of, 684–85; governors defending enemy towns, killing of, 546–49; noncombatants, treatment of, 550–51; postliminium, right of, 606–8

trade. See commerce

trading companies, 138, 232–33. See also East Indies companies

traite foraine, 318

traitors, 584–85, 627–28, 707–10

Trajan (Roman emperor), 125

treason, 584–85, 627–28, 707–10

treaties and conventions, 77, 338–65; alienation of public property by, 239–40; asseverations used in, 392; authority to make, 338–39, 372–73; auxiliary, 512; boundaries and territories settled by, 77; commercial, 136–37, 275–78, 360; conflicts between, 443–47; deposed sovereigns, made by, 363–65; dissolution due to destruction of contracting power, 369–70; dissolution due to mutual consent, 371–72; dissolution due to violation of terms, 367–69; duties owed to self, conflicting with, 345–46; between enemies, 576–77; equal treaties, 346–48; existing treaties, agreements contrary to, 343–44; expiration of, 366; faith or sacredness of, 386–95, 411; interpretation of (see interpretation of treaties); lawful vs. unlawful, necessary law of nations as means of distinguishing, 70–71; maritime rights, 251; on migration rights, 224; with multiple nations toward same end, 344; nations bound by, 83; nations under protection of foreign power (see under voluntary submission to foreign power); natural law, things already due by, 345–46; of neutrality, 525–26; nullification, grounds for, 341–42, 419–20, 435, 440; oaths, use of, 390–92; obligation to observe terms of, 342–43; of peace (see peace treaties); perfect treaties, 360; personal treaties and alliances, 355, 362–64; as positive law, 78; on postliminium, 611; precedence of more ancient allies regarding, 344; prescription, 338; private contracts made by sovereign, 382–86; by proxies or plenipotentiaries, 339–40; real treaties, 355–59, 364–65; religion, difference of, 342, 392; renewal of, 366–67; securities (see

treaties and conventions (*continued*)
security given for observance of
treaties); sovereigns, treaties made
by, 338–39, 356–57, 372, 382–86;
sponsio (treaties made by subordinate powers without proper permission), 379–82, 481–82;
subordinate powers with proper
permission, treaties made by, 372–
73; successors bound by, 359–62;
suspension of hostilities, 618–19
(*see also* truces); temporary vs. perpetual or long-term, 338; truces (*see*
truces); types of, 345, 355; unequal
treaties, 349–55; unjust war, no assistance owed in, 344; usucaption,
338; validity of, 340–41, 392; violation of terms, consequences of,
367–69; violation of terms, as violation of law of nations, 387–91;
war, treaties relative to, 512; wording of, 393
Trente, treaty of, 341
Tribbechov, Adam, 176n, 810
tributary states, 83
Trimouille (Trémoille), Louis II de
La, viscount of Thouars, 382–83,
403
Trollius, archbishop of Upsal, 172
troops. *See* entries at military
truces, 618–33; authority to conclude,
619–21; civil revolts during, 627;
contravention or violation of, 622–
23; dead, burial of, 626; expiration,
renewal of war at end of, 629; general effects of, 624–25; intercourse
and travel between enemy countries during, 628; military actions
during, 624–28; partial and general, 619; particular conditions of,
628–29; penalties for violation of,
622–23; postliminium, 628; publication of, 621–22; suspension of
hostilities vs., 618–19; time of, 619,

623–24; treasonous offers during,
627–28; war not terminated by, 619
trumpeters, ambassadorial, 702–5
Tschudi, Aegidius (Giles), 155n, 206n,
212n, 327n, 402n, 455n, 810
Tucker, Dean, 137n
Turenne, Henri de la Tour d'Auvergne,
Vicomte de, 205, 415, 419
Turkish empire: ambassadors, respect
for, 721; capitulation, 631; general
truce with, 619; limitations on obligations and rights between nations and, 270; Malta, siege of,
547; Vienna, siege of, 263; war
made without reason or motive by,
487
Turretini (Turretin or Turretinus),
François, 171n, 182n, 810
Twelve Tables, 780, 781n
tyrants, right to overthrow, 101n,
103–9

Uladislaus or Ladislaus (king of
Naples), 255
Uladislaus or Vladislaus III (king of
Poland), 388
Ulpian (Domitius Ulpianus), 356
Ulysses, 523
Unam sanctam, 171
uncultivated land, domain over,
306–7
unequal treaties and alliances, 83,
349–55, 683–85
United Provinces. *See* Netherlands
universality of natural law, 775
universal monarchy in Europe,
Vattel's fear of, 491–99
unjust war: alliances denied in, 515;
both sides, war not just on, 489–
90; defensive, 487–88; defined,
484; liberty of unjustly conquered
people, restoring, 603; passage of
troops denied in cases of, 541; postliminium, 604; treaties of assis-

tance not required to be honored regarding, 344; voluntary law of nations on, 592–93

unlawful and informal wars, 507–8

unlawful means used to obtain good ends, 202

Urban VI (pope), 177n

Urban VIII (pope), 177, 280

urban environments. *See* towns and cities

Usbecks, 301

Usipetes, 329n

usucaption, 331–38

usurpers: embassy with, 688–90; peace treaties with, 660–61

Utrecht, treaty of, 308, 662

vagrants, 220

Valens (Flavius Julius Valens, Roman emperor), 328

Valerian (Roman emperor), 394–95

Valerius Maximus, 82n, 394n, 558n, 583–84, 810

Valette, Cardinal De la, 474–75n

valor, national reputation for, 200–201

van Beuningen, Coenraad, 296n, 665n

van Bynkershoek, Cornelius, 463n, 717n, 730n, 732n, 736, 799

Vandals, 329

Varro (Marcus Terrentius Varro), 7n, 810–11

Varus (Publius Quinctilius Varus), 561

Vassor, Michel Le, 291n, 804

Vattel, David, ix

Vattel, Emer de: biographical information, xi–xii; *Défense* of Leibniz's philosophy, x; dialogues, xi (*see also Dialogue Between the Prince of* **** *and His Confidant*); essays and essay collections, x–xii (*see also Can Natural Law Bring Society to Perfection Without the Assistance of Po-*

litical Laws? and *Essay on the Foundation of Natural Law*); illustration, iii; *Law of Nations* (*see Law of Nations*); *Loisir Philosophique*, 186n; Swiss heritage, influence of, xii–xiii, xix, 20

Vaud, Swiss possession of, 399–400

Vega, Garcilaso (Garcillaso) de la, 290n, 802

Veii, 629

Velly, Paul François, 97n, 125n, 183n, 341n, 728n, 811

Venice: commerce of, 280; embassy, 716; maritime laws of, 254–55; papacy, power of, 172; ranking and precedence of nations, effect of form of government on, 282; War of the Austrian Succession and, 534

Vera, Antony de, 707n

Vertot, René-Aubert de, 172n, 179n, 401n, 811

Vervins, peace of, 532

Vespasian (Roman emperor), 431n

vice and virtue: moral science or ethics, defined, 747–48; national love of virtue and abhorrence of vice, fostering, 150

Victor Amadeus II, duke of Savoy, 428–29, 525

Vienna, council of, ix, xviii–xix

Vienna, treaty of, 347

Vienna, Turkish siege of, 263

Villeroy, minister, 689

Virgil (Publius Vergilius Maro), 397n, 449n, 455n, 553n, 581n, 618n, 811

Viriatus, 583

virtue and vice: moral science or ethics, defined, 747–48; national love of virtue and abhorrence of vice, fostering, 150

Vladislaus or Uladislaus III (king of Poland), 388

Vogel, Franz Adam, 173n, 206n, 811
Volcatius Gallicanus, 616n
voluntary law of nations, 16–17, 75–76; on dispute resolution, 456–57; enemy property, treatment of, 574–75; necessary law distinguished from, 78–79; as positive law, 78; on property acquired by war, 594; usucaption and prescription, 337; on war, 589–93
voluntary submission to foreign power, 83–85, 207–10; authority to make treaties, 339; effect on existing treaties, 370–71; embassy, right of, 683–85; unequal treaties, 349–55
volunteer soldiers, 615
von Wattenwyl, Alexander Ludwig. See Wattenwyl (De Watteville), Alexander Ludwig von
Vopiscus (Flavius Vopiscus), 320n

Waldemar I (king of Denmark), 474n
war, 469–71; aggrandizement of neighboring power, 491–99; allies, between, 517; capitulation of towns and cities, 629–32; civil (see civil war); commencement of hostilities, 504–5; commerce between neutral states and states at war, 528–34; compelling assistance from another nation, 266; conquest, 308, 568, 593, 596–603, 606–9; declarations of, 500–506, 522–23; defensive, 471, 487–88, 503, 515; defined, 469; disputes leading to right to wage, 455–57; doubtful causes, 489; embassy in, 686–88; equitable conditions of peace offered after declarations of, 502; faith between enemies in, 575–85; foreigners, treatment of, 505, 506n; government of another nation, no right to interfere in, 289–93; government's duty to protect nation against, 198–203; horrors of, 653–54; informal and unlawful wars, 507–8; instruments of (armies, troops, and commanders), 472–82, 500, 513; just (see just war); lawful wars in due form, 507–8; mischievous nations and sovereigns, coalitions against, 289; motives for, 483, 484–87; natural law of nations on, 589–90; necessary law of nations on, 589; necessity, right of, 320–21; obligations and rights in (see obligations and rights in just wars); offensive, 471, 488–89, 503; passage of troops through neutral country leading to acts of, 534–41; perfection, no entitlement of one nation to forcibly obtrude upon another for purposes of, 265; postliminium, 603–11, 628; preparation for war, responding to, 499–500; pretexts for, 486–87; prisoners of (see prisoners of war); property acquired by, 568–69, 593–603; public vs. private, 469; punishment, right of, 289; reparations, right to, 289; reprisals leading to, 466–67; resistance, right of, 288–89; right of making, 469–71; safe-conducts during, 633–37; stratagems and artifices in, 579–81; terror, right to use, 614; treaties, violation of, 287–88; treaties relative to, 512; unjust (see unjust war); voluntary law of nations on, 589–93. See also alliances; enemies; neutrality and neutral states; peace; peace treaties; truces
warlike associations vs. alliances, 512
War of the Austrian Succession, 425, 481n, 521n, 534n, 554, 573n, 614, 616
War of the Polish Succession, 666

War of the Spanish Succession, 365, 493–94, 525

wastage of enemy property, 570–73

Wattenwyl (De Watteville), Alexander Ludwig von: biographical information, 811; on embassy, 684n; on glory of nation, 206n; on postliminium, 603n; on settling disputes between nations, 455n, 463n; on treaties, 381n, 383n; on voluntary submission of nation to foreign power, 209n, 212n; on war, 564n

wealth of nations, 201–2, 228–29, 788–96

weapons, poisoned, 562–63

Westphalia, peace of, 286n, 389, 684, 701, 726n

Whitehall, treaty of, 529

Wicquefort, Abraham de: on consuls, 280; on honors due ambassadors, 695n; on immunity of ambassadors, 707n, 712n, 714n, 741n, 742; passage, ambassadorial right of, 701n, 702n, 703n; on right of embassy, 687n

William I (the Silent) of Orange, 560

William III of Orange (king of England), 290, 365, 373, 573, 580, 689–90

William VIII (pope), 177n

wills: of foreigners, 315–17; of prisoners of war, 611

wine trade, 137n, 139

Winkelried, Arnold de, 154–55

Witt, Johan de, 296n, 461n, 530n, 532n, 665n, 811–12

Wolff (Wolf), Christian: on allies and associates, 518n; biographical information, 812; on embassy, 705n; on hostages, 401n; on inalienable rights, 321n; on natural law, 10–16, 748n, 751n, 752n, 757n; on peace treaties, 659n, 678n; on prescription, 331; on treaties, 368n, 408n; Vattel influenced by, xi, xii, xiv–xv, 10–16; on voluntary law of nations, 76

Wolsius, Johannes, 333

women: ambassadors, wives of, 741; as enemies, 510, 549; as prisoners of war, 551; right to carry off, 321–22; safe-conducts for individuals not covering wives, 635; as soldiers, 474

wrecks, right to, 256

Xenophon, 146n, 545n, 550n, 564n, 583n, 812

Young Pretender (James Stuart), 364–65, 689–90

Zenobia (queen of Armenia), 394

This book is set in Adobe Garamond, a modern adaptation by
Robert Slimbach of the typeface originally cut around 1540 by the
French typographer and printer Claude Garamond. The Garamond
face, with its small lowercase height and restrained contrast between
thick and thin strokes, is a classic "old-style" face and has long been
one of the most influential and widely used typefaces.

Printed on paper that is acid-free and meets the requirements of
the American National Standard for Permanence of Paper for
Printed Library Materials, z39.48-1992. ♾

Book design by Louise OFarrell
Gainesville, Florida
Typography by Apex CoVantage
Madison, Wisconsin
Printed and bound by Sheridan Books, Inc.,
Chelsea, Michigan